AMERICAN HISTORY VOLUME I

Pre-Colonial through Reconstruction

Fourteenth Edition

Editor

Robert James Maddox
Pennsylvania State University
University Park

Robert James Maddox, distinguished historian and professor of American history at Pennsylvania State University, received a B.S. from Fairleigh Dickinson University in 1957, an M.S. from the University of Wisconsin in 1958, and a Ph.D. from Rutgers in 1964. He has written, reviewed, and lectured extensively, and is widely respected for his interpretations of presidential character and policy.

A Library of Information from the Public Press
Dushkin/McGraw-Hill
Sluice Dock, Guilford, Connecticut 06437

*Visit us on the Internet—*http://www.dushkin.com/

The Annual Editions Series

ANNUAL EDITIONS, including GLOBAL STUDIES, consist of over 70 volumes designed to provide the reader with convenient, low-cost access to a wide range of current, carefully selected articles from some of the most important magazines, newspapers, and journals published today. ANNUAL EDITIONS are updated on an annual basis through a continuous monitoring of over 300 periodical sources. All ANNUAL EDITIONS have a number of features that are designed to make them particularly useful, including topic guides, annotated tables of contents, unit overviews, and indexes. For the teacher using ANNUAL EDITIONS in the classroom, an Instructor's Resource Guide with test questions is available for each volume. GLOBAL STUDIES titles provide comprehensive background information and selected world press articles on the regions and countries of the world.

VOLUMES AVAILABLE

ANNUAL EDITIONS
Abnormal Psychology
Accounting
Adolescent Psychology
Aging
American Foreign Policy
American Government
American History, Pre-Civil War
American History, Post-Civil War
American Public Policy
Anthropology
Archaeology
Astronomy
Biopsychology
Business Ethics
Child Growth and Development
Comparative Politics
Computers in Education
Computers in Society
Criminal Justice
Criminology
Developing World
Deviant Behavior
Drugs, Society, and Behavior
Dying, Death, and Bereavement
Early Childhood Education
Economics

Educating Exceptional Children
Education
Educational Psychology
Environment
Geography
Geology
Global Issues
Health
Human Development
Human Resources
Human Sexuality
India and South Asia
International Business
Latin America
Macroeconomics
Management
Marketing
Marriage and Family
Mass Media
Microeconomics
Multicultural Education
Nutrition
Personal Growth and Behavior
Physical Anthropology
Psychology
Public Administration
Race and Ethnic Relations

Social Problems
Social Psychology
Sociology
State and Local Government
Teaching English as a Second
    Language
Urban Society
Violence and Terrorism
Western Civilization,
    Pre-Reformation
Western Civilization,
    Post-Reformation
Women's Health
World History, Pre-Modern
World History, Modern
World Politics

GLOBAL STUDIES
Africa
China
India and South Asia
Japan and the Pacific Rim
Latin America
Middle East
Russia, the Eurasian Republics,
    and Central/Eastern Europe
Western Europe

Cataloging in Publication Data
Main entry under title: Annual Editions: American history, vol. one: Pre-Colonial through reconstruction. 14/E.
    1. United States—History—Periodicals. 2. United States—Historiography—Periodicals. 3. United States—Civilization—Periodicals. I. Title: American history, vol. one: Pre-Colonial through reconstruction.
E171.A75   973'.5   74—187540
ISBN 0–697–36303–1

Fourteenth Edition

Cover: © 1996, Granger Collection

Printed in the United States of America

Printed on Recycled Paper

Editors/Advisory Board

Members of the Advisory Board are instrumental in the final selection of articles for each edition of ANNUAL EDITIONS. Their review of articles for content, level, currentness, and appropriateness provides critical direction to the editor and staff. We think that you will find their careful consideration well reflected in this volume.

EDITOR

Robert James Maddox
Pennsylvania State University
University Park

ADVISORY BOARD

Staff

To the Reader

In publishing ANNUAL EDITIONS we recognize the enormous role played by the magazines, newspapers, and journals of the *public press* in providing current, first-rate educational information in a broad spectrum of interest areas. Many of these articles are appropriate for students, researchers, and professionals seeking accurate, current material to help bridge the gap between principles and theories and the real world. These articles, however, become more useful for study when those of lasting value are carefully *collected, organized, indexed,* and *reproduced* in a *low-cost format,* which provides easy and permanent access when the material is needed. That is the role played by ANNUAL EDITIONS. Under the direction of each volume's *academic editor,* who is an expert in the subject area, and with the guidance of an *Advisory Board,* each year we seek to provide in each ANNUAL EDITION a current, well-balanced, carefully selected collection of the best of the public press for your study and enjoyment. We think that you will find this volume useful, and we hope that you will take a moment to let us know what you think.

The increasing interest scholars have shown in studying nontraditional areas of American history has vastly increased the number of available subjects, as well as the number of journals, we considered in putting together this fourteenth edition of *Annual Editions: American History, Volume I.*

As we reviewed the numerous comments and suggestions that we received from previous users of this anthology, we determined that there is a lack of consensus among respondents. Articles that rated high with some users were rated poor by others. Interestingly, several readers complained that *Annual Editions: American History, Volume I* has become too "politically correct" in offering selections on women, blacks, Native Americans, and environmental history. They urge a return to the more conventional topics of political, economic, and military history. Still, others would like to have race, class, and gender emphasized throughout. We can only hope to strike a balance for those who think students should be exposed to both types of history.

This volume contains a number of features designed to be helpful to students, researchers, and professionals. These include a *topic guide* for locating articles on specific subjects; the *table of contents abstracts* that summerize each essay, with key concepts in bold italics; and a comprehensive *in-dex.* Articles are organized into four units, each preceded by an overview that provides a background for informed reading of the articles, emphasizes critical issues, and presents *challenge questions.*

Every edition of *Annual Editions: American History, Volume I* includes new articles to replace some old ones. We continue to strive to update and improve the quality of the selections, and we would like the opportunity to consider alternatives that we might have missed. If you find an article that you think merits inclusion in the next edition, please send it to us (or at least mention it, so that the editor can track it down for consideration). We welcome your comments about the readings in this volume, and a postage-paid reader response card is included in the back of the book for your convenience. Your suggestions will be carefully considered and greatly appreciated.

Robert James Maddox
Editor

Contents

UNIT 1

The New Land

Eight selections discuss the beginnings of America, the new land from pre-Columbian times, early life of the colonists, and religious intolerance, to the stirrings of liberty and independence.

The concepts in bold italics are developed in the article. For further expansion please refer to the Topic Guide and the Index.

UNIT 2

Revolutionary America

Seven articles examine the start
of the American Revolution.
The new land offered opportunities for new ideas that
led to the creation of an
independent nation.

UNIT 3

National Consolidation and Expansion

Fifteen selections examine the developing United States, the westward movement of people seeking a new life, and the realities of living in early nineteenth-century America.

The concepts in bold italics are developed in the article. For further expansion please refer to the Topic Guide and the Index.

The concepts in bold italics are developed in the article. For further expansion please refer to the Topic Guide and the Index.

UNIT 4

The Civil War and Reconstruction

Ten articles discuss the tremendous effects of the Civil War on America. With the abolishment of slavery, the United States had to reconstruct society.

The concepts in bold italics are developed in the article. For further expansion please refer to the Topic Guide and the Index.

Topic Guide

This topic guide suggests how the selections in this book relate to topics of traditional concern to American history students and professionals. It is useful for locating articles that relate to each other for reading and research. The guide is arranged alphabetically according to topic. Articles may, of course, treat topics that do not appear in the topic guide. In turn, entries in the topic guide do not necessarily constitute a comprehensive listing of all the contents of each selection.

TOPIC AREA	TREATED IN	TOPIC AREA	TREATED IN
Adams, John Quincy	19. John Quincy Adams and American Continental Expansion	Culture	1. Mighty Cahokia 3. Laboring in the Fields of the Lord 6. Entertaining Satan 7. How British Are You? 20. Indians in the Land 22. Secret Life of a Developing Country (Ours) 23. Fenimore Cooper's America 28. Christmas in 19th Century America 30. Walt Whitman's Different Lights
African American	8. Slavery and Insurrections in the Colonial Province of New York 14. Founding Fathers, Conditional Antislavery, and the Nonradicalism of the American Revolution 21. Lives of Slave Women 31. Dred Scott in History 33. Struggle for Black Freedom before Emancipation 40. New View of Reconstruction		
		Environment	20. Indians in the Land 29. Eden Ravished
American Revolution	9. Editing the Declaration 10. *Radical* Revolution 11. Hessians	Exploration	2. Columbus—Hero or Villain?
Articles of Confederation	12. 'It Is Not a Union'	Government	12. 'It Is Not a Union' 13. "To Form a More Perfect Union..." 14. Founding Fathers, Conditional Antislavery, and the Nonradicalism of the American Revolution 15. Bill of Rights in Its Context 16. Hamilton's Legacy 17. Whiskey Rebellion 18. Great Chief Justice 19. John Quincy Adams and American Continental Expansion 31. Dred Scott in History 40. New View of Reconstruction
Civil War	32. First Blood to the South 33. Struggle for Black Freedom before Emancipation 34. Combat Trauma in the American Civil War 35. Who Was Lincoln? 37. Why the South Lost the Civil War 38. War That Never Goes Away		
Colonial America	4. Bearing the Burden? Puritan Wives 5. Colonists in Bondage 6. Entertaining Satan 7. How British Are You? 8. Slavery and Insurrections	Hamilton, Alexander	16. Hamilton's Legacy
		Hessians	11. Hessians
Constitution	13. "To Form a More Perfect Union..." 14. Founding Fathers, Conditional Antislavery, and the Nonradicalism of the American Revolution 15. Bill of Rights in Its Context	Hispanics	2. Columbus—Hero or Villain? 3. Laboring in the Fields of the Lord
		Homosexuality	30. Walt Whitman's Different Lights

The New Land

The first people who populated what later would be called North, Central, and South America came from Asia tens of thousands of years ago. They crossed a land bridge between Asia and Alaska and spread out over huge areas of previously uninhabited land. Over the years they established a large number of communites that varied widely with regard to languages, technological levels, and social organizations. The first unit article, "Mighty Cahokia," describes a town that was established near what is now St. Louis, Missouri. At its peak, about 1050 to 1150 A.D., it became an important trading community for a vast region.

The first Europeans to encounter the "new world" were Norseman who landed as early as the tenth century. Their settlements eventually disappeared, and they had no real influence on subsequent developments. Then, a combination of political, economic, and technological developments in western Europe led to the "age of exploration" in the fifteenth century.

Christopher Columbus "discovered" the New World only in the sense that he discovered it for Europeans. He was lionized for his achievement, and later explorers charted and occupied vast new regions. American history books used to celebrate these men, even while admitting that they often treated peoples they encountered with great harshness. They also brought with them, unknowingly, diseases that ravaged local populations who lacked immunities. Instead of a stunning achievement of great benefit, recent historians see the "invasion of paradise" as an alloyed holocaust, the unfortunate results of which are still with us. The essay "Columbus—Hero or Villain?" acknowledges both aspects. Jerald Milanich, in "Laboring in the Fields of the Lord," describes Spanish efforts to establish missions in what is now Georgia and Florida and the catastrophic results that followed the highly motivated acts of many of the friars.

The English were relative latecomers to the New World. Many of the earliest arrivals came in search of wealth, just as the Spanish had done. Others came to settle, whether to escape religious persecution or merely to get a new start in life. "Bearing the Burden? Puritan Wives" by Martha Saxton tells of the changing roles of women in Puritan communities and how they were able to attain moral and spiritual authority despite their subordination to men.

There were chronic shortages of labor in the English colonies. Importing black slaves from Africa was one means of obtaining labor, and using indentured servants was another. The indentured servants agreed to work for a stipulated period in return for passage across the ocean, food, clothing, and shelter. In "Colonists in Bondage: Indentured Servants in America," Barbara Bigham describes this arrangement.

Most early colonists believed in witchcraft. The Salem witch trials of 1692 have received great attention because of the sheer number of people involved. John Demos, in "Entertaining Satan," analyzes the more ordinary accusations of witchcraft and shows how ideas have changed over time. Colonists in exposed areas lived under a far more deadly threat: attacks by the French and their Native American allies during frequent wars with England.

The United States is a nation of immigrants. Successive waves of immigrants came from various parts of Europe, and more recently they have come from Asia and Latin America. In "How British Are You? An Interview with David Hackett Fischer," Bertram Wyatt-Brown evaluates the beliefs of noted historian David Hackett Fischer that four great migrations from Britain during the colonial period greatly shaped the course of American history.

The institution of slavery is usually associated with the American South. This was true only after northern communities had prohibited slavery. "Slavery and Insurrections in the Colonial Province of New York" by Marc Newman describes how harsh laws against slaves led to insurrections in the early 1700s that caused widespread fear in the New York province.

Looking Ahead: Challenge Questions

Although many people are at least dimly aware of the elaborate civilizations created by groups such as the Incas and Aztecs, the perception remains that most other tribes scratched out bare existences in the most primitive forms. Evaluate the evidence against this notion with regard to the settlement of Cahokia in Missouri.

In the long run, did Columbus and other Europeans who came to the New World have a positive or negative effect on the course of history? Defend your answer.

Indenturing oneself for a stated period of time would be repugnant to most Americans today. What purpose did it serve in the past, and why might it have seemed necessary to those who devised it?

Why did the belief in witchcraft appear perfectly reasonable to people during the colonial period?

Does the idea that emigrations from Britain exerted such an enormous influence on American history seem persuasive to you? Why or why not?

Tomo Chachi Mico or King of Yamacran. and
Tooanahowi his Nephew Son to the Mico of the Etchitas.

Mighty Cahokia

A major trading center whose influence extended throughout much of North America, Cahokia was in its day the greatest settlement north of Mexico.

William R. Iseminger

William R. Iseminger is an archaeologist and curator at Cahokia Mounds State Historic Site.

It is the time of the annual harvest festival celebrating the fall equinox. *Traders from distant territories have brought precious offerings for the lords of Cahokia. Ramadas have been erected everywhere to shelter the merchants and their goods: beads and other ornaments shaped from native copper; drinking vessels and gorgets cut from large whelk and conch shells, many engraved with symbolic designs; baskets of tiny marginella shells; bangles cut from sheets of mica; quivers of arrows tipped with gemlike points; galena, hematite, and ocher from which to make pigments for pottery, clothing and body paint; and salt from springs and seeps to the south. In exchange the Cahokians offer their own goods: feathered capes; freshwater pearls; finely woven fabrics; fur garments made from otter, mink, and beaver; chert hoes and axes; and corn, dried squash, pumpkin, and seeds from many other plants. These will be taken back to distant places, some in polished black ceramic vessels bearing incised designs of interlocking scrolls, forked eyes, and nested chevrons, symbols of power and prestige because of their place of origin—mighty Cahokia.*

This fanciful yet fairly accurate description of Cahokia's harvest celebration is drawn from archaeological studies and early historical accounts of remnant Mississippian cultures in the Southeast. Eight miles east of St. Louis, Cahokia was in its day the largest and most influential settlement north of Mexico. Its merchants traded with cultures from the Gulf Coast to the Great Lakes, from the Atlantic coast to Oklahoma, and they helped spread Mississippian culture across much of that vast area. Some 120 earthen mounds supporting civic buildings and the residences of Cahokia's elite were spread over more than five square miles—perhaps six times as many earthen platforms as the great Mississippian site of Moundville, south of Tuscaloosa, Alabama. At its core, within a log stockade ten to 12 feet tall, was the 200-acre Sacred Precinct where the ruling elite lived and were buried. Atop a massive earthen mound stood a pole-framed temple more than 100 feet long, its grass roof possibly decorated with carved wooden animal figures festooned with glimmering beads, feathers, and cloth. Here Cahokia's rulers performed the political and religious rituals that united the realm. Estimates of the city's population at its zenith, ca. A.D. 1050–1150, range from 8,000 to more than 40,000, though most fall between 10,000 and 20,000. Around A.D. 1200, perhaps having exhausted its natural resources, Cahokia went into a decline that left it virtually empty by 1400.

In 1810 the lawyer and journalist Henry Marie Brackenridge, while surveying the Mississippi and Missouri valleys, visited the site and marveled at the "stupendous pile of earth" at its center. At the time a colony of Trappist monks was growing wheat and fruit trees on the earthen structure, soon to be known as Monks Mound. Their plans to build a monastery atop it were abandoned when fever and a shortage of money forced them to leave the site in 1813. The first archaeological excavations at Cahokia took place in the 1920s under the direction of Warren K. Moorehead of the R. S. Peabody Museum in Andover, Massachusetts. Moorehead's work confirmed that the mounds were neither natural hills nor

Today Collinsville Road passes in front of Monks Mound, which is 100 feet high, covers 14 acres at its base, and contains 22 million cubic feet of earth.

WILLIAM R. ISEMINGER, COURTESY CAHOKIA MOUNDS STATE HISTORIC SITE

Reconstruction of Cahokia at its apex shows (1) the 40-acre Grand Plaza, surrounded by temples and elite residences, within (2) a wooden stockade. Bordering the plaza are (3) Monks Mound and (4) the Twin Mounds. Outside the stockade is (5) the Woodhenge, where Cahokia's priests may have observed solstice and equinox sunrises, as well as houses of elite and less well-to-do inhabitants.

the work of a mysterious race of Mound Builders or Precolumbian colonists from Europe—as imagined by nineteenth-century amateur historians but had been built by American Indians. In the 1940s and 1950s archaeologists from the University of Michigan, the Illinois State Museum, the Gilcrease Institute of Tulsa, and elsewhere conducted scattered excavations at the site, but the most intensive work began in the early 1960s when Interstate 55–70 was routed through it. Over the years many of Cahokia's mounds have been lost to the bulldozer and the plow, to subdivisions, highways, and discount stores. Today fewer than 80 remain, 68 of which are preserved within the 2,200-acre Cahokia Mounds State Historic Site, managed by the Illinois Historic Preservation Agency.

Cahokia owed its existence to a floodplain 80 miles long at the confluence of the Mississippi and Missouri rivers. Known as the American Bottom, the plain was interlaced with creeks, sloughs, lakes, and marshes. With fertile soil, extensive forests, and plentiful fish and game, the region was an ideal place to settle. During

the Palaeoindian (ca. 9500–8000 B.C.) and Archaic (ca. 8000–600 B.C.) periods transient hunter-gatherers set up temporary camps or seasonal villages here. During the Woodland period (ca. 600 B.C.–A.D. 800) the population grew, cultivation of native crops began, and larger and more settled communities, including Cahokia, were established. Settlements spread slowly and grew in size throughout the Emergent Mississippian period (ca. A.D. 800–1000), then expanded rapidly in the Mississippian (ca. A.D. 1000–1400) as more intense farming, especially of corn, made fast population growth possible. Cahokia reached its apex during this period, when it was surrounded by dozens of satellite settlements (see box, "East St. Louis Yields a Satellite Settlement") and scores of smaller villages.

In time, Cahokia's influence spread far beyond the American Bottom. Artifacts made there, including Ramey Incised pottery and hoes of Mill Creek chert from southern Illinois, have been found at sites as far north as Minnesota, as far west as eastern Kansas and Oklahoma, and as far south as the lower Ohio

River Valley, Arkansas, and Mississippi. Local imitations of Cahokia's wares, especially pottery, have also been unearthed in these regions. At Cahokia itself we have found copper from the area of Lake Superior; mica from the southern Appalachian Mountains; shells from the Atlantic and Gulf coasts; and galena, ocher, hematite, chert, fluorite, and quartz from throughout the Midwest. Finely made ceramics from the lower Mississippi Valley, perhaps used to carry exotic commodities such as shells from that area, have also been discovered at Cahokia, along with local copies of many of these forms.

The most visible remains of the ancient city are its mounds. Most are rectangular with flat tops (platform mounds) that supported civic buildings and the homes of the elite. Somewhat rarer are conical mounds that may have contained elite burials, as they did in the earlier Woodland period. During the 1920s Moorehead excavated several such burials, but it is often difficult to tell from his records whether they were found in the mounds themselves or in earlier layers. Rarest of

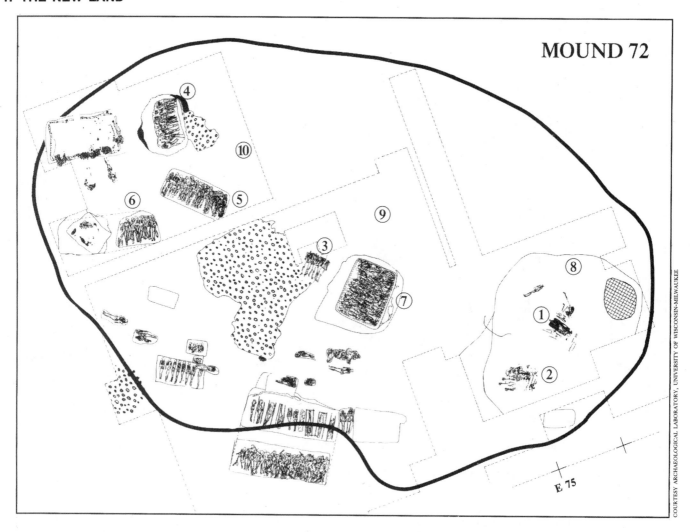

MOUND 72

COURTESY ARCHAEOLOGICAL LABORATORY, UNIVERSITY OF WISCONSIN–MILWAUKEE

Excavated between 1967 and 1971, Mound 72 contained the burials of about 280 people, including an elite male laid on a bed of some 20,000 shells (1). Nearby six people were interred with hundreds of arrowheads, beads, and other items (2). Four men buried without their heads and hands (3) and four mass graves of women (4–7) suggest human sacrifice. Mound 72 was originally three separate smaller mounds (8–10) that were later incorporated into a single structure about 140 feet long, 70 feet wide, and six feet tall.

all are rectangular ridgetop mounds that may have marked important locations such as community boundaries or mortuary complexes. The destruction of one such mound by farmers in 1931 revealed mass burials laid upon platforms of shell beads and cedar bark.

Monks Mound stands at the center of the site, on the northern edge of the 40-acre Grand Plaza. Covering 14 acres at the base and rising in four terraces to a height of 100 feet, it is the largest prehistoric earthen structure in the New World. Some 19 million man-hours of labor would have been required to excavate, carry, and deposit the estimated 22 million cubic feet of earth needed for this project. Excavations and soil cores indicate that it was built in stages between ca. A.D. 900 and 1200, each pos-

sibly related to the accession of a new leader. Probes on the summit have revealed wall trenches for a wooden building 104 feet long and 48 feet wide. Here the leader of Cahokia governed his domain, performed ceremonies, consulted with the spirit world, and may have resided as well. The bones of deceased chiefs may also have been stored here, as was the custom among some historical tribes in the Southeast.

One of the most fascinating discoveries at Cahokia came during the 1967–1971 excavation of Mound 72, a ridgetop one-half mile south of Monks Mound. Measuring 140 feet long, 70 feet wide, and barely six feet high, Mound 72 is oriented along a northwest-southeast axis, one end pointing toward the winter solstice sunrise and the other toward the

summer solstice sunset. Excavations revealed that it had originally been three separate, smaller mounds, two platforms and one conical. Around and beneath these three mounds were some 280 burials dating to Cahokia's initial development between ca. A.D. 1000 and 1050. Some of the dead had been borne to their graves on litters or wrapped in mats or blankets, while others had simply been tossed into pits, suggesting that people of different statuses were buried at the same place. Soon after the burials the three mounds were fused into a single ridgetop mound with a final mantle of earth.

In one opulent burial a man about 40 years old, perhaps one of Cahokia's early leaders, was laid upon a bird-shaped platform of nearly 20,000 marine-shell beads. Around him were several other bodies, perhaps of retainers or relatives, some interred for the first time and others reburied from elsewhere. Heaped atop six nearby burials were two caches of more than 800 newly made arrowheads, whose Midwestern cherts and hafting styles suggest possible origins in Wisconsin, Illinois, Missouri, Tennessee, Arkansas, and Oklahoma. One cache included 15 large concave ground-stone discs, sometimes known as "chunkey" stones, after a game played with similar stones by historical tribes in the Southeast. Also found were a large pile of unprocessed mica from the southern Appalachian Mountains, a three-foot-long roll of copper (possibly a ceremonial staff) hammered from Lake Superior nuggets, and more marine-shell beads.

Further excavations under Mound 72 revealed several mass burials, most of females between 15 and 25 years old, suggesting human sacrifice. The largest pit held more than 50 women laid out in two rows and stacked two and three deep; two others contained 22 and 24 women. A fourth pit, with 19 women, had been partially redug, and more than 36,000 marine-shell beads, another cache of unused arrowheads (more than 400 of chert and a few hundred more of bone and antler), and several broken ceramic vessels had been deposited there. Another burial, of four males whose heads and hands had been removed, may represent the ritual sacrifice of vassals or retainers, perhaps to accompany their leader in death. How and why these people were sacrificed remain mysteries, but there

may be parallels with rituals performed by the Natchez Indians of seventeenth- and eighteenth-century Mississippi, where individuals often volunteered to be sacrificed upon a leader's death to raise their own or their family's status.

In the early 1960s archaeologists working in the remains of a residential area outside the stockade, to the west of Monks Mound, discovered a number of postholes at regular intervals along the circumferences of at least five circles of different diameters. Four of these constructions are thought to have been complete circles, with 24, 36, 48, and 60 posts, respectively. The fifth seems only to have had 12 posts standing along a portion of the circle; if complete it would have had 72. Why all five circles were formed of multiples of twelve posts is unknown, though some scholars have speculated that the number may have been related to lunar cycles. Because of their resemblance to the famous English megalithic monument of Stonehenge, Cahokia's circles of standing wooden posts became known as "woodhenges." One, with a large center post and 48 evenly spaced perimeter posts, was 410 feet in diameter and dates to just after A.D. 1100. It is the most completely excavated of the woodhenges and has been reconstructed in its original location. From a platform atop the central post a priest might have observed sunrises along the eastern horizon aligning with particular perimeter posts at the equinoxes and solstices. On the equinoxes the sun would have risen over the front of Monks Mound, perhaps symbolizing the bond between earthly

ruler and solar deity. Other posts may have marked other important dates, such as harvest festivals or moon and star alignments.

Most of the work at Cahokia has dealt with the everyday life of its people, many of whom lived outside the stockade in small, rectangular one-family pole-and-thatch dwellings with walls covered with mats or sometimes daub. Compounds of these dwellings grouped around small courtyards may have housed kinfolk. Each compound also included buildings used for storage, food processing, and cooking. Excavation of refuse pits around the houses has revealed that the Cahokians ate mainly cultivated corn, squash, and pumpkin, as well as the seeds of cultivated sunflower, lambs' quarters, marsh elder, little barley, and may grass. This diet was supplemented by hundreds of different wild plants and mammals, birds, fish, reptiles, and amphibians.

Household groups were in turn arranged around larger communal plazas that may have defined neighborhoods. Other structures found in each neighborhood included small circular sweat lodges, where water sprinkled upon heated rocks produced steam for ritual cleansing of the body and spirit; community meeting lodges, granaries, and storage buildings; and possibly huts to which women would have been restricted during menstruation.

Ceremonial structures, special-use buildings, and the dwellings of the elite were generally larger versions of the basic house. Many of the elite must have lived within the stockade, but so far none of their residences has been excavated. Elite areas outside the wall include a plaza mound group to the west; another group to the east; Rattlesnake Mound (named for the snakes in the area) to the south; and the North Plaza and Kunnemann (named after a family that once owned the land) groups to the north. We do not know whether the elite living outside the stockade differed from those living inside, although relationship to the leader by lineage or clan affiliation may have been a factor.

Evidence for warfare at Cahokia remains largely circumstantial. A stockade was erected around the Sacred Precinct ca. A.D. 1150 and rebuilt at least three times during the next hundred years. The defensive nature of the wall is suggested by the regular spacing of bastions at 85-foot intervals along its length. From elevated platforms in these projections, warriors could launch arrows at

Archaeologists excavate Mound 72, whose ends point to the winter solstice sunrise and the summer solstice sunset.

East St. Louis Yields a Satellite Settlement

John E. Kelly

Once a thriving industrial city, East St. Louis had by the 1970s been abandoned by many of the companies that had long sustained it, becoming a wasteland of worn-out factories and vacant lots. Today a general cleanup is under way as part of a long-term effort to attract new business. In 1987 historical archaeologist Bonnie Gums and I began excavations in advance of the widening of Interstate 55–70, which runs through the city. Beneath one to two feet of historical trash we uncovered traces of earthen mounds and small wooden buildings—remains of a satellite of Cahokia. Many of the mounds had supported wooden temples and elite residences, but by the end of the twelfth century the site lay abandoned. One hundred years later Cahokia, too, was empty.

Some 45 mounds still stood in 1810 when the lawyer and journalist Henry Marie Brackenridge visited the site. Brackenridge climbed 40 feet to the top of the largest mound, about 200 by 300 feet at its base, later known as Cemetery Mound for the graveyard atop it used by settlers. From here he looked out over an ancient plaza and across the Mississippi to another group of mounds, remnants of another satellite settlement where St. Louis now stands. East St. Louis' mounds remained largely undisturbed for another 40 or 50 years until many were mined to build levees or demolished to make way for railroad tracks. When local dentist John Patrick mapped the site after the Civil War, only 15 mounds remained. A century later they had been buried beneath factories and Interstate 55–70.

In what was once an alley next to the highway we found remnants of small mounds. Soil stains atop them indicated where wooden structures had stood. Excavations nearby revealed the corner of a small, rectangular platform

Excavations in East St. Louis have yielded remains of a satellite settlement of Cahokia.

mound two feet tall linked to a long, low natural ridge. Stains left in the ground by wooden posts indicated that a structure atop this mound had been rebuilt at least ten times. Later a wooden post three feet in diameter had been driven ten feet into the top of the mound, a practice also known from two mounds at Cahokia, perhaps to mark the end of its life as a ritual structure. At its base were the remains of other large wooden buildings. These extended east toward Cemetery Mound, which had been demolished in 1870 by contractors using its earth in construction projects. On its site we uncovered remains of a low platform that had served as a foundation for Cemetery Mound. Atop this we found traces of a sequence of buildings and an unusual elliptical enclosure of square wooden posts unlike anything at Cahokia. On three occasions the platform had been renovated with a new coat of earth six to 12 inches thick, and each time the posts had been replaced. These rejuve-

nations of platform and ellipse may have symbolically linked earthly rituals of fertility, purification, and renewal with the cosmic cycles of the stars and planets.

Buildings and fences had marked the southeastern corner of the plaza, now along the highway shoulder. In a clayey depression, once a shallow marsh, we found broken ceramics, animal bones, and carbonized plant remains. Flood deposits lay above the trash, and atop these stood a twelfth-century mound. Although we only exposed one corner, several constructions and reconstructions were visible, perhaps symbols of renewal like the layers of soil applied to other mounds. Later small, tightly packed houses had been built on the mound's edges. Here we found celts, knives, hoes, and ceramic vessels, some largely intact. Just beyond the last group of structures, two parallel rows of postholes marked where a palisade, similar to that at Cahokia, had stood alongside a moat. The palisade stretched north, but we were unable to find its extension on the other side of the highway. We did, however, discover another area in which small huts had been built amid the remains of earlier, grander buildings about the same time as the first building of the stockade at Cahokia. Clearly something happened across the region that forced people to take refuge in crowded enclaves behind defensive walls, and eventually to desert the settlement altogether.

As East St. Louis' abandoned factories give way to new businesses, its residents can take pride in the emergence of an ancient city in their midst.

JOHN E. KELLY *is the American Bottom survey coordinator for the Illinois Transportation Archaeological Research Program at the University of Illinois, Urbana-Champaign.*

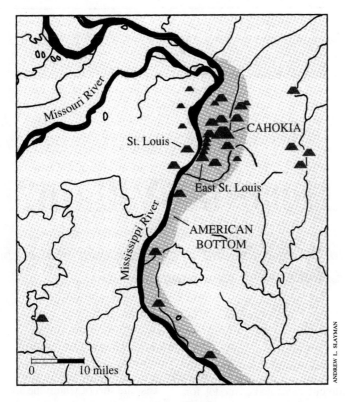

Map shows regional settlements with mounds; not included are scores of smaller villages without mounds.

attackers and protect the narrow L-shaped entryways between some bastions. The everyday function of the wall may have been more social, to isolate and protect the Sacred Precinct. Free access may have been limited to the elites who lived there, probably members of the ruling lineage, with the general population admitted only for ceremonial occasions or markets, or in times of war.

The stockade was a monumental construction, built at a great cost of time, labor, and materials. Much of my own fieldwork at Cahokia has involved excavations along the lines of the stockade east of Monks Mound. Based on that work I have estimated that builders would have used nearly 20,000 logs each time the wall was built, and conservatively 130,000 man-hours to fell, trim, debark, transport, and place the posts in excavated trenches. Construction of the stockade, itself designed to protect the city center, may have contributed to Cahokia's decline beginning ca. A.D. 1200. The demands for wood would have been staggering, even for such a renewable resource. Wood was also needed for fires and construction, and people from nearby communities

would have been competing for the same resources. The forests around Cahokia, and the animals and plants living there, would have been affected. Soil eroding from deforested slopes may have clogged streams and lakes with silt, increasing localized flooding of valuable farmland.

Beginning in the thirteenth century, a cooling of the climate and concomitant floods, droughts, and early and late frosts may have led to more crop failures and reduced yields. As food and other natural resources became scarce, economic disruption and social unrest could have become problems, perhaps even leading to wars between Cahokia and its neighbors. Eventually its political and economic power base eroded as nearby groups became more autonomous. Although increases in contagious diseases and nutritional deficiencies caused by a heavily corn-based diet may have affected Cahokia's population, more data are needed to determine the role of such health problems in Cahokia's decline.

Where the people of Cahokia went is one of the site's many mysteries. There is no evidence that the city was destroyed in a single catastrophe. It appears that its

people slowly dispersed, breaking up into smaller groups, some establishing new communities and perhaps new ways of life elsewhere. Many small Late Mississippian villages and hamlets have been found in the uplands surrounding the American Bottom and at higher elevations in the bottomlands themselves. Other people may have been absorbed into existing groups elsewhere, possibly where kinship ties already existed. In any event Cahokia was abandoned by 1400, and no positive ties have been established between the great city and any historical tribe.

Because of limited funding and the site's enormous size, only a small percentage of Cahokia has been excavated. Research continues through small field-school programs that include nondestructive remote-sensing projects using electromagnetic conductivity, electrical resistivity, and magnetometry, as well as soil coring. These efforts help locate manmade features underground, providing direction for future small-scale excavations. Detailed mapping projects, combined with soil-core studies, are helping identify the original forms of mounds that have suffered from heavy plowing or erosion. Unpublished data from earlier excavations are being analyzed or reexamined and the results published. In addition, salvage projects at contemporary sites in the American Bottom such as East St. Louis, are providing insight into Cahokia's interactions with these outlying sites.

Though I have worked at Cahokia for 25 years, I still marvel at what I see. It is an awesome site, massive and mysterious, especially in the predawn hours as I drive past the dark shapes of mounds poking through ground-hugging mist on my way to greet modern-day solstice and equinox observers at the reconstructed woodhenge. Cahokia, the largest prehistoric community north of Mexico, was one of the crowning achievements of the American Indians. Here they established a complex social, political, religious, and economic system and influenced a large portion of the midcontinent. Today, as then, the climb to the top of Monks Mound is breathtaking, literally as well as figuratively, and looking out from the summit one can only imagine what this truly extraordinary place must have been like.

Columbus—Hero or Villain?

Felipe Fernández-Armesto *weighs up the case for and against the man of the hour and finds a Columbus for all seasons.*

Felipe Fernández-Armesto

Felipe Fernández-Armesto is a member of The Faculty of Modern History of Oxford University.

This year, his statue in Barcelona exchanged symbolic rings with the Statue of Liberty in New York; meanwhile, the descendants of slaves and peons will burn his effigy. In a dream-painting by Salvador Dali, Columbus takes a great step for mankind, toga-clad and cross-bearing—while a sail in the middle distance drips with blood. The Columbus of tradition shares a single canvas with the Columbus of fashion, the culture-hero of the western world with the bogey who exploited his fellow-man and despoiled his environment. Both versions are false and, if historians had their way, the quincentennial celebrations ought to stimulate enough educational work and research to destroy them. Instead, the polemical atmosphere seems to be reinforcing *à parti pris* positions.

It is commonly said that the traditional Columbus myth—which awards him personal credit for anything good that ever came out of America since 1492—originated in the War of Independence, when the founding fathers, in search of an American hero, pitched on the Genoese weaver as the improbable progenitor of all-American virtues. Joel Barlow's poem, *The Vision of Columbus,* appeared in

1787. Columbus remained a model for nineteenth-century Americans, engaged in a project for taming their own wilderness. Washington Irving's perniciously influential *History of the Life and Voyages of Christopher Columbus* of 1828—which spread a lot of nonsense including the ever-popular folly that Columbus was derided for claiming that the world was round—appealed unashamedly to Americans' self-image as promoters of civilisation.

Yet aspects of the myth are much older—traceable to Columbus' own times and, to a large extent, to his own efforts. He was a loquacious and indefatigable self-publicist, who bored adversaries into submission and acquired a proverbial reputation for using more paper than Ptolemy. The image he projected was that of a providential agent, the divinely-elected 'messenger of a new heaven', chosen to bear the light of the gospel to unevangelised recesses of the earth—the parts which other explorers could not reach. His plan for an Atlantic crossing 'God revealed to me by His manifest hand'. Playing on his christian name, he called himself 'Christo ferens' and compiled a book of what he said were biblical prophecies of his own discoveries. Enough contemporaries were convinced by his gigantic self-esteem for him to become literally a legend in his own lifetime. To a leading astrological guru at the court of Spain, he was 'like a new apostle'. To a humanist from Italy who taught the would-be Renaissance men of Castile, he

was 'the sort of whom the ancients made gods'.

From his last years, his reputation dipped: writers were obliged to belittle him in the service of monarchs who were locked in legal conflict with Columbus' family over the level of reward he had earned. Yet his own self-perception was passed on to posterity by influential early books. Bartolomé de Las Casas—Columbus' editor and historian—professed a major role for himself in the apostolate of the New World and heartily endorsed Columbus' self-evaluation as an agent of God's purpose. Almost as important was the *Historie dell'Ammiraglio,* which claimed to be a work of filial piety and therefore presented Columbus as an unblemished hero, with an imputed pedigree to match his noble soul.

Claims to having access to a divine hot-line are by their nature unverifiable. Demonstrably false was the second element in Columbus' self-made myth: his image of tenacity in adversity—a sort of *Mein Kampf* version of his life, in which he waged a long, lone and unremitting struggle against the ignorance and derision of contemporaries. This theme has echoed through the historical tradition. That 'they all laughed at Christopher Columbus' has been confirmed by modern doggerel. Vast books have been wasted in an attempt to explain his mythical perseverance by ascribing to him 'secret' foreknowledge of the existence of America. Yet almost all the evidence which underlies it comes straight out of Columbus' own propaganda, according to which he was isolated, ignored, victimised and persecuted, usually for the numinous span of 'seven' years; then, after fulfilling his destiny, to the great profit of his detractors he was returned to a wilderness of contumely and neglect, unrewarded by the standard of his deserts, in a renewed trial of faith.

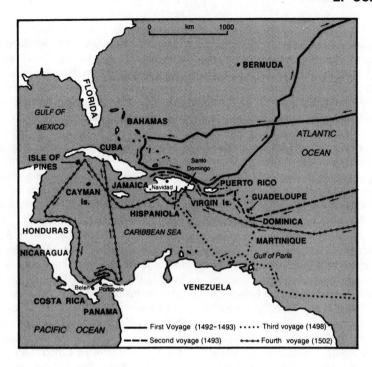

The image of Columbus-as-victim of the Spanish courts is explained by his relishing his own misfortunes as good copy and good theatre.

These passages of autobiography cannot be confirmed by the facts. The documented length of his quest for patronage was less than five years. Throughout that time he built up a powerful lobby of moral supporters at the Castilian court and financial backers in the business community of Seville. His own protestations of loneliness are usually qualified by an admission that he was unsupported 'save for' one or two individuals. When added together, these form an impressive cohort, which includes at least two archbishops, one court astrologer, two royal confessors, one royal treasurer and the queen herself. In his second supposed period of persecution, he was an honoured figure, loaded with titles, received at court, consulted by the crown and—depite his woebegone protestations of poverty—amply moneyed.

The explanation of the image of Columbus-as-victim must be sought in his character, not in his career. He was what would now be called a whinger, who relished his own misfortunes as good copy and good theatre. When he appeared at court in chains, or in a friar's habit, he was playing the role of victim for all it was worth. His written lamentations—which cover many folios of memoranda, supplications and personal letters—are thick with allusions to Jeremiah and Job. The notions of patience under suffering and of persecution for righteousness' sake fitted the hagiographical model on which much of his

self-promotional writing was based: a flash of divine enlightenment; a life transformed; consecration to a cause; unwavering fidelity in adversity.

The images of Columbus-as-hero and Columbus-as-villain has a long historical and literary tradition.

The most successful promotional literature is believed by its own propagators. To judge from his consistency, Columbus believed in his own image of himself. It is not surprising that most readers of his works, from Las Casas onwards, have been equally convinced. Columbus seems to have been predisposed to self-persuasion by saturation in the right literary models: saints, prophets and heroes of romance. Despite his astonishing record of achievement, and his impressive accumulation of earthly rewards, he had an implacable temperament which could never be satisfied, and an unremitting ambition which could never be assuaged. Such men always think themselves hard done by. His extraordinary powers of

persuasion—his communicator's skills which won backing for an impossible project in his lifetime—have continued to win followers of his legend ever since his death.

Like Columbus-the-hero, Columbus-the-villain is also an old character in a long literary tradition. Most of the denunciations of him written in his day have not survived but we can judge their tenor from surviving scraps. The usual complaints against servants of the Castilian crown in the period are made: he acted arbitrarily in the administration of justice; he exceeded his powers in enforcing his authority; he usurped royal rights by denying appeal to condemned rebels; he alienated crown property without authorisation; he deprived privileged colonists of offices or perquisites; he favoured his own family or friends; he lined his pockets at public expense. In the course of what seems to have been a general campaign against Genoese employees of the crown in the late 1490s, he was 'blamed as a foreigner' and accused of 'plotting to give the island of Hispaniola to the Genoese'.

Other allegations attacked his competence rather than his good faith, generally with justice. It was true, for instance, that he had selected an unhealthy and inconvenient site for the settlement of Hispaniola; that he had disastrously misjudged the natives' intentions in supposing them to be peaceful; and that his proceedings had so far alienated so many colonists that by the time of his removal in 1500 it was a missionary's opinion that the colony would never be at peace if he were allowed back. All these complaints reflect the priorities of Spaniards and the interests of the colonists and of the crown. There were, however, some charges against Columbus which anticipated the objections of modern detractors, who scrutinise his record from the natives' point of view, or who look at it from the perspective of fashionably ecological priorities.

First, there was the issue of Columbus' activities as a slaver. Coming from a Genoese background, Columbus never understood Spanish scruples about slavery, which had been characterised as an unnatural estate in the most influential medieval Spanish law-code, and which the monarchs distrusted as a form of intermediate lordship that reserved subjects from royal jurisdiction. Castilian practice was, perhaps, the most fastidious in Christendom. The propriety of slavery was acknowledged in the cases of captives of just war and offenders against natural law; but such cases were reviewed with rigour and in the royal courts, at least, decision-making tended to be biased in favour of the alleged slaves.

Shortly before the discovery of the New World, large numbers of Canary Islanders, enslaved by a conquistador on the pretext that they were 'rebels against their natural lord' had been pronounced free by a judicial inquiry commissioned by the crown, and liberated, in cases contested by their 'owners', in a series of trials. This does not seem, however, to have alerted Columbus to the risks of slap-happy slaving.

Although the ferocious Caribs of the Lesser Antilles were generally deemed to be lawful victims of enslavement (since the cannibalism imputed to them seemed an obvious offence against natural law) Columbus' trade was chiefly in Arawaks, who, by his own account, were rendered exempt by their amenability to evangelisation. By denying that the Arawaks were idolatrous, Columbus exonerated them of the one possible charge which might, in the terms of the time, be considered an 'unnatural' offence. Even when the monarchs reproved him and freed the Arawaks he sold, Columbus was astonishingly slow on the uptake. In a colony where the yield of other profitable products was disappointing, he traded slaves to allay the colony's grievous prob-

lems of supply. 'And although at present they die on shipment,' he continued, 'this will not always be the case, for the Negroes and Canary Islanders reacted in the same way at first'. In one respect, contemporary criticisms of the traffic differed from those made today. The friars and bureaucrats who denounced Columbus for it did so not because it was immoral, but because it was unlawful.

Slavery was only one among many ills which Columbus was said to have inflicted on the natives. The current myth incriminates him with 'genocide'. In the opinion of one *soi-disant* Native American spokesman, 'he makes Hitler look like a juvenile delinquent'. This sort of hype is doubly unhelpful: demonstrably false, it makes the horrors of the holocaust seem precedented and gives comfort to Nazi apologists by making 'genocide' an unshocking commonplace. Though he was often callous and usually incompetent in formulating indigenist policy, the destruction of the natives was as far removed from Columbus' thoughts as from his interests. The Indians, he acknowledged, were 'the wealth of this land'. Their conservation was an inescapable part of any rational policy for their exploitation. Without them the colony would have no labour resources. At a deeper level of Columbus' personal concerns, they were the great glory of his discovery: their evangelisation justified it and demonstrated its place in God's plans for the world, even if the material yield was disappointing to his patrons and backers. And Columbus had enough sense to realise that a large and contented native population was, as the monarchs said, their 'chief desire' for his colony. 'The principal thing which you must do,' he wrote to his first deputy,

is to take much care of the Indians, that no ill nor harm may be done them, nor anything taken from them against their will, but rather that they be honoured and feel secure and so should have no cause to rebel.

Though no contemporary was so foolish as to accuse Columbus of wilfully exterminating Indians, it was widely realised that his injunctions were often honoured in the breach and that his own administrative regulations sometimes caused the natives harm. The missionaries almost unanimously regarded him as an obstacle to their work, though the only specific crime against the natives to survive among their memoranda—that

'he took their women and all their property'—is otherwise undocumented. The imposition of forced labour and of unrealistic levels of tribute were disastrous policies, which diverted manpower from food-growing and intensified the 'culture-shock' under which indigenous society reeled and tottered, though Columbus claimed they were expedients to which he was driven by economic necessity.

Columbus was a man of extraordinary vision with a defiant attitude to what was possible; he could not anticipate the consequences of his discovery.

Some contemporaries also condemned the sanguinary excesses of his and his brother's punitive campaigns in the interior of Hispaniola in 1495–96. It should be said in Columbus' defence, however, that he claimed to see his own part as an almost bloodless pacification and that the 50,000 deaths ascribed to these campaigns in the earliest surviving account were caused, according to the same source, chiefly by the Indians' scorched-earth strategy. The outcome was horrible enough, but Columbus' treatment of the Indians inflicted catastrophe on them rather by mistakes than by crimes. In general, he was reluctant to chastise them—refusing, for instance, to take punitive measures over the massacre of the first garrison of Hispaniola; and he tried to take seriously the monarchs' rather impractical command to 'win them by love'.

It would be absurd to look for environmental sensitivity of a late twentieth-century kind in Columbus' earliest critics. Yet the accusation of over-exploitation of the New World environment, which is at the heart of the current, ecologically-conscious anti-Columbus mood, was also made before the fifteenth century was quite over. According to the first missionaries, members of Columbus' family were 'robbing and destroying the land' in their greed for gold. Though he declined to accept personal responsibility, Columbus detected a similar problem when he denounced his fellow-colonists' exploitative attitude: unmarried men, with no stake in the success of the colony and no intention of permanent residence, should be excluded, he thought. They merely mulcted the island for what they could get before rushing home to Castile.

The danger of deforestation from the demand for dyestuffs, building materials and fuel was quickly recognised. The diversion of labour from agriculture to gold-panning aroused friars' moral indignation. The usefulness of many products of the indigenous agronomy was praised by Columbus and documented by the earliest students of the pharmacopoeia and florilegium of the New World. The assumption that there was an ecological 'balance' to be disturbed at hazard was, of course, impossible. On the contrary, everyone who arrived from the Old World assumed that the natural resources had to be supplemented with imported products to provide a balanced diet, a civilised environment and resources for trade. The modifications made by Columbus and his successors were intended, from their point of view, to improve, not to destroy. They introduced sources of protein—like livestock; comforts of home—like wheat and grapes; and potential exports—like sugar, whether these changes were really disastrous is hard to judge dispassionately. The loss of population in the early colonial period was probably due to other causes. In the long run, colonial Hispaniola proved able to maintain a large population and a spectacular material culture.

Since it was first broached in Columbus' day, the debate about the morality of the colonisation of the New World has had three intense periods: in the sixteenth century, when the issues of the justice of the Spanish presence and the iniquity of maltreatment of the natives were raised by religious critics and foreign opportunists; in the late eighteenth century, when Rousseau and Dr Johnson agreed in preferring the uncorrupted wilderness which was thought to have preceded colonisation; and in our own day. Until recently, Columbus managed largely to avoid implication in the sins of his successors. Las Casas revered him, and pitied, rather than censured, the imperfections of his attitude to the natives. Eighteenth-century sentimentalists regretted the colonial experience as a whole, generally without blaming Columbus for it. This was fair enough. Columbus' own model of colonial society seems to have derived from Genoese precedents: the trading factory, merchant quarter and family firm. The idea of a 'total' colony, with a population and environment revolutionised by the impact and image of the metropolis, seems to have been imposed on him by his Castilian masters. In making him personally responsible for everything which followed—*post hunc ergo propter hunc*—his modern critics have followed a convention inaugurated by admirers, who credited Columbus with much that [h]as nothing to do with him—including, most absurdly of all—the culture of the present United States. Columbus never touched what was to become US territory except in Puerto Rico and the Virgin Islands. The values which define the 'American ideal'—personal liberty, individualism, freedom of conscience, equality of opportunity and representative democracy—would have meant nothing to him.

Columbus deserves the credit or blame only for what he actually did: which was to discover a route that permanently linked the shores of the Atlantic and to contribute—more signally, perhaps, than any other individual—to the long process by which once sundered peoples of the world were brought together in a single network of communications, which exposed them to the perils and benefits of mutual contagion and exchange. Whether or not one regards this as meritorious achievement, there was a genuine touch of heroism in it—both in the scale of its effects and in the boldness which inspired it. There had been many attempts to cross the Atlantic in central latitudes, but all—as far as we know—failed because the explorers clung to the zone of westerly winds in an attempt to secure a passage home. Columbus was the first to succeed precisely because he had the courage to sail with the wind at his back.

Historians, it is often said, have no business making moral judgements at all. The philosophy of the nursery-school assembly, in which role-models and culprits are paraded for praise or reproof seems nowadays to belong to a hopelessly antiquated sort of history, for which the reality of the past mattered less than the lessons for the present and the future. A great part of the historian's art is now held to consist in what the examiners call 'empathy'—the ability to see the past with the eyes, and to re-construct the feelings, of those who took part in it. If value judgements are made at all, they ought at least to be controlled by certain essential disciplines. First, they must be consistent with the facts: it is unhelpful to accuse of 'genocide', for instance, a colonial administrator who was anxious for the preservation of the native labour force. Secondly, they should be made in the context of the value-system of the society scrutinised, at the time concerned. It would be impertinent to expect Columbus to regard slavery as immoral, or to uphold the equality of all peoples. Conquistadors and colonists are as entitled to be judged from the perspective of moral relativism as are the cannibals and human-sacrificers of the indigenous past. Thirdly, moral judgements should be expressed in language tempered by respect for the proper meanings of words. Loose talk of 'genocide' twists a spiral to verbal hype. Useful distinctions are obliterated; our awareness of the real cases, when they occur, is dulled.

Finally, when we presume to judge someone from a long time ago, we should take into account the practical constraints under which they had to operate, and the limited mental horizons by which they were enclosed. Columbus was in some ways a man of extraordinary vision with a defiant attitude to the art of the possible. Yet he could not anticipate the consequences of his discovery or of the colonial enterprise confided to him. Five hundred years further on, with all our advantages of hindsight, we can only boast a handful of 'successful' colonial experiments—in the United States, Siberia, Australia and New Zealand—in all of which the indigenous populations have been exterminated or swamped. The Spanish empire founded by Columbus was strictly unprecedented and, in crucial respects, has never been paralleled. The problems of regulating such vast dominions, with so many inhabitants, so far away, and with so few resources, were unforeseeable and proved unmanageable. Never had so many people been conquered by culture-shock or their immune-systems invaded by irresistible disease. Never before had such a challenging environment been so suddenly transformed in an alien image. In these circumstances, it would be unreasonable to expect Columbus' creation to work well. Like Dr Johnson's dog, it deserves some applause for having performed at all.

So which was Columbus: hero or villain? The answer is that he *was* neither but has *become* both. The real Columbus was a mixture of virtues and vices like the rest of us, not conspicuously good or just, but generally well-intentioned, who grappled creditably with intractable problems. Heroism and villainy are not, however, objective qualities. They exist only in the eye of the beholder.

In images of Columbus, they are now firmly impressed on the retinas of the upholders of rival legends and will never be expunged. Myths are versions of the past which people believe in for irrational motives—usually because they feel good or find their prejudices confirmed. To liberal or ecologically conscious intellectuals, for instance, who treasure their feelings of superiority over their predecessors, moral indignation with Columbus is too precious to discard. Kinship with a culture-hero is too profound a part of many Americans' sense of identity to be easily excised.

Thus Columbus-the-hero and Columbus-the-villain live on, mutually sustained by the passion which continuing controversy imparts to their supporters. No argument can dispel them, however convincing; no evidence, however compelling. They have eclipsed the real Columbus and, judged by their effects, have outstripped him in importance. For one of the sad lessons historians learn is that history is influenced less by the facts as they happen than by the falsehoods men believe.

FOR FURTHER READING:

J. H. Elliott, *The Old World and the New* (Cambridge University Press, 1970); A. W. Crosby, *Columbian Exchange: Biological and Cultural Consequences of 1492* (Greenwood, 1972); J. Larner 'The Certainty of Columbus', *History*, lxxiii (1987); F. Fernández-Armesto, *Columbus* (Oxford University Press, 1991).

Laboring in the Fields of the Lord

The Franciscan missions of seventeenth-century Florida enabled Spain to harness the energies of tens of thousands of native people.

Jerald T. Milanich

Jerald T. Milanich is curator of archaeology in the department of anthropology at the Florida Museum of Natural History, Gainesville.

Beginning in the 1590s Franciscan friars established dozens of missions in what is today southern Georgia and northern Florida, but by the time Spain relinquished its Florida colony to Great Britain in 1763 only two missions remained. Spain regained control of the colony in 1783, only to cede it to the United States 38 years later. With the Spaniards

This quartz pendant, nearly three inches long, was found at San Luís, a late seventeenth-century Apalachee mission.

FLORIDA DIVISION OF HISTORICAL RESOURCES

gone, memories of their missions faded. Their wood-and-thatch buildings, like the native peoples they had served, simply disappeared from the landscape.

In the late 1940s archaeologists began searching for the north Florida missions. By the end of the 1970s fieldwork and historical research had, it was thought, closed the book on the history of the settlements. My own research and that of my colleagues has reopened that book, adding new chapters to the history of the Spanish colony.

The missions of La Florida were an integral part of Pedro Menéndez de Avilés' master plan for his colony, whose first town, St. Augustine, was established in 1565. By converting the native peoples to Catholicism, as required by contract between him and his sovereign, Philip II, Menéndez hoped to insure loyal, obedient subjects. He initially arranged for Jesuit friars to establish a handful of missions along the Atlantic and Gulf coasts. The Jesuits, however, failed to build support among the native peoples and returned to Spain in 1572. They were replaced by Franciscans subsidized by the Spanish Crown. At first the hardships of mission work—the rigors of travel, climate, and lack of supplies—sent them packing as well. By 1592 only two friars and one lay brother remained, but three years later 12 new friars arrived, and missionary efforts began in earnest. The friars were assigned to *doctrinas,* missions with churches where native people were instructed in religious doctrine.

The first Franciscan missions were established along the Atlantic coast, from St. Augustine north to Santa Elena

J.T. MILANICH

This Guale Indian grasping a cross was interred in a shallow grave on the floor of the church at mission Santa Catalina on Amelia Island, Florida. The piety of the Christian Indians was, in the eyes of the mission friars, extraordinary.

on Parris Island, South Carolina. In 1587, however, raids by unfriendly Indians forced the abandonment of Santa Elena, and the chain of coastal missions serving the Timucuas and their northern neighbors, the Guale, stopped just short of present-day South Carolina. During the next 35 years a second chain of missions was established on the *camino real,* or royal road, that led westward about 350 miles from St. Augustine through the provinces of Timucua and Apalachee in northwestern Florida. Over time, these missions were moved or aban-

FLORIDA DIVISION OF HISTORICAL RESOURCES

In this pencil drawing by Edward Jonas, the mission church at San Luís, in modern Tallahassee, Florida, faces a central plaza. Size and construction details—the walls, thatched roof, position of the front door, and presence of two bells—are based on data from excavations by Bonnie McEwan, an archaeologist with the San Luís project, Florida Division of Historic Resources.

doned and new ones founded. Historian John Hann of the Florida Bureau of Archaeological Research estimates that as many as 140 existed at one time or another.

After the British settled Charleston in 1670—in territory that had once been under Spanish control—they began to challenge Spain's hold on La Florida. Through its Carolinian colonists, the British began to chip away at the Spanish presence. One effective way was to destroy the Franciscan missions. In the 1680s Carolinian militia and their native allies raided several missions in north Florida and the Georgia coast. Timucuas and Guale were captured and taken to Charleston where they were sold into slavery to work plantations in the Carolinas and the West Indies. The raids on the Georgia coastal missions grew so intense that by the late 1680s all of the missions north of Amelia Island were abandoned.

In 1702 and 1704 Carolinian raids on the Apalachee and Timucuan missions in northern Florida effectively destroyed the mission system west of the St. Johns River. Churches were burned and their contents smashed. Villagers were scattered, tortured, and killed. Nearly 5,000 Indians were sold into slavery, while others fled west to the Gulf of Mexico. Of some 12,000 original mission Indians fewer than 1,000 remained, and they fled to refugee villages that grew up around St. Augustine. When Spain turned La Florida over to Britain in 1763, only 63 Christian Indians remained, and the retreating Spanish took them to Cuba.

By the early 1980s archaeologists had found the remains of perhaps a dozen missions. In doing so, they had relied on an important document written by a seventeenth-century bishop of Cuba, Gabriel Díaz Vara Calderón. The bishop had vis-

ited La Florida from 1674 to 1675 to witness firsthand what the Franciscan friars had accomplished. His report lists 24 missions along the camino real and provides the distances between them:

Ten leagues [1 league = 3.5 miles] from the city of Saint Augustine, on the bank of the river Corrientes [the St. Johns], is the village and mission of San Diego de Salamototo. It [the river] is very turbulent and almost a league and a half in width. From there to the village and mission of Santa Fe there are some 20 uninhabited leagues. Santa Fe is the principal mission of this province. Off to the side [from Santa Fe] toward the southern border, at a distance of 3 leagues, is the deserted mission and village of San Francisco. Twelve leagues from Santa Fe is the mission of Santa Catalina, with Ajohica 3 leagues

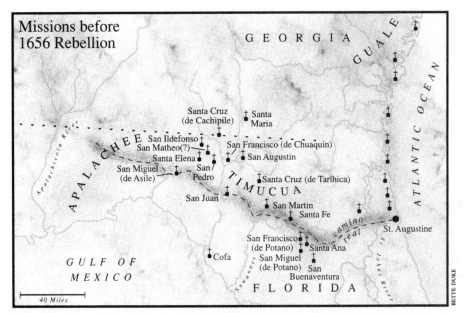

Beginning in 1595 Franciscan missions were built along the Atlantic coast from St. Augustine to just short of present-day South Carolina. In 1606 a second chain of missions was started north and south of the camino real, or royal road, that led westward about 350 miles from St. Augustine through the provinces of Timucua and Apalachee in northwestern Florida.

northern Florida (see ARCHAEOLOGY, May/June 1989). My field crews did indeed find de Soto-era native villages, but they also discovered two seventeenth-century Spanish missions, both north of the camino real. Again, neither was listed by Bishop Calderón. The good news was that we had an excellent idea of de Soto's route; the bad news was that something was terribly wrong with our understanding of the history and geography of the missions.

I needed dates for the three mysterious sites. One way to get them was to study Spanish majolica pottery, a tin-glazed tableware that is common at Spanish colonial sites in the Americas and abundant at all three missions. Majolicas can be divided into types based on differences in vessel shapes, colors of glazes, and glazed designs. Because some types were popular mainly before ca. 1650 and others mainly after that date, we can date collections to the early or late seventeenth century. Analysis of majolicas from the mystery missions showed that all three were occupied only before 1650. Had something occurred in the mid-seventeenth century that led to their abandonment two decades before Bishop Calderón's visit?

Since the 1930s historians have known of Spanish accounts documenting a 1656 Indian rebellion at the Timucuan missions. The governor of Spanish

away and Santa Cruz de Tarihica 2. Seven leagues away, on the bank of the large river Guacara [the Suwannee], is the mission of San Juan of the same name. Ten [further on] is that of San Pedro de Potohiriba, 2 that of Santa Helena de Machaba, 4, that of San Matheo, 2, that of San Miguel de Asyle, last in this . . . province.

What made this guide especially valuable was the discovery and publication in 1938 of a map of the camino real drawn by a British surveyor in 1778, when the road was still a major route across northern Florida. Some names of Spanish missions appear on the map. It seemed that it would only be a matter of time until we had discovered all of the sites.

The first clue that the accepted history of the missions needed a major overhaul came in 1976. Excavating a seventeenth-century Spanish-Indian site in north Florida, I had uncovered the burnt remains of a small wooden church and an earth-floored friars' quarters, both adjacent to a Timucuan village. The evidence suggested that the site was one of the missions along the camino real. But which mission was it? Its position on the road did not match any of the locations mentioned in Bishop Calderón's account.

It was too far east to be mission San Juan and too far west to be Santa Cruz.

More questions about the geography of the missions surfaced in the late 1980s when I was looking for archaeological traces of the Spanish conquistador Hernando de Soto's 1539 march across

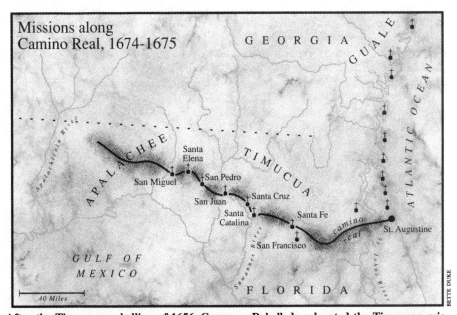

After the Timucuan rebellion of 1656, Governor Rebolledo relocated the Timucuan missions along the camino real, roughly a day's travel apart, where they functioned as way stations between Apalachee province and St. Augustine. The relocation also reflected the demographic devastation caused by epidemics, especially smallpox and measles.

These native ceramics from Apalachee are typical of the mission period. Each Indian culture had its own style of pottery.

Villagers were paid in glass beads and trinkets, which were exchanged for hides and furs for trading back to the Spanish.

Florida, Diego de Rebolledo, sent troops to put down the rebellion. Ten native leaders were rounded up and hanged. The governor was subsequently charged with having displayed great cruelty and was slated to answer for his actions, but he died before a hearing could be held.

What was not known until the early 1990s was that an investigation took place after Rebolledo's death. In the Archivo General de Indias in Seville, Spain, John Worth, then a doctoral student at the University of Florida, found lengthy testimony taken at the hearing and related documents that described the rebellion and its aftermath. They also rewrote what we had known abort mission geography.

The documents recount how the rebellion began in the spring of 1656, when Lúcas Menéndez, one of the major chiefs in Timucua, and other chiefs defied Governor Rebolledo's orders. Hear-

ing a report that the British were planning a raid on St. Augustine, the governor had commanded the chiefs of Apalachee and Timucua to assemble 500 men and march to St. Augustine. The Indians were ordered to carry food for a stay of at least a month. Because construction of fortifications was still under way and the number of soldiers stationed in the colony was well below its full complement, the town was poorly prepared to withstand an attack. The governor wanted to reinforce its defenses with Indian warriors.

But the chiefs of Timucua refused to go, a decision that grew out of dissatisfaction with treatment they had received from the governor on previous visits to St. Augustine. Rebolledo had not properly feasted the chiefs, nor had he given them gifts, as was customary. The chiefs also refused to carry their own food and

supplies or to provide warriors to defend the town without compensation. The power of native leaders in Timucua had already been threatened by nearly a century of Spanish colonization, and Rebolledo's 1656 order was seen by the Timucuan chiefs as demeaning and an attempt to undercut their authority.

Chief Lúcas Menéndez told his followers and the other chiefs to kill Spaniards, though not the mission friars. The first deaths occurred at San Miguel and San Pedro in western Timucua. At each site a Spanish soldier, part of the small military presence in the province, was slain. A Spanish servant and a Mexican Indian who by chance had camped in Timucua while traveling the camino real were the next to die. Warriors led by Lúcas Menéndez then raided a Spanish cattle ranch near modern Gainesville, killing a third Spanish soldier and two African

Painting by John LoCastro depicts the Apalachee Indian council house at San Luís. The 120-foot diameter building was at one end of a central plaza which served as a field for a game in which teams tried to kick a ball into an eagle-nest target atop a pole.

J.T. MILANICH

Remains of 59 villagers buried in a corner of Amelia Island's Santa Catalina church attest the decimation of native people. A 1659 report states that 10,000 people died in one measles epidemic.

workers. All across northern Florida Timucuas abandoned their missions.

Knowing the Spanish would retaliate, some of the rebellious Timucuas gathered at mission Santa Elena, which they converted into a palisaded fort. Rebolledo sent 60 Spanish infantry and several hundred Apalachee Indians to capture the rebels. After extended negotiations the Timucuas came out. Their leaders were seized along with several Timucuas who had participated in the murders. One man confessed almost immediately and was executed, probably by hanging. Other prisoners were taken to Apalachee and held while word was sent to the governor.

In late November Rebolledo and a small entourage marched from St. Augustine, capturing several chiefs along the way. A trial was held in Apalachee. Ten of the prisoners were sentenced to forced labor in St. Augustine, while ten others, most of whom were chiefs, were sentenced to death. Rebolledo ordered the men hanged at various places along the camino real as grim reminders of the power of the Spaniards and the fate that awaited those who rebelled against the Crown.

Rebolledo also seized the opportunity to reorganize the province and its missions so they would better serve the needs of the colony and its Spanish overlords. Missions were relocated roughly a day's travel apart so they could function as way stations between Apalachee prov-

ince and St. Augustine. This arrangement of missions was what Bishop Calderón had observed in 1674 and 1675. That explained two of our three mystery sites. One of the northern two was the pre-1656 mission of Santa Cruz, which was moved south to the camino real after the rebellion. The site we had excavated in 1976 was the mission of San Juan which, after the rebellion, was moved six miles west to a point on the camino real that intersected the Suwannee River. The identity of our third mission remains a mystery, although it seems certain it too was abandoned after the rebellion.

Worth's research led us to believe there were two mission systems in Timucua, one before and one after 1656. What made it necessary for the governor to reorganize the missions? To answer that question we began to reexamine other Spanish documents discovered by Hann and Worth. They indicated that by 1656 epidemics had devastated the population of Timucua province. Although the occurrence of epidemics—especially smallpox and measles—had long been recognized by scholars, we had no inkling that demographic devastation had occurred so quickly in Timucua. The Spanish sources indicate that by the 1620s Timucuan mission villages had been hard hit, some so reduced in population that their chiefs could not send men to St. Augustine to provide labor

for the Spaniards. The documents also indicate that epidemics struck soon after the first missions were founded. In 1595 an unknown epidemic hit the coastal missions. Between 1612 and late 1616 epidemics killed as many as 10,000 mission Indians. Another epidemic struck in 1649–1650, and in 1655 smallpox ravaged Timucua and Guale. In 1657, following the rebellion, Governor Rebolledo wrote that the Indians of Guale and Timucua were few in number "because they have been wiped out with the sickness of the plague [*peste*] and smallpox which have overtaken them in the past years." Two years later a new governor, Francisco de Corcoles y Martínez, reported that 10,000 mission Indians had died in a measles epidemic.

The decimation of mission Indians is grimly reflected in the archaeological record. The remains of hundreds of native villagers have been found in shallow graves under the floors of more than ten mission churches excavated in Apalachee, Guale, and Timucua. At some churches bodies were found stacked in layers three deep. Many older burials had been pushed aside to make room for new ones. The depopulation of Timucua is what apparently led Rebolledo to convert the missions into way stations on the camino real. With its larger native population, Apalachee province would be the focus of Spanish farming and ranching efforts, the colony's breadbasket, and the main source of labor.

The severity of the epidemics and the geographical reorganization of the Timucuan missions has provided a basis for reinterpreting the role of the missions in Spanish Florida. Now more than ever we see that missions and colonization were integrally related. Christianized Indians enabled the colony to function. In return for providing religious education for native people, the Spanish could harness them as workers in support of colonial interests. Religious instruction converted villagers to Catholicism and made them obedient, productive members of Spain's empire. One should not underestimate the hold the new beliefs and customs had on these people. The piety of converted Indians was, even in the eyes of the friars, extraordinary. In 1614 Father Francisco Pareja, a Franciscan friar at mission San Juan (north of modern-day Jacksonville), described the intensity of that devotion:

T. DE BRY, BREVIS NARRATIO EORUM QUAE IN FLORIDA AMERICAE, 1591

Sick and dying Timucuas are depicted in this sixteenth-century etching by the Flemish engraver Theodor de Bry.

Among them are Indian men who have sufficient knowledge to give instructions while there are Indian women who catechize other Indian women, preparing them for the reception of Christianity. They assist at Masses of obligation on Sundays and feastdays in which they take part and sing; in some districts that have their confraternities and the procession of Holy Thursday, and from the mission stations they come to the principal mission to hear the Salve [the Salve Regina] which is sung on Saturdays. . . . They take holy water and recite their prayers in the morning and evening. They come together in the community house to teach one another singing and reading. . . . Do they confess as Christians? I answer yes. . . . Many persons are found, men and women, who confess and who receive [Holy Communion] with tears, and who show up advantageously with many Spaniards. And I shall make bold and say and sustain my contention by what I have learned by experience that with regard to the myster-ies of the faith, many of them answer better than the Spaniards.

Father Pareja also noted the effectiveness of conversion, writing that Catholicism had vanquished many of the native superstitions so effectively that the mission Indians "do not even remember them . . . so much so that the younger generation which has been nourished by the milk of the Gospel derides and laughs at some old men and women. . . ."

Faith was an efficient tool for organizing native people who, now laboring in the fields of the Lord, performed a variety of tasks for the Spaniards. Adult males carried corn from Apalachee and Timucua to the Gulf Coast, where it was shipped to St. Augustine or exported to Cuba or other nearby Spanish colonies. Villagers also drove cattle over the camino real to St. Augustine. Supplies for the missions—lamp and cooking oil for the friars and construction hardware for repairing buildings—were shouldered from St. Augustine back to the mis-sions. Indians tended fields and harvested crops for the soldiers stationed at St. Augustine. They helped build forts and other fortifications; they cut and transported logs used for lumber; and they quarried coquina stone on Anastasia Island to build the town gates and the massive castillo that still dominates St. Augustine's waterfront. As many as 300 Christian Indians were involved in the construction of the castillo when it was begun in the 1670s.

Native laborers were paid in hawks' bells, knives, colorful glass beads, pieces of sheet brass, razors, cloth, and scissors. Some of these items were then traded to non-mission Indians to the north who did not have access to the much sought-after European imports. Mission Indians received deer hides and, perhaps, furs in exchange. These could be traded back to the Spaniards for more trinkets. The Spaniards, in turn, exported these hides, which were far more valuable than the trinkets they handed out.

Pedro Menéndez de Avilés, founder of La Florida, believed converting natives to Catholicism would ensure loyal subjects.

Spanish ceramics, made throughout the seventeenth century, are useful in dating mission sites across northern Florida.

Native people also labored for the Spaniards in the mission provinces. They maintained the camino real, clearing brush, repairing creek crossings, and even building bridges. Where roads crossed rivers too deep to ford, they operated ferries, probably little more than rafts or canoes lashed together. At the missions men, women, and children labored in support of the friars. They cooked, tended gardens, looked after farm animals, did household chores, hunted and fished, collected firewood, made charcoal, carried burdens, and paddled canoes when the friars traveled. Cornfields were planted, hoed, and harvested; the corn husked, shelled, ground into meal, and stored. Any surplus was sold by the friars to St. Augustine when times were hard in town,

a clever way to generate credit against which Franciscans, who had taken vows of poverty, could charge items needed to maintain the missions. In Spanish Florida corn was money, whether it was taken to St. Augustine for use there or shipped out of the colony. Mission Indians were encouraged to increase production, aided by iron tools such as the hoes found at several missions. Increased production of corn for export resulted in huge numbers of ears being shelled, producing an equally large number of cobs that were used as fuel. Hundreds of charred corncobs have been found at every Spanish mission excavated thus far.

Lifetimes of labor in support of the Spaniards are reflected in bioanthropological analyses of the mission Indians

themselves. The native workers enjoyed better living conditions than did their Precolumbian ancestors, but the stresses of labor resulted in more broken bones and injuries. Was this a benign system that improved the lot of the native people of Apalachee, Guale, and Timucua? Hardly. Although individual friars went to La Florida to bring a better life to the native people, in reality the missions provided the means for compelling the Indians to serve the Spanish Empire. In the end the process proved catastrophic. Tens of thousands of Apalachee, Guale, and Timucuas were destroyed by disease and war. By the time the British took over the territory, they had ceased to exist. Archaeology and history are now giving voice to that forgotten past.

Bearing the Burden?
Puritan Wives

Obedience, modesty, taciturnity—all hallmarks of the archetypal 'good woman' in colonial New England. But did suffering in silence invert tradition and give the weaker sex a new moral authority in the community? Martha Saxton investigates, in the first piece from a mini series examining women's social experience in the New world.

Martha Saxton

Martha Saxton teaches Colonial History at Columbia University. She is author of Louisa May Alcott *(Andre Deutsch, 1977) and is currently working on a study of American women's moral standards—those prescribed for them and those they fashioned for themselves.*

Seventeenth-century American Puritans subordinated female to male, wife to husband, and mother to father, insisting on obedience, modesty, and taciturnity for women. They justified this arrangement by emphasising woman's descent from Eve and her innate irrationality, both of which made her more vulnerable to error and corruption than man. Because of this she was to view her husband as God's representative in the family. He would mediate her religious existence and direct her temporal one. She would produce children and care for them, but he would have the ultimate authority over them.

At the same time, the experience of Puritans of both sexes in the second half of the seventeenth century undermined this clearly defined system of authority in which the allocation of secular power flowed from a presumed moral and spiritual hierarchy. After 1660, women began outnumbering men in the churches, and by the end of the century the numerical difference was sufficient to prompt Cotton Mather to attempt to account for the demonstrated female proclivity for spirituality. Mather ascribed enhanced female religiosity precisely to that subordination that Puritan men insisted upon as well as mothers' suffering during childbirth.

Long before Mather published his conclusions at the end of the seventeenth century, other Puritan men anticipated his thinking about female virtue, and many identified its sources in female suffering. Men praised the patient endurance of wives with abusive husbands. Others granted to childbirth pain the power to enhance goodness. Some saw the sacrifices of mothering, rather than childbirth *per se,* as a source of virtue and testified to the moral significance of their mothers in the conduct of their lives. And still others simply acknowledged their mothers, wives, or other female relatives as inspirational or spiritually influential to them.

In the Puritan world then, women could and did earn respect for their moral stature in the family, and this was meaningful to women deprived of public recognition in a society run by men. It would be an important heritage to women of a later era. Pious women would pass on the idea that their principled expressions of conscience could shape morally, both family and society.

Before looking at the way women achieved moral authority, let us look at how Puritan men elaborated beliefs about the propriety of subordinating women to men. John Winthrop, Governor of Massachusetts, who was happily married to three submissive women, writing in the mid-seventeenth century put the ideal case:

> A true wife accounts her subjection her honor and freedom and would not think her condition safe and free but in her subjection to her husband's authority. Such is the liberty of the church under the authority of Christ, her king and husband; his yoke is so easy and sweet to her as a bride's ornaments; and if through forwardness or wantonness, etc., she shakes it off at any time, she is at no rest in her spirit until she take it up again; and whether her lord smiles upon her and embraceth her in his arms, or whether he frowns and rebukes her, or smites her, she comprehends the sweetness of his love in all, and is refreshed, and instructed by every such dispensation of his authority over her.

While not all American Puritans saw female obedience in such a cheerful light as Winthrop did, all agreed that it was essential to marital satisfaction and should exist regardless of the husband's comportment. John Cotton compared wifely obedience to the excellence and inevitability of the universe, the air we breathe, and the clouds that shower rain upon the earth. Benjamin Wadsworth, in a book published in 1712, wrote that a woman should 'reverence' her husband, as the bible commanded. He was God's representative in the family, and even if he should 'pass the bounds of wisdom and kindness; yet must not she shake off the bond of submission but must bear patiently the burden, which God hath laid upon the daughters of Eve'. And Cotton Mather, writing before his final, tempestuous marriage to Lydia Lee George would give these words a wistful ring, insisted that though the husband be 'ever so much a Churl, yet she treats him considerately'.

An important facet of this unanimous male insistence on female submission was the envy and fascination Puritan men felt for womanly meekness and obedience. Salvation demanded that men, as well as women, submit to God's will in all things. For women, submission to God's will and the will of the men around them made their lives, ideally, a continuum of obedience.

Men, however, enjoyed considerable social power during their lifetime as husbands and, depending upon their status, as community leaders. Submission and the self-suppression that it required, was, therefore, a more prickly and intractable issue for men than for women. Furthermore, as husbands, men determined how heavily or lightly the yoke of marriage would rest on their wives' shoulders. Men's direct responsibility for the suffering that their domination might cause women was likely to make them particularly alive to the issue.

Cotton Mather, who had openly linked woman's tendency to spiritual excellence with her subordination and suffering, wrote 'But if thou hast an Husband that will do so, [beat his wife] bear it patiently; and know thou shalt have—Rewards—hereafter for it, as well as *Praises* here...'. And Puritan men since the settlement of Plymouth had praised women for remaining uncomplainingly with husbands who were violent and/or unfaithful. Mrs Lyford, of Plymouth endured—and sometimes witnessed—her husband's sexual escapades for years in silence. Eventually, she testified against him. But, wrote the governor of the colony, William Bradford, approvingly, 'being a grave matron, and of good carriage... spoke of those things out of the sorrow of her harte, sparingly'.

The wife of Jared Davis submitted to years of her husband's cruelty, drunkenness, lies, scandalous behaviour, and indolence. He had, according to John Winthrop, neither compassion nor humanity toward his wife, insisted on sex with her when she was pregnant (which

Puritans regarded as dangerous) and did not provide for her. The governor admired Mrs Davis who, under all these provocations, continued to try to help her husband. As Winthrop had written elsewhere, Mrs Davis was able to find in her husband's blows, God's love and correction. Winthrop and Bradford believed that the Christlike acceptance of lengthy, undeserved abuse endowed women with a unique moral vantage point from which they might even venture to criticise their victimisers.

Men were also fascinated by—and implicated in—the crisis of child labour and delivery, which combined submission to physical suffering as well as the more difficult task: resignation to the possibility of death. Husbands were awed by their wives' apparent conquest of mortal fear. Puritans believed that pregnancy rendered women more fearful than usual. The Reverend Peter Thacher wrote in his diary in February 1680, that his wife had fallen on a chair, and was 'soe frighted with it that shee had like to have fainted away' because she feared she had hurt the child in her womb. When normally timid women, rendered even more so by pregnancy, triumphed over the terror of death, they reassured the whole community of its ability to conquer its fear of the hereafter through submission to God. As Mather said at the funeral of seventeen-year-old Mrs Rebeckah Burnel in 1724:

But when it pleases Him, to take *children*, and those of that *Sex* which *Fear* is most incident and enslaving to; and make such *Babes and Sucklings* to triumph over the Enemy,—Oh! The *Wondrous Power* of our God!...

Thirteen years earlier, Cotton Mather's sister, Jerusha, decided when she was five months pregnant that it was time to get herself ready for death. She acknowledged that she was a fearful creature, and especially so because of her pregnancy, and wished to give herself up completely to God. She vowed that if God gave her an easy and short labour that she would dedicate herself to bringing up her child in fear of Him. She petitioned for a 'resigned will' and to be made fit for whatever God demanded for her. When her labour approached she prayed to be delivered from the sin of fear. As it happened, her labour was

easy, but she and her baby died a short time later.

Mather, in recording his sister's death, assured his readers that Jerusha, while exceptionally joyous, said 'nothing that look'd at all Delirious', lest they discount the God-given courage with which she had faced her end. He quoted her as saying that when she was healthy 'Death was a Terror to me. But now I know, I shall Dy, I am not at *all afraid of it. This* is a Wonderful *Work of God!* I know *that I am* going to Christ... *I see things that are Unutterable!*'. Her father, Increase Mather, asked her if she were not afraid of death. 'She replied with great Earnestness; "Not in the least! Not in the least! Not in the least!"' Mather ended his memoir with what he said were her last words, 'Eye has not seen, Ear has not heard, neither entered into the Heart of Man, the things which God has prepared for them that Love Him!' Mather's text pointed out in many ways that if a frail, sickly and frightened (i.e. womanly) woman lived as a Puritan woman should, she would die blissfully; hence, ran the implicit parallel, how much easier would it be for a strong man to do the same.

Similarly, Barbara Ruggles, an inhabitant of Roxburg, was able, according to the Roxburg Church records, to 'shine in her life & death' because of the way she dealt with her afflictions, including a fatal delivery. She had a 'stone chollik in which sicknesse she manifested much patiens, and faith; she dyed in childbed... & left a godly savor behind her'.

When a woman lost the mortal battle of birth graciously, she acquired unhesitating male praise. When she won, her husband's admiration might be muted by feelings of competition or guilty ambivalence about the pleasure in which such suffering originated. In journal accounts, husbands often expropriated the religious significance of their wives' brushes with death to themselves. They mingled their admiration with a vision of their *own* sins as the origin of their wives' agonies.

When, in the late 1660s, God visited upon the wife of the Reverend Joseph Thompson of Billerica such a weakness as made the couple fear her pregnancy might end badly, Thompson took a lesson in submission to the Lord's will from his wife's peril. He acknowledged that nothing could happen without God's intervention. The Lord further let him see that he had not been sufficiently grateful for the health, companionship, and work of his wife. He therefore feared that God might punish him by taking her away—although one can imagine that Mrs Thompson probably saw the punishment as hers. He prayed that the Lord would restore his wife's health and vowed perpetual gratitude for her. When his wife recovered, he charged himself with a return to indifference toward his blessings in her and a 'vile hart'. Mrs Thompson's near-death underlined to Thompson the sinful contrast between his unthankful acceptance of his spouse and his brief, divinely-inspired awareness of her value. And uncertainty and fear gave Thompson an all-too-brief reminder of the level of active, spiritual struggle on which he should be conducting more of his life.

The Reverend Thomas Shepard, in ruminating about the imminent birth of his child in the 1640s, wondered what would happen if the labour did not go well 'and her pains be long and [the] Lord remember my sin? And I began to trouble my heart with fear of the worst'. When he learned that his wife had delivered a baby safely, '. . . I saw the Lord's mercy and my own folly, to disquiet my heart with fear of what never shall be nor will be, and not rather to submit unto the Lord's will, and, come what can come, to be quiet there'. Like Thompson, Shepard's wife's mortal risk made him acutely conscious of his own sins. When his fears went unrealised he attempted to learn the lesson of peaceful resignation to God's will. He could not avoid seeing that his wife, in giving herself up to the miseries and uncertain outcome of travail, embodied this lesson.

In the same period the Reverend Michael Wigglesworth described his intimate involvement in his wife's labour. When she had pain, he:

lay sighing, sweating, praying, almost fainting through weakness before morning. The next day, the spleen much enfeebled me, and setting in with grief took away my strength, my heart was smitten within me, and as sleep departed from myne eyes my stomach abhored meat, I was brought very low and knew not how to pass away another night.

He then described feeling hasty and impatient', presumably with the excessive duration of their labour, and he prayed that the Lord make him want to 'stoop to his will'. His wife's endurance taunted him with the patience and submission he lacked. And although he portrayed his wife's labour as his own, it was she who demonstrated uncomplaining fortitude in the face of pains which he likened to 'the pangs of eternal death'.

If women who were courageous in childbirth accrued complicated, competitive admiration from men, energetically religious mothering produced more straightforward praise. Sons whose mothers had toiled over their salvation knew from their own deep experience of maternal force what such efforts entailed. Unlike husbands who had impregnated their wives but been excluded from the redemptive suffering of labour, sons had been the object of mothers' strenuous efforts and sacrifices. Cotton Mather described a good mother 'travail[ing] for her children more than once' to save them from the abominable sinfulness with which human birth had infected them. She was to work as hard as she could, instilling the principles of religion in her babies and catechising them as soon as they could speak.

Perhaps the most fearsome aspect of a righteous mother was that she would rather see her children dead than living outside the grace of God. In Michael Wigglesworth's famous epic, *The Day of Doom,* (1662) 'The tender mother will own no other/of all her numerous brood/But such as stand at Christ's right hand/acquitted through his blood'. Mothers with this unique spiritual ferocity, who gave more importance to their children's salvation than to their physical lives, were exhibiting the highest form of human love a Puritan could imagine. And yet, it could engender the starkest fear.

Of all imagery pertaining to females, Puritans had the most positive associations with the lactating breast. In sermons, ministers used metaphors giving God, the father, the capacity to nurse his children. This potent symbol of security, warmth and joy—the union of loving mother and nursing infant stood in stark contrast to the mother who would repudiate her unsaved offspring. In the eyes of a small child, the mother's immense power to give peace and happiness was paired with her ability to destroy forever the ease and hope of the unrepentant child.

These contrasting childhood images of perfect love and total terror persisted in the imaginations of children of such fervent mothers. In childbirth husbands saw wives resigned to God's will to sacrifice their own lives to create life. But the sons of deeply pious women remembered their mothers' seeming willingness to sacrifice *them* if their wickedness demanded it. Such fearsome, Janus-faced mothers undoubtedly contributed to men's admiration for female virtue at the same time that they implanted an abiding fear of powerful women.

Thomas Shepard recalled admiringly that his second wife cried and prayed in secret for her son, requesting that 'if the Lord did not intend to glorify himself by thee, that he would cut thee off by death rather than to live to dishonour him by sin'. His first wife, on the other hand, displayed the other ultimate motherly virtue. In explaining to his son his mother's death, Shepard said that she 'died in the Lord, departing out of this world to another, who did lose her life by being careful to preserve thine, for in the ship thou wert so feeble and froward both in the day and night that hereby she lost her strength and at last her life'. The first Mrs Shepard had sacrificed her life so that her child could live, and the second Mrs Shepard was willing to sacrifice her *son* if his soul became corrupt. A mighty Puritan mother elicited both veneration and terror.

The sons of other spiritually influential women came up with more tranquil memories, formed from less terrifying maternal images. These men recalled prayerful women to whom love meant hawklike watchfulness for their sons' salvation. Thomas Shepard remembered that his own mother, who died when he was still young, bore 'exceeding great love to me and made many prayers for me'. In Increase Mather's *Autobiography* he called his mother, Cotton's grandmother, 'a very Holy, praying woman. She desired two things for him, he remembered: grace and learning. As a boy he learned to read from his mother. His father taught him to write, 'who also instructed me in grammar learning' in Latin and Greek. But, as Cotton later remembered, Increase's mother taught her son, his father, 'all that was Good . . . among her Instructions . . . she mightily Inculcated the lesson of *Diligence*'.

Mather had often heard about his grandmother's potent combination of love and exhortation. He proudly recounted family lore: when Increase was very little his mother told him, that he was 'very much her *Darling*', and that all she wished for him was to be a good Christian and a good scholar. She pleaded successfully on her deathbed that her fifteen-year-old son go into the ministry. She had been most 'honourable... for her *Vertue*, ... that for which a *Woman* is most of all *to be Praised*'. She was Mather's model for his twice-travailing mother. He wrote, 'She was a Woman of Uncommon Devotion, and in her Importunate Prayers for this her son, she ... became *Twice a Mother* to him'. Mather's own mother had similar moral structure, challenging the family to live up to her example. Mather remembered her as 'a Godly, an Humble, and a Praying Woman, and one that often set apart *Whole Days* for prayer and Secret Interviews with Heaven'.

Frances Boland arrived in America from Scotland in 1682. In his journal he gave special thanks for the 'pious nurture and example of my godly mother.... She was a praying woman and prayed much for her children'. He went on to say what a blessing it was for the young to have parents such as his.

John Dane, a surgeon in Ipswich, Massachusetts, remembered with respect that his mother had been a 'serious woman'. He recalled that she had once had a dream in which she heard a certain minister deliver a sermon; according to Dane's account she accurately foresaw the date, the place, and the text of that preacher's talk. Dane prudently did not praise his mother as a seer and mystic, which would have unsettled New World Puritans. Instead, he portrayed her as a sober student, indifferent to her gift of prophecy and desirous only to make 'good improvement of that sermon', which, thanks to her vision, she was able to enjoy twice.

The zealous mother was an exacting conscience to her children and, by extension, to the community. Embedded in the Puritan notion of community was mutual moral responsibility and the notion that the sin of one member stained the whole society. Boys and girls both grew up cultivating the ability to spot a sin in themselves and others. Cotton Mather wrote approvingly that his sister, Jerusha, recorded in her journal judgments on the activities and behaviour of

people in the community. He wrote that in her journal:

> She Remarks on the Dealings of God with Others; Especially if anything either Good or Bad were observable in the condition of the Town; But most of all what occur'd Joyful or Grievous, unto her nearest *Relatives,* and their Families; and she employes agreeable *Meditations* and *Supplications* there-upon.

Wives, in particular, were supposed to watch their husbands' spiritual state. Benjamin Wadsworth had written that 'If Husbands that call themselves Christian, are vain, wicked, ungodly; their pious Wives (if such they have) should by a meek winning Conversation, indeavour their spiritual & eternal Good'. Christopher Lawson sued his wife for divorce in 1669, accusing her of failing in her duty as a converted Puritan to attend to the spiritual needs of her unconverted husband. 'The unbelieving husband', he wrote, 'should be wonn by the good conversation of the believing wife ...'.

The Reverend John Ward praised his wife for being an 'accusing conscience' and letting him know when he was acting in an ungodly manner. Mather extolled Ward's wife who had lived happily with her husband for forty years:

> Although she would so faithfully tell him of everything that might seem amendable in him ... yet she ever pleased him wonderfully. And she would oft put him upon the duties of secret fasts, and when she met with anything in reading that she counted singularly agreeable, she would still impart it unto him.

The marriage of the Wards was an active spiritual partnership in which Mrs Ward not infrequently gave her husband direction.

Women often achieved the role of conscience by becoming shadow ministers, absorbing, sometimes writing down (as Jerusha Mather did), and acting upon the weekly sermons of their husbands and/or pastors. Thomas Shepard commended his wife for her 'excellency to reprove for sin and discern the evils of men'. He went on to say that she loved the words of the Lord exceedingly and was, therefore, glad to read his notes for

his sermons every week and ponder the thoughts therein.

Cotton Mather memorialised the second Mrs Whiting for her 'singular piety and gravity', who prayed in her closet every day to God. He commended her for writing down the sermons that she heard 'on the Lord's days with much dexterity', while living by their messages all week.

Although Puritan traditions cast doubt on women's capacity for goodness and prohibited them from exercising concrete authority, Puritan women did achieve moral stature from quietly enduring suffering, intense dedication to the salvation of their children, and gentle correction of the behaviour of their spouses and neighbours. The blessing Puritan men bestowed on notably virtuous women registered the conflict in which it was born. Women had to criticise, suggest, and direct others—particularly men—with extreme caution as Puritan men were deeply alarmed when women presumed to judge them. Nonetheless, Puritan women, inclined to religious depth, would find respect and deference in their communities, no small treasures in a male-dominated world. And they would bequeath to later generations of women a tradition of moral criticism and the conviction that zealous effort on behalf of the salvation of others was part of their human responsibility. This belief would empower women to turn their moral energies upon their husbands, families, and, in time, the world around them.

FOR FURTHER READING

Laurel Thacher Ulrich, *Goodwives: Image and Reality in the Lives of Women of Northern New England, 1650–1750* (Knopt, 1982); Carol Karlsen, *The Devil in the Shape of a Woman* (Norton, 1987; David Leverenz, *The Language of Puritan Feeling* (Rutgers University Press, 1980); Perry Miller, *The American Puritan* (Doubleday/Anchor, 1956); Lyle Koehler, *A Search for Power, The "Weaker Sex" in Seventeenth Century New England* (University of Illinois Press, 1980); Kenneth Silverman, *The Life and Times of Cotton Mather* (Harper & Row, 1970).

Colonists in Bondage: Indentured Servants in America

Barbara Bigham

A ship docked at a Virginia harbor in 1635, and from its decks emerged nearly two-hundred newcomers from England, among them twenty-five-year-old Thomas Carter. For some the voyage had cost over £5 sterling. For others, the price was higher still: several years of their lives. Carter, like thousands of other penniless Europeans, had sold himself into bondage as an indentured servant to pay his passage to the colonies. Once there, he lived the life of a virtual slave— the property of his master. But when his indenture was over, he became a free man, and with his "freedom dues" of some clothes and tools, he worked to rise above his humble beginnings and serve as a respected member of the community. Eventually, he had four servants indentured under him at his estate in Isle of Wight County, Virginia. His descendants took an active part in colonial affairs and went on to fight in the Revolution. Some were involved in noble pursuits, others in scandalous incidents, and one—a ninth-generation grandson—became the thirty-ninth president of the United States.

Land was plentiful in the New World, and fertile, but without a large number of laborers to fell trees and work the soil, it was as useless as a desert. Few new settlers could afford to hire a work force of free men, nor could they afford to buy slaves. Of the several schemes employed to entice workers to the colonies, none worked so well as the system of indentured servitude, which established itself almost as soon as the first colonists landed.

The earliest surviving indenture contract is dated 1619, when four owners of a Virginia plantation signed an agreement with Robert Coopy, of Gloucestershire, England. Coopy promised "faythfully to serve . . . for three years from the daye of his landing in the land of Virginia" in return for his benefactors' promise to "transport him (with gods assistance) with all convenient speed into the said land of Virginia at their costs and charges in all things, and there to maintayne him with convenient diet and apparell meet for such a servant, And in the end of the said terme to make him a free man of the said Cuntry . . . And to grant to the said Robert thirty acres of land within their Territory . . ."

The system caught on immediately, and by 1625 there were 487 indentured servants out of a population of 1,227 in the Virginia Company. During the next decade the wording of indenture contracts became fairly uniform, and by 1636, printed forms were available with blank spaces for the names of the servant and master and the details of the contract.

Indentured servitude grew as thousands of men and women in England crammed into cities competing for the few low-paying jobs open to them and for a precariously short food supply. Religious and political pressures, aggravated by famine and disease, made people restless and receptive to the prospect

Few Germans arriving in America under indenture knew the English language. This indenture, written in German, is dated 1736. Courtesy of the Pennsylvania Historical and Museum Commission, Harrisburg, Pennsylvania.

of a better existence elsewhere. Handbills and broadsides written by promoters (many of whom had never been to America) to stimulate migration painted the rosiest possible picture of the American colonies, promising abundant land for all and high wages for craftsmen. They neglected to mention the hardships of living in the still-wild country. As the colonies grew, those who had already made the transition sent tantalizing letters home. Robert Parke wrote to his sister in 1725, "There is not one of the family but what likes the country very well and would if we were in Ireland again come here directly; it being the best country for working folk and tradesmen in the world." With such encouragement, "emigration fever" swept through Europe, keeping ships filled with would-be settlers. Those who could afford to do so paid their own passages, arriving in the colonies as free men. Thousands more, with a yearning for the colonies, but no gold in their pockets to pay for the trip, were satisfied by enterprising colonists willing to invest in their passage and maintenance in return for several years of labor.

These early capitalists usually hired an agent (a ship captain was a frequent choice, as were merchants who traveled between the two continents) to contact discouraged workers in England and sign them on as indentured servants. An agreement written in duplicate on a large sheet of paper was signed by both master and servant, then "indented" or cut, in two—one copy for each party. The terms of the contract seldom varied; besides transporting the servant, the master agreed to feed, clothe, and house him for a certain number of years, usually between four and fourteen. At the end of the stipulated time, he was to pay the servant with a small stake and his freedom. Details of the treatment the servant could expect, the rules governing his life, and the freedom dues were rarely set down in writing. They were, instead, to be "according to the custom of the country," which could change with the prosperity, or the personality, of the master.

It was soon evident that great profits were to be made, and many a "middle man" turned professional agent and combed the cities and farm regions in England for men and women willing to become bound servants. He signed their indentures as master and transported them, a shipload at a time, to the colonies. The total cost, including transporta-tion and a few pieces of clothing per person, was seldom more than £10 per head. In the colonies the agent could count on getting £15 to £30 for each servant "set over." (The word sell was consciously avoided when it referred to white men, yet the new owner bought a servant in much the same way he bought a slave.)

Substantial profits to be made in the servant trade led to notoriously deceitful, as well as illegal, methods of recruitment. Agents came to be known as "spirits," with reputations for having no qualms about lying to a man or getting him so drunk that he would put his mark on any piece of paper shoved in front of him. If lies and gin didn't work, a whack on the head usually would. Many men and women were forced to the ship and shoved into the hold not to see daylight again until the shores of England were out of sight.

JUST ARRIVED, *in the* Ship JOHN, *Capt.* ROACH, *from* DUBLIN,
A NUMBER of HEALTHY, INDENTED MEN and WOMEN SERVANTS :
AMONG THE FORMER ARE,
A Variety of TRADESMEN, with some good FAR-MERS, and stout LABOURERS: Their Indentures will be disposed of, on reasonable Terms, for CASH, by
GEORGE SALMON.

Many Europeans could afford to come to America only by offering themselves as indentured servants or redemptioners. Newspaper advertisements like the one above regularly announced the arrival of indentured servants.

Public outrage over such forced migration, particularly when it involved children, spurred Parliament to enact laws that protected the citizen from the spirits and, at the same time, protected the honest agent from false accusations of kidnapping by a servant with second thoughts about honoring his indenture. Agents and servants were required to sign the contract before a magistrate, a registry of servants being transported to the colonies was kept, and in some cases, outbound ships were searched so that any passengers with a change of mind could return home. Although these measures were not entirely successful, they helped ensure that most men and women who bound themselves as servants and sailed for America did so because they wanted to.

The English Parliament used indentured servitude to rid the country of vagrants roaming England in that time of social upheaval. Frequently these rootless vagabonds were farmers who had been dispossessed of their lands; and unable to find work, they turned in desperation or bitterness to lives of petty crime and theft. Convicted criminals, many from Newgate Prison, were sent by the state to the colonies as bound servants. Most had a choice of sorts: hanging or America. America was the favored alternative. Prior to 1717, forced exile did not exist in England, but convicts who would ordinarily be sentenced to die (and a large number of minor crimes were punishable by that harsh sentence) could be pardoned on condition that they leave the country. After 1717, most offenders could be legally transported to America or the West Indies as indentured servants for not less than seven years.

Besides clearing out overcrowded English jails, bondage supplied much needed labor for the colonies. Of the prisoners convicted at Old Bailey from 1729 to the American Revolution, at least 70 percent were sent to America. Such deportation of criminals did not win favor with colonists who likened it to having England "emptying their jakes (privies) on our tables." Maryland and Virginia, destinations for most criminal-immigrants, passed restrictive laws forbidding convict ships to land, but such laws were quashed by the British crown. Although they complained bitterly, colonists desperate for cheap labor could not afford to be too particular about the past indiscretions of available servants: convict indentures never lacked buyers. About 30,000 convicts (in reality a small part of those who arrived under indenture) were transported to the colonies, many for petty crimes.

Whether the ships crossing the Atlantic were filled with convicts or willing bondsmen, they were filled to overflowing. As many as 800 persons might be crowded aboard a single vessel, and even the smaller ships often carried 200 or 300 people. One ship, measured for a safe load of 223, made the crossing with 322 on board; when criticized, the ship owner claimed his craft was far less crowded than many others.

Except for the convict ships, servants rarely had to endure the horrors common on slavers. Still, the voyage was unpleasant at best. Food supplies were as limited as space, and although ships were usually provisioned for a twelve-week voyage, many crossings delayed by bad weather or poor navigation ended as the last rations of wormy food and rancid water were being handed out. Less fortunate voyagers came to the end of provisions before they sighted land.

RUN away the 27th of *August* laſt, from *James Anderſon* Miniſter of the Goſpel in *Donigal*, in the County of *Lancaſter* in *Penſilvania*, a Servant Man named *Hugh Wier*, aged about 30 Years of a middle Stature and freſh Complexion, ſandy Beard, and ſhort dark brown Hair, he went off very bear in Cloathing, and is ſuppoſed to have got himſelf dreſs'd in *Indian* Habit, (He having been uſed among *Indians*, when he run away from other Maſters before) He is by Trade a Flax-dreſſer, Spinſter and Woolcomber, and it is ſuppoſed he can Weave; He alſo does moſt ſort of Women Work, ſuch as waſhing of Cloaths or Diſhes, milking of Cows, and other Kitchen Work, and uſually changes his Name. Whoever takes up ſaid Servant and ſecures him either in this or any of the neighbouring Provinces and let his Maſter know of it, by Poſt or otherways, ſo as his ſaid Maſter may have him again, ſhall have *Three Pounds* as a Reward, and all reaſonable Charges paid by me, *James Anderſon*

Advertisement for a runaway indentured servant in the "American Weekly Mercury" of Philadelphia, December 14, 1733.

Ship captains were notoriously neglectful of cleanliness. Even when they did periodically wash out the ship with vinegar, the vessels were normally steeped in filth. Jammed into cargo holds with few sanitary facilities, the mass of passengers suffered from diseases and sickness made worse by the lack of ventilation. Although they were free to go above deck for fresh air during fair weather, when rough seas or stormy skies threatened, all were sent below the battened-down hatches. One German immigrant cataloged the suffering of fellow passengers during a 1751 crossing as "terrible misery, stench, fumes, horror, vomiting, many kinds of seasickness, fever, dysentery, headache, heat, constipation, boils, scurvy, cancer, mouthrot, and the like." Another voyager reported that "we had enough in the day to behold the miserable sight of blotches, pox, others devoured with lice til they almost at death's door. In the night fearful cries and groaning of sick and distracted persons. . . ."

By the time the servants reached the colonies they were dirty, sick, and weak. Those with prearranged indentures were taken off the ship by their new masters, while those indentured to agents were readied for sale. Fresh clothing, clean water, and good food were enough to erase most of the visible ill effects of the voyage, and within a few days the cargo was ready for sale. Newspaper advertisements or broadsides announced the arrival of "a number of healthy indented men and women servants . . . a variety of tradesmen, good farmers, stout laborers . . . whose indentures will be disposed of, on reasonable terms, for cash."

The buyers arrived on the day of the sale, and the servants were brought out for inspection. Strong young men, skilled workers, and comely women sold quickly, but the sick or old were harder to dispose of, and at times were given away as a bonus with more desirable servants. In later years, it was not uncommon for one buyer to purchase the indentures of all, or a large part, of the human cargo. These "soul-drivers" loaded their merchandise on wagons and drove through the countryside selling it door-to-door the way the drummer sold sewing needles.

A Pennsylvania soul-driver named McCullough got more than he bargained for when he bought a group of servants in Philadelphia and began a circular swing through the farmlands and towns of the backcountry. He sold all but one of the servants, an Irishman whose rowdy behavior frightened away any potential buyers. The two men stayed one night at an inn but the Irishman woke early and, passing himself off as the master, sold McCullough—still asleep upstairs—to the innkeeper. Before he left the inn he warned the innkeeper that his newly acquired servant was a clever rascal, fond of telling lies and even of persuading gullible people that he was the master.

There were other passengers on those ships who found their way into servitude, although they had not begun their voyages with that in mind. Whole families of German and Swiss immigrants left home to build new lives in the American colonies, making their way down the Rhine to book passage in Rotterdam. But overly-enthusiastic recruitment pamphlets didn't mention the opportunists who overcharged for provisions along the route, or the long waits at the docks until space could be found on some America-bound vessel. Many found that their

money would not stretch far enough to pay their passage. An agent, merchant, or ship captain would step forward to advance the money needed for the voyage, granting the prospective colonist a period of time, usually two weeks, to raise the balance due when he arrived in the colonies. Some managed to find friends or relatives to redeem them, or had the good fortune to fall into the hands of one of the relief societies set up by their countrymen for the unwary victims. Many did not and so, to repay the agent, were sold into servitude. The redemptioner was in no position to quibble over the terms of his indenture, and often had to accept a situation no willing servant would have agreed to before leaving home.

Willing servant, transported convict, or disappointed redemptioner—once bound to a master he was his property, like his house, or horse, or slave. Yet his status was a curious mixture of slave and free man. His services could be bought or sold, rented or even inherited, but the terms of his contract remained the same under each master. He could own property but could not engage in trade. Marriage without his master's consent was strictly forbidden, and fornication and illegitimate pregnancy were serious offenses. Runaway servants were tracked down like runaway slaves and punished just as severely, although a white complexion made eluding capture much more possible. Posters and advertisements offered rewards for their return and warned of the consequences of harboring fugitives. Corporal punishment, including whipping, was accepted practice, often accompanied by a punishment even more hated: the addition of months or even years to the indenture period. A thwarted runaway could expect one month to be added to his term for every week he was gone. Sometimes the extension was confirmed with a whipping or the gift of a heavy iron collar engraved with the master's initials.

But indentured servants were not black slaves—they were white and Christian and as such had an edge over their African counterparts. The most important difference was the right to petition the courts against abuse, a right that was exercised freely and frequently.

At first, the rules regulating the lives of the servants and their treatment were governed by local custom. As the number of servants soared, many of these customs were incorporated into law. Any servant who felt his master was defying a 'custom of the country' or breaking a law could visit the local magistrate and file a petition of grievance.

In 1700, Catherine Douglas of Lancaster County, Virginia, learned that the courts would listen to and judge a case impartially, without bias against a penniless bonded servant. She filed a petition claiming that in England she had signed a four-year indenture with John Gilchrist in exchange for her passage, Gilchrist in turn sold her to Mottron Wright for a seven-year term. Although her own copy of the indenture had been destroyed, Catherine was able to produce three witnesses who testified that they had seen the original and that it had indeed specified four years. Wright argued that his seven-year contract had to be upheld, but the court decided in Catherine's favor; she was set free after serving her four years.

Until the middle of the 17th century, when laws governing black slavery began to be passed, Africans were also imported into the colonies under indenture. Until then, and occasionally after, redress was afforded blacks through the courts. In 1691, a Stafford County, Virginia, court heard an unusual case when black servant Benjamin Lewis petitioned for his freedom, claiming that before leaving England he had been indentured for four years. His term was over but his master refused to set him free, saying that as a Negro, Lewis was not a servant but a slave. The master produced another indenture signed by Lewis for a fourteen year term, but admitted it had been written while the first contract was still in effect. The jury ruled that the original contract was valid and proclaimed Lewis a free man.

Most cases brought before the courts by servants dealt with poor treatment and physical abuse. As with black slaves, the treatment of bonded servants was as var-

ied as the personalities of their masters. Most were dealt with fairly and well, for humanitarian as well as practical reasons, but for some servants, life became a nightmare. Elizabeth Sprigs, indentured in Maryland, wrote of "toiling day and night, and then [being] tied up and whipped to that degree you would not beat an animal, scarce anything but Indian corn and salt to eat and that even begrudged." Some observers reported that when white servants worked side by side with black slaves, the slaves were often fed better and treated with more care since they represented a life-time investment.

The relatively minor charge of providing insufficient clothing was brought against William Miller by his servant William Hust. Court officials in Spotsylvania, Virginia, heard the case in 1758 and issued detailed orders to Miller. "The said Miller [shall] give him one cotton and kersey jacket and britches, 3 Ozanb shirts and sufficient diet and 1 pair of shoes and stockings, 1 hat. . . ." Usually the court found it adequate to reprimand the master and instruct him to properly provide for his servant.

A more serious charge was filed against plantation owners Francis Leaven and Samuel Hodgkins. Their servant, John Thomas, had committed some minor offense, and for punishment, the two hung him up by his hands and placed lighted sticks between his fingers, permanently injuring his hands. The court awarded Thomas not only his freedom, but 5,000 pounds of cotton from each of the masters, who were jailed for the assault.

Most indentured servants lived out their indenture periods without having need to petition the courts, and without the inclination to abscond. They worked hard, as did the free settlers, often learning a trade and gaining valuable experience. When their indenture period ended, freedom dues helped them begin life as

free men. The dues varied with locale, but its intent was to give the servant a stake to start out on his own. In 1640, Maryland law required a freedom dues of "one good cloth suit of kersey or broadcloth, a shift of white linen, one new pair of stockings and shoes, two hoes, one axe, 3 barrells of corn and fifty acres of land. . . ." Land as part of the freedom dues was an important incentive for immigration, but as the more desirable tracts were taken up in populated areas, the promise of acreage virtually ended except for wilderness or scrub land. In 1683, the Maryland law dropped the land requirement. In Virginia, a 1748 law gave freed servants a freedom dues of three pounds, ten shillings. The tendency toward cash increased as the colonies prospered.

With his freedom dues, the former servant could make his way in the colonies as a hired laborer or even as a landowner. No stigma attached to his past bondage; with diligent hard work he could become as prosperous and respected as any settler who had paid his own way from Europe with cash. Those who had been lazy and dishonest in Europe before they were bound out probably continued to be so after they were free. Former convicts often ended up on American rather than English gallows, but many others became distinguished citizens and property holders. Seven burgesses in the Virginia assembly of 1629 had been indentured servants, as had fifteen members of the 1637 Maryland Assembly. Charles Thomas, later to serve as Secretary of the Continental Congress, started his American life in bondage, as did Matthew Thornton, a signer of the Declaration of Independence for the colony of New Hampshire. Like many other Americans who could trace their roots to humble beginnings, they had bought their dreams with the most precious commodity they owned: themselves.

Entertaining Satan

John Demos

John Demos is a professor of history at Brandeis University and is currently working on a book on witchcraft in colonial America.

The place is the fledgling community of Windsor, Connecticut: the time, an autumn day in the year 1651. A group of local militiamen has assembled for training exercises. They drill in their usual manner through the morning, then pause for rest and refreshment. Several of the younger recruits begin a moment's horseplay; one of these—a certain Thomas Allen—cocks his musket and inadvertently knocks it against a tree. The weapon fires, and a few yards away a bystander falls heavily to the ground. The unfortunate victim is an older man, also a trainee, Henry Stiles by name. Quickly, the group converges on Stiles, and bears him to the house of the local physician. But the bullet has fatally pierced his heart.

One month later the "particular court" of the Connecticut colony meets in regular session. On its agenda is an indictment of Thomas Allen: "that . . . [thou] didst suddenly, negligently, carelessly cock thy piece, and carry the piece . . . which piece being charged and going off in thine hand, slew thy neighbor, to the great dishonor of God, breach of the peace, and loss of a member of this commonwealth." Allen confesses the fact, and is found guilty of "homicide by misadventure." For his "sinful neglect and careless carriages" the court orders him to pay a fine of twenty pounds sterling. In addition he is bound to good behavior for the ensuing year, with the special proviso "that he shall not bear arms for the same term."

But this is not the end of the matter. Stiles's death remains a topic of local conversation, and three years later it yields a more drastic result. In November, 1654, the court meets in special session to try a case of witchcraft—against a woman, Lydia Gilbert, also of Windsor: "Lydia Gilbert, thou art here indicted . . . that not having the fear of God before thine eyes, thou hast of late years or still dost give entertainment to Satan, the great enemy of God and mankind, and by his help hast killed the body of Henry Stiles, besides other witchcrafts, for which according to the law of God and the established law of this commonwealth thou deservest to die." The court, in effect, is considering a complicated question: did Lydia Gilbert's witchcraft *cause* Thomas Allen's gun to go off, so as to kill Henry Stiles? Evidence is taken on various points deemed relevant. Henry Stiles was a boarder in the Gilbert household for some while before his death. The arrangement was not a happy one; neighbors could recall the sounds of frequent quarreling. From time to time Stiles loaned money and property to his landlord, but this served only to heighten the tension. Goodwife Gilbert, in particular, violated her Christian obligation of charitable and peaceable behavior. A naturally assertive sort, she did not conceal her sense of grievance against Goodman Stiles. In fact, her local reputation has long encompassed some unfavorable elements: disapproval of her quick temper, envy of her success in besting personal antagonists, suspicion that she is not above invoking the "Devil's means." The jury weighs the evidence and reaches its verdict—guilty as charged. The magistrates hand down the prescribed sentence of death by hanging. A few days thereafter the sentence is carried out.

On the next succeeding Sabbath day, and with solemn forewarning, the pastor of the Windsor church climbs to the pulpit to deliver his sermon. Directly he faces the questions that are weighing heavily in the minds of his parishioners. Why has this terrible scourge of witchcraft been visited on their little community? What has created the opportunity which the Devil and his legions have so untimely seized? For what reason has God Almighty condoned such a tragic intrusion on the life of Windsor? The pastor's answer to these questions is neither surprising nor pleasant for his audience to hear, but it carries a purgative force. The Windsor townsfolk are themselves at least partially to blame. For too long they have strayed from the paths of virtue: overvaluing secular interests while neglecting religious ones, tippling in alehouses, "nightwalking," and—worst of all—engaging one another in repeated strife. In such circumstances the Devil always finds an opening; to such communities God brings retribution. Thus the recent witchcraft episode is a lesson to the people of Windsor, and a warning to mend their ways.

Lydia Gilbert was not the first witch to have lived at Windsor, nor would she be the last. For so-called Puritans, the happenstance of everyday life was part of a struggle of cosmic dimensions, a struggle in which witchcraft played a logical part. The ultimate triumph of Almighty God was assured. But in particular times and places Satan might achieve some temporary success—and claim important victims. Indeed he was continually adding earthly recruits to his nefarious cause. Tempted by bribes and blandishments, or frightened by threats of torture, weak-willed persons signed the "Devil's Book" and enrolled as witches. Thereafter they were armed with his power and obliged to do his bidding. God, meanwhile, opposed this onslaught of evil—and yet He also permitted it. For errant men and women there was no more effective means of "chastening."

In a sense, therefore, witchcraft was part of God's own intention. And the element of intention was absolutely central, in the minds of the human actors. When a man lay dead from a violent accident on a training field, his fellow townspeople would carefully investigate how events had proceeded to such an end. But they sought, in addition, to understand the *why* of it all—the motives, whether human or supernatural (or both), which lay behind the events. The same was true for other forms of everyday mischance. When cows took strangely ill, when a boat capsized in a sudden storm, when bread failed to rise in the oven or beer went bad in the barrel, there was cause for careful reflection. Witchcraft would not necessarily provide the best explanation, but it was always a possibility—and sometimes a most convenient one. To discover an unseen hand at work in one's life was to dispel mystery, to explain misfortune, to excuse incompetence. Belief in witchcraft was rooted in the practical experience no less than the theology of the time.

A single shocking episode—the Salem "hysteria" of 1692—has dominated the lore of this subject ever since. Yet the Salem trials were distinctive only in a quantitative sense—that is, in the sheer numbers of the accused. Between the late 1630's and 1700 dozens of New England towns supported proceedings against witchcraft; some did so on repeated occasions. The total of cases was over a hundred (and this includes only actual trials from which some record survives today). At least forty of the defendants were put to death; the rest were acquitted or convicted of a lesser charge. Numerous additional cases went unrecorded because they did not reach a court of law; nonetheless they generated much excitement—and distress. "Witches" were suspected, accused informally, and condemned in unofficial ways. Gossip and rumor about such people constituted a staple part of the local culture.

The typical witch was a woman of middle age. Like Lydia Gilbert, she was married, had children, and lived as a settled member of her community. (However, widows and childless women were also suspected, perhaps to an extent disproportionate to their numbers in the

population at large.) Some of the accused were quite poor and a few were given to begging; but taken altogether they spanned the entire social spectrum. (One was the wife of a leading magistrate in the Massachusetts Bay Colony.) Most seemed conspicuous in their personal behavior: they were cantankerous, feisty, quick to take offense, and free in their expression of anger. As such they matched the prevalent stereotype of a witch, with its emphasis on strife and malice and vengeance. It was no accident, in a culture which valued "peaceableness" above all things, that suspected witches were persons much given to conflict. Like deviant figures everywhere, they served to mark the accepted boundaries between Good and Evil.

Their alleged victims, and actual accusers, are much harder to categorize. Children were sometimes centrally involved—notoriously so at Salem—but witchcraft evidence came from people of both sexes and all ages. The young had their "fits"; older witnesses had other things of which to complain. Illness, injury, and the loss of property loomed largest in such testimony; but there were reports, too, of strange sights and sounds, of portents and omens, of mutterings and curses—all attributable in some way to the supposed witch. The chances for conviction were greatest when the range of this evidence was wide and the sources numerous. In some cases whole neighborhoods joined the ranks of the accusers.

Usually a trial involved only a single witch, or perhaps two; the events at issue were purely local. A finding of guilt would remove the defendant forever from her community. An acquittal would send her back, but with a clear warning to watch her step. Either way tension was lowered.

Occasionally the situation became more complicated. In Connecticut, during the years from 1662 to 1665, the courts heard a long sequence of witchcraft cases—perhaps as many as a dozen. Some of the accused were eventually executed; others fled for their lives to neighboring colonies. Almost none of the legal evidence has survived; it is known, however, that Connecticut was then experiencing severe problems of religious factionalism. The witch trials may well have bean a direct result.

The context for the other wide-scale outbreak is much clearer. Salem, in the closing decades of the seventeenth cen-

tury, was a town notorious for internal contention. An old guard of village farmers was arrayed against newly prosperous merchants and townsmen. For years, indeed decades, local governance was disrupted: town meetings broke up with important issues unresolved, ministers came and left (out of favor with one side or the other), lawsuits filled the court dockets. Thus when the first sparks of witchcraft were fanned, in a small group of troubled girls, they acted like tinder on a dried-out woodpile. Suspicion led immediately to new suspicion, and accusation to accusation—with results that every schoolchild knows. Soon the conflagration burst the boundaries of Salem itself; eventually it claimed victims throughout eastern Massachusetts. By the time cooler heads prevailed—especially that of the new governor, Sir William Phips—twenty witches had been executed and dozens more were languishing in local jails.

But the Salem trials—to repeat—were highly unusual in their sheer scope: witch-hunting gone wild. In the more typical case, events moved slowly, even carefully, within a limited and intensely personal framework. This dimension of the witchcraft story also deserves close attention.

October, 1688. A cart stops by the roadside in the south part of Boston. A tall man alights and hurries along a pathway toward a small house. A door opens to admit him and quickly closes again. The visitor is Rev. Cotton Mather, a young but already eminent clergyman of the town. The house is occupied by the family of a mason named John Goodwin.

Immediately upon entering, Mather becomes witness to an extraordinary scene. On the parlor floor in front of him two small human forms are thrashing about. A girl of thirteen (named Martha) and a boy of eleven (John, Jr.) are caught in the throes of agonizing fits. Their bodies contort into strange, distended shapes. Their eyes bulge. Their mouths snap open and shut. They shriek uncontrollably. From time to time they affect the postures of animals, and crawl about the room, barking like dogs or bellowing like frightened cows. Their father and several neighbors look on in horror, and try by turns to prevent serious damage to persons or property.

Mather waits for a moment's lull; then he opens a Bible, kneels, and begins to pray. Immediately the children stop their ears and resume their shrieking. "*They say we must not listen*," cries the girl, while hurling herself toward the fireplace. Her father manages to block the way; briefly he catches her in an awkward embrace. But she reels off and falls heavily on her brother.

Soon it is time for supper. The children quiet temporarily, and come to the table with their elders. However, when food is offered them, their teeth are set as if to lock their mouths shut. Later there are new troubles. The children need assistance in preparing for bed, and they tear their nightclothes fearfully. At last they quiet and pass into a deep sleep.

Mather sits by the fireside and reviews the history of their affliction with the distraught parents. The family is a religious one, and until the preceding summer the children were unfailingly pious and well behaved. Martha's fits had begun first, John's soon thereafter; indeed, two still younger children in the family have also been affected from time to time. A physician had been summoned, but he could discover no "natural maladies" at work.

The parents recall an episode that had directly preceded the onset of Martha's fits. The girl was sent to retrieve some family linen from a laundress who lived nearby. Several items had disappeared, and Martha complained—intimating theft. The laundress angrily denied the charges, and was joined in this by her own mother, an Irishwoman named Glover. Goodwife Glover was already a feared presence in the neighborhood; her late husband, on his deathbed, had accused her of practicing witchcraft. Now she poured out her retaliative anger on young Martha Goodwin. The girl has not been the same since.

Late in the evening, having listened with care to the entire story, Mather prepares to leave. John Goodwin explains that several neighbors have been urging the use of "tricks"—countermagic—to end his children's difficulties. But Goodwin prefers a strategy based on orthodox Christian principles.

In this Cotton Mather is eager to cooperate. He returns to the Goodwin house each day for a week, and on one particular afternoon he is joined by his fellow clergymen from all parts of Boston. Eventually he invites Martha Goodwin into his own home for a period of intensive pastoral care. (Martha's younger brother is taken, at the same time, into

the home of the minister at Watertown.) Their afflictions continue, though with lessened severity.

Meanwhile the courts intervene and Goodwife Glover is put on trial for her alleged crimes. She has difficulty answering the prosecutor's questions; she can speak only in her native tongue (Gaelic), so the proceedings must involve interpreters. Her house is searched, and "poppets" are discovered—small images, made of rags, believed to be instrumental in the perpetration of witchcraft. Eventually she confesses guilt and raves wildly in court about her dealings with the Devil. The judges appoint six physicians to assess her sanity; they find her compos mentis. The court orders her execution.

On her way to the gallows Goodwife Glover declares bitterly that the children will not be cured after her death, for "others had a hand in it as well." And in fact, the fits suffered by Martha and young John increase immediately thereafter. Winter begins, and suspicion shifts to another woman of the neighborhood. However, the new suspect dies suddenly, and under strange circumstances, before she can be brought to trial. At last the children show marked improvement, and by spring they are virtually their former selves. Meanwhile a relieved, and triumphant, Cotton Mather is spending long days in his study, completing a new book that will soon be published under the title *Memorable Providences, Relating to Witchcrafts and Possessions*. A central chapter deals at length with selected "examples," and includes the events in which Mather himself has so recently participated. The Goodwin children will be leading characters in a local best seller.

Goodwife Glover was relatively rare, among those accused of witchcraft in early New England, in confessing guilt. Only at Salem did any considerable number choose to convict themselves—and there, it seemed confession was the strategy of choice if one wished to avoid the gallows. Were Goody Glover's admissions, in effect, forced out of her? Was she perhaps seriously deranged (the opinion of the court-appointed physicians notwithstanding)? Did she truly believe herself guilty? Had she, in fact, sought to invoke the power of the Devil, by stroking poppets with her spittle—or whatever?

We have no way now to answer such questions; the evidence comes to us entirely through persons who believed—

and prosecuted—the case against her. It does seem likely, in a community where virtually everyone accepted the reality of witchcraft, that at least a few would have tried to practice it. In a sense, however, it no longer matters whether specific individuals were guilty as charged. What does matter is that many of them were believed guilty—and that this belief was itself efficacious. As anthropologists have observed in cultures around the world, people who regard themselves as objects of witchcraft are vulnerable to all manner of mischance. They blunder into "accidents," they lose their effectiveness in work and social relations, they occasionally sicken and die.

No less was true in early New England. The victims of witchcraft—whatever the variety of their particular afflictions—had this in common: they believed *beforehand* that they had been marked as targets for attack. Their fearful expectation became, at some point, incapacitating—and yielded its own directly feared result. Thus the idea of witchcraft served both as the *ad hoc* cause of the victim's troubles and as the *post hoc* explanation. The process was neatly circular, for each explanation created a further cause—which, in turn, required additional explanation. In the language of modern medicine, these episodes were "symptoms," and their basis was "psychogenic."

The seizures of the afflicted children were but the extreme end of the symptomatic continuum. When Martha Goodwin had been drawn into a bitter exchange with a suspected witch, she was left deeply unsettled. She feared retaliation; she wished to retaliate herself; she felt acutely uncomfortable with the anger she had already expressed. Henceforth an anguished "victim" of witchcraft, she was, in effect, punished for her own vengeful impulse. Yet, too, she *had* her revenge, for her accusations led straight to the trial and conviction of her antagonist. The same inner processes, and a similar blend of wish and fear, served to energize fits in victims of witchcraft all across New England.

But fits could be explained in other ways—hence the requirement that all such victims be examined by medical doctors. Only when natural causes had been ruled out was a diagnosis of witchcraft clearly justified. Normally, beyond this point, clergymen would assume control of the proceedings, for they were "healers of the soul" and experts in the struggle against Evil. Long sessions of prayer, earnest conversation with the afflicted, occasional periods of fasting and humiliation—these were the preferred methods of treatment.

At least they were the *Christian* methods. For—much to the chagrin of the clergy—there were other ways of combating witchcraft. From obscure sources in the folk culture of pre-Christian times the New Englanders had inherited a rich lore of countermagic—including, for example, the tricks which John Goodwin refused to try. Thus a family might decide to lay branches of "sweet bays under their threshold. ("It would keep a witch from coming in.") Or a woman tending a sick child would perform elaborate rituals of protection. ("She smote the back of her hands together sundry times, and spat in the fire; then she . . . rubbed [herbs] in her hand and strewed them about the hearth.") Or a man would hurl a pudding into a fire in order to draw a suspect to the scene of his alleged crimes. ("To get hay was no true cause of his coming thither, but rather the spirit that bewitched the pudding brought him.") All this was of a piece with other strands of belief and custom in seventeenth-century New England: fortunetelling, astrology, healing charms, love potions and powders—to mention a few. Witchcraft, in short, belonged to a large and complex world of interest in the supernatural.

Beyond the tricks against witches, besides the efficacy of prayer, there was always legal recourse. Witchcraft was a capital crime in every one of the New England colonies, and thus was a particularly solemn responsibility of the courts. Procedure was scrupulously observed: indictment by a grand jury, depositions from qualified witnesses, verdict by a jury of trials, sentencing by the magistrates. Some features of witchcraft trials seem highly repugnant today—for example, the elaborate and intimate body searches of defendants suspected of having "witch's teats" (nipplelike growths through which the witch or wizard was believed to give suck to Satan). But in the context of the times, such procedures were not extraordinary. Contrary to popular belief, physical torture was *not* used to obtain evidence. Testimony was taken on both sides, and character references favorable to the defendant were not uncommon. Guilt was never a foregone conclusion; most trials ended in acquittal. Perhaps *because* the crime was a

capital one, many juries seemed reluctant to convict. Some returned verdicts like the following: "[We find her] not legally guilty according to indictment, but [there is] just ground of vehement suspicion of her having had familiarity with the Devil."

At Salem, to be sure, such caution was thrown to the winds. The creation of special courts, the admission of "spectral evidence" (supplied by "shapes" visible only to the afflicted victims), the strong momentum favoring conviction—all this marked a decided tilt in the legal process. But it brought, in time, its own reaction. Magistrates, clergymen, and ordinary participants eventually would see the enormity of what they had done at Salem in the name of law and religion. And they would not make the same mistakes again.

Thus the eighteenth century, in New England, was essentially free of *legal* action against witchcraft. However, the belief which had sustained such action did not evaporate so quickly.

Hampton, New Hampshire: March 26, 1769. The finest house in the town, a mansion by any standard, is destroyed in a spectacular fire. The owner is General Jonathan Moulton—scion of an old family, frequent town officer, commander of the local forces in various Indian wars, businessman of extraordinary skill and energy. Yet despite these marks of eminence, Moulton is no favorite of his fellow townsmen. To them he seems ruthless, crafty, altogether a "sharp dealer." Indeed, the local gossips have long suggested that Moulton is in league with the Devil. There is no easier way to explain, among other things, his truly prodigious wealth.

The ashes of Moulton's house are barely cold when a new story circulates in the town: the fire was set by the Devil, because the General had cheated him in a bargain. The details are told as follows. Moulton had pledged his soul to the Devil, in exchange for regular payments of gold and silver coins. The payments were delivered down his chimney and into his boot, which was hung there precisely for this purpose. The arrangement went smoothly for awhile, but then came a time when the boot took far more coins than usual. The Devil was perplexed, and decided to go down the chimney to see what was wrong. He found that the General had cut off the foot of the boot; the room was so full of

money that there was scarcely air to breathe.

The fire—and this account of it—notwithstanding, Moulton quickly recoups. He builds a new mansion even more grand than the first one. His business enterprises yield ever greater profit. He serves with distinction in the Revolutionary War and also in the convention which draws up the constitution of the state of New Hampshire. Yet his local reputation shows little change with the passage of years. When he dies, in 1788, the news is carried to the haymakers on the Hampton marsh: "General Moulton is dead!" they call to one another in tones of evident satisfaction. And there is one final peculiarity about his passing. His body, prepared for burial, is suddenly missing from the coffin. The people of Hampton are not surprised. "The Devil," they whisper knowingly to one another, "has got his own at last."

Similar stories are preserved in the lore of many New England towns. Through them we can trace an enduring interest in the idea of witchcraft—and also an unmistakable change. The figure of the witch gradually lost its power to inspire fear. In many towns, for many generations, there were one or two persons suspected of practicing the black arts, but the effects of such practice were discounted. Witches were associated more and more with simple mischief—and less with death and destruction. There was even, as the Moulton story shows, an element of humor in the later lore of witchcraft. In our own time the wheel has turned full circle. There are many new witches among us—self-proclaimed, and proud of the fact. They haunt our television talk-shows and write syndicated columns for our newspapers. Their witchcraft is entirely constructive—so they assure us—and we are all invited to join in their celebration of things occult. Meanwhile some of the old witches have been rehabilitated.

Hampton, New Hampshire: March 8, 1938. A town meeting considers the case of a certain Eunice Cole, whose witchcraft was locally notorious three centuries before. The following motion is made: "*Resolved,* that we, the citizens . . . of Hampton . . . do hereby declare that we believe that Eunice (Goody) Cole was unjustly accused of witchcraft and familiarity with the Devil in the seventeenth century, and we do hereby restore to the said Eunice

(Goody) Cole her rightful place as a citizen of the town of Hampton." The resolution is passed unanimously. In fact, the legend of Goody Cole has become a cherished part of the local culture. A bronze urn in the town hall holds material purported to be her earthly remains. A stone memorial on the village green affirms her twentieth-century rehabilitation. There are exhibits on her life at the local historical society. There are even some *new* tales in which she plays a ghostly, though harmless part: an aged figure, in tattered shawl, seen walking late at night along a deserted road, or stopping in the early dawn to peer at gravestones by the edge of the green. And now an author's postscript:

Hampton, New Hampshire: October, 1972. The living room in a comfortable house abutting the main street. A stranger has come there, to examine a venerable manuscript held in this family through many generations. Laboriously his eyes move across the page, straining to unravel the cramped and irregular script of a bygone era. Two girls, aged nine or ten, arrive home from school; after a brief greeting they move off into an alcove and begin to play. Awash in the sounds of their game, the stranger looks up from his work and listens. "I'll be Goody Cole!" cries one of the girls. "Yes," responds the other, "and I'll be the one who gives you a whipping—you mean old witch!"

It is a long way from their time to ours, but at least a few of the early New England witches have made the whole journey.

How British Are You?

*Very. The legacy of British traits in America is deeper and
more significant than we knew.*

An Interview with David Hackett Fischer by Bertram Wyatt-Brown

As one of the most imaginative historians in contemporary America, David Hackett Fischer has produced a work that may put his fellow scholars' teeth on edge. Historians, rather conservative in temperament, are reluctant converts when their choice ideas are thrown into question. Yet Fischer's latest book, *Albion's Seed: Four British Folkways in America* (Oxford University Press) will fascinate them as well as the general reading public. Lucid, dramatic, and always entertaining, the thick, handsomely illustrated volume may safely be called a modern classic, and comparisons to Tocqueville are inevitable. The historian Gordon Wood declared that the Brandeis University professor has delivered a "revisionist blockbuster" that "has uncovered America's political and cultural roots in the countryside of Britain." The title suggests as much. Albion was the ancient Greek name for the island.

Fischer shows how particular religious persuasions, coupled with certain regional habits in four distinct areas of the kingdom, helped build four equally separate cultures in seventeenth- and eighteenth-century America. Each British district and its American counterpart had special ways of doing things and thinking about them. This broad-sweeping reinterpretation flies in the face of long-standing scholarly assumptions and even popular myths. Neither the early frontier nor the ethnic mix of later centuries can alone explain who we are and why Americans so cherish liberty. According to Fischer, these British roots, long neglected in the textbooks, require reexamination. And he provides it.

Fischer has an infectious smile and cherubic face that belie a steely intelligence and a no-nonsense approach to historical verification. Trained at City College, Baltimore, Fischer graduated from Princeton and later from Johns Hopkins, where he earned his Ph.D. in 1962. The young Brandeis teacher gained quick notice—even notoriety—for *Historians' Fallacies* (1970). This irreverent exposure of his elders' scholarly sins sent professors scurrying to find their names in the index. A steady outpouring of other books, articles, and edited works established him as a major figure. As a History Book Club Main Selection, *Albion's Seed,* however, reaches a much wider audience and arouses more praise than anything he has written before. It inaugurates an ambitious design to reinterpret, rather than merely retell, the whole of American history. (This interview took place in May at the National Humanities Center, Research Triangle Park, North Carolina.)

What led you to write the series of books on American history of which *Albion's Seed* is the first?

The effort comes out of a dissatisfaction with the state of history writing today. Many of my colleagues feel the same way. Some three generations ago scholars confined their interests to what we might call old political history—the study of Presidents, parties, wars, treaties, and the like. Then, in the sixties, something new called social history arose: a "total" history of ordinary people. Then it fragmented into such special areas as ethnicity, sexuality, and race. But the new school of historians calls to mind the man who mounted his horse and rode off in all directions. The great French scholar Fernand Braudel wrote that the new social history was overwhelmed by its own success. I am merely one of many historians who are looking for ways to bring the various components together in a form of cultural history that might unite the old political with the new social history.

How do you answer those who claim that material circumstances rather than ideas or cultural habits generate not only economic life but pretty much everything else in the social order? Marxist scholars adopt this position.

It strikes me that there is an irony here. Marxism is collapsing everywhere in the world. Its policies, appeal, and theories are thoroughly discredited. At the same time, a good many young American and British historians call themselves Marxists! Perhaps it helps them get a larger perspective, but the materialist model simply does not work. People and societies are more complicated than that. In fact, ideas and habits often predetermine economic choices rather than the other way around. For instance, most historians—even non-Marxist ones—believe that the culture of early Virginia, as well as the rest of the South later on, was created out of the introduction of slavery. But when did the slaves first appear in really significant numbers? Not until the colony was nearly a century old.

That gets us to the main arguments of *Albion's Seed*. What regions of Britain and America bear the kinds of affinities you describe?

There were at least four great migrations. From the Puritan East of England came the pious families of Massachu-

From *American Heritage*, November 1990, pp. 59–62, 66–68, 70, 73. © 1990 by Forbes, Inc. Reprinted by permission of *American Heritage* magazine, a division of Forbes, Inc.

The four migratory groups had much in common. But they also differed, and those differences perpetuated in our regional cultures to this day.

setts Bay. Their numbers were small. But the twenty-one thousand emigrants who arrived between, roughly, 1629 and 1640 were sufficient to dominate the social, religious, and political life of the Northeast. Eastern England was close to the Netherlands. Dutch influences can be found in the region's architecture and religion, in its burgher life of small towns and crafts and devotion to learning. This heritage is still very much alive in New England today. Much of the Massachusetts economy is based on educational institutions that grew out of the Puritan tradition.

Virginia's character stems not from the frail founding of Jamestown but rather from a later time: 1640–80. During and after the English Civil War, younger sons of gentry households tried to create in Virginia an aristocratic order, to reproduce the style of life in which they had been raised. Historians still have it wrong: They deny any validity to the Old South legend of shining knights and "Cavaliers." Of course, there was nothing very glorious about these Royalists, but they did set the style for Virginia life. They also imported large numbers of indentured servants—

about 70 percent of the population—from the South of England.

The Quakers of the Delaware Valley appeared later in the same century. Unlike the Puritans, who belonged to the middling ranks, Quakers came from the lower end of the social order. But not from the very bottom. Like the Puritans and the Cavaliers, they sought a haven from an unsympathetic government. They chiefly emigrated from the English North Midlands and Wales.

The fourth great migration brought people from the British borderlands—Ireland, Scotland, the North of England, and Wales. Hundreds of thousands poured in from 1720 to the American Revolution. These people endowed the hinterlands with a culture that Americans associate with the Wild West—the frontier spirit.

The map below charts the four folkways of *Albion's Seed:* **The Puritan migration from East Anglia peaked between 1629 and 1641; Cavalier Royalists from the southern counties settled around Chesapeake Bay, 1642 to 1675; North Midland Quakers arrived in Delaware Valley between 1675 and 1725; and immigrants from the borderlands of England, Scotland, and northern Ireland populated the Carolinas and Appalachia from 1717 to the eve of the Revolution.**

Ever since the seventeenth century New Englanders have cultivated an indifference to high fashions, preferring "sadd" colors and sensible shoes.

All these groups had much in common. They all spoke English, lived under British laws, and cherished British liberties. But they also differed in many ways: their separate dialects; wedding, child-naming, and child-rearing customs; attitudes about rank, age, gender, work, and leisure. These discrete folkways, as I call them, are perpetuated in our own regional cultures.

How about some specific examples for each of these regions?

Take speech, for example—something we all are aware of. New Englanders have a noticeable twang. It is a way of speaking that developed from the dialects of eastern England, such as the "Norfolk whine." Or clothing. New Englanders have long cultivated an indifference toward high fashions, preferring "sadd" colors, sensible shoes, and so on. This attitude was brought to Massachusetts in the seventeenth century. It survives in the famous Harvard crimson. It's really a muddy color, not blood red at all.

Now contrast these two patterns with Virginia's. Yankees chose to say "I am," "You are," "She isn't," "I haven't." Virginians, even the wealthy, preferred to say "I be," "You be," "She ain't," "I hain't." They often dropped the "as if" in favor of "like": "He looks like he's dead." They dropped or softened their R's. No respectable Puritan would say "book learning," but in Virginia, where intellectuality was not so highly regarded, that was the preferred term for education. These peculiarities of vocabulary, syntax, grammar, and accent were derived from the South and West of England. In dress the Virginia elite mimicked the styles of London. Women wore bright red cloaks, men seldom went without a sword. It was a symbol of their claim to being "gentlemen." Commoners were denied that equipage.

Many upper-class Virginians displayed coats of arms and stamped their books, silver, and coaches with these emblems of their genealogical lines.

Most interesting is the speech of the Delaware Valley. It was here that arose the flat accent, which linguists call midland speech, stretching from mid-New Jersey all the way across Middle America to Utah and beyond. Appropriately enough, that dialect is derived from the North Midlands of England—Nottinghamshire, Yorkshire, Lancashire, Cheshire, et cetera. An amusing example is the way people translated the noise their horses made. In East Anglia and New England they *neighed*—related to the Dutch *neijen*. In Wessex and the Chesapeake they *whickered*, but in midlands of both countries they *whinnied*.

Finally, the backcountry. The clothing of this culture underscored manliness for men, femininity for women. Bodices were cut low, and the dresses

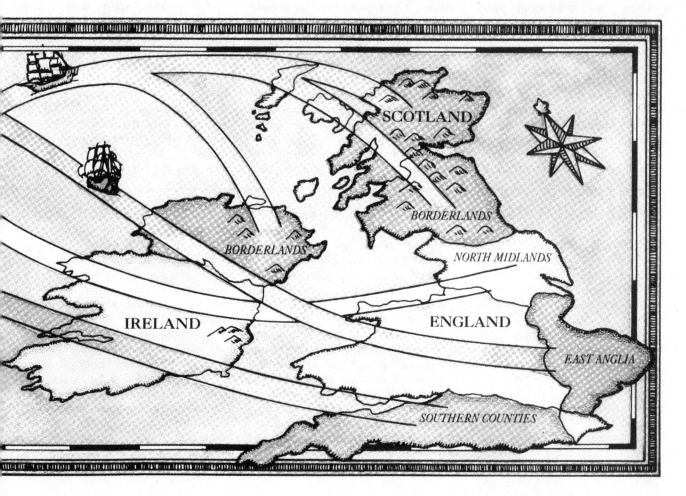

New Englanders thought that one should always be working hard; to Virginians the "gentleman of leisure" was a figure of high respectability.

were comparatively short. They were thought to be immodest by Quaker, Puritan, or even Anglican standards. Backwoodsmen wore clothes that emphasized muscularity, with the broad seams running horizontally. The shirt was "cinched" tightly at the waist. This style enlarged the shoulders and narrowed the hips. We like to think that this attire sprang from the frontier life of these people. Not so. It was a direct importation from the borderlands. As for speech, do you remember Lyndon Johnson's speech with its *whar* for *where, far* for *fire, narrer* for *narrow?* This is typical of the British borderlands, especially Northern Ireland. Double negatives abound: "He don't do nothin'." Of course, linguistically and sartorially much has changed in both America and Great Britain. Yet the persistence of many old patterns of speech and even of clothing is striking.

What about other contrasting patterns, such as sports, for example?

Let me make a comment before doing so. These topics—I have about twenty-five or so categories—are important in themselves but also in their cumulative and integrative capacity. They dovetail and reinforce each other. In other words, you won't find housing styles out of line with modes of social ranking or clothing habits out of alignment with religious and magical beliefs

and so on. To illustrate: Virginia's upper-class houses were designed like the manor houses of southern England. In both countries they were built with a distinct public function in mind: In the great center halls the gentry conducted their business, entertained their guests with balls, administered local justice, and so forth. That form of vernacular architecture was suited to the kind of life and culture the big planters developed.

But to answer your question. Sport is a very good indicator. New Englanders, for instance, were very organized in all things, even the kinds of games they played. They especially liked team sports. In early America football was called the Boston game, and baseball the New England game.

In Virginia *sport* meant a hierarchy of blood sports. Every rank was encouraged to kill animals of a size proportionate to their status—a great chain of slaughter. Commoners were not allowed to race their mounts against those of the elite. Even their betting was prohibited. Whereas anyone, high or low, could be fined in New England for gambling, in the Tidewater commoners alone were punished for violating their social position by gaming. Virginia gentlemen wagered enormous sums to demonstrate their wealth and power and to defy the fates. The Virginians were obsessed with fortune and astrology. Gambling was a

testing of one's fortune. In fact, Virginians often cast their sense of social order in terms of fortune. That is, it was fortune that placed one rank over another. The New Englanders had a very different way of thinking about the world, dividing it between the forces of good and the forces of evil. So their obsession was with witchcraft, the same as in eastern England. But back to sports. Sundays and court days in Virginia were favorite times for a horse race that often ended in bloody melees over the outcome. Jockeys lashed each other as well as their horses.

In stark contrast were the quiet habits of the Quakers. They preferred gardening. In the backcountry the Scots and Irish imported those sports that suited the warrior mode of their life. Our modern field sports—the javelin, foot race, broad jump, weight throwing, and so on—derive directly from the so-called Caledonian games. Also boxing and wrestling. These sports were a hardy business in the seventeenth and eighteenth centuries. Eye gouging was common. Some backwoodsmen let their nails grow long and hard, the better to spring an eye from its socket.

It sounds as if there were differences as well with regard to more serious matters, such as the proper use of time and the concept of work.

Massachusetts and East Anglia: Taxes and Town Government

This and the other boxes in this article are adapted from Albion's Seed.

A distinctive pattern of participation in town meetings developed at an early date in Massachusetts. It was normally characterized by very low levels of turnout—normally in the range of 10 to 30 percent of adult males. But when controversial questions came up, participation sometimes approached 100 percent.

This pattern of very low participation, punctuated by sudden surges of very high turnout, has been characteristic of New England town govern-

ment for three centuries—and very different . . . from voting patterns in other regions.

New England town governments tended to become very active in the life of their communities. The inhabitants voted to tax themselves heavily by comparison with other parts of British America. On a per capita basis, levels of spending by local government in Massachusetts were two to four times higher than in many other colonies, though much below the cost of government in Europe. These relative patterns have also persisted.

Town meeting government in early New England was not really democratic in our majoritarian sense. The object was not rule by majority, but by consensus. The purpose of a town meeting was to achieve that consensual goal by discussion, persuasion and mutual adjustment of differences. The numbers of votes were rarely counted, but merely recorded as the "will of the town." This system was unique to New England, and nearly universal within it. It was the combined product of East Anglian experiences, Puritan ideas, and the American environment.

Virginians spoke of *killing* time, backwoodsmen of *passing* time, New Englanders believed in *improving* time, Quakers in *redeeming* time.

"Time ways" is a superb marker of cultural distinctiveness. As you might expect, New Englanders believed in the idea of *improving* time. Virginians spoke of *killing* time; Quakers, *redeeming* time. Backwoodsmen thought in terms of *passing* the time. Each of these concepts reflected the deepest values of their culture. By improvement New Englanders had in mind personal and spiritual advancement. "Killing time" was not a phrase that appeared in any New England diary I have ever read. After all, it was a native of Boston who invented daylight savings time and an English Puritan who invented the alarm clock. New Englanders thought that one should be working hard at either mental or physical labor, not leaving it to others so that one could simply relax and enjoy. Study—especially religious study—was a high priority for self-enhancement.

On the other hand, very different were the Virginians. Of course, they could hardly avoid disagreeable work in the wilderness setting. But for both commoner and rich landholder, leisure was to be prized. Virginians had to engage in all sorts of commercial activities, but their attitudes toward work were ambivalent. Although no one admired the spendthrift, the "gentleman of leisure" was a figure of high respectability.

Quakers were less dedicated to the life of the intellect than were the Puritans. They also believed that the Puritans made an idolatry of time. The Quakers' neat farms, attention to business, and stolid sobriety revealed a sense of godly orderliness.

Backcountry folk had a different economy and a different sense of time's utility. Their cabins and farms were almost impromptu affairs, compared with those of the Quakers and German pietists who settled in Pennsylvania. These border and backcountry attitudes were a response to insecurity: There was no point in building forever when a conquering army or band of brigands could abruptly destroy your handiwork. In some respects, conditions in frontier America, especially where Native Americans were powerful, seemed little different from the old borderlands. So, idling away time in gossip, storytelling, sipping spirits, or singing ballads was a particular pleasure. Hogs and cattle, foraging in the unclaimed forests, were the prime source of livelihood and required little concentrated labor.

From the way you describe it, it sounds as if these Britons deliberately chose sites for settlement that would duplicate the conditions they knew at home. Or was it just happenstance to lead East Englishmen to rocky New England soils, borderers to the foothills, South Englishmen to the Southern lowlands, midlanders to a fertile valley?

Well, take the Quakers for an example. They were looking for a very special environment. What they wanted was a place to live in peace, a matter of profound importance to them. George Fox, the great Quaker leader, found in Pennsylvania that the local "Indians were loving," as he put it. He thought there would be less hostility, less conflict with natives than would be the case elsewhere.

How about the border people? why did they choose the hinterlands, where the Native Americans were not at all so "loving"?

By the time the border folk reached America, the coastal areas were pretty well occupied and the lands too expensive. Many arrived through Philadelphia. The Quakers disliked their alien ways and hurried them on to settlements inland. The backcountrymen migrated south along the Appalachian ridge. They did not have a lot of choice, but after

Virginia and Rural England: Cavalier Rape

The abolitionist indictment of slavery for its association with predatory sex had a solid foundation in historical fact. One thinks of Mary Boykin Chesnut's response to the antislavery movement in the nineteenth century: "Like the patriarchs of old our men live in one house with their wives and their concubines, and the mulattoes one sees in every family exactly resemble the white children—and every lady tells you who is the father of all the mulatto children in everybody's household, but those in her own she seems to think drop from the clouds. . . . You see, Mrs. Stowe did not hit on the sorest spot. She makes Legree a bachelor." Mrs. Chesnut knew whereof she spoke, and was haunted by her knowledge of sexual predators within her own family. But she (and the abolitionists, and many historians too) were very much mistaken in thinking that the "peculiar institution" of race slavery itself was the first cause of this behavior. The same pattern had appeared in Virginia before slavery was widespread. It had also existed in rural England.

The cultural idea of the predatory male was carried very far in early Virginia—even to the point of condoning rape. The diaries and commonplace books of Anglo-American gentlemen often recorded a complaisant and even jocular attitude toward rape that differed very much from prevailing mores in Puritan New England. The founders of New England made rape a hanging crime. In the courts of the Chesapeake colonies, it was sometimes punished less severely than petty theft—a different attitude from the Puritan colonies.

The sex ways of the southern colonies differed from New England in other ways as well. The people of Virginia thought less of the biblical commandment to increase and multiply and replenish the earth which so obsessed the Puritans, and more of breeding stocks and bloodlines. The gentry of Virginia studied one another's genealogies as closely as a stockman would scrutinize his stud books.

The Revolution was a cultural conflict. A *fifth* British culture had emerged, united and bureaucratized, and it became the common enemy.

all, the harsh life of the herdsman was what they knew. By the way, these people were not all Scots-Irish, as popular opinion has it. Ulster could not have produced the numbers. There were many Lowland Scots, more from Northern Ireland, and some from Southern Ireland, largely nominal Anglicans. We like to think that the backwoods revival camp-meeting was a strictly American experience. It was not. The encampment for worship and fellowship was a border practice, long predating the famous pioneer revivals.

Two points, somewhat related. where do we get our ideas of liberty? And how does your four-regions approach explain our polity today?

Each of the regions in Britain and America had a different understanding of liberty. New Englanders believed in *ordered* liberty. Consensus was a prime requirement. The whole community was an entity to itself, enjoying a freedom of association, but that did not allow for much internal dissent. Quakerism, witchcraft, and other alien heresies or blasphemies had no place at all but were to be suppressed without mercy. Yet in a curious paradox the Puritans were sincere in defending what they called liberty of conscience—even as they failed to see contradictions in their persecutions of those practicing it.

Virginians had a hegemonic or hierarchical notion of liberty—the right to rule others and themselves without in-

terference from outside authorities. Hence, liberty for some—the elite—involved subordination of others. Slaveholding was a right, not just a convenience.

Quakers were the most egalitarian group and saw freedom as a more universal commodity, as a reciprocal matter. Although Quakers recognized the primacy of men, they allowed women to speak at church meetings, for instance, and children were tender plants to be nurtured as if in a garden. Quakers did not resort to the customary cuffings and spankings by which Puritans sought to break the will of a child, naturally evil or amoral. So the Quakers' sense of liberty eventually brought them in the mid-eighteenth century to the then revolutionary idea that enslavement of Africans was a sin against God.

Backcountry folk saw liberty as a natural endowment. It had an individualistic and familial character—the right of a man to protect himself and his loved ones from enemies outside the clan (or even, in feuds, within it).

The critic might complain that such a view suggests that American Revolutionary unity was based on false premises. If there were so many versions of liberty, how could the colonists have coalesced to seek a single goal, independence?

I understand the Revolution as a cultural conflict, developing mainly from the challenge of a *fifth* British culture.

Over the years Britain itself had become increasingly united—subduing the Jacobite Scots and Irish—and more bureaucratized. A new national elite emerged with its own distinctive dialect, which we call Oxford English. This imperial elite tried to impose on Americans a new cultural order along with unprecedented modes of taxation—an unworthy, demeaning form of "slavery," as the Patriots saw it. The people of the four regions had long enjoyed their distinguishable liberties, many of them for nearly two centuries. A common enemy made for a common cause.

What does your interpretation tell us about today?

A very important purpose of this book is to study the past in a way that speaks to the present. Too many historians are antiquarians. They think the past is separate from the present. Still others see the past as merely prologue to the present, without its own integrity. Neither is correct. I am looking for a way of writing history without falling into either error.

It's interesting that many Americans feel that early colonial history is irrelevant to things happening in the United States today. We differ in this respect from other cultures in the world. In Latin America, for example, the memory of the colonial period is urgently important in debates about public questions. The same is true for Canada and South Africa or the current ethnic

---

Pennsylvania and the North Midlands: A Loving Neighborhood

On the day after William Penn arrived in Pennsylvania, he called his colonists together, and solemnly pledged to protect their full "spiritual and temporal rights." In return, he asked only two things. The first was that they should try to stay sober. The second was that they should keep up a "loving neighborhood" with one another.

This notion of "loving neighborhood" was an ideal of high importance in the Delaware Valley. It became the cultural cement of a special type of

comity which combined Quaker ideas and North Midland traditions. This Delaware comity differed from those of New England and the Chesapeake in many ways—in patterns of settlement, migration, association and social bonding.

The ideal settlement in the Delaware Valley was one where every family lived separately upon its farmstead, but was not entirely isolated from others. Houses were to be built in small clusters which became the nuclei of rural neighborhoods—a pattern still to be

seen through the Pennsylvania countryside.

This form of settlement had long existed in the north of England—a pattern equally distinct from the town life of East Anglia and the manorial villages of Wessex. Nucleated towns were comparatively rare in the North Midlands. So also were landed estates with a great house surrounded by a cluster of close-built cottages. The economy of the northern counties required smaller units and more open settlements.

Backcountry folk saw liberty as a natural endowment—the right of a man to protect himself and his loved ones from enemies outside the clan.

troubles in the Soviet Union. But in America our colonial past has been sanitized. This is partly because Americans think of history as change. We tend to be less conscious of continuities. History, we assume, is something that happens to less fortunate people. I think this is wrong.

But how can the colonial past seem pertinent when so few Americans today have even a drop of "British blood"?

It's true that only 19 percent of us have British ancestry. Nonetheless, most Americans are "Albion's seed" in a cultural sense. Take the Kennedys of Massachusetts, for example. Though Irish and Catholic, John F. Kennedy and his family were also New Englanders. When he pronounced "Americer" and "Cuber," he demonstrated the old New England twang. Another example is Franklin Roosevelt. He was three-quarters Yankee, despite his Dutch New York name. His New England culture profoundly influenced his political beliefs.

So, in other words, these cultural factors not only demonstrate the survival of old tendencies but also affect national politics.

Very much so. We have had forty Presidents, and all but two, Martin Van Buren and Kennedy, descended from one or more of the four great migrations. Surprisingly, the borderers have supplied the greatest number—some eighteen—from Andrew Jackson and James Polk to Gerald Ford, Jimmy Carter, and Ronald Reagan. Next came the sixteen Presidents from Puritan roots. They include George Bush. Ten can be traced to the "distressed Cavalier" tradition—the early Virginia Presidents down to Harry Truman. Only seven arose from the Quaker-German Pietist background, most notably Herbert Hoover and Dwight Eisenhower, a soldier-hero who hated war. Isn't it curious that, apart from Kennedy, only those of early colonial extraction have reached the White House?

If we turn to major national policy questions, we find that region was the single most salient factor—quite apart from the obviously sectional character of the Civil War. Richard Bensel, the political scientist, has demonstrated that between 1880 and 1908 congressional voting was based more on region than on party, class, or any other factor. Even today political struggles arise from old folk ideas of order, power, and freedom, all of which still define our regional cultures. For instance, the retributive and every-man-his-own-master principles of the border legacy help to explain the Southern and Western opposition to gun control. In contrast, those states most affected by settlement of New Englanders have a low rate of homicide when compared with the statistics of the South and Southwest. On the women's suffrage and equal rights amendments, where has been the strongest support or challenge? The answers lie in those sections of the land affected by their roots in the colonial past.

How will your series develop hereafter?

Albion's Seed is the first of other works designed to fill out many questions left unanswered here. For instance, the next book will explain four distinctive African-American cultures that developed in various regions of the United States. Volume three is about Dutch, German, and Spanish cultures in North America. But the first, *Albion's Seed,* suggests that the colonial period of American history has left us a rich and dynamic legacy. That bequest continues to be a vital part of our contemporary culture.

Bertram Wyatt-Brown is a professor of history at the University of Florida and a fellow at the National Humanities Center. One of his books, Southern Honor: Ethics and Behavior in the Old South, *was a finalist for both the Pulitzer Prize and the National Book Award.*

Virginia, Pennsylvania, and the Scottish Border: Backcountry Squalor

Cabin architecture was striking for its roughness and impermanence. It was a simple style of building, suitable to a migratory people with little wealth, few possessions and small confidence in the future. It was also an inconspicuous structure, highly adapted to a violent world where a handsome building was an invitation to disaster. In that respect, cabin architecture was an expression of the insecurity of life in the northern borders.

The cabin was also the product of a world of scarcity. It was a style of vernacular architecture created by deep and grinding poverty through much of north Britain during the late seventeenth and early eighteenth centuries. In that barren country, cabins made of earth and stone were an adaptation to an environment in which other building materials were rare.

Cabin architecture was also a style of building well suited to a people who had a strong sense of family and a weak sense of individual privacy. Travelers from the south of England expressed horror at the lack of respect for privacy. Much the same observations were also made in the American backcountry. "They sleep altogether in common in one room, and shift and dress openly without ceremony," Woodmason wrote, " . . . nakedness is counted as nothing." Sometimes there was not even a bed. William Byrd described one backcountry family that "pigged lovingly together" on the floor.

In the eighteenth century, these cabins began to rise throughout the American backcountry wherever migrants from North Britain settled. The strong resemblance of these houses to the vernacular architecture of the borders was noted by travelers who knew both places. One English traveler noted of a Scots-Irish settlement in the backcountry of Pennsylvania that the people lived in "paltry log houses, and as dirty as in the north of Ireland, or even Scotland."

Slavery and Insurrections in the Colonial Province of New York

Marc Newman

Marc Newman teaches history for grades 11 and 12 at the Valley Central High School, Montgomery, New York. He has been the recipient of many national and state awards for historical instruction.

Many school systems are committed to developing curriculum materials on slavery. Teaching and research dealing with slavery have, however, focused more on the South of this country than the North. Yet in the first part of the eighteenth century, slavery was an important feature of the social structure of the North, including the Province of New York, which is the focus of this article.

The rapid commercial growth of both the City and the Province of New York in the eighteenth century was partly attributable to the increased use of slave labor. Slavery existed both in rural and urban areas and slaves performed functions ranging from unskilled manual labor to skilled work in trades and crafts.

The rapid expansion of the slave population worried officials concerned with maintaining order. They attempted to control the population through a series of repressive ordinances known as the "Laws of Bondage and Servitude." However, the rigidity of these laws convinced slaves that only open armed revolt could eradicate the evils of the system. The result was two black slave insurrections, in 1712 and 1741, which created mass fear and hysteria in the Province.

THE GROWTH OF THE SLAVE POPULATION

In the first part of the eighteenth century, the demand for slave labor exceeded the supply. In 1701, only thirty-six slaves were imported to New York from the West Indies and the African coast. Eleven years later the number of black slaves imported by private traders in a year had increased to four hundred and thirty.[1] After this, the slave population expanded dramatically. Although in 1712, there were 1775 slaves in the Province of New York, by 1746 that number had almost reached 10,000, and was close to 20 percent of the population (Table 1).

Most of these inhabitants resided in the urbanized areas of New York City, Albany and Queens counties.

This population increase meant not only that a significant minority of the population were resentful of the system which enslaved them; it may also have provided a sense of "safety in numbers" for the slaves, should the decision be made to revolt violently against the slave system.

While black slaves were retained for the menial labor of the New York "plantations," or "patroons" (estates), many were sent into towns and urban areas to be employed in skilled trades and crafts. The rise in the number of slaves residing

---

Table 1

Inhabitants of The Province of New York, June 4, 1746

County	Number of Whites	Number of Slaves
New York	9,273	2,444
Kingston	1,686	645
Albany *		
Queens	7,996	1,647
Dutchess	8,306	500
Suffolk	5,855	1,399
Richmond	1,691	382
Orange	2,958	310
West Chester	8,563	682
Ulster	4,154	1,122
Total *(except Albany)**	50,482	9,131

Source: E.B. O'Callaghan, *Documentary History of the State of New York* (Albany, New York, 1849-1851) I: 693-95.

* *A count could not be made in Albany County because of French-British hostilities in North America resulting from the War of the Austrian Succession. In a count made in 1723, there had been 808 slaves in Albany County, which made it the county with the fourth largest slave population.*

From *Social Education*, March 1995, pp. 125–129. © 1995 by the National Council for the Social Studies. Reprinted by permission.

in the urban areas provided an opportunity for them to converse with other black slaves. Channels of communication between the slaves were further enhanced through the architectural construction of the cities themselves, whose many buildings, and twisting and turning streets and alleys, allowed encounters that could not be closely monitored by slaveowners.

THE LEGAL REGULATION OF SLAVERY

Because of fears of slave maneuverability, laws and regulations aimed not merely at defining the master-slave relationship, but also at controlling and restricting the freedom of movement of slaves. The major corpus of law during this period, the Laws of Bondage and Servitude passed in the first part of the eighteenth century, defined the nature of the institution of slavery and delegated authority to the slaveowner and white community to regulate the slave. These laws built on earlier legislation in New York, consisting mainly of several laws and statutes passed between 1664 and 1702 to prescribe the nature of "indentured servitude." Slaves were subjected to these laws until their numbers were sufficiently large that laws explicitly dealing with slavery were enacted.

The first legislation in the province consisted of the "Duke of Yorks Laws, 1665 to 1675." The Law of 1665 required, among other things, that "all labourers and servants shall work in their callings being thereunto required the whole day,"[2] whether they worked in the fields, crafts, or as domestics.

Freedom from indentured servitude could be sought at first through conversion to Christianity. In 1664, Christianity became a pre-requisite for exclusion from indentured servitude, with the exception of cases in which people had sold themselves into servitude. The realization that a conversion of faith would result in the gradual diminution of a cheap labor force brought legislative revision in 1706 by the Governor's Council and Assembly, as the slave population became larger. According to the new provisions, "the Baptizing of any Negro, Indian, or Mulatto Slave shall not be any cause for the setting them or any of them at liberty."[3]

In 1683, a law was enacted to prevent more than three slaves meeting together at any time or place away from the service of their master in the City. The fear of slave conspiracies prompted the white inhabitants of New York to demand the restriction of slave assemblage and armament.

> And that noe such Slave doe goe Armed att Any tyme with gunns, Swords, Clubs, Staves Or Any Other kind of weapons Wt Soever, under the Penalty of being whipped at the Public whipping poste. Ten lashes, unless the Master or Owners of Such Slave will Pay Six Shillings to Excuse the Same[4]

Slave owners in New York feared slave uprisings, especially during the period 1680 to 1708 when there was slave unrest in a number of colonies: South Carolina, Virginia, New Jersey and Maryland. The masters were also concerned with the loss of their "chattel property" through flight. Governor Thomas Dongan enacted a bill against fugitive servants in 1684, which made clear that runaway servants would be caught and serve double their time for such an absence. When war broke out between England and France between 1702 and 1713, slaves tried to leave New York and cross to Canada, which was under French occupation, to seek their freedom. The result was a new law in 1705: An Act to Prevent the Running Away of Negro Slaves Out of the City, and County of Albany to the French at Canada.

The same Act of 1706 that barred conversion to Christianity as a means for slaves to obtain their freedom further stated that the status of the mother, slave or free, would determine the status of the child born to the mother. Thus the "Barbados Code" of the West Indies was transplanted to New York to perpetuate the system of slavery there. A child who was the product of a sexual union between a female slave and a white freeman was therefore deemed a slave.

The provincial laws on miscegenation were harsh and the penalties severe for any white women who had sexual relations with a Negro slave. Although most children born of miscegenation were predominantly dark pigmented, there were many who could "pass as white" due to their light color. The hereditary characteristic of dark pigmentation became a mark of distinction barring the "black colonial" from entering white colonial New York society.

To prevent the possibility of social assimilation, white political leaders enacted two important laws defining and organizing the system of slavery within the province. The laws of 1702 and 1712 determined the method and means of punishing blacks who sought freedom. The Act for Regulating Slaves of 1702 delegated authority to the master, or mistress, to punish their slaves at their discretion as long as the punishment did not extend to life, or member. An Act regulating slavery after the insurrection of 1712 prescribed methods of punishment for criminal offenses committed by the slave. It granted authority to the community to appoint a "Common Whipper," whose job was to lash the back of any person in violation of provincial, or community laws, especially slaves. The number of lashes inflicted was determined by the severity of the crime.

Punishment was often arbitrary, and could in large measure be based on the color of skin and the religious affiliation of the accused. Although the whip became the prescribed method of punishment, and a vital means of securing the slave's obedience to the institution of slavery, the death penalty could also be inflicted on any slave who committed a serious felony. The laws of 1702 and 1712 regulated any attempt of a slave to defend himself against the brutality of the white slave owner.

SLAVERY AND DEHUMANIZATION

Although the workmanship and expertise exhibited by slaves in the trades and crafts were comparable to those of white skilled laborers, the black slave was a "chattel possession" bought and sold on New York's Slave Market. Many black laborers who did menial work on the plantations, or patroons, were hired out by their master to work as apprentices or journeymen in the skilled crafts of the towns, villages and cities. Some of the slaves who were employed under this "hiring system" would be given tips by their city, village, or town craft employer to keep. Eventually, by saving sufficient money, the slaves could strike a bargain with their master for their freedom in exchange for the money they accumulated through this system. Eventually, the "hiring system" was abandoned because it became a means of liberty and freedom for the slave.

The sale of slaves was advertised in the various journals and newspapers of the day. New York, Massachusetts and Pennsylvania were leading centers of the printed word, and their records are revealing. The following advertisement in a New York weekly typifies the value placed on the Negro slave:

To be sold by Obadiah Wells, in Prince Street A LIKELY NEGRO BOY, about 20 years of Age, is well recommended, and suitable for either Town or Country; also a parcel of Corrage, Spuryarn, Iron Pots, and sundry sorts of European Goods.[5]

The purchase of one or more slaves became an ever-widening practice accepted and perpetuated by middle and upper class whites. Representative of this attitude is a letter dated December 7, 1721, in which Mr. Cadwallader Colden, the future governor of New York, expresses his desire to purchase domestics:

I am oblidged to you for your kinde offer of buying me three or four slaves and that in so doing you will particularly consider my interest. Please to buy mee two negro men, about eighteen years of age. I designe them for labor and would have them strong and well made. Please likewise to buy mee a Negro girl about 13 years old my wife has told you that she designes her chiefly to keep the children & to sow & therefore would have her likely & one that appears to be good natured. Pray send them upon my account & risque as soon as you can purchase them.[6]

A TALE OF TWO INSURRECTIONS

On April 6, 1712, the fear and frustrations of a disenchanted people reached its full expression within the City of New York. The urban development of the city, with its many areas concealed from public view, had provided a haven for slaves to meet together In Mr. Cook's orchard, near the middle of the town, twenty-three slaves assembled to rebel against the institution of slavery, a system symbolized in the person of the white slaveowner.

In a letter dated June 23, 1712, Governor Robert Hunter affirmed that the Negro slaves "had resolved to revenge themselves for some hard usage they Apprehended to have received from their Master."[7] Several of the slaves were armed with firearms, swords, knives, and hatchets. The signal to begin the revolt began when Coffee, a slave of a Mr. Vantilburgh, set fire to an outhouse of his master. Once Coffee returned to the orchard, the insurrectionists rallied with their arms and marched to the site of the fire.

The flames of the fire were immediately detected and attracted the attention of a large number of white inhabitants. While many of the whites were attempting to extinguish the flames, they were fired upon by the insurgents. Nine white people were shot and killed, and some five others were seriously wounded. A detachment of militia, stationed at Fort George, was sent to the scene, but the slaves dispersed into the neighboring woods. The next morning, several whites began to search the area for the rebels and on the afternoon of April 7, the rebels were captured and then brought to trial.

The trial of the insurgents was held immediately, with the testimony of several eyewitnesses to the crimes of arson and murder. Of the twenty-seven slaves tried for the crime, twenty-three were convicted and executed. The majority of these slaves suffered the penalty of death by hanging, or by being burned at the stake.

One direct consequence of the slave insurrection of 1712 was that the fear and anxiety of future plots stimulated the passage of additional laws to strengthen those that existed. A more repressive slave code was enacted in December 1712. Another code in 1717 dissuaded slaveowners from setting their slaves free by the unusual device of making the owner pay two hundred pounds annually to the freed slave, as well as twenty pounds to the Colony of New York.

During the era from 1716 to 1734, laws were passed to derive revenue from the importation of slaves, as well [as] to attempt to dissuade whites from importing slaves on too large a scale. To ensure gradual diminution of the number of slaves imported, a revenue tax was levied on each slave in 1716. When the importation of slaves increased rather than decreased, a further duty was legislated in 1734 on goods, and another tax was levied on imported slaves.

In the years that followed, fear and anxiety about slave reprisals resulted in the stricter enforcement of the slave system through the implementation of the laws previously mentioned. New York slave owners became harsher and more brutal in their treatment of slaves in an attempt to instill obedience and quell any desires for freedom. The brutality of the system did not, however, dampen the fires of rage and insurrection, but rather became a catalyst for another revolt in 1741.

That year, the first outbreak of violence occurred on February 28 in the City of New York. On this particular Saturday night, a robbery was committed at the shop of a merchant, Robert Hogg. Several articles of cloth and silver coins were taken. While the police and magistrates of the city were investigating the theft, a fire broke out at the Governor's mansion, the Chapel, and other buildings in the area. During the months of March and April, fires broke out throughout parts of the City, destroying nine edifices (Table 2). Although the fires were suppressed, the white community believed that slaves were plotting to destroy the city.

The day before the robbery in Hogg's shop, Wilson, a Negro youth seventeen years of age, and a Spanish Negro sailor had entered the shop to purchase some check linens. Mrs. Hogg sold the merchandise to the customers. While exchanging the large amount of currency given to her, Wilson and the sailor inspected the contents of the bureau drawer of the shop, which contained a considerable quantity of milled Spanish pieces-of-eight. The following day, Mr. Hogg's shop was robbed of linens and silver coins.

Upon reflection, Mrs. Hogg remembered the visit of Wilson and his friend. Through an intense search for the stolen items and the whereabouts of Wilson, the authorities recovered several stolen items in the home of a John Hughson. It seemed that the Hughsons were in some way participants in the robbery, and received the stolen merchandise from a black slave, Caesar. Upon further investigation it appeared that John Hughson was not only responsible for the robbery, but could also have been implicated in the succession of fires that broke out in February. The association of the Hughsons and their servant, Margaret Kerry, a woman of "immoral character," with two slaves, Caesar and Prince, led the white population to believe that the Hughsons and a majority of the slaves were conspiring to murder the white inhabitants of the city.

Table 2
A List of Fires in New York City, 1741

Date	Location
March 18, 1741	Governor's House and Chapel
March 25, 1741	Captain Warren's House
April 1, 1741	Storehouse of Mr. Van Zant
April 4, 1741	Cow Stables near Quick's House
April 4, 1741	Ben Thomas' House
April 5, 1741	Haystack near the Coach House
April 5, 1741	Stables of Joseph Murray, Esq.
April 6, 1741	Sargent Burns' House
April 6, 1741	Mrs. Hilton's House

Source: Daniel Horsemanden, *The New York Conspiracy: History of the Negro Plot, 1741-1742* (New York, 1810): 19-36.

I am humbly of the opinion that such confessions unless some certain Overt Act appear to confirm the same are not worth a straw; for many time they are obtain'd by foul means, by force or torment, by Surprise, by Flattery, by Distraction, by Discontent with their Circumstances, through envy that they may bring others in to the same condemnation; or in hopes of a longer time to live, or to dye an easier death &c.[10]

Such views were, however, in the minority. Slavery continued to be legal in New York until late in the eighteenth century. Those studying or teaching the history of the period may find it enlightening to examine slavery in New York and northern cities, as well as the more commonly studied southern plantations. The slave rebellions and the fears they generated offer dramatic insights into the instability of a socio-economic system based on humiliation and degradation.

In March 1741, the Hughsons, Margaret Kerry, Caesar and Prince were arraigned for the crimes of arson and robbery. On April 17, a proclamation was offered by the Governor, offering one hundred pounds for any information about the identity of those involved in setting the fires in town. This proclamation provided a major incentive for whites and blacks to testify in the court. Although the defendants pleaded not guilty, the testimony of Mary Burton, a sixteen-year-old servant of the Hughsons, and John Varrack, a baker and slaveowner of Caesar and Prince, was sufficient evidence to convict the defendants of the crimes of robbery, arson and conspiracy. On May 11, 1741, John Hughson, Caesar and Prince were convicted and executed in the City of New York.

The evidence supporting the validity of a slave conspiracy was never substantiated in detail. Although Hughson and his wife admitted they were the recipients of stolen goods, they pleaded innocent to arson and conspiracy. The fear and anxiety of the white populace was reminiscent of the insurrection of 1712.

From May 11 to March 13, 1742, approximately one hundred and sixty slaves were accused and arraigned on charges of conspiracy against the City of New York. While it is impossible to trace the outcome of all cases, the records show that forty-one slaves were convicted of conspiracy, while seventy-seven confessed either at the stake or in court. Approximately thirteen slaves were burned alive at the stake, eighteen were hanged, and seventy-one were exported to islands in the Caribbean Sea.[8] Seventeen were acquitted.

Injustice triumphed as a result of the reactions of a white community fearful of its slaves, who had ample reason and provocation to rebel. A predominantly white society not only prejudged the defendants, but failed to provide them legal counsel for their defense, since "the lawyers of the City refused to a man to assist the slaves in their trials on this occasion."[9] The resulting inability to present an adequate defense, as well as the testimony of Mary Burton and Arthur Prince, resulted in mass convictions.

It was a sign of hope for the future that there were members of society who believed the trials and judicial procedures were violations of English law. In an unsigned letter to Cadwallader Colden, a member of the Governor's Council, on June 23, 1741, the following viewpoint was expressed:

Notes

1. See E. B. O'Callaghans *Documentary History of the State of New York* (Albany, New York, 1849–1851) I: 693.
2. *Colonial Laws of New York from the Year 1664 to the Revolution,* 5 vol. (Albany, New York, 1894) I: 47.
3. *Colonial Laws of New York from the Year 1664 to the Revolution,* I: 598.
4. *Minutes of The Common Council of the City of New York, 1675–1776.* 8 vol. (New York: Dodd, Mead and Co., 1905) I: 134. In this quotation, as in other direct quotations cited in this article, the original language and spelling have been retained.
5. *The New York Weekly Post Boy,* January 30, 1749.
6. *Letters and Papers of Cadwallader Colden, 1711–1775,* 9 vol. (New York: New York Historical Society) V: 51.
7. Daniel Parish, *Transcripts of Material On Slavery, 1688–1760, 1695–1713, and 1740–1747.* New York Historical Society Collections, Collection 1695–1713: 163.
8. See Daniel Horsmanden's *The New York Conspiracy: History of The Negro Plot, 1741–1742* (New York, 1810): 19–36. Daniel Horsmanden was one of three New York Justices appointed to preside over the case. His account appears to be an attempt to justify the verdicts and mass executions in 1741 and 1742.
9. David T. Valentine, ed. *Manual of the Corporation of New York* (New York: Francis P. Harper, 1900): 449.
10. *Letters and papers of Cadwallader Colden,* VII: 41.

Revolutionary America

The American colonies were but one part of a vast British empire. They were expected to serve as sources for raw materials, especially strategic goods such as shipbuilding materials, and to provide a market for British manufactured goods. As time passed, London permitted the colonies to exercise a great deal of control over their own internal affairs so long as they played their designated economic role. This was less by design than by what became known as "benign neglect." The British were too preoccupied with other matters to attempt day-to-day involvement in matters that meant little to them. Some commercial regulations were deemed necessary to regulate the flow of trade, but these were only loosely applied.

Benign neglect, the passage of time, and the distance from Britain wrought changes in colonists' attitudes. Although most counted themselves loyal British subjects, they also came to assume the autonomy they enjoyed as the natural state of affairs and also to think of themselves more and more as "Americans."

What colonists called the French and Indian War ended after seven long years in 1763, with the British acquiring French possessions in North America. The British people were suffering under staggering tax burdens to pay for the war, and the government thought it only equitable that colonists should bear their fair share. Many Americans did not see it that way, especially since they no longer had to rely on British troops to protect them from the French.

The new taxes and tightened shipping regulations, together with the means London employed to see that they were carried out, seemed to the colonists an almost revolutionary assault on the rights and privileges they had long enjoyed. Economic matters quickly became entangled with quarrels over rights and freedoms in other areas. Some colonists who prevously had regarded themselves as loyal subjects of the crown now began calling for separation from the motherland. The British, of course, meant to keep their possessions. This conflict resulted in the Revolutionary War.

In "Editing the Declaration," Joseph Ellis examines the creation of the Declaration of Independence. Usually attributed almost solely to Thomas Jefferson, Ellis explores the numerous revisions made by others to this important document. "The *Radical* Revolution" by Fredric Smoler presents an interview with author Gordon Wood. This noted scholar's rebuttal of the view that the French Revolution was radical, while its American counterpart was a conservative attempt merely to overthrow British rule is examined by Smoler. Wood argues that our revolution was crucial in leading to the most democratic society in the world. In "The Hessians," Debra Brill examines the part played by the German soldiers, frequently referred to as Hessians, who fought for the British during the rebellion of the American colonies. Brill also presents American efforts to alienate these soliders from the British.

Victory over the British during the revolution did not bring on the golden age that some of the American participants anticipated. Within a few years after the struggle, as Peter Onuf shows in " 'It Is Not a Union,' " there were serious economic problems and a number of disputes among the former colonies under the Articles of Confederation. Dissatisfaction with the existing system led to the Constitutional Convention of 1787. In " 'To Form a More Perfect Union,' " Robin Russin analyzes the many divisive issues the Founding Fathers confronted at the convention and describes how compromises were reached. William Freehling, in "The Founding Fathers, Conditional Antislavery, and the Nonradicalism of the American Revolution," concludes that although the Founders did not intend to bring about a radical change in the institution of slavery, they did take steps that would undermine its future. "The Bill of Rights in Its Context" analyzes what the authors of these amendments intended as contrasted to more recent interpretations of what rights are protected.

Looking Ahead: Challenge Questions

Evaluate the Declaration of Independence, particularly with regard to the revisions of Jefferson's draft. Did these changes strengthen the document or dilute it? Why?

Analyze Gordon Wood's argument (see "The *Radical* Revolution") that the American Revolution had far more radical implications than usually is assumed.

Why was the system established by the Articles of Confederation scrapped instead of merely revised?

What were those who took part in the Constitutional Convention trying to accomplish, and what were the main points of contention that divided them?

Why did the issue of slavery prove so difficult to resolve, and how effective were efforts to modify the institution?

Why did so many people believe a Bill of Rights was necessary, and what rights did the authors intend to protect?

Editing the Declaration

Jefferson's original text provided the inspiration, but early drafts make clear that the document was not the creation of one man

Joseph J. Ellis

Joseph J. Ellis is a professor of history at Mount Holyoke College and a contributing editor of Civilization.

Handwritten historical documents speak across the gap of time in a distinctive voice that print cannot duplicate. The yellowed paper and the slant of the scrawl connect us in a personal way with the dead. When the handwriting is Thomas Jefferson's and the document is the Declaration of Independence, well, the effect can be inspirational. We feel, in the primal American sense, "present at the creation."

During the middle of June 1776, on the second floor of his temporary lodgings at Seventh and Market streets in Philadelphia, Jefferson applied his quill pen to paper on a custom-made portable desk and wrote the magic phrases of American history. Here, in just 55 words, is the seminal statement of the American Creed, the poetry of our political culture:

> We hold these truths to be self-evident; that all men are created equal; that they are endowed by their creator with certain inalienable rights; that among these are life, liberty, & the pursuit of happiness; that to secure these rights, governments are instituted among men, deriving their just powers from the consent of the governed.

When asked, as he often was in later years, what sources he drew on when drafting the declaration, he explained that his purpose was "not to find out new principles, or new arguments, never before thought of, not merely to say things which had never been said before; but to place before mankind the common sense of the subject, in terms so plain and firm as to command their assent. . . ." As he recalled the drafting process, he did not refer to any books or pamphlets, but took inspiration from what he called "the harmonizing sentiments of the day" and intended his words simply as "an expression of the American mind."

When we imagine Jefferson sitting alone at his desk, receiving the message from the gods and sending it along to us, the urge to depict him as an oracle is almost irresistible. No less an authority than Abraham Lincoln, who also changed history with words, expressed with characteristic eloquence this quasi-religious view of Jefferson:

> All honor to Jefferson—to the man who, in the concrete pressure of a struggle for national independence by a single people, had the coolness, forecast, and capacity to introduce into a merely revolutionary document, an abstract truth, . . . and so to embalm it there, that to-day, and in all coming days, it shall he a rebuke and a stumbling-block to the very harbingers of re-appearing tyrany and oppression.

As a statement of what the Declaration of Independence has come to mean, Lincoln's eulogy to the oracular Jefferson makes perfect sense. (The phrase "a merely revolutionary document" is also pure Lincoln poetry.) After all, the declaration is the American version of the Magna Carta. It served as the inspiration for Lincoln at Gettysburg and Martin Luther King on the steps of the Lincoln Memorial. Even Ho Chi Minh quoted from it when declaring Vietnam independent of the French, and several other emerging nations followed suit when announcing their break with colonial rule. Every significant reform movement in American history—from the feminists at Seneca Falls, to the civil-rights workers in Mississippi, to the founders of SDS at Port Huron, Michigan—has harked back to its liberal message. Although legal scholars who embrace the doctrine of "original intent" are usually referring to the Constitution, it is in fact the declaration that captures the essence of America's original promise to itself and the world. The English writer G. K. Chesterton put it succinctly:

> America is the only nation in the world that is founded on a creed. That creed is set forth with dogmatic and even theological lucidity in the Declaration of Independence, perhaps the only piece of practical politics that is also theoretical politics and also great literature.

But when we view the four different versions of the document, on display at the Library of Congress from June 29 through July 4, the sense of quiet communion is quickly displaced by a cacophony of human voices. The multiple cross-outs, insertions and faded smudges transport us back to the Pennsylvania State House (now Independence Hall), where we hear real people arguing like modern-day editors about language, punctuation and the difference between what is essential and what is peripheral. The exhibit makes it clear that the dec-

 From *Civilization*, July/August 1995, pp. 58–63. © 1995 by Joseph J. Ellis. Reprinted by permission.

A Declaration by the Representatives of the UNITED STATES OF AMERICA, in General Congress assembled.

When in the course of human events it becomes necessary for one people to dissolve the political bands which have connected them with another, and to assume among the powers of the earth the separate and equal station to which the laws of nature & of nature's god entitle them, a decent respect to the opinions of mankind requires that they should declare the causes which impel them to the separation.

We hold these truths to be self-evident, that all men are created equal, that they are endowed by their creator with inherent & inalienable rights, that among these are life, liberty, & the pursuit of happiness; that to secure these rights, governments are instituted among men, deriving their just powers from the consent of the governed; that whenever any form of government becomes destructive of these ends, it is the right of the people to alter or to abolish it, & to institute new government, laying it's foundation on such principles & organising it's powers in such form, as to them shall seem most likely to effect their safety & happiness. prudence indeed will dictate that governments long established should not be changed for light & transient causes: and accordingly all experience hath shewn that mankind are more disposed to suffer while evils are sufferable, than to right themselves by abolishing the forms to which they are accustomed. but when a long train of abuses & usurpations [begun at a distinguished period, &] pursuing invariably the same object, evinces a design to reduce them under absolute Despotism, it is their right, it is their duty, to throw off such government & to provide new guards for their future security. such has been the patient sufferance of these colonies; & such is now the necessity which constrains them to expunge their former systems of government. the history of the present king of Great Britain is a history of unremitting injuries and usurpations, among which appears no solitary fact to contradict the uniform tenor of the rest, but all have in direct object the establishment of an absolute tyranny over these states. to prove this, let facts be submitted to a candid world, for the truth of which we pledge a faith yet unsullied by falsehood.

The Congress's first deletion contained an emotional passage condemning "our British brethren." Jefferson went to his grave regretting the change

laration was not the creation of one man. Eighty-six substantive or stylistic changes were made in Jefferson's draft, most of them by the members of the Continental Congress, who also excised about one-quarter of his original text. If the semisacred character of the Declaration of Independence depends in part on sustaining a blurry image of a solitary Jefferson, gazing presciently into the middle distance while pondering self-evident truths, this exhibit has sacrilegious potential. For it exposes the drafting of the declaration as a profane and political process.

The great text was crafted in a specific context. Although claims and counterclaims about what really happened began to surface immediately, to be repeated and inflated in later accounts, the essential facts are beyond dispute. The story goes like this:

On May 15, 1776, Virginia took the lead in instructing its delegates in the Continental Congress to propose complete American independence from Britain. By then British and American forces had clashed at Bunker Hill, Lexington and Concord. Various committees throughout the 13 colonies were busy drafting resolutions and manifestoes in favor of independence (perhaps Jefferson was referring to them when he spoke of "the harmonizing sentiments of the day"). On June 7, Richard Henry Lee of Virginia moved the resolution "that these United Colonies are, and of right ought to be, free and independent States. . . ." The Congress delayed a vote

on Lee's resolution until July 1, in deference to several delegations that were still divided or that needed to confer with their state governments. In the meantime, the delegates appointed a committee to draft a document implementing the resolution so that, if and when it was approved, the Congress could proceed without pause to publicize the decision.

John Adams convened that committee on June 11. In addition to Adams, the committee included Benjamin Franklin, Thomas Jefferson, Robert Livingston and Roger Sherman. The other members immediately delegated the drafting to Adams and Jefferson, and Adams then turned it over to Jefferson. Years later, in his autobiography, Adams recalled that he chose Jefferson because of his reputation as a stylist and also because Adams's own prominence as a leader of the radical faction in the Congress would have subjected the document to greater scrutiny and criticism. Jefferson, according to this account, was more appropriate because he was more innocuous.

Jefferson wrote the first draft of the Declaration of Independence quickly—Adams later claimed it took him only a "day or two"—then showed the draft to Adams and Franklin because "they were the two members of whose judgments and amendments I wished most to have the benefit." They made only a few minor revisions—replacing "sacred & undeniable" truths with "self-evident" truths, for example—before the full committee approved the revised draft

and placed the document before the Congress on June 28. (This event is immortalized in the famous painting by John Trumbull, which is often mistakenly described as the signing ceremony.) After two days of debate, the Congress passed Lee's resolution on July 2. It then began two more days of debate over the wording of the declaration. After making several major changes in the text, the Congress approved the final version on July 4 and sent it to the printer for publication. Jefferson later recalled that the declaration was signed by the members of the Congress on that day, but his memory was almost surely incorrect. The parchment copy was not signed by most members until August 2.

Jefferson was extremely distressed, and remained indignant about the revisions for the remaining 50 years of his life. Throughout the debate over language, he suffered and simmered in silence, leaving the defense of his version to Adams. At one point, Franklin noticed his agitation, sat down beside him and tried to calm him down with a joke: A sign painter was commissioned by the proprietor of a hat shop to prepare a placard spelling out the excellence of the hats in his store; but when the critics had finished excising all the words and ornate lettering, all that was left next to the hatter's name was the picture of a hat.

Jefferson, however, was not amused. In letters to friends in Virginia he endorsed the charge that the Congress had "mangled" the manuscript. And in his autobiography he went to great lengths to print his original text alongside the version adopted by Congress, commenting sarcastically on the revisions. Despite his lifelong sensitivity on this question, the overwhelming majority of historians and biographers who have studied the different drafts, including Jefferson's most avid advocates, have concluded that the changes improved the overall cogency and crispness of the prose and helped make the declaration the lyrical statement we all know.

The section of the document that we care most about—the early evocation of the natural-rights doctrine—came through the editing process almost unscathed. The Congress merely dropped "inherent &" before "inalienable rights." The delegates focused their attention on the long list of grievances against George III, primarily because that section spelled out the "long train of abuses" that justified the action they were about to take. And since that section attempted to provide a summary of England's policy toward the Colonies for the previous 15 years, albeit from the Colonists' point of view, there was considerable room for disagreement among the different state delegations about what to emphasize. In retrospect, the relative silence of the Congress on what has turned out to be the most resonant words in the declaration is the equivalent of "the dog that did not bark" in the editorial debate. In that sense Lincoln was right. Jefferson smuggled an abstract truth past the censors. Instead of indignation about the changes, he should have felt sly satisfaction as the hounds went baying down the false trail of the long indictment against the king.

Meanwhile, down in Williamsburg, where the Virginia Convention was simultaneously drafting a new state constitution, George Mason had proposed the following Declaration of Rights:

That all men are born equally free and independant, and have certain inherent natural Rights, . . . among which are the Enjoyment of Life and Liberty, with the Means of acquiring and possessing Property, and pursueing and obtaining Happiness and Safety.

These words provoked a spirited debate among the delegates at Williamsburg, some of whom read them as a recipe for anarchy and others as a direct attack on the institution of slavery. Exactly why the delegates in Philadelphia remained silent on this matter has never been satisfactorily explained. (Perhaps it was because the prospect of a debate over slavery was too threatening to Colonial unity; they chose to deflect this discussion by raising the tangential issue of the slave trade in the grievances section of the document.) At any rate, we know that Jefferson was being kept apprised of the Williamsburg debate by courier, and Mason's draft was also published in two Philadelphia newspapers at the same time Jefferson was drafting the declaration. What Jefferson meant by "the pursuit of happiness" remains controversial. But the fact that he got the phrase itself from George Mason is virtually certain.

The motives of the delegates in making the three major changes in Jefferson's draft are less obvious but within the range of our understanding. The Library of Congress exhibit includes the sole surviving fragment of his earliest and roughest draft. That first version, eventually submitted to the Congress on June 28, contained a rousingly emotional passage that condemned "our British brethren" for sending over "not only soldiers of our common blood, but Scotch & foreign mercenaries to invade & destroy us." It went on:

These facts have given the last stab to agonizing affection, and manly spirit bids us to renounce for ever these unfeeling brethren. We must endeavor to forget our former love for them, and to hold them as we hold the rest of mankind, enemies in war, in peace friends. We might have been a free & a great people together; but a communication of grandeur & of freedom it seems is below their dignity. Be it so, since they will have it: the road to happiness & to glory is open to us too; we will tread it apart from them.

The members of the Congress deleted this entire passage; Jefferson went to his grave regretting the change. "The pusillanimous idea that we had friends in England worth keeping terms with, still haunted the minds of many," he recalled in 1821 in his autobiography, and "for this reason, the passages which conveyed censures on the people of England were struck out, lest they should give them offence." What is most striking today, however, is not the Congress's timidity for excising the passage so much as Jefferson's melodramatic sentimentalism in composing it. The passage also makes the mistake of transforming the indictment of George III and the British government into a repudiation of the British people. For strategic as well as stylistic reasons, its deletion was a major improvement.

A second significant change was prompted by another of Jefferson's fondest idiosyncrasies. This is the passage in which he claimed that:

In the second major deletion, Jefferson incorrectly claimed that the Colonists had never acknowledged the authority of Parliament

The longest deletion delivered a mixed message: the king was being blamed for establishing slavery in America and condemned for liberating slaves to fight for him

the circumstances of our emigration & settlement here . . . were effected at the expense of our own blood & treasure, unassisted by the wealth or the strength of Great Britain: that in constituting indeed our several forms of government, we had adopted one common king . . . but that submission to their parliament was no part of our constitution, nor ever in idea, if history may be credited.

The problem here was that Jefferson's revisionist version of Colonial history was too obviously at odds with the tangled truth of Anglo-American relations. His explicit claim that the Colonists had never acknowledged the authority of Parliament was factually inaccurate. His implicit claim that the original act of emigrating to America had severed all political connections with British rulers was a useful fiction. It suggested that American separation from the British Empire was not a radical act at all, but rather a simple recognition of a longstanding reality. Several members of the Continental Congress, including Adams and James Wilson of Pennsylvania, knew that Jefferson's argument simply did not fit the facts. Its deletion preserved the credibility of what was already an inflated case against George III.

Similar motives probably explain the longest deletion from Jefferson's draft, which also generated the lengthiest and most spirited debate within the Congress. This is the passage in which Jefferson blamed the British monarch for initiating the slave trade, thereby implying that slavery was an evil imposed on the unwilling Colonists by a diabolical king. Here are the most salient sentences:

He has waged cruel war against human nature itself violating it's most sacred rights of life & liberty in the persons of a distant people who never offended him, captivating & carrying them into slavery in another hemisphere, or to incur miserable death in their transportation thither . . . and that this assemblage of horrors might want no fact of distinguished die, he is now exciting those very people to rise in arms among us, and to purchase that liberty of which he has deprived them, by murdering the people upon whom he also obtruded them.

Jefferson subsequently claimed that he was attempting to make a principled moral stand against slavery and the slave trade but that certain factions in the Congress blocked his effort. In his autobiography he recalled that the passage:

was struck out in complaisance to South Carolina and Georgia, who had never attempted to restrain the importation of slaves. . . . Our northern brethren also, I believe, felt a little tender under those censures; for though their people had very few slaves themselves, yet they had been pretty considerable carriers of them to others.

Here our hearts must go with Jefferson, since the retention of his linkage between slavery and a corrupt British government opened up the possibility of an early end to the slave trade and a serious debate over the extinction of slavery itself. Clearly, his fellow delegates were not ready for that debate in 1776 and were prepared to threaten the unity of the independence movement to get their way. Jefferson's daring decision to see this moment as a golden opportunity to pin slavery on the evil king represented a noble fabrication that deserves our salute.

On the other hand, we need to give equal notice to two inconvenient pieces of evidence. First, a close reading of the excised passage reveals a tortured logic and a mixed moral message, for the king was simultaneously being blamed for establishing slavery in America and being condemned for liberating slaves to fight on the British side. Jefferson was a genius at having it both ways (as his later equivocations on slavery proved), but here the contradiction was too glaring; it actually called greater attention to the inherent paradox of slave owners fighting on behalf of "life, liberty & the pursuit of happiness." Second, the main thrust of the deleted section explicitly condemned only the slave trade and merely insinuated that slavery itself must die. Jefferson knew from his experience in the Virginia legislature that many established slave owners in the Tidewater region supported an end to slave imports because their own plantations were already full and new arrivals only reduced the value of their existing slave populations. For most Virginians, ending the slave trade had nothing whatsoever to do with ending slavery.

Perhaps the final version of the declaration has become so familiar to our eyes and ears, so self-evidently the right combination of words and ideas, that any alterations—including any restoration of Jefferson's original language—would now strike a false note. But if that is the price that all classic works impose on present-day sensibilities, then we should regard the declaration as a decidedly collaborative creation, with the members of the Continental Congress standing one step behind Jefferson on the stage as we applaud their mutual achievement. If a miracle happened that summer in Philadelphia, it was an editorial rather than a supernatural experience. The muses who spoke to Jefferson were his colleagues in the Continental Congress.

The Library of Congress exhibit includes Jefferson's "last letter," written on June 24, 1826, in response to an invitation to attend the declaration's 50th anniversary celebration in Washington. Although suffering with an intestinal disorder that would ultimately carry him off on the anniversary itself (Adams would expire a few hours later on the same day, prompting memorialists to claim that divine providence was making a statement and causing historians to wonder if they were not right), Jefferson polished and revised the letter with the same attention to detail that he had brought to the original draft of the declaration. The result was one of the most inspired renditions of the Jeffersonian message, his final statement on what the declaration meant to him:

May it be to the world, what I believe it will be (to some parts sooner, to others later, but finally to all), the signal of arousing men to burst the chains under which monkish ignorance and superstition had persuaded them to bind themselves, and to assume the blessings and security of self-government. . . . All eyes are opened, or opening, to the rights of man. The general spread of the light of science has already laid open to every view the palpable truth, that the mass of mankind has not been born with saddles on their backs, nor a favored few booted and spurred, ready to ride them legitimately, by the grace of God. These are grounds of hope for others. For ourselves, let the annual return of this day forever refresh our recollections of these rights, and an undiminished devotion to them.

The lyrical language and melodic cadences were vintage Jefferson, as was the uplifting message. But the memorable image of mankind being born without "saddles on their backs," and the passage about "a favored few booted and spurred, ready to ride them," came right out of an oration delivered by a Puritan soldier executed for treason in 1685. Jefferson owned copies of several English histories that reprinted the speech. Certain phrases had obviously lodged themselves in his memory, or perhaps had been consulted silently. But even if the felicity of the style was in part secondhand, the same could be said for the declaration itself. And it is still Jefferson whom we remember.

FURTHER READING ON INTERPRETING THE DECLARATION

Readers interested in pursuing the different meanings historians have discovered in the Declaration of Independence can find the major interpretive traditions in three books. The classic account is Carl Becker's *The Declaration of Independence: A Study in the History of Political Ideas* (1922), which emphasizes the influence of Locke and sees the Jeffersonian message as the essence of liberalism. Garry Wills's *Inventing America: Jefferson's Declaration of Independence* (1978) challenges the liberal interpretation and locates the source of Jefferson's thinking in Scottish philosophers who espoused the doctrine of the moral sense. Jay Fliegelman's *Declaring Independence: Jefferson, Natural Language, & the Culture of Performance* (1993) claims that Jefferson intended that his words be spoken rather than merely read and develops an intriguing if somewhat idiosyncratic interpretation from that premise. All three books are available in paperback.

The *Radical* Revolution

For years people have argued that France had the real *revolution and that ours was mild by comparison. But now a powerful new book says the American Revolution was the most sweeping in all history. It alone established a pure commercial culture—a culture that makes America the universal society we are today.*

An Interview with Gordon Wood by Fredric Smoler

Fredric Smoler's discussion with Arthur Schlesinger, Jr., on multi-culturalism appeared in the February/March issue.

The French Revolution followed American independence by six years, but it was the later event that went into the books as "the Great Revolution" and became the revolutionary archetype. It is not only the contrast of the conspicuously greater political violence of the French Revolution that has led historians to play down the comparative radicalism of its American counterpart but the fact that the French Revolution swiftly became the model for radical political transformation. For more than a century successful revolutionaries no sooner took power than they designed tricolors and located themselves to the "left" or "right," terms that originally denoted where the delegates sat in the French Convention; the French taught succeeding generations the revolutionary drill. Until the Russian Revolution displaced it, the French Revolution formed the dominant modern political myth, the distorting mirror in which posterity located its dreams and dreads.

The American Revolution, on the other hand, was distinguished by its alleged conservatism; historians have generally held that we didn't kill enough people, engender enough proto-Bolsheviks, or produce a sufficient social upheaval to achieve true revolutionary significance—a failure lamented in some quarters and celebrated in others.

Gordon Wood's impressive new book *The Radicalism of the American Revolu-* tion takes sharp issue with this consensus. American society is generally thought to embody cultural extremes of both egalitarian idealism and materialist vulgarity. Professor Wood thinks that these cultural characteristics are the direct—and thoroughly unintended—consequence of the Revolution, which made us for good and ill the most democratic culture on the planet. Thus our revolution was the most radical one imaginable, for it entirely discredited the older forms of paternalistic authority that everywhere else delayed the coming of capitalist modernity, and resulted in the construction of the first and so far the most completely commercial society the world has seen. If the measure of radicalism is the totality of the destruction of the old order, we are for Professor Wood's money the heirs of the most radical revolution in history.

The revolutionaries not only destroyed the old ties but were unable to establish the kind of new ties they would have liked. They wound up with a very different society from the one they anticipated.

I spoke with Gordon Wood in his office at Brown University in Providence, Rhode Island, where he is University Professor and Professor of History.

• **You argue that our Revolution's true radicalism lies in its destruction of an older hierarchical order. But just what was that order?**

It was a society characterized by a particular kind of hierarchy, a monarchy. This meant certain kinds of social relationships, mainly ones of dependency, with people tied together by patronage, blood, and kinship. Our revolution destroyed these kinds of monarchical relationships; that's what it was designed to do. But what makes it even more radical is the fact that the revolutionaries not only destroyed these ties but were unable to establish the kinds of ties they would have liked. They wound up in a very different society from the one they anticipated.

• **And you believe that one of the things they hadn't taken into account was religion.**

Yes. The old order was at the top rationalist, but ordinary people in the eighteenth century were still very much engaged with religion. It was the way they made fundamental sense of the world. What happens in the Revolution is that with the rise of ordinary people into dominance—which I suppose is a one-sentence summary of what the book is saying—they bring their religiosity with them. These people make sense of the world through religion, as ordinary people have done for centuries. People like Jefferson and Franklin were simply not religious in that sense; they did not use religion to explain the world, any more than most educated people today use religion to explain the world. But ordinary people did, and when they emerged into cultural, social, and political dominance in the early nineteenth century, they brought that religiosity with them, and that's what gives the nineteenth century such striking religious coloration.

•**You've quoted the Founders on their distress at the decline of secularism and rationalism.**

The ones who saw what was happening. Jefferson, for example, was very optimistic, as late as 1820 he thought that every person alive would eventually die a Unitarian. He saw the society becoming more like him, and he couldn't have been more wrong. The Founding Fathers were at most deists—they believed God created the world, then left it alone to run— but they were a very thin veneer on their society, and I think they misinterpreted what was going to happen. They certainly never intended to create the kind of evangelical Protestant world that emerged by the 1820s in the Second Great Awakening. This is true, I think, even for those who are always associated with Puritanism, like John Adams, for whom the Second Great Awakening was an unanticipated consequence, and for someone like Jefferson, for whom, when he finally caught on to what was happening, it was absolutely a horror show. It was just unbelievable; he could only blame the New England Puritan Federalists, who he decided had caused it all. This of course didn't help him explain the rise of evangelical Protestantism in Virginia.

•**And we're still the most religious of the industrial societies.**

I think that's because we are a society in which ordinary people continue to dominate the culture to a greater extent than in the societies of Western Europe. Our religiosity is a function of the democratic cast of our culture, which is, of course, the source of our vulgarity, our materialism, and all the other things that lots of people don't like about America.

•**No gentlemen, right?**

No gentlemen. And that's important. The whole phenomenon of the gentleman is important because it's about a lot more than just manners. The gentleman was not only somebody who knew how to behave but also somebody who knew how to rule. I think the idea of the gentleman and what happened to it is a fantastically interesting subject. The eighteenth century was the high point of the Anglo-American culture of the gentleman. It was a concept of increasing importance from the Renaissance on, and in the eighteenth century people were really wrestling with it. Jane Aus-

ten was fascinated with the subject; all her novels consider the definition of a proper gentleman. I think this examination was also occurring in the Colonies, where there was less and less emphasis on blood, family, wealth as being the proper measure of a gentleman and more on moral behavior, which made it possible for the Founders, who had by English aristocratic standards very little wealth and who could make very little appeal to the criterion of blood, to aspire to gentility.

•**What made someone qualify as a gentleman?**

A certain amount of wealth, giving one independence, was a prerequisite. Jane Austen, along with many other people, thought of a gentleman as someone who had, at a minimum, so many hundred pounds of income; Darcy had ten thousand pounds a year. Such an income would certainly constitute independence. Of course, you could not be a shopkeeper or manual laborer, but the more controversial question was, What is the relation of the professions to gentility? This was a period of transition in the ideal of gentility and the conception of the professions, but members of the professions were for the most part still regarded as primarily gentlemen, not as professionals. This is, of course, very confusing for historians, because we look at the period and notice growing numbers of lawyers and doctors, and we assume they're like modern professionals, but it's a mistake to anticipate the future.

Someone like Benjamin Rush was a doctor, but first he's a gentleman, then he practices medicine, and he doesn't practice the way a modern practitioner would. He's not at the hospital ten or twelve hours a day; he has a lot of time for doing the kinds of things that people in Jane Austen's world did, which is to visit and be genteel. And the same is true of lawyers. They're not working so many billable hours to get their salaries from their law firms; they are much more independent and leisured than that.

•**And you believe that the purpose of such leisure is to allow a gentleman to specialize in the art of ruling?**

That's the traditional view. Jefferson took it very seriously; so did Franklin. They felt they had a responsibility to devote themselves to philosophy, the arts, or public service. Now in the old order people were deferred to because they had power; they could command

those who were in a condition of dependence and reward them with patronage, or wealth, or whatever. The Founding Fathers, despite their reputation for hardheaded realism, were naive enough to believe that the people would follow and obey them simply because they were more talented, and because they had been elected. They had tremendous confidence in elections; the people, having chosen them, would naturally follow their leadership.

We are indeed a materialistic capitalist society. That can be seen pejoratively, or it can be seen as a sign of equality. There's something peculiarly egalitarian about the cash nexus.

Those who doubted this became the Federalists as they emerged in the 1790s. John Adams is the archetype; his famous exchange with Jefferson late in his life explored this issue. And I think Adams has the better of the argument. Jefferson remained a Pollyanna, naive about the sociology of democracy. Adams in effect said: "Don't kid yourself, Mr. Jefferson, the people who get elected aren't going to be the best and most talented. They're going to be the prettiest, the most handsome, the wealthiest, the people who can attract the attention of a television audience with the best sound bite." Jefferson remained committed to the revolutionary dream that talent would win out.

•**You talk about America as the first commercial society, a political order sustained by the new idea that men's calculations of their own economic interest constitute the sole social bond.**

That's why I think our revolution was so radical. Obviously commerce had existed from the beginning of history, and so one gets into all kinds of arguments with people who will say, "Well, look, there was commerce already." But a commercial society doesn't mean merely one in which commerce occurs. In the North—the South remained closer to the eighteenth century, and I think this helps explain the sectional split—you have a society that increasingly comes to regard

In a business allegory from an 1808 map of Philadelphia, the goddess Minerva, seated on Trade, instructs youth in navigation and commerce.

the business of America as business, buying and selling, with exchange for monetary gain as the basic adhesive of society. And it's that preoccupation that startled Tocqueville and everybody else who came here. Observers with traditional attitudes came and condemned, because the cash nexus is not supposed to be a nice way to tie people together. We are indeed a materialistic capitalist society.

That can be seen pejoratively, or it can be seen in another way, as a sign of equality. There's something peculiarly egalitarian about the cash nexus. From the nineteenth century up to the present, we have come to regard the cash nexus as an unjust and wicked way to tie people together. But in the context of the old order the cash nexus was regarded as an egalitarian achievement, as a better way to connect people than through blood or patronage, who your father was or whom you married. It seemed better for a person to be assessed in terms of "What can I buy?" or "What can my money buy for me?"

•Well, it certainly wasn't Jefferson's intent. How did the Revolution produce such a pure, expansive, inclusive commercial regime?
It destroyed the older ties and discredited them in a way that has simply never happened in England. The Revolution made blood and patronage ties dishonorable in this new world. There were attempts made to construct new utopian arrangements, with varying degrees of success, but ultimately they weren't sufficient. What emerged to fill the vacuum, to tie people together, was commercial exchange, and this came about because this was what ordinary people were doing, and they thrived in this kind of environment. They didn't need justifications for relationships that the Founding Fathers might have needed. They certainly didn't feel the need for old-fashioned republican virtue; they simply wanted to get ahead, and pursue happiness. They took Jefferson's pursuit of happiness quite literally.

The way you do that is by making money. In that sense a commercial society is a victory for those very ordinary, self-interested people, the kinds of people who political philosophers from the beginning of time have said are ill equipped to run any government. They're too self-interested, too preoccupied with the pursuit of their private interests.

•**Interestedness plays a very big role in your book, and this brings us back to the gentleman. Gentlemen are by definition disinterested, and their disinterestedness is the justification for their political authority. The gentlemen remained a powerful force in every other European society; the old order survived. The American victory** over the gentlemen was the least savage—we weren't guillotining them—but in some sense it's the most complete.

Yes. Except in the South there was no traditional aristocracy left. And that's why there has never been a real working-class movement in America. Everybody claimed to work; everybody was saying, "Yes, I'm a workingman too." It was very difficult for a separate group of workingmen to establish their autonomy. There's no labor party that can develop when everybody says, "I'm a laborer." No socialist movement or workingman's movement can develop without the aristocracy at the other end to act as a foil. Now, obviously, the notion of disinterestedness doesn't die out entirely, and in fact it re-emerges later in the century, with members of the professions and academics and scientists coming to claim some of the disinterested qualities of gentlemen. But the ideal was much diminished when compared with what had existed earlier. Interest seems to conquer all. That's what Tocqueville saw, and that's what any outside observer would have seen, this dominance of interest in the culture. Many Americans would not have accepted this description of their society and would have been horrified by the notion that they were concerned only with interest.

But there was a realization that this was what democracy meant: the emergence of ordinary people who by definition have economic interest; that's what it means to have an occupation. To be a shoemaker or a businessman or a shopkeeper is to have an interest, and it's precisely because they aren't independent of the marketplace that they have these interests. In a democratic society these people are running the show, and they're bringing their interests with them; they can't shed them, they are inherent in their being businessmen. Nobody doubted that. Adam Smith understood it as well as anyone: These kinds of people do not make good legislators because they have private interests. That is why Smith always accepted the landed gentry's dominance in the House of Commons. They alone could be free of these kinds of interests.

Gentlemen don't have to exert themselves for their income. But anybody who worked for a living was going to have interests and was going to bring them into the political arena. Some sought to resist this by denying the real-

ity. But others, like Madison, accepted the reality of interests. He said, in effect, "Well, that's the way it is, but we're going to deal with it by trying to keep these people out of political leadership by elevating and extending the national government." That was his solution, and it failed.

•**You're rather harsh on Madison. You certainly don't think much of his prophetic powers as a political theorist.**

Madison still conceived of public interest that transcends private interest, and in his Federalist Paper number ten he said, in effect, "Look, there are interests everywhere in society; I understand that. What we'd like to do is devise a political structure that will keep these interests from getting into government, or at least dominating government, and the way to do that is to expand the sphere of government so that these interests counteract

one another and allow disinterested gentlemen to rule." His model was always religion; he understood that the secret of America's success in creating religious liberty and separating church and state, which is what allowed him and Jefferson and those other secular humanists or deists to run the show, was the fact that there were so many religious groups competing with one another that they negated one another, neutralized the state in religious matters, and allowed rationalist thinkers to predominate.

He hoped the same thing would happen in the larger sphere of interest-group politics. Let the interests collide and compete with one another in the society; let's erect a government on a national level that will be dominated by the likes of James Madison and Thomas Jefferson, people who were free of interest. I think he really saw himself as a disin-

The apotheosis of commerce: a Philadelphia store ablaze with incentives, 1850s.

terested person, capable of rising above narrow marketplace interests, and hoped to create a government that would be more or less dominated by his kind of person. Now it didn't work out quite like that, and I think that was part of the problem of the Federalists in the 1790s. There weren't enough James Madisons or Alexander Hamiltons or George Washingtons. There were too many Federalists who had interests to promote, even though they were presumably an aristocracy. They were an aristocracy caught up in interests.

I think the intriguing person in all of this is Aaron Burr. Burr was the one aristocrat among the Founding Fathers who never made any claims for virtue. He was just a real American politician.

I think the intriguing and revealing person in all of this is Aaron Burr. Burr was the one aristocrat among the Founding Fathers who never made any claims for virtue and had no visions of an America based on virtue and republican idealism. The explanation may be that he was a more authentic aristocrat who never needed to justify himself; his father was the second president of Princeton. He had as much aristocratic lineage as anybody in New England.

Burr never had the insecurity of the rest of the Founding Fathers, many of whom had to justify themselves in terms of achievement. In New York and even when he was Vice President, his behavior was very different from that of someone like Jefferson or John Adams. He was always writing letters to people promoting some kind of interest, trying to make money. He was an aristocrat, but he never had enough money to bring it off, and his correspondence is very revealing; it's full of "See if you can get a job for so-and-so. I owe him something. Burn this letter." You never find Thomas Jefferson saying, "Burn this letter." Burr sounds like a ward politician of the 1880s.

As a consequence he comes to be feared by both ends of the political spectrum. Both Hamilton and Jefferson fear Burr long before his ventures in the West. He's frightening to them because he's supposed to be the kind of person the Republic will need as a leader. He's a natural aristocrat, he has a Princeton education, he's got money, he's got all the pose and status of a gentleman, yet he's behaving in this interested way, conniving at land deals and banking deals in New York and persisting even when he gets to be Vice President. He had the gall to wonder if it would be possible for him to continue to practice law while he was Vice President. People talked about Hillary Clinton's continuing to practice law when her husband became President. Burr was actually hoping to practice law while Vice President. One of his confidants had to say to him, No, it's improper, you can't have the Vice President walking into court as an attorney; you would overawe the court.

What really scared his contemporaries, the real treason of Aaron Burr, is that he was a traitor to his class. They expected more from him. He had all the promise of leadership, which is why he got elevated so quickly, first to the Senate and then to the Vice Presidency at a time when you had to be somebody to be Vice President. Think of who his predecessors were: Jefferson and Adams. Then there's Burr. He was expected to be one of the shining lights of the new Republic. He had a distinguished war record, he had everything going for him—looks, charm, extraordinary abilities—but he failed the test of disinterested leadership, and he scared the bejesus out of the other Founding Fathers.

And what was Burr? He was just an anticipation of a real American politician. Gore Vidal in his novel *Burr* makes him the natural father of Martin Van Buren. That's one of the invented sections of the book; there's no real evidence of that at all, though it was a scurrilous rumor at the time. But Vidal's choice is interesting because Van Buren does emerge as the first great modern politician, still a gentleman, but a nineteenth-century version, a type simply unanticipated by the Founding Fathers, a victorious candidate who had done nothing notable to deserve office. He had written no great documents, he had won no battles, he had no great distinctions. But he had built the best political machine the country had ever seen. He was the most astute politician of his era and a great champion of the legitimacy of parties and interest groups in politics. There is a kind of spiritual tie between Burr and Van Buren, which Vidal hit upon.

•**You seem to suggest that self-interest is unchallengeable in American politics, that government can never stand above it but must merely accommodate as many interests as possible. And yet our politicians are always decrying "special interests."**

Sure. That's our conventional rhetoric, and we continue to hope against hope that there is somebody out there who might stand above interests. One of the appeals of Perot is that he had so much money he would not be beholden to special interests. Perot in this sense has that independence that gentleman are supposed to possess in classical political theory. But when you get down to it, everybody has interests. Press them, and people say, "Well, I mean special interest . . . that other interest, not this one." There's a certain amount of fiction and incoherence that is involved in our rhetoric of "special interests."

•**But surely there is a persisting sense that the use of political power for economic purposes is illegitimate.**

I do agree that there is a dream of a leader out there who stands above interest. That persists in American life, and it accounts for our periodic election of military heroes and accounts as well for our anti-partyism, which continues right up to the present. We're seeing an indication of it in our systematic destruction of our political parties, most conspicuously in the weakening of the Democratic party over the last thirty years.

The liberal Republican movement, the Mugwump movement, and the Progressive movement were all anti-party. A party necessarily suggests interests; the term *party* does, after all, mean just that: taking a partial view. So despite our so-called acceptance of interests and parties, there's always been, perhaps as a consequence of the republican emphasis in the Founding Fathers' dream, a high level of rhetoric that condemns parties and interests, whether special or not.

•**Later in your book you argue that in the world created by the Revolution great disparities of wealth are not considered antithetical to a democratic order. But didn't the successive waves of American populism have a strong and recurring hostility to concentrations of wealth—take the New Deal term *economic royalists,* for instance?**

Sure. But what's extraordinary is the extent to which Americans have put up with and continue to put up with great disparities of wealth as long as they see the wealth as achieved. There's very little resentment of rich ballplayers and rock stars. In any event, I'm less concerned with what happened later than with explaining the 1820s and 1830s. Americans then clearly accepted—at least for a while—unprecedented disparities of wealth, disparities far greater than those of the eighteenth century, and nonetheless called their era the age of equality. This has led some historians to think that the first post-revolutionary generations misunderstood their own culture, that theirs was the age of the uncommon man, not the common man. I think the historians are wrong and the contemporaries were right when they called it the age of the common man, because differences of wealth are the least mortifying and least humiliating of the various ways in which people on top have made those on the bottom feel their inferiority. If you think about it a bit, that's true even today; if you're told that the reason you're inferior is your race or your bloodline or your father's ethnicity, that's not something you can do anything

about. But if you're told that you're inferior because you haven't got as much money as someone else, that's something that you *can* theoretically do something about. To have wealth become the only source of distinction is to place only a weak social barrier between classes.

Everybody's here. No race or nationality hasn't got somebody in the United States living as a citizen. It's extraordinary, and it's the product of our being so pure a commercial society.

That gave a lot of encouragement to a lot of ambitious people.

•**One of the great nineteenth-century hopes—it was John Stuart Mill's—is that people who are not used to exercising political power will get better at it by doing so; they will become more rational. You don't put much stock in that, do you?**

I suppose there may be some evidence

here and there, but I don't have much confidence. I suppose you can work at educating people to be more disinterested; that's what a liberal arts education is supposed to be about. But I don't think it's working all that well, except perhaps in environmental matters. Not much suggests that we are becoming more disinterested.

•**Your book seems to say, Look, this is what we've got. This is a very stable commercial culture in its political habits, and there are some very lovely things and some rather nasty things about it.**

I think that's true. That's how I feel. I think we need to see all of the sides of what we've got. There are tawdry and unattractive sides, but American society is an extraordinary thing, now more than ever. We have a truly universal society; everybody's here. No race, nationality, or ethnic group hasn't got somebody in the United States living as a citizen. It's an extraordinary thing, and it is a product of our being so pure a commercial society without any particular claims of ethnicity or race. I think that every once in a while we ought to acknowledge that this democratic inclusiveness remains immensely impressive.

The Hessians

***The almost 30,000 German troops hired to help Great Britain fight the
rebellious American colonies are frequently misnamed and unfairly maligned.***

Debra Brill

*Debra Brill is a freelance writer with a
special interest in the American Revolution.*

Ambrose Serle, a civilian secretary
to General William Howe during
the American Revolution, described
the German troops who fought with the
British in that war as "a dirty, cowardly
set of contemptible miscreants." It was
not a very nice way to refer to one's allies.

A negative opinion of the German
force—frequently referred to as Hessians—has
persisted for so long that
even today they are commonly spoken
of with disdain and, despite the fact that
they composed nearly half of the British
fighting force in America in 1776, they
receive scant attention in general histories
of the conflict. King George III's
decision to hire foreign troops was not
a popular one in England. It was, however,
a necessity if Britain was to put
down the rebellion in its American colonies.
The Seven Years' War that ended
in 1763 had reduced the army's numbers,
and new recruits were hard to find
among the war-weary British populace.
The king applied to Empress Catherine
of Russia for troops, but she refused.

In desperation, King George turned to
the German principalities in Europe, as had
other British monarchs before him. He
struck deals with the rulers of Hesse-
Cassel, Hesse-Hanau, Brunswick-Lüne-
burg, Anspach-Bayreuth, Anhalt-Zerbst,
and Waldeck. The two Hesses provided
about two-thirds of the almost 30,000
German soldiers hired out to King George,
hence the common appellation, "Hessians,"
for all the Germans.

The treaties, which were drawn up to
look like reciprocal agreements rather
than bargains for hired soldiers, generated
a political battle in the British Parliament.
"Is there one of your Lordships," Lord

Camden asked, "who does not perceive
most clearly that the whole is a mere
mercenary bargain for the hire of troops
on one side and the sale of human blood
on the other; and that the devoted
wretches thus purchased for slaughter
are mere mercenaries, in the worst sense
of the word?"

The British Prime Minister, Sir Frederick
North, took the opposite view reasoning
that mere numbers of combined
British and German troops would cow
the Americans into submission and that the
rebellion would, therefore, be short-lived
and relatively bloodless. In the end, the
treaties were easily approved—100–32
in the House of Lords and 252–88 in the
Commons.

The terms of the agreements varied.
The Duke of Brunswick, for example,
was to be paid a levy of about £7 per
recruit, an annual subsidy of £11,517
until the war's end, and twice that
amount annually for two years thereafter.

Of the six princes, however, the Landgrave
of Hesse-Cassel profited the most.
While it is true that he supplied more
troops to the British—more than 16,000—
than the others, he also drove a harder
bargain, receiving nearly £3,000,000 for
the use of his soldiers.

The Landgrave, for all his astuteness
in negotiating for the use of his men,
did not insist on a "blood money" clause
by which a prince would receive a sum
equal to the levy for each man killed
(three wounded warriors were considered
equal to one dead soldier). This
clause, which was part of four of the six
treaties riled even the Americans. Not
only were German troops being sold to
fight in a war that in no way concerned
them, but their avaricious princes were
to reap a profit from their deaths!

Benjamin Franklin attacked the blood-
money clause after the capture of some

nine hundred Germans at the 1776 Battle
of Trenton, during which twenty-two
of their number died. In a satirical letter
from the "Count de Schaumbergh" to
the "Baron Hohendorf," Franklin had
the Count express his "joy on being told
that of the 1,950 Hessians engaged in
the fight but 345 escaped. There were
just 1,605 men killed, and I cannot sufficiently
commend your prudence in
sending an exact list of the dead to my
minister in London. This precaution was
the more necessary as the report sent to
the English ministry does not give but
1,455 dead. This would make 483,450
florins instead of 643,500 which I am
entitled to demand under our convention."

Just as "Hessian" fails to convey adequately
their place of origin, the term
"mercenary" is an inaccurate reflection
of the German troops' status. Mercenaries
hire themselves out. In this case,
however, the rulers profited, while the
soldiers did the fighting.

Indeed, some of the German troops—
far from being mercenaries—were kidnap
victims, impressed into service. One such
was Johann Seume, a theological student
at the University of Leipzig. Having
left the university due to a religious
dispute, he was headed for Paris when
the Landgrave's recruiting agents arrested
him. Seume later wrote in his
autobiography that "No one was [then]
safe from the grip of this seller of souls.
Persuasion, cunning, deception, force—
all.... Strangers of all sorts were arrested,
imprisoned, then sent off."

Seume was held in a fortress in Ziegenhain
with some 1,500 other conscripts,
who plotted to escape. Their attempt
failed when they were betrayed. Later,
while en route from Ziegenhain to Munden,
they planned a second attempt, but
this too was foiled.

Unhappy conscripts such as these formed a larger proportion of the army as the war dragged on. In their negotiations with the British, the princes had promised more men than they could easily deliver. Having dispatched the best-trained, regular soldiers to America in the conflict's first years, the princes were forced to resort more and more to ruthless conscription—even beyond their own borders—in order to meet their quotas.

In November of 1776, only seven months after the first German division sailed for America, the Landgrave of Hesse-Cassel petitioned several German principalities and free cities for permission to recruit within their territory. Some acquiesced as a means of weeding out undesirables. In March 1777, a London newspaper quoted a letter writer from Hamburg: "I have long wondered [why] the magistracy have not put a stop to recruiting here, but I am told it is a political stroke of theirs, for as Hamburgh [sic.] is a free city, it is the reservoir of all the rogues, rascals and runaways in Germany and as the army and the gallows refuse none, they by that means get rid of them."

Before they set sail for America, the German troops were reviewed by Colonel William Faucitt, King George's minister plenipotentiary in Germany. In his early reports to Lord Suffolk, the British Minister of State, Faucitt described the hirelings as an "exceedingly fine body of men . . . fit for any service whatever."

As time passed, however, the quality of troops declined, and by April 1778, Faucitt was finding that "the Hessian recruits, as usual, appeared raw and undisciplined; some few of whom, moreover, I found it necessary to reject, on account of old age and other infirmities." A year later, his report noted that many recruits were "very raw and clownish, and will require a good deal of drilling." Even some the elite *Jägers*—German hunters who were excellent marksmen—were found to be of poor quality. A *Jäger* captain called one batch sent to him in America "the dregs of society."

The first groups of Germans to leave for Britain's rebellious colonies, expecting peculiarities of wildlife, terrain, and climate quite remote from anything they had known, expressed apprehension about what they would find. They believed the Indians to be cannibals and had heard that the colonists ate horse meat and cats. Before learning the accuracy of these notions, these men, reared in landlocked countries, had to cross more than three thousand miles of unpredictable ocean.

The voyage behind them, however, they found America surprisingly like their native lands and praised it in their letters home. "On the whole," wrote one, "nearly everything here is the same as with us at home—the same kinds of bushes and trees; but as the soil is richer here, the leaves grow larger and the wood thicker." Another described Charleston, South Carolina as "more beautiful than I had imagined. The wealth of the inhabitants was apparent everywhere."

"At the present time," yet another declared, "I can form no mental picture of an earthly paradise without including in the jerseys and Long Island." But, this same writer thought Pennsylvania an undesirable place to live because never had he "met anywhere with more crazy people than in [Philadelphia] . . . [N]early all of the people are quietly mad—a sort of mental aberration caused by a compression rather than a heating of the blood." He attributed this singular state of affairs to the non-nutritious quality of Pennsylvania food and milk.

Having come from relatively poor states, the German troops found the abundance of wealth in America quite astonishing. Some of the officers, who had at first felt sympathy for the colonists, came to feel that the Americans did not appreciate their good fortune. A Major Baurmeister concluded that Americans were the greediest people on earth, while another Hessian officer wrote, "When I was in Europe, I had pity of them, but now no more. They have been the happiest people under the sun."

Although the American women were much admired for their beauty the population in general was variously described as indolent, fearless, good-for-nothing, and haughty. The German officers felt a great deal of contempt for their American counterparts, who were not officers by profession, but merely tailors, cobblers, bankers, and other low types. Coming from a society that put a premium on rank and status, the Germans of the officer class could not readily accept the American philosophy that all men are created equal. One German captain complained that "what we have seen so far brings us little honor to fight against these."

For their part, Americans did not hold a high opinion of the Germans. From the first, when news of the British-German alliance reached the colonies, the Germans were portrayed as fearsome and vicious savages. One American newspaper expected their participation in the fighting to result in "such a scene of cruelty, death and devastation, as will fill those of us who survive the carnage, with indignation and horror." A German lieutenant colonel reported that Americans believed that his troops ate small children, and another officer wrote that when spectators gathered to see captured German soldiers, they found it hard to accept that these normal-looking men were the "monsters" about whom they had heard.

As Germans and Americans became familiar with each other, their opinions changed. German prisoners, in fact, were generally better treated than the British, partly due to a propaganda campaign directed at instigating desertions within their ranks.

It was a strategy that some Englishmen had foreseen. Indeed, during the original debate on the treaties, Major General Sir Henry Clinton—later to command the British troops and their auxiliaries—had recommended procuring Russian troops since there were few in America able to communicate with them. People of German ancestry by contrast, represented the second largest ethnic group in America at the war's outset.

The Americans seized every opportunity to try to wrest the German troops from the British. On the August 1776 day that the first German contingent set foot on American soil, a broadside—translated into German—offered to any "foreigners who shall leave the armies of his Britannic majesty in America and shall chuse to become members of any of these states; that they shall be protected in the free exercise of their respective religions, and be invested with the rights, privileges and immunities of natives, as established by the laws of these states...." Further, Congress would provide any such deserters with fifty acres of unappropriated land.

The capture of almost a thousand Germans at Trenton further fueled the propaganda effort. The Pennsylvania Council of Safety issued a proclamation stating that General George Washington, in turning the prisoners over to its care, recommended they "have such principles instilled into them, whilst they remain prisoners, that when they return on being exchanged they may fully open the eyes of their countrymen" as to their error in fighting such people as the Americans.

These tactics met with a measure of success; on many occasions exchanged prisoners did praise the Americans and their way of life. But the beauty of the land needed no advertising, and the apparent equality of all levels of society appealed to many among the German rank and file. Of the almost 30,000 Germans who fought for the British in the Revolution, approximately 5,000 deserted or were given permission by their sovereigns to remain in America after the war.

Although many of the German soldiers had been forced to fight in America, others—mostly officers—were professional soldiers who saw the war as an opportunity to seek promotion. They anticipated an easy victory which would assure them glory and advancement.

In his journal, Lieutenant John Charles Philip von Krafft, a mercenary in the true sense, frequently complained of the delays of his promotion. Overlooked on several occasions when promotions were announced, he threatened to leave his regiment and join the British. He had earlier thrown his lot with the Americans, but when General Washington refused him a captaincy, von Krafft, joined a Hessian regiment.

Some officers were particularly irked when they still had not received promotion by war's end. Even Seume, the reluctant soldier, praised by his superiors, became ambitious. "When finally the news of the concluded peace arrived," he wrote, "we were not exactly happy because young, energetic men do not like to have their careers thus abruptly changed."

The relationship between the British and their auxiliary troops was not particularly good, although no serious rift occurred between the two armies. The Germans proved convenient scapegoats for the British since everyone seemed inclined to think ill of them. General Friedrich Adolphus Riedesel, commander of the Brunswick troops, wrote that he was "surrounded only by Englishmen who are drunk with haughtiness. With these people I have to get along; if something disadvantageous happens, it will be all my fault."

German soldiers participated in every major and most minor battles from the summer of 1776 to the war's end, from Brunswick forces in Canada (later to be captured at Saratoga with General John Burgoyne) to the Waldeckers in the Floridas. Their previous experience had not prepared them for the American terrain or style of fighting. Trained as they were in the highly-disciplined European manner, the Germans were surprised by and disapproved of, American guerrilla tactics.

The Americans claimed that the Germans were vicious fighters and would give no quarter. This was, in fact, generally true early in the war; the Germans had been told by the British, who hoped to goad them into enthusiastic combat, that they would be especially targeted by the rebels, who would show them no mercy.

By war's end, however, many of the Germans had fought against and lived amongst the Americans for eight years. They never fully comprehended—some from lack of interest, others due to the language barrier—the issues at stake or the consequences of an American victory (Baron Riedesel felt the rebels themselves did not know why they were fighting.)

Nonetheless, when the German soldiers returned home, they carried with them memories of a new people and a rich and beautiful land. As the final transports of soldiers prepared to leave, Americans waved to the departing troops. "During [it] all," a Hessian captain wrote, "there was a deep silence on board the ships that were lying at anchor with troops, as if everyone were in deep mourning because of the loss of the thirteen beautiful provinces."

'It Is Not a Union'

Peter Onuf

Peter Onuf, 40, is associate professor of history at Worcester Polytechnic Institute. Born in New Haven, Connecticut, he received an A.B. (1967) and a Ph.D. (1973) from Johns Hopkins University. He is the Author of The Origins of the Federal Republic: Jurisdictional Controversies in the United States 1775–87 *(1983), and* Statehood and Union: A History of the Northwest Ordinance *(1987).*

When news of the Peace of Paris reached the United States in the spring of 1783, war-weary Americans marked the event with jubilant parades. In Philadelphia, a writer in the *Pennsylvania Gazette* pleaded with his fellow citizens to restrain their revels during the celebratory "illumination of the city." It was the end of seven long years of deprivation and sacrifice, and an occasion for much pride: The United States (with crucial help from France) had just bested the mightiest power on earth.

Patriots looked forward to a new epoch of prosperity and growth. In a Fourth of July oration in 1785, a prominent Boston minister named John Gardiner declared that "if we make a right use of our natural advantages, we soon must be a truly great and happy people." The hinterland would become "a world within ourselves, sufficient to produce whatever can contribute to the necessities and even the superfluities of life."

Many Americans shared Gardiner's optimism. Their land was inherently rich in natural resources, still barely exploited. Virtually all of its three million inhabitants (including some 600,000 black slaves) still lived within 100 miles of the Atlantic Ocean, in a band of settlement stretching some 1,200 miles from Maine to Georgia. In 1790, the first U.S. census would establish the nation's demographic center at a point 25 miles *east* of Baltimore. At the time of the Revolution, that Maryland city with a population of some 6,000, was the nation's fifth largest, behind Philadelphia (30,000), New York (22,000), Boston (16,000), and Charleston (14,000).

Directly or indirectly, city folk depended upon trade for their livelihood. Merchant ships set sail for Europe bearing wheat, corn, fur pelts, dried fish—or headed down the coast to pick up cargoes of tobacco, indigo, and rice from Southern plantations before crossing the Atlantic. They returned carrying calico, velvet, furniture, brandy, machinery, and often with new immigrants. Labor shortages in the cities pushed wages for servants, stevedores, and carpenters far higher than those prevailing in the cities of Europe. Many foreign visitors remarked on the new nation's general good fortune. "Nor have the rich the power of oppressing the less rich," said Thomas Cooper, a British scientist, "for poverty such as in Great Britain is almost unknown." (Such reports were not always reliable. One traveler wrote home about the amazing American Wakwak tree, with fruit that grew in the shape of a young woman.)

A CHRISTIAN SPARTA?

But the overwhelming majority of Americans—more than 90 percent—lived on farms. On a tract of 90 to 160 acres, the typical American farmer grew corn and other staples for home consumption, and raised chickens, pigs, and a dairy cow or two for his family with perhaps a few extra animals to be bartered in the village market. Visits to town were weekly events at best; anyone who journeyed more than 50 miles from home was probably heading west, leaving for good. People and news traveled slowly. It took about a month for a Philadelphia newspaper to reach Pittsburgh, then a crude frontier outpost 250 miles inland.

Despite the general sparsity of population, local crowding and worn-out cropland in New England produced growing numbers of migrants. They crossed the Appalachians over rough wagon trails to the frontier in western Pennsylvania and Virginia, or to the future states of Kentucky, Tennessee, and Ohio. Other settlers moved South, to Georgia and the Carolinas. And all during the 1780s modest numbers of new immigrants from Europe continued to arrive at East Coast ports, chiefly from Ireland, Scotland, and Germany.

And yet, despite the outward signs of economic vitality during the mid-1780s, there was a growing alarm among many of the new nation's leaders—men such as George Washington, John Jay, and Alexander Hamilton. The states, only loosely bound together under the Articles of Confederation of 1781, were constantly bickering over conflicting territorial claims beyond the Appalachians, and Congress was powerless to mediate. Near Wilkes-Barre, Pennsylvania militiamen had even opened fire on Connecticut settlers.

Spain and Great Britain were poised to take advantage of the frontier's "anarchy." To the north, British troops still garrisoned forts along the Great Lakes, a violation of the Treaty of Paris. To the south, the Spaniards, who held New Orleans and claimed all the lands west of the Mississippi, had closed the great river to American shipping below Natchez. King Charles III's officers were actively encouraging American settlers in Kentucky to break away from the Union and establish political and commercial relations with Spain.

Washington worried about the nation's fragmentation and decline into a state of degrading neocolonial dependency.

Washington and his allies worried less about America's outright conquest by a foreign power than the nation's fragmentation and decline into a state of degrading neocolonial dependency. A postwar consumer spree deepened that concern. Samuel Adams, the austere Bostonian, fretted that his countrymen's hunger for "luxury" goods imported from England—glassware, clocks, rugs—was "prostituting all our glory, as people." Few of his peers shared Adams's vision of a future America reigning as a virtuous "Christian Sparta," but they worried that the expensive imports would drain the nation of scarce hard currency and hinder the growth of domestic industry.

The states themselves were badly divided over these and other issues. The merchants, farmers, and fishermen of the North regarded the slave-owning plantation proprietors of the South with deep suspicion. Geographically and culturally, great distances separated them. Thomas Jefferson once drew up a list comparing the people of the two regions, describing Northerners as "chicaning," "jealous of their liberties and those of others," and "hypocritical in their religion." Southerners, he said, were "candid," "zealous for their own liberties but trampling on those of others," and devoted only to the religion "of the heart."

Economic issues were also divisive. Many Northern traders and politicians were angered by British laws that banned American merchantmen from the lucrative trade with the British West Indies, involving the exchange of Southern tobacco and rice for Caribbean sugar, molasses, and rum. But the Southerners feared a Northern monopoly on that traffic more than they did the relatively benign British one. Pierce Butler, later a South Carolina delegate to the Federal Convention, declared that the interests of North and South were "as different as the interests of Russia and Turkey."

DO-NOTHING CONGRESS

None of these challenges would have proved insurmountable for a strong national government. But the Continental Congress, operating under the Articles of Confederation, was ineffective. The Confederation was but "a firm league of friendship," as the 1781 document put it, that left the states their "sovereignty, freedom and independence, and every Power, Jurisdiction and right" not expressly delegated to the Continental Congress.

Among the many powers left to the states was that of taxing the citizenry. Congress received its revenues by levies on the state governments—"a timid kind of recommendation from Congress to the States," as George Washington described it. If a state chose not to pay, as often happened, Congress could do nothing.

Not only did the Articles grant Congress few powers, but they made it difficult for the legislature to exercise those that it did possess. There was no real executive, only a largely ceremonial president of Congress. The congressmen voted by states (there was thus no fixed number of legislators), and most important measures required the assent of nine of the 13 states to become law. Substantive amendments of the Articles could be adopted only by a unanimous vote in Congress and by the state legislatures. Every effort to strengthen the Confederation failed.

The history of the Articles themselves illustrates the difficulty of organizing concerted action by the states. A year after the Declaration of Independence, the Continental Congress, as-

sembled in Philadelphia, had finally endorsed a draft of the Articles and sent it to the new state legislatures for ratification. Each of the ex-Colonies had strong objections, but, amid the pressures of wartime, they all swallowed their misgivings—except Maryland. It held out for four years, until March 1781. Meanwhile, the Continental Congress was forced to carry on the war effort without any constitutional authority. Laboring under enormous handicaps, it gave George Washington's beleaguered forces in the field little in the way of coherent support.

THE 'DOGS OF WAR'

By the mid-1780s, Congress was hard-pressed even to muster a quorum, and it suffered numerous indignities. In June 1783, after the Treaty of Paris, a band of mutinous soldiers surrounded the Pennsylvania State House in Philadelphia, where Congress was meeting, holding the legislators captive for a day. After the Pennsylvania authorities refused to call out the militia and restore order, the legislators decamped for Princeton, New Jersey, then moved to Annapolis, Maryland, before settling in New York City in 1785. The *Boston Evening Post* mocked the politicians for "not being stars of the *first* magnitude, but rather partaking of the nature of *inferior* luminaries, or *wandering* comets."

Victory, in short, had shredded many of the old wartime bonds. Without a common enemy to fight, Americans seemed incapable of preserving their Union. "Lycurgus," a pseudonymous writer in the *New Haven Gazette,* complained that the Union under the Articles "is not a union of sentiment;—it is not a union of interest;—it is not a union to be seen—or felt—or in any manner perceived."

Many local politicians—Congressman Melancton Smith of New York, Luther Martin of Maryland, George Mason of Virginia—dismissed such worries. The Antifederalists, as they were later called, believed that the preservation of republican liberties won by the Revolution depended on maintaining the sovereignty and independence of the states. They held, with Montesquieu, the great French *philosophe,* that republican government could survive only in small countries, where citizens could be intimately involved in politics. Maryland planter John Francis Mercer spoke for the Antifederalists when he declared that he was "persuaded that the People of so large a Continent, so different in Interests, so distinct in habits," could not be adequately represented in a single legislature.

With some justice, the Antifederalists could also claim that the states were managing quite well. Their citizens enjoyed the benefits of the most progressive constitutions the world had ever known and, by and large, they were prospering. Patrick Henry dismissed all the talk of trouble in the land. Had *Virginia* suffered, he asked?

The weakness of the central government handicapped American diplomats.

But Washington, Virginia's James Madison, and other advocates of an "energetic" central government warned that the 13 states would not survive for long on their own, at least not as republics. These nationalists (later called Federalists) viewed the growing power of the states as a threat to peace. The state governments had begun to fill the vacuum left by Congress, adopting their own commercial policies, ignoring national treaties, and, at the behest of wealthy citizens who feared that they would never otherwise be repaid, even assuming some debts incurred by Congress. The nationalists feared that increasing conflicts among the states would unleash what the Old Dominion's Edmund Randolph called the "dogs of war."

WHISPERING REASON

Such warnings were not easily dismissed. In New York, Governor George Clinton was enriching the state treasury by taxing merchandise shipped through New York between New Jersey and Connecticut.

Feelings ran so high that Congressman Nathaniel Gorham of Massachusetts worried that "bloodshed would very quickly be the consequence."

The weakness of the central government handicapped America diplomats. Britain had refused to abandon its outposts on U.S. soil, arguing (correctly) that Congress had failed to enforce some of *its* obligations under the Treaty of Paris, namely guarantees that prewar debts owed to British creditors would be repaid and that American loyalists would be reimbursed for their confiscated property.* Several states had simply ignored these provisions.

On the frontier, the threats from foreign powers were a constant worry. Rufus King, a Massachusetts congressman, observed that if the nation's disputes with Spain over the Mississippi and other matters were not settled, "we shall be obliged either wholly to give up the western settlers, or join *them* in an issue of force with the Catholic king." Both prospects, he concluded, were unthinkable.

More troubling still to the nationalists were the activities of the American frontiersmen themselves. From the Maine District of Massachusetts to western North Carolina, various separatists since the time of the Revolution had been petitioning Congress for admission to the Union as new states. But the older states refused to relinquish their claims. Vermont, legally a part of New York, was the most durable—and dangerous—of these rebellious territories. Rebuffed by Congress during the Revolution, the Vermonters, led by a group including Governor Thomas Chittenden and Ethan Allen, hero of the Green Mountain Boys, had entered into not-so-secret negotiations with London to rejoin the British empire.

The nationalists were dismayed when these talks resumed in 1786. Washington wrote that the Vermonters might "become a sore thorn in our sides," adding, "the western settlements without good and wise management . . . may be equally troublesome."**

The Westerners, in Kentucky and Tennessee, were understandably frustrated by the weakness of the central government. Chief among their complaints was the absence of congressional help in fending off constant attacks by marauding Indians, often

instigated by the British and the Spaniards. Nor could the state governments, they argued, effectively govern distant territories. "Nature has separated us," wrote Judge David Campbell of the would-be state of Franklin in western North Carolina. The frontiersmen's anger grew during 1786 and 1787 as rumors circulated that Congress was negotiating with Spain, offering to relinquish American claims to free navigation of the Mississippi in exchange for trade advantages. (These suspicions were justified, but the talks collapsed.) Kentucky's General James Wilkinson and other Westerners talked openly about leaving the Union and forming alliances with the Old World.

A RAT AND A GAMBLE

All of the nationalists' apprehensions were dramatized by a shock in the summer of 1786: the outbreak of Shays's Rebellion.

The rebels were farmers in economically depressed western Massachusetts who faced ruinous new state taxes imposed to help retire the state's wartime debt. As distress turned to anger, Captain Daniel Shays, a veteran of the Revolution, emerged as the leader of a ragtag mob that gathered to close down the Massachusetts courthouses that oversaw farm foreclosures and sent debtors to jail.

Thomas Jefferson, serving abroad as the American minister to France, was unperturbed. "I like a little rebellion now and then," he wrote to Abigail Adams. "It is like a storm in the Atmosphere." But in the United States, the uprising could not be so airily dismissed. It sparked the first general alarm about the future of the Union. "I never saw so great a change in the public mind," observed Boston merchant Stephen Higginson that autumn.

---

*During the Revolution, some 100,000 Loyalists fled to Britain, Canada, and the British West Indies. Many of the exiles were well-to-do farmers or merchants, and they claimed to have left behind more than $40 million worth of property, which the state governments seized.
**Vermont finally gained statehood in 1791.

2. REVOLUTIONARY AMERICA

Word of the insurrection spread quickly In Annapolis, Maryland, the news came during the first week of September, just as delegates from five states were meeting to discuss the condition of the Confederation's commerce. Among them were two of the country's most ardent nationalists—James Madison and New York's Alexander Hamilton—who were desperately seeking ways to strengthen the central government.

The stage for the Annapolis Convention had been set two years earlier at Mount Vernon, at a meeting hosted by George Washington. There, in March 1785, commissioners from Virginia and Maryland had met to resolve their disputes over tolls and fishing rights on the Potomac River. The success of the meeting led the two state legislatures to call for a larger meeting of all the states, to be held at Annapolis, to consider granting Congress broader powers to regulate interstate commerce.

The Annapolis Convention was a failure. Eight of the 13 states sent no representatives. More out of desperation than careful forethought, Hamilton and Madison proposed yet another meeting to consider strengthening the Confederation, to be held in Philadelphia in May 1787.

So clear to the Annapolis delegates was the case for reform that they might well have agreed to the Philadelphia meeting even without the shocking news from Massachusetts. The six-month rebellion was effectively ended in January 1787, in a battle near the federal armory at Springfield. Four Shaysites lost their lives. But the insurrection had already persuaded many state and local leaders to put aside their doubts about the need for a stronger central government.

In February 1787, after several states had already elected delegates to the Philadelphia Convention, the Continental Congress in New York City endorsed the gathering, with the stipulation (added at the insistence of Massachusetts) that it meet "for the sole and express purpose of revising the Articles of Confederation."

Patrick Henry, the fierce opponent of a stronger Union, had already declined to be a delegate from Virginia, declaring that he "smelt a rat." Indeed, few of the American political leaders who recognized the need for reform harbored any illusions about merely patching up the Confederation. They did not know what would happen at Philadelphia, or even if, like the Annapolis meeting, it would prove to be a failure, but they were now prepared to gamble. As Madison put it one month before the Federal Convention, the hurdles confronting any reform were so great that they "would inspire despair in any case where the alternative was less formidable."

"To Form a More Perfect Union . . ."

The creation of the Constitution was nothing less than the second American revolution.

Robin U. Russin

Robin U. Russin is a freelance writer and artist who graduated from Harvard College in 1979. He is currently living in Los Angeles.

Less than ten years after the signing of the Declaration of Independence, the loose confederation of ex-colonies that formed the United States was in chaos, threatened by internal strife and foreign intrigue. In the wake of the Revolution Washington had marveled, "Who, that was not a witness, could imagine that the most violent local prejudices would cease so soon; and that men who came from different parts of the continent, strongly disposed by the habits of education to despise and quarrel with one another, would instantly become but one band of brothers?" And yet, with the shots of Lexington and Concord still ringing in their ears, but without an enemy presence or a sense of common purpose to bind them, the men who had spoken and fought so bravely for the cause of liberty in the New World were now in danger of losing everything.

The Revolution had in fact been a civil war and had left deep and bitter divisions in the country, a legacy of bad blood and distrust. In government there was no president, no Supreme Court, only a Congress so weak that most of its members never bothered to attend. The country was hopelessly in debt, unable to pay even the interest on its loans, with the original Articles of Confederation allowing no national powers of trade regulation, taxation, or even effective military defense. Drastic action was

needed and yet none seemed possible. The new experiment in freedom drifted ever closer to destruction.

In retrospect we have come to take the Constitution for granted as a natural outcome of the Revolution. It hardly seems possible that it was the product of debate and compromise—struggled over, endlessly revised and rewritten—and not gifted to us as an eternal mandate from some higher power. The Constitutional Convention is known to most Americans, if at all, as hardly more than a procedural formality, a footnote in our history. In truth it was a daring and uncertain venture, in fact almost treasonous, since its implied purpose was the overthrow of the existing government. Perhaps that is why the Constitution has endured so well; the tensions it addresses and embodies are largely still with us—the challenges to human rights, the financial struggles of farmers and tradesmen, the difficulty of giving each and every person his or her "inalienable" chance to live and prosper as an "equal" citizen under the law. As we approach the Constitution's bicentennial birthday, it is hard to imagine how new, how visionary was that agenda two hundred years ago.

The new nation's problems were legion. For one thing, the states were far from united; each viewed itself as a sovereign power, with disastrous consequences. Between them, jealousies and economic battles arose. States such as New York and Rhode Island were actually drifting toward a secessionist stance, hoping to go it alone.

Traders who wanted to engage in interstate commerce often had to pay two tariffs, one going and one returning, stifling an already ruinous economy. Northerners were embarrassed by the presence of slavery in the South; Southern states, their economies dependent on "the Africans," resented any interference. Travel and communications were difficult—news of the Declaration had crossed the Atlantic almost before it had crossed the Alleghenies. The Carolinas and Georgia were so different from even the middle states that to some they seemed like strange tropical fiefdoms, more West Indian than "American." And states were often torn by internal strife, as the Tennessee area sought to split away from North Carolina, Kentucky from Virginia, and New York and New Hampshire wrestled over what is now Vermont. There was no central authority to adjudicate what course expansion into the West would take.

The financial situation was a nightmare. Without a common currency or set of standards, merchants tore their hair over interstate exchange: French sovereigns and Spanish pieces of eight were traded alongside doubloons, British sterling, gold johannes, moidores, pistoles, and hundreds of independent state mintings, creating chaos in the marketplace. Pieces of eight and dollars were worth six shillings in New England, eight in New York, seven in Pennsylvania, and 32 in South Carolina. Good hard currency was in short supply, and coins were commonly "shaved" to stretch their value, the shavings melted down for the precious metals. Forgery was such a problem that when Rufus King, of the Massachusetts legislature, received a shipment of supposedly safe, newly minted money, all of it was counterfeit.

To make things worse, a number of states without sufficient hard assets were independently experimenting with paper money, in a situation that prefigured events in Weimar Germany, the market was flooded with paper in the hope of paying off debt, making farmers and manufacturers afraid to sell their products in return for currency that was devalued daily. The old Continental dollar bills were so useless that one satirical fellow used them to wallpaper his barbershop; in Philadelphia, a mob of men and boys festooned their hats with money one day and paraded an unhappy mutt they had tarred and feathered in worthless bills.

Common citizens especially found themselves longing for the good old days of British stability. Farm foreclosures became commonplace, and class tensions ran high. The jails were overflowing with debtors and the dispossessed, and conditions were terrible; one prisoner described himself as "alive, and that is all, as I am full of boils and putrefied sores all over my body and they make me stink alive, besides having some of my feet froze." In Massachusetts, Shays's Rebellion, an uprising of desperate farmers, threatened to bring down the state government. The farmers surrounded courthouses from Northampton to Worcester in order to dramatize the poverty that worthless money and legal manipulation had inflicted on them, green sprigs in their hatbands to symbolize "natural" law. For these people, democracy had failed.

The Revolutionary veterans themselves, unpaid and restive, posed a grave threat. In 1783 inflammatory, "anonymous pamphlets, circulated by those discontented with the current leadership, urged the army to throw down the new government. "Imagine," wrote Finance Minister Robert Morris, "an army ready to disband or mutiny," threatening "a government whose sole authority consists in the power of framing recommendations." In one of the great dramatic moments in our history, Washington called for a meeting of the army and spoke to the hostile crowd. "Gentlemen, you will permit me to put on my spectacles," he said, "for I have grown not only gray, but almost blind, in the service of my country." As had happened

before and would again, Washington turned the tide, leaving the assembly in tears when he begged them not to "deluge our rising empire in blood." Even so, a band of eighty troops from Pennsylvania marched on Philadelphia and humiliated the Congress, which could do nothing to stop the harassment.

The bold men who had faced and beaten the British empire were paralyzed by their distrust of a strong central government.

Europe was only too happy to contribute to the confusion. In vain did John Adams attempt to enforce the Treaty of Peace worked out at the end of the Revolution. Britain, still America's chief trading partner, insisted on allowing only business using British ships and actually kept illegal military posts along the major American waterways to enforce its monopoly, citing America's inability to pay off the war debt and refusal to return confiscated Tory property as its excuse. Largely dependent on the shipping trade, the hard-hit northern states attempted an embargo against England, only to find the middle and southern states stabbing them in the back by declaring free ports for trade with the British. Those American shippers who tried to break the British stranglehold were victimized by Barbary pirates who, backed by France, Spain, and Morocco, stole their cargoes and demanded huge extortion fees. France, after all, had supported America during the war largely to humiliate its old enemy, England. Algiers actually declared war on America to further its demands, and sold captured Americans into slavery, where they were confined to vermin-infested dungeons, shackled and worked on treadmills, whipped, beaten, and traded in the marketplaces—hostages apparently forgotten by an impotent government at home.

In violation of the treaty, the British navy refused to help. Congress had no power to pay ransom, or to form a navy,

and was unable to provide protection. Adams and Thomas Jefferson were laughed at while representing America in England and France. At home there was fear that some of the states might actually be sold, and in Europe the expectation was that the ex-colonies soon would come begging. Spain owned Florida, controlled the mouth of the Mississippi, and was eager to take on the Carolinas as well. Under intense pressure from Spain, John Jay, a brilliant statesman and secretary of foreign affairs under the Confederation, was almost forced in 1784 to bargain away America's right to use the Mississippi, which would have left the new country in ruins.

The root of the problem was that the bold men who had faced and beaten the British Empire were paralyzed by their distrust of the power of a strong central government and their fear of its becoming a tyranny; no successful republic on such a scale had existed since the days of ancient Rome, and even that had degenerated quickly into a monarchy. It therefore fell to the younger generation, raised on the blood of the Revolution, to save the United States. In particular, it fell to James Madison and his fiery counterpart, Alexander Hamilton.

Madison and Hamilton were a study in contrast. James Madison, the son of a wealthy Virginia plantation family, had initially planned to enter the clergy. Frail and unambitious in his youth, he developed his talents only over time. He was an earnest, methodical man—devoted to the country for which his father had actively campaigned—with a calm manner that disguised an iron will and a determination to finish what he started. This cost him dearly in personal terms: early in his career, before he met and married Dolley Payne Todd, his neglected sixteen-year-old fiancée abandoned him for someone who could romance her more properly.

Elected to the Continental Congress, Madison experienced firsthand the frustrations of working for an impotent government in conflict with the selfish and often contradictory demands of the various states. His nationalism made him bitter enemies with Patrick Henry, governor of his home state of Virginia, a passionate states'-rights advocate who did not approve of Madison's efforts to create a strong Continental army. He also lost the financial support of his family, who would have preferred that he return to the plantation. Since the states often neglected to pay the salaries of their congressmen, Madison found himself in the same severe financial bind faced by many legislators. Indeed, Madison and others were often saved from poverty only by the generosity of the local Jewish moneylender, Haym Salomon, a little man with a big heart whose belief in the new country precluded any thought of accepting repayment from the destitute lawmakers.

While Madison was the even-tempered, well-connected gentleman, Alexander Hamilton was an explosive West Indian whose meteoric rise from poverty could be attributed to nothing but his own genius and drive. Growing up in the Leeward Islands, he was "the bastard brat of a Scots pedlar" and a fiery, independent woman who was the scandal of the region. A brilliant soldier, financier, and philosopher, he became lieutenant-colonel on Washington's staff in 1777, when barely into his twenties.

Where Madison failed in love, the handsome, flashy Hamilton charmed Elizabeth Schuyler and thereby married into one of New York's leading families. But his engagement didn't hinder his ongoing affairs, one of which was with Elizabeth's sister Angelica, a witty, worldly girl who had a longstanding crush on the handsome statesman. In a letter to Angelica written before he was to be married, Hamilton joked that Elizabeth would be "much less dangerous when she has a rival equal in charms to dispute the place with her. I solicit your aid."

It was in Congress that Hamilton met Madison, when the two men worked closely on a fruitless and discouraging effort to create a national revenue and pay the mutinying army in the face of states' opposition. Disgusted with the quagmire into which the country was sinking, they seized the first opportunity to work on a solution. A meeting had been called between a few states to discuss the use of the Potomac; Madison and Hamilton engineered it into a general convention, at Annapolis, for delegates from all the states to discuss the issue of commerce. They arrived to discover that only twelve delegates had shown up, their number awkwardly dwarfed by the hall in which the peace treaty with Britain had been ratified.

Rather than give in to disappointment, Hamilton drew up a ringing pamphlet calling for another, even more ambitious convention. This one, to be held at Independence Hall in Philadelphia the following May, would go far beyond commerce to address the central questions of if and how America was going to survive. It was not an easily achieved proposal. Many states, including Hamilton's home state of New York, were against a stronger national government, and many delegates were unhappy at the prospect of a long, hot summer in Philadelphia wrestling with impossible problems. But Madison and Hamilton were not to be denied. Together with two allies from Annapolis—Governor Randolph of Virginia and the wise old Scotsman James Wilson—they built support for the convention state by state. Only Rhode Island, blindly destroying itself with paper currency, refused to send delegates.

A significant absentee would be Patrick Henry, Madison's old foe, who violently opposed the convention and stayed home to organize opposition to it. Elected governor of Virginia for a time, the fiery orator who in 1775 had challenged, "Give me liberty or give me death," now directed the same salvo at the Congress. The Declaration had been Henry's goal, a separation of Virginia from England; he had no desire to see his state resubjugated to a new national master. His inflexible, radical views appeared oddly reactionary in the postwar context as he proved unwilling to abandon the patchwork of institutions left over from colonial days. A tragic, illness-ridden figure who lived to see his hour come and go, Henry ironically became the devil's advocate, unable to admit that revolution alone was not enough to secure the liberty in which he so passionately believed.

Madison did not content himself with politicking. He knew that without a solid plan to consider, the delegates would lose precious time and energy and he wanted more than just a rehash of the Articles of Confederation. Writing to Jefferson, who was serving in Paris, he asked for every book available in English, French, or Latin on natural law and the history of republican governments. Jefferson sent him two trunks full, and Madison threw himself into his studies day and night, working by candlelight to try to create out of the ghosts of the past a unique, vital reality for the future. Not that he was a novice: he had already helped the great libertarian George Mason draw up Virginia's Bill of Rights. Madison set to writing up the structure he envisioned for the government in what became known as the Virginia Plan. With various modifications, it formed the basis of the Constitution, the skeleton on which the living document was built.

The planning was progressing well. George Washington, it was assumed would be elected president of the assembly. Washington was almost universally considered the greatest living American, and Madison and Hamilton needed no less to keep the convention alive. Indeed, eighty-one-year-old Benjamin Franklin was deliberately not invited in order to avoid conflict in the election. The strategy seemed to be working—then, catastrophe. Washington declined to attend.

Washington was not against the idea of the convention, but he had intended to retire from public life. He had just declined an invitation to be honored by the Society of the Cincinnati in Philadelphia that same week; uncomfortable with presiding over this elite officers' association. Washington had several times threatened to resign unless reforms in its aristocratic doctrines were made. However, he did not wish to snub the many friends he had in the society by instead showing up for such an unlikely enterprise. The time for the convention drew near. With only a week to go, Washington still had not been persuaded. Fearing all would be lost, Madison and Hamilton at last invited Franklin to step in. On May 14, 1787, the moment arrived. Braving poor weather and muddy roads, the delegates began to assemble.

At the final hour Washington changed his mind, descending from Mount Vernon in his carriage like an Old Testament prophet. The militia—youngsters to whom he was just a legend and veterans who had actually served under his command—lined the streets as he rode through, giving him a full military salute. As the greatest soldier of the age dismounted, he was met by Ben Franklin, one of the greatest intellects. The prestige of these two grand old men, unquestioned heroes, proved vital to the success of the convention and later to the adoption of the Consti-

A Constitutional Add-On: Ten Amendments to Protect the Individual Rights of Citizens

Of the delegates present at the end of the convention, all but three signed the Constitution. Madison was saddened that two of these three were his old colleagues from Virginia, Governor Edmund Randolph and George Mason. They had come so far, and yet still they withheld their approval—in large part because while the document outlined the powers of government, it did not specify its limitations. The Constitution was without that ultimate guarantee of personal liberties, a bill of rights: the idea had been proposed in committee but was voted down as unnecessary. Most of the delegates reasoned that the extent of government was clearly limited by the enumeration of its powers—how could it exceed them? Eight states already had bills of rights, which were not affected by the Constitution as it stood. Perhaps Mason, as principal author of the Virginia Bill of Rights—the first in the colonies—was simply being too cautious. Yet, as before, his wisdom proved prophetic.

The absence of a bill of rights from the Constitution became the major stumbling block for subsequent ratification by the states. This issue went right to the heart of the fears many revolutionaries had about establishing a strong central government, because guaranteed rights were at the heart of the Revolution itself. The infamous Stamp and Quartering acts had been outrageous precisely because they had violated central tenets of the British Declaration of Rights: "No taxation without representation," and protection of the civilian populace from abuse by the military.

> *"A Bill of Rights is what the people are entitled to,"* declared Jefferson, *"against every government on earth, general or particular."*

The explicit preservation of individual liberties, the freedom from fear of the capricious or immoderate use of power by the government, were matters that few raised in the English tradition took lightly. Such freedoms had been hard won through hundreds of years of struggle, dating back at least to the summer of 1215, when King John put his forced signature to the Magna Charta on the field of Runnymede. The rights of the people, represented by an elected governing body, had been tested again and again, as the English suffered through a brutal civil war and the execution of a monarch in the seventeenth century; less than half a century later came the banishment of another. A Dutch ruler was imported only on condition that he submit to a new and much more extensive Declaration of Rights. It was a Hanoverian, George III, who broke this covenant again.

There was no way the colonists, having fought so hard to regain their rights, were going to gamble them away now. Led by Patrick Henry and joined by Mason, the anti-Federalists blasted the unamended Constitution as a model for tyranny. In vain Madison and Hamilton argued their case: it was absurd, a bill of rights would be redundant. "Why declare that things shall not be done, which there is no power to do?" Hamilton wrote in frustration. But the counterarguments were strong. It was suggested, for example, that while the state was not entitled to unreasonable search and seizure, this could be the unforeseen result of the new provision to collect taxes.

James Wilson pursued another tack in questioning the need for a bill: the very act of detailing rights would have

---

tution. Heightening the sense of drama was the fact that the assembly had decided to work in secrecy, a trust that, incredibly, no one broke. Although many spoke of amending the existing articles, and although few would have admitted it, they were engaged in a coup d'état, a peaceful, second revolution. Throughout the period of the convention the press was reduced to speculation: even the delegates' closest friends were kept in the dark. So were the antinationalists like Henry, who had boycotted the convention.

Philadelphia, the city upon which Franklin had lavished the best of his genius, was itself particularly colorful. America's largest metropolitan center, in the middle of a building boom brought on by the immigration of Irish, Germans, and Scots, Philadelphia was a mixture of raw energy and elegant high society that perfectly reflected the men who had come to decide the nations future—"an assembly of demigods," as Jefferson described them.

While most of the delegates stayed at a local inn, Washington was the guest of the richest man in America, Robert Morris, who lived in the grand manner and hosted Philadelphia's high-society affairs. Round and amiable, he was nevertheless a man of iron whose financial magic had managed to keep the wolf away from America's door in spite of all its problems. As "The Financier" of the Continental Congress, he had struggled against the disastrous flood of paper monies and tried along with his associate Gouverneur Morris, to found a central mint and a stable currency. When the disgruntled army, unpaid and in tatters, had confronted him, he and Gouverneur Morris had actually advocated the march on Congress, to demonstrate that the army's desperation (and their threat) was real. Should they fail and be forced to disband, he had said, "I will feed them." But even Morris, willing to invest his own enormous personal fortune and talents, was unable to make up for a fundamentally flawed central government. With Congress unable to raise taxes or stem its flow of debt, he had resigned, stating, "I will never be minister of injustice."

(Box continued from previous page.)

the effect of limiting them. "Who will be bold enough to enumerate all the rights of the people? And . . . if the enumeration is not complete, everything not expressly mentioned will be presumed to be purposely omitted." Washington agreed: liberty was too dynamic to be bounded by definition. But Jefferson's words sounded a stubborn reaction. "A Bill of Rights," he declared, "is what the people are entitled to, against every government on earth, general or particular."

In the end, the Federalists realized that without the inclusion of a bill of rights, the Constitution would not be ratified. And so they promised to amend the document once the government had been elected and installed. Even so, the contest was close when it reached the states. Fistfights broke out in the Pennsylvania legislature when the Federalists forcibly kept those opposed in the hall in order to fix a quorum. In Massachusetts, out of 355 votes, the Constitution passed by only nineteen. In Virginia Madison faced the fury of Patrick Henry and the vote was uncertain—until Randolph, satisfied at last, rose and declared, "I am a friend to the Union." It passed by a mere ten votes, but pass it did.

The convention, circumventing the Continental Congress, had decided that the approval of nine states was required for ratification, and by 1788 ten had been won over. After a bitter battle fought by Hamilton and Jay against Clinton and his men, New York, the "eleventh pillar," finally went along by a margin of three votes. James Wilson wrote to his wife: "Last night they fired thirteen cannon . . . over the funeral of the Confederation, and this morning they saluted the new government with eleven cannon." North Carolina and Rhode Island, still committed to local paper currencies, refused to ratify but were not long in changing direction.

The Federalists kept their promise. In his inaugural address, penned by Madison, Washington asked for suggested amendments. Out of the hundreds of submissions, Madison narrowed the field to seventeen, working in the Congress with the help of Jefferson, Mason, and others. Twelve amendments were adopted by the Congress and sent out to the states. The first two dealt with congressional details and were voted down; the other ten were adopted. Generally based on Mason's bill for Virginia, the amendments fell into four categories: the first was essentially a Jeffersonian restatement of the "open society"; the second, third, and fourth grew directly out of the military and political struggles of recent history and prevented military infringement on the rights and privacy of the people; the fifth through eighth went back to the "Law of the Land," passed down from the Magna Charta, and protected the rights of the individual from abuse by the legal system; the ninth and tenth disposed of Wilson's objections, by guaranteeing to the people and the states any and all rights not expressly curtailed by the Constitution.

As it turns out, the colonists' wary insistence on explicit protection of individual liberties proved to be brilliantly farsighted; throughout our history people have found refuge from injustice in the provisions that were then laid out. Nor did the impulse toward freedom stop with the first ten amendments. As the late Justice William O. Douglas suggested, the Bill of Rights now also includes the thirteenth, fourteenth, fifteenth, and nineteenth amendments, which abolish slavery and guarantee citizenship, the right to vote, and equal protection under the law regardless of race, color, or sex. "Our Bill of Rights . . . subjects all departments of government to a rule of law and sets boundaries beyond which no official may go," observed Douglas. "It emphasizes that in this country man walks with dignity and without fear, that he need not grovel before an all-powerful government."

—R.U.R.

Morris's former counsel and another key figure at the convention was James Wilson of Pennsylvania. A tall, erudite Scotsman, Wilson came to the New World at the age of 23 to seek his fortune, became a lawyer, and was a signer of the Declaration. He, like Morris, had experienced firsthand the anger of the mob when his own house was attacked. Known as the "Fort Wilson Riot," the attack was spurred on by impoverished radicals resentful of what they viewed as the vested interests of the lawyers and bankers. Rallying at a nearby tavern, the mob descended while Wilson and about thirty of his friends, barricaded inside, sent for help. Before the militia could arrive, one man was dead on either side. The incident was a sign that the law itself was under fire, and it made Wilson one of the most committed delegates at the convention.

Washington, as everyone had expected, was elected president of the assembly. Madison, working behind the scenes, had Edmund Randolph introduce his Virginia Plan. The hard work had begun. Although everyone in the company was civil, strong animosities, which often went beyond difference of opinion, were present. Essentially, four sets of difficulties had to be overcome: the conflict in interests between the larger, more populous states and the smaller, more vulnerable ones; the balance of power between the nation as a whole and the individual states; the issue of slavery; and the creation of an executive branch strong enough to be effective and yet incapable of hardening into a dictatorship. In every instance the convention was exploring uncharted waters.

In every instance the convention was exploring uncharted waters.

The Virginia Plan ran into immediate opposition from small states, both northern and southern, because it called for representation in Congress, whether composed of one house or two, based on population. The existing Congress instead gave one vote to each state. The idea of a popular national government, even then, was so daring, so untried, that it took a great leap of the imagination to see how it could work. Furthermore, such a system would mean a permanent underdog position for the less populous states. The southern delegates proposed that if this plan were adopted, they would accept it only if slaves were counted as part of the population, even though slaves had no vote. The small northern states objected because they feared domination by always-devious New York, and formed an unnatural alliance with the slave states.

The chief spokesmen for these interests and Madison's most vocal and aggressive opponents, were Luther Martin of Maryland and William Paterson of New Jersey. Martin had arrived in a storm of doubt, continued throughout in a storm of discontent, and left at the end in a storm of disgust. This stocky, untidy figure, with his loud voice and back-country manners, was the sore thumb of the convention, sure to voice opposition to anything he believed threatened the self-determination of small communities, whether it involved taxes, representation, or legal jurisdiction. From a poor, rural background, Martin had become rich through his talents as an attorney, but unlike Hamilton he had no aspirations to aristocracy. He was the shrewd country lawyer, distrustful of national politicians, and he fought tirelessly for the preservation of states' rights. Martin had married the daughter of a man Jefferson had accused of slaughtering the family of a friendly Indian chief; Martin never forgave Jefferson, using his name as a curse. He was also a lusty drinker who could distress and astonish his colleagues and clients by getting rip-roaring drunk only a few hours before a trial and then showing up and giving a masterful performance.

Paterson was more genteel. Born in Ireland but educated at Princeton, he had been in all the right places and met all the right people. He was "a man of great modesty, with looks that bespeak talents of no great extent, but whose powers break in on you." Paterson's motives in opposing Madison's efforts were not entirely selfless, since after the Revolution he had invested heavily in undervalued,

confiscated loyalist properties. Under the Treaty of Peace, these holdings were to be returned lawfully to their former owners, something only a strong national government could enforce. Together he and Martin introduced a proposal to counter Madison's, the New Jersey Plan, aimed at forming a federation more in keeping with the existing articles and preserving a great deal of state autonomy—but it was too little, too late, and was rejected.

While the New Jersey Plan had failed, Martin and Paterson's arguments against centralization had succeeded in putting Madison's nationalist Virginia Plan in jeopardy. Hamilton saw they were losing ground fast, and tensions arose between him and Madison. Using his own considerable skills as a writer and orator, he took the surprising step of drafting yet another proposal only this one was for a national government so strong that the states would have almost no say whatsoever. The Congress would be elected for life, and it in turn would elect a president-for-life whose power approached that of a monarch. The convention, shocked by the extremism of Hamilton's proposal, voted it down. It had very likely been a ploy. The delegates returned with renewed appreciation to the Virginia Plan, which now seemed reasonably moderate. Martin again responded with a long and impassioned plea for states' rights, but his moment had passed. He and Paterson were forced into a position they held to the end, that of embittered nay-sayers.

Although Hamilton had helped achieve a tactical victory his relations with Madison were still strained. He had also been continuously opposed in his efforts by the other New York delegates, men hand-picked by his enemy, George Clinton, governor of New York. Clinton was a huge brawler of a man, a pork-barrel politician determined to keep New York independent (and under his thumb), and was personally antagonistic to Hamilton. He had prevented John Jay, Madison and Hamilton's ally and partner in writing the *Federalist* papers, from being a delegate to the convention. Although he could not bar Hamilton, given his role at Annapolis, Clinton hamstrung him by sending two violently antinationalist delegates to accompany him. Respected for his force and geniality, Clinton also had a brutal streak, and he evidenced his contempt for the national government by decimating a lo-

cal tribe of Iroquois Indians in disregard of a treaty they had signed with Congress in 1784. When Clinton's delegates withdrew in protest from the assembly, New York was left without an effective vote. At the end of June, tired and disgusted, Hamilton left the convention and returned home to be with his wife and resume his neglected law practice.

His withdrawal did not improve the mood of the assembly, who would all have loved to follow his example. The summer was hot and sticky and everyone was anxious to get back on track, frustrated by the long and fruitless debates. Tensions were running so high, in fact, that Franklin stunned the company by suggesting each session begin with a prayer to God for help. The suggestion was not taken up, but the point was made; with or without prayer, there was business to be done. Over the Independence Day hiatus, Franklin helped Roger Sherman and his Connecticut delegation forge the Great Compromise, without which there would have been no Constitution: Congress would have two houses, one of which would represent the general population, and one of which would represent the states in equal measure. Madison was not happy with it, fearing the parochialism of the states, but it was compromise or lose the whole fight. To his pleasant surprise, after winning this victory, many of his former opponents from the smaller states outdid one another in working for a stronger national government.

Over the Independence Day hiatus, Franklin helped forge the Great Compromise, without which there would have been no Constitution.

A major obstacle overcome, it was decided that a short break would help restore energy and good humor to the assembly. With the exception of a small committee assigned to record what had been accomplished so far, the delegates took a ten day vacation. Washington and fellow delegate Gouverneur Morris decided to go fishing at Valley Forge. There, in the heat of the summer, among the decaying remains of fortifications, they reminisced about the fateful, freezing winter of a decade before.

In the arguments that followed this peaceful interlude, one can already sense the coming storm of the Civil War. The delegates returned to find their progress drafted up, with an unexpected addition. In the drafting committee, the South Carolina delegation had inserted a provision prohibiting any form of taxation on imports, or exports, including slaves. It was a direct move to maintain the slave trade, something most of the northern and middle states had abolished, and was particularly significant since it had implications for the spread of slavery throughout the unchartered western provinces.

One of the Massachusetts delegates, Rufus King, violently objected to having slavery actually codified into the structure of the new government. After all, even the feeble Continental Congress had managed to forbid the spread of slavery above the Ohio River, acting independently on the Northwest Ordinance just the month before. Gouverneur Morris, a Pennsylvanian of Huguenot ancestry—usually one of the most charming and politic of the delegates—stood up on his peg leg and in an uncharacteristic rage gave one of the most stirring antislavery speeches on record, eighty years ahead of its time. "It is a nefarious institution," he cried. "It is the curse of Heaven on the states where it prevails!" Even Martin added his thunder to this protest. But the South, already in financial straits and almost totally dependent on a slave population that often exceeded one third of the total census, was not to be denied. In the sweltering August weather, the majority of the delegates, impatient to move on to other issues, agreed to a fence-straddling compromise. The issue of slave ownership was essentially left up to the individual states, with restrictions imposed on its spread into free western territories, partial inclusion of nonvoting slaves in determining the population census allowed, and a stipulation ending the importation of slaves after 1808.

In retrospect, the inability to define a solid position in regard to slavery and the commercial conflicts between North and South was perhaps the greatest failing of the convention, putting off a confrontation that would only grow worse until it eventually erupted in war. George Mason, as always the standard-bearer for individual liberty, sounded a prophetic warning: "Providence punishes national sins by national calamities."

The challenges of working out an executive and an independent judiciary put the talents of the convention to the test. How could a presidency be created that effectively administered the laws, provided military leadership, and offered a unified political vision without instituting a dictatorship? There was no precedent for it: every previous historical effort to consolidate power in one or a few men had led to disaster. Debate on how the president should be elected was lengthy: direct popular vote was technically unfeasible, and no one trusted the state legislatures. Finally, following a brilliant suggestion from Wilson, a new democratic process—the electoral college—was invented, striking a balance between the demands of the states and the rights of the voters.

The convention was aided in mid-August by the return of Hamilton, who, his temper restored, was anxious to contribute. But it was Washington's presence that was essential. As the assembly hammered out the powers and limitations of the executive, they knew full well who the first man to fill the office would be. More than Hamilton's brilliant rhetoric, it was their personal trust in Washington that led to the creation of a much stronger executive than any of them, particularly, the states' righters, had expected—a true Commander in Chief. They modeled the presidency on Washington, and Washington was to serve as the model for all future presidents. At the same time they worked out the structure and responsibilities of the judiciary branch, a less threatening and hence less divisive issue for this gathering of lawyers.

At last, a full four months after they had begun, the document was complete. It was given to Gouverneur Morris, a magnificent stylist, to be translated into the elegant language that has resounded throughout our history. A brief debate ensued on whether or nor to put the various parts of it to Congress or to the individual states for ratification, but the idea was dismissed. The document had been written in secrecy, without consulting the Confederation or the separate legislatures, and it would be presented for adoption as it stood, whole, a new beginning for a troubled land. On September 17, the final vote taken, the Constitution was adopted by the assembly and was signed by the majority of the delegates.

Franklin, the patriarch of the convention, wrote the stirring closing speech, which he asked fellow Pennsylvanian James Wilson, with his genteel burr, to read. As the delegates began to file out of Independence Hall, their great labor ended, Franklin turned his gaze to a painting of a sun at the back of Washington's chair. "I have," he said to those around him, "often and often in the course of the session . . . looked at that behind the President without being able to tell whether it was rising or setting. But now at length I have the happiness to know that it is a rising and not setting sun."

The United States Constitution, celebrating its two hundredth birthday this year, is regarded with almost religious reverence by most Americans. While it makes no claim to divine authorship, we turn to it for guidance and answers with the same devotion the Greeks once showed their oracles at Delphi and Olympia. It is the shrine containing the best wisdom of our best men; our sense of what is right or wrong has become virtually indistinguishable from what is, or is not, constitutional.

Oracles are mystical creatures, and so perhaps it is not remarkable how little most of us know about how and why the Constitution came to be written, about what America was in the tumultuous decade between the Declaration of Independence and the drafting of this great document. Our Constitution seems to have come down to us from the mountain like the tablets of Moses, written in blazing letters to announce the doctrines we now equate with enlightened civilization. And yet it was, and is, a human document, and was anything but a natural consequence of the Revolution. It was the brainchild of extraordinary men living in extraordinary times, an astonishing, unique compromise among contending ideologies, a mosaic patterned to bring humane order to the fragmentation the war had left in its wake. It was, in fact, the manifesto of a second revolution, whose vital momentum continues to affect us to this day. The convention in Philadelphia that long, hot summer two centuries ago was a gamble against seemingly impossible odds on the part of a few dedicated, desperate patriots, a now-or-never move that John Adams described as "the greatest single effort of national deliberation that the world has ever seen."

The Founding Fathers, Conditional Antislavery, and the Nonradicalism of the American Revolution

William W. Freehling

By 1972, two years after publishing "The Editorial Revolution," I more clearly understood that the story of the events of 1860 must begin with the Founding Fathers. But I still hoped that my narrative of disunion could begin in 1850. I thus decided to publish my thoughts on the earlier history separately. The resulting first version of this essay, entitled "The Founding Fathers and Slavery," appeared in the American Historical Review in 1972.[1] "Founding Fathers" has been widely republished. I nevertheless regret its overemphasis on antislavery accomplishment. My changed title reflects my partial disenchantment. I am grateful to the American Historical Review for permission to republish some of the previous essay in this much-altered form.

When I wrote the original essay, historians were increasingly scoffing that the Founding Fathers ignored the Declaration of Independence's antislavery imperatives.[2] That denunciation has continued to swell despite my countervailing emphasis, indeed partly because of my overstated argument.[3] My original essay, as David Brion Davis pointed out, too much conflated Thomas Jefferson and the Founding Fathers.[4] The essay also erroneously portrayed the Founding Fathers as pragmatic reformers, eager to assault slavery whenever political realities permitted. They were in truth skittish abolitionists, chary of pouncing on antislavery opportunity. The Founding Fathers freed some slaves but erected obstacles against freeing others. They also sometimes moved past those obstacles for crass rather than ideological reasons. Thus historians who dismissed the Founding Fathers as antislavery reformers could easily dismiss my argument.

I have come to be more unhappy about the historians who appropriated "Founding Fathers." They have used my contention that the Founding Fathers chipped away at slavery to support their contention that the Declaration of Independence inspired a true American social revolution.[5] I find that argument unpersuasive, even about the white male minority. The notion is still less persuasive about African Americans and about other members of the nonwhite and nonmale majority, which means that the contention mischaracterizes American society writ large. Neither women nor African Americans nor Native Americans conceived that the American Revolution revolutionized their lives. Their position is relevant if we are to widen American history beyond Anglo-Saxon males, to write the story of a multicultural civilization.

Some historians answer that the majority's definition of a proper social revolution is irrelevant for judging the American Revolution, since only the white male minority had the power to define the event and the society. Such positions tend to narrow American history into solely a history of the white male power structure. But in the specific case of slavery, the elite's standard for judgment widens perspectives. Wealthy revolutionaries' criterion, no less than poorer Americans' criterion and posterity's criterion, required a proper American Revolution to include the slaves. By that universal yardstick, the Founding Fathers achieved no social revolution.

The Founding Fathers instead set us on our nonrevolutionary social history. Despite their dismay at slavery, America's worst multicultural dislocation, they both timidly reformed and established towering bulwarks against reform, not least because many of them preferred a monoracial America. I have revised this essay to include more of the bulwarks against antislavery, in company with those who think the Founding Fathers did nothing to further abolition. But I hope the revision will yield more tolerance for my continued belief, and latter-day slaveholders' worried conviction, that the Founding Fathers also did a most nonrevolutionary something to weaken slaveholders' defenses. For without that ambivalent perspective on the nation's founders, we can understand neither the subsequent meandering road toward emancipation nor America's persistently nonradical road toward a radically new multicultural social order, based on the ethics of the Declaration of Independence.

The American Revolutionaries intended to achieve a political revolution. They brilliantly succeeded. They split the British Empire, mightiest of the world's powers. They destroyed monarchical government in what became the United States. They recast the nature of republican ideology and structure with the federal Constitution of 1787. Over the next generation, their revolution helped undermine their own aristocratic conception of republicanism, leading to Andrew Jackson's very different egalitarian republicanism.

With a single exception, the men of 1776 intended no parallel revolution in the culture's social institutions. The Founders had no desire to confiscate property from the rich and give it to the poor. They gave no thought to appropriating familial power from males and giving it to females, or seizing land from whites and returning it to Native Americans. They embraced the entire colonial white male system of social power—except for slave holders' despotism over slaves. That they would abolish. To judge them by their standards, posterity must ask whether this, their sole desired social revolution, was secured.

The Founding Fathers partially lived up to their revolutionary imperative: They barred the African slave trade from American ports; they banned slavery from midwestern territories; they dissolved the institution in northern states; and they diluted slavery in the Border South. Yet the Founding Fathers also backed away from their revolutionary imperative: They delayed emancipation in the North; they left antislavery half accomplished in the Border South; they rejected abolition in the Middle South; and they expanded slaveholder power in the Lower South. These retreats both inhibited final emancipation where slavery had been damaged and augmented slave holders' resources where slavery had been untouched. The advances and retreats set off both an antislavery process and a proslavery counteroffensive. Slavery would eventually be abolished, partly because the Founding Fathers shackled the slaveholders. But emancipation would be so long delayed—partly because the Founders rearmed the slavocracy—that the slavery issue would epitomize the social nonradicalism of the American Revolution.

1

Since every generation rewrites history, most historians achieve only fading influence. One twentieth-century American historical insight, however, seems unlikely to fade. In his multivolume history of slavery as a recognized problem, David Brion Davis demonstrated that throughout most of history, humankind failed to recognize any problem in slavery.[6] Then around the time of the American Revolution, Americans suddenly, almost universally, saw the institution as a distressing problem. Davis showed that throughout the Western world, a changed Enlightenment mentality and a changing industrial order helped revolutionize sensibility about slavery. The American political revolution quickened the pace of ideological revolution. Slavery, as the world's most antirepublican social system, seemed particularly hypocritical in the world's most republican nation. Most American Revolutionaries called King George's enslavement of colonists and whites' enslavement of blacks parallel tyrannies. "Let us either cease to enslave our fellow-men," wrote the New England cleric Nathaniel Niles,

"or else let us cease to complain of those that would enslave us."[7]

Yet the Founding Fathers' awareness of slavery as a problem never deepened into the perception that slavery's foundations were a problem. A slaveholder's claim to slaves was first of all founded on property rights; and the men of 1776 never conceived of redistributing private property or private power to ensure that all men (or women!) were created equal. They believed that governments, to secure slaves' natural right to liberty, must pay slaveholders to surrender the natural right to property. That conviction put a forbidding price tag on emancipation.

The price escalated because these discoverers of slavery as a problem (and nondiscoverers of maldistributed property as a problem) also failed to see that other foundation of slavery, racism, as problematic.[8] Thomas Jefferson, like most of his countrymen, suspected that blacks were created different, inferior in intellectual talents and excessive in sexual ardency. Jefferson also worried that freed blacks would precipitate racial warfare. He shrank from abolition, as did most Americans who lived amidst significant concentrations of slaves, unless the freedmen could be resettled outside the republic.[9]

That race removal condition, like the condition that seized property required compensation, placed roadblocks before emancipation. To colonize blacks in foreign lands would have added 25 percent to the already heavy cost of compensated abolition. To coerce a million enslaved humans to leave a republic as a condition for ending coercive slavery could also seem to be a dubious step toward government by consent.

The Founding Fathers' conditional aspiration to free black slaves furthermore had to compete with their unconditional aspiration to build white republics. It was no contest. The American Revolutionaries appreciated all the problems in establishing free government; but that appreciation energized them, inspired them, led to sustained bursts of imaginative remedies. In contrast, these propertied racists exaggerated all the problems in freeing blacks; and that exaggeration paralyzed them, turned them into procrastinators, led to infrequent stabs at limited reforms.

The inhibitions built into the conditional antislavery mentality could be seen even in the Virginia abolitionist who scorned the supposedly necessary

conditions. Edward Coles, James Madison's occasional secretary, intruded on Thomas Jefferson's mailbox with demands that the ex-President crusade for emancipation without waiting for slaveholder opposition to relent. Coles himself acted on antislavery imperatives without waiting for action on deportation imperatives. He migrated with his Virginia slaves to almost entirely free-soil Illinois, manumitted all of them, gave each family a 160-acre farm, and provided for the education of those who were underage. After that rare demonstration of how to turn conditional antislavery into unconditional freedom, Coles advised his ex-slaves to return to Africa! The black race, said Coles, might never prosper in the bigoted white republic. That message, coming from that messenger, well conveyed the national mentality that rendered an antislavery revolution impossible.[10]

2

In conditionally antislavery post-Revolutionary America, the more blacks in a local area, the less possibility of emancipation. Where blacks formed a high percentage of the labor force, as in the original Middle South states of North Carolina and Virginia (35 percent enslaved in 1790) and in the original Lower South states of Georgia and South Carolina (41 percent enslaved in 1970), whites' economic aspirations and race phobias overwhelmed conditional antislavery.[11] In contrast, where blacks were less dense and the slavebased economy was noncrucial, as in the original northern states (all under 5 percent enslaved in 1790) and in the original Border South states of Delaware and Maryland (25 percent enslaved in 1790), the inhibiting conditions for antislavery could be overcome—but after revealing difficulties.

In northern states, the sparse numbers of blacks made slavery seem especially unimportant, both economically and racially, to the huge majority of nonslaveholders. The low percentage of blacks, however, made abolition equally unimportant, economically and racially, to most northern citizens. For the Founders to secure emancipation in the North, an unimportant set of economic/racial antislavery imperatives and a conditional strategy for solving the newly perceived slavery problem had to supplement each other, for neither tepid crass motives nor a compromised ideological awakening could, by itself, overwhelm a vigorous proslavery minority.[12]

That vigor will come as a shock to those who think slavery was peculiar to the South. Yet northern slaveholders fought long and hard to save the institution in temperate climes. Although neither slavery nor emancipation significantly influenced the northern economy, the ownership of humans vitally influenced northern slaveholders' cash flow. Slaveholders made money using slavery up North, and they could always sell slaves for several hundred dollars down South. These crass motives of a few could never have held back an ideological surge of the many had a disinterested majority passionately believed that illegitimate property in humans must be unconditionally seized. But since northern nonslaveholders conceded that this morally suspect property had legal sanction, the struggle for emancipation in the North was long a stalemate.

The only exception was far northward, in New Hampshire, Vermont, and Massachusetts. In those upper parts of New England, the extreme paucity of blacks, a few hundred in each state, led to the phenomenon conspicuously absent elsewhere: total abolition, achieved with revolutionary swiftness, soon after the Revolution. But in the more southerly New England states of Connecticut and Rhode Island, and in the mid-Atlantic states of Pennsylvania, New Jersey, and New York, where percentages of blacks were in the 1 to 5 percent range, emancipation came exceedingly gradually, with antirevolutionary evasions.

Blacks' creeping path to northern freedom commenced in Pennsylvania in 1780, where the Western Hemisphere's first so-called post-nati emancipation law was passed.[13] Post-nati abolition meant freedom for only those born after the law was enacted and only many years after their birth. The formula enabled liberty-loving property holders to split the difference between property rights and human rights. A post-nati law required that no then-held slave property be seized. Only a property not yet on earth was to be freed, and only on some distant day. Accordingly, under the Pennsylvania formula, emancipation would eventually arrive only for slaves thereafter born and only when they reached twenty-eight years of age. Slaveholders thus could keep their previously born slaves forever and their fu-

ture-born slaves throughout the best years for physical labor. That compromised emancipation was the best a conditional abolition mentality could secure, even in a northern Quaker state where only 2.4 percent of the population was enslaved.

Connecticut and Rhode Island passed post-nati edicts soon after Pennsylvania set the precedent. New York and New Jersey, the northern states with the most slaves, delayed decades longer. New York slaveholders managed to stave off laws freeing the future-born until 1799, and New Jersey slaveholders, until 1804. So it took a quarter century after the revolution for these northern states to enact post-nati antislavery—in decrees that would free no one for another quarter century.

Slaves themselves injected a little revolutionary speed into this nonrevolutionary process. Everywhere in the Americas, slaves sensed when mastery was waning and shrewdly stepped up their resistance, especially by running away. An increase of fugitive slaves often led to informal bargains between northern masters and slaves. Many northern slaveholders promised their slaves liberty sooner than post-nati laws required if slaves provided good service in the interim. Thus did perpetual servitude sometimes shade gradually into fixed-time servitude and more gradually still into wage labor, with masters retaining years of forced labor and slaves gaining liberty at a snail's pace. In 1817, New York's legislature declared that the weakening system must end by 1827.[14] Although New Jersey and Pennsylvania never followed suit, by 1840 only a few slaves remained in the North. By 1860, thirteen New Jersey slaves were the last vestige of northern slavery.

For thousands of northern slaves, however, the incremental post-nati process led not to postponed freedom in the North but to perpetual servitude in the South. When New York and New Jersey masters faced state laws that would free slaves on a future date, they could beat the deadline. They could sell a victimized black to a state down south, which had no post-nati law. One historian estimates that as many as two-thirds of New York slaves may never have been freed.[15]

Despite this reactionary outcome for some northern slaves and the long delay in liberation of others, the post-nati tradition might still be seen as a quasi-

revolutionary movement if it had spread to the South. But every southern state rejected post-nati conceptions, even Delaware, and even when President Abraham Lincoln offered extra federal inducements in 1861. Instead of state-imposed gradual reform, the two original Border South states, Delaware and Maryland, experimented with an even less revolutionary process: voluntary manumission by individual masters. Delaware, which contained 9,000 slaves and 4,000 free blacks in 1790, contained 1,800 slaves and 20,000 free blacks in 1860. Maryland, with 103,000 slaves and 8,000 free blacks in 1790, contained 87,000 slaves and 84,000 free blacks in 1860. The two states' proportions of black freedmen to black slaves came to exceed those of Brazil and Cuba, countries that supposedly had a monopoly on Western Hemisphere voluntary emancipation.

Just as fugitive slaves accelerated post-nati emancipation in Pennsylvania, New York, and New Jersey, so the threat of runaways sometimes speeded manumissions in Delaware and Maryland. Especially in border cities such as Baltimore and Wilmington, masters could profitably agree to liberate slaves at some future date if good labor was thereby secured before manumission. A hardworking slave for seven years was a bargain compared to a slave who might run away the next day, especially since the slavemaster as republican, upon offering a favorite bondsman future freedom, won himself a good conscience as well as a better short-term worker. This combination of altruism and greed, however, ultimately lost the slaveholder a long-term slave. That result, portending a day when no slaves would remain in northern Maryland, was deplored in southern Maryland tobacco belts, where manumission slowed and blacks usually remained enslaved.[16]

The Maryland-Delaware never-completed manumission movement failed to spread south of the Border South, just as the long-delayed northern post-nati movement never spread south of the mid-Atlantic. True, in Virginia, George Washington freed all his many slaves. But that uncharacteristically extensive Middle South manumission came at a characteristic time. President Washington profited from his slaves while living and then freed them in his last will and testament. President Thomas Jefferson freed a more characteristic proportion of his many Middle South slaves—10 percent. Meanwhile, Jefferson's luxurious life-style piled up huge debts, which prevented the rest of his slaves from being manumitted even after his death.

South of Virginia, Jefferson's 10 percent manumission rate exceeded the norm. A master who worked huge gangs of slaves in the pestilential Georgia and South Carolina lowlands rarely freed his bondsmen before or after he died. By 1830, only 2 percent of the South Carolina/Georgia blacks were free, compared to 8.5 percent of the Virginia/North Carolina blacks and 39 percent of the Maryland/Delaware blacks. The revolutionary U.S. sensibility about slavery had, with nonrevolutionary speed, emancipated the North over a half century and compromised slavery in the original two Border South states. But the institution remained stubbornly persistent in the Border South and largely intact in the Middle South; and Lower South states had been left unharmed, defiant, and determined to confine the Founding Fathers' only desired social revolution to the American locales with the lowest percentages of slaves.

3

National considerations of slavery in the Age of the Founding Fathers repeated the pattern of the various states' considerations. During national debates on slavery, many South Carolina and Georgia Revolutionary leaders denounced the new conception that slavery was a problem. Their arguments included every element of the later proslavery polemic: that the Bible sanctioned slavery, that blacks needed a master, that antislavery invited social chaos. They warned that they would not join or continue in an antislavery Union. They sought to retain the option of reopening the African slave trade. In the first Congress after the Constitution was ratified, they demanded that Congress never debate abolition, even if silence meant that representatives must gag their constituents' antislavery petitions.[17]

The Georgians and South Carolinians achieved congressional silence, even though other Southerners and all Northerners winced at such antirepublican intransigence. North of South Carolina, almost every Founding Father called slavery a deplorable problem, an evil necessary only until the conditions for abolition could be secured. The conditions included perpetuating the Union

(and thus appeasing the Lower South), protecting property rights (and thus not seizing presently owned slave property), and removing freed blacks (and thus keeping blacks enslaved until they could be deported). The first step in removing blacks from the United States was to stop Africans from coming, and the last step was to deport those already in the nation. In between, conditional antislavery steps were more debatable, and the Upper South's position changed.

The change involved whether slavery should be allowed to spread from old states to new territories. In the eighteenth century, Virginians presumed, to the displeasure of South Carolinians and Georgians, that the evil should be barred from new territories. In 1784, Thomas Jefferson's proposed Southwest Ordinance would have banned slavery from Alabama and Mississippi Territories after 1800. The bill would theoretically have prevented much of the nineteenth-century Cotton Kingdom from importing slaves. The proposal lost in the Continental Congress by a single vote, that of a New Jerseyite who lay ill at home. "The fate of millions unborn," Jefferson later wrote, was "hanging on the tongue of one man, and heaven was silent in that awful moment."[18]

The bill, however, would not necessarily have been awful for future Mississippi and Alabama cotton planters. Jefferson's bill would have allowed planters in these areas to import slaves until 1800. The proposed delay in banning imports into Mississippi and Alabama stemmed from the same mentality, North and South, that delayed emancipation in Pennsylvania, New York, and New Jersey for decades. In Mississippi and Alabama, delay would have likely killed antislavery. Eli Whitney invented the cotton gin in 1793. By 1800, thousands of slaves would likely have been picking cotton in these southwestern areas. Then the property-respecting Founding Fathers probably would not have passed the administrative laws to confiscate Mississippi and Alabama slaves, since the conditional antislavery mentality always backed away from seizing slaves who were legally on the ground. Probabilities aside, the certainty about the proposed Southwestern Ordinance of 1784 remains. The Founding Fathers defeated its antislavery provisions. Nationally no less than locally, they preserved slavery in Lower South climes.

They also retained their perfect record, nationally no less than locally, in very gradually removing slavery from northern habitats. Just as state legislators abolished slavery in northern states, with nonrevolutionary slowness, so congressmen prevented the institution from spreading into the nation's Northwest Territories, with yet more nonradical caution. Although the Continental Congress removed Jefferson's antislavery provisions from the Southwest Ordinance of 1784, congressmen attached antislavery clauses to the Northwest Ordinance of 1787. Slavery was declared barred from the area of the future states of Illinois, Indiana, Michigan, Wisconsin, and Ohio. Antislavery consciousness helped inspire the ban, as did capitalistic consciousness. Upper South tobacco planters in the Continental Congress explicitly declared that they did not wish rival tobacco planters to develop the Northwest.[19]

The history of the Northwest Ordinance exemplified not only the usual combination of selfishness and selflessness, always present whenever the Founders passed an antislavery reform, but also the usual limited and slow antislavery action whenever conditional antislavery scored a triumph. Just as northern postnati laws freed slaves born in the future, so the national Northwest Ordinance barred the *future* spread of slavery into the Midwest. But had the Northwest Ordinance emancipated the few slaves who presently lived in the area? Only if congressmen passed a supplemental law providing administrative mechanisms to seize present property. That a property-protecting Congress, led by James Madison, conspicuously failed to do, just as property-protecting northern legislatures usually freed only future-born slaves. Congressmen's failure to enforce seizure of the few midwestern slaves indicates again the probability that they would have shunned mechanisms to confiscate the many slaves in Alabama and Mississippi in 1800 had the Southwest Ordinance of 1784 passed.

The few midwestern slaveholders, their human property intact, proceeded to demonstrate, as did New York slaveholders, that slavery could be profitable used on northern farms. Slaveholding farmers soon found allies in midwestern land speculators, who thought more farmers would come to the prairies if more slaves could be brought along. These land speculators, led by the future president William Henry Harrison of Indiana, repeatedly petitioned Congress in the early nineteenth century to repeal the Northwest Ordinance's prohibition on slave imports. But though congressmen would not confiscate present slave property, they refused to remove the ban on future slaves.

Although frustrated, a few stubborn Illinois slaveholders imported black so-called indentured servants who were slaves in all but name. Once again, Congress did nothing to remove these de facto slaves, despite the de jure declaration of the Northwest Ordinance. So when Illinois entered the Union in 1818, Congress had massively discouraged slavery but had not totally ended it. The congressional discouragement kept the number of indentured black servants in Illinois to about nine hundred, compared to the over ten thousand slaves in neighboring Missouri Territory, where Congress had not barred slavery. But those nine hundred victims of the loopholes in the Northwest Ordinance kept the reality of slavery alive in the Midwest until Illinois was admitted to the Union and Congress no longer had jurisdiction over the midwestern labor system.

Then slaveholders sought to make Illinois an official slave state. In 1824, a historic battle occurred in the prairies over a statewide referendum on legalizing slavery. The leader of Illinois's antislavery forces was none other than now-Governor Edward Coles, that ex-Virginian who had moved northward to free his slaves. Coles emphasized that slavery was antithetical to republicanism, while some of his compatriots pointed out that enforced servitude was antithetical to free laborers' economic interests. Once again, as in the Baltimore masters' decisions to manumit slaves and in the congressional decision to ban slavery from the Midwest, economic and moral motives fused. The fusion of selfish and unselfish antislavery sentiments secured 58 percent of Illinois electorate. That too-close-for-comfort margin indicated how much conditional antislavery congressmen had risked when they failed to close those indentured servant loopholes. But in the Midwest as in the North, the new vision of slavery as a problem had finally helped secure abolition—half a century after the American Revolution.

4

While the Founding Fathers belatedly contained slavery from expanding into the Midwest, Thomas Jefferson and his fellow Virginians ultimately abandoned the principle of containment. In 1819–20, when Northerners sought to impose post-nati antislavery on the proposed new slave state of Missouri, Jefferson called the containment of slavery wrong. Slaves should not be restricted to old areas, he explained, for whites would never free thickly concentrated slaves. Only if slaves were thinly spread over new areas would racist whites free them.[20]

Given many Founding Fathers' conviction that emancipation must be conditional on the removal of concentrations of blacks, their latter-day argument that slaves should be diffusely scattered made more sense than their earlier argument that slaves must be prevented from diffusing. Still, the Upper South's retreat from containment of slavery illuminates the forbidding power of that race removal condition. If Upper South Founding Fathers had opted for diffusion of blacks rather than containment in 1787, as they did in 1819–20, even the diluted antislavery provision in the Northwest Ordinance probably would not have passed. Then the already almost-triumphant Illinois slaveholders probably would have prevailed, and slavery would have had a permanent toehold in the North. On the subject of the expansion of slavery into new areas, as in the matter of the abolition of slavery in old states, the Founding Fathers had suffered a total loss in the South, had scored a difficult victory in the North, and had everywhere displayed the tentativeness of so conditional a reform mentality.

5

To posterity, the Virginians' switch from containing slavery in old American areas to diffusing slavery over new American areas adds up to a sellout of antislavery. The Thomas Jeffersons, however, considered the question of whether slavery should be contained or diffused in America to be a relatively minor matter. The major issues were whether blacks should be prevented from coming to America and whether slaves should be deported from America. On these matters, conditional antislavery men never wavered.

In the letter Jefferson wrote at the time of the Missouri Controversy in which he first urged diffusion of blacks within America, he repeated that blacks should eventually be diffused outside the white republic. Four years later, in his final statement on antislavery, Jefferson stressed again his persistent conditional antislavery solution. His "reflections on the subject" of emancipation, Jefferson wrote a northern Federalist, had not changed for "five and forty years." He would emancipate the "afterborn" and deport them at "a proper age," with the federal government selling federal lands to pay for the deportations. Federal emancipation/colonization raises "some constitutional scruples," conceded this advocate of strict construction of the government's constitutional powers. "But a liberal construction of the Constitution," he affirmed, may go "the whole length."[21]

Jefferson's "whole length" required not only federal funding but also an organization that would resettle blacks outside the United States. That need found fruition in the Upper South's favorite conditional antislavery institution, the American Colonization Society, founded in 1817.[22] William Lloyd Garrison would soon denounce the society as not antislavery at all. But to Jefferson's entire Virginia generation, and to most mainstream Americans in all parts of the country in the 1817–60 period, the American Colonization Society was the best hope to secure an altogether liberated (and lily-white) American populace.

The only significant southern opponent of the society concurred that colonization of blacks could undermine slavery. South Carolinians doubted that the American Colonization Society would remove millions of blacks to its Liberian colony. (The society, in fact, rarely resettled a thousand in one year and only ten thousand in forty-five years.) But South Carolina extremists conceded that an Upper South-North national majority coalition could be rallied for colonization. They also realized that once Congress voted for an emancipation plan, whatever the absurdity of the scheme, abolition might be near. Capitalists would never invest in the property. Slaves would sense that liberation was imminent. Only a suicidal slaveholding class, warned the Carolinians, would take such a chance. Carolinians threatened to secede if Congress so much as discussed the heresy. So congressional colonization discussion halted in the late 1820s, just as South Carolina's disunion threats had halted antislavery discussions in the First Congress.[23]

A few historians have pronounced these South Carolinians to be but bluffers, cynical blusterers who never meant to carry out their early disunion threats.[24] The charge, based solely on the opinion of the few Founding Fathers who wished to defy the Carolinians, does not ring true. Many South Carolina coastal planters lived among 8:1 concentrations of blacks to whites, a racial concentration unheard of elsewhere. The Carolinians farmed expensive miasmic swamplands, unlike the cheaper, healthier slaveholding areas everywhere else. Unless black slaves could be forced to endure the pestilential Carolina jungle, the lushest area for entrepreneurial profits in North America would become economically useless. So enormous a percentage of blacks might also be racially dangerous if freed. South Carolinians' special stake in slavery engendered understandable worry when Northerners and Southerners called slavery an evil that must be removed.

So South Carolinians threatened disunion. Posterity cannot say whether they would have had the nerve to secede if an early national Congress had enacted, for example, Jefferson's conditional antislavery plan of using federal land proceeds to deport slaves. South Carolinians might have early found, as they later discovered, that their nerves were not up to the requirements of bringing off a revolution against every other state. But though they might not have been able to carry out their threats, that hardly means they were bluffing. Their threats were credible because these sincere warriors intended to act, if the nation defied their non-bluff.

Still, the larger point is that so conditional an antislavery mentality was not equipped to test South Carolinians' capacity to carry out their threats, any more than that mentality's compromised worldview was equipped to seize presently owned property from recalcitrant slaveholders. The master spirit of the age was a passion to build white republics, not an inclination to deport black slaves; and South Carolinians threatened to splinter the Union unless congressmen ceased to talk of deporting blacks. The Founding Fathers' priorities prevailed. South Carolina's threats effec-

tively shut off congressional speculation about removing slaves from America. That left only the other major conditional antislavery aspiration still viable: shutting off the flow of Africans to America.

6

South Carolinians long opposed closure of the African slave trade, too. But their opposition to stopping future slaves from traveling to America was mild compared to their opposition to deporting slaves from America. Like the northern slaveholders who could accept emancipation if they had fifty more years to use slaves, South Carolinians could accept the end of the African slave trade if they had twenty more years to import Africans.

Their potential interest in more African imports first surfaced at the beginning of the American national experience. When drafting the Declaration of Independence and cataloging King George's sins, Thomas Jefferson proposed condemning the tyrant for supposedly foisting Africans on his allegedly slavery-hating colonies. South Carolinians bridled at the language. Jefferson deleted the draft paragraph. Although Jefferson was not present at the 1787 Philadelphia Constitutional Convention, history repeated itself. When northern and Upper South delegates proposed that Congress be empowered to end the African slave trade immediately, South Carolinians warned that they would then refuse to join the Union. The issue was compromised. Congress was given authority to close the overseas trade only after 1807. South Carolinians had a guaranteed twenty-year-long opportunity to import African slaves.

In the early nineteenth century, with the emerging Cotton Kingdom avid for more slaves, Carolinians seized their expiring opportunity. In 1803, the state officially opened its ports for the importation of Africans. Some 40,000 Africans landed in the next four years. Assuming the normal course of black natural increase in the Old South, these latest arrivals in the land of liberty multiplied to 150,000 slaves by 1860, or almost 4 percent of the southern total.

Jefferson was President at the moment when Congress could shutter South Carolina's twenty-year window of opportunity. "I congratulate you, fellow-citizens," Jefferson wrote in his annual

message of December 2, 1806, "on the approach of the period when you may interpose your authority constitutionally" to stop Americans "from all further participation in those violations of human rights which have been so long continued on the unoffending inhabitants of Africa, and which the morality, the reputation, and the best interests of our country have long been eager to proscribe.[25] Closure of the African slave trade could not take effect until January 1, 1808, conceded Jefferson. Yet the reform, if passed in 1807, could ensure that no extra African could legally land in a U.S. port. In 1807 Congress enacted Jefferson's proposal.

Prompt enactment came in part because almost all Americans beyond South Carolina shared Jefferson's ideological distaste for slavery. The African slave trade seemed especially loathsome to most white republicans. But neither the loathing nor the enactment came wholly because of disinterested republican ideology. Jefferson and fellow racists hated the African slave trade partly because it brought more *blacks* to America. So too South Carolina planters were now willing to acquiesce in the prohibition partly because they considered their forty thousand imports to be enough so-called African barbarians. So too Upper South slave sellers could gain more dollars for their slaves if Cotton South purchasers could buy no more blacks from Africa. With the closure of the African slave trade—as with the Northwest Ordinance and as with the abolition of northern slavery and as with the manumission of Baltimore slaves—republican selflessness came entwined with racist selfishness; and no historian can say whether the beautiful or the ugly contributed the stronger strand.

The closure of the African slave trade emerges in the textbooks as a nonevent, worthy of no more than a sentence. Whole books have been written on the Founding Fathers and slavery without a word devoted to the reform.[26] Yet this law was the jewel of the Founding Fathers' antislavery effort, and no viable assessment of that effort can ignore this far-reaching accomplishment. The federal closure's impact reached as far as Africa. Brazil and Cuba imported over 1.5 million Africans between 1815 and 1860, largely to stock sugar and coffee plantations.[27] Slaveholders in the United States could have productively paid the then-prevailing price for at least that many black imports to stock southwestern sugar and cotton plantations.

The effect of the closure of the African slave trade also reached deep into the slaves' huts and the masters' Big Houses. If the South had contained a million newly landed "raw Africans," as Southerners called those human folk, southern slaveholders would have deployed more savage terror and less caring paternalism to control the strangers. The contest between the United States, where the nineteenth-century overseas slave trade was closed, and Cuba and Brazil, where it was wide open, makes the point. Wherever Latin Americans imported cheap Africans, they drove down slave life expectancies. In the United States, alone among the large nineteenth-century slavocracies, slaves naturally increased in numbers, thanks to less fearful, more kindly masters and to more acculturated, more irreplaceable blacks.

The closure of the African trade also changed the demographical configuration of the South and the nation, to the detriment of slaveholders' political power. When white immigrants shunned the Slave South and voyaged to the free-labor North, the South could not import Africans to compensate. The North grew faster in population, faster in labor supply, faster in industrialization, faster in the ability to seize agricultural territories such as Kansas, and faster in the ability to control congressional majorities. Worse, after African slave trade closure, the Cotton South could race after the free-labor North only by draining slaves from the Border South. The combination of manumissions and African slave trade closure doubly hindered slavery in the most geographically northern slave states. In 1790 almost 20 percent of American slaves had lived in this Border South tier. By 1860 the figure was down to 11 percent. On the other hand, in 1790 the Lower South states had 21 percent of American slaves, but by 1860, the figure was up to 59 percent. From 1830 to 1860 the percentage of slaves in the total population declined in Delaware from 4 to 1 percent; in Maryland from 23 to 13 percent; in Kentucky from 24 to 19 percent; in Missouri from 18 to 10 percent; and in the counties that would become West Virginia from 10 to 5 percent. By 1860 Delaware, Maryland, Missouri, and the area that would become West Virginia had a lower percentage of slaves than New York had

possessed at the time of the Revolution, and Kentucky did not have a much higher percentage. The goal of abolition had become almost as practicable in these border states as it had been in New York in 1776, twenty-five years before the state passed a post-nati law and fifty years before the New York slave was freed. Had no Civil War occurred, fifty years after 1860 is a good estimate for when the last Border South slave might have been freed. Then slavery would have remained in only eleven of the fifteen slave states.

To sum up the antislavery accomplishments in the first American age that considered slavery a problem: When the Founding Fathers were growing up, slavery existed throughout Great Britain's North American colonies. The African slave trade was open. Even in the North, as John Jay of New York reported, "very few ... doubted the propriety and rectitude" of slavery.[28] When the Founders left the national stage, slavery had been abolished in the North, kept out of the Midwest, and placed on the defensive in the South. A conditional antislavery mentality, looking for ways to ease slavery and blacks out of the country, prevailed everywhere except in the Lower South. If the Founders had done none of this—if slavery had continued in the North and expanded into the Northwest; if a million Africans had been imported to strengthen slavery in the Lower South, to retain it in New York and Illinois, to spread it to Kansas, and to preserve it in the Border South; if no free black population had developed in Delaware and Maryland; if no conditional antislavery ideology had left Southerners on shaky moral grounds; if, in short, Jefferson and his contemporaries had lifted not one antislavery finger—everything would have been different and far less worrisome for the Lower South slavocracy.

7

But the Founding Fathers also inadvertently empowered a worried Low South to wage its coming struggle. "Inadvertent" is the word, for most American Revolutionaries did not wish to strengthen an intransigent slavocracy, any more than they wished to delay African slave trade closure or to silence congressional consideration of colonization. The problem, again, was that these architects of republicanism cared more about building

white republics than about securing antislavery. So opportunities to consolidate a republican Union counted for much and the side effects on slavery counted for little—when side effects on slavery where even noticed.

Thus at the Constitutional Convention, Lower South slaveholders, by threatening not to join the Union unless their power was strengthened, secured another Union-saving compromise. Slaves were to be counted as three-fifths of a white man, when the national House of Representatives was apportioned. This constitutional clause gave Southerners around 20 percent more congressmen than their white numbers justified. Since the numbers of members in the president-electing electoral college were based on the numbers of congressmen, the South also gained 20 percent more power over the choice of chief executive. An unappetizing number illustrates the point. The South received one extra congressman and presidential elector throughout the antebellum years as a result of South Carolina's 1803-07 importation of Africans.

The Founding Fathers also augmented Lower South territory. In 1803, Thomas Jefferson's Louisiana Purchase from France added the areas of Louisiana, Arkansas, and Missouri to the Union. In 1819, James Monroe's treaty with Spain secured the areas of Florida, Southern Alabama, and Southern Mississippi. A desire to protect slavery was only marginally involved in the Florida purchase and not at all involved in the Louisiana Purchase. Presidents Jefferson and Monroe primarily sought to protect national frontiers. But they were so determined to bolster national power and gave so little thought to the consequences for slaveholder power that their calculations about blacks could not offset their diplomatic imperatives. Their successful diplomacy yielded territories already containing slaves. Then their antislavery mentality was too conditional to conceive of confiscating slave property. The net result: The Founding Fathers contributed four new slave states and parts of two others to the eventual fifteen slave states in the Union. That increased the South's power in the U.S. Senate 27 percent and the Lower South's economic power enormously.

If the Founding Fathers had done none of this—if they had not awarded the South the extra congressmen and presidential electors garnered from the three-fifths clause; if they had not allowed South Carolina to import forty thousand more Africans; if they had not acquired Florida, Louisiana, Arkansas, Missouri, southern Mississippi, and southern Alabama; if in short they had restricted the slavocracy to its pre-1787 power and possessions—the situation would have been far bleaker for the Cotton Kingdom. Indeed, without the Founding Fathers' bolstering of slaveholder power, their antislavery reforms, however guarded, might have been lethal. As it was, the American Revolutionaries made the slave system stronger in the South, where it was already strongest, and weaker in the North, where it was weakest. That contradictory amalgam of increased slaveholder vulnerabilities and increased slaveholder armor established the pattern for everything that was to come.

8

In the 1820–60 period, and on the 1861–65 battlefields, the slaveholders fought their added vulnerabilities with their added power. By 1860, the slaveholders had fifteen states against the North's sixteen. But if the four Border South states fell away, the North's margin would widen to twenty against eleven. Then all sorts of dangers would loom for a once-national institution, which in the wake of the Founding Fathers was slowly becoming more defensively and peculiarly southern.

Southern proslavery campaigns, ideological and political, could be summed up as one long campaign to reverse the Founding Fathers' conditional antislavery drift. The conditional antislavery ideology, declaring emancipation desirable *if* blacks could be removed and *if* the Union could be preserved, persisted in the North and the Upper South throughout the antebellum period. That predominant national apologetic attitude toward slavery, Lower South zealots persistently feared, could inspire a national political movement aimed at removing blacks and slaves from the nation unless the Lower South deterred it.

Deterrence began with a determined proslavery campaign aimed at showing Southerners that slavery was no problem after all. In its extreme manifestations in the 1850s, proslavery visionaries, led by Virginia's George Fitzhugh, called wage slavery the unrecognized problem. The impolitic implication (although Fitzhugh disavowed it): Even white wage earners should be enslaved.[29] Proslavery polemicists more commonly called freedom for blacks the unrecognized problem. The common message: Black slaves should never be freed to starve as free workers in or out of America.

While proslavery intellectuals took aim at the Founding Fathers' revolutionary awareness that slavery was a problem, proslavery politicians sought to counter the waning of slavery in the Border South. With the Fugitive Slave Law of 1850, particularly aimed at stopping border slaves from fleeing to permanent liberty in the North, and the Kansas-Nebraska Act of 1854, originally urged by its southern advocates to protect slavery in Missouri, Southerners endeavored to fortify the border regime which the Fathers had somewhat weakened. So too the most dramatic (although unsuccessful) Lower South political movement of the 1850s, the campaign to reopen the African slave trade, sought to reverse the Fathers' greatest debilitation of the slavocracy.

The minority's persistent proslavery campaigns and frequent congressional victories eventually convinced most Northerners that appeasement of a slaveholding minority damaged rather than saved white men's highest priority: majority rule in a white men's republic. That determination to rescue majority rule from the Slavepower minority underrode Abraham Lincoln's election in 1860; and with Lincoln's election came the secession of the Lower South minority. Secessionists feared not least that the President-elect might build that long-feared North-Upper South movement to end slavery by deporting blacks, especially from the compromised Border South.

The ensuing Civil War would prove that latter-day Southerners had been right to worry about slavery's incremental erosion in the borderlands. The four Border South states would fight for the Union, tipping the balance of power against the Confederacy. Abraham Lincoln would allegedly say that though he hoped to have God on his side, he *had* to have Kentucky. He would retain his native Kentucky and all the borderlands, including his adopted Illinois, which the Founders had at long last emancipated.

He would also obtain, against his initial objections, black soldiers, who would again sense an opportunity to read themselves into the Declaration of Independence. Just as fugitive slaves had pushed reluctant Pennsylvania, New York, and Maryland slaveholders into faster manumissions, so fugitive blacks should push a reluctant Great Emancipator to let them in his army and thereby make his victory theirs. Black soldiers would help win the war, secure emancipation, and thus finally defeat the slaveholders' long attempt to reverse the Founding Fathers' conditional antislavery drift.

To omit the Fathers' guarded contributions to America's drift toward the Civil War and emancipation in the name of condemning them as hypocrites is to miss the tortuous way black freedom came to the United States. But to omit the Fathers' contributions to Lower South proslavery power in the name of calling them social revolutionaries is to deny the very meaning of the word *revolution.*

9

More broadly and more significantly, the American Revolutionaries' stance on blacks illuminated their ambivalent approach to the one truly radical social implication of the Revolution. As the historian Jack P. Greene has brilliantly shown, nothing was radical about the Declaration's affirmation of an American right to life, liberty, and the pursuit of happiness, so long as only white males' pursuits counted as American.[30] Whatever the poverty in urban slums and tenants' shacks, American colonials had long since developed a radically modern social order, dedicated to white males' pursuit of happiness and rooted in unprecedented capitalist opportunity. The Revolution, while expanding political opportunity and political mobility, only a little further widened an economic doorway already unprecedentedly open—but labeled "white males only."

For the others who peopled America—the women, the Native Americans, the blacks, in short, the majority—opportunity was closed. To include these dispossessed groups in the American Revolution—to open up a world where *all* men and women were at liberty to pursue their happiness—was the Declaration's truly radical social implication. No such color-blind, ethnically blind, gender-blind social order had ever existed, not on these shores, not anywhere else.

The Founding Fathers caught an uneasy glimpse of this potential social revolution. Despite their obsession with white republics and white property, they recognized that the Declaration applied to blacks, too. But their racism led them to take a step backward from the revolutionary promise of the Declaration of Independence. Most of them were no advocates of an egalitarian multicultural society *in* America. The Virginia Dynasty especially would extend quality to black Americans by moving them *out* of America. That reactionary black-removal foundation of antislavery statecraft, peculiar among all the New World slavocracies to these North Americans, did not a progressive social revolution portend.

Thomas Jefferson had captured the nonradicalism of the American Revolution in one of the great American phrases. "We have the wolf by the ears," he wrote at the time of the Missouri Controversy, "and we can neither hold him, nor safely let him go."[31] The Founding Fathers had more wolves by the ears than Jefferson had in mind: blacks, slaves, their own antislavery hopes, their implication, that *all* people must be included in the Declaration of Independence. They propounded those ideals, but they quailed before their own creation. Someday, the ideals may prevail and Americans may cease to recoil from the Declaration's implications. But it would not happen to the Founders, not with revolutionary speed, not to men who equipped a nation to hang on to slavery's slippery ears for almost a century.

Notes

1. William W. Freehling, "The Founding Fathers and Slavery," *American Historical Review,* 77 (1972): 81–93.
2. See, for example, Robert McColley, *Slavery and Jeffersonian Virginia* (Urbana, Ill., 1964); Donald L. Robinson, *Slavery in the Structure of American Politics, 1765–1820* (New York, 1971); William Cohen, "Thomas Jefferson and the Problem of Slavery," *Journal of American History,* 56 (1969): 503–26.
3. Later writers have also extended the blame for failure to emancipate to encompass Northerners as well as Southerners. See, for example, Larry E. Tise, *Proslavery: A History of the Defense of Slavery in America, 1701–1840* (Athens, Ga., 1987), and Gary B. Nash, *Race and Revolution* (Madison, Wisc., 1990).
4. David Brion Davis, *The Problem of Slavery in the Age of Revolution, 177–1823* (Ithaca, N.Y., 1975), 168.
5. Most recently and notably in Gordon S. Wood, *The Radicalism of the American Revolution* (New York, 1992), 186–87, 401 *n* 43. For an estimate of this matter very close to my own, see Drew R. McCoy in *Journal of American History,* 79 (1993): 1563–64.
6. David Brion Davis, *The Problem of Slavery in Western Culture* (Ithaca, N.Y., 1966), and Davis, *The Problem of Slavery in the Age of Revolution.*
7. Quoted in ibid., 292.
8. A phenomenon splendidly illustrated in Winthrop D. Jordan, *White over Black: American Attitudes toward the Negro, 1550–1812* (Chapel Hill, N.C., 1968).
9. For further discussion of Jefferson's conditional antislavery position, see William W. Freehling, *The Road to Disunion,* Vol. 1, *Secessionists at Bay, 1776–1854* (New York, 1990), 123–31. For further discussion of the black-removal condition, see below, ch. 7.
10. For an excellent discussion of this episode, see Drew R. McCoy, *The Last of the Fathers: James Madison and the Republican Legacy* (New York, 1989), 310–16.
11. All demographic statistics in this essay derive from *The Statistics of the Population of the United Sates,* comp. Francis A. Walker (Washington, D.C., 1872), 11–74, and U.S. Bureau of the Census, *A Century of Population Growth; From the First Census of the United States to the Twelfth, 1790–1900* (Washington, D.C., 1909).
12. The classic study of emancipation in the North is Arthur Zilversmit, *The First Emancipation: The Abolition of Slavery in the North* (Chicago, 1967).
13. For an excellent discussion of the Pennsylvania episode, see Gary B. Nash and Jean R. Soderlund, *Freedom by Degrees: Emancipation and Its Aftermath in Pennsylvania* (New York, 1991).
14. For a fine recent study of the New York phase, see Shane White, *Somewhat More Independent: the End of Slavery in New York City, 1770–1810* (Athens, Ga., 1991).
15. Claudia Dale Golden, "The Economics of Emancipation," *Journal of Economic History, 33* (1973): 70.
16. Torrey Stephen Whitman, "Slavery, Manumission, and Free Black Workers in Early National Baltimore," Ph.D. diss., Johns Hopkins University, 1993, expertly develops these themes. On the broader Maryland milieu, see Barbara J. Fields, *Slavery and Freedom on the Middle Ground: Maryland during the Nineteenth Century* (New Haven, Conn., 1985).
17. Joseph C. Burke, "The Pro-Slavery Argument in the First Congress," *Duquesne Review,* 16 (1969): 3–15; Howard Ohline, "Slavery, Economics, and Congressional Politics," *Journal of Southern History,* 46 (1980): 335–60; Richard Newman, "The First Gag Rule," forthcoming. I am grateful to Mr. Newman for allowing me to use his excellent essay before its publication.
18. Quoted in Merrill D. Peterson, *Thomas Jefferson and the New Nation: A Biography* (New York, 1970), 283.
19. William Grayson to James Monroe, August 8, 1787, in *Letters of Members of the Continental Congress,* ed. Edmund C. Burnett, 8 vols. (Washington, D.C., 1921–36), 8:631–33. The following account of the Northwest Ordinance and its Illinois aftermath has been much influenced by the salutary notes of cynicism in Peter Onuf's fine *Statehood and Union: A History of the Northwest Ordinance* (Indianapolis, Ind., 1987) and in Paul Finkelman's several illuminating essays, especially "Slavery and the Northwest Ordinance: A Study in Ambiguity," *Journal of the Early Republic, 6* (1986): 343–70, and "Evading the Ordinance: The Persistence of Bondage in Indiana and Illinois," *Journal of the Early Republic, 9* (1989): 21–51. But for a cautionary note, see David Brion Davis's judicious "The Significance of Excluding Slavery from the Old Northwest in 1787," *Indiana Magazine of History,* 84 (1988); 75–89.
20. Jefferson to John Holmes, April 22, 1820, in *The Writings of Thomas Jefferson,* ed. Paul Leicester Ford, 10 vols. (New York, 1892–99), 10:157–58.
21. Jefferson to Jared Sparks, February 24, 1824, ibid., 10:289–92.
22. Phillip J. Staudenraus, *The African Colonization Movement, 1816–1865* (New York, 1961).
23. The theme is discussed at length in William W. Freehling, *Prelude to Civil War: The Nullification Controversy in South Carolina, 1816–1836* (New York, 1966).
24. See, for example, Paul Finkelman's otherwise illuminating "Slavery and the Constitutional Convention: Making a Covenant with Death," in *Beyond Confederation: Origins of the Constitution and National Identity,* ed. Richard Beeman et al. (Chapel Hill, N.C., 1987), 188–225.
25. A *Compilation of the Messages and Papers of the Presidents,* comp. James D. Richardson, 10 vols. (Washington, D.C., 1900), 1:408.
26. See, for example, Nash, *Race and Revolution.*
27. David Eltis, *Economic Growth and the Ending of the Transatlantic Slave Trade* (New York, 1987).
28. John Jay to the English Anti-Slavery Society, [1788], in *The Correspondence and Public Papers of John Jay,* ed. Henry P. Johnston, 4 vols. (New York, 1890–93), 3:342.
29. See below, pp. 98–100.
30. Jack P. Greene, *Pursuits of Happiness: The Social Development of Early Modern British Colonies and the Formation of American Culture* (Chapel Hill, N.C., 1988).
31. Jefferson to John Holmes, April 22, 1820, in *Jefferson's Writings,* ed. Ford, 10:157–58.

The Bill of Rights in Its Context

Oscar Handlin

Oscar Handlin, Carl M. Loeb University Professor at Harvard University, is the author, with Lilian Handlin, of the four-volume History of Liberty in America.

As its bicentennial commemoration recedes, the American Bill of Rights remains as puzzling as ever—more puzzling than ever.

Such celebrations no doubt satisfy some deep need for a periodic reminder of the advance of time and of continuity with the past—saints' days, birthdays, and anniversaries of longer duration—centennial or bicentennial, even quincentennial. The advance of knowledge, however, is rarely among the rewards of such celebrations, which more often than not serve to advance some particular cause of the celebrants.

The United States has enjoyed a good clutch of such occasions since 1976, when memorials of the American Revolution spread their share of ignorance; and a big one came up in 1992, when it became time to consider whether Columbus discovered, vanquished, or despoiled the New World. And for 1791, Chief Justice Burger led a distinguished committee in celebration of the Bill of Rights, an occasion certainly worthy of note, especially in a decade upbeat on rights, worldwide, a time when a multitude of causes, often contradictory, enlisted the concept of rights—right to life for the unborn fetus, for instance, as well as right to death for the incurably mori-bund, right to leisure and right to work, but also right to unionize.

Hence the prudent must approach the event with caution. Two warnings are particularly appropriate.

First, the lawyers are in on it, and they play a game of their own. They are, after all, each trained to make a case, to advance the client's interests, not to discover or expound the truth. Therefore lawyers operate with procedures hostile to historical accuracy. In making a case, they proceed from the present backward to the past. A search for the most recent case leads to its precedents, and those in turn become the threads on which attorneys hang their arguments. In the nature of the procedure, furthermore, legal training encourages the practitioner to tear phrases, concepts, and events out of context. Since present relevance is all-important, the actual bygone circumstances recede into a background of little consequence. The use to the litigant becomes far more significant than the meaning or intent of the old phrasemakers.

Surely enough, recent discussions of the Bill of Rights focusing on the present issue distort the text almost beyond recognition. Discussions of the First Amendment emanate from such issues as flag burning, panhandling on the subways, and obscenity, and they lead to debates over whether those actions deserve the protection of the 1791 safeguards of free speech. So, too, arguments such as those over the Mapplethorpe exhibition hang upon the question of whether government has the right to censor art, and they lead to the even more general issue of subsidies for the arts, so that deprivation of a grant becomes a measure that restricts freedom of expression. More recently, learned judges have debated the degree of nudity guaranteed topless dancers by the First Amendment. For five years, the federal courts pondered the constitutionality of an Indiana law that prohibited stripteasers at the Kitty Kat Lounge in South Bend from removing their G-strings. In June 1992, the Supreme Court finally upheld the statute by a five-to-four vote that rested upon four separate opinions (*Barnes v. Glen Theatre*). It requires generous exercise of the arts of debate to make these connections; but we have not been wanting in that respect.

Again, the Bill of Rights has entered into the abortion issue. The majority decision in *Roe v. Wade* pivoted on the right to privacy, infringement of which, the Court held, violated guarantees assured by the Bill of Rights.

Finally, litigants drag the broad issue of religious freedom, touched off by school prayer, back to the separation of church and state, also presumably a feature of the First Amendment. These efforts provide evidence of legal ingenuity; they do not further an understanding of the meaning of the Bill of Rights.

First warning, therefore: beware of the instrumental fallacy that tailors the past to the present use to which debaters put it.

A second warning concerns the disposition to regard the Founding Fathers, the authors of the Bill of Rights, as demigods. The very figure of speech—*Fathers*—exemplifies exaggerated respect and devotion. So, too, does the iconography: the surviving portraits show faces in repose, above the turmoil of immediate conflict, as do the statues in conventional relaxed postures. Yet it ought not surprise us to learn that the authors of the first ten amendments, like their contemporaries, were not objects of marble or paint on canvas, but human beings, flesh and bones—inconsistent, prone to mistakes, and often fallible in their judgments. The observation seems obvious, yet requires explanation.

While their countrymen debated the Constitution, Thomas Jefferson and John Adams—the ablest American theorists of their generation—lived abroad (probably a good thing that they did). Had they been present, the convention would have had much more difficulty in attaining the compromises embraced in that document. Jefferson lived in Paris and John Adams in London. Time hung heavily on their hands. With the treaties of peace signed, the emissaries had little business to transact. In Paris, Jefferson sought companionship and launched a discreet flirtation, first with Maria Cosway and then with Angelica Schuyler Church, both married and therefore both safe recipients of amorous letters.

No, however they bottled up emotions, these men were not devoid of passion—no, not the most intellectual of them. Jefferson, infuriated by a reference to someone else as author of the Declaration of Independence, laboriously composed an anonymous letter to the *Journal de Paris,* then refrained from sending it when it became clear that he could not conceal his identity. John Adams seethed with resentment at imagined slights, seethed with jealousy of rivals, and seethed with bitterness at real or fancied enemies. Young Alexander Hamilton, for a fancied slight, quit General George Washington's staff, foregoing opportunities for service and advancement. For a reflection on his honor he challenged the Reverend William Gordon to a duel in a wearisome correspondence. Like a country bumpkin he fell into the clutches of an English strumpet bent on blackmail.

These all-too-human traits explain the suspicion with which Jefferson and Adams viewed the Constitutional Convention at a distance.

Dribbles of information reached them (from Madison to Jefferson and from Abigail to John Adams). Their attention focused obsessively on one danger. They feared that the Constitution writers, meeting in secrecy in Philadelphia, would create a monarchy with Washington as king. Only the reflection that Washington had no children and therefore no incentive to establish a royal line somewhat eased their trepidation.

Supreme Court judges, then and later, were human too. In the bench and in posed photos, indeed in any public presence, they appear robed, immobile, inscrutable. Yet beneath those robes breathed men and women, living creatures of passion and prejudice as well as of learning and reason. We know more about past than about present occupants of the bench—John Marshall, given to fits of furious anger; Roger B. Taney, who in 1852 wrote a charming renewal of his pledge of love—to his wife, forty-six years after their wedding; Oliver Wendell Holmes, whose life the Civil War touched with fire and whose imagination flourished in correspondence and encounters with Lady Claire Castletown; Louis D. Brandeis and Felix Frankfurter, who pursued deeply held, although not publicly expressed, political agendas. We can wonder also whether Hugo L. Black's transformation from Klan member to liberal owed something to his friendship with Mrs. Clifford (Virginia) Durr while he served in the Senate. In other words, no impenetrable barrier of law shielded these creatures of flesh and blood from the influences about them, any more than legislators, congressmen, governors, or presidents. None of them argued about rights in isolation from life.

Behold, in this context, the Bill of Rights. Recall first that it did not form an integral part of the Constitution composed in Philadelphia and ratified by the states. Rather it consists of ten amendments (1791–1794) added at the request of some of the ratifying conventions. Why? Why did the framers not insert these provisions in the body of the Constitution?

Contemporaries clearly understood the answer: they needed no provisions of this sort. The Constitution formed a government of delegated powers. What it did not delegate, it did not grant; what it did not delegate, therefore, lay beyond the competence of president, Congress, and courts. Lest there be any doubt on this score, the Ninth and Tenth Amendments would make the point doubly clear. The enumeration of certain rights in the Constitution was not to deny or disparage others retained by the people; and the powers not delegated to the United States nor prohibited to the states were reserved to the states or to the people.

More important, Americans of the revolutionary generation believed that rights, the sacred rights of humankind, were not to be rummaged for among old parchments or musty records. Alexander Hamilton explained that they were inscribed in the whole volume of human nature rather than in arbitrary clauses. Writing to Thomas Jefferson in 1788, James Madison pointed out that experience proved how ineffective a Bill of Rights was when it was most needed. Overbearing majorities in every state, past and present, repeatedly ran roughshod over these parchment barriers. Wherever the real power in government lies, Madison stated, there is the danger of oppression; and formal statements would do nothing to prevent such oppression. Experience would prove him right.

The extent to which the issue of rights arose, therefore, depended less on the phrases engrossed on parchment or inscribed in formal judicial opinions than upon the structure and the views of the community. The small town tolerated the village atheist, and Concord raised no objection to the abstract anarchist Thoreau. Dissent expressed in acceptable terms presented no threat to established order. So, too, the Quakers thrived in nineteenth-century, but not in seventeenth-century, Boston, and the federal government took ruthless action to extirpate Mormon polygamy regardless of the right to religious freedom. The First World War raised more drastic issues of sedition, and neither the people nor the legislatures nor the courts acquitted themselves well in that period. And during the Second World War, whatever the Constitution said about rights did not protect the Japanese-American citizens from being hustled off to concentration camps. Experience justified the belief of Hamilton and Madison that, although prefatory statements could do no harm, they were unnecessary and fallible and did little good.

These basic conditions explain the characteristic features of the Bill of Rights, which stands not as a distinct section or article of the Constitution, but as ten amendments added later. From the state ratifying conventions and from concerned citizens, dozens of suggested amendments poured in upon the congressional committee charged with making order of them, some proposals sincerely concerned with the substance of the matter, others from anti-federalists simply eager to torpedo the Constitution, and still others from perfectionists who hoped that endless squabbling would lead to the summons to a new constitutional convention in which abler theorists would devise a superior product. Jefferson very likely had some such prospect in view. Although Madison, charged with reviewing the proposals, did his best to make order of them, in the end, the Congress put those amendments together in a casual manner, by a hit-or-miss process, in no logical or coherent order. These propositions did not therefore form a reasoned catalogue of rights. Moreover, they contained no enforcement procedures, although their compilers recognized that there could be no right without a statement of a remedy.

Two amendments, Nine and Ten, dealt with the issue of delegated powers. The enumeration of specific rights shall not be construed to deny others retained by the people; and reserving to the states and to the people powers not specifically delegated to the United States. These statements spelled out one of the Constitution's basic assumptions.

Most of the other amendments (Two through Eight), residues of the Revolution, rested upon recollections of abuses that seemed worth guarding against in the future. They dealt with the militia, with the right to bear arms, with the power of the government to quarter troops in homes, with unreasonable searches and seizures, with jury trials, self-incrimination, and due process. Even references to these familiar matters were vague and imprecise, sometimes inconsistent, and sometimes in conflict with one another. *Jury* could have meant grand or petit, acting by majority or unanimity. Startling omissions reflected the haphazard fashion in which the compilers put the list of rights together. For instance, Americans valued no liberty more than the freedom of movement—a stark contrast with the situation in Europe, where barriers marked off every province and walled off every city. Silence about this right did not diminish its worth in more than a century's spread of settlement. Much later, it blocked California's effort to bar the entry of Okies and the attempts of cities to keep out newcomers who threatened to crowd the welfare rolls. Yet the Constitution and its

amendments did not mention that right. Or the right to privacy—which was, no doubt, taken for granted. Yet the right to property did receive attention, not because it seemed more important or more threatened, but because the revolutionary experience brought it to mind.

Hence later efforts to make out the original intent of the framers miss the point: whose intent? The members of the state conventions who suggested the amendments, or the congressmen who framed them, or the conventions that ratified them, or the voters who elected those bodies? A hopeless task!

The crux of the contemporary issue, however, lay in the First Amendment—a statement more often referred to than remembered, and therefore worth quoting specifically.

Congress shall make no law respecting an establishment of religion or prohibiting the free exercise thereof; or abridging the freedom of speech, or of the press, or the right of the people peaceably to assemble and to petition the government for a redress of grievances.

Note that the amendment and the rights safeguarded shackle Congress and not the states. Taken at face value, the First Amendment thus did not extend to a Texas law that forbade flag burning, which the Court struck down in 1987.

Furthermore the loosely phrased First Amendment left considerable latitude in practice. The Massachusetts Constitution of 1780 safeguarded the rights of conscience, but also expected taxes to support churches. Many other states did so, too, and also retained test oaths for service as public officials. Jefferson and Madison in the Virginia statute on religious liberty wished a total separation of church and state, but the Northwest Ordinance of 1787 also stated that "religion, morality, and knowledge were necessary to good government." And even the federal Congress encountered no complaints when it appointed chaplains, opened sessions with prayers, and utilized religious emblems such as In God We Trust.

There was no reason why the references to freedom of speech and of the press restrained Congress, not the states, and applied to the use of words, not to art or to other forms of expression. Americans assumed that the protection served reasonable citizens capable of persuasion by rational argu-

ment, not flag burners blowing off steam or artists letting it all hang out. Francis Mezzara, a temperamental French portrait painter, discovered that free speech did not extend to art in 1817. When a subject who considered the likeness he painted insufficiently flattering refused to pay for it, Mezzara adorned the portrait with a pair of long ears usually worn by a stupid animal and put it on public exhibition. A plea of free speech did not spare him conviction of criminal libel. As late as 1968 in *U.S. v. O'Brien* (391 U.S. 367), Chief Justice Warren, speaking for the Court, held, "We cannot accept the view that an apparently limitless variety of conduct can be labelled 'speech' whenever a person intends thereby to express an idea." His colleagues would soon drift away from that sensible proposition.

For the same reason, the Founders did not believe that freedom of the press created a right to print lies, slanders, and sedition; and the conflict with other rights such as that to privacy troubled them. Orators and editors enjoyed the right to speak or print but not immunity from the consequences of abuses. John Adams's administration, after all, enacted a sedition act, and Jefferson as president did not hesitate to launch prosecutions under its provisions. Therein they followed the advice of Benjamin Franklin, himself a printer, publisher, and editor, who in 1789 made it clear that he would resort to the liberty of the cudgel against an impudent writer who went too far—break his head or tar and feather him. And he meant it.

The press was far from sacrosanct. Annoyed by the journalism of the early Republic, Jefferson expressed the view that the citizen who never saw a newspaper was better informed than a regular reader "inasmuch as he who knows nothing is nearer to the truth than he whose mind is filled with falsehoods." Justice Joseph Story summed it up for the next generation: The supposition that the First Amendment gave every citizen the absolute right to speak, to write, or to print whatever he might please, he considered too wild to be indulged by a rational man. To allow every citizen the right to destroy the reputation, the peace, the property, and even the personal safety of others would end civil society, with private vengeance compensating for the deficiency of law. Truth, he argued, was not alone sufficient to justify publication. In an orderly society, legislation would define the areas excluded, among them, he believed, obscenity and blasphemy.

Much has changed in the twentieth century, indeed in the last four decades. Rather than trace the wearisome steps by which those changes came about, it will be more enlightening to comment briefly on the consequences and the context of change.

First, the courts have applied the restraints of the Bill of Rights to the states by incorporating them under the Fourteenth Amendment, which held:

No state shall make or enforce any law which shall abridge the privileges or immunities of citizens of the United States; nor shall any state deprive any person of life, liberty, or property, without due process of law; nor deny to any person within its jurisdiction the equal protection of the laws.

The amendment did not succeed in its primary objective—protection of the freed slaves. And the justices who broadened its scope ironically did so initially in order to limit local police power, striking down, for instance, laws limiting the labor of women and children. But gradually after 1920 the courts also invalidated restraints upon Catholic schools and upon proselytizing by Jehovah's Witnesses, upon obscenity, and upon some forms of expression. The phrase "due process" could apply in unpredictable fashion.

Second, the transformation came not by legislation or executive order or by constitutional amendment, but by judicial interpretation, with consequences still unfolding.

It requires no strenuous stretch of the imagination to understand the deficiencies of judge-made law. Rulings from the bench are not etched in stone; what the Court holds in one case, its successors can reverse in another. *Plessy v. Fergusson* upheld the constitutionality of Jim Crow laws; *Brown v. Topeka* struck them down. Stare decisis, precedent, is a convenient strategem, not a binding principle. *Roe v. Wade* reversed venerable practices by which states regulated sexual conduct; another court could evade, modify, or nullify its position.

Recall further that judges are human, too—guided by their own foibles, prejudices, and limited knowledge. And among the most insidious of human traits is the desire to *do something,* to make a mark on history, be more than a rubber

stamp affirming the judgments of the past. In every ruling, the Supreme Court can choose broad or narrow grounds for its decision. It can refuse to hear a case, and it needs give no reason at all for doing so. It can rule on the narrow grounds of the case in hand and needs to announce its decision in no more than a curt statement. Or, it can take the occasion to soar in a broad decision that will earn a place in the history books. John Marshall did so in *Marbury* and Roger Taney in *Dred Scott.* The grand, sweeping rulings do not often have the dire consequences that *Dred Scott* did. But they all too often, nonetheless, carry the seeds of future trouble.

Nevertheless, the reach for the broad memorable opinion remains tempting. In the *Brown* case, certainly one of the most historic of the century, the Court could have rendered a narrow decision. It could have ruled unconstitutional a state law establishing segregation in the public schools of Topeka. Instead, the decision took a broad view and held segregation, whether by law or de facto, inherently unconstitutional; any separation created inequality contrary to the Fourteenth Amendment. The Court thereupon ordered the federal district courts, with all deliberate speed, to desegregate the nation's educational system. All good-hearted friends of the public schools and advocates of racial peace joined in hailing the decision, as I myself did at the time.

In the four decades that have elapsed since *Brown,* all its gallant expectations have faded. Education has not improved, indeed very likely it has deteriorated. Urban schools are not less segregated than before; they are probably more so. And racial peace is as elusive as ever. Furthermore, experience has demonstrated the incorrectness of the social psychological research on which *Brown* drew. Schools with student bodies drawn from a single group as often as not provide a more congenial setting for learning and better preparation for social mobility than those with students artificially commingled.

The problems with *Roe* also originated in excessive judicial activism that began with efforts to circumvent anachronistic state laws designed to prevent the use of contraceptives. Connecticut's statute simply forbade the employment of any such device, even by consenting married couples. It dealt with *use*—that is, with action and behavior—not with informa-

tion or speech within the purview of the First Amendment. What detection techniques could have harried out offenders is not clear. Nevertheless, a contrived test brought the issue to the Supreme Court. The judges did not like the statute at all but were hard put to find constitutional grounds for its invalidation.

A concerted drive for change then began, directed less at public opinion or at the legislatures than at the judiciary. The Planned Parenthood League, in the forefront of the campaign, drew support from the American Civil Liberties Union, which interpreted the issue as one of free speech, and of the National Council of Churches, which published *Responsible Parenthood* (New York, 1961), a powerful polemic in favor of planning. The doctrine of stare decisis, however, formed a great obstacle to change. In 1961 in the case of *Poe v. Ellman,* the Court refused to overturn the Connecticut statute, a decision without serious practical consequences except insofar as it demonstrated the difficulties in the way of judicial action.

Four years later in *Griswold v. Connecticut* (381 U.S. 479, 1965), the Court abandoned precedent and invalidated the Connecticut statute insofar as it applied to the behavior of married couples. In achieving the about-face, the Court drew upon argument in the briefs submitted to it, and spoke of the changed climate of opinion that left the statue out of accord with modern reality. To arrive at that conclusion the justices had to disregard the fact that the Connecticut legislature, presumably in touch with public opinion, had refused to act, and furthermore that two referenda that also reflected opinion had also opposed change. Those subtleties did not matter. The Court's view had hardened. Justice William O. Douglas, a cowboy willing to take risks on behalf of justice, pushed to strike down the silly law. Grounds? The right to marital privacy. The state could not intrude upon the privacy of the conjugal pair.

Now search as you will the text of the first ten amendments and all the commentaries upon them, and you will not find a reference to privacy. In a general sense, Americans had vaguely believed in the right to privacy but had not formulated it in any constitutional guarantee. And, in any case, the states had frequently regulated personal and family behavior without challenge.

To support his position, Douglas stated that the guarantees of the Bill of Rights went beyond their specific content. They included "penumbras" formed by emanations from those specified guarantees—a dangerous argument indeed, for it rested upon subjective judgments; one observer's penumbra may be the nightmare of another.

Nevertheless, the right of privacy in due course became central to the decision in *Roe v. Wade,* which dealt not with contraception but with the more inflammable issue of abortion, and which did not confine itself to the conjugal pair but extended to any couple, indeed to any female.

We have scarcely begun to explore the pitfalls of the right to privacy thus conceived. Does it apply to the relationship of parents to offspring—parental discipline ("Spare the rod and spoil the child"), battered children? Or to spousal relations, including traditional conjugal chastisement, wife beating? And a recent book by a distinguished professor of law criticizes affirmative action as an invasion of privacy. We may not yet have seen the end of that line of argument.

The effort to anchor the right to choice in the Bill of Rights by way of privacy did not settle the matter, which continues to divide citizens; for it rested upon exaggerated respect for the parchment barriers erected by judicial opinions. The citizens of the revolutionary era regarded theirs as a government by consent of the governed. And the governed respected the rights of others, not as defined by judges but as defined by their own experience and reason.

National Consolidation and Expansion

The Constitution necessarily was skeletal—it could establish the broad outlines of the system, but it could not afford prescriptions for its day-to-day operations. This meant that when the new government got under way, there would be great concern shown over precedents that would be set each step of the way. This extended to such relatively minor matters as to how to address the president. It also meant there would be a number of individuals and groups within the government trying to advance their programs based on what the Constitution most nearly "intended."

Although there were variations across the board, two competing groups began to emerge during the early years of George Washington's first administration. One group, concentrated primarily in the northeast, represented commercial and manufacturing interests and came to be led by Alexander Hamilton. The other group, based in the South and West, favored agricultural and rural interests and was represented by Thomas Jefferson and James Madison. These two groups had strong differences about what the federal government could and could not do under the Constitution, what sources of revenue should be tapped, and a host of other matters.

President George Washington quite frequently agreed with Hamilton's recommendations. Though the president despised what he called "factions," his actions eventually led to the formation of a two-party system. In "Hamilton's Legacy," Michael Lind argues that Hamilton's prescription for government was sound and that his influence continues to this day.

The next essay, "The Whiskey Rebellion" by Robert Kyff, shows how a federal tax on whiskey caused a serious internal crisis that involved a number of disputes between interest groups in 1794. This event also helped to spawn the two-party political system in the United States.

The Constitution provided for a balanced government of three branches: executive, legislative, and judicial. But how, in practice, was an equilibrium to be achieved? At first the Supreme Court was distinctly subordinate to the other two branches, but Chief Justice John Marshall changed all that. How his enormous influence helped establish the principle of judicial review, which prevails as part of the system to this day, is examined in "The Great Chief Justice" by Brian McGinty.

There are two essays about western expansion in this unit. In "John Quincy Adams and American Continental Expansion," Stanley Underdal reviews how Adams, as secretary of state and as president, helped acquire enormous territories for the United States. "1846: The Way We Were—and the Way We Went" by Timothy Foote describes a watershed year in the history of American expansionism.

Those who bemoan the quality and actions of Congress today should look at the past. A description of the sometimes outlandish behavior of congressmen during the first half of the nineteenth century is presented by James Chiles in "Congress Couldn't Have Been *This* Bad, or Could It?"

Environmentalism is emphasized in two articles. William Cronon and Richard White, in "Indians in the Land," treat the great differences between the way whites and Native Americans regarded nature. "Eden Ravished" by Harlan Hague tells how, despite warnings to the contrary, many Americans acted as though natural resources were inexhaustible and accepted wasteful practices as the norm.

Three selections deal specifically with women. In "The Lives of Slave Women," Deborah Gray White recounts both the common experiences they shared with men and the differences. "Forgotten Forty-Niners" by JoAnn Levy describes the participation of women in the great California Gold Rush of 1849. How the development of public transportation gave women more independence and altered their relationships with men is examined by Patricia Cline Cohen in "Women at Large: Travel in Antebellum America."

Four essays concentrate on pre–Civil War society. The essay "The Secret Life of a Developing Country (Ours)" by Jack Larkin describes the everyday lives of people during the early nineteenth century. Then, Alan Taylor, in "Fenimore Cooper's America," suggests that the reason that this author became so popular was because he celebrated the nation's cultural worth. How changing social conditions after 1850 helped standardize the celebration of Christmas is demonstrated by Penne Restad in "Christmas in 19th-Century America." "Walt Whitman's Different Lights" by Robert Martin tells how this poet and activist responded to social issues, many of which concern us today.

Looking Ahead: Challenge Questions

What were the basic issues over which the Hamiltonians and Jeffersonians disagreed? What kind of society did each group envision? How did the whiskey rebellion symbolize this conflict?

What were the contributions of Chief Justice John Marshall in establishing a balance of power within the government?

Evaluate westward expansion across the continent. What were the benefits to those who settled the West, and for the nation as a whole? What were the costs to the environment within which it took place?

Discuss the various roles of women during the first half of the nineteenth century. How did these change as the period wore on?

Hamilton's Legacy

He was George Washington's right-hand man, an abrasive genius and ruthless political infighter. As America's first secretary of the treasury, Alexander Hamilton worked hard to implement his vision of government, economy, and foreign policy—a vision that merits renewed attention in these uncertain times.

Michael Lind

Michael Lind, a senior editor of Harper's, *is the author of* The Next American Nation, *published by the Free Press.*

After the revolutions of 1989 brought down communism in Eastern Europe, many of the political and intellectual leaders of the emerging democracies turned for guidance to the United States. Americans of all political persuasions recommended the writings of such sages as Thomas Jefferson, James Madison, and Abraham Lincoln. Alexander Hamilton was seldom mentioned, even though his contributions to that compendium of political wisdom, *The Federalist,* far outweigh those of his co-authors Madison and John Jay. No one suggested that the theories and example of Hamilton might be far more relevant to the new democratic regimes struggling to consolidate their rule and build new governmental, financial, and military institutions on the remnants of Soviet colonialism.

This oversight is puzzling, if not tragic, because Hamilton was perhaps the most practical nation builder among the Founding Fathers. Thanks largely to his vision and energy, the United States became what it is today: a relatively centralized nation-state with a military second to none in the world, a powerful presidency, a strong judiciary, and an industrial capitalist economy. John Marshall, the first chief justice of the Supreme Court, who did so much to fix Hamilton's expansive view of federal authority in law, thought that Hamilton and his mentor George Washington were the greatest of the Founders. One contemporary acquaintance, Judge Ambrose Spencer, who

had clashed with Hamilton, nevertheless declared that he was "the greatest man this country ever produced.... He, more than any man, did the thinking of the time." The great French diplomat and statesman Talleyrand, who worked with Hamilton during the Revolution and the early years of the republic, put his "mind and character ... on a par with [those of] the most distinguished statesmen of Europe, not even excepting Mr. Pitt and Mr. Fox."

Such praise was anything but fulsome. As well as serving as George Washington's valued aide-de-camp during most of the Revolutionary War (and successfully reorganizing the Continental Army as one of his tasks), Hamilton

Alexander Hamilton (by Ezra Ames)

helped to initiate the move toward a more centralized union that resulted in the Philadelphia convention of 1787 and the federal constitution. His view of the Constitution as the source of implied as well as enumerated powers became the dominant interpretation, thanks to his admirers and students John Marshall, Joseph Storey, and Daniel Webster, and his conception of expansive presidential war and foreign policy powers would prevail in the 20th century. As secretary of the treasury (1789–95), Hamilton established the fiscal infrastructure of the new republic, including the Bank of the United States, precursor of the Federal Reserve. He not only articulated the theory of tariff-based industrial policy (an inspiration to later American, German, and Japanese modernizers) but organized the Society for Useful Manufactures (SUM), the first American research institute and industrial conglomerate, sited on 38 acres by the Passaic River falls in Paterson, New Jersey.

Today, however, those who remember the mastermind of the Washington administration (1789–97) tend to know only a caricature of Hamilton as a champion of the rich—the prototype of such Wall Street wizards as Andrew Mellon and Michael Milken. Now and then Hamilton's ideas are invoked by those seeking to justify policies of economic nationalism, but more often "Hamiltonianism" is used as shorthand for a blend of plutocracy and authoritarianism, the antithesis of democratic idealism associated with his lifelong political rival Thomas Jefferson. (Jefferson placed a bust of Hamilton on the right side of

From *The Wilson Quarterly,* Summer 1994, pp. 40–52. © 1994 by the Woodrow Wilson International Center for Scholars. Reprinted by permission.

the entrance hall at Monticello, across from his own portrait on the left. He explained to visitors: "Opposed in death as in life.") Regardless of political orientations, American politicians all claim to be Jeffersonians. Few, if any, will admit to being Hamiltonians. In the late 20th century, it appears, the consensus holds that Noah Webster was right to name Hamilton "the evil genius of this country."

It is far easier to understand why Hamilton has been maligned than why he has been forgotten. His life was as dramatic as any in the annals of the early American republic. The only non-native among the Founding Fathers, he was born in the British West Indies, probably in 1755, the illegitimate son of an aristocratic Scot and a French Huguenot. Orphaned at 13, he supported himself as a clerk in the St. Croix office of a New York import-export firm, acquiring a head for commerce that would further distinguish him from all the other Founders but Franklin. Hamilton so impressed his employers with his intelligence and industry that they, and other sponsors, sent him to the North American colonies to further his education. He enrolled in King's College (later Columbia) in 1773, but academic pursuits were cut short by his involvement in the writing of anti-British pamphlets and the subsequent outbreak of war. Nevertheless, wide and thorough reading kept Hamilton abreast of intellectual developments in Britain and continental Europe. Perhaps one of the strongest influences on his thought was the work of the Scottish philosopher David Hume, whose skepticism about classical republicanism and yeoman virtues made him anathema to Jefferson and other American republican idealists.

Psychobiographers eager to explain away Hamilton's devotion to the principle of a strong military need look no farther than his years in the inner circle of Washington's headquarters. As a member of what Washington called his "family," Hamilton made himself so indispensable that he almost missed his chance for martial glory. (That finally came at the Battle of Yorktown, where the slight, still boyish-looking officer personally led his battalion in an assault on a British position.) The bond forged with Washington, though subject to strains, would eventually bring Hamilton

into the first president's administration. But between the war's end and Washington's inauguration, Hamilton was never idle. He read and practiced the law, started a family with Elizabeth Schuyler (a New York patrician's daughter whom he had married in 1780), and became increasingly involved in New York and national politics. To the latter he brought his strong conviction that the weakly knit confederation could not work, a conviction that spurred his cogent defense of the proposed constitution in the essays that he and his collaborators Madison and Jay wrote between October 1787 and May 1788. (At least two-thirds of the 85 essays eventually published as *The Federalist* came from Hamilton's pen.)

As an immigrant, Hamilton lacked any ties to a particular region that might have qualified his intense devotion to the American nation in its entirety. Installed as Washington's secretary of the treasury, he took decisive steps to strengthen the standing and power of the federal government. To that end, and to make the nation creditworthy, he arranged for the federal government to assume the debts accumulated by the states during and after the Revolution and devised a system of taxation to pay off the debt. (A political pragmatist, he won support for his plan, a bitterly contested assertion of sovereignty by the federal government, by agreeing to back Thomas Jefferson and other southerners in their ambition to move the nation's capital to a site on the Potomac River.) Though at first opposed to political parties because of their disruptive character, Hamilton helped to create and then took the helm of the Federalist Party to push his policies through the legislature. His rivals in the newly formed Republican Party, including Secretary of State Thomas Jefferson, fought just as hard to thwart Hamilton's agenda, which they labeled crudely as probusiness, antidemocratic, and monarchical. Hamilton's disposition to favor England over France—and to hold up England's powerful civil administration as a model—only stoked his enemies' animosity. The Republicans' efforts to drive their foe from office, including unfounded accusations of wrongdoing, finally succeeded in 1795, two years before the end of Washington's second term.

Still wielding power in private life—among other ways, through the *New York Post,* which he founded (and which survives to this day)—Hamilton began to make enemies even among his fellow Federalists, opposing John Adams's reelection to the presidency in 1800 and supporting the Louisiana Purchase in 1803. Hamilton, who, like Napoleon, preferred to make war on allies, enraged another Federalist by speaking ill of his candidacy for the governorship of New York. The offended party, Aaron Burr, demanded satisfaction. Hamilton accepted, though in the resulting duel he took care to aim away from his challenger. Burr was not so gracious. Hamilton, who as a boy had hoped to become a physician, offered an immediate evaluation of his condition: "This is a mortal wound, Doctor." He died the next day—July 14, 1804.

His ideas could not be so easily extinguished. Like his rival Jefferson, Hamilton was a theorist as well as a statesman. His premature death prevented him from writing the "full investigation of the history and science of civil government and the various modifications of it upon the freedom and happiness of mankind," to which he had planned to devote his later years, according to his admirer Chancellor Joseph Kent, an early chief justice of the Supreme Court of New York. Though he never wrote his treatise on government, Hamilton lived to see the republication of *The Federalist* and his polemical *Pacificus* letters defending presidential authority in foreign affairs. These and other occasional writings, together with the three great reports he made to Congress as secretary of the treasury—*The Report on the Public Credit* (1790), *The Report on the Bank of the United States* (1790), and *The Report on Manufactures* (1791)—constitute a substantial body of work explicating the principles of Hamiltonianism.

As Hamilton saw it, the United States was (and should always remain) a nation-state in which the states are clearly subordinated to a strong but not oppressive federal government. The federal government must possess the military force not only to secure America's interests abroad but to suppress domestic insurrection quickly and effectively—a lesson he learned in the Whiskey Rebellion, which President Washington, with Hamilton's aid, put down in 1794. The success of the federal government, for Hamilton and his followers, depends

A cartoon of 1793 ridicules the Anti-Federalists' overheated attacks on Hamilton.

upon an efficient and competent executive branch and a powerful federal judiciary, both insulated to a degree from the popularly elected legislature. "The test of good government," Hamilton wrote, "is its aptitude and tendency to produce a good administration." Holding that good administration requires first-rate officers with long tenure, Hamilton firmly rejected the Jeffersonian notion that a great and powerful state can be administered by amateur politicians and short-term, inexperienced appointees.

One of the duties of the federal government, in Hamilton's view, is the active promotion of a dynamic, industrial capitalist economy—not by government ownership of industry (which Hamilton favored only for military contractors) but by establishment of sound public finance, public investment in infrastructure, and promotion of new industrial sectors unlikely to be profitable in their early stages. "Capital is wayward and timid in lending itself to new undertakings, and the State ought to excite the confidence of capitalists, who are ever cautious and saga-

cious, by aiding them to overcome the obstacles that lie in the way of all experiments," Hamilton wrote in *The Report on Manufactures.*

Hamilton, who had studied Adam Smith's *Wealth of Nations,* agreed with the Scottish philosopher on most points but criticized two of his ideas. He rejected Smith's notion that agriculture was preferable to manufacturing industry. And though Hamilton saw many benefits in trade and foreign investment, he believed that free trade was a mistaken policy in some circumstances. Hamilton had learned during the Revolutionary War how important it was for a country not to depend on others for "the manufactories of all the necessary weapons of war." He also advocated protection of infant American industries such as textiles, at least until they were capable of competing on an equal basis with foreign products. Finally, Hamilton thought it foolish for a country to open its markets to countries that protected theirs. In short, Hamilton held that economic policymakers should be guided by results rather than by dogmas in promoting state interests such as national

security and the diversification of the national economy.

With the collapse of the Federalist Party a few years after Hamilton's death in 1804, his philosophy of a strong, centralized national government promoting industrial capitalism and defending America's concrete interests abroad with an effective professional military passed into partial eclipse for a couple of generations. Quite different conceptions—states' rights, minimal government, agrarianism, isolationism, a militia-based defense—inspired the Jeffersonian and Jacksonian Democrats who dominated antebellum American politics. "National Republicans" such as John Quincy Adams, and later Whigs such as Daniel Webster and Henry Clay, kept the Hamiltonian legacy alive. The Whigs, fusing with anti-slavery Jacksonian Democrats in the 1850s, formed the new Republican Party, which under Lincoln and his successors crushed the Confederacy, abolished slavery, and made America into a strong union linked by a federally sponsored railroad infrastructure and industrializing behind high tariff walls.

The triumph of the Union was in many ways a vindication of Hamilton's vision, as was the rise of the United States as one of the world's great powers by the time of the Spanish-American War. "For many decades after the Civil War," Hamilton biographer Forrest McDonald writes, "his niche in the pantheon of American demigods was beneath only Washington's, if indeed it was not at Washington's right hand." Even so, the industrial magnates of the Gilded Age—the Jay Goulds and Edward H. Harrimans and J. P. Morgans—were not as a rule Hamiltonian in their philosophy. They tended to follow Herbert Spencer, the English philosopher of laissez-faire Social Darwinism. Moreover, many American business leaders were pacifists, believing that international capitalism, by increasing interdependence, would render war and economic rivalry between states obsolete.

The intellectual and political heirs of Hamilton operated largely outside the realm of business. Harvard political scientist Samuel P. Huntington, in *The Soldier and the State* (1957), describes the rise and fall of a neo-Hamiltonian school between 1890 and 1920. It included politicians such as Theodore Roosevelt and Massachusetts Senator Henry Cabot Lodge as well as intellectuals such as Herbert Croly, Brooks Adams, and Alfred Thayer Mahan, the prophet of American navalism and great-power politics. This congeries of like-minded men often combined *realpolitik* in foreign policy with support for progressive reforms at home—more in the interest of national efficiency than of abstract social justice. They rejected the Gilded Age's celebration of the entrepreneur in favor of the patrician-military ideal of an elite that serves the public by serving the state. According to Huntington, "Brooks Adams even went so far as to suggest openly that America would do well to substitute the values of West Point for the values of Wall Street." (It should come as no surprise to learn that West Point was a scaled-down version of Hamilton's grandiose vision of a comprehensive military academy.)

At the beginning of this century, Hamilton's reputation reached its peak. The most influential of his proponents was Herbert Croly, the founding editor of the *New Republic*. In

The Promise of American Life (1909), Croly contrasted Hamilton's view that "the central government is to be used, not merely to maintain the Constitution, but to promote the national interest and to consolidate the national organization" with the Jeffersonian theory that "there should be as little government as possible." The latter view rested on what Croly considered a naive belief in "the native goodness of human nature." To Croly and his allies, Jeffersonian doctrines, if they had ever been relevant, were obsolete in the new era of national and multinational corporations, mass organizations, technological warfare, and imperialism. Croly conceded that Hamilton's version of American nationalism had been inadequate because of its excessive distrust of popular democracy, but he held that the basic conception of an activist national government promoting the common good was as compatible with egalitarian as with aristocratic notions of a good social order.

Croly's beau ideal of an American statesman was Theodore Roosevelt, whom he praised for emancipating "American democracy from its Jeffersonian bondage." TR united progressive nationalism in domestic policy with an assertive realism, based on military power, in foreign affairs—a realism seen in his seizure of Panama and his mediation of the Russo-Japanese War in the interest of the Pacific balance of power, for which he won the Nobel Peace Prize in 1904. Roosevelt, like his friend Henry Cabot Lodge, chairman of the Senate Foreign Relations Committee, favored U.S. intervention in World War I but opposed Wilson's League of Nations Treaty because it committed the United States to a vague collective security arrangement rather than a traditional limited alliance. In his own biography of Hamilton, published in 1883, Lodge predicted that "so long as the people of the United States form one nation, the name of Alexander Hamilton will be held in high and lasting honor, and even in the wreck of governments that noble intellect would still command the homage of men."

Lodge spoke too soon. After World War I, Hamilton's reputation, along with Hamiltonianism, went into sudden decline. The defeat of the progressive TR–Robert La Follette wing of the Republican Party by the representatives of the conventional business elite made the Republicans hostile to overseas mili-

tary intervention, high levels of military spending, and ideas of government activism in the economy, even on behalf of business. The liberal wing of the Democratic Party inherited the legacy of Hamiltonian progressivism. But New Deal liberalism, as it evolved in the 1930s, was quite different from the nationalism of earlier Progressives such as TR and Croly.

The claim is often made that the New Deal resulted in a fusion of the two great American traditions of government—the pursuit of Jeffersonian ends by Hamiltonian means. The historian Merrill D. Peterson writes that during the New Deal, "national power and purpose grew without disturbing the axis of the democratic faith. For all practical purposes, the New Deal ended the historic Jefferson-Hamilton dialogue in American history." One might more plausibly argue that New Deal liberals abandoned the democratic and technocratic Hamiltonianism of Herbert Croly in favor of the ideal of the lobby-based broker state.

Partly to shield themselves from accusations that the New Deal was the American version of fascism or communism, New Dealers stressed the *absence* of centralized state direction of the economy. The journalist John Chamberlain described Roosevelt's broker state as a liberal-democratic alternative to the directive state of the Progressives (and totalitarians). Interest-group liberalism was seen as a pragmatic, democratic, American version of corporatism or syndicalism. "We have equilibrated power," theologian Reinhold Niebuhr wrote. "We have attained a certain equilibrium in economic society itself by setting organized power against organized power" in the form of unions, corporations, and professional associations.

New Deal liberals found a patron saint for interest-group liberalism not in Hamilton but in Madison, particularly in his *Federalist* no. 10, with its theory of factions in a democracy. They reinterpreted Madison to stress the idea not of conflict but of harmony and equilibrium through pluralism. In the 1940s and '50s, Madison was elevated to the status of a patron saint of interest-group liberalism, while Hamilton, the moving force behind *The*

Federalist, was denounced by, among others, historian Douglass Adair for favoring "an overruling, irresponsible, and unlimited government."

Franklin D. Roosevelt himself played an important role in expelling Hamilton from the American pantheon. FDR, a tory Democrat from the landed gentry of the Hudson River, saw himself in the tory democrat from the Virginia Tidewater. In his mind, Jefferson stood for popular government, not necessarily for weak or decentralized government, while Hamilton was a forerunner of Andrew Mellon and identified with the worst excesses of callous plutocracy. Reviewing a book by Claude G. Bowers, *Jefferson and Hamilton: The Struggle for Democracy in America,* Roosevelt suggested in 1925 that the common people needed a champion against the forces of plutocracy: "I have a breathless feeling, too, as I wonder if, a century and a quarter later, the same contending forces are not mobilizing." At the 1928 Democratic national convention, FDR, the keynote speaker, declared, "Hamiltons we have today. Is a Jefferson on the horizon?" Soon enough, Jefferson—or at least a sanitized Jefferson, whose racial views and small-government, states' rights preferences were conveniently underplayed—came to stand at the head of a line leading, by way of Andrew Jackson, to President Franklin D. Roosevelt himself. The work of rewriting American history as a prelude to the New Deal was completed by the moderate-liberal consensus historians of the 1950s and '60s, including Arthur Schlesinger, Jr., and Richard Hofstadter. At least one dissenting historian, Samuel Eliot Morison, considered this dismissal of the Federalist-Whig-Republican tradition "unbalanced and unhealthy, tending to create a neoliberal stereotype." But Hamilton's stock remained low.

To the extent that the Hamiltonian tradition lived on, it was in foreign policy. The logic of the broker state did not apply to the centralized national-security state that was assembled during World War II and consolidated into a permanent structure during the Korean War. Samuel Huntington notes "the curious way in which Theodore Roosevelt was the intellectual godfather of Democratic administrations after 1933" in foreign policy, and he

sees a "clear line" from such neo-Hamiltonians as TR and Elihu Root to "Stimson to Marshall, Lovett, and McCloy."*

One might have expected the leaders of the civil rights movement of the 1950s and '60s to have looked to Hamilton for inspiration. The civil rights struggle, after all, was largely carried out in the name of federal authority by federal judges, whose power and independence Hamilton strenuously defended (notably in *Federalist* no. 76). What is more, Hamilton was one of the more ardent opponents of slavery and racism among the Founding Fathers. When he was aide-de-camp to Washington, Hamilton favored giving blacks their freedom and citizenship and arming them as soldiers: "The contempt we have been taught to entertain for the blacks, makes us fancy many things that are founded neither in reason nor experience. . . . [T]he dictates of humanity and true policy equally interest me in favour of this unfortunate class of men." After the war, Hamilton—who had grown up in the slave society of the West Indies—helped organize the Society for Promoting the Manumission of Slaves. Jefferson, by contrast, opposed emancipation if it could not be accompanied by the immediate colonization of black Americans abroad, and his speculations about alleged black racial inferiority in his *Notes on the State of Virginia* (1784–85) made him a hero to generations of pseudoscientific racists. Nevertheless, the modern habit of attributing everything good in American life to the inspiration of Jefferson alone has resulted in his being given credit for convictions about black equality and freedom that are, in fact, closer to those of Hamilton.

The New Left and the modern conservative movement both draw on Jeffersonian distrust of concentrated authority, whether commercial or governmental, and on Jeffersonian individualism. The Jeffersonian Left stresses sexual rights, while the Jeffersonian Right stresses property rights; Left-Jeffersonians attack big business, while Right-Jeffersonians attack big government. For all that, there is a striking similarity in the paeans to the virtue of the people and the suspicion of authority and organization shared by the leaders of both the sexual revolution and the tax revolt—and a common dislike of Alexander Hamilton, the socially conservative proponent of big business *and* big government.

While liberals were redefining their tradition as one that stretched from Jefferson to Lincoln to FDR, leaving out Hamilton and TR, the conservatives of the 1950s were reading Hamilton out of the lineage of the contemporary Right. Conservative writer Russell Kirk, who repeated the hoary Jeffersonian libel that Hamilton sought to ensure that the rich and well born "could keep their saddles and ride . . . like English squires," criticized him as an unwitting precursor of the New Deal welfare state. "A man on the Right," according to historian Clinton Rossiter in 1955, "is not necessarily a conservative, and if Hamilton was a conservative, he was the only one of his kind." The McCarthy-Buckley-Goldwater conservative movement owed more to the old southern Democrats than to the Federalist-Whig-Republican tradition. Its philosophical roots sank deep in Jeffersonian antistatism, states' rights, and free-market libertarianism, and its antielitism and anti-intellectualism originated in southern and western populism. The defense of the Hamiltonian tradition fell to northeastern moderate Republicans such as Senator Jacob Javits of New York. In *Order of Battle (1964),* Javits sought to defend his conception of the Republican Party against the ex-Democratic Goldwaterite conservatives of the South and West: "This is the spirit which has represented the most dominant strain in Republican history. Hamilton-Clay-Lincoln-Theodore Roosevelt: they represent the line of evolution embodying this tradition." Arguably the last great Hamiltonians in American politics were Richard Nixon—a foreign-policy realist who admired TR—and John Connally, who, as one of Hamilton's distant successors as secretary of the treasury, shocked foreign governments and American critics with his unapologetic economic nationalism.

By the time Ronald Reagan was elected in 1980, the Republican Party had become a completely libertarian, antistatist party in econom-

---

*The theory of Cold War American realism, however, owed little to Hamilton, TR, Lodge, or Mahan, and far more to European émigré intellectuals such as Nicholas Spykman and Hans Morgenthau (the exception being the perennial critic of foreign policy utopianism, Walter Lippmann, Croly's fellow *New Republic* editor).

ics, with serious disagreements in its ranks only over social issues such as abortion and school prayer. Though Kevin Phillips, a graduate of the Nixon-Connally wing of the GOP, published a book, *Staying on Top: The Business Case for National Industry Strategy* (1984), advocating a conservative industrial policy that would target federal aid to "basic industries like steel or automobiles, or high-technology industry," his was an isolated voice. (Phillips was decisively read out of the Right for attacking its plutocratic tendencies in his 1990 best seller, *The Politics of Rich and Poor*.) Former Reagan trade negotiator Clyde Prestowitz founded the Economic Strategy Institute (ESI) to contest orthodox laissez-faire notions and advocate government-business partnership and a results-oriented trade policy.

Nevertheless, the dominant group in the Republican Party today consists of southern and western Jeffersonians in the Dixiecrat tradition, along with ex-Democratic intellectuals who, while retaining a strong cultural nationalism, have repudiated the New Deal and the Great Society for laissez-faire economics and the libertarian ideal of minimal government. In 1990, George Will named Jefferson the "Person of the Millennium," writing that Jefferson "is what a free person looks like—confident, serene, rational, disciplined, temperate, tolerant, curious." Ronald Reagan, himself an apostate Democrat, recommended that we "pluck a flower from Thomas Jefferson's life and wear it in our soul forever."

Hamilton probably would have thought as little of the contemporary Republican Right as it thinks of him. Reagan's brand of populist conservatism, contrasting the virtue of the people with the evils of the elite, would have found no favor with the elitist Hamilton. He despised politicians concerned with "what will *please* (and) not what will *benefit* the people." Though often maligned as a champion of plutocracy, Hamilton favored imposts on the luxuries of the rich as a means of "taxing their superior wealth," praised inheritance laws that would "soon melt down those great estates which, if they continued, might favor the power of the few," and denounced the poll tax in order "to guard the least wealthy part of the community from oppression." Though Hamilton was not alarmed by a moderate

deficit, he would have been shocked by deficits produced, like Reagan's, by an unwillingness to levy taxes to match spending. In his *Second Report on the Public Credit* (1795), he noted that runaway debt is "the natural disease of all governments" and that it is difficult "to conceive anything more likely than this to lead to great and convulsive revolutions of empire." The first and greatest secretary of the treasury, who during the Whiskey Rebellion helped President Washington to mobilize the militia to collect excise taxes, would not have smiled upon the tax-revolt rhetoric of Howard Jarvis and Ronald Reagan.

Having seen the consequences of feeble government during the Revolutionary War and the years of the Articles of Confederation, Hamilton would have been appalled by Reagan's assertion that "government is not part of the solution; it is the problem." Indeed, during the French Revolution, Hamilton contemptuously dismissed the "pernicious system" that maintained "that but a small portion of power is requisite to Government . . . and that as human nature shall refine and ameliorate by the operation of a more enlightened plan, government itself will become useless, and Society will subsist and flourish free from its shackles."

"The American nation reached the peak of its greatness in the middle of the 20th century," historian Forrest McDonald has lamented. "After that time it became increasingly Jeffersonian, governed by coercion and the party spirit, its people progressively more dependent and less self-reliant, its decline candy-coated with the rhetoric of liberty and equality and justice for all: and with that decline Hamilton's fame declined apace." Repudiated by *ersatz* Jeffersonians and Jacksonians of the Left and Right alike, Hamilton, by the mid-20th century, was even being cast as a villain in American fiction and poetry. In his book-length poem *Paterson* (1946–58) William Carlos Williams, one of America's leading midcentury modernist poets, chose the site of Hamilton's early industrial experiments as a symbol of the blighting of the American spirit in the era of centralized government and concentrated industry. (The poem is interlarded with quotations from a pamphlet Williams had read attacking Hamilton and the Federal Reserve, entitled "Tom Edison on the Money Subject.") In the ultimate insult—from an eccentric

populist perspective—Gore Vidal's best selling historical novel *Burr* (1986) cast Hamilton as a sinister foil to the man who murdered him in a duel. Never had Hamilton's reputation been lower.

In recent years, Hamiltonianism has been reintroduced into American political debate by way of Japan. Whereas the neo-Hamiltonians of the late 19th century looked to Hamilton as a guide to power politics, the Hamiltonians of today are more likely to view him as the patron saint of industrial policy and economic nationalism.

The architects of the postwar Japanese economic miracle in the Ministry of International Trade and Industry (MITI) and the Ministry of Finance (MOF) were inspired not only by the examples of 19th-century Germany and America, but by the theories of the 19th-century German economic nationalist Friedrich List, who, when he lived for a time in Pennsylvania, absorbed Hamilton's ideas about the protection of infant industries. By the late 1970s, the remarkable success of modern Japan in promoting its high-tech industry and banking sectors by combining protectionism and industrial policy with the targeting of open foreign markets—including that of the United States—was presenting a challenge to orthodox American economists and politicians, who had been committed to free trade since the aftermath of World War II. Working within the neoclassical paradigm, architects of "the new trade theory" (which is little more than a recycling of the old Hamilton-List theory of tariff-driven industrial policy) began to question the orthodox view that free trade is always beneficial to a country.

By the early 1980s, a growing number of American thinkers and politicians was advocating the emulation, in the United States, of aspects of Japanese industrial policy. It would be a mistake to describe all American proponents of industrial policy as Hamiltonian. Most of the industrial-policy advocates were Left-liberals such as Robert Reich, Robert Kuttner, and Lester Thurow, whose interest in different (and sometimes conflicting) versions of industrial policy grew out of a desire to help American workers threatened by foreign competition. Also in this school is Laura Tyson, who left the Berkeley Roundtable on the International Economy, an influential forum for the new trade theory, to chair President Clinton's Council of Economic Advisers. Many of these liberals are reluctant nationalists. Given a choice, they would prefer a "global New Deal" regulating the excesses of transnational capitalism to American economic nationalism in the service of American self-sufficiency and geopolitical preeminence. They are better described as neo-Keynesians than as Hamiltonians. As for Ross Perot's brand of economic nationalism, it owes more to southwestern populism than to Hamilton's principles.

The genuine Hamiltonians, one can argue, are the politicians and national-security experts more concerned about the U.S. defense industrial base than about union jobs in Detroit. The United States has long had its own military-led industrial policy, in the form of Pentagon-funded research and development. Military procurement has been largely responsible for the postwar U.S. lead in industries characterized by high risk and high research costs requiring government support: computers, aircraft, and communications equipment. The chief Pentagon agency—the American MITI—was the Defense Advanced Research Projects Agency (DARPA).* During the 1980s, DARPA funded R&D in sectors including very high speed integrated circuits (VHSIC), fiber optics, advanced lasers, computer software, and composite materials, which promised to have commercial applications as well as military uses.

The leading Hamiltonians to emerge from the military-industrial complex have not fared well in politics or in the private sector. DARPA director Craig Fields, an advocate of industrial policy, was forced out of his job by the Bush administration in 1990. The view that prevailed in that administration was one attributed to Michael J. Boskin, chairman of the Council of Economic Advisers: "It doesn't matter whether the United States makes computer chips or potato chips." Admiral Bobby Ray Inman, the former National Security Agency (NSA) director who grew concerned about American technological dependence in the mid-'80s, left government for an unsuccessful stint as the head of a government-backed computer consortium, Microelectronics and Computer Technology Corporation (MCC), in Austin, Texas. (It might be useful to

(NATIONAL ARCHIVES)

The first page of Hamilton's Report on a National Bank (1790)

recall, however, that Hamilton failed both in his political efforts to promote an industrial policy and in his private attempt to jump-start American industrialization with his Society for Useful Manufactures in Paterson—only to be posthumously vindicated by later generations that adopted certain aspects of his program for national development.)

Among recent American politicians, only the "Atari Democrats," led by Gary Hart and Al Gore, combined interests in military innovation and domestic technology policy in true Hamiltonian fashion. Gore's advocacy of military intervention in the Persian Gulf, technology policy, and the building of an "information highway"—the modern version of canals and railroads—makes this southern Democrat the philosophical descendant of northern Federalists, Whigs, and Republicans. One influential thinker among the neoliberal Democrats, journalist James Fallows, is the author of a book on high-tech military reform, *National Defense* (1981) as well as a study of the

application of the Hamilton-List economic theory in modern Japan, *Looking at the Sun* (1994). Hamiltonian economic ideas, currently out of favor, can be expected to make a comeback if the contemporary panacea of free-trade agreements such as the North American Free Trade Agreement (NAFTA) and the General Agreement on Tariffs and Trade (GATT) fails to produce the promised results in terms of employment and the revitalization of the American industrial base.

If the neo-Hamiltonians of the 1890s gave a one-sided emphasis to Hamilton's foreign policy realism, the Hamiltonians of today may be overstressing his approach to trade and industry. To Hamilton, foreign policy and economic policy alike were mere means to achieving the goal to which he devoted his life—the unity of the American nation and the competence of its agent, the na-

---

*President Clinton has since dropped the word "Defense" from the agency's name.

tional state. The circumstances of the 1990s are far different from those of the 1890s, and the United States is a far different country—thanks, in no small part, to Hamilton and his successors. And yet the questions of national unity and competent government are as important in our day as in his.

Today the greatest threat to national unity comes not from sectionalism but from multiculturalism—from the idea that there is no single nation comprising Americans of all races, ancestries, and religions but only an aggregate of biologically defined "cultures" coexisting under a minimal framework of law. Neither Hamilton nor any of his contemporaries gave any thought to the necessity of a multiracial but unicultural society. Still, Hamilton's impassioned vision of a "continentalist" American society can inspire us indirectly as we seek to integrate the American nation in the aftermath of both segregation and multiculturalism.

When it comes to the problem of effective democratic government, Hamilton's legacy is more relevant today than ever. For a generation, the United States has suffered from political gridlock, symbolized by, but not limited to, an inability to make tax revenues match spending. What Jonathan Rauch has called "demosclerosis" is a lethal byproduct of the interest-group liberalism of the New Deal, a system now in advanced decay. Rauch, along with other conservatives and libertarians, argues for a "Jeffersonian" solution involving the radical reduction of government at all levels and the dispersal of authority from the central government to the states. However, in the conditions of the 21st century, when the United States will likely face geopolitical competition with rising technological powers, mercantilist economic rivalries, and the threat of mass immigration from the Third World, minimal government will almost certainly not be a realistic alternative. Because the quantity of national government will not be significantly reduced, the quality of national governance will have to be improved. That will mean repudiating the ideal of the directionless broker state—now three-quarters of a century old—and attempting to realize the Hamiltonian and Progressive ideal of a strong but not authoritarian executive branch that is led by a meritocratic elite and capable of resisting interest-group pressures without ceasing to be ultimately accountable to elected representatives.

The 1992 campaigns of Clinton and Perot—both of whom, in essence, promised more "businesslike" government rather than less government—are signs that the American public is disenchanted with New Deal interest-group liberalism and with the nostalgic antigovernment libertarianism of the Reagan Right. Journalist David Frum sees American politicians on both Left and Right slowly returning to "the political formula that has won more presidential elections than any other: active government intervention in the economy to promote welfare and assist private business, conservative moral reform at home, and the assertion of American nationality." If Frum is right, then in the decades ahead Hamiltonian nationalism may once again define the political mainstream.

Elsewhere in the world, the Hamiltonian approach to building democratic capitalism in ex-communist and Third World societies could not be more timely. In the immediate aftermath of the Cold War, Americans urged a "Jeffersonian" model of reconstruction on societies everywhere, thinking that immediate elections and rapid marketization of statist economies would solve all problems. The result, in Russia and much of Eastern Europe and the Third World, has been economic collapse, popular disillusionment with democracy and capitalism, and the acquisition of local industries by foreigners at fire-sale prices. The leaders of new democracies can learn from Hamilton and his mentor Washington that it is not enough to hold elections and establish free markets. A struggling new democratic government must be able to defend its borders against foreign enemies, suppress insurrection and criminality, gradually construct a system of sound finance, and guide industrial reform and development in the nation's interest—if necessary, at the expense of free trade.

Not only contemporary Americans, then, but people everywhere have much to learn from Hamilton and Hamiltonianism in the century ahead. In the words of Clinton Rossiter, Hamilton "was conservative and radical, traditionalist and revolutionary, reactionary and visionary, Tory and Whig all thrown into one. He is a glorious source of inspiration and instruction to modern conservatives, but so is he to modern liberals." Earlier in this century, when the threats were totalitarian imperialism and domestic conformity and repression, Americans and freedom-loving peoples around the world may have been right to look for inspiration to apostles of revolution and individualism such as Thomas Jefferson. In the aftermath of successful revolutions, however, a quite different kind of leadership is called for. The task of the coming generation is not to tear down, but to rebuild and build anew. In that task, Alexander Hamilton, the master architect among America's Founders, must be our pre-eminent guide.

The Whiskey Rebellion

Two hundred years ago a federal tax on distilled spirits led to our young nation's greatest internal crisis.

Robert S. Kyff

Robert S. Kyff teaches history at Kingswood-Oxford School in West Hartford, Connecticut, and writes a syndicated newspaper column. His article on frontier historian Frederick Jackson Turner appeared in the July/August issue of American History Illustrated.

On August 1, 1794, a motley army assembled at Braddock's Field on the Monongahela River near Pittsburgh. Nearly seven thousand armed militiamen—some dressed in regimental uniforms, others wearing the yellow hunting shirts of Indian fighter—mustered on the plain where, thirty-nine years before, British General William Braddock had been mortally wounded and his forces defeated during the French and Indian War.

To the casual observer the assembly might have appeared to be a celebration, given the holiday atmosphere that prevailed as military drums beat loudly, soldiers marched and countermarched, and riflemen took target practice, filling the air with thick gray smoke. But the purpose of the gathering was deadly serious. These were the "Whiskey Rebels"—backwoods citizens of Pennsylvania's four western counties (Allegheny, Westmoreland, Fayette, and Washington*) who had assembled to demonstrate their defiance of the federal government's excise tax on whiskey and to coerce others into joining them in opposition. Many of the rebels advocated outright independence from the United States, and several of the units displayed a six-striped flag representing the six defiant counties of western Pennsylvania and Virginia.

The insurgents' immediate plan was to seize nearby Fort Fayette and then occupy and burn Pittsburgh, which in their eyes exemplified the haughty eastern patricians who had imposed this unfair tax. The rationale at the time, according to an 1859 defense of a key figure in the events, was that "as old Sodom had been burned by fire from heaven, this second Sodom should be burnt by fire from earth!"

The ardent force was led by "Major General" David Bradford, a wealthy lawyer who fancied himself the "George Washington of the West." As the troops assembled, Bradford, dressed in military attire and mounted on a "superb horse in splendid trappings," dashed across the field "with plumes floating in the air and sword drawn." The ostentatious Bradford (prudently deciding to bypass well-defended Fort Fayette) then led his forces eight miles west toward Pittsburgh for what was euphemistically described as a "visit." Relishing the upcoming plunder of Pittsburgh's fancy shops, one upcountry soldier twirled his hat on his rifle barrel and boasted, "I have a bad hat now but I expect to have a better one soon."

The advance of such a lawless, anti-aristocratic mob terrified the citizens of Pittsburgh, even though many sympathized with the rebel cause. The residents' apprehension was heightened by an eerie apparition: a lone horseman riding through the streets holding a tomahawk above his head and warning that revocation of the excise tax would be only the beginning of a larger revolution. "A great deal more is yet to be done," he chanted ominously.

Fearing the worst, Pittsburgh's twelve hundred citizens deployed a shrewd strategy to protect their town. Rather than greeting the insurrectionists with guns, they instead offered the soldiers hams, dried venison, bear meat, and, of course, casks of whiskey. Through these conciliatory actions, and by agreeing to banish known Federalist sympathizers from their limits, the Pittsburgh residents saved their town from destruction. Although the occupying force did burn a few farm buildings and steal some livestock, it soon dispersed, leaving "Sodom" largely undamaged and its populace shaken but unharmed.

The rally at Braddock's Field and the occupation of Pittsburgh marked the high point of what has since become known as the "Whiskey Rebellion." Perhaps because of its bibulous nickname—conjuring up images of a comical, pop-gun skirmish involving moonshining hillbillies—the uprising, regarded by nineteenth-century historians as the most important national crisis between the Revolutionary and Civil wars, today is

---

*At that time Washington County included what is today Greene County in the southwest corner of the state. Although not playing a central role in the actual insurrection, two other Pennsylvania counties—Bedford and Somerset—are today also associated with the Whiskey Rebellion. Residents of these two counties, which until 1795 comprised Bedford Country, shared their western neighbors' opposition to the excise tax and witnessed the assembling of the army called in to quell the rebellion.

From *American History,* August 1994, pp. 36–43, 65–66. © 1994 by Cowles Magazines, Inc. Reprinted through the courtesy of Cowles Magazines, Inc., publishers of *American History.*

more often remembered as a minor bump on the road to national consolidation.

Such an interpretation, however, overlooks the true significance of the crisis, which, more than any in the nation's formative years, defined the nature of the new federal government and its relationship to its citizens. This single event embodied nearly all of the fundamental issues and conflicts facing the young American republic and its new Constitution: the clash between liberty and order in a democracy; western versus eastern interests; agriculture versus industry; the nature of taxation; the duties and rights of citizens; relations with European powers such as Great Britain and Spain; the influence of the French Revolution; the rise of political parties; and the meaning of the American Revolution itself.

While some historians have dismissed the suppression of the rebellion as "duck soup" for the federal government, the outcome of this Constitutional crisis was, in fact, far from a foregone conclusion. It might well have resulted in the establishment of new states, fully independent of the government in Philadelphia, or perhaps in the alliance of trans-Appalachian counties with British Canada to the north or New Spain to the south. Moreover, the uprising was fraught with fascinating ironies: the requirements of the excise tax that triggered the revolt were relaxed just prior to the largest protest against it; the insurrection itself seemed to be dying out just when the federal government decided to suppress it; and President Washington, who had led the American rebellion against British taxation, now found himself on the opposite side, crushing a revolt against a similar internal tax.

The roots of this complex and intriguing episode lay in the unique character of life on the western frontier during the 1780s and '90s. Separated from the coastal regions by vast stretches of rugged wilderness, westerners lived an isolated and dangerous existence that was characterized by violence, economic uncertainty, and physical hardship. Despite frequent appeals to the federal government for protection, people all along the frontier lived in constant fear of massacre. Between 1783 and 1790 alone, fifteen hundred settlers in the Ohio Valley were killed, wounded, or captured by hostile Native Americans.

PHOTOGRAPH BY STEVEN P. MASON

The Whiskey Rebellion is the subject of fond annual (and during 1994, bicentennial) commemorations in parts of western Pennsylvania. Re-enactors gather around an authentic rebellion-era still at the Oliver Miller Homestead near Pittsburgh.

Many settlers who had moved west in pursuit of economic opportunity and personal liberty now found themselves living in lice-infested hovels and scratching out a bare subsistence on land owned by absentee landlords. Geography and politics made it difficult for farmers to ship their commodities to larger markets: overland transportation of goods to eastern cities was costly while Spanish control of New Orleans prevented shipment via the Ohio and Mississippi Rivers. The settlers begged the federal government to negotiate with Spain for transportation rights, but by 1791 no agreement had been reached.

Amid such poverty and economic isolation, many backwoodsmen fell into a life of crudity and dissipation. Squalid living conditions, excessive drinking, and random violence were common. Headstrong settlers—many recently arrived from Scotland, Ireland, and Germany—grew increasingly frustrated by the disparity between their expectations of prosperity in America and the harsh realities of frontier life. Increasingly they blamed their troubles on a presumed conspiracy between the federal government, which had proved unable or unwilling to control the Indians or to secure westerners access to Mississippi River trade rights, and the eastern elite.

It was against this background of economic impoverishment, political frustration, and social unrest in the trans-Appalachian West that, in March of 1791, the federal government imposed an excise tax on whiskey. Seeking to put the new nation on a sound financial footing, Treasury Secretary Alexander Hamilton convinced Congress and President Washington that the whiskey tax was needed to pay off the debts, now assumed by the federal government, that had been incurred by the former colonies during the Revolutionary War.

The new excise law required that each rural distiller pay either an annual rate of sixty cents for each gallon of his still's capacity or nine cents per gallon produced. Distillers also were expected to keep accurate records of production and to gauge and label each cask before shipment—stipulations that placed a particular burden on part-time, small-scale distillers not accustomed to such strict accounting. Federal excisemen were empowered to inspect stills and search property for contraband goods and illegal distilling operations. And, even more disturbing to westerners, the law called for accused tax evaders to be tried in federal courts at Philadelphia, necessitating a costly time-consuming journey that could ruin a distiller financially even if he were found innocent.

The concept of an excise tax—an internal, direct tax on products produced—was especially odious to western Pennsylvanians. Numerous attempts to levy such taxes within the late colony of Pennsylvania had met with failure. Many recent immigrants from the British Isles had experienced first-hand the oppressive practices of the Crown's hated excise collectors, who often confiscated property and employed paid informers. And, of course, it had been an excise tax—the Stamp Tax—that had angered and turned American colonists against Britain, leading to the late war for independence. That the infamous tax of 1765 had been imposed by a government in which they enjoyed no representation, while the tax on whiskey was enacted by their duly elected representatives, mattered little to a populace not yet used to the federal system of government created only a few years before. Finally citizens feared that, once the federal government got its foot in the door with the whiskey tax, it would soon pass internal taxes on other goods. "I plainly perceive," a Georgian predicted, "that the time will come when a shirt shall not be washed without an excise."

Hamilton dismissed many of the objections raised against the whiskey tax. The imposition of the duty he believed, did not unfairly burden whiskey-producing areas because the tax rates—only a few dollars a year for the average small distiller—seemed quite low. And, reasoned Hamilton, if distillers did not want to pay the duty they could simply produce less whiskey. What the Treasury Secretary failed to grasp was the centrality of whiskey to frontier life.

On the nation's western perimeter, whiskey was more than a luxury item or an incidental distraction from the rigors of survival. It was the lifeblood of the backwoods economy and culture. Virtually cut off as they were from eastern markets and the Mississippi River trade, farmers found it more efficient to distill their rye grain into whiskey that could easily be sold or bartered. While the average pack horse, for instance, could carry only four bushels of grain, it could haul the equivalent of twenty-four bushels if that grain were converted into two casks of whiskey. Thus, in this more portable liquid form, "Monongahela Rye" became the "coin of the realm"

in western Pennsylvania, used to pay hired workers or to buy everything from salt to nails to gunpowder.

But whiskey was much more than just commodity or currency on the frontier; it was a way of life. Whether sweetened with tansy, mint, or maple sugar or swallowed straight, whiskey lubricated nearly every rite of frontier existence. No marriage, baptism, contract signing, brawl, trial, election, meal, or funeral took place without generous helpings of the local brew. Doctors prescribed it for nearly every ill; ministers sipped it before services, field workers demanded it as refreshment; and the United States Army issued a gill each day to soldiers.

Docents at the restored David Bradford house—the Washington, Pennsylvania home of the insurrection's most militant firebrand—display a replica of the only surviving Whiskey Rebellion flag. Bradford reportedly jumped from the second-story window at right and disappeared into the night when federal militiamen arrived to arrest him. He fled to Louisiana, where he became a wealthy planter—finally to be pardoned by President John Adams in 1799.

PHOTOGRAPH BY STEVEN P. MASON

This insatiable thirst for whiskey rendered the still a "necessary appendage of every farm" that could afford it. "In many parts of the country" wrote one observer, you could scarcely get out of sight of the smoke of a still-house." while perhaps only ten to twenty percent of western Pennsylvania farmers actually owned whiskey stills, many neighbors purchased stills together and shared their use. And, even those farmers who performed no distilling had a direct stake in whiskey production because they sold their rye grain to the local distillers.

Given the importance of whiskey on the frontier, it is not surprising that residents of the trans-Appalachian counties violently opposed the federal excise tax. The federal government in far-away Philadelphia—the same government that could not protect them from the Indians and could not secure them trade rights on the Mississippi—was asking westerners to shoulder a disproportionate financial burden by taxing their region's dominant product. Worse yet, in a society based on a barter economy where coin and currency were scarce, the government demanded that its excise be paid not in whiskey or other commodities, but in hard specie.

It soon became clear that, in its search for the sweet honey of revenue, the federal government had stuck its hand into a beehive. Shortly after the whiskey tax went into effect on July 1, 1791, western Pennsylvanians responded with protest meetings, petitions, and outright assaults on revenue agents. In September 1791, sixteen Washington County men dressed in women's clothing seized excise collector Robert Johnson, cut off his hair, then tarred and feathered him. When John Connor tried to serve warrants to those accused of the assault, he himself was whipped, tarred and feathered, and tied to a tree.

Mobs burned revenue collectors in effigy and attacked their offices and lodgings. To show that the backwoodsmen equated the excise tax with British colonial oppression, dissidents erected "liberty poles," familiar icons of the Revolutionary War, and set up committees of correspondence similar to those that had kept protestors informed of developments in the struggle against the former mother country.

PHOTOGRAPH BY STEVEN P. MASON

Re-enactors at the Oliver Miller Homestead demonstrate how eigthteenth-century Pennsylvania whiskey-makers checked the proof of their product: the persistence and size of bubbles formed by shaking a small sample of the brew were proportional to its alcohol content.

Inspired by the French Revolution as well as the American, tax resisters formed numerous democratic societies modeled after the Jacobin Clubs, righteously vowing to "erect the temple of LIBERTY on the ruins of palaces and thrones." These extra-legal organizations particularly irked President Washington, who, with France's upheavals in mind, viewed them as a direct challenge to Constitutional authority. They masked, he said, "diabolical attempts to destroy the best fabric of human government."

In May 1792, Secretary Hamilton, hoping to defuse the protests that rendered the whiskey revenue virtually uncollectible, persuaded Congress to reduce the tax rates and allow for monthly payments. When this failed to discourage the assemblies and quell the violence, Washington, in September 1792, issued a proclamation ordering the dissolution of any organization or meeting designed to obstruct the enforcement of any federal law. This action, however, also effectively silenced the moderates who sought a peaceful solution to the controversy, thus leaving radical leaders free to pursue their violent tactics.

Sporadic attacks on revenue collectors continued through 1793, completely shutting down the collection of whiskey tax in all frontier regions. Meanwhile, the federal government in Philadelphia—

already preoccupied by the Reign of Terror in France, Indian attacks on the frontier, and threats by Spain and Britain—was brought to a near-standstill by a yellow fever epidemic that killed more than four thousand people in that city. Mistaking the federal government's distraction for lack of resolve on excise enforcement, tax protestors pressed their demands for its repeal.

In early 1794, radical leaders took a new tack. Instead of directing violence only against collectors and their offices, they now targeted anyone who complied with the tax or cooperated with its enforcement. Law-abiding distillers were visited by "Tom the Tinker" who "mended" their stills by riddling them with bullets. In Allegheny County for example, mobs destroyed the 120-gallon still of William Cochran and dismantled the grist mill of James Kiddoe simply because both men had registered their stills with authorities as the law required.

Seeking to pacify the insurgents, Congress on June 5, 1794 further amended the excise law to provide accused tax evaders with local trials and small distillers with a special license for temporary operations. But on that same day Congress passed a new revenue act extending excise levies to snuff and sugar—a move that confirmed protestors' fears that the excise on whiskey would inevitably expand to other products.

When federal agents began serving arrest warrants on alleged tax evaders during the summer of 1794, violence erupted anew. At dawn on July 16, forty rebels arrived at Bower Hill, the home of distinguished Revolutionary War officer John Neville, to demand his resignation as Inspector of Revenue for western Pennsylvania. Before his appointment as supervisor of excise collection, Neville—a wealthy whiskey producer whose clapboard mansion boasted such luxuries as mirrors, carpets, and an eight-day clock—had adamantly opposed the whiskey tax, leading rebels to suspect that he had taken a large bribe to assume his federal office. The once-respected Neville now was detested as a turncoat by the insurgents.

When the mob in his front yard ignored an order to disband, Neville fired into their midst, mortally wounding Oliver Miller. The rebels shot back and were closing in on the house when some of Neville's slaves, armed in anticipation of attack, opened fire from the rear, wounding four more militiamen. After a twenty-five-minute gun battle, the posse retreated.

The next day an army of five to seven hundred men led by Captain James McFarlane showed up at Bower Hill, which was now defended by ten federal soldiers from Fort Pitt, under the command of Major James Kirkpatrick. After brief negotiations, the rebels set several of the estates' outbuildings on fire and began an exchange of gunfire with the defending troops. During a lull in the fighting, McFarlane, thinking he had heard a call to parley, stepped out from behind a tree and was shot dead by the regulars. Smoke and heat from the burning structures subsequently filled the house, forcing the soldiers to surrender. The insurrectionists pillaged Neville's home and estate, liberating the mirrors and fancy clock. But Neville, who had been secreted in a nearby ravine by the soldiers before the rebels appeared on his property, escaped, as did his family.

With the death of McFarlane—who was a respected Revolutionary War hero—the insurgents now had a martyr. Radical leader David Bradford denounced McFarlane's "murder" and called

for the rendezvous of militia forces at Braddock's Field. As it turned out, this dramatic show of force on August 1 marked the rebellion's zenith and helped to provoke its violent suppression.

On learning of the rebels' "visit" to Pittsburgh, President Washington and Secretary Hamilton decided that time for military action had come. The nascent federal government, they believed, could no longer tolerate such blatant defiance of its laws. Although most residents of upcountry Georgia, Kentucky, North Carolina and Virginia also refused to pay the excise tax, the opposition in western Pennsylvania was more visible and violent than in these states, and its suppression would send a strong message to all of the dissidents.

Moreover, it was unthinkable to allow such treason to flourish in the very state that held the nation's capital. Exaggerated rumors of attacks on federal arsenals and invasions of towns by armed mobs swept through eastern cities. With Britain and Spain seeking to bully the young nation and France grappling with its revolution, this was no time for conciliation. At issue, Washington and Hamilton believed, was the very integrity and credibility of the federal government—perhaps even its survival.

Although he had made up his mind to wage war, Washington, hoping to appear conciliatory, in late August went through the motions of sending peace commissioners to seek a non-military solution. Thinking these negotiations legitimate, moderate leaders like Albert Gallatin, who himself later served as Secretary of the Treasury, persuaded many of the dissidents to cease their violence. Ironically evidence suggests that opposition to the tax was waning just as Washington was preparing for military operations.

By early October, Washington had assembled a 12,950-man army from the state militias of Pennsylvania, New Jersey, Virginia, and Maryland. In many ways these forces were no more disciplined or well-organized than the dissidents they opposed. A curious blend of lower-class and gentlemen volunteers, the impromptu army suffered from high desertion rates, squabbles over chains of command, and persistent rumors that it was really being sent to fight Indians or seasoned British regulars.

But the militiamen's spirit was aroused when rebels derided their fighting prowess. "Brother, you must not think to frighten us," wrote one "Captain Whiskey" in a western Pennsylvania newspaper, "with . . . your watermelon armies from the Jersey shores; they would cut a much better figure in warring with the crabs and oysters about the Cape of Delaware." A "Jersey Blue" angrily retorted that "the watermelon army of New Jersey [had] ten-inch howitzers for throwing a species of melon very useful for curing a gravel occasioned by whiskey!" From then on this combined federal force would be known, both affectionately and derisively, as the "watermelon army."

General Henry "Light Horse Harry" Lee, then governor of Virginia, commanded the force, whose ranks included the governors of Pennsylvania and New Jersey Revolutionary General Dan Morgan, future explorer Meriwether Lewis, five nephews of President Washington, and Alexander Hamilton himself. The southern wing of the army marched north-westward toward Pennsylvania from Virginia and Maryland, while the right flank proceeded westward from New Jersey and eastern Pennsylvania.

On October 4, President Washington reviewed the northern contingent at Carlisle, Pennsylvania, and his charisma greatly boosted morale. Soldiers and townspeople alike gave the hero of the Revolution a royal welcome. One observer noted that "when I saw the President lift his hat to the troops as they passed along, I thought I caught a glimpse of the Revolutionary Scene."

After traveling to Fort Cumberland, Maryland, to review the southern wing of the army, the president returned to Philadelphia. Soon after, the two contingents converged in Bedford, Pennsylvania. Although Lee was left in charge of military operations, Hamilton served as the force's unofficial civilian leader. Officers familiar with Hamilton's ambition noted that the Secretary's tent was bigger than Lee's and that he sometimes gave orders directly to soldiers.

The army's march westward during those brilliant autumn days proved part picnic and part pogrom. As the column crossed the Alleghenies, the Whiskey Rebellion seemed to evaporate ahead of it. Encountering no military opposition, the troops plundered plump chickens, butchered hogs, and imbibed generous portions of the notorious taxable liquid.

The officers' diaries and letters read like tourist brochures, noting, for instance, that while Newtown was a poor place for acquiring hay it boasted "mountains of beef and oceans of whiskey."

But the army encountered—and inflicted—hardship as well. Because the huge force constantly out-marched its provisions, rations ran short. The troops' poorly made shoes disintegrated on cold, muddy roads. And the many liberty poles erected along the route served notice of the local citizens' hostility, which often manifested itself in taunts aimed at the soldiers or refusal of food or lodging.

In apprehending suspected leaders of the insurgency for interrogation, the troops could be brutal. On November 13, in what came to be known as the 'dreadful night," the New Jersey cavalry dragged 150 suspects from their beds, marched them—some half-clothed and barefooted—through snow and sleet, and incarcerated them in a roofless outdoor pen. General Andrew White, dubbed "Black-beard" for his cruelty, kept his forty captives tied back-to-back in an unheated cellar for two days without food, then herded them like animals through twelve miles of mud and rain.

Because David Bradford* and as many as two thousand die-hard rebels fled westward into the wilderness, most of the suspects seized for questioning were not the ringleaders of the uprising. Hamilton and Lee, for instance, interrogated the moderate Hugh Brackenridge intensely for hours before concluding that their prisoner had been trying to temper the rebellion rather than incite it.

---

*After fleeing Pennsylvania, Bradford settled permanently in the Louisiana Territory.

In late November, twenty obscure rebels—none of whom had actually been key figures in the uprising—were shipped to Philadelphia for trial. Paraded through the capital's streets on Christmas Day the prisoners looked so wretched that even Presley Neville, son of the besieged excise inspector, felt sorry for them. Ultimately only two suspects were found guilty of treason, and Washington, seeking to appear magnanimous, pardoned both.

Leaving fifteen hundred troops in Pittsburgh to maintain order, the bulk of the watermelon army began its return home in late November. The entire expedition had cost $1,500,000—about one third of the revenues raised by the whiskey tax during its entire life. But cost mattered little given the principles at stake. On January 1, 1795, a "gravely exultant" Washington proclaimed February 19 as a day of thanksgiving for "the reasonable control which has been given to a spirit of disorder in the suppression of the late insurrection."

Indeed, Washington and the Federalists had much to be thankful for. With a relatively painless and largely bloodless military excursion, they had asserted the supremacy of the federal Constitution and ensured that the trans-Appalachian west would remain part of the United States.

The Whiskey Rebellion was a personal triumph for Washington as well. He had placed his political reputation and prestige on the line—and had prevailed. His actions would serve as precedent for John Adams in his handling of the Fries Rebellion in 1799, Andrew Jackson's response to the nullification crisis of the 1830s, and Abraham Lincoln's reaction to secession in 1861.

Ironically the defeat of western Pennsylvanians in the Whiskey Rebellion brought with it the alleviation of many of the region's problems. By spending so much money during its invasion, the watermelon army seeded western Pennsylvania with enough currency to germinate a prosperous commercial economy there. And in the single year following the rebellion, the Jay Treaty reduced Great Britain's Indian agitation and interference on the American western frontier, the Pinckney Treaty secured free trade on the Mississippi from Spain, and the Treaty of Greenville reduced the threat of Indian attack.

Finally by dramatically defining the key political issues of the day—East versus West, agriculture versus commerce, plutocracy versus democracy, order versus liberty—the Whiskey Rebellion fostered the development of a two-party system in American politics. By 1801, with the election of Thomas Jefferson as president, the Republican Party representing many of the principles advocated by insurgents, would gain control of the national government.

Thus, when the Republican Congress in 1802 repealed the hated excise that had started all the fuss, the Whiskey Boys could hoist their first untaxed jugs in ten years and savor sweet victory.

Recommended additional reading: Two excellent book-length narratives of the events described in this article are Thomas P. Slaughter's *The Whiskey Rebellion: Frontier Epilouge to the American Revolution* (Oxford University Press, 1986) and *The Whiskey Rebellion: Southwestern Pennsylvania's Frontier People Test the American Constitution* by Jerry A. Clouse (Pennsylvania Historical and Museum Commission, 1994).

The Great Chief Justice

Under the leadership of John Marshall, the nation's highest tribunal became a court supreme in fact as well as in name.

Brian McGinty

Brian McGinty is a California attorney and writer.

He was a tall man with long legs, gangling arms, and a round, friendly face. He had a thick head of dark hair and strong, black eyes—"penetrating eyes," a friend called them, "beaming with intelligence and good nature." He was born in a log cabin in western Virginia and never wholly lost his rough frontier manners. Yet John Marshall became a lawyer, a member of Congress, a diplomat, an advisor to presidents, and the most influential and respected judge in the history of the United States. "If

American law were to be represented by a single figure," Supreme Court Justice Oliver Wendell Holmes, Jr., once said, "sceptic and worshipper alike would agree without dispute that the figure could be but one alone, and that one John Marshall."

To understand Marshall's preeminence in American legal history it is necessary to understand the marvelous rebirth the United States Supreme Court experienced after he became its chief justice in 1801. During all of the previous eleven years of its existence, the highest judicial court in the federal system had been weak and ineffectual—ignored by most of the nation's lawyers and judges and scorned by its principal politicians. Un-

der Marshall's leadership, the court became a strong and vital participant in national affairs. During his more than thirty-four years as Chief Justice of the United States, Marshall welded the Supreme Court into an effective and cohesive whole. With the support of his colleagues on the high bench, he declared acts of Congress and of the president unconstitutional, struck down laws that infringed on federal prerogatives, and gave force and dignity to basic guarantees of life and liberty and property. Without John Marshall, the Supreme Court might never have been anything but an inconsequential junior partner of the executive and legislative branches of the national government. Under his guid-

PROFILE PORTRAITS
BY M. FEVRET DE SAINT MEMIN
AMERICAN HISTORY ILLUSTRATED COLLECTION

Jefferson and Marshall: Two Great Minds in Conflict

Fellow Virginians Thomas Jefferson and John Marshall (next page) had contrasting philosophies regarding the roles of government. Jefferson believed in state sovereignty and in a limited role for national government.

ance and inspiration, it became what the Constitution intended it to be—a court system in fact as well as in name.

Born on September 4, 1755, in Fauquier County, Virginia, John Marshall was the oldest of fifteen children born to Thomas Marshall and Mary Randolph Keith. On his mother's side, the young Virginian was distantly related to Thomas Jefferson, the gentlemanly squire of Monticello and author of the Declaration of Independence. Aside from this kinship, there was little similarity between Marshall and Jefferson. A son of the frontier, Marshall was a backwoodsman at heart, more comfortable in the company of farmers than intellectuals or scholars. Jefferson was a polished aristocrat who liked to relax in the library of his mansion near Charlottesville and meditate on the subtleties of philosophy and political theory.

The contrast between the two men was most clearly drawn in their opposing political beliefs. An advocate of limiting the powers of central government, Thomas Jefferson thought of himself first and foremost as a Virginian (his epitaph did not even mention the fact that he had once been president of the United States). Marshall, in contrast, had, even

as a young man, come to transcend his state roots, to look to Congress rather than the Virginia legislature as his government, to think of himself first, last, and always as an American. Throughout their careers, their contrasting philosophies would place the two men at odds.

Marshall's national outlook was furthered by his father's close association with George Washington and his own unflinching admiration for the nation's first president. Thomas Marshall had been a schoolmate of Washington and, as a young man, helped him survey the Fairfax estates in northern Virginia. John Marshall served under Washington during the bitter winter at Valley Forge and later became one of the planter-turned-statesman's most loyal supporters.

Years after the Revolution was over, Marshall attributed his political views to his experiences as a foot soldier in the great conflict, recalling that he grew up "at a time when a love of union and resistance to the claims of Great Britain were the inseparable inmates of the same bosom;—when patriotism and a strong fellow feeling with our suffering fellow citizens of Boston were identical;—when the maxim 'united we stand, divided we

fall' was the maxim of every orthodox American . . ." "I had imbibed these sentiments so thoughroughly [sic] that they constituted a part of my being," wrote Marshall. "I carried them with me into the army where I found myself associated with brave men from different states who were risking life and everything valuable in a common cause believed by all to be most precious; and where I was confirmed in the habit of considering America as my country, and Congress as my government."

After Washington's death, Marshall became the great man's biographer, penning a long and admiring account of Washington's life as a farmer, soldier, and statesman, expounding the Federalist philosophy represented by Washington and attacking those who stood in opposition to it. Jefferson, who detested Federalism as much as he disliked Marshall, was incensed by the biography, which he branded a "five-volume libel."

Frontiersman though he was, Marshall was no bumpkin. His father had personally attended to his earliest schooling, teaching him to read and write and giving him a taste for history and poetry (by the age of twelve he had already transcribed the whole of Alexander Pope's

Marshall believed in a strong central government, in the Constitution as the key to the laws of the land, and in courts as the supreme custodians of those laws— views that would influence his shaping of the Supreme Court.

Essay on Man). When he was fourteen, Marshall was sent to a school a hundred miles from home, where future president James Monroe was one of his classmates. After a year, he returned home to be tutored by a Scottish pastor who had come to live in the Marshall house. The future lawyer read Horace and Livy, pored through the English dictionary, and scraped at least a passing acquaintance with the "Bible of the Common Law," William Blackstone's celebrated *Commentaries on the Laws of England.*

In 1779, during a lull in the Revolution, young Marshall attended lectures at the College of William and Mary in Williamsburg. He remained at the college only a few weeks, but the impression made on him by his professor there, George Wythe, was lasting. A lawyer, judge, and signer of the Declaration of Independence, Wythe is best remembered today as the first professor of law at any institution of higher learning in the United States. As a teacher, he was a seminal influence in the development of American law, counting among his many distinguished students Thomas Jefferson, John Breckinridge, and Henry Clay.

Marshall did not remain long at William and Mary. It was the nearly universal custom then for budding lawyers to "read law" in the office of an older lawyer or judge or, failing that, to appeal to the greatest teacher of all—experience—for instruction. In August 1780, a few weeks before his twenty-fifth birthday, Marshall appeared at the Fauquier County Courthouse where, armed with a license signed by Governor Thomas Jefferson of Virginia, he was promptly admitted to the bar.

His first cases were not important, but he handled them well and made a favorable impression on his neighbors; so favorable that they sent him to Richmond in 1782 as a member of the Virginia House of Delegates. Though he retained a farm in Fauquier County all his life, Richmond became Marshall's home after his election to the legislature. The general courts of Virginia held their sessions in the new capital, and the commonwealth's most distinguished lawyers crowded its bar. When Marshall's fortunes improved, he built a comfortable brick house on the outskirts of the city, in which he and his beloved wife Polly raised five sons and one daughter (four other offspring died during childhood).

Marshall's skill as a lawyer earned him an enthusiastic coterie of admirers

and his honest country manners an even warmer circle of friends. He liked to frequent the city's taverns and grog shops, more for conviviality than for refreshment, and he was an enthusiastic member of the Barbecue Club, which met each Saturday to eat, drink, "josh," and play quoits.

Marshall liked to do his own shopping for groceries. Each morning he marched through the streets with a basket under his arm, collecting fresh fruits, vegetables, and poultry for the Marshall family larder. Years after his death, Richmonders were fond of recalling the day when a stranger came into the city in search of a lawyer and found Marshall in front of the Eagle Hotel, holding a hat filled with cherries and speaking casually

---

"If American law were to be represented by a single figure . . . the figure could be but one alone, and that one John Marshall."

---

with the hotel proprietor. After Marshall went on his way, the stranger approached the proprietor and asked if he could direct him to the best lawyer in Richmond. The proprietor replied quite readily that the best lawyer was John Marshall, the tall man with the hat full of cherries who had just walked down the street.

But the stranger could not believe that a man who walked through town so casually could be a really "proper barrister" and chose instead to hire a lawyer who wore a black suit and powdered wig. On the day set for the stranger's trial, several cases were scheduled to be argued. In the first that was called, the visitor was surprised to see that John Marshall and his own lawyer were to speak on opposite sides. As he listened to the arguments, he quickly realized that he had made a serious mistake. At the first recess, he approached Marshall and confessed that he had come to Richmond with a hundred dollars to hire the best lawyer in the city, but he had chosen the wrong one and now had only five dollars left. Would Marshall agree to represent him for such a small fee? Smiling good-naturedly, Marshall accepted the five

dollars, then proceeded to make a brilliant legal argument that quickly won the stranger's case.

Marshall was not an eloquent man; not eloquent, that is, in the sense that his great contemporary, Patrick Henry, a spellbinding courtroom orator, was eloquent. Marshall was an effective enough speaker; but, more importantly, he was a rigorously logical thinker. He had the ability to reduce complex issues to bare essentials and easily and effortlessly apply abstract principles to resolve them.

Thomas Jefferson (himself a brilliant lawyer) was awed, even intimidated, by Marshall's powers of persuasion. "When conversing with Marshall," Jefferson once said, "I never admit anything. So sure as you admit any position to be good, no matter how remote from the conclusion he seeks to establish, you are gone. . . . Why, if he were to ask me if it were daylight or not, I'd reply, 'Sir, I don't know, I can't tell.' "

THOUGH MARSHALL'S LEGAL PROWESS and genial manner won him many friends in Richmond, his political views did little to endear him to the Old Dominion's political establishment. While Jefferson and his followers preached the virtues of agrarian democracy, viewing with alarm every step by which the fledgling national government extended its powers through the young nation, Marshall clearly allied himself with Washington, Alexander Hamilton, and John Adams and the Federalist policies they espoused.

Marshall was not a delegate to the convention that met in Philadelphia in 1787 to draft a constitution for the United States, but he took a prominent part in efforts to secure ratification of the Constitution, thereby winning the special admiration of George Washington. After taking office as president, Washington offered Marshall the post of attorney general. Marshall declined the appointment, as he did a later offer of the prestigious post of American minister to France, explaining that he preferred to stay in Richmond with his family and law practice.

He did agree, however, to go to Paris in 1798 as one of three envoys from President John Adams to the government of revolutionary France. He did this, in part, because he was assured that his duties in Paris would be temporary only, in part because he believed he could perform a real service for his country, helping to preserve peaceful relations between it and France during a time of unusual diplomatic tension.

After Marshall joined his colleagues Elbridge Gerry and Charles Pinckney in Paris, he was outraged to learn that the French government expected to be paid before it would receive the American emissaries. Marshall recognized the French request as a solicitation for a bribe (the recipients of the payments were mysteriously identified as "X," "Y," and "Z"), and he refused to consider it.

Thomas Jefferson, who was smitten with the ardor and ideals of the French Revolution, suspected that Marshall and his Federalist "cronies" were planning war with France to promote the interests of their friends in England. But the American people believed otherwise. When they received news of the "XYZ Affair," they were outraged. "Millions for defense," the newspapers thundered, "but not one cent for tribute!" When Marshall returned home in the summer of 1798, he was welcomed as a hero. In the elections of the following fall, he was sent to Congress as a Federalist representative from Richmond.

Jefferson was not pleased. He declined to attend a dinner honoring Marshall in Philadelphia and wrote worried letters to his friends. Though he deprecated his fellow Virginian's popularity, alternatively attributing it to his "lax, lounging manners" and his "profound hypocrisy," Jefferson knew that Marshall was a potentially dangerous adversary. A half-dozen years before the Richmonder's triumphal return from Paris, Jefferson had written James Madison a cutting letter about Marshall that included words he would one day rue: "I think nothing better could be done than to make him a judge."

In Congress, Marshall vigorously supported the Federalist policies of President John Adams. Adams took note of the Virginian's ability in 1800 when he appointed him to the important post of secretary of state, a position that not only charged him with conduct of the country's foreign affairs but also left him in effective charge of the government during Adams's frequent absences in Massachusetts.

John Marshall's future in government seemed rosy and secure in 1800. But the elections in November of that year changed all that, sweeping Adams and the Federalists from power and replacing them with Jefferson and the Democratic Republicans.

After the election, but before Adams's term as president expired, ailing Supreme Court Chief Justice Oliver Ellsworth submitted his resignation. Casting about for a successor to Ellsworth, Adams sent John Jay's name to the Senate, only to have Jay demand that it be withdrawn. The thought of leaving the appointment of a new chief justice to Jefferson was abhorrent to Adams, and the president was growing anxious. He summoned Marshall to his office to confer about the problem.

"Who shall I nominate now?" Adams asked dejectedly. Marshall answered that he did not know. He had previously suggested that Associate Justice William Paterson be elevated to the chief justiceship, but Adams had opposed Paterson then and Marshall supposed that he still did. The president pondered for a moment, then turned to Marshall and announced: "I believe I shall nominate you!"

Adams's statement astounded Marshall. Only two years before, Marshall had declined the president's offer of an associate justiceship, explaining that he still hoped to return to his law practice in Richmond. "I had never before heard myself named for the office," Marshall recalled later, "and had not even thought of it. I was pleased as well as surprised [sic], and bowed my head in silence."

Marshall's nomination was sent to the Senate and promptly confirmed, and on February 4, 1801, he took his seat as the nation's fourth chief justice. As subsequent events would prove, it was one of the most important dates in American history.

WITH THOMAS JEFFERSON IN THE EXECUTIVE Mansion and John Marshall in the chief justice's chair, it was inevitable that the Supreme Court and the executive branch of the government should come into conflict. Marshall believed firmly in a strong national government and was willing to do all he could to strengthen federal institutions. Jefferson believed as firmly in state sovereignty and the necessity for maintaining constant vigilance against federal "usurpations." In legal matters, Jefferson believed that the Constitution should be interpreted strictly, so as to reduce rather than expand federal power.

Marshall, in contrast, believed that the Constitution should be construed fairly so as to carry out the intentions of its framers. Any law or executive act that violated the terms of the Constitution was, in Marshall's view, a nullity, of no force or effect; and it was the peculiar prerogative of the courts, as custodians of the laws of the land, to strike down any law that offended the Supreme Law of the Land.

Jefferson did not question the authority of the courts to decide whether a law or executive act violated the Constitution, but he believed that the other branches of the government also had a duty and a right to decide constitutional questions. In a controversy between the Supreme Court and the president, for example, the Supreme Court could order the president to do whatever the Court thought the Constitution required him to do; but the president could decide for himself whether the Supreme Court's order was proper and whether or not it should be obeyed.

As he took up the duties of the chief justiceship, Marshall contemplated his role with uncertainty. The Supreme Court in 1801 was certainly not the kind of strong, vital institution that might have been expected to provide direction in national affairs. There were six justices when Marshall joined the Court, but none (save the chief justice himself) was particularly distinguished. One or two men of national prominence had accepted appointment to the Court in the first eleven years of its existence, but none had remained there long. John Jay, the first chief justice, had resigned his seat in 1795 to become governor of New York. During the two years that John

John Marshall's Richmond home, completed in 1790, still survives and is open to the public. Completely restored and furnished following extensive archaeological and historical research, the elegant Federal-style two-story residence—the only eighteenth-century brick house still standing in Richmond—retains its original woodwork, floors, and paneling. Ninety percent of the home's furnishings, silver, and china are original to the Marshall family, and John Marshall's judicial robes and his wife Polly's wedding dress are also on display. Located at 818 Marshall Street, the John Marshall House is administered by the Association for the Preservation of Virginia Antiquities and is open Tuesday through Saturday, 11:00 AM to 4:00 PM. For further information, call (804) 648-7998.

Rutledge was an associate justice, he had regarded the Court's business as so trifling that he did not bother to attend a single session, and he finally resigned to become chief justice of South Carolina. The Court itself had counted for so little when the new capitol at Washington was being planned that the architects had made no provision for either a courtroom or judges' chambers, and the justices (to everyone's embarrassment) found that they had to meet in a dingy basement room originally designed for the clerk of the Senate.

How could Chief Justice Marshall use his new office to further the legal principles in which he believed so strongly? How could he strengthen the weak and undeveloped federal judiciary when most of the nation's lawyers and judges regarded that judiciary as superfluous and unnecessary? How could he implement his view of the Supreme Court as the final arbiter of constitutional questions when the President of the United States—his old nemesis, Thomas Jefferson—disagreed with that view so sharply? It was not an easy task, but John Marshall was a resourceful man, and he found a way to accomplish it.

His opportunity came in 1803 in the case of *Marbury v. Madison*. William Marbury was one of several minor federal judges who had been appointed during the closing days of John Adams's administration. When Jefferson's secretary of state, James Madison, refused to deliver the commissions of their offices, the judges sued Madison to compel delivery. In 1789, Congress had passed a law granting the Supreme Court authority to issue writs of mandamus, that is, legally enforceable orders compelling public officials to do their legal duties. Following the mandate of Congress, Marbury and the other appointees filed a petition for writ of mandamus in the Supreme Court.

Marshall pondered the possibilities of the case. He was sure that Marbury and his colleagues were entitled to their commissions, and he was just as sure that Jefferson and Madison had no intention of letting them have them. He could order Madison to deliver the commissions, but the secretary of state would certainly defy the order; and, as a practical matter, the Court could not compel obedience to any order that the president refused to acknowledge. Such an impasse would weaken, not strengthen, the federal union, and it would engender un-

precedented controversy. No, there must be a better way. . . .

All eyes and ears in the capitol were trained on the lanky chief justice as he took his seat at the head of the high bench on February 24, 1803, and began to read the Supreme Court's opinion in *Marbury v. Madison.*

The evidence, Marshall said, clearly showed that Marbury and the other judges were entitled to their commissions. The commissions had been signed and sealed before John Adams left office and were, for all legal purposes, complete and effective. To withhold them, as Jefferson and Madison insisted on doing, was an illegal act. But the Supreme Court would not order the secretary of state to deliver the commissions because the law authorizing it to issue writs of mandamus was unconstitutional: the Constitution does not authorize the Supreme Court to issue writs of mandamus; in fact, it prohibits it from doing so. And any law that violates the Constitution is void. Since the law purporting to authorize the Supreme Court to act was unconstitutional, the Court would not—indeed, it could not—order Madison to do his legal duty.

If historians and constitutional lawyers were asked to name the single most important case ever decided in the United States Supreme Court, there is little doubt that the case would be *Marbury v. Madison*. Though the dispute that gave rise to the decision was in itself insignificant, John Marshall used it as a springboard to a great constitutional pronouncement. The rule of the case—that the courts of the United States have the right to declare laws unconstitutional—was immediately recognized as the cornerstone of American constitutional law, and it has remained so ever since.

MORE THAN A HALF-CENTURY WOULD pass before the Supreme Court would again declare an act of Congress unconstitutional, but its authority to do so would never again be seriously doubted. Marshall had made a bold stroke, and he had done so in such a way that neither Congress, nor the president, nor any other public official had any power to resist it. By denying relief to Marbury, he had made the Supreme Court's order marvelously self-enforcing!

Predictably, Thomas Jefferson was angry. If the Supreme Court could not issue writs of mandamus, Jefferson asked, why did Marshall spend so much time

discussing Marbury's entitlement to a commission? And why did the chief justice lecture Madison that withholding the commission was an illegal act?

The president thought for a time that he might have the chief justice and his allies on the bench impeached. After a mentally unstable federal judge in New Hampshire was removed from office, Jefferson's supporters in the House of Representatives brought a bill of impeachment against Marshall's colleague on the Supreme Court, Associate Justice Samuel Chase. Chase was a Federalist who had occasionally badgered witnesses and made intemperate speeches, but no one seriously contended that he had committed an impeachable offense (which the Constitution defines as "treason, bribery, or other high crimes and misdemeanors"). So the Senate, three-quarters of whose members were Jeffersonians, refused to remove Chase from office. Marshall breathed a deep sigh of relief. Had the associate justice been impeached, the chief had no doubt that he himself would have been Jefferson's next target.

Though he never again had occasion to strike down an act of Congress, Marshall delivered opinions in many cases of national significance; and, in his capacity as circuit judge (all Supreme Court justices "rode circuit" in the early years of the nineteenth century), he presided over important, sometimes controversial, trials. He was the presiding judge when Jefferson's political arch rival, Aaron Burr, was charged with treason in 1807. Interpreting the constitutional provision defining treason against the United States, Marshall helped to acquit Burr, though he did so with obvious distaste. The Burr prosecution, Marshall said, was "the most unpleasant case which has been brought before a judge in this or perhaps any other country which affected to be governed by law."

On the high bench, Marshall presided over scores of precedent-setting cases. In *Fletcher v. Peck* (1810) and *Dartmouth College v. Woodward* (1819), he construed the contracts clause of the Constitution so as to afford important protection for the country's growing business community. In *McCulloch v. Maryland* (1819), he upheld the constitutionality of the first Bank of the United States and struck down the Maryland law that purported to tax it. In *Gibbons v. Ogden* (1824), he upheld federal jurisdiction over interstate commerce and lectured those (mainly Jeffersonians) who persistently sought to enlarge state powers at the expense of legitimate federal authority.

Though Marshall's opinions always commanded respect, they were frequently unpopular. When, in *Worcester v. Georgia* (1832), he upheld the treaty rights of the Cherokee Indians against encroachments by the State of Georgia, he incurred the wrath of President Andrew Jackson. "John Marshall has made his decision," "Old Hickory" snapped contemptuously "Now let him enforce it!" Marshall knew, of course, that he could not enforce the decision; that he could not enforce any decision that did not have the moral respect and acquiescence of the public and the officials they elected. And so he bowed his head in sadness and hoped that officials other than Andrew Jackson would one day show greater respect for the nation's legal principles and institutions.

Despite the controversy that some of his decisions inspired, the chief justice remained personally popular; and, during the whole of his more than thirty-four years as head of the federal judiciary, the Court grew steadily in authority and respect.

WELL INTO HIS SEVENTIES, MARSHALL continued to ride circuit in Virginia and North Carolina, to travel each year to his farm in Fauquier County, to attend to his shopping duties in Richmond, and to preside over the high court each winter and spring in Washington. On one of his visits to a neighborhood market in Richmond, the chief justice happened on a young man who had been sent to fetch a turkey for his mother. The youth wanted to comply with his mother's request, but thought it was undignified to carry a turkey in the streets "like a servant." Marshall offered to carry it for him. When the jurist got as far as his own home, he turned to the young man and said, "This is where I live. Your house is not far off; can't you carry the turkey the balance of the way?" The young man's face turned crimson as he suddenly realized that his benefactor was none other, than the chief justice of the United States.

Joseph Story, who served as an associate justice of the Supreme Court for more than twenty years of Marshall's term as chief justice, spent many hours with the Virginian in and out of Washington. Wherever Story observed Marshall,

he was impressed by his modesty and geniality. "Meet him in a stagecoach, as a stranger, and travel with him a whole day," Story said, "and you would only be struck with his readiness to administer to the accommodations of others, and his anxiety to appropriate the least to himself. Be with him, the unknown guest at an inn, and he seemed adjusted to the very scene, partaking of the warm welcome of its comforts, wherever found; and if not found, resigning himself without complaint to its meanest arrangements. You would never suspect, in either case, that he was a great man; far less that he was the Chief Justice of the United States."

In his youth, Marshall had been fond of corn whiskey. As he grew older, he lost his appetite for spirits but not for wine. He formulated a "rule" under which the Supreme Court judges abstained from wine except in wet weather, but Story said he was liberal in allowing "exceptions." "It does sometime happen," Story once said, "the the Chief Justice will say to me, when the cloth is removed, 'Brother Story, step to the window and see if it does not look like rain.' And if I tell him that the sun is shining brightly, Judge Marshall will sometimes reply, 'All the better; for our jurisdiction extends over so large a territory that it must be raining somewhere.'" "You know," Story added, "that the Chief was brought up upon Federalism and Madeira, and he is not the man to outgrow his early prejudices."

In Richmond, Marshall held regular dinners for local lawyers, swapped stories with old friends, and tossed quoits with his neighbors in the Barbecue Club. An artist named Chester Harding remembered seeing the chief justice at a session of the Barbecue Club in 1829. Harding said Marshall was "the best pitcher of the party, and could throw heavier quoits than any other member of the club." "There were several ties," he added, "and, before long, I saw the great Chief Justice of the United States, down on his knees, measuring the contested distance with a straw, with as much earnestness as if it had been a point of law; and if he proved to be in the right, the woods would ring with his triumphant shout."

In 1830, a young Pennsylvania congressman and future president of the United States commented on Marshall's enduring popularity among his neighbors. "His decisions upon constitutional

questions have ever been hostile to the opinions of a vast majority of the people in his own State," James Buchanan said, "and yet with what respect and veneration has he been viewed by Virginia? Is there a Virginian whose heart does not beat with honest pride when the just fame of the Chief Justice is the subject of conversation? They consider him, as he truly is, one of the great and best men which this country has ever produced."

MARSHALL WAS NEARLY EIGHTY YEARS old when he died in Philadelphia on July 6, 1835. His body was brought back to Virginia for burial, where it was met by the longest procession the city of Richmond had ever seen.

In the contest between proponents of strong and weak national government, Marshall had been one of the foremost and clearest advocates of strength. The struggle—between union and disunion, between federation and confederation, between the belief that the Constitution created a nation and the theory that it aligned the states in a loose league—was not finally resolved until 1865. But the struggle *was* resolved. "Time has been on Marshall's side," Oliver Wendell Holmes, Jr., said in 1901. "The theory for which Hamilton argued, and he decided, and Webster spoke, and Grant fought, is now our cornerstone.

Justice Story thought that Marshall's appointment to the Supreme Court contributed more "to the preservation of the true principles of the Constitution than any other circumstances in our domestic history." "He was a great man," Story said. "I go farther; and insist, that he would have been deemed a great man in any age, and of all ages. He was one of those, to whom centuries alone give birth."

John Adams and Thomas Jefferson both lived long and distinguished lives, but neither ever gave an inch in their differences of opinion over Marshall. Jefferson went to his grave bemoaning the "cunning and sophistry" of his fellow Virginian. Adams died secure in the belief that his decision to make Marshall chief justice had been both wise and provident. Years later, Adams called Marshall's appointment "the pride of my life." Time has accorded Thomas Jefferson a great place in the affections of the American people; but, in the controversy over John Marshall, the judgment of history has come down with quiet strength on the side of John Adams.

John Quincy Adams and American Continental Expansion

Stanley J. Underdal

Dr. Stanley J. Underdal is a lecturer in the Department of History at San Jose State University, San Jose, CA. He was formerly a consultant in National Security Affairs (1983–1984) and Coordinator of Graduate Studies and Assistant Dean for Graduate Programs at the Defense Intelligence College, Washington, D.C. (1978–1983). He received his M. Phil. and Ph.D. from Columbia University (1974, 1977).

When John Quincy Adams died on 21 February 1848, two days after suffering a stroke while voting in the House of Representatives, few Westerners wept for the former President. By that time, frontier Americans saw the cranky New Englander as an obstacle holding up their exploitation of the vast new American territories west of the Mississippi River. Adams had opposed the annexation of Texas after it had won independence from Mexico in 1836. He stubbornly insisted on raking up the deadly divisive issue of the extension of slavery every time Western frontiersmen sought to establish territorial government. His campaign to wipe out the "gag rule" imposed by the House of Representatives in 1836 to prevent the hearing of anti-slavery petitions stirred up increasing tension over the nature of new territories and states carved out of the Western lands. Finally, he led the Whig opposition to the Mexican War which was to cost Mexico one-third of its territory and gave the United States the vast resources and Pacific harbor of the Southwest.[1]

It certainly would have been difficult to imagine Adams as a frontiersman. Compared to his great and detested rival, the charismatic, tobacco-chewing, gun-toting, barroom-brawling, Indian-hating, knife-wielding, dueling Andrew Jackson of Tennessee, Adams seemed a ludicrous figure. But Westerners misjudged Adams.

Although he was slight of stature (about five feet, seven inches tall) and sported a slight pot belly, a nearly bald head from an early age, red and watery eyes that seemed to cry out for glasses (which he would never wear), a constantly-recurring cough, and periodic touches of lumbago and rheumatism, he had surprising stamina. In fact, he was something of a health nut, or at least his contemporaries thought so. Reminiscent of a later President, Harry Truman, Adams loved to take long, brisk walks. While President, he regularly walked back and forth from the White House to Capitol Hill. He also was an avid swimmer all his life. In Washington, he loved to swim in the Potomac River, usually clad only in a cap (one can hardly imagine a skinny-dipping George Bush), against the tide of the river sometimes for 90 minutes at a stretch. Even in later temporary retirement in Quincy, Massachusetts, he would regularly swim the one-half mile back and forth between the wharfs of a neighbor in a time he was proud to record as 16 minutes.[2]

Westerners also misjudged his contributions to the creation of the continental empire that they were so eager to exploit. No one labored longer or more successfully to extend the continental limits of the United States. It is but little exaggeration to say that the United States became a geographic giant because of the zeal of the little New Englander. Adams's public career comprised three phases, two glorious in accomplishment (although in different ways), and the

John Quincy Adams at 16. Engraving by Sidney L. Smith after a drawing by Schmidt made at The Hague in 1783. (Courtesy of The New York Historical Society, New York City)

third decidedly less so. As diplomat and as congressman, Adams distinguished himself, but his record as President was marked by futility, though not always of his doing. And in all three career phases Adams deeply affected the West.

ADAMS, THE DIPLOMATIST

Adams's diplomatic accomplishments from 1814 to 1828, during those years generally known as the Era of Good Feelings (though "good feelings" were hard to find in American politics then), mark the era as what historian Walter Lafeber has called the Golden Age of

John Quincy Adams as Secretary of State, 1819. Engraving by Francis Kearney *ca.* **1824 from the Charles Bird King portrait of 1819. (Courtesy of The New York Historical Society, New York City)**

American diplomacy.[3] Adams played a key, and sometimes central, role in negotiating the Treaty of Ghent that ended the nearly disastrous War of 1812; the Rush-Bagot agreement of 1817 which limited American and British warships on the Great Lakes and began more than a century and one-half of peaceful border relations between Canada and the United States; agreements ensuring the right of American fishermen to work the rich banks off Labrador and Newfoundland; the Convention of 1818 which established the 49th parallel as the northern boundary of the Louisiana Purchase and protected American claims to the Pacific Northwest by providing for joint occupation of Oregon Territory by the United States and Great Britain; and an agreement with Tsar Alexander of Russia that extinguished Russian claims south of the present-day border of Alaska and set in train the diplomatic friendship that eventually culminated in the purchase of Alaska and the removal of Russian influence from the Western Hemisphere. Perhaps the most important success of Adams's career, and of vital importance to Westerners and to Southern frontiersmen, was the Transcontinental Treaty (also called the Adams-Onís Treaty) of 1819 which made Florida part of the Union and strengthened American claims to the Pacific Coast by defining the border with Spain all the way to the Pacific,

thus paving the way for American expansion into the Far West.[4]

Adams also was influential in establishing American relations with the newly independent nations of South America, undercutting a potential commercial monopoly by the British. His tact in dealing both with Spain and with the revolutionary Latin American governments helped to establish the paramount economic position that the United States now enjoys in the Western Hemisphere. Adams was an unabashed expansionist and was among the first government officials to declare openly that Providence intended that the United States ultimately possess the entire continent of North America. This premise underlay one of his chief contributions to the famous doctrine which bears the name of President Monroe, but which could be known as the Adams Doctrine because of his persuasive powers with the President: the non-colonization principle. This principle stated that the New World no longer was to be regarded as an area for the establishment of European colonies. Henceforth, America was to be the province of Americans only, and Adams intended, of course, that the greatest power in the Hemisphere was to be the United States.[5]

A child of the American Revolution, Adams was better prepared for the position of Secretary of State and of President than anyone in history, with the possible exception of Thomas Jefferson whom he grudgingly admired despite the long rivalry between Jefferson and his father, John Adams. At the age of eight, he stood with his mother on a hill on the family farm near Braintree, Massachusetts, and watched in horror the burning of Charlestown by the British and listened to the roar of cannon in the Battle of Bunker Hill. From that day on, he pulled the beard of the British lion at every possible occasion.[6]

At ten and one-half years of age, he began his exposure to diplomatic relations when in 1778 he accompanied his father who had been appointed to replace Silas Deane as one of three commissioners (with Benjamin Franklin and Arthur Lee) at the French court. Three years later, young Adams officially entered public life as secretary to Francis Dana, who had been the secretary of the American commission in France but was now appointed representative to the court of Empress Catherine II of Russia. Dana could not speak French, the official diplomatic language of the Russian court,

so the budding linguist Adams was invaluable. In late 1782 he returned to Paris to become his father's personal secretary during the negotiations for the end of the war. After his father was appointed the first United States minister to Great Britain, Adams returned home to attend Harvard College and, in 1787, to begin the practice of law, at which he was decidedly unhappy and unsuccessful. He fared better at politics and gained a degree of notoriety as the author of the Publicola Papers, which criticized Thomas Paine's *The Rights of Man* for its laudatory celebration of the French Revolution as more liberal and democratic than that of the United States. He came to the attention of President George Washington when, in 1793, he published a series of articles under the *nom de plume* of Columbus that discredited the French Jacobin minister to the United States, Edmond Genet. That led to his first official diplomatic appointment as minister resident to The Hague at age 28, as minister to Portugal briefly in 1797, and then as minister to the King of Prussia.[7]

When his father was swept from office in the election of 1800, Adams returned home and in 1803 was elected by the Massachusetts legislature as a U.S. senator. Senator Adams displayed his lifelong political independence first by becoming the only Federalist senator to vote in favor of the treaty completing the Louisiana Purchase which nearly doubled the size of the United States, and then by supporting President Jefferson's efforts to defend American maritime rights during the Napoleonic Wars. Ever a believer in the importance of principle over pragmatic opportunism, he was so disturbed by his party's willingness to placate Britain in order to keep New England shipping interests profitable that he voted in favor of Jefferson's embargo that shut down the nation's ports. For that apostasy, he was drummed out of the Federalist Party and in 1808 forced to resign his position as Senator. Nearly a year before Adams's term was to expire, the Massachusetts legislature selected as his successor, a former Harvard classmate.[8]

Adams was rescued from the political icebox by the newly elected President James Madison who, as Secretary of State, had appreciated Adams's support in the Senate. Although it was rumored that Madison would appoint him as Secretary of War, Adams was pleased to be asked to become the first Minister Plenipotentiary to Russia in 1809. For the next five years, Adams courted good relations with Tsar Alexander I and Chancellor Rumiantsev. Both men shared Adams's concern over Britain's growing dominance of world maritime trade and over the expansion of the new French Empire under Napoleon whose Continental System also threatened economic development. Adams's anti-British, free trade stance perfectly matched the current feelings of the Russian court. The American minister described the young Tsar as handsome, personally elegant, and both affable and condescending in manner; what he found most attractive was the Tsar's spirit of benevolence and humanity. The republican and the autocrat got along famously. The future Secretary of State was able to take advantage of the goodwill developed during those years, when much later he would respond to Alexander's claim of territory in America so far south as Oregon country by declaring for the first time that the Western Hemisphere no longer was open to European colonization.[9]

In late 1810 and early 1811, Alexander, increasingly angry over the trade demands of Napoleon, issued a ukase, or imperial decree, very favorable to American shipping. Enraged, Napoleon recalled the French ambassador and both countries prepared for war. Earlier that year, Adams had turned down an appointment to the U.S. Supreme Court pleading that, though he had been trained as a lawyer, he never was comfortable in the law and therefore felt unqualified for such a position; he preferred to stay in Russia for the time being, even if as a private citizen.[10]

When France invaded Russia in 1812, the Tsar allied with Great Britain, which put Adams into an embarrassing situation when the United States declared war on that country over the violation of maritime rights. But President Monroe made it clear that the United States' quarrel was limited to Britain and that the Tsar's arrangements with Britain should have no effect on friendly Russo-American relations. In response, Alexander offered to mediate between the two belligerents. With Napoleon's crushing defeat in Russia, the way was clear to settle the Anglo-U.S. dispute. Without waiting to hear Britain's response to Alexander's mediation offer, President Madison appointed Albert Gallatin to head a peace commission composed of

Henry Clay, James Bayard, Jonathan Russell, Albert Gallatin, and John Quincy Adams. Ironically, the British turned down the mediation effort, but agreed to direct negotiations with the Americans at the Flemish city of Ghent.[11]

Fortunately for the United States, the American commissioners were far more competent and intelligent than were the British emissaries. When negotiations began, the Britons insisted that peace could be had only upon certain conditions; foremost was the creation of an independent Indian barrier state between British Canada and the United States, which would have encompassed the present states of Ohio, Michigan, Indiana, Illinois, and Wisconsin. Henry Clay of Kentucky, then the leading political spokesman of the West, was enraged at such a suggestion; even Adams, who was more concerned about retaining American access to the rich fishing banks off Newfoundland and Labrador than about Indians on the Western frontier, could not accept such an idea. He wrote to Secretary of State James Monroe that the Indian question was basic to America's future. The Indians should be compensated for their land and moved to areas less likely to be the object of frontier expansion, but to claim that a hunting people somehow had possessory rights to the land was "incompatible with the moral as well as the physical nature of things." To keep fertile land out of the hands of the tillers of the earth would be "an outrage upon Providence, which gave the earth to man for cultivation, and made the tillage of the ground the condition of his nature and the law of existence."[12]

Next, the British negotiators demanded peace based on the current military position; each nation would keep what its armies then occupied. That was unacceptable to Adams, for it would have cost much of Maine and other territory claimed by the United States as a result of the War of Independence. The Americans held out for the status quo ante-bellum. In the end, that is what they got. In the Peace of Christmas Eve signed at Ghent in 1814, the Americans preserved their Western territories for future frontier expansion. Still unresolved, however, were the precise northeast boundaries, control of armaments on the Great Lakes, and the claims of Great Britain to free navigation up and down the Mississippi River; those issues

Adams in 1826. Engraving by Thomas Gimbrede. J. Q. Adams' seal appears under the portrait. Its motif of the eagle and lyre has been used by the artist on the draperies and the chair. (Courtesy of The New York Historical Society, New York City)

were left for later commissions to wrangle over.[13]

After the war, Adams was appointed as minister to Great Britain and charged with negotiating a commercial treaty with that erstwhile enemy. His relations with Lord Castlereagh, the British foreign minister, were difficult; they developed mutual respect, but no warmth. The resultant treaty resolved none of the major differences between the two nations, other than elimination of some discriminatory tariff duties and American access to a few East Indian ports, but the process of negotiation established the basis for later agreements. In 1817 Adams was recalled from England by the new President, James Monroe, to become Secretary of State. His period of greatness, and of direct impact on the West, was about to begin.

As Secretary of State, Adams virtually created the concept of Manifest Destiny, long before it was trumpeted by John L. O'Sullivan and other supporters of James K. Polk. A deeply moral and religious man, Adams was convinced that Providence had created the United States for a special purpose: to inhabit and civilize the entire North American continent and, through example, to stamp out all traces of monarchical European colonialism from the face of the earth. He would devote his entire en-

Adams in 1834. Painting by Asher B. Durand. (Courtesy of The New York Historical Society, New York City)

ergies as Secretary of State to those propositions.

According to the Treaty of Ghent, the British were to return all seized territories to the United States and revert only to possessions held before the war; the trick was in getting them to abide by that decision. During the war, British agents and traders had seized control of much of the Old Northwest region of the Upper Mississippi and Ohio Rivers. In the Pacific Northwest, the American trading post at the mouth of the Columbia River, Astoria, had fallen to a ragged band of men sent by the British North West Company. Afraid of losing everything to the British without compensation, the American partners sold Astoria to the North West Company just before its formal capture in 1813 by the British frigate HMS *Racoon* during the War of 1812. Because it was simply a commercial transaction, the selling of Astoria had no effect on American political claims to the territory. As the United States saw matters, by the terms of the Treaty of Ghent Astoria should have been returned and all British traders cleared out of the region. However, the treaty was silent on this and several other disputed matters, and Adams determined to resolve them if he could.

In 1818 Adams dispatched Albert Gallatin, then minister to France, to join Richard Rush, minister to Britain, to negotiate a treaty to replace the one Adams had obtained in 1815 that would deal

with commercial matters, the Canadian fisheries, compensation for slaves taken away by the British during the War of 1812, and the Northwest boundary. On the whole, the Americans won substantial concessions. Great Britain, in this Anglo-American Convention of 1818, agreed to give up its irritating claim to navigation rights on the Mississippi and Missouri Rivers, much to the satisfaction of St. Louis fur interests, who insisted that Britain be locked out of that profitable region. The British negotiators also accepted a U.S.-Canadian border that ran from the Lake of the Woods along the 49th parallel to the crest of the Rocky Mountains. This achievement ensured that large sections of Minnesota, North Dakota, and Montana would remain in American hands and preserved the rich Mesabi iron ore deposits for the later development of the American iron and steel industry.[14]

Both Thomas Hart Benton, of Missouri, and Adams coveted Oregon, for control of the mouth of the Columbia would make that river and the future overland Oregon Trail a "highway" for commerce between the Mississippi Valley and the Pacific Coast with its plentiful sea otter trove and access to trade with China. In August 1818, Astoria was restored to American control, but Britain refused to admit American title to the entire territory. Gallatin and Rush finally convinced the British commissioners to agree to a ten-year joint Anglo-American occupation of the disputed area and free use of the Columbia River by both nations. Adams had won what he could; he protected American claims to Oregon and waited for a more convenient time, and a flood of American immigrants, to settle the matter. In the meantime, he would extinguish all Spanish claim to the area north of California.[15]

Adams's greatest achievement as Secretary of State undoubtedly was the Transcontinental Treaty of 1819 negotiated with the Spanish minister to the United States, Don Luis de Onís. The treaty dealt with three major issues: Florida, Texas, and the border of the Louisiana Purchase with Spanish Mexico and California. Long before the Revolution, Americans had coveted Spanish-controlled Florida, and the language of the Louisiana Purchase of 1803 seemed to give the United States reasonable claim to a portion of West Florida, at least from the Mississippi River eastward to the Pearl River. Spain never recognized

such a right, so in 1810 and in 1813, after a series of rather disreputable raids tacitly authorized by President Madison, the United States occupied and annexed all of West Florida up to the Perdido River near Pensacola. Spain was too weak to do anything but protest, and the stage was set for the purchase of the rest of Florida for which the United States had no legitimate claim. Florida was becoming increasingly important as its rivers provided convenient outlets to the Gulf of Mexico for the growing American settlements in Georgia, Alabama, and Mississippi. It was decidedly inconvenient that Spanish Florida also provided a haven for escaped slaves and for Seminole Indians forced out of the American Southeast. Using these enclaves as sanctuaries, Indians raided American settlements.[16]

In 1817 Adams opened negotiations with Onís to obtain Florida, but the resolute Spaniard demanded that the United States also surrender all claim to Texas, which might have been obtained from France in the Louisiana Purchase. This Adams was reluctant to do and the negotiations dragged on.

In the spring of 1817, the War Department received news that a band of Indians on the Georgia-Florida border had killed a white woman and her two children and were likely to cause more trouble. The military commander in Georgia, General Edmund Gaines, called a conference of the local Seminole leaders to berate them for not stopping the murders. The Indians replied that Americans had killed many Indians and the attack on Mrs. Garrett was to settle the score. Gaines then accused them of harboring runaway slaves, to which they replied that their harboring and marrying former slaves was none of the General's business. Relations between white settlers and the Indians continued to deteriorate, and by fall the Army moved to enforce the provisions of the Treaty of Fort Jackson imposed by General Andrew Jackson at the close of the Creek Indian War in 1815: the cession of some 23 million acres by the Indians. When General Gaines ordered the Indians of Fowltown near the Florida border to vacate, they refused, explaining that they had not signed the treaty. Gaines sent a detachment to clear the town and burn it to the ground; the troops also killed several of the villagers. The Indians retaliated on 30 November by killing nearly 50 people on

Lithograph of John Quincy Adams by B. F. Butler made in 1848 from an 1843 daguerreotype by Philip Haas. (Courtesy of The New York Historical Society, New York City)

a supply boat commanded by Lieutenant R. W. Scott as it ascended the Appalachicola River. In the midst of this crisis, General Gaines was ordered to take command of Amelia Island, a former base for pirates and smugglers situated in the St. Mary's River between Georgia and East Florida. On 26 December, General Jackson was appointed to replace him on the border.[17]

Both Adams and Jackson believed that there could be no real security on America's Southern borders until all of Florida was under U.S. sovereignty. Neither was happy about foreign adventurers, runaway slaves, and hostile Indians having a sanctuary from which to raid the expanding American settlements. They knew that Spain had neither the will nor the force to control them, even though the Pinckney Treaty of 1795 obliged Spain to restrain Indians and adventurers from raiding across the border. That slaves were allowed to remain unchecked on Spanish soil was far more outrageous to the Southern slaveowner Jackson than to Adams who personally was repelled by the very notion of slavery, but as Secretary of State Adams had to guard against any foreign threat, and he felt that he could not allow American laws to be violated without retribution. So these two seemingly mismatched nationalists, the flamboyant and emotional Jackson and the reserved, ascetic Adams, joined forces unwittingly to force Spain to give up much of its claim to North America.

Shortly before his transfer to Amelia Island, General Gaines had received from Secretary of War John C. Calhoun orders to follow the Seminole Indians across the border into Florida if they "should still refuse to make reparations for the outrages and depredations on the citizens of the United States. . . ." However, if they should seek shelter within a Spanish fort, Gaines was to "immediately notify this department." Jackson inherited those orders and immediately began to question any limitations on his actions. His original orders from Calhoun instructed him to "adopt the necessary measures to terminate" the conflict. President Monroe, in a letter two days later, informed Jackson that his campaign would "bring you on a theatre where you may possibly have other services to perform. Great interests are at issue. . . . This is not a time for repose . . . until our cause is carried triumphantly thro'." What did this mean? Was Jackson free to do whatever he felt justified?

In a secret note to President Monroe of 6 January 1818, Jackson declared that all of Florida should be seized and held as an indemnity for Spain's permitting outrages on American citizens. To his very deathbed, Monroe insisted that, though he had read the note, he simply passed it on to the Secretary of War with no comment—he had never authorized the seizure of Florida. Jackson insisted thereafter that he had received unofficial, but unmistakable, permission to invade and take possession. What is clear is that neither Calhoun nor Monroe gave Jackson direct orders *not* to engage the Spanish.[18]

Jackson invaded Florida, burned several Indian villages, pursued the fleeing survivors to the Spanish fort of St. Mark's, occupied it, and court-martialed and executed two British adventurers together with two Seminole chiefs. He then seized Pensacola, the seat of the Spanish provincial government. After permitting the Spanish governor to embark for Havana, Jackson appointed one of his officers as acting governor of Florida and returned to Tennessee.[19]

Monroe and the members of the Cabinet were startled to learn the extent of Jackson's actions. Onís, with whom Adams had begun negotiations over boundary matters, was outraged and demanded that Florida be returned and that Jackson be publicly disavowed and punished. In a series of July Cabinet meetings, Monroe and everyone but Adams at first insisted that Florida should be returned immediately and Jackson disavowed. That would be a terrible mistake, argued Adams. As an experienced and crafty diplomat, Adams realized that to censure Jackson would cause Onís to be intransigent at the bargaining table where power and determination were the ultimate determinants. He also argued that Jackson was so popular that the Monroe administration would be heavily criticized for "trucking" to Spain, and likely would pay a heavy price at the polls. No doubt Jackson's actions were embarrassing as they risked war with Spain and might be interpreted at home as a presidential act of war without congressional approval, but "defensive acts of hostility may be authorized by the Executive . . . [and] Jackson was authorized to cross the Spanish line in pursuit of the Indian enemy." Besides, to back down would be a sign of national weakness, and it would be unjust to punish an officer "when in principle he is strictly justifiable." He also thought to himself that the ease of Jackson's victory might be turned to advantage in negotiations with Onís. How then could both Spain and Jackson be assuaged and the negotiations speeded?[20]

Adams won reluctant acquiescence to his position. In a letter of 19 July to Jackson, Monroe explained that though he realized the General thought the circumstances justified his actions, the President was going to return Florida to Spain. To retain the Spanish posts would be tantamount to a declaration of war, a power exclusively the province of Congress. However, restoration would work to the advantage of the United States in the Adams-Onís discussions, for Spain could feel free to bargain away Florida without suffering the humility of admitting that it was unable to hold off American conquest.[21] On 23 July, Adams responded officially to Onís by defending Jackson's actions as necessary upon the immutable principles of self-defence." He reminded the Spanish minister of Spain's treaty obligations to restrain the Indians on Spanish soil. "By the ordinary laws and usages of nations, the right of pursuing an enemy, who seeks refuge from actual conflict within a neutral territory, incontestable. But, in this case the territory of Florida was not even neutral." The United States returned Florida, but "the preservation of peace . . . indispensably requires that henceforth the stipulations by Spain to restrain by force her Indians from all hostilities against the United States should be faithfully and effectually fulfilled." If Spain couldn't manage its territory, the United States would.[22]

Onís was temporarily quieted, but political pressure for disavowal of Jackson by the General's enemies, led by Henry Clay, and British anger over Jackson's execution of British citizens threatened the negotiations over Oregon and led to one of the most remarkable diplomatic notes of Adam's career. Taking advantage of the situation, Onís renewed his demand that the United States recognize Spanish sovereignty over the West as far north as the Missouri River, thus severely limiting what the Americans thought had been gained through the Louisiana Purchase. Adams responded with a note to the American minister to Spain, George Erving, that he also sent to the British foreign minister and to newspapers that supported the Monroe administration. The letter not only defended Jackson, but it was a virtual manifesto of Manifest Destiny justifying American expansionism into areas that European governments could not control. Adams traced the roots of the Seminole War to British machinations in Florida during the War of 1812. After the war, Spain failed either to control British agents remaining there, or to restrain the Indians whom those agents stirred up. Consequently, Jackson was fully justified in punishing both the Indians and the renegade British agents as an act of national self-defense. The audacious Adams declared that the Spanish colonial officials should be punished for their dereliction and that Spain should pay "a just and reasonable indemnity" for Jackson's expenses incurred while doing what Spain itself should have done. What is more, "if the necessities of self-defence should again compel the United States to take possession of the Spanish forts and places in Florida . . . another unconditional restoration of them must not be expected."

Publication of this note ended domestic criticism of Jackson, satisfied the British government that the United States was doing nothing more than Britain would have done under like cir-

cumstances, and prompted Onís and the Spanish government to seek quick resolution of border matters before the Americans turned greedy eyes on even more territory.[23]

The result was the Transcontinental Treaty of 1819 which gained for the United States all of Florida and a stairstep Western border with Spanish territory using the Sabine, Red, and Arkansas Rivers as north-south lines and included a straight line from the headwaters of the Arkansas along the 42nd parallel all the way to the Pacific Ocean. By this treaty, Spain had transferred all claim to Oregon territory to the United States. The only remaining claimants to the rest of North America were Great Britain and Russia, and Adams would soon seek to limit Russia. Although Adams had no way of knowing it, the Spanish government was so eager to settle the dispute before it lost Florida with no compensation at all that Onís was instructed to give up claim to most of Texas, if necessary. Partisan political criticism for his failure to obtain Texas would dog Adams all his life, but he felt justified by the overall success of the negotiations, by the general ignorance of Spain's negotiating position, and by the fact that though he tried to convince the Cabinet to hold out for Texas, no one had supported him.[24]

When discussing John Quincy Adams and the West, it is significant to note that the non-colonization principle of the Monroe Doctrine, authored by Adams, stemmed from his attempt to extinguish Russian claims to the Pacific Northwest. In 1812 a Russian expedition landed at Bodoga Bay north of present-day San Francisco and established its Fort Ross fur trading post. Soon after taking office as Secretary of State in 1817, Adams was told that Russian activity in the area was expanding. He initially discounted the rumor but became alarmed in late 1818 when an agent in California incorrectly reported that Russia was about to seize San Francisco Bay from Spain. The Russian government denied that Spain was about to cede her claims to California, but Adams, then negotiating the Transcontinental Treaty with Spain, was not pleased to have the Russians muddy the waters. On 4 September 1821, Tsar Alexander signed an edict declaring Russia's right to the Pacific Northwest all the way south to the 51st parallel, barring all foreign traders and fishermen from the area, and forbidding any non-Russian vessel to come within 115 miles of the coast.

Adams advised the Russian minister that Alexander's pretension to authority so far south was a bit surprising, as was his claim to jurisdiction on the high seas

The United States Senate Chamber in 1846. Painting by Thomas Doney. John Quincy Adams is the fourth figure to the left of the Speaker.

"beyond the ordinary distance." Russia replied that there were 500 miles between America's settlement with Spain on the 42nd parallel and the Russian claim in the north. So far as the high seas restrictions were concerned, they were necessary because the United States would not control its illegal traders; if Russia owned the land on both sides of the ocean, why could not it declare the sea in between to be closed? Adams did not press the issue vigorously at the time, for the Tsar was arbitrating a dispute between Great Britain and the United States over slave compensation arising from the provisions of the Treaty of Ghent.[25]

The United States had little concern for Spain's domestic turbulence in 1823, nor for the French intrusion, but what would be the effect on the rebellious Spanish colonies in the New World of French dominance in Spain? Would France send armies to quell the rebellions and then create a new French empire in South America? Not likely. But would some other country take advantage of Spain's distress to establish political or commercial domination in the region? And what about Cuba and Puerto Rico which had not yet declared their independence from Spain. Might they be transferred by Spain to some other power such as France or, horrors, to Great Britain? It seemed to Monroe and his advisors that the United States must clarify its position regarding European colonies, and the Russian claims provided a way to do it.

When the cabinet met on 28 June 1823 to discuss instructions for Henry Middleton, U.S. minister to Russia, in response to Alexander's 1821 ukase, Adams took the position that no other country should be permitted to establish territorial rights on the North American continent; but the Cabinet finally toned down Middleton's instructions by proposing that the entire region be open and free to both Russians and Americans for a specified number of years (similar to the arrangement with Britain over Oregon); if that were turned down, Russia should be offered a line at the 55th parallel, provided that Americans be permitted to trade with Indians all along the Pacific Coast. Several days later Baron Tuyll, the Russian minister, called on Adams to inquire about the American position on the Northwest boundary. Adams told him frankly that the United States would contest the right of Russia

"to any territorial establishment on this continent. . . . We should assume distinctly the principle that the American continents are no longer subjects for any new European colonial establishments." Here was a direct statement of the noncolonization principle adopted later that year in the Monroe Doctrine. The real target was not Russia, for Adams' was convinced that Alexander had no real intention of seeking to extend his empire just for the sake of a declining sea otter trade. Adams meant to send a signal to Great Britain. He stated the substance of his no-further-colonization principle once more that same day in a letter to Richard Rush, the American minister to Britain, declaring that American claims to the continent were not by conquest or exploration, but "by the finger of nature." "A necessary consequence of this state of things will be, that the American continents, henceforth, will no longer be subjects of colonization."[26]

The rest of the story of the Monroe Doctrine is familiar. The United States rejected a proposal by Britain's George Canning for a joint statement opposing further attempts by European powers to colonize the Western Hemisphere. At Adams's suggestion, President Monroe, in his State of the Union address on 2 December 1823, set forth three basic principles: no new European colonies in America; no European political meddling in the New World; and no American interference in the politics of the Old World.

Tsar Alexander was unruffled either by Adams's first declaration of the noncolonization doctrine to Baron Tuyll or by Monroe's presidential address. As Adams anticipated, Alexander, who had no plans either to help Spain recover its colonies or to extend his dominions in America, realized that the true target of the Monroe Doctrine was Great Britain which hoped to use its maritime power to dominate the markets of the world. A slap in the face of the British Lion suited him just fine, particularly if it came from someone else. In 1824 Russia concluded a treaty with the United States setting the southern boundary of Alaska at 54°40′ and setting the stage for the ultimate sale of Alaska to the United States after the Civil War.[27] Years later Adams summarized his view of the matter in a letter to Richard Rush:

Mr. Monroe's declaration in the message of 2 December 1823, to

which you allude, was my own work. I wrote that paragraph of the message, and I think he adopted it without alteration. The Declaration itself was first made in a secret communication from me to Baron Tuyll, the Russian Minister. I proposed to Mr. Monroe that it should be made, and after some hesitation and deliberate reflection he agreed to it—Your secret conferences with Mr. Canning and mine with Baron Tuyll both concurred in leading to it—its first object was to present to the Emperor Alexander a prevailing *motive,* to recede from his pretensions on the Northwest Coast of America by presenting a principle which he would consider a bearing chiefly upon Great Britain, and which would fall in with his feelings towards her at that time. Its Second purpose was as you judged—a warning to Great Britain herself. . . . You know what its effect was upon Canning.[28]

It is probably correct to say that Adams's greatest years of achievement and the years in which he had the greatest impact upon the West were before he became President. It is customary to call his a failed presidency. Despite his great aspirations for the nation, he lacked the charisma and congressional political organization to carry out his dreams. It did not help that Adams had become President despite having fewer popular votes and fewer electoral votes than Andrew Jackson, the choice of most frontiersmen. He also could have demonstrated more political skill than to appoint Henry Clay as Secretary of State, the position most Americans believed to be heir-designate to the presidency. Clay not only was Jackson's chief rival as spokesman for the Western and Southern exponents of expansion, but he ensured Adams's election by throwing his support to Adams in the House of Representatives when that body voted to determine the new president. Thereafter, the charges of "corrupt bargain" cursed Adams.

Adams was never comfortable with the notion that the president should be the leader of a political party. In that sense, he was a true eighteenth-century Enlightenment intellectual, like his friend James Madison who warned of the dangers of political "factionalism" during the debate over the ratification of the Constitution. His long experience overseas, his rigorous and eclectic edu-

John Quincy Adams in 1848. Stipple engraving by Richard Soper from a sketch made by Arthur J. Stansbury of Adams a few hours before his death. (Courtesy of The New York Historical Society, New York City)

cation, and his passionate belief in the principles of the American Revolution made him one of the least sectional or party-oriented politicians of his or any time. Unfortunately, he was fighting the tide of political change. After the first quarter of the nineteenth century, successful politicians courted the favor of the rising popular democracy and built support through the rigorous and deliberate use of patronage. Adams believed that government should be an agency for useful action, and he frequently criticized the waste and abuse that underlay the actions of many who trumpeted the principles of individual liberty and commercial competition. His sponsorship of a national law in 1828 to protect a beautiful live-oak forest near Pensacola, Florida, in the interest of science and conservation, presages the efforts of twentieth-century environmentalists. But the proposal was defeated by his Jacksonian enemies in Congress who acted, as he saw it, out of "stolid ignorance and stupid malignity," yet defended their actions in the name of liberty, free enterprise, and necessary expansion. He was clearly out of step with his times.[29]

He had an agenda, a remarkable agenda, but one for the twentieth century, not for his own. In a remarkably farsighted State of the Union address, Adams expressed a broad, positive concept of national leadership. Despite objections by his Cabinet members that he

was proposing far more than the citizens wanted or that Congress would accept, Adams insisted in his December 1825 address that since Liberty had been won in 1776 and the Union assured by 1825, it was now time to use both Liberty and Union in the public interest. "The great object of the institution of civil government," he lectured an unreceptive Congress, "is the improvement of the condition of those who are parties to the social compact, and no government in whatever form constituted, can accomplish the lawful ends of its institutions but in proportion as it improves the condition of those over whom it is established." And how did he propose to improve their conditions? By an extensive system of internal improvements—a nationally planned and financed network of railroads, canals, and roads to tie the nation together—that made Henry Clay's American System seem modest in comparison and that would be financed by the sale of Western lands. He also proposed creation of a national university to prepare the best American minds for public and private service, and a national military academy to train future military leaders to protect American democracy. He called for the development of geographic science through surveys of natural resources and scientific explorations of the West. Adams also suggested that Indians should be treated more fairly, helped perhaps to assimilate

into the general population instead of just being robbed of their lands. He proposed a uniform system of weights and measures, reformation of the patent system to encourage invention, and the fostering of astronomical science through the creation of a national observatory.

Viewed from the late twentieth century when most of his proposals have long since been implemented and taken for granted, it is hard to believe that Westerners, and Americans in general, not only failed to support Adams but ridiculed him for such notions. Americans particularly guffawed at his characterization of astronomical observatories as "light-houses of the skies." Today, Westerners are justifiably proud of their many observatories manned by scientists probing a new frontier.

The nationalist tone of his address did not sit well with the growing number of States Righters and party politicians in the country. Adams was talking about a powerful central government at a time when sectional and state interests were in the ascendance. Adams's notion of liberty with power did not sound like democracy to them. Adams's presidency failed almost as it began and his State of the Union address has been described by George Dangerfield as a prime example of the art of suicide by manifesto.[30]

Were the year 1961 and the speaker John F. Kennedy, his speech might have been greeted with applause and national determination to best their European protagonists. But in 1825 there were no Sputniks, missile races, or Cold Wars, and Adams's call to national greatness fell on deaf ears. So also fell his presidency.

From 1831 to 1848, ex-president Adams served in eight successive Congresses where he won a reputation as "Old Man Eloquent." Representative Adams is best remembered there for his protracted fight, ultimately victorious, to eliminate the "gag rule" under which anti-slavery petitions were tabled without discussion. He opposed the annexation of Texas as well as the war with Mexico fearing that each meant the expansion of slavery. Feisty to the end, Congressman Adams's last public act on 21 February 1848, the very day President James K. Polk received the text of the Treaty of Guadalupe Hidalgo, was to stand on the floor of the House with young Abraham Lincoln and a few other diehard opponents of the Mexican War to oppose a resolution tendering thanks and awarding medals to the victorious American generals. A few minutes after voting "No!" Adams suffered a stroke, collapsed, and was carried into the Speaker's office. Two days later he died.

Notes

1. For an excellent brief survey of his career see Maldwyn A. Jones, "John Quincy Adams," *History Today*, 30 (Nov. 1980): 5–8. The standard biography of Adams is the two-volume study by Samuel Flagg Bemis, *John Quincy Adams and the Foundations of American Foreign Policy* (New York, 1949) and *John Quincy Adams and the Union* (New York, 1956). See also the more recent Marie B. Hecht, *John Quincy Adams: A Personal History of an Independent Man* (New York, 1972), Mary W. M. Hargreaves, *The Presidency of John Quincy Adams* (Lawrence, KS, 1985), and Leonard L. Richards, *The Life and Times of Congressman John Quincy Adams* (New York, 1986).

2. Richards, *Life and Times*, 3.

3. Walter Lafeber, ed., *John Quincy Adams and American Continental Empire* (Chicago, 1965), 13; see also in *passim* George Dangerfield, *The Era of Good Feelings* (London, 1953).

4. Samuel Flagg Bemis called this treaty "the greatest diplomatic victory won by any single individual in the history of the United States," Bemis, *Foundations*, 340.

5. Jones, "John Quincy Adams," 6.

6. Hecht, *A Personal History*, 11.

7. *Ibid.*, 19–31, 42–53, 65–69, 73–76, 104, 115.

8. *Ibid.*, 136–137, 144, 148–152, 177–180; William H. Goetzmann, *When the Eagle Screamed: The Romantic Horizon in American Diplomacy, 1800–1860* (New York, 1966), 2–3.

9. Norman E. Saul, *Distant Friends: The United States and Russia, 1763–1867* (Lawrence, KS, 1991), 48–61; Hecht, *A Personal History*, 192–193.

10. Hecht, *A Personal History*, 199–200.

11. Saul, *Distant Friends*, 71–78; Hecht, *A Personal History*, 206–207, 212–217.

12. Quoted in Hecht, *A Personal History*, 228.

13. For a wonderfully written narrative of the negotiations at Ghent, see Fred L. Engelman, *The Peace of Christmas Eve* (New York, 1962); see also Harry L. Coles, *The War of 1812* (Chicago, 1965), 246–255, and Dangerfield, *The Era of Good Feelings*, 64–73, 83–89.

14. Lafeber, *Adams and American Continental Empire*, 22.

15. Goetzmann, *When the Eagle Screamed*, 11–13; Dexter Perkins, "John Quincy Adams" in Samuel Flagg Bemis, ed., *The American Secretaries of State and Their Diplomacy*, (New York, 1928), 4: 86–90; Frederick Merk, *The Oregon Question: Essays in Anglo-American Diplomacy and Politics* (Cambridge, MA, 1967), 30–45.

16. Bemis, *Foundations*, 300–307.

17. James Chace and Caleb Carr, "The Odd Couple Who Won Florida and Half the West," *Smithsonian*, 19 (Apr. 1988): 143–145.

18. William Earl Weeks, "John Quincy Adams's 'Great Gun' and the Rhetoric of American Empire," *Diplomatic History*, 14 (Winter 1990): 27–28; Chace and Carr, "The Odd Couple," 148.

19. Robert V. Remini, *Andrew Jackson and the Course of American Empire, 1767–1821* (New York, 1977), 344–366; Michael Paul Rogin, *Fathers and Children: Andrew Jackson and the Subjugation of the American Indian* (New York, 1975), 193–200.

20. Bemis, *Foundations*, 313–316.

21. Harry Ammon, *James Monroe: The Quest for National Identity* (New York, 1971), 423–424; Remini, *Course of American Empire*, 367–368.

22. The letter to Onís and selections from Adams's diary about the July Cabinet meetings are reprinted in Lafeber, *Adams and American Continental Empire*, 72–77, and Allan Nevins, ed., *The Diary of John Quincy Adams, 1794–1845* (New York, 1951), 199–201.

23. Weeks, " 'Great Gun' and the Rhetoric," 25–42; the standard treatment of the Transcontinental Treaty is Philip C. Brooks, *Diplomacy and the Borderlands: The Adams-Onís Treaty of 1819* (New York, 1970).

24. Robert H. Ferrell, *American Diplomacy* (New York, 1977), 171–183; Bemis, *Foundations*, 317–334; Brooks, *Diplomacy and the Borderlands*, 146–147, 193–196. The text of the treaty is reprinted in Brooks, 205–214.

25. Williams Appleman Williams, *American-Russian Relations, 1781–1947* (New York, 1971 [c. 1952]), 10–12; *Saul, Distant Friends*, 96–98.

26. Hecht, *A Personal History*, 349–353; Williams, *American-Russian Relations*, 12–16; Saul, *Distant Friends*, 96–100.

27. Saul, *Distant Friends*, 99–105; see also two articles by Harold E. Bergquist, Jr., "John Quincy Adams and the Promulgation of the Monroe Doctrine, October–December 1823," *Essex Institute Historical Collections*, 3 (Jan. 1975): 37–52, and "The Perkins-Bemis Interpretation of the Monroe Doctrine Questioned," *SHAFR Newsletter*, 18 (Dec. 1987): 1–12.

28. Reprinted in Edward P Crapol, "John Quincy Adams and the Monroe Doctrine: Some New Evidence," *Pacific Historical Review*, 48 (Aug. 1979): 413–418.

29. Ralph Ketcham, *Presidents Above Party: The First American Presidency, 1789–1829* (Chapel Hill, NC, 1984), 132–133.

30. Dangerfield, *The Era of Good Feelings*, 346–353; Bemis, *The Union*, 60–70; Hecht, *A Personal History*, 425–426; Hargreaves, *The Presidency of John Quincy Adams*, 165–168.

Indians in the Land

Did the Indians have a special, almost noble, affinity with the American environment—or were they despoilers of it? Two historians of the environment explain the profound clash of cultures between Indians and whites that has made each group almost incomprehensible to the other.

A conversation between William Cronon and Richard White

When the historian Richard White wrote his first scholarly article about Indian environmental history in the mid–1970s, he knew he was taking a new approach to an old field, but he did not realize just how new it was. "I sent it to a historical journal," he reports, "and I never realized the U.S. mail could move so fast. It was back in three days. The editor told me it wasn't history."

Times have changed. The history of how American Indians have lived in, used, and altered the environment of North America has emerged as one of the most exciting new fields in historical scholarship. It has changed our understanding not only of American Indians but of the American landscape itself. To learn more about what historians in the field have been discovering, American Heritage asked two of its leading practitioners, Richard White and William Cronon, to meet and talk about their subject.

White, who is thirty-nine, teaches at the University of Utah. While earning his B.A. from the University of California at Santa Cruz in the late 1960s, he became involved in Indian politics. He wrote his doctoral dissertation at the University of Washington on the environmental history of Island County, Washington. That work, which became his first book—*Land Use, Environment, and Social Change*—earned him the Forest History Society's prize for the best book published in 1979-1980. This was followed by *The Roots of Dependency*, an environmental history of three Indian tribes: the Choctaws of the Southeast, the Pawnees of the Great Plains, and the Navajos of the Southwest. In it he showed how each had gradually been forced into economic dependency on the now-dominant white society.

William Cronon, thirty-two, teaches history at Yale University. His first book, *Changes in the Land: Indians, Colonists, and the Ecology of New England*, examined the different ways Indians and colonists had used the New England landscape. It won the Francis Parkman Prize in 1984. Cronon recently became a MacArthur Fellow, and is working on several projects in environmental history and the history of the American West.

This conversation, which was arranged and edited by William Cronon, took place late last year at Richard White's home in Salt lake City.

William Cronon   If historians thought about the environment at all up until a few years ago, they thought of it in terms of an older school of American historians who are often called "environmental determinists." People like Frederick Jackson Turner argued that Europeans came to North America, settled on the frontier, and began to be changed by the environment.

Richard White   In a delayed reaction to Turner, historians in the late 1960s and early 1970s reversed this. They began to emphasize a series of horror stories when they wrote about the environment. The standard metaphor of the time was "the rape of the earth," but what they were really describing was the way Americans moving west cut down the forests, ploughed the land, destroyed the grasslands, harnessed the rivers—how they in effect transformed the whole appearance of the North American landscape.

WC   Since then, I think, we've realized that both positions are true, but incomplete. The real problem is that human beings reshape the earth as they live upon it, but as they reshape it, the new form of the earth has an influence on the way those people can live. The two reshape each other. This is as true of Indians as it is of European settlers.

RW   My first connections with Indians in the environment was very immediate. I became interested because of fishing-rights controversies in the Northwest, in which the Indians' leading opponents included several major environmental organizations. They argued that Indians were destroying the fisheries. What made this odd was that these same groups also held up Indians as sort of primal ecologists. I remember reading a Sierra Club book which claimed that Indians had moved over the face of the land and when they left you couldn't tell they'd ever been there. Actually, this idea demeans Indians. It makes them seem simply like an animal species, and thus deprives them of culture. It also demeans the environment by so simplifying it that all changes come to seem negative—as if somehow the ideal is never to have been here at all. It's a crude view of the environment, and it's a crude view of Indians.

WC   Fundamentally, it's an historical view. It says not only that the land never changed—"wilderness" was always in this condition—but that the people who lived upon it had no history, and existed outside of time. They were "natural."

RW That word *natural* is the key. Many of these concepts of Indians are quite old, and they all picture Indians as people without culture. Depending on your view of human nature, there are two versions. If human beings are inherently evil in a Calvinistic sense, then you see Indians as inherently violent and cruel. They're identified with nature, but it's the nature of the howling wilderness, which is full of Indians. But if you believe in a beneficent nature, and a basically good human nature, then you see Indians as noble savages, people at one with their environment.

WC To understand how Indians really did view and use their environment, we have to move beyond these notions of "noble savages" and "Indians as the original ecologists." We have to look instead at how they actually lived.

RW Well, take the case of fire. Fire transformed environments all over the continent. It was a basic tool used by Indians to reshape landscape, enabling them to clear forests to create grasslands for hunting and fields for planting. Hoe agriculture—as opposed to the plow agriculture of the Europeans—is another.

WC There's also the Indians' use of "wild" animals—animals that were not domesticated, not owned in ways Europeans recognized. Virtually all North American Indians were intimately linked to the animals around them, but they had no cattle or pigs or horses.

RW What's hardest for us to understand, I think, is the Indians' different way of making sense of species and the natural world in general. I'm currently writing about the Indians of the Great Lakes region. Most of them thought of animals as a species of *persons*. Until you grasp that fact, you can't really understand the way they treated animals. This is easy to romanticize—it's easy to turn it into a "my brother the buffalo" sort of thing. But it wasn't. The Indians *killed* animals. They often overhunted animals. But when they overhunted, they did so within the context of a moral universe that both they and the animals inhabited. They conceived of animals as having, not rights—that's the wrong word—but *powers*. To kill an animal was to be involved in a social relationship with the animal. One thing that has impressed me about Indians I've known is their realization that this is a harsh planet, that they survive by the deaths of

other creatures. There's no attempt to gloss over that or romanticize it.

WC There's a kind of debt implied by killing animals.

RW Yes. You incur an obligation. And even more than the obligation is your sense that those animals have somehow surrendered themselves to you.

WC There's a gift relationship implied . . .

RW . . . which is also a *social* relationship. This is where it becomes almost impossible to compare Indian environmentalism and modern white environmentalism. You cannot take an American forester or an American wildlife manager and expect him to think that he has a special social relationship with the species he's working on.

WC Or that he owes the forest some kind of gift in return for the gift of wood he's taking from it.

RW Exactly. And it seems to me hopeless to try to impose that attitude onto Western culture. We distort Indian reality when we say Indians were conservationists—that's not what conservation means. We don't give them full credit for their view, and so we falsify history.

Another thing that made Indians different from modern Euro-Americans was their commitment to producing for *security* rather than for maximum yield. Indians didn't try to maximize the production of any single commodity. Most tried to attain security by diversifying their diet, by following the seasonal cycles: they ate what was most abundant. What always confused Europeans was why Indians didn't simply concentrate on the most productive part of the cycle: agriculture, say. They could have grown more crops and neglected something else. But once you've done that, you lose a certain amount of security.

WC I like to think of Indian communities having a whole series of ecological nets under them. When one net failed, there was always another underneath it. If the corn died, they could always hunt deer or gather wild roots. In hard times—during an extended drought, for instance—those nets became crucial.

All of this was linked to seasonal cycles. For me, one of the best ways of understanding the great diversity of environmental practices among Indian peoples is to think about the different ways they moved across the seasons of the year. Because the seasons of North America differ markedly between, say, the Eastern forests and the Great Plains

and the Southwestern deserts, Indian groups devised quite different ways of life to match different natural cycles.

New England is the region I know best. For Indians there, spring started with hunting groups drawing together to plant their crops after having been relatively dispersed for the winter. While women planted beans, squash, and corn, men hunted the migrating fish and birds. They dispersed for summer hunting and gathering while the crops matured, and then reassembled in the fall. The corn was harvested and great celebrations took place. Then, once the harvest was done and the corn stored in the ground, people broke up their villages and fanned out in small bands for the fall hunt, when deer and other animals were at their fattest. The hunt went on until winter faded and the season of agriculture began again. What they had was agriculture during one part of the year, gathering going on continuously, and hunting concentrated in special seasons. That was typical not just of the Indians of New England but of eastern Indians in general.

To regard Indians as primal ecologists is a crude view.

RW For me the most dramatic example of seasonal changes among Indian peoples would be the horticulturists of the eastern Great Plains. The Pawnees are the example I know best. Depending on when you saw the Pawnees, you might not recognize them as the same people. If you came upon them in the spring or early fall, when they were planting or harvesting crops, you would have found a people living in large, semi-subterranean earth lodges and surrounded by scattered fields of corn and beans and squash. They looked like horticultural people. If you encountered the Pawnees in early summer or late fall, you would have thought you were seeing Plains nomads—because then they followed the buffalo, and their whole economy revolved around the buffalo. They lived in tepees and were very similar, at least in outward appearance, to the Plains nomads who surrounded them.

For the Pawnees, these cycles of hunting and farming were intimately connected. One of my favorite examples is a conversation in the 1870s between the

Pawnee Petalesharo and a Quaker Indian agent who was trying to explain to him why he should no longer hunt buffalo. Suddenly a cultural chasm opens between them, because Petalesharo is trying to explain that the corn will not grow without the buffalo hunt. Without buffalo to sacrifice at the ceremonies, corn will not come up and the Pawnee world will cease. You see them talking, but there's no communication.

WC It's difficult for a modern American hearing this to see Petalesharo's point of view as anything other than alien and wrong. This notion of sacrificing buffalo so corn will grow is fundamental to his view of nature, even though it's utterly different from what *we* mean when we call him a conservationist.

RW And yet, if you want to understand people's actions historically, you have to take Petalesharo seriously.

WC Environmental historians have not only been reconstructing the ways Indians used and thought about the land, they've also been analyzing how those things changed when the Europeans invaded. A key discovery of the last couple of decades had been our radically changed sense of how important European disease was in changing Indian lives.

RW It was appalling. Two worlds that had been largely isolated suddenly came into contact. The Europeans brought with them diseases the Indians had never experienced. The resulting death rates are almost impossible to imagine: 90 to 95 percent in some places.

WC The ancestors of the Indians came to North America from ten to forty thousand years ago. They traveled through an Arctic environment in which many of the diseases common to temperate and tropical climates simply couldn't survive. They came in groups that were biologically too small to sustain those diseases. And they came without the domesticated animals with which we share several of our important illnesses. Those three circumstances meant that Indians shed many of the most common diseases of Europe and Asia. Measles, chicken pox, smallpox, and many of the venereal diseases vanished during migration. For over twenty thousand years, Indians lived without encountering these illnesses, and so lost the antibodies that would ordinarily have protected them.

RW Most historians would now agree that when the Europeans arrived, the Indian population of North America was between ten and twelve million (the old

estimate was about one million). By the early twentieth century it had fallen to less than five hundred thousand. At the same time, Indian populations were also under stress from warfare. Their seasonal cycles were being broken up, and they were inadequately nourished as a result. All these things contributed to the tremendous mortality they suffered.

WC Part of the problem was biological; part of it was cultural. If a disease arrived in mid-summer, it had quite different effects from one that arrived in the middle of the winter, when people's nutrition levels were low and they were more susceptible to disease. A disease that arrived in spring, when crops had to be planted, could disrupt the food supply for the entire year. Nutrition levels would be down for the whole subsequent year, and new diseases would find readier victims as a result.

RW The effects extended well beyond the original epidemic—a whole series of changes occurred. If Indian peoples in fact shaped the North American landscape, this enormous drop in their population changed the way the land looked. For example, as the Indians of the Southeast died in what had once been a densely populated region with a lot of farmland, cleared areas reverted to grassy woodland. Deer and other animal populations increased in response. When whites arrived, they saw the abundance of animals as somehow natural, but it was nothing of the sort.

Disease also dramatically altered relationships among Indian peoples. In the 1780s and 1790s the most powerful and prosperous peoples on the Great Plains margins were the Mandans, the Arikaras, the Hidatsas, the Pawnees, all of whom raised corn as part of their subsistence cycles. Nomadic, nonagricultural groups like the Sioux were small and poor. Smallpox changed all that. Those peoples living in large, populous farming villages were precisely those who suffered the greatest death rates. So the group that had once controlled the region went into decline, while another fairly marginal group rose to historical prominence.

WC That's a perfect example of biological and cultural interaction, of how complex it is. A dense population is more susceptible to disease than a less dense one: that's a biological observation true of any animal species. But which Indian communities are dense and which are not, which ones are living in clustered

settlements and which ones are scattered thinly on the ground—these aren't biological phenomena but *cultural* ones.

RW Perhaps the best example of this is the way different Plains Indians responded to the horse, which, along with disease, actually preceded the arrival of significant numbers of Europeans in the region. The older conception of what happened is that when the horse arrived, it transformed the world. That may have been true for the Sioux, but not for the Pawnees. The Sioux became horse nomads; the Pawnees didn't. They were not willing to give up the security of raising crops. For them, the horse provided an ability to hunt buffalo more efficiently, but they were not about to rely solely on buffalo. If the buffalo hunt failed, and they had neglected their crops, they would be in great trouble. As far as I know, there is no agricultural group, with the exception of the Crows and perhaps the Cheyennes, that *willingly* gave up agriculture to rely solely on the buffalo. The people like the Sioux who became Plains nomads had always been hunters and gatherers, and for them horses represented a *more* secure subsistence, not a less secure one.

WC It's the ecological safety net again. People who practiced agriculture were reluctant to abandon it, because it was one of their strongest nets.

RW And they didn't. When given a choice, even under harsh circumstances, people tried to integrate the horse into their existing economy, not transform themselves.

The horse came to the Sioux at a time when they were in trouble. Their subsistence base had grown precarious: the buffalo and beavers they'd hunted farther east were declining, and the decline of the farming villages from disease meant the Sioux could no longer raid or trade with them for food. The horse was a godsend: buffalo hunting became more efficient, and the buffalo began to replace other food sources. Having adopted the horse, the Sioux moved farther out onto the Plains. By the time they had their famous conflicts with the United States in the 1860s and 1870s, they were the dominant people of the Great Plains. Their way of life was unimaginable without the horse and buffalo.

WC The result was that the Sioux reduced the number of ecological nets that sustained their economy and way of life. And although the bison were present in enormous numbers when the Sioux began to adopt the horse, by the 1860s the bison were disappearing from the Plains; by the early eighties they were virtually gone. That meant the Sioux's main ecological net was gone, and there wasn't much left to replace it.

RW To destroy the buffalo was to destroy the Sioux. Of course, given time, they might have been able to replace the buffalo with cattle and become a pastoral people. That seems well within the realm of historical possibility. But they were never allowed that option.

WC Disease and the horse are obviously important factors in Indian history. But there's a deeper theme underlying these things. All North American Indian peoples eventually found themselves in a relationship of dependency with the dominant Euro-American culture. At some point, in various ways, they ceased to be entirely autonomous peoples, controlling their own resources and their own political and cultural life. Is environmental history fundamental to explaining how this happened?

RW I think it's absolutely crucial. Compare the history of European settlement in North America with what happened in Asia and Africa. Colonialism in Asia and Africa was very important, but it was a passing phase. It has left a strong legacy, but Africa is nonetheless a continent inhabited by Africans, Asia a continent inhabited by Asians. American Indian peoples, on the other hand, are a small minority in North America. Part of what happened was simply the decline in population, but as we've said, that decline was not simple at all. To understand it, we have to understand environmental history.

Many Indians were never militarily conquered.

Many Indians were never militarily conquered. They nonetheless became dependent on whites, partly because their subsistence economy was systematically undercut. Virtually every American Indian community eventually had to face the fact that it could no longer feed or shelter itself without outside aid. A key aspect of this was the arrival of a market economy in which certain resources came to be overexploited. The fur trade is the clearest example of this.

WC No question. The traditional picture of the fur trade is that Europeans arrive, wave a few guns and kettles and blankets in the air, and Indians come rushing forward to trade. What do they have to trade? They have beaver pelts, deerskins, bison robes. As soon as the incentive is present, as soon as those European goods are there to be had, the Indians sweep across the continent, wipe out the furbearing animals, and destroy their own subsistence. That's the classic myth of the fur trade.

RW It simply didn't happen that way. European goods often penetrated Indian communities slowly; Indian technologies held on for a long time. Indians wanted European goods, but for reasons that could be very different from why *we* think they wanted them.

WC One of my favorite examples is the kettle trade. Indians wanted kettles partly because you can put them on a fire and boil water and they won't break. That's nice. But many of those kettles didn't stay kettles for long. They got cut up and turned into arrowheads that were then used in the hunt. Or they got turned into high-status jewelry. Indians valued kettles because they were such an extraordinarily flexible resource.

RW The numbers of kettles that have turned up in Indian graves proves that their value was not simply utilitarian.

WC The basic facts of the fur trade are uncontestable. Europeans sought to acquire Indian furs, food, and land; Indians sought to acquire European textiles, alcohol, guns, and other metal goods. Indians began to hunt greater numbers of furbearing animals, until finally several species, especially the beaver, were eliminated. Those are the two end points of the fur-trade story. But understanding how to get from one to the other is very complicated. Why did Indians engage in the fur trade in the first place? That's the question.

RW We tend to assume that exchange is straightforward, that it's simply giving one thing in return for another. That is not how it appeared to Indian peoples.

WC Think of the different ways goods are exchanged. One is how we usually perceive exchange today: we go into the local supermarket, lay down a dollar, and get a candy bar in return. Many Europeans in the fur trade thought that was what they were doing—giving a gun, or a blanket, or a kettle and receiving a number of furs in return. But for the

Indians the exchange looked very different.

RW To see how Indians perceived this, consider two things we all know, but which we don't ordinarily label as "trade." One is gifts. There's no need to romanticize the giving of gifts. Contemporary Americans exchange gifts at Christmas or at weddings, and when those gifts are exchanged, as anybody who has received one knows, you incur an obligation. You often have relatives who never let you forget the gift they've given you, and what you owe in return. There's no *price* set on the exchange, it's a gift, but the obligation is very real. That's one way Indians saw exchange. To exchange goods that way, the two parties at least had to pretend to be friends.

At the other extreme, if friendship hadn't been established, goods could still change hands, but here the basis of exchange was often simple theft. If you had enemies, you could rob them. So if traders failed to establish some friendship, kinship, or alliance, Indians felt perfectly justified in attacking them and taking their goods. In the fur trade there was a fine line between people who sometimes traded with each other and sometimes stole from each other.

WC To make that more concrete, when the Indian handed a beaver skin to the trader, who gave a gun in return, it wasn't simply two goods that were moving back and forth. There were *symbols* passing between them as well. The trader might not have been aware of all those symbols, but for the Indian the exchange represented a statement about their friendship. The Indian might expect to rely on the trader for military support, and to support him in return. Even promises about marriage, about linking two communities together, might be expressed as goods passed from hand to hand. It was almost as if a language was being spoken when goods were exchanged. It took a long time for the two sides to realize they weren't speaking the same language.

RW Right. But for Indians the basic meanings of exchange were clear. You gave generously to friends; you stole from enemies. Indians also recognized that not everybody could be classified simply as a friend or an enemy, and this middle ground is where trade took place.

But even in that middle ground, trade always began with an exchange of gifts. And to fail to be generous in your gifts, to push too hard on the price—Indians read that as hostility. When Europeans tried to explain the concept of a "market" to Indians, it bewildered them. The notion that demand for furs in London could affect how many blankets they would receive for a beaver skin in Canada was quite alien to them. How on earth could events taking place an ocean away have anything to do with the relationship between two people standing right here who were supposed to act as friends and brothers toward each other?

WC So one thing Indian peoples had trouble comprehending at certain stages in this dialogue was the concept of *price:* the price of a good fluctuating because of its abundance in the market. Indian notions were much closer to the medieval "just price." This much gunpowder is always worth this many beaver skins. If somebody tells me they want twice as many skins for the same gunpowder I bought last year at half the price, suddenly they're being treacherous. They're beginning to act as an enemy.

RW Or in the words Algonquians often used, "This must mean my father doesn't love me any more." To Europeans that kind of language seems ludicrous. What in the world does love have to do with giving a beaver skin for gunpowder? But for Indians it's absolutely critical.

The concepts of price and market bewildered Indians.

Of course, exchange became more commercial with time. Early in the fur trade, Indians had received European goods as gifts, because they were allies against other Indians or other Europeans. But increasingly they found that the only way to receive those goods was through direct economic exchange. Gift giving became less important, and trading goods for set prices became more important. As part of these commercial dealings, traders often advanced loans to Indians before they actually had furs to trade. By that mechanism, gifts were transformed into debts. Debts could in turn be used to coerce greater and greater hunting from Indians.

WC As exchange became more commercial, the Indians' relationship to animals became more commercial as well. Hunting increased with the rise in trade, and animal populations declined in re-

sponse. First the beaver, then the deer, then the bison disappeared from large stretches of North America. As that happened, Indians found themselves in the peculiar position of relying more and more on European goods but no longer having the furs they needed to acquire them. Worse, they could no longer even *make* those same goods as they once had, in the form of skin garments, wild meat, and so on. That's the trap they fell into.

RW And that becomes dependency. That's what Thomas Jefferson correctly and cynically realized when he argued that the best way for the United States to acquire Indian lands was to encourage trade and have government storehouses assume Indian debts. Indians would have no choice but to cede their lands to pay their debts, and they couldn't even renounce those debts because they now needed the resources the United States offered them in order to survive. Not all tribes became involved in this, but most who relied on the fur trade eventually did.

Of course, the effects go both ways. As whites eliminated Indians and Indian control, they were also, without realizing it, eliminating the forces that had shaped the landscape itself. The things they took as natural—why there were trees, why there weren't trees, the species of plants that grew there—were really the results of Indian practices. As whites changed the practices, those things vanished. Trees began to reinvade the grassland, and forests that had once been open became closed.

WC Once the wild animals that had been part of the Indians' spiritual and ecological universe began to disappear, Europeans acquired the land and began to transform it to match their assumptions about what a "civilized" landscape should look like. With native animals disappearing, other animals could be brought in to use the same food supply that the deer, the moose, and the bison had previously used. And so the cow, the horse, the pig—the animals so central to European notions of what an animal universe looks like—began to move across the continent like a kind of animal frontier. In many instances the Indians turned to these domesticated European species to replace their own decreasing food supply and so adopted a more pastoral way of life. As they lost their lands, they were then stuck with the problem of feeding their animals as well as themselves.

RW The Navajos are a good example of this. We tend to forget that Indians don't simply vanish when we enter the twentieth century. The Navajos are perhaps the group who maintained control over their own lands for the longest time, but their control was increasingly subject to outside pressures. They very early adopted European sheep, which became more and more important to their economy, both because wild foods were eliminated and because the government strongly encouraged the Navajos to raise more sheep. They built up prosperous herds but were gradually forced to confine them to the reservation instead of the wider regions they had grazed before.

The result was a crisis on the Navajo reservation. The land began to erode. By the 1920s and 1930s the Navajos had far more sheep than could be sustained during dry years. And here's where one of the more interesting confrontations between Indians and conservationists took place. The government sought to reduce Navajo stock, but its own motives were mixed. There was a genuine fear for the Navajos, but the main concern had to do with Boulder Dam. Conservationists feared Lake Mead was going to silt up, and that the economic development of the Southwest would be badly inhibited.

What they didn't understand were the causes of erosion. They blamed it all on Navajo sheep, but it now appears that there was a natural gullying cycle going on in the Southwest. Anybody familiar with the Southwest knows that its terrain is shaped by more than sheep and horses, no matter how badly it is overgrazed. So the result of government conservation policy for the Navajos was deeply ironic. Having adjusted to the European presence, having prospered with their sheep, they found their herds being undercut by the government for the good of the larger economy. It's a classic case of Indians—as the poorest and least powerful people in a region—forced to bear the brunt of economic-development costs. So the Navajo economy was again transformed. As the Navajos became poorer and poorer, they grew more willing to lease out oil and allow strip mining on the reservation. They found themselves in the familiar situation of being forced to agree to practices that were harmful, even in their view, to the land. They had to do it in order to survive, but they were then attacked by white conservationists for abandoning their own values.

3. NATIONAL CONSOLIDATION AND EXPANSION

WC A real no-win situation.

RW There are lessons in all this. We can't copy Indian ways of understanding nature, we're too different. But studying them throws our own assumptions into starker relief and suggests shortcomings in our relationships with nature that could cost us dearly in the long run.

WC I think environmental history may be capable of transforming our perspective, not just on Indian history, but on all human history. The great arrogance of Western civilization in the industrial and postindustrial eras has been to imagine human beings existing somehow apart from the earth. Often the history of the industrial era has been written as if technology has liberated human beings so that the earth has become increasingly irrelevant to modern civilization—when in fact all history is a long-standing dialogue between human beings and the earth. It's as if people are constantly speaking to the earth, and the earth is speaking to them. That's a way of putting it that Indians would be far more capable of understanding than most modern Americans. But this dialogue, this conversation between earth and the inhabitants of earth, is fundamental to environmental history. With it we can try to draw together all these pieces—human population changes, cultural changes, economic changes, environmental changes—into a complicated but unified history of humanity upon the earth. That, in rather ambitious terms, is what environmental historians are seeking to do.

The Lives of Slave Women

Deborah Gray White

Deborah Gray White is associate professor of history and Africana studies at Rutgers University, New Brunswick, New Jersey. This chapter is adapted from her book, Ar'nt I a Woman? Female Slaves in the Plantation South, *published in 1985 by W. W. Norton.*

Slave women have often been characterized as self-reliant and self-sufficient, yet not every black woman was a Sojourner Truth or a Harriet Tubman. Strength had to be cultivated. It came no more naturally to them than to anyone else, slave or free, male or female, black or white. If slave women seemed exceptionally strong it was partly because they often functioned in groups and derived strength from their numbers.

Much of the work slaves did and the regimen they followed served to stratify slave society along sex lines. Consequently slave women had ample opportunity to develop a consciousness grounded in their identity as females. While close contact sometimes gave rise to strife, adult female cooperation and dependence of women on each other was a fact of female slave life. The self-reliance and self-sufficiency of slave women, therefore, must be viewed in the context not only of what the individual slave woman did for herself, but what slave women as a group were able to do for each other.

It is easy to overlook the separate world of female slaves because from colonial times through the Civil War black women often worked with black men at tasks considered by Europeans to be either too difficult or inappropriate for females. All women worked hard, but when white women consistently performed field labor it was considered temporary, irregular, or extraordinary, putting them on a par with slaves. Actress Fredericka Bremer, visiting the ante-bellum South,

noted that usually only men and black women did field work; commenting on what another woman traveler sarcastically claimed to be a noble admission of female equality, Bremer observed that "black [women] are not considered to belong to the weaker sex."[1]

Bremer's comment reflects what former slaves and fugitive male slaves regarded as the defeminization of black women. Bonded women cut down trees to clear lands for cultivation. They hauled logs in leather straps attached to their shoulders. They plowed using mule and ox teams, and hoed, sometimes with the heaviest implements available. They dug ditches, spread manure fertilizer, and piled coarse fodder with their bare hands. They built and cleaned Southern roads, helped construct Southern railroads, and, of course, they picked cotton. In short, what fugitive slave Williamson Pease said regretfully of slave women was borne out in fact: "Women who do outdoor work are used as bad as men."[2] Almost a century later Green Wilbanks spoke less remorsefully than Pease in his remembrances of his Grandma Rose, where he implied that the work had a kind of neutering effect. Grandma Rose, he said, was a woman who could do any kind of job a man could do, a woman who "was some worker, a regular man-woman."[3]

It is hardly likely, though, that slave women, especially those on large plantations with sizable female populations, lost their female identity. Harvesting season on staple crop plantations may have found men and women gathering the crop in sex-integrated gangs, but at other times women often worked in exclusively or predominantly female gangs.[4] Thus women stayed in each other's company for most of the day. This meant that those they ate meals with, sang work songs with, and commiserated with during the work day were people who by virtue of their sex had the same kind of

responsibilities and problems. As a result, slave women appeared to have developed their own female culture, a way of doing things and a way of assigning value that flowed from their perspective as slave women on Southern plantations. Rather than being squelched, their sense of womanhood was probably enhanced and their bonds to each other strengthened.

Since slaveowners and managers seemingly took little note of the slave woman's lesser physical strength, one wonders why they separated men and women at all. One answer appears to be that gender provided a natural and easy way to divide the labor force. Also probable is that despite their limited sensitivity regarding female slave labor, and the double standard they used when evaluating the uses of white and black female labor, slaveowners did, using standards only they could explain, reluctantly acquiesce to female physiology. For instance, depending on their stage of pregnancy, pregnant women were considered half or quarter hands. Healthy nonpregnant women were considered three-quarter hands. Three-quarter hands were not necessarily exempt from some of the herculean tasks performed by men who were full hands, but usually, when labor was being parceled out and barring a shortage of male hands to do the very heavy work or a rush to get that work completed, men did the more physically demanding work. A case in point was the most common differentiation where men plowed and women hoed.[5]

Like much of the field labor, nonfield labor was structured to promote cooperation among women. In the Sea Islands, slave women sorted cotton lint according to color and fineness and removed cotton seeds crushed by the gin into the cotton and lint. Fence building often found men splitting rails in one area and women doing the actual construction in another. Men usually shelled corn, threshed peas, cut potatoes for planting, and platted

From *Southern Exposure*, November/December 1984, pp. 32-39. Adapted from *Ar'n't I a Woman? Female Slaves in the Plantation South* by Deborah Gray White. © 1984 by Deborah Gray White. Reprinted by permission of W. W. Norton & Company, Inc.

shucks. Grinding corn into meal or hominy was women's work. So too were spinning, weaving, sewing, and washing.[6] On Captain Kinsler's South Carolina plantation, as on countless others, "old women and women bearin' chillun not yet born, did cardin' wid handcards." Some would spin, others would weave, but all would eventually learn from some skilled woman "how to make clothes for the family . . . knit coarse socks and stockins."[7]

"When the work in the fields was finished women were required to come home and spin one cut a night," reported a Georgian. "Those who were not successful in completing this work were punished the next morning."[8] Women had to work in the evenings partly because slaveowners bought them few ready-made clothes. On one South Carolina plantation each male slave received annually two cotton shirts, three pairs of pants, and one jacket. Slave women, on the other hand, received six yards of woolen cloth, six yards of cotton drilling, and six yards of cotton shirting a year, along with two needles and a dozen buttons.[9]

A great deal of both field labor and nonfield labor was structured to promote cooperation among slave women.

Perhaps a saving grace to this "double duty" was that women got a chance to interact with each other. On a Sedalia County, Missouri plantation, women looked forward to Saturday afternoon washing because, as Mary Frances Webb explained, they "would get to talk and spend the day together."[10] Quiltings, referred to by former slaves as female "frolics" and "parties," were especially convivial. Anna Peek recalled that when slaves were allowed to relax, they gathered around a pine wood fire in Aunt Anna's cabin to tell stories. At that time "the old women with pipes in their mouths would sit and gossip for hours."[11] Missourian Alice Sewell noted that sometimes women would slip away and hold their own prayer meetings. They cemented their bonds to each other at the end of every meeting when they walked around shaking hands and singing, "fare you well my sisters, I am going home."[12]

The organization of female slave work and social activities tended not only to separate women and men, but also to generate female cooperation and interdependence. Slave women and their children could depend on midwives and "doctor women" to treat a variety of ailments. Menstrual cramps, for example, were sometimes treated with a tea made from the bark of the gum tree. Midwives and "doctor women" administered various other herb teas to ease the pains of many ailing slaves. Any number of broths—made from the leaves and barks of trees, from the branches and twigs of bushes, from turpentine, catnip, or tobacco—were used to treat whooping cough, diarrhea, toothaches, colds, fevers, headaches, and backaches.[13] According to a Georgia ex-slave, "One had to be mighty sick to have the services of a doctor." On his master's plantation "old women were . . . responsible for the care of the sick."[14] This was also the case on Rebecca Hooks's former Florida residence. "The doctor," she noted, "was not nearly as popular as the 'granny' or midwife, who brewed medicines for every ailment."[15]

Female cooperation in the realm of medical care helped foster bonding that led to collaboration in the area of resistance to abuses by slaveholders. Frances Kemble could attest to the concerted efforts of the black women on her husband's Sea Island plantations. More than once she was visited by groups of women imploring her to persuade her husband to extend the lying-in period for childbearing women. On one occasion the women had apparently prepared beforehand the approach they would take with the foreign-born and sympathetic Kemble, for their chosen spokeswoman took care to play on Kemble's own maternal sentiments, and pointedly argued that slave women deserved at least some of the care and tenderness that Kemble's own pregnancy had elicited.[16]

Usually, however, slave women could not be so outspoken about their needs, and covert cooperative resistance prevailed. Slaveowners suspected that midwives conspired with their female patients to bring about abortions and infanticides, and on Charles Colcock Jones's Georgia plantation, for example, this seems in fact to have been the case. A woman named Lucy gave birth in secret and then denied that she had ever been pregnant. Although the midwife attended her, she too claimed not to have delivered a child,

as did Lucy's mother. Jones had a physician examine Lucy, and the doctor confirmed what Jones had suspected, that Lucy had indeed given birth. Twelve days later the decomposing body of a full-term infant was found, and Lucy, her mother, and the midwife were all hauled off to court. Another woman, a nurse, managed to avoid prosecution but not suspicion. Whether Lucy was guilty of murder, and whether the others were accessories, will never be known because the court could not shatter their collective defense that the child had been stillborn.[17]

The inability to penetrate the private world of female slaves is probably what kept many abortions and infanticides from becoming known to slaveowners. The secrets kept by a midwife named Mollie became too much for her to bear. When she accepted Christianity these were the first things for which she asked forgiveness. She recalled, "I was carried to the gates of hell and the devil pulled out a book showing me the things which I had committed and that they were all true. My life as a midwife was shown to me and I have certainly felt sorry for all the things I did, after I was converted."[18]

Health care is not the only example of how the organization of slave work and slave responsibilities led to female cooperation and bonding; slave women also depended on each other for child-care. Sometimes, especially on small farms or new plantations where there was no extra woman to superintend children, bondswomen took their offspring to the field with them and attended to them during pre-scheduled breaks. Usually, however, infants and older children were left in the charge of an elderly female or females. Josephine Bristow, for example, spent more time with Mary Novlin, the nursery keeper on Ferdinand Gibson's South Carolina plantation, than she spent with her mother and father, who came in from the fields after she was asleep: "De old lady, she looked after every blessed thing for us all day long en cooked for us right along wid de mindin'."[19] In their complementary role as nurses, they ministered to the hurts and illnesses of infants and children.[20] It was not at all uncommon for the children's weekly rations to be given to the "grannies" as opposed to the children's parents.[21] Neither the slaveowner nor slave society expected the biological mother of a child to fulfill all of her child's needs. Given the circumstances, the responsibilities of motherhood had to be shared, and this required close female cooperation.

Cooperation in this sphere helped slave women overcome one of the most difficult of predicaments—who would provide maternal care for a child whose mother had died or been sold away? Fathers sometimes served as both mother and father, but when slaves, as opposed to the master, determined maternal care, it was usually a woman who became a child's surrogate mother. Usually that woman was an aunt or a sister, but in the absence of female relatives, a non-kin woman assumed the responsibility.[22] In the case of Georgian Mollie Malone, for example, the nursery superintendent became the child's substitute mother.[23] When Julia Malone's mother was killed by another Texas slave, little Julia was raised by the woman with whom her mother had shared a cabin.[24] On Southern plantations the female community made sure that no child was truly motherless.

Because black women on a plantation spent so much time together, they inevitably developed some appreciation of each other's skills and talents. This intimacy enabled them to establish the criteria by which to rank and order themselves. The existence of certain "female jobs" that carried prestige created a yardstick by which bondswomen could measure each other's achievements. Some of these jobs allowed for growth and self-satisfaction, fringe benefits that were usually out of reach for the field laborer. A seamstress, for example, had unusual opportunities for self-expression and creativity. On very large plantations the seamstress usually did no field work, and a particularly good seamstress, or "mantua-maker," might be hired out to others and even allowed to keep a portion of the money she earned.[25] For obvious reasons cooks, midwives, and female folk doctors also commanded the respect of their peers. Midwives in particular often were able to travel to other plantations to practice their art. This gave them an enviable mobility and also enabled them to carry messages from one plantation to the next.

Apart from the seamstresses, cooks, and midwives, a few women were distinguished as work gang-leaders. On most farms and plantations where there were overseers, managers, foremen, and drivers, these positions were held by men, either black or white. Occasionally, however, a woman was given a measure of authority over slave work, or a particular aspect of it. For instance Louis Hughes noted that each plantation he saw had a "forewoman who . . . had charge of the female slaves and also the boys and girls from twelve to sixteen years of age, and all the old people that were feeble."[26] Similarly, a Mississippi slave remembered that on his master's Osceola plantation there was a "colored woman as foreman."[27]

Clearly, a pecking order existed among bondswomen—one which they themselves helped to create. Because of age, occupation, association with the master class, or personal achievements, certain women were recognized by other women—and also by men—as important people, even as leaders. Laura Towne met an aged woman who commanded such a degree of respect that other slaves bowed to her and lowered their voices in her presence. The old woman, Maum Katie, was according to Towne a "spiritual mother" and a woman of "tremendous influence over her spiritual children."[28]

> *A slaveowner lamented that Big Lucy, one of his oldest slaves, had more control over his female workers than he did.*

Sometimes two or three factors combined to distinguish a particular woman. Aunt Charlotte was the aged cook in John M. Booth's Georgia household. When Aunt Charlotte spoke, said Booth, "other colored people hastened to obey her."[29] Frederick Douglass's grandmother wielded influence because of her age and the skills she possessed. She made the best fishnets in Tuckahoe, Maryland, and she knew better than anyone else how to preserve sweet potato seedlings and how to plant them successfully. She enjoyed what Douglass called "high reputation," and accordingly "she was remembered by others."[30] In another example, when Elizabeth Botume went to the Sea Islands after the Civil War, she employed as a house servant a young woman named Amy who performed her tasks slowly and sullenly, until an older woman named Aunt Mary arrived from Beaufort. During slavery Amy and Aunt Mary had both worked in the house but Amy had learned to listen and obey Aunt Mary. After Aunt Mary arrived the once obstreperous Amy became "quiet, orderly, helpful and painstaking."[31]

The leadership of some women had a disruptive effect on plantation operations. Bennet H. Barrow repeatedly lamented the fact that Big Lucy, one of his oldest slaves, had more control over his female workers than he did: "Anica, Center, Cook Jane, the better you treat them the worse they are. Big Lucy the Leader corrupts every young negro in her power."[32] A self-proclaimed prophetess named Sinda was responsible for a cessation of all slave work for a considerable period on Butler Island in Georgia. According to a notation made by Frances Kemble in 1839, Sinda's prediction that the world would come to an end on a certain day caused the slaves to lay down their hoes and plows in the belief that their final emancipation was imminent. So sure were Sinda's fellow slaves of her prediction that even the lash failed to get them into the fields. When the appointed day of judgment passed uneventfully Sinda was whipped mercilessly. Yet, for a time, she had commanded more authority than either master or overseer.[33]

Bonded women did not have to go to such lengths in order to make a difference in each other's lives. The supportive atmosphere of the female community was considerable buffer against the depersonalizing regimen of plantation work and the general dehumanizing nature of slavery. When we consider that women were much more strictly confined to the plantation than men, that many women had husbands who visited only once or twice a week, and that slave women outlived slave men by an average of two years, we realize just how important the female community was to its members.

If we define a stable relationship as one of long duration, then it was probably easier for slave women to sustain stable emotional relationships with other bondswomen than with bondsmen. This is not to say that male-female relationships were unfulfilling or of no consequence. But they were generally fraught with more uncertainty about the future than female-to-female relationships, especially those existing between female blood kin. In her study of ex-slave interviews, Martha Goodson found that of all the relationships slaveowners disrupted, through either sale or dispersal, they were least likely to separate mothers and daughters.[34] Cody found that when South Carolina cotton planter Peter Gaillard divided his estate among his eight children, slave women in their twenties and thirties were twice as likely to have a sister with them, and women over 40 were four times more likely to have sisters with them than brothers. Similarly, daughters were less likely than sons to be separated from their mother. Over 60 percent of women aged 20 to 24 remained with their mothers when the estate was divided, as did 90 percent of those aged 25 to 29.[35] A slave song reflected the bonds between female siblings by indicating who took responsibility for the motherless female slave child. Interestingly enough, the one designated was neither the father nor the brother:

A motherless chile see a hard time.
  Oh Lord, help her on de road.
Er sister will do de bes' she kin,
  Dis is a hard world, Lord, fer a motherless chile.[36]

If female blood ties did indeed promote the most enduring relationships among slaves, then we should probably assume that like occupation, age, and personal achievement these relationships helped structure the female slave community. This assumption should not, however, obscure the fact that in friendships and dependency relationships women often treated non-relatives as if a consanguineous tie existed. This is why older women were called Aunt and Granny, and why unrelated women sometimes called each other Sister.[37]

While the focus here has been on those aspects of the bondswoman's life that fostered female bonding, female-to-female conflict was not uncommon. It was impossible for harmony always to prevail among women who saw so much of each other and who knew so much about one another. Lifelong friendships were founded in the hoe gangs and sewing groups, but the constant jockeying for occupational and social status created an atmosphere in which jealousies and antipathies smoldered. From Jesse Belflowers, the overseer of the Allston rice plantation in South Carolina, Adele Petigru Allston heard that "mostly mongst the Women" there was a "goodeal of quarling and disputing and telling lies."[38] The terms of a widely circulated overseer's contract advised rigorous

punishment for "fighting, particularly amongst the women."[39] Some overseers followed this advice. According to Georgian Isaac Green, "Sometimes de women uster git whuppin's for fightin'."[40]

Occasionally, violence between women could and did get very ugly. Molly, the cook in James Chesnut's household, once took a red hot poker and attacked the woman to whom her husband had given one of her calico dresses.[41] Similarly, when she was a young woman in Arkansas, Lucretia Alexander came to blows with another woman over a pair of stockings that the master had given Lucretia.[42] In another incident on a Louisiana cotton plantation, the day's cotton chopping was interrupted when a feisty field worker named Betty lost her temper in the midst of a dispute with a fellow slave named Molly and struck her in the face with a hoe.[43]

The presence of conflict within interpersonal relationships between female slaves should not detract from the more important cooperation and dependence that prevailed among them. Conflict occurred *because* women were in close daily contact with each other and because the penalties for venting anger on other women were not as severe as those for striking out at men, either black or white. It is not difficult to understand how dependency relationships could become parasitical, how sewing and washing sessions could become "hanging courts," how one party could use knowledge gained in an intimate conversation against another.

Just how sisterhood could co-exist with discord is illustrated by the experience of some black women of the South Carolina and Georgia Sea Islands between 1862 and 1865. On November 7, 1861, Commodore S. F. DuPont sailed into Port Royal Sound, quickly defeated the Confederates, and put Union troops ashore to occupy the islands. Almost before DuPont's guns ceased firing, the entire white population left the islands for the mainland. A few house servants were taken with the fleeing whites but most of the slaves remained on the islands. The following year they and the occupying army were joined by a host of government agents and Northern missionaries. Several interest groups were gathered in the islands and each had priorities. As Treasury agents concerned themselves with the cotton, and army officers recruited and drafted black soldiers, and missionaries went about "pre-

paring" slaves for freedom, the black Sea Islanders' world was turned upside down. This was true for young and middle-aged men who served in the Union army, but also for the women who had to manage their families and do most of the planting and harvesting in the absence of the men.[44]

During the three years of upheaval, black female life conformed in many ways to that outlined here. Missionaries' comments indicate that certain women were perceived as leaders by their peers. Harriet Ware, for instance, identified a woman from Fripp Point on St. Helena Island named Old Peggy as "the leader." This woman was important because she, along with another woman named Binah, oversaw church membership. Ware's housekeeper Flora told her, "Old Peggy and Binah were the two whom all that came into the Church had to come through, and the Church supports them."[45]

On the Coffin's Point Plantation on St. Helena Island, a woman named Grace served her fellow women at least twice by acting as spokeswoman in disputes over wages paid for cotton production. On one occasion the women of the plantation complained to Mr. Philbrick, one of the plantation superintendents, that their wages were not high enough to permit them to purchase cloth at the local store. They were also upset because the molasses they bought from one of the other plantation superintendents was watered down. As Grace spoke in their behalf, the women shouted words of approval. At least part of the reason for Grace's ascendancy stemmed from the fact that she was among the older women of the island. She was also a strong and diligent worker who was able despite her advanced age to plant, hoe, and harvest cotton along with the younger women.[46]

Ample evidence exists of dependency relationships and cooperation among Sea Island women throughout the war years. In slavery sick and "lying-in" women relied on their peers to help them, and the missionaries found this to be the case on the islands during the Union occupation as well. For instance, Philbrick observed that it was quite common for the blacks to hire each other to hoe their tasks when sickness or other inconveniences kept an individual from it. In 1862 some of the Coffin's Point men were recruited by government agents to pick cotton elsewhere in the Sea Islands. This left many of the women at Coffin's Point completely responsible for hoeing the land allotted to each. Women who were sick or pregnant stood to lose their family's allotment since neglected land was reassigned to others. However, the women saw to it, according to Philbrick, that "the tasks of the lying-in women [were] taken care of by sisters or other friends in the absence of their husbands." No doubt these "other friends" were women, since in the same letter Philbrick noted that the only men left on the plantation were those too old to work in the cotton.[47]

Another missionary, Elizabeth Hyde Botume, related similar episodes of female cooperation. Regardless of the circumstances surrounding a pregnancy, it was common for the women of Port Royal to care for, and keep company with, expectant and convalescing mothers. Several times Botume was approached by a spokeswoman seeking provisions for these mothers. Sometimes she gave them reluctantly because many of the women were not married. Usually, however, she was so impressed by the support that the pregnant women received from their peers that she suspended judgment and sent clothes and groceries for the mothers and infants. On one occasion she was approached by several women who sought aid for a woman named Cumber. The women were so willing to assist one of their own that Botume remarked abashedly: " . . . their readiness to help the poor erring girl made me ashamed."[48] These were not the only instances of cooperation among the black women. Some moved in with each other and shared domestic duties; others looked after the sick together.[49] With so many of the men away, women found ways of surviving together and cooperating. Predictably, however, along with the "togetherness" went conflict.

Many situations held possibilities for discord. Charles P. Ware, a missionary from Boston, wrote that the work in the crops would go more smoothly if only he could get the women to stop fighting. At least some of the fights were caused by disputes over the distribution of the former mistress's wardrobe. According to Ware, when a woman said, "I free, I as much right to ole missus' things as you," a fight was sure to erupt.[50] Harriet Ware witnessed a fight in which the women "fired shells and tore each other's clothes in a most disgraceful way." The cause of the fight was unknown to her but she was sure it was the "tongues of the women." Jealousy, she noted, ran rampant among the women, and to her mind there was "much foundation for it."[51]

The experiences of the Sea Islands women in the early 1860s comprised a special episode in American history, but their behavior conformed to patterns that had been set previously by bonded women on large plantations. Historians have shown that the community of the quarters, the slave family, and slave religion shielded the slave from absolute dependence on the master and that parents, siblings, friends, and relatives served in different capacities as buffers against the internalization of degrading and dependent roles. The female slave network served as a similar buffer for black women, but it also had a larger significance. Treated by Southern whites as if they were anything but self-respecting women, many bonded females helped one another to forge their own independent definitions of womanhood, their own notions about what women should be and how they should act.

NOTES

1. Fredericka Bremer, *Homes of the New World*, 2 vols. (New York, 1853), 2: 519; Frances Anne Kemble, *Journal of a Residence on a Georgian Plantation*, ed. John A. Scott (New York, 1961 [1863]), p. 66. See also: Harriet Martineau, *Society in America*, 3 vols. (London, 1837), 2: 243, 311-12.

2. Benjamin Drew, *The Refugees: A North Side View of Slavery*, in *Four Fugitive Slave Narratives* (Boston, 1969), p. 92.

3. George Rawick, ed., *The American Slave, A complete Autobiography*, 19 vols. (Westport, CT, 1972), Ga., vol. 13, pt. 4: 139.

4. Frederick Olmsted, *A Journey in the Seaboard Slave States* (New York, 1856), pp. 430-32; Olmsted, *The Cotton Kingdom*, ed. David Freeman Hawke (New York, 1971), p. 176; William Howard Russell, *My Diary North and South (Canada, Its Defenses, Condition and Resources)*, 3 vols. (London, 1865), 1: 379-80; Solomon Northup, *Twelve Years a Slave, Narrative of Solomon Northup* in Gilbert Osofsky, ed., *Puttin' on Ole Massa* (New York, 1969), pp. 308-09; Rawick, *American Slave*, Ark., vol. 10, pt. 5: 54; Ala., vol. 6: 46, 336; Newstead Plantation Diary 1856-58, entry Wednesday, May 6, 1857, Southern Historical Collection (SHC), University Of North Carolina at Chapel Hill; Adwon Adams Davis, *Plantation Life in the Florida Parishes of Louisiana 1836-1846 as Reflected in the Diary of Bennet H. Barrow* (New York, 1943), p. 127; Frederick Olmsted, *A Journey in the Back Country* (New York, 1907), p. 152; *Plantation Manual*, SHC, p. 4; Eugene Genovese, *The Political Economy of Slavery: Studies in the Economy and Society of the Slave South* (New York, 1961), p. 133; Stuart Bruchey, ed., *Cotton and the Growth of the American Economy: 1790-1860* (New York, 1967), pp. 176-80.

5. See note 4.

6. J. A. Turner, ed., *The Cotton Planters Manual* (New York, 1865), pp. 97-98; Guion B. Johnson, *A Social History of the Sea Islands* (Chapel Hill, NC, 1930), pp. 28-30; Jenkins Mikell, *Rumbling of the Chariot Wheels* (Columbia, SC, 1923), pp. 19-20; Bruchey, *Cotton and the Growth of the American Economy*, pp. 176-80.

7. Rawick, *American Slave*, S.C., vol. 2, pt. 2: 114.

8. Ibid., Ga., vol. 13, p. 3: 186.

9. *Plantation Manual*, SHC, p. 1.

10. Rawick, *American Slave*, Ok., vol. 7: 315.

11. George P. Rawick, Jan Hillegas, and Ken Lawrence, ed., *The American Slave: A Composite Autobiography, Supplement, Series 1*, 12 vols. (Westport, CT, 1978), Ga., Supp. 1, vol. 4: 479.

12. Rawick, *American Slave*, Mo., vol. 11: 307.

13. For examples of cures see: Ibid., Ark., vol. 10, pt. 5: 21, 125; Ala., vol. 6: 256, 318; Ga., vol. 13, pt. 3: 106.

14. Ibid., Ga., vol. 12, pt. 1: 303.

15. Ibid., Fla, vol. 17: 175; see also: Rawick et al., *American Slave, Supplement*, Miss. Supp. 1, vol. 6: 317; Ga. Supp. 1, vol. 4: 444; John Spencer Bassett, *The Southern Plantation Overseer, as Revealed in His Letters* (Northampton, MA, 1923), pp. 28, 31.

16. Kemble, *Journal of a Residence on a Georgian Plantation*, p. 222.

17. Robert Manson Myers, ed., *The Children of Pride: A True Story of Georgia and the Civil War* (New Haven, CT, 1972), pp. 528, 532, 542, 544, 546.

18. Charles S. Johnson, ed., *God Struck Me Dead: Religious Conversion Experiences and Autobiographies of Negro Ex-Slaves* in Rawick, *American Slave*, vol. 19: 74.

19. Rawick, *American Slave*, S.C., vol. 2, pt. 1: 99.

20. Ibid., Ga., vol. 12, pt. 2: 112; S.C., vol. 2, pt. 2: 55; Fla., vol. 17: 174; see also Olmsted, *Back Country*, p. 76.

21. See, for instance, *Plantation Manual*, SHC, p. 1.

22. Rawick, *American Slave*, Ala., vol. 6: 73.

23. Rawick et al., *American Slave, Supplement*, Ga. Supp. 1, vol. 4, pt. 3: 103.

24. Rawick, *American Slave*, Tex., vol. 5, pt. 3: 103.

25. Hughes, *Thirty Years a Slave*, p. 39; Rawick, *American Slave*, Fla., vol. 17: 158; S.C., vol. 2, pt. 1: 114; White Hill Plantation Books, SHC, p. 13.

26. Hughes, *Thirty Years a Slave*, p. 22.

27. Ophelia Settle Egypt, J. Masuoha, and Charles S. Johnson, eds., *Unwritten History of Slavery: Autobiographical Accounts of Negro Ex-Slaves* (Washington, 1968 [1945]), p. 41.

28. Laura M. Towne, *Letters and Diary of Laura M. Towne Written from the Sea Islands of South Carolina 1862-1884*, ed. Rupert Sargent Holland (New York, 1969 [1912]), pp. 144-45. See also: Kemble, *Journal of a Residence on a Georgian Plantation*, p. 55.

29. Rawick, *American Slave*, Ga. vol. 13, pt. 3: 190.

30. Frederick Douglass, *My Bondage and My Freedom* (New York, 1968 [1855]), p. 36.

31. Elizabeth Hyde Botume, *First Days Amongst the Contrabands* (Boston, 1893), p. 132.

32. Davis, *Plantation Life in the Florida Parishes*, p. 191. See also pp. 168, 173.

33. Kemble, *Journal of a Residence on a Georgian Plantation*, pp. 118–19.

34. Martha Graham Goodson, "An Introductory Essay and Subject Index to Selected Interviews from the Slave Narrative Collection," (Ph.D. diss., Union Graduate School, 1977), p. 33.

35. Cheryll Ann Cody, "Naming, Kinship, and Estate Dispersal: Notes on Slave Family Life on a South Carolina Plantation, 1786 to 1833," *William and Mary Quarterly* 39 (1982): 207–09.

36. Rawick, *American Slave*, Ala., vol. 7:73.

37. Herbert G. Gutman, *The Black Family in Slavery and Freedom, 1750–1925* (New York, 1976), pp. 216–22.

38. J. H. Easterby, ed., *The South Carolina Rice Plantations as Revealed in the Papers of Robert W. Allston* (Chicago, 1945), p. 291.

39. Bassett, *The Southern Plantation Overseer*, pp. 19–20, 32.

40. Rawick, *American Slave*, Ga., vol. 12, pt. 2: 57.

41. C. Vann Woodward, ed., *Mary Chesnut's Civil War* (New Haven, CT, 1981), pp. 33–34.

42. Norman Yetman, *Voices from Slavery* (New York, 1970), p. 13.

43. J. Mason Brewer, *American Negro Folklore* (New York, 1968), p. 233.

44. Willie Lee Rose, *Rehearsal for Reconstruction: The Port Royal Experiment* (New York, 1964), p. 11.

45. Elizabeth Ware Pearson, ed., *Letters from Port Royal: Written at the Time of the Civil War* (New York, 1969 [1906]), p. 44.

46. Ibid., pp. 250, 303–04.

47. Ibid., p. 56.

48. Botume, *First Days Amongst the Contrabands*, p. 125.

49. See for instance: Ibid., pp. 55–56, 58, 80, 212.

50. Pearson, *Letters from Port Royal*, p. 1133.

51. Botume, *First Days Amongst the Contrabands*, pp. 210–11.

The Secret Life of a Developing Country

(Ours)

Forget your conventional picture of America in 1810. In the first half of the nineteenth century, we were not at all the placid, straitlaced, white-picket-fence nation we imagine ourselves to have been. By looking at the patterns of everyday life as recorded by contemporary foreign and native observers of the young republic and by asking the question that historians often didn't think to ask of another time—what were people really like? how did they greet one another on the street? how did they occupy their leisure time? what did they eat?—Jack Larkin brings us a detailed portrait of another America, an America that was so different from both our conception of its past life and its present-day reality as to seem a foreign country.

Jack Larkin

Jack Larkin is Chief Historian at Old Sturbridge Village. This article is adapted from his book The Reshaping of Everyday Life in the United States, 1790-1840, *published by Harper & Row.*

WE LOOKED DIFFERENT

Contemporary observers of early-nineteenth-century America left a fragmentary but nonetheless fascinating and revealing picture of the manner in which rich and poor, Southerner and Northerner, farmer and city dweller, freeman and slave presented themselves to the world. To begin with, a wide variety of characteristic facial expressions, gestures, and ways of carrying the body reflected the extraordinary regional and social diversity of the young republic.

When two farmers met in early-nineteenth-century New England, wrote Francis Underwood, of Enfield, Massachusetts, the author of a pioneering 1893 study of small-town life, "their greeting might seem to a stranger gruff or surly, since the facial muscles were so inexpressive, while, in fact, they were on excellent terms." In courtship and marriage, countrymen and women were equally constrained, with couples "wearing all unconsciously the masks which custom had prescribed; and the onlookers who did not know the secret would think them cold and indifferent."

Underwood noted a pervasive physical as well as emotional constraint among the people of Enfield; it was rooted, he thought, not only in the self-denying ethic of their Calvinist tradition but in the nature of their work. The great physical demands of unmechanized agriculture gave New England men, like other rural Americans, a distinctively ponderous gait and posture. Despite their strength and endurance, farmers were "heavy, awkward and slouching in movement" and walked with a "slow inclination from side to side."

Yankee visages were captured by itinerant New England portraitists during the early nineteenth century, as rural storekeepers, physicians, and master craftsmen became the first more or less ordinary Americans to have their portraits done. The portraits caught their caution and immobility of expression as well as recording their angular, long-jawed features, thus creating good collective likenesses of whole communities.

The Yankees, however, were not the stiffest Americans. Even by their own impassive standards, New Englanders found New York Dutchmen and Pennsyl-

From *American Heritage*, September/October 1988, pp. 44-46, 50, 52, 54-56, 58-62, 64, 66-67. Adapted from *The Reshaping of Everyday Life in the United States, 1790-1840* by Jack Larkin. © 1988 by Jack Larkin. Reprinted by permission of HarperCollins Publishers, Inc.

A dour face of the early 1800s.

vania German farmers "clumsy and chill" or "dull and stolid." But the "wild Irish" stood out in America for precisely the opposite reason. They were not "chill" or "stolid" enough, but loud and expansive. Their expressiveness made Anglo-Americans uncomfortable.

The seemingly uncontrolled physical energy of American blacks left many whites ill at ease. Of the slaves celebrating at a plantation ball, it was "impossible to describe the things these people did with their bodies," Frances Kemble Butler, an English-born actress who married a Georgia slave owner, observed, "and above all with their faces. . . ." Blacks' expressions and gestures, their preference for rhythmic rather than rigid bodily motion, their alternations of energy and rest made no cultural sense to observers who saw only "antics and frolics," "laziness," or "savagery." Sometimes perceived as obsequious, childlike, and dependent, or sullen and inexpressive, slaves also wore masks—not "all unconsciously" as Northern farm folk did, but as part of their self-protective strategies for controlling what masters, mistresses, and other whites could know about their feelings and motivations.

American city dwellers, whose daily routines were driven by the quicker pace of commerce, were easy to distinguish from "heavy and slouching" farmers attuned to slow seasonal rhythms. New Yorkers, in particular, had already acquired their own characteristic body language. The clerks and commercial men

who crowded Broadway, intent on their business, had a universal "contraction of the brow, knitting of the eyebrows, and compression of the lips . . . and a hurried walk." It was a popular American saying in the 1830s, reported Frederick Marryat, an Englishman who traveled extensively in the period, that "a New York merchant always walks as if he had a good dinner before him, and a bailiff behind him."

Northern and Southern farmers and city merchants alike, to say nothing of Irishmen and blacks, fell well short of the standard of genteel "bodily carriage" enshrined in both English and American etiquette books and the instructions of dancing masters: "flexibility in the arms . . . erectness in the spinal column . . . easy carriage of the head." It was the ideal of the British aristocracy, and Southern planters came closest to it, expressing the power of their class in the way they stood and moved. Slave owners accustomed to command, imbued with an ethic of honor and pride, at ease in the saddle, carried themselves more gracefully than men hardened by toil or preoccupied with commerce. Visiting Washington in 1835, the Englishwoman Harriet Martineau contrasted not the politics but the postures of Northern and Southern congressmen. She marked the confident bearing, the "ease and frank courtesy . . . with an occasional touch of arrogance" of the slaveholders alongside the "cautious . . . and too deferential air of the members of the North." She could recognize a New Englander "in the open air," she claimed, "by his deprecatory walk."

Local inhabitants' faces became more open, travelers observed, as one went west. Nathaniel Hawthorne found a dramatic contrast in public appearances only a few days' travel west of Boston. "The people out here," in New York State just west of the Berkshires, he confided to his notebook in 1839, "show out their character much more strongly than they do with us," in his native eastern Massachusetts. He compared the "quiet, silent, dull decency . . . in our public assemblages" with Westerners' wider gamut of expressiveness, "mirth, anger, eccentricity, all showing themselves freely." Westerners in general, the clergyman and publicist Henry Ward Beecher observed, had "far more freedom of manners, and more frankness and spontaneous geniality" than did the city or country people of the New England and Middle

In marriage, couples wore "all unconsciously the masks which custom had prescribed."

Atlantic states, as did the "odd mortals that wander in from the western border," that Martineau observed in Washington's political population.

WE WERE DIRTY AND SMELLY

Early-nineteenth-century Americans lived in a world of dirt, insects, and pungent smells. Farmyards were strewn with animal wastes, and farmers wore manure-spattered boots and trousers everywhere. Men's and women's working clothes alike were often stiff with dirt and dried sweat, and men's shirts were often stained with "yellow rivulets" of tobacco juice. The locations of privies were all too obvious on warm or windy days. Unemptied chamber pots advertised their presence. Wet baby "napkins," today's diapers, were not immediately washed but simply put by the fire to dry. Vats of "chamber lye"—highly concentrated urine used for cleaning type or degreasing wool—perfumed all printing offices and many households. "The breath of that fiery bar-room," as Underwood described a country tavern, "was overpowering. The odors of the hostlers' boots, redolent of fish-oil and tallow, and of buffalo-robes and horse-blankets, the latter reminiscent of equine ammonia, almost got the better of the all-pervading fumes of spirits and tobacco."

Densely populated, but poorly cleaned and drained, America's cities were often far more noisome than its farmyards. Horse manure thickly covered city streets, and few neighborhoods were free from the spreading stench of tanneries and slaughterhouses. New York City accumulated so much refuse that it was generally believed the actual surfaces of the streets had not been seen for decades. During her stay in Cincinnati, the English writer Frances Trollope followed the practice of the vast majority of American city housewives when she threw her household "slops"—refuse food and dirty dishwater—out into the street. An irate neighbor soon informed her that

Freely moving pigs fed on the city's trash.

municipal ordinances forbade "throwing such things at the sides of the streets" as she had done; "they must just all be cast right into the middle and the pigs soon takes them off." In most cities hundreds, sometimes thousands, of free-roaming pigs scavenged the garbage; one exception was Charleston, South Carolina, where buzzards patrolled the streets. By converting garbage into pork, pigs kept city streets cleaner than they would otherwise have been, but the pigs themselves befouled the streets and those who ate their meat—primarily poor families—ran greater than usual risks of infection.

PRIVY MATTERS

The most visible symbols of early American sanitation were privies or "necessary houses." But Americans did not always use them; many rural householders simply took to the closest available patch of woods or brush. However, in more densely settled communities and in regions with cold winters, privies were in widespread use. They were not usually put in out-of-the-way locations. The fashion of some Northern farm families, according to Robert B. Thomas's *Farmer's Almanack* in 1826, had long been to have their "necessary planted in a garden or other conspicuous place." Other countryfolk went even further in turning human wastes to agricultural account and built their out-houses "within the territory of a hog yard, that the swine may root and ruminate and devour the nastiness thereof." Thomas was a longstanding critic of primitive manners in the countryside and roundly condemned these traditional sanitary arrangements as demonstrating a "want of taste, decency, and propriety." The better arranged necessaries of the prosperous

emptied into vaults that could be opened and cleaned out. The dripping horsedrawn carts of the "nocturnal goldfinders," who emptied the vaults and took their loads out for burial or water disposal—"night soil" was almost never used as manure—were a familiar part of nighttime traffic on city streets.

The humblest pieces of American household furniture were the chamber pots that allowed people to avoid dark and often cold nighttime journeys outdoors. Kept under beds or in corners of rooms, "chambers" were used primarily upon retiring and arising. Collecting, emptying, and cleaning them remained an unspoken, daily part of every housewife's routine.

Nineteenth-century inventory takers became considerably more reticent about naming chamber pots than their predecessors, usually lumping them with miscellaneous "crockery," but most households

Chamber pots were dumped in the streets.

probably had a couple of chamber pots; genteel families reached the optimum of one for each bedchamber. English-made ceramic pots had become cheap enough by 1820 that few American families within the reach of commerce needed to go without one. "Without a pot to piss in" was a vulgar tag of long standing for extreme poverty; those poorest households without one, perhaps more common in the warm South, used the outdoors at all times and seasons.

The most decorous way for householders to deal with chamber-pot wastes accumulated during the night was to throw them down the privy hole. But more casual and unsavory methods of disposal were still in wide use. Farm families often dumped their chamber pots out the most convenient door or window. In densely settled communities like York, Pennsylvania, the results could be more serious. In 1801, the York

diarist Lewis Miller drew and then described an event in North George Street when "Mr. Day an English man [as the German-American Miller was quick to point out] had a bad practice by pouring out of the upper window his filthiness . . . one day came the discharge . . . on a man and wife going to a wedding, her silk dress was fouled."

LETTING THE BEDBUGS BITE

Sleeping accommodations in American country taverns were often dirty and insect-ridden. The eighteenth-century observer of American life Isaac Weld saw "filthy beds swarming with bugs" in 1794; in 1840 Charles Dickens noted "a sort of game not on the bill of fare." Complaints increased in intensity as travelers went south or west. Tavern beds were uniquely vulnerable to infestation by whatever insect guests travelers brought with them. The bedding of most American households was surely less foul. Yet it was dirty enough. New England farmers were still too often "tormented all night by bed bugs," complained *The Farmer's Almanack* in 1837, and books of domestic advice contained extensive instructions on removing them from feather beds and straw ticks.

Journeying between Washington and New Orleans in 1828, Margaret Hall, a well-to-do and cultivated Scottish woman, became far more familiar with intimate insect life than she had ever been in the genteel houses of London or Edinburgh. Her letters home, never intended for publication, gave a graphic and unsparing account of American sanitary conditions. After sleeping in a succession of beds with the "usual complement of fleas and bugs," she and her party had themselves become infested: "We bring them

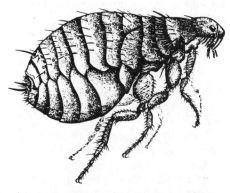

Insects infested many American beds.

along with us in our clothes and when I undress I find them crawling on my skin, nasty wretches." New and distasteful to her, such discoveries were commonplace among the ordinary folk with whom she lodged. The American children she saw on her Southern journey were "kept in such a state of filth," with clothes "dirty and slovenly to a degree," but this was "nothing in comparison with their heads . . . [which] are absolutely crawling!" In New Orleans she observed women picking through children's heads for lice, "catching them according to the method depicted in an engraving of a similar proceeding in the streets of Naples."

Davy Crockett, like many Americans, preferred to wash himself in the great outdoors.

BIRTH OF THE BATH

Americans were not "clean and decent" by today's standards, and it was virtually impossible that they should be. The furnishings and use of rooms in most American houses made more than the most elementary washing difficult. In a New England farmer's household, wrote Underwood, each household member would "go down to the 'sink' in the lean-to, next to the kitchen, fortunate if he had not to break ice in order to wash his face and hands, or more fortunate if a little warm water was poured into his basin from the kettle swung over the kitchen fire." Even in the comfortable household of the prominent minister Lyman Beecher in Litchfield, Connecticut, around 1815 all family members washed in the kitchen, using a stone sink and "a couple of basins."

Southerners washed in their detached kitchens or, like Westerners in warm weather, washed outside, "at the doors . . . or at the wells" of their houses. Using basins and sinks outdoors or in full view of others, most Americans found anything more than "washing the face and hands once a-day," usually in cold water, difficult, even unthinkable. Most men and women also washed without soap, reserving it for laundering clothes; instead they used a brisk rubbing with a coarse towel to scrub the dirt off their skins.

Gradually the practice of complete bathing spread beyond the topmost levels of American society and into smaller towns and villages. This became possible as families moved washing equipment out of kitchens and into bedchambers, from shared space to space that could

be made private. As more prosperous households furnished one or two of their chambers with washing equipment—a washstand, a basin, and a ewer, or large-mouthed pitcher—family members could shut the chamber door, undress, and wash themselves completely. The daughters of the Larcom family, living in Lowell, Massachusetts, in the late 1830s, began to bathe in a bedchamber in this way; Lucy Larcom described how her

We were not "clean and decent" by today's standards; washing was difficult.

oldest sister started to take "a full cold bath every morning before she went to her work . . . in a room without a fire," and the other young Larcoms "did the same whenever we could be resolute enough." By the 1830s better city hotels and even some country taverns were providing individual basins and pitchers in their rooms.

At a far remove from "primitive manners" and "bad practices" was the genteel ideal of domestic sanitation embodied in the "chamber sets"—matching basin and ewer for private bathing, a cup for brushing the teeth, and a chamber pot with cover to minimize odor and spillage—that American stores were beginning to stock. By 1840 a significant minority of American households owned chamber

sets and wash-stands to hold them in their bedchambers. For a handful there was the very faint dawning of an entirely new age of sanitary arrangements. In 1829 the new Tremont House hotel in Boston offered its patrons indoor plumbing: eight chambers with bathtubs and eight "water closets." In New York City and Philadelphia, which had developed rudimentary public water systems, a few wealthy households had water taps and, more rarely, water closets by the 1830s. For all others flush toilets and bathtubs remained far in the future.

The American people moved very slowly toward cleanliness. In "the back-country at the present day," commented the fastidious author of the *Lady's Book* in 1836, custom still "requires that everyone should wash at the pump in the yard, or at the sink in the kitchen." Writing in 1846, the physician and health reformer William Alcott rejoiced that to "wash the surface of the whole body in water daily" had now been accepted as a genteel standard of personal cleanliness. But, he added, there were "multitudes who pass for models of neatness and cleanliness, who do not perform this work for themselves half a dozen times—nay once—a year." As the better-off became cleaner than ever before, the poor stayed dirty.

WE DRANK AND FOUGHT WHENEVER WE COULD

In the early part of the century America was a bawdy, hard-edged, and violent land. We drank more than we ever had

136

Backwoodsmen have a "knock down" in this 1841 woodcut from *Crockett's Almanack*.

races or bet on cockfights and wrestling matches.

Drink permeated and propelled the social world of early-nineteenth-century America—first as an unquestioned presence and later as a serious and divisive problem. "Liquor at that time," recalled the builder and architect Elbridge Boyden, "was used as commonly as the food we ate." Before 1820 the vast majority of Americans considered alcohol an essential stimulant to exertion as well as a symbol of hospitality and fellowship. Like the Kentuckians with whom Daniel Drake grew up, they "regarded it as a duty to their families and visitors . . . to keep the bottle well replenished." Weddings, funerals, frolics, even a casual "gathering of two or three neighbors for an evening's social chat" required the obligatory "spirituous liquor"—rum, whiskey, or gin—"at all seasons and on all occasions."

Northern householders drank hard cider as their common table beverage, and all ages drank it freely. Dramming—taking a fortifying glass in the forenoon and again in the afternoon—was part of the daily regimen of many men. Clergymen took sustaining libations between services, lawyers before going to court, and physicians at their patients' bedsides. To raise a barn or get through a long day's haying without fortifying drink seemed a virtual impossibility. Slaves

To get through a long day's haying without drink seemed an impossibility.

enjoyed hard drinking at festival times and at Saturday-night barbecues as much as any of their countrymen. But of all Americans they probably drank the least on a daily basis because their masters could usually control their access to liquor.

In Parma, Ohio, in the mid-1820s, Lyndon Freeman, a farmer, and his brothers were used to seeing men "in their cups" and passed them by without comment. But one dark and rainy night

before or ever would again. We smoked and chewed tobacco like addicts and fought and quarreled on the flimsiest pretexts. The tavern was the most important gateway to the primarily male world of drink and disorder: in sight of the village church in most American communities, observed Daniel Drake, a Cincinnati physician who wrote a reminiscence of his Kentucky boyhood, stood the village tavern, and the two structures "did in fact represent two great opposing principles."

The great majority of American men in every region were taverngoers. The printed street directories of American cities listed tavernkeepers in staggering numbers, and even the best-churched parts of New England could show more "licensed houses" than meetinghouses. In 1827 the fast-growing city of Rochester, New York, with a population of approximately eight thousand, had nearly one hundred establishments licensed to sell liquor, or one for every eighty inhabitants.

America's most important centers of male sociability, taverns were often the scene of excited gaming and vicious fights and always of hard drinking, heavy smoking, and an enormous amount of alcohol-stimulated talk. City men came to their neighborhood taverns daily, and "tavern haunting, tippling, and gaming," as Samuel Goodrich, a New England historian and publisher, remembered, "were the chief resources of men in the dead and dreary winter months" in the countryside.

City taverns catered to clienteles of different classes: sordid sailors' grog-shops near the waterfront were rife with brawling and prostitution; neighborhood taverns and liquor-selling groceries were visited by craftsmen and clerks; well-appointed and relatively decorous places were favored by substantial merchants. Taverns on busy highways often specialized in teamsters or stage passengers, while country inns took their patrons as they came.

Taverns accommodated women as travelers, but their barroom clienteles were almost exclusively male. Apart from the dockside dives frequented by prostitutes, or the liquor-selling groceries of poor city neighborhoods, women rarely drank in public.

Gambling was a substantial preoccupation for many male citizens of the early republic. Men played billiards at

In the 1820s America was a bawdy and violent land. We drank more than we ever would again.

tavern tables for money stakes. They threw dice in "hazard," slamming the dice boxes down so hard and so often that tavern tables wore the characteristic scars of their play. Even more often Americans sat down to cards, playing brag, similar to modern-day poker, or an elaborate table game called faro. Outdoors they wagered with each other on horse they discovered something far more shocking, "nothing less than a *woman beastly drunk . . .* with a flask of whiskey by her side." American women drank as well as men, but usually much less heavily. They were more likely to make themselves "tipsy" with hard cider and alcohol-containing patent medicines than to become inebriated with rum or whiskey. Temperance advocates in the late 1820s estimated that men consumed fifteen times the volume of distilled spirits that women did; this may have been a considerable exaggeration, but there was a great difference in drinking habits between the sexes. Americans traditionally found drunkenness tolerable and forgivable in men but deeply shameful in women.

By almost any standard, Americans drank not only nearly universally but in large quantities. Their yearly consumption at the time of the Revolution has been estimated at the equivalent of three and one-half gallons of pure two-hundred-proof alcohol for each person. After 1790 American men began to drink even more. By the late 1820s their imbibing had risen to an all-time high of almost four gallons per capita.

Along with drinking went fighting. Americans fought often and with great relish. York, Pennsylvania, for example, was a peaceable place as American communities went, but the Miller and Weaver families had a long-running quarrel. It had begun in 1800 when the Millers found young George Weaver stealing apples in their yard and punished him by "throwing him over the fence," injuring

In isolated areas it was not uncommon to meet men who had lost an eye in a fight.

him painfully. Over the years hostilities broke out periodically. Lewis Miller remembered walking down the street as a teenaged boy and meeting Mrs. Weaver, who drenched him with the bucket of water she was carrying. He retaliated by "turning about and giving her a kick, laughing at her, this is for your politeness." Other York households had their quarrels too; in "a general fight on Beaver Street," Mistress Hess and Mistress Forsch tore each other's caps from their heads. Their husbands and then the neighbors interfered, and "all of them had a knock down."

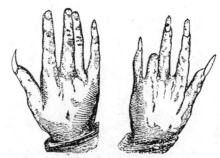

The hands of a celebrated gouger.

When Peter Lung's wife, Abigail, refused "to get up and dig some potatoes" for supper from the yard of their small house, the Hartford, Connecticut, laborer recalled in his confession, he "kicked her on the side . . . then gave her a violent push" and went out to dig the potatoes himself. He returned and "again kicked her against the shoulder and neck." Both had been drinking, and loud arguments and blows within the Lung household, as in many others, were routine. But this time the outcome was not. Alice Lung was dead the next day, and Peter Lung was arrested, tried, and hanged for murder in 1815.

In the most isolated, least literate and commercialized parts of the United States, it was "by no means uncommon, wrote Isaac Weld, "to meet with those who have lost an eye in a combat, and there are men who pride themselves upon the dexterity with which they can scoop one out. This is called *gouging."*

THE SLAVE'S LOT

Slaves wrestled among themselves, sometimes fought one another bitterly over quarrels in the quarters, and even at times stood up to the vastly superior force of masters and overseers. They rarely, if ever, reduced themselves to the ferocity of eye gouging. White Southerners lived with a pervasive fear of the violent potential of their slaves, and the Nat Turner uprising in Virginia in 1831, when a party of slaves rebelled and killed whites before being overcome, gave rise to tighter and harsher controls. But in daily reality slaves had far more to fear from their masters.

Margaret Hall was no proponent of abolition and had little sympathy for black Americans. Yet in her travels south she confronted incidents of what she ironically called the "good treatment of slaves" that were impossible to ignore. At a country tavern in Georgia, she summoned the slave chamber-maid, but "she could not come" because the mis-

tress had been whipping her and she was not fit to be seen. Next morning she made her appearance with her face marked in several places by the cuts of the cowskin and her neck handkerchief covered with spots of blood."

Southern stores were very much like Northern ones, Francis Kemble Butler observed, except that they stocked "negro-whips" and "mantraps" on their shelves. A few slaves were never beaten at all, and for most, whippings were not a daily or weekly occurrence. But they were, of all Americans, by far the most vulnerable to violence. All slaves had, as

A white master takes a baby from its mother.

William Wells Brown, an ex-slave himself, said, often "heard the crack of the whip, and the screams of the slave" and knew that they were never more than a white man's or woman's whim away from a beating. With masters' unchecked power came worse than whipping: the mutilating punishments of the old penal law including branding, ear cropping, and even occasionally castration and burning alive as penalties for severe offenses. In public places or along the road blacks were also subject to casual kicks, shoves, and cuffs, for which they could retaliate only at great peril. "Six or seven feet in length, made of cow-hide, with a platted wire on the end of it," as Brown recalled it, the negro-whip, for sale in most stores and brandished by masters and overseers in the fields, stood for a pervasive climate of force and intimidation.

PUBLIC PUNISHMENT

The penal codes of the American states were far less blood-thirsty than those of England. Capital punishment was not often imposed on whites for crimes other than murder. Yet at the beginning of the nineteenth century many criminal offenses were punished by the public infliction of pain and suffering. "The whipping post and stocks stood on the green near the meetinghouse" in most of the towns of New England and near courthouses everywhere. In Massachusetts before 1805 a counterfeiter was liable to have an ear cut off, and a forger to have one cropped or partially amputated, after spending an hour in the pillory. A criminal convicted of manslaughter was set up on the gallows to have his forehead branded with a letter M. In most jurisdictions town officials flogged petty thieves as punishment for their crime. In New Haven, Connecticut, around 1810, Charles Fowler, a local historian, recalled seeing the "admiring students of [Yale] college" gathered around to watch petty criminals receive "five or ten lashes . . . with a rawhide whip."

A man in the stocks awaits a flogging.

Throughout the United States public hangings brought enormous crowds to the seats of justice and sometimes seemed like brutal festivals. Thousands of spectators arrived to pack the streets of courthouse towns. On the day of a hanging near Mount Holly, New Jersey, in the 1820s, the scene was that of a holiday: "around the place in every direction were the assembled multitudes—some in tents, and by-wagons, engaged in gambling and other vices of the sort, in open day." In order to accommodate the throngs, hangings were usually held not in the public square but on the outskirts of town. The gallows erected on a hill or set up at the bottom of a natural amphitheater allowed onlookers an unobstructed view. A reprieve or stay of execution might disappoint a crowd intent on witnessing the deadly drama and

provoke a riot, as it did in Pembroke, New Hampshire, in 1834.

RISE OF RESPECTABILITY

At a drunkard's funeral in Enfield, Massachusetts, in the 1830s—the man had strayed out of the road while walking home and fallen over a cliff, "his stiffened fingers still grasping the handle of the jug"—Rev. Sumner G. Clapp, the Congregationalist minister of Enfield, mounted a log by the woodpile and preached the town's first temperance sermon before a crowd full of hardened drinkers. In this way Clapp began a campaign to "civilize" the manners of his parishioners, and "before many years there was a great change in the town; the incorrigible were removed by death, and others took warning." Drinking declined sharply, and along with it went "a general reform in conduct."

Although it remained a powerful force in many parts of the United States, the American way of drunkenness began to lose ground as early as the mid-1820s. The powerful upsurge in liquor consumption had provoked a powerful reaction, an unprecedented attack on all forms of drink that gathered momentum in the Northeast. Some New England clergymen had been campaigning in their own communities as early as 1810, but their concerns took on organized impetus with the founding of the American Temperance Society in 1826. Energized in part by a concern for social order, in part by evangelical piety, temperance reformers popularized a radically new way of looking at alcohol. The "good creature" became "demon rum"; prominent physicians and writers on physiology, like Benjamin Rush, told Americans that alcohol, traditionally considered healthy and fortifying, was actually a physical and moral poison. National and state societies distributed anti-liquor tracts, at first calling for moderation in drink but increasingly demanding total abstinence from alcohol.

To a surprising degree these aggressive temperance campaigns worked. By 1840 the consumption of alcohol had declined by more than two-thirds, from close to four gallons per person each year to less than one and one-half. Country storekeepers gave up the sale of spirits, local authorities limited the number of tavern licenses, and farmers even abandoned hard cider and cut down their

apple orchards. The shift to temperance was a striking transformation in the everyday habits of an enormous number of Americans. "A great, though silent change," in Horace Greeley's words, had been "wrought in public sentiment."

But although the "great change" affected some Americans everywhere, it had a very uneven impact. Organized temperance reform was sharply delimited by geography. Temperance societies were enormously powerful in New England and western New York and numerous in eastern New York, New Jersey, and Pennsylvania. More than three-fourths of all recorded temperance pledges came from these states. In the South and West, and in the laborers' and artisans' neighborhoods of the cities, the campaign against drink was much weaker. In many places drinking ways survived and even flourished, but as individuals and families came under the influence of militant evangelical piety, their "men of business

---

Liquor consumption provoked a powerful reaction: an unprecedented attack on drinking.

---

and sobriety" increased gradually in number. As liquor grew "unfashionable in the country," Greeley noted, Americans who wanted to drink and carouse turned increasingly to the cities, "where no one's deeds or ways are observed or much regarded."

Closely linked as they were to drink, such diversions as gambling, racing, and blood sports also fell to the same forces of change. In the central Massachusetts region that George Davis, a lawyer in Sturbridge, knew well, until 1820 or so gaming had "continued to prevail, more and more extensively." After that "a blessed change had succeeded," overturning the scenes of high-stakes dice and card games that he knew in his young manhood. Impelled by a new perception of its "pernicious effects," local leaders gave it up and placed "men of respectable standing" firmly in opposition. Racecourses were abandoned and "planted to corn." Likewise, "bear-baiting, cock-fighting, and other cruel amusements" began to dwindle in the Northern countryside. Elsewhere the rude life of

AMERICAN ANTIQUARIAN SOCIETY

A popular temperance print of 1826 shows a drunkard's progress from a morning dram to loss of his home.

the tavern and "cruel amusements" remained widespread, but some of their excesses of "sin and shame" did diminish gradually.

Over the first four decades of the nineteenth century the American people increasingly made churchgoing an obligatory ritual. The proportion of families affiliated with a local church or Methodist circuit rose dramatically, particularly after 1820, and there were fewer stretches of the wholly pagan, unchurched territory that travelers had noted around 1800. "Since 1830," maintained Emerson Davis in his retrospect of America, *The Half Century, "* . . . the friends of the Sabbath have been gaining ground. . . . In 1800, good men slumbered over the desecration of the Sabbath. They have since awoke. . . ." The number of Sunday mails declined, and the campaign to eliminate the delivery of mail on the Sabbath entirely grew stronger. "In the smaller cities and towns," wrote Mrs. Trollope in 1832, worship and "prayer meetings" had come to "take the place of almost all other amusements." There were still communities near the edge of settlement where a traveler would "rarely find either churches or chapels, prayer or preacher," but it was the working-class neighborhoods of America's larger cities that were increasingly the chief strongholds of "Sunday dissipation" and "Sabbath-breaking."

Whipping and the pillory, with their attentive audiences, began to disappear from the statute book, to be replaced by terms of imprisonment in another new American institution, the state penitentiary. Beginning with Pennsylvania's abolition of flogging in 1790 and Massachusetts's elimination of mutilating pun-

ishments in 1805, several American states gradually accepted John Hancock's view of 1796 that "mutilating or lacerating the body" was less an effective punishment than "an indignity to human nature." Connecticut's town constables whipped petty criminals for the last time in 1828.

Slaveholding states were far slower to change their provisions for public punishment. The whipping and mutilation of blacks may have become a little less ferocious over the decades, but the whip remained the essential instrument of punishment and discipline. "The secret of our success," thought a slave owner, looking back after emancipation, had been "the great motive power contained in that little instrument." Delaware achieved notoriety by keeping flogging on the books for whites and blacks alike through most of the twentieth century.

Although there were important stirrings of sentiment against capital punishment, all American states continued to execute convicted murders before the mid-1840s. Public hangings never lost their drawing power. But a number of American public officials began to abandon the long-standing view of executions as instructive communal rituals. They saw the crowd's holiday mood and eager participation as sharing too much in the condemned killer's own brutality. Starting with Pennsylvania, New York, and Massachusetts in the mid-1830s, several state legislatures voted to take executions away from the crowd, out of the public realm. Sheriffs began to carry out death sentences behind the walls of the jailyard, before a small assembly of representative onlookers. Other states clung much longer to tradition and continued

public executions into the twentieth century.

SEX LIFE OF THE NATIVES

Early-nineteenth-century Americans were more licentious than we ordinarily imagine them to be.

"On the 20th day of July" in 1830, Harriet Winter, a young woman working as a domestic in Joseph Dunham's household in Brimfield, Massachusetts, "was gathering raspberries" in a field west of the house. "Near the close of day," Charles Phelps, a farm laborer then living in the town, "came to the field where she was," and in the gathering dusk they made love—and, Justice of the Peace Asa Lincoln added in his account, "it was the Sabbath." American communities did not usually document their inhabitants' amorous rendezvous, and Harriet's tryst with Charles was a commonplace event in early-nineteenth-century America. It escaped historical oblivion because she was unlucky, less in

> *Early-nineteenth-century Americans were more licentious than we imagine them to be.*

becoming pregnant than in Charles's refusal to marry her. Asa Lincoln did not approve of Sabbath evening indiscretions, but he was not pursuing Harriet for immorality. He was concerned instead with economic responsibility for the child. Thus he interrogated Harriet about the baby's father—while she was in labor, as was the long-customary practice—in order to force Charles to contribute to the maintenance of the child, who was going to be "born a bastard and chargeable to the town."

Some foreign travelers found that the Americans they met were reluctant to admit that such things happened in the United States. They were remarkably straitlaced about sexual matters in public and eager to insist upon the "purity" of their manners. But to take such protestations at face value, the unusually candid Englishman Frederick Marryat thought, would be "to suppose that human nature is not the same everywhere."

The well-organized birth and marriage records of a number of American communities reveal that in late-eighteenth-century America pregnancy was frequently the prelude to marriage. The proportion of brides who were pregnant at the time of their weddings had been rising since the late seventeenth century and peaked in the turbulent decades during and after the Revolution. In the 1780s and 1790s nearly one-third of rural New England's brides were already with child. The frequency of sexual intercourse before marriage was surely higher, since some couples would have escaped early pregnancy. For many couples sexual relations were part of serious courtship. Premarital pregnancies in late-eighteenth-century Dedham, Massachusetts, observed the local historian Erastus Worthington in 1828, were occasioned by "the custom then prevalent of females admitting young men to their beds, who sought their company in marriage."

Pregnancies usually simply accelerated a marriage that would have taken place in any case, but community and parental pressure worked strongly to assure it. Most rural communities simply accepted the "early" pregnancies that marked so many marriages, although in Hingham, Massachusetts, tax records suggest that the families of well-to-do brides were considerably less generous to couples who had had "early babies" than to those who had avoided pregnancy.

"Bundling very much abounds," wrote the anonymous author of "A New Bundling Song," still circulating in Boston in 1812, "in many parts in country towns." Noah Webster's first *Dictionary* of *the American Language* defined it as

Lovers await Cupid's dart in this woodcut.

the custom that allowed couples "to sleep on the same bed without undressing"—with, a later commentator added, "the shared understanding that innocent endearments should not be exceeded." Folklore and local tradition, from Maine south to New York, had American mothers tucking bundling couples into bed with special chastity-protecting garments for the young woman or a "bundling board' to separate them.

In actuality, if bundling had been intended to allow courting couples privacy and emotional intimacy but not sexual contact, it clearly failed. Couples may have begun with bundling, but as courtship advanced, they clearly pushed beyond its restraints, like the "bundling maid" in "A New Bundling Song" who would "sometimes say when she lies down/She can't be cumbered with a gown."

Young black men and women shared American whites' freedom in courtship and sexuality and sometimes exceeded it. Echoing the cultural traditions of West Africa, and reflecting the fact that their marriages were not given legal status and security, slave communities were somewhat more tolerant and accepting of sex before marriage.

Gradations of color and facial features among the slaves were testimony that "thousands," as the abolitionist and former slave Frederick Douglass wrote, were "ushered into the world annually, who, like myself, owe their existence to white fathers, and those fathers most frequently their own masters." Sex crossed the boundaries of race and servitude more often than slavery's defenders wanted to admit, if less frequently than

the most outspoken abolitionists claimed. Slave women had little protection from whatever sexual demands masters or overseers might make, so that rapes, short liaisons, and long-term "concubinage" all were part of plantation life.

As Nathaniel Hawthorne stood talking with a group of men on the porch of a tavern in Augusta, Maine, in 1836, a young man "in a laborer's dress" came up and asked if anyone knew the whereabouts of Mary Ann Russell. "Do you want to use her?" asked one of the bystanders. Mary Ann was, in fact, the young laborer's wife, but she had left him and their child in Portland to become "one of a knot of whores." A few years earlier the young men of York, Pennsylvania, made up a party for "overturning and pulling to the ground" Eve Geese's "shameful house" of prostitution in Queen Street. The frightened women fled out the back door as the chimney collapsed around them; the apprentices and young journeymen—many of whom had surely been previous customers—were treated by local officials "to wine, for the good work."

From medium-sized towns like Augusta and York to great cities, poor American women were sometimes pulled into a darker, harsher sexual world, one of vulnerability, exploitation, and commerce. Many prostitutes took up their trade out of poverty and domestic disaster. A young widow or a country girl arrived in the city and, thrown on her own resources, often faced desperate economic choices because most women's work paid too poorly to provide decent food, clothing, and shelter, while other women sought excitement and independence from their families.

As cities grew, and changes in transportation involved more men in long-distance travel, prostitution became more visible. Men of all ages, married and unmarried, from city lawyers to visiting country storekeepers to sailors on the docks, turned to brothels for sexual release, but most of the customers were young men, living away from home and unlikely to marry until their late twenties. Sexual commerce in New York City was elaborately graded by price and the economic status of clients, from the "parlor houses" situated not far from the city's best hotels on Broadway to the more numerous and moderately priced houses that drew artisans and clerks, and finally to the broken and dissipated women who haunted dockside grogshops in the Five Points neighborhood.

From New Orleans to Boston, city theaters were important sexual market-places. Men often bought tickets less to see the performance than to make assignations with the prostitutes, who sat by custom in the topmost gallery of seats. The women usually received free admission from theater managers, who claimed that they could not stay in business without the male theatergoers drawn by the "guilty third tier."

Most Americans—and the American common law—still did not regard abortion as a crime until the fetus had "quickened" or began to move perceptibly in the womb. Books of medical advice actually contained prescriptions for bringing on delayed menstrual periods, which would also produce an abortion if the woman happened to be pregnant. They suggested heavy doses of purgatives that created violent cramps, powerful douches, or extreme kinds of physical activity, like the "violent exercise, raising great weights . . . strokes on the belly . . . [and] falls" noted in William Buchan's *Domestic Medicine,* a manual read widely through the 1820s. Women's folklore echoed most of these prescriptions and added others, particularly the use of two American herbal preparations—savin, or the extract of juniper berries, and Seneca snake-root—as abortion-producing drugs. They were dangerous procedures but sometimes effective.

REINING IN THE PASSIONS

Starting at the turn of the nineteenth century, the sexual lives of many Americans began to change, shaped by a growing insistence on control: reining in the passions in courtship, limiting family size, and even redefining male and female sexual desire.

Bundling was already on the wane in rural America before 1800; by the 1820s it was written about as a rare and antique custom. It had ceased, thought an elderly man from East Haddam, Connecticut, "as a consequence of education and refinement." Decade by decade the proportion of young women who had conceived a child before marriage declined. In most of the towns of New England the rate had dropped from nearly one pregnant bride in three to one in five or six by 1840; in some places prenuptial pregnancy dropped to 5 per-

Every Body's Album (PHILADELPHIA, 1836)

Just say no: Quaker lovers hold back.

cent. For many young Americans this marked the acceptance of new limits on sexual behavior, imposed not by their parents or other authorities in their communities but by themselves.

These young men and women were not more closely supervised by their parents than earlier generations had been; in fact, they had more mobility and greater freedom. The couples that courted in the new style put a far greater emphasis on control of the passions. For some of them—young Northern merchants and professional men and their intended brides—revealing love letters have survived for the years after 1820. Their intimate correspondence reveals that they did not give up sexual expression but gave it new boundaries, reserving sexual intercourse for marriage. Many of them were marrying later than their parents, often living through long engagements while the husband-to-be strove to establish his place in the world. They chose not to risk a pregnancy that would precipitate them into an early marriage.

Many American husbands and wives were also breaking with tradition as they began to limit the size of their families. Clearly, married couples were renegotiating the terms of their sexual lives together, but they remained resolutely silent about how they did it. In the first two decades of the nineteenth century, they almost certainly set about avoiding childbirth through abstinence; coitus interruptus, or male withdrawal; and perhaps sometimes abortion. These contraceptive techniques had long been traditional in preindustrial Europe, although previously little used in America.

As they entered the 1830s, Americans had their first opportunity to learn, at least in print, about more effective or

less self-denying forms of birth control. They could read reasonably inexpensive editions of the first works on contraception published in the United States: Robert Dale Owen's *Moral Physiology* of 1831 and Dr. Charles Knowlton's *The Fruits of Philosophy* of 1832. Both authors frankly described the full range of contraceptive techniques, although they solemnly rejected physical intervention in the sexual act and recommended only douching after intercourse and coitus interruptus. Official opinion, legal and religious, was deeply hostile. Knowlton, who had trained as a physician in rural Massachusetts, was prosecuted in three different counties for obscenity, convicted once, and imprisoned for three months.

But both works found substantial numbers of Americans eager to read them. By 1839 each book had gone through nine editions, putting a combined total of twenty to thirty thousand copies in circulation. An American physician could write in 1850 that contraception had "been of late years so much talked of." Greater knowledge about contraception surely played a part in the continuing decline of the American birthrate after 1830.

The sexual lives of Americans began to change, reshaped by a new emphasis on self-control.

New ways of thinking about sexuality emerged that stressed control and channeling of the passions. Into the 1820s almost all Americans would have subscribed to the commonplace notion that sex, within proper social confines, was enjoyable and healthy and that prolonged sexual abstinence could be injurious to health. They also would have assumed that women had powerful sexual drives.

Starting with his "Lecture to Young Men on Chastity" in 1832, Sylvester Graham articulated very different counsels about health and sex. Sexual indulgence, he argued, was not only morally suspect but psychologically and physiologically risky. The sexual overstimulation involved in young men's lives produced anxiety and nervous disorders, "a shocking state of debility and excessive irritability." The remedy was diet, exercise, and a regular routine that pulled the mind away from animal lusts. Medical writings that discussed the evils of masturbation, or "solitary vice," began to appear. Popular books of advice, like William Alcott's *Young Man's Guide,* gave similar warnings. They tried to persuade young men that their health could be ruined, and their prospects for success darkened, by consorting with prostitutes or becoming sexually entangled before marriage.

A new belief about women's sexual nature appeared, one that elevated them above "carnal passion." Many American men and women came to believe during the nineteenth century that in their true and proper nature as mothers and guardians of the home, women were far less interested in sex than men were. Women who defined themselves as passionless were in a strong position to control or deny men's sexual demands either during courtship or in limiting their childbearing within marriage.

Graham went considerably farther than this, advising restraint not only in early life and courtship but in marriage itself. It was far healthier, he maintained, for couples to have sexual relations "very seldom."

Neither contraception nor the new style of courtship had become anything like universal by 1840. Prenuptial pregnancy rates had fallen, but they remained high enough to indicate that many couples simply continued in familiar ways. American husbands and wives in the cities and the Northern countryside were limiting the number of their children, but it was clear that those living on the farms of the West or in the slave quarters had not yet begun to. There is strong evidence that many American women felt far from passionless, although others restrained or renounced their sexuality. For many people in the United States, there had been a profound change. Reining in the passions had become part of everyday life.

SMOKING AND SPITTING

Everyone smokes and some chew in America," wrote Isaac Weld in 1795. Americans turned tobacco, a new and controversial stimulant at the time of colonial settlement, into a crucially important staple crop and made its heavy use a commonplace—and a never-ending source of surprise and indignation to

---

After 1800, in public and private it became nearly impossible to avoid tobacco chewers.

---

visitors. Tobacco use spread in the United States because it was comparatively cheap, a homegrown product free from the heavy import duties levied on it by European governments. A number of slave rations described in plantation documents included "one hand of tobacco per month." Through the eighteenth century most American smokers used clay pipes, which are abundant in colonial archeological sites, although some men and women dipped snuff or inhaled powdered tobacco.

Where the smokers of early colonial America "drank" or gulped smoke through the short, thick stems of their seventeenth-century pipes, those of 1800 inhaled it more slowly and gradually; from the early seventeenth to the late eighteenth century, pipe stems became steadily longer and narrower, increasingly distancing smokers from their burning tobacco.

In the 1790s cigars, or "segars," were introduced from the Caribbean. Prosperous men widely took them up; they were the most expensive way to consume tobacco, and it was a sign of financial security to puff away on "long-nines or principe cigars at three cents each" while the poor used clay pipes and much

cheaper "cut plug" tobacco. After 1800 in American streets, barrooms, stores, public conveyances, and even private homes it became nearly impossible to avoid tobacco chewers. Chewing extended tobacco use, particularly into workplaces; men who smoked pipes at home or in the tavern barroom could chew while working in barns or workshops where smoking carried the danger of fire.

An expert spitter takes aim.

"In all the public places of America," wrote Charles Dickens, multitudes of men engaged in "the odious practice of chewing and expectorating," a recreation practiced by all ranks of American society. Chewing stimulated salivation and gave rise to a public environment of frequent and copious spitting, where men every few minutes were "squirting a mouthful of saliva through the room."

Spittoons were provided in the more meticulous establishments, but men often ignored them. The floors of American public buildings were not pleasant to contemplate. A courtroom in New York City in 1833 was decorated by a "mass of abomination" contributed to by "judges, counsel, jury, witnesses, officers, and audience." The floor of the Virginia House of Burgesses in 1827 was "actually flooded with their horrible spitting," and even the aisle of a Connecticut meetinghouse was black with the "ejection after ejection, incessant from twenty mouths," of the men singing in the choir. In order to drink, an American man might remove his quid, put it in a pocket or hold it in his hand, take his

On the home front: a smoker indulges.

glassful, and then restore it to his mouth. Women's dresses might even be in danger at fashionable balls. "One night as l was walking upstairs to valse," reported Margaret Hall of a dance in Washington in 1828, "my partner began clearing his throat. This I thought ominous. However, I said to myself, 'surely he will turn his head to the other side.' The gentleman, however, had no such thought but deliberately shot across me. I had not courage enough to examine whether the result landed in the flounce of my dress."

The segar and the quid were almost entirely male appurtenances, but as the nineteenth century began, many rural and lower-class urban women were smoking pipes or dipping snuff. During his boyhood in New Hampshire, Horace Greeley remembered, "it was often my filial duty to fill and light my mother's pipe."

After 1820 or so tobacco use among women in the North began to decline. Northern women remembered or depicted with pipe or snuffbox were almost all elderly. More and more Americans adopted a genteel standard that saw tobacco use and womanliness— delicate and nurturing—as antithetical, and young women avoided it as a pollutant. For them, tobacco use marked off male from female territory with increasing sharpness.

In the households of small Southern and Western farmers, however, smoking and snuff taking remained common. When women visited "among the country people" of North Carolina, Frances Kemble Butler reported in 1837, the "proffer of the snuffbox, and its passing from hand to hand, is the usual civility." By the late 1830s visiting New Englanders were profoundly shocked when they saw the women of Methodist congregations in Illinois, including nursing mothers, taking out their pipes for a smoke between worship services.

FROM DEFERENCE TO EQUALITY

The Americans of 1820 would have been more recognizable to us in the informal and egalitarian way they treated one another. The traditional signs of deference before social superiors—the deep bow, the "courtesy," the doffed cap, lowered head, and averted eyes—had been a part of social relationships in colonial America. in the 1780s, wrote the American

poetess Lydia Huntley Sigourney in 1824, there were still "individuals . . . in every grade of society" who had grown up "when a bow was not an offense to fashion nor . . . a relic of monarchy." But in the early nineteenth century such signals of subordination rapidly fell away. It was a natural consequence of the Revolution, she maintained, which, "in giving us liberty, obliterated almost every vestige of politeness of the 'old school.'" Shaking hands became the accustomed American greeting between men, a gesture whose symmetry and mutuality signified equality. Frederick Marryat found in 1835 that it was "invariably the custom to shake hands" when he was introduced to Americans and that he could not carefully grade the acknowledgment he would give to new acquaintances according to their signs of wealth and breeding. He found instead that he had to "go on shaking hands here, there and everywhere, and with everybody." Americans were not blind to inequalities of economic and social power, but they less and less gave them overt physical expression. Bred in a society where such distinctions were far more clearly spelled out, Marryat was somewhat disoriented in the United States; "it is impossible to know who is who," he claimed, "in this land of equality."

Well-born British travelers encountered not just confusion but conflict when they failed to receive the signs of respect they expected. Margaret Hall's letters home during her Southern travels outlined a true comedy of manners. At every stage stop in the Carolinas, Georgia, and Alabama, she demanded that country tavernkeepers and their households give her deferential service and well-prepared meals; she received instead rancid bacon and "such an absence of all kindness of feeling, such unbending frigid heartlessness." But she and her family had a far greater share than they realized in creating this chilly reception. Squeezed between the pride and poise of the great planters and the social debasement of the slaves, small Southern farmers often displayed a prickly insolence, a considered lack of response, to those who too obviously considered themselves their betters. Greatly to their discomfort and incomprehension, the Halls were experiencing what a British traveler more sympathetic to American ways, Patrick Shirreff, called "the democratic rudeness which assumed or presump-

tuous superiority seldom fails to experience."

LAND OF ABUNDANCE

In the seventeenth century white American colonials were no taller than their European counterparts, but by the time of the Revolution they were close to their late-twentieth-century average height for men of slightly over five feet eight inches. The citizens of the early republic towered over most Europeans. Americans' early achievement of modern stature—by a full century and more—was a striking consequence of American abundance. Americans were taller because they were better nourished than the great majority of the world's peoples.

Yet not all Americans participated equally in the nation's abundance. Differences in stature between whites and blacks, and between city and country dwellers, echoed those between Europeans and Americans. Enslaved blacks were a full inch shorter than whites. But they remained a full inch taller than European peasants and laborers and were taller still than their fellow slaves eating the scanty diets afforded by the more savagely oppressive plantation system of the West Indies. And by 1820 those who lived in the expanding cities of

AMERICAN ANTIQUARIAN SOCIETY

Possum and other game were dietary staples.

the United States—even excluding immigrants, whose heights would have reflected European, not American, conditions—were noticeably shorter than the people of the countryside, suggesting an increasing concentration of poverty and poorer diets in urban places.

Across the United States almost all country households ate the two great American staples: corn and "the eternal pork," as one surfeited traveler called it, "which makes its appearance on every American table, high and low, rich and poor." Families in the cattle-raising, dairying country of New England, New York, and northern Ohio ate butter,

Families began to sit down at mealtime.

Americans were better nourished than the great majority of the world's peoples.

---

cheese, and salted beef as well as pork and made their bread from wheat flour or rye and Indian corn. In Pennsylvania, as well as Maryland, Delaware, and Virginia, Americans ate the same breadstuffs as their Northern neighbors, but their consumption of cheese and beef declined every mile southward in favor of pork.

Farther to the south, and in the West, corn and corn-fed pork were truly "eternal"; where reliance on them reached its peak in the Southern uplands, they were still the only crops many small farmers raised. Most Southern and Western families built their diets around smoked and salted bacon, rather than the Northerners' salt pork, and, instead of wheat or rye bread, made cornpone or hoecake, a coarse, strong bread, and hominy, pounded Indian corn boiled together with milk.

Before 1800, game—venison, possum, raccoon, and wild fowl—was for many American households "a substantial portion of the supply of food at certain seasons of the year," although only on the frontier was it a regular part of the diet. In the West and South this continued to be true, but in the Northeast game became increasingly rare as forests gave way to open farmland, where wild animals could not live.

Through the first half of the eighteenth century, Americans had been primarily concerned with obtaining a sufficiency of

meat and bread for their families; they paid relatively little attention to foodstuffs other than these two "staffs of life," but since that time the daily fare of many households had grown substantially more diverse.

COMING TO THE TABLE

Remembering his turn-of-the-century Kentucky boyhood, Daniel Drake could still see the mealtime scene at the house of a neighbor, "Old Billy," who "with his sons" would "frequently breakfast in common on mush and milk out of a huge buckeye bowl, each one dipping in a spoon. Old Billy" and his family were less frontier savages than traditionalists; in the same decade Gov. Caleb Strong of Massachusetts stopped for the night with a country family who ate in the same way, where "each had a spoon and dipped from the same dish." These households ate as almost all American families once had, communally partaking of food from the same dish and passing around a single vessel to drink from. Such meals were often surprisingly haphazard affairs, with household members moving in and out, eating quickly and going on to other tasks.

But by 1800 they were already in a small and diminishing minority. Over the eighteenth century dining "in common" had given way to individualized yet social eating; as families acquired chairs and dining utensils, they were able to

make mealtimes more important social occasions. Most Americans expected to eat individual portions of food at a table set with personal knives, forks, glasses, bowls, and plates. Anything that smacked of the old communal ways was increasingly likely to be treated as a sin against domestic decency. The clergyman Peter Cartwright was shocked at the table manners of a "backward" family who ate off a "wooden trencher," improvised forks with "sharp pieces of cane," and used a single knife, which they passed around the table.

"One and all, male and female," the observant Margaret Hall took note, even in New York's best society, ate "invariably and indefatigably with their knives." As a legacy of the fork's late arrival in the colonies, Americans were peculiar in using their "great lumbering, long, two-pronged forks," not to convey food to the mouth, as their English and French contemporaries did, but merely to keep their meat from slipping off the plate while cutting it. "Feeding yourself with your right hand, armed with a steel blade," was the prevalent American custom, acknowledged Eliza Farrar's elaborate *Young Lady's Friend* of 1836. She added that it was perfectly proper, despite English visitors' discomfort at the sight of a "prettily dressed, nice-looking young woman ladling rice pudding into her mouth with the point of a great knife" or a domestic helper "feeding an infant of seventeen months in the same way.

Mrs. Farrar acknowledged that there were stirrings of change among the sophisticated in the 1830s, conceding that some of her readers might now want "to imitate the French or English . . . and put every mouthful into your mouth with your fork." Later in the nineteenth century the American habit of eating with the knife completely lost its claims to gentility, and it became another relic of "primitive manners." Americans gradually learned to use forks more dexterously, although to this day they hold them in the wrong hand and "upside down" from an Englishman's point of view.

The old ways, so startlingly unfamiliar to the modern reader, gradually fell away. Americans changed their assumptions about what was proper, decent, and nor-

Primitive manners succumbed to campaigns for temperance and gentility.

mal in everyday life in directions that would have greatly surprised most of the men and women of the early republic. Some aspects of their "primitive manners" succumbed to campaigns for temperance and gentility, while others evaporated with the later growth of mass merchandising and mass communications.

Important patterns of regional, class, and ethnic distinctiveness remain in American everyday life. But they are far less powerful, and less central to understanding American experience, than they once were. Through the rest of the nineteenth century and into the twentieth, the United States became ever more diverse, with new waves of Eastern and Southern European immigrants joining the older Americans of Northern European stock. Yet the new arrivals—and even more, their descendants—have experienced the attractiveness and reshaping power of a national culture formed by department stores, newspapers, radios, movies, and universal public education. America, the developing nation, developed into us. And perhaps our manners and morals, to some future observer, will seem as idiosyncratic and astonishing as this portrait of our earlier self.

Fenimore Cooper's America

Alan Taylor examines how the social concerns and ambitions of the new republic and those of the author of Last of the Mohicans intertwined—and how they gave him the canvas to become the United States' first great novelist

Alan Taylor

Alan Taylor is Professor of American history at the University of California, Davis. He is the author of William Cooper's Town *(Alfred A. Knopf, 1995).*

Twentieth-century readers know the American novelist James Fenimore Cooper as the author of the five 'Leatherstocking Tales', including *The Last of the Mohicans,* set in the North American forest and prairie during the late eighteenth and early nineteenth centuries. These novels of frontier violence and adventure helped define the American experience and identity, especially for European readers. Although his narrative voice conveys a powerful self-assurance, James Fenimore Cooper, in fact, became a novelist during the early 1820s at the same time that his inherited estate in New York State collapsed under the weight of unpaid debts and court-ordered foreclosures.

Despite a boyish love for 'reading novels and amusing tales', he did not begin to write fiction until he was thirty and only after the frustration of his ambitions as a gentleman farmer, frontier landlord, and mercantile investor.

His father, Judge William Cooper, had become rich by founding, as a land speculation, the frontier village of Cooperstown in central New York State. In 1809 the Judge died, leaving an apparently immense fortune to his widow and six children. But he had saddled the estate with debts that proved crushing during the economic depression of the late 1810s. Unable to cope with the financial crisis, James Fenimore Cooper fled from

Cooperstown in 1817, taking refuge with his wife's wealthy and aristocratic family, the DeLanceys of Westchester County, in the Hudson Valley. To his chagrin, they concluded that Cooper was a reckless spendthrift who would inevitably squander his wife's patrimony. Insulted, in late 1822 he angrily removed his family to a rented house on Broadway in New York City.

Cooper might flee from the DeLanceys, but he could not escape his debts. Acting on behalf of a creditor, in 1823 the New York City sheriff impounded and inventoried Cooper's household goods. However, the creditor decided to release the goods when his agent reported that they would fetch very little if auctioned: 'I have seen his household goods. They are of no very great value; they are few and of a cheap kind'. This dismissive judgement must have infuriated Cooper who took pride in his exquisite taste and so resented his ebbing fortunes.

According to Susan Fenimore Cooper, her father began his first novel in response to a challenge from his wife:

He always read a great deal, in a desultory way. Military works, travels, Biographies, History—and novels! He frequently read aloud at that time to my Mother, in the quiet evenings at Angevine. Of course the books were all English. A new novel had been brought from England in the last *monthly packet;* it was, I think, one of Mrs. Opie's, or one of that school. My Mother was not well; she was lying on the sofa, and he was read-

(MANSELL COLLECTION)

The myth-maker: James Fenimore Cooper exorcised his own bittersweet experiences of rural life by writing about an idealised frontier, and in doing so created a fortune for himself and a national identity for Americans.

ing this newly imported novel to her; it must have been very trashy; after a chapter or two he threw it aside, exclaiming, 'I could write you a better book than that myself!' Our Mother laughed at the idea, as the height of absurdity—he who disliked writing even a letter, that he should write a book!! He persisted in his declaration, however, and almost immediately wrote the first pages of a tale, not yet named, the scene laid in England, as a matter of course.

The story is plausible, especially in Susan's claim that Cooper turned to fiction as a lark rather than as a career decision. Because no previous American novelist had enjoyed sustained commercial success, Cooper could not have begun writing with any expectation that he would make money.

Prior to 1820 American readers and publishers preferred to import or pirate their books from England—because English texts were, at once, less expensive and more fashionable. Moreover, English novels offered more romantic characters and exotic settings—lords and ladies in castles or grand estates—than seemed possible in the common and commercial American republic. Professing themselves a people of equality and common sense, Americans doubted that their society could ever inspire a novelist. So doubting, they continued to read the imports from aristocratic England. Consequently, the most famous and promising American novelist of the previous generation, Charles Brockden Brown, had failed to support or sustain himself as a writer.

In early 1820, after one false start, Cooper enthusiastically and rapidly fabricated a novel of manners set in England and entitled *Precaution,* but he balked at publishing it for fear of embarrassment. Because women prevailed among both the writers and readers of novels, many gentlemen did not respect the genre. Leading Americans ordinarily considered novels to be trivial, feminine, and vaguely dishonourable, because they appealed to the emotions and aroused the imagination—impulses profoundly distrusted by gentlemen dedicated to self-control. Because Cooper took his gentility and masculinity so very seriously, he feared that publishing a novel would be unbecoming to one of his dignity and station.

Before launching into print, Cooper first sought approval from the gentleman he most admired—the former governor of New York, John Jay, who lived nearby. Pretending to present the work of an anonymous friend, Cooper read his manuscript to a small group of ladies and gentlemen gathered in Jay's parlour. Pleasantly surprised by their eager interest and avid approval, Cooper hired a New York City publisher who produced *Precaution* in November. Still not daring to hazard his name and reputation on a novel, Cooper published anonymously, but the secret did not keep for very long. In July of 1821 a Cooperstown newspaper reported as common knowledge that *Precaution* came 'from the pen of James Cooper, Esq., late of this Village, now a resident of Westchester Co., youngest son of the Hon. William Cooper, deceased'.

Badly edited and inferior to its English models, *Precaution* sold poorly in the United States, and Cooper probably lost money on its publication—as he was losing money on all of his investments in 1820. But Cooper had fallen in love with writing—with crafting an imagined world. In fiction he discovered a reassuring power to control characters and plot, a power that was especially intoxicating because he was so impotent in the real world to preserve his cherished position as a landed gentleman. Cooper took to the genre so readily because its prevailing conventions perfectly served his own concerns and needs. As a dispossessed son, he shared with other novelists a preoccupation with safeguarding a genteel reputation and inheritance. Distrusted and scorned by his DeLancey in-laws, Cooper felt drawn to novels because they tended to vindicate a mysterious and misunderstood protagonist by ultimately revealing his hidden but true nobility of breeding and spirit, thereby dumbfounding rivals and critics.

He delighted in the gamesmanship and business of publishing and promoting a novel. In submitting *Precaution,* Cooper assured his publisher:

Urban Americans saw the frontier as a place of danger, but a danger they could overcome, a feeling Cooper's writing reinforced, as this illustration from the 1832 edition of *The Pioneers* shows.

No book was ever written with less thought and more rapidity. I can make a much better one—am making a much better one. I send this out as a pilot balloon. I made it English to impose on the public—and merely wish'd to see myself in print—and honestly own [that] I am pleased with my appearance—considering that from fourteen to twenty-eight pages of the book were written between nine o'clock in the morning and nine at night.

Apparently, the shock of his collapsing fortunes and the novelty of writing fiction combined to jar Cooper's mind into new powers. A friend noted, '[Cooper's] loss of property called forth the slumbering energies of his mind'.

Upon completing (and before publishing) *Precaution*, Cooper plunged into writing a new, more innovative and ambitious novel with an American setting and a patriotic theme: *The Spy*. This time he explicitly took on the daunting 'task of making American manners and American scenes interesting to an American reader'. He based his new novel on a story John Jay told of a selfless but misunderstood American spy active in bitterly-contested Westchester County during the American Revolutionary War.

Published in December, Cooper's second novel proved instantly and phenomenally popular. Although highly priced at two dollars apiece, the first 1,000 copies sold out within a month. By the end of the year, bookstores had ordered and retailed at least 6,000 copies and Cooper had reaped royalties worth nearly $4,000—an unprecedented success for an American novelist. A popular play based on *The Spy* began a long run in New York City in March 1822.

Cooper discovered that there was a great new public demand for an adventure tale derived from memories of the American Revolution. In the early 1820s, as the revolutionary generation relinquished public control and life, their heirs eagerly read a novel that constructed a national identity rooted in a romanticised past. Fearful of losing touch with the heroic, patriotic age, the new generation sought, by reading *The Spy*, a vicarious participation in their Revolution.

Cooper also benefited from the precedent provided by the English historical romances written by Sir Walter Scott that proved so immensely popular

on both sides of the Atlantic. Scott's novels were sufficiently 'manly' and moral to disarm any opposition to the genre by leading Americans. In particular, the publication in 1819 of Scott's *Ivanhoe* established the new popularity and respectability of the historical romance in America as well as England. In effect, Scott convened the American audience that enthusiastically greeted Cooper's similar works. Moreover, those readers responded so enthusiastically to Cooper because they longed for an American who could compete with Scott in creating characters and describing landscapes. They especially cherished *The Spy* because they believed that Cooper had so precisely and patriotically captured American manners, character and setting.

Addicted to writing and heady with success, James Cooper quickly wrote a third novel entitled *The Pioneers, or the Sources of the Susquehannah,* published in January 1823. Primed by the sensational popularity of *The Spy* and by a steady succession of newspaper teasers for the new novel, readers immediately purchased 3,500 copies, an unprecedented first-day sale for an American book. Although sales later slowed and never quite matched the remarkable commercial success of *The Spy*, Cooper made a substantial profit and reaped widespread critical applause for *The Pioneers*.

The Pioneers offers an especially deep entry into James Cooper's troubles and desires. Because Cooper wrote rapidly and spontaneously, with minimal revision, his novels express more immediate impulse than careful reconsideration. In late 1822 Cooper confessed to his English publisher:

I ought in justice to myself say, that in opposition to a thousand good resolutions, *The Pioneers* has been more hastily and carelessly written than any of my books. Not a line has been copied, and it has gone from my desk to the printers. I have not to this moment been able even to *read* it.

The novel is also especially revealing because, for its setting, Cooper returns to the place and time of his boyhood: Otsego County in central New York State during the early 1790s when American settlers occupied and transformed the region. To craft the character of Judge Marmaduke Temple and the

imaginary village of Templeton, Cooper drew upon his memories of his father the land-speculating founder of the frontier village of Cooperstown.

Because Cooper wrote *The Pioneers* as a mature but troubled man in his thirties, he does not, and could not, offer a simple, straightforward account of the village that he had known as a boy. The novel speaks primarily in witness to Cooper's predicament in the 1820s and only secondarily to the Cooperstown of the 1790s. He describes characters, buildings, and the landscape with a vivid, dream-like intensity. He seems to take inventory of his most powerful memories as if determined to embed and perpetuate them. He lingers lovingly over scenes and characters, indulging in the melancholia of his lost childhood and legacy in Otsego. Indeed, he spends the first fifteen chapters describing the events of a single day.

In this book Cooper reaffirms his self-worth and reclaims his legacy by imagining and crafting an improved past—where property and power flow from a well-meaning but flawed father to his perfectly genteel heirs: his daughter Elizabeth and her lover Oliver Effingham. In the novel's penultimate chapter, Judge Temple flourishes a will which dispels all illusions and assures a just and stable transition of his estate to his heirs—in stark contrast to William Cooper's will which had proved so deceptive and destabilising. In the end, Oliver marries Elizabeth and obtains possession of the Judge's entire estate—the novelist's fondest wish. As a mysterious young gentleman who overcomes adversity and misunderstanding to secure his proper inheritance and esteem, Oliver is the author's protagonist and proxy. In his imaginary Otsego, James Fenimore Cooper enjoyed a mastery denied him in the real world.

Through his novel, Cooper also promoted his social vision of a more stable and genteel republic governed by its natural aristocracy. He tried to quiet his own fears—and those of other genteel Americans—that the nation's revolutionary upheaval and frontier disorder would prove permanent. He had grown up in a country engaged in the continuing conquest and dispossession of the native peoples in a nation riven with competition to control and own the lands wrested from the Indians; and in a country bitterly divided between political parties contesting for power and competing to control the meaning of the American Revolution. By the 1820s leading Americans hoped for national unity, wished to set aside the bitter political conflicts of the preceding four decades, and longed to consolidate the Revolution into enduring institutions. Cooper succeeded so quickly and spectacularly as a novelist because he was so sensitive to the ideological tensions within America *and* to the powerful desire for consensus.

In *The Pioneers* Templeton appears precariously poised on the verge either of maturing into a stable, prosperous and just social order or of lapsing into a purgatory of demagoguery, deceit, hypocrisy and turmoil. Cooper insisted that the fate of the American republic hinged upon the resolution of the contest between law and chaos in the hundreds of new settlements along the expanding frontier arc.

Superficially, *The Pioneers* seems to question the rule of law by sympathising wit—the plight and arguments of Natty Bumppo, a squatter and hunter. Capable of governing himself in the wilderness free from legal and political institutions, Natty suffers when surrounded and overpowered by the invasive, crowded, complicated and commercialised society brought into Otsego by Judge Temple and his settlers. Caught in the trammels of the laws introduced and enforced by the judge, Natty eloquently denounces the inflexibility of the new system.

The novelist permits Natty a full and sympathetic hearing, but ultimately insists that his asocial way of life is doomed and properly so. Like most American gentlemen, Cooper believed that English common and equity law had gradually perfected the principles of universal, timeless justice—the very essence of civilisation and the key to perpetuating property, order and liberty. By remaining true to English law, the American republic could achieve its potential as the social culmination of human history. The novel's glowing description of the New York rural landscape and society of the 1820s conveys Cooper's confidence that the law had triumphed and had produced the greatest good for the greatest number.

Until the novel's conclusion, it seems that Judge Temple had exploited the American Revolution to defraud the Effinghams—Loyalist gentry who had been driven into exile by the war—of their Otsego estate. But Judge Temple

(NEW YORK HISTORICAL ASSOCIATION)

Judge William Cooper by Henry Stuart (*c.* 1800). James' father was the model for Judge Temple in *The Pioneers*—but the fictional judge's death and generous will, when compared to his own father's impecunious end, represents one of the author's many rewrites of his own past.

ultimately reaffirms his enduring fealty to the Effinghams as Otsego's rightful owners. The marriage of Oliver and Elizabeth symbolically binds the Revolution's wounds, reconciling Loyalist and Whig, in one reunited American gentry. The reconciliation legitimises Temple's enterprise, and by extension the American Revolution, on conservative terms—by asserting the republic's continuity from its colonial past. In his subsequent *Notions of the Americans,* published in 1828, Cooper insisted, 'We have ever been reformers rather than revolutionists. Our own struggle for independence was not in its aspect a revolution. We contrived to give it all the dignity of a war, from the first blow.'

In *The Pioneers,* Cooper vividly displays division and violence, only to confine and suffocate them as providence mandates the inevitable triumph of harmony and stability. As Otsego's preeminent family, the Effinghams will exercise a unified authority—at once social, economic, cultural and political—over an increasingly deferential and harmonious community: the very antithesis of what had actually transpired

in post-Revolutionary America. Cooper's narrative ultimately suppresses the economic and political conflicts that generated his need to write.

Through the novel, Cooper reassures himself and his class that the contentious competition for new wealth and power associated with the revolutionary frontier would quickly pass, giving way to peaceful communities governed by the natural elite at the pinnacle of a stable hierarchy. He expected Americans freely to bestow honour and electoral office upon gentlemen distinguished by their good manners, great property, liberal education and commitment to public service: 'So long as society shall be governed by its ordinary and natural feelings, it is not possible to deprive money, intelligence and manners, of their influence.' In sum, during the 1820s Cooper wishfully imagined an America where he securely belonged to an honoured, ruling class—defying the actual instability of fortune and authority in the new republic.

Cooper hoped to hasten the conservative consolidation of the revolutionary frontier by persuading Americans that it was inevitable and just. In *The Pioneers*

(HT ARCHIVES)

The final frontier: Tennessee's Andrew Jackson, from 1828 America's seventh president, and the first 'backwoodsman' to achieve that office following a string of 'aristocratic' Virginians. Cooper may have had mixed feelings on this result—his books perhaps paved the way for Jackson's success, whilst he himself was an advocate of 'aristocratic' rule.

Cooper crafted a reassuring past intended to secure the republic's future stability. He understood that people sought the future based upon a collective identity derived from narratives that made sense of their past; histories shaped the trajectory of the nation's future. In 1820 he remarked, 'Books are, in a great measure, the instruments of controlling the opinions of a nation like ours. They are an engine alike powerful to save or destroy.' For Cooper, truth was morally didactic; it was what ought to be in a moral universe; and it was what would come to prevail through the influence of moral texts. By writing a reassuring and popular fiction he meant to make his social vision the American reality.

In combination, *The Spy* and *The Pioneers* persuaded American readers that at last their republic had produced a novelist who could refute the British scoff that no one bothered to read an American book. The extraordinarily popular success of Cooper's novels reassured anxious publishers, painters and writers that there was a public for American arts. Most of the cultural élite considered Cooper, not merely as a successful novelist, but as their great champion in a struggle for domestic self-respect and for international regard. He suddenly became *the* American novelist, the new nation's counterpart to the celebrated Sir Walter Scott. A grateful reader in Charleston, South Carolina, wrote to Charles Wiley, Cooper's publisher:

My eyes are scarcely yet sufficiently dry to enable me to write you, requesting that you will convey to the author of *The Pioneers* my heartiest thanks for the pleasure he has given me. The book is certainly the greatest literary honour yet conferred on the country.

So read, Cooper's novels became freighted with patriotic significance as vindications of the new republic's cultural worth and potential. Warming to the role, Cooper grandly announced that he meant to 'rouse the sleeping talents of the nation, and in some measure clear us from the odium of dullness'.

Cooper had become a national celebrity. In April of 1823 the American Philosophical Society honoured Cooper with election to membership and in Au-

gust 1824 he received an honorary degree from Columbia College in New York City. In 1824 Cooper gathered his growing circle of prestigious and talented admirers into 'the Bread and Cheese Club'. The members included Chancellor James Kent, the artists Asher B. Durand, John Wesley Jarvis and Samuel F.B. Morse, and the poets Fitz-Greene Halleck and William Cullen Bryant. Although surrounded by talent, Cooper's lively, witty, forceful and boastful conversation usually dominated their gatherings in New York City. After a dinner party, Bryant grumbled, 'Mr Cooper engrossed the whole conversation, and seems a little giddy with the great success his works have met with'. A more indulgent friend observed:

Mr Cooper was in person solid, robust, athletic: in voice, manly; in manner, earnest, emphatic, almost dictatorial—with something of self-assertion, bordering on egotism. The first effect was unpleasant, indeed repulsive, but there shone through all this a heartiness, a frankness, which excited confidence, respect, and at last affection.

Never bashful, his personality fed on new praise to grow more overpowering. Long frustrated in his dreams of playing the influential landed gentleman, Cooper exuberantly wallowed in his new-found prestige and fame as a popular novelist and literary statesman.

Cooper's prestige and purpose as a writer gradually took shape in the early 1820s as a consequence of three interacting processes: the practice of writing; feedback from his audience and peers; and the collapse of his inherited estate. First, by writing three novels, he became steadily more intrigued by, skilled at, and ambitious for his craft as a novelist. Second, popularity and critical applause combined to offer Cooper the role of patriotic spokesman as the new nation's premier novelist. Third, that new role helped him cope with his failure as a landlord and investor. The utter collapse of his inheritance and the simultaneous triumph of *The Spy* and *The Pioneers* determined that Cooper would rely on his pen for a living and for self-esteem. No longer able to play the landed gentleman, he withdrew to the city and threw himself into his new identity as the great American novelist.

3. NATIONAL CONSOLIDATION AND EXPANSION

Cooper had failed as a conventional gentleman and capitalist only to succeed, beyond anyone's wildest imagination, at the most implausible and risky of ventures: writing and publishing novels set in America. Against all odds, Cooper arose from the ashes of his paternal estate to become the first American to prosper as a professional novelist. He found writing so entrancing and fulfilling because, to his initial surprise, it satisfied his deep, but long frustrated, hunger for public influence and power. Unable to replicate his father's success as a politician and developer, Cooper found his own prestige and primacy as a popular novelist and literary spokesman for the nation.

Indeed, he became the most influential American writer of the nineteenth century. In particular, Cooper created the stock characters—the noble but doomed Indian, the resourceful frontiersman and the loyal slave—as well as the favourite settings, especially the violent frontier, that characterised most historical romances through the nineteenth century and into the twentieth. In Harvey Birch, of *The Spy* and Natty Bumppo of *The Pioneers,* James Fenimore Cooper created the essential American hero of innumerable novels, stories and films: the socially marginal and rootless loner operating in a violent no-man's land beyond the rule of law, but guided by his own superior code of justice.

Whether imitating or deriding Cooper, his rivals and successors could never escape the long shadow of his most popular romances nor fully transcend the expectations that he planted in the minds of their readers.

FOR FURTHER READING:

James Franklin Beard, ed., *The Letters and Journals of James Fenimore Cooper,* 6 vols. (Harvard University Press, 1960–1968); James Fenimore Cooper, *Notions of the Americans, Picked Up by a Travelling Bachelor* (Frederick Ungar, 1963); James Fenimore Cooper, *The Pioneers, or the Sources of the Susquehannah; A Descriptive Tale* (State University Press of New York, 1980); Wayne Franklin, *The New World of James Fenimore Cooper* (University of Chicago Press, 1982); Warren Motley, *The American Abraham: James Fenimore Cooper and the Frontier Patriarch* (Columbia University Press, 1987); James D. Wallace, *Early Cooper and His Audience* (Columbia University Press, 1986).

Congress Couldn't Have Been *This* Bad, or Could It?

If you think things are pretty messy on Capitol Hill today, just take a look at what was going on up there a century and a half ago

James R. Chiles

James Chiles is a frequent contributor. His most recent article (July 1994) dealt with the arduous digging of New York City's latest water tunnel.

When Charles Dickens visited the U.S. Congress in 1842, he found "some men of high character and great abilities." But many, the noted English novelist reported, practiced "despicable trickery at elections; underhanded tamperings with public officers; cowardly attacks upon opponents," not to mention "aidings and abettings of every bad inclination in the popular mind."

During his visit, Dickens heard one Congressman threaten to cut another's throat, and was surprised that the House did nothing to discipline the scoundrel. "There he sat among them," the stunned novelist wrote, "not crushed by the general feeling of the assembly—but as good a man as any."

Members of the House, Dickens also noted, sat at their desks with their feet propped up, lavishly spitting tobacco juice. "Both houses are handsomely carpeted; but the state to which these carpets are reduced by the universal disregard of the spittoon . . . do not admit of being described." Strangers, he continued, should be wary of picking up any article from the floor "with an ungloved hand."

Anyone inclined to dismiss Dickens as a snobbish and sarcastic Briton with heightened powers of description need only consult other local sources. In 1837, according to a contemporary newspaper reporter, you could easily slip on the "disgusting compound of tobacco juice, wafers and sand" that coated the floor of the House of Representatives. Young messengers often slid down the aisles on the loose papers that accumulated there. "Not all the soap and scrubbing-brushes in christendom," the reporter wrote of the chamber, "would make it fit for a peasant's hut."

It was at about this time, too, that the House found itself reduced to fining members who missed roll call. To avoid the $2 fine, some Honorable Members were not above scooting in through open windows or sliding down columns from the gallery.

Indeed, voters who share the current dissatisfaction with the goings-on of the people's representatives on Capitol Hill, or deplore the current levels of partisanship in American politics, should take a measure of comfort from a look at how things used to be in the good old days.

In the first half of the 19th century, members of Congress, untroubled by the relentless gaze of C-SPAN, were not under the direct scrutiny of the public eye. Like many Americans in a rough-and-tumble new nation, they indulged in bad manners, unruly behavior and sometimes outright violence. Long before Representative Preston Brooks of South Carolina beat Senator Charles Sumner of Massachusetts into unconsciousness in a celebrated 1856 dispute over slavery, Congressmen regularly attacked one another—with words and, on occasion, weapons.

There was much to get violent about. Every time a new territory clamored for statehood, it threatened the balance of Congressional power between the various rival regions (East versus West, North versus South) and eventually between slave states and free states. Congressmen battled tooth and nail over tariffs—the federal government's main source of income—which helped the commercial Northeast at the expense of the agricultural South, and gave more power to the federal government than the states' rights followers of Thomas Jefferson thought tolerable.

Long before the Civil War, South Carolina talked hotly of nullifying the Constitution on this issue, even of outright secession from the Union. The question of whether or not to have a national bank sundered state from state and brother from brother at a time when many Americans still thought lending money at interest was not only unchristian but akin to theft. And farmers (circa 1830, about 70 percent of the population) just knew that people who didn't plant and harvest—that is, urban stockjobbers and Northern moneymen—were not to be trusted.

A good deal of Congressional exacerbation had to do with conditions in the nation's new capital, a muggy, barren spot regarded for years as a provincial and unhealthy outpost by the diplomatic corps of European nations. For decades the capital city seemed raw and only half-built, with weed-choked bare lots and streets of yellow clay. To keep carriages from foundering in heavy rains, logs had to be thrown into the deepest mudholes of Washington's unpaved roads. One Representative who ventured out at night for a social visit in 1818 complained that he slipped into gutters, fell over dirt piles and tripped over bricks and barrels—because the District of Columbia, then as now, fiscally feckless, hadn't supplied the streetlamps with fuel. Hogs got to be such a nuisance that in 1828 the police issued a stern warning: any porker found running loose in the streets would be arrested—and promptly sold.

Like their modern-day counterparts, early Congressmen had to wrangle together and somehow pass the expanding nation's laws. But their lifestyles, like those of most Americans, were totally different from today's. Forget about weekend jaunts home to campaign or see friends. Until the completion of the Erie Canal in 1825 and the arrival of rail connections in the mid-1830s, members rarely got home at all during the session, which began in December and lasted from four to six months. The journey from Washington to Boston took 11 days by coach in 1807, and sometimes coaches could not get through at all. Until the early 1850s, most of the members did not bring their wives and families to Washington.

Today, staff for 535 Senators and Representatives runs to about 18,000 people, with an annual payroll of more than $1 billion. But for the first century of Congress, our public servants had little or no personal staff to help draft legislation or answer letters. And they did receive letters; in those days citizens took their right of petition seriously. During a two-year term starting in 1817, Delegate John Scott from the Territory of Missouri received more than 1,000 petitions on subjects ranging from widows' woes to patent applications to damage claims for property destroyed during Indian raids. At the time, the entire population of Missouri was something like 65,000.

Without staff, Congressmen had no need for the suites of offices their successors have today. In fact, most had no offices at all. They spent their days at assigned desks in the House or Senate chamber. At night there was still no privacy from politically hostile colleagues. Until the mid-1840s, most Congressmen lived together in boardinghouses and were sometimes obliged to bunk two to a room.

Finding a boardinghouse was a Congressman's first job on arriving in Washington. Dozens of these establishments were advertised in city papers like the *National Intelligencer.* ("Mrs. Cottringer, in Ninth street a few doors South of E street," read an 1831 notice, "can accommodate a Mess of Members of Congress, or other strangers visiting the City.")

THE WORKS—FOR EIGHT BUCKS A WEEK

Congressional boardinghouses clustered in three places around town. Some of the oldest were in Georgetown, a long, bumpy carriage ride from the Capitol, but already well established by 1800, the year when the capital was moved from Philadelphia to the raw, new city of Washington. Another clutch of House and Senate hostelries sat back on Capitol Hill, where today's Supreme Court and Library of Congress now stand. A third group ranged itself along the base of the Hill, facing what are now the Mall and the Washington Monument.

In 1835, $8—a full day's pay for House members—bought Representative John Fairfield of Maine a room and his meals for a week, fuel for his fireplace and two spermaceti candles to read by. Meals were substantial: Fairfield commonly sat down to a breakfast of coffee, beefsteak, mutton, sausage, hominy and buckwheat cakes, corncakes or biscuits. At meals, Congressmen sat like schoolboys at assigned places, with the proprietor at the head of the table.

Boarders slept and lived upstairs but often gathered as at an English inn, in first-floor common rooms. Such gatherings were not always congenial. "At Capt. Coyle's . . . there are 16 of us," Senator William Plumer of New Hampshire complained to his diary in 1806. "This is too many—We have too much noise. . . . In each chamber there are two lodgers—This is very inconvenient. 'Tis difficult to obtain an hour's quiet. . . . your papers are too much exposed or you must constantly be on you guard. I believe I have kept mine secret."

A Republican allied with President Jefferson (who had lived in a boardinghouse himself when he was Washington's Vice President), poor Plumer found himself outnumbered by Federalist housemates who opposed Jefferson's attempts to limit federal power: hence his care in guarding his papers. "I dare not invite a gentleman to call upon me whose politics are different," he wrote, "lest these violent inmates should treat him with rudeness & insult." Plumer once asked his Federalist housemates to notify him before they invited a certain Federalist to dinner, because, he said, he couldn't stand to eat with the gentleman.

A few years earlier, at a dinner in Miss Shields' boardinghouse, Representative John Randolph of Virginia, another Jeffersonian, and Representative Willis Alston, a Federalist from North Carolina, ended an evening of verbal insult by throwing glassware at each other. They managed not to interact for the next six years—until Alston insulted Randolph one day on their way out of session. Randolph whacked Alston on the head with his riding crop, drawing blood, and paid a fine of $20 for the privilege.

If tempers did not noticeably improve, eventually the supply of Congressional boardinghouses did, enough so that single bedrooms became the norm. Congressmen also got better at sorting themselves out into more or less congenial groups. Over the years, predominantly Republican or Federalist houses evolved, as well as houses that catered to highly partisan political tastes. Quite early, there was a "War Hawks" boardinghouse (for supporters of the War of 1812) and, starting in the 1830s, a hostelry known as "Abolition House" for those opposing slavery (who, for years, tended to be dismissed as crackpots and political madmen).

Of course, parties and political allegiances evolved over time. A Representative who started out in 1800 as a Federalist conceivably might have joined Madison and Jefferson's new "Republican" Party (which later became the Democratic Party) after the Federalist Party petered out in 1814, supported Andrew Jackson as a Democrat in the late 1820s, and finally bolted to the Whigs after Jackson destroyed the Bank of the United States by removing federal funds from it in 1833. But whatever his political views, he could still find a "mess" of boarders somewhere who agreed with him.

Thus organized, the boardinghouses became the political "war rooms" of the day. Following a plan hatched in the boardinghouse known as the "war mess," a number of War Hawks burst into the House one night in June 1812. A group of Federalists had held the floor nonstop for three days, trying to fend off a vote on the declaration of war against Britain. The intruders grabbed brass spittoons from the floor, banging on the metal and flinging them around the room. The Federalist speaker, startled, abruptly shut up and sat down. A War Hawk instantly moved to cut off debate, and the fateful measure shot through the House like the proverbial hot knife through butter.

When the declaration came up for a vote in the Senate on June 18, the War Hawks apparently rounded up a drunken member, usually absent from important sessions, to help carry the vote. The nation was at war. When the news reached the war mess on New Jersey Avenue, 30-year-old Representative John C. Calhoun of South Carolina—often described as somber and humorless—reportedly threw his arms around the neck of Speaker of the House Henry Clay and joined his comrades in a Shawnee war dance around the boardinghouse table. ("I don't like Henry Clay," Calhoun once said. "He is a bad man, an imposter, a creator of wicked schemes. I wouldn't speak to him, but, by God, I love him.")

The camaraderie of boardinghouse life mattered enormously, too, because for decades there were few respectable things to do in Washington at night. Social life picked up over the years—and so did the social reputation of politicians, particularly members of the House, who were initially snubbed as yokels by such few Washington hostesses as there were. (Senators, always more staid than Congressmen, got a bit more respect.) But for years, by far the biggest nighttime diversion was cards—whist, faro and brag—played at those boarding-houses whose rules permitted it. One unhappy Congressman reported losing $3,500—more than a year's salary circa 1856—in a single evening.

Whenever they really got fed up, Congressmen agitated to move the nation's capital (it had been moved twice already), claiming that anywhere would be better than Washington in summer. During an early debate on the question of moving the capital, when citizens opposing the move turned up in the gallery, Senator James Jackson of Georgia threatened to call in the military and have them all shot. Threats of violence, however, were usually directed at other Congressmen. The House, particularly, was rough and raucous. The chamber's high, elliptical ceiling echoed and amplified every stray sound, from mild chatter and rustling newspapers to shouts. With all the noise, it was said at the time, no more than one-third of the members had any idea what was going on. With little chance, compared with today, of being instantly heard, either by colleagues or constituents, some members saw no need to curb their language. According to Augustus Foster, aide to England's minister to the United States, to

"judge from their Congress, one should suppose the nation to be the most blackguard society that was ever brought together."

Whether they acted well or badly, Congressmen didn't expect to stay around very long. There were no term limits, but voters, then as now, were a fickle lot. More important, before the great increase in federal power that set in after FDR and World War II, much of the political action was back in the state capitals. During the first four decades of Congress' existence, 41 percent of the House, on average, dropped out every two years.

Even so, both houses had their share of memorable and often contentious characters, some short-run, many very long-run indeed. A relative short-runner was Davy Crockett, "fresh from the backwoods, half-horse, half-alligator," who served as Representative from Tennessee for three terms. Starting in 1827, Crockett made quite an impression, but he never managed to pass the bill he cared about, opening government land in Tennessee to poor settlers. After losing his seat in 1835 Crockett told voters they could all go to hell. For his part, he was going to Texas (where he died—at the Alamo—within a year).

South Carolina's John C. Calhoun had been in the House for five years when, in 1816, Congress voted to give itself a substantial pay increase. The public was outraged, so the next year the measure was reversed. Calhoun, who predicted that men of high caliber would no longer seek Congressional office if salaries were not raised to equal or exceed those of Presidential appointees, resigned—to take on the higher-paying job of Secretary of War. Eventually, though, he returned to Congress, becoming one of those men who spent entire careers—or significant chunks of them—on Capitol Hill. After serving as Vice President from 1825 to 1832 under both John Quincy Adams and Andrew Jackson, Calhoun went to the Senate, and remained there, minus one year as Secretary of State to President John Tyler, until his death in 1850.

Daniel Webster, the renowned legal orator who could outwit the Devil himself, chose not to run in 1816. Seven years later, he was reelected to the House, went on to a seat in the Senate, where—despite being famously eloquent on the subjects of the sacredness of the Union and the need for aboli-

tion—he remained, off and on (mostly on), until 1850.

Calhoun's and Webster's careers resemble those of today's Congressional stars—rising from the House to the Senate or positions in the Cabinet—but their careers were unusual for their time. Today, most Senators voted out of office would sooner retire from politics than run for a seat in the lower house. But back then, the House of Representatives was where the real political power in Washington lay, and there were no high-paying lobbying firms, consulting groups or think tanks to absorb out-of-work politicians.

A spectacular example was John Quincy Adams, who got himself elected to the House after leaving the Presidency in 1829. Adams, a great public servant and defender of the citizen's right of petition, was appalled when, in 1836, Congress imposed a ban on the reading of abolitionist petitions—or any petition regarding slavery—in session. In protest, for nine years running, Adams opened each new session by reading aloud petitions he had received on the issue. "Nothing daunts him," said an observer at the time; "the House may ring with the cries of 'Order, order!'—unmoved, contemptuous, he stands amid the tempest, and, like an oak that knows his gnarled and knotted strength, stretches his arms forth, and defies the blast." Adams' dramatic brand of civil disobedience led to the repeal of the gag rule in 1844.

John Randolph of Virginia, another career Congressman, also took full advantage of his freedom of speech. Tall and pale, with black hair, Randolph dressed in buckskin riding clothes, carried a riding crop and often strode into the House with one or two hunting dogs at heel. But what truly distinguished him was his savage wit. He had a habit of pointing an index finger like grim Death while hurling remarks at adversaries. He once described a colleague as "the most contemptible and degraded of beings, whom no man ought to touch, unless with a pair of tongs."

First elected to Congress in 1799, Randolph was a brilliant orator, a strong defender of states' rights and a political maverick, holding seats in the House or Senate for most of the years until his death in 1833. Eventually, his language grew so sarcastic and abusive that many Senators simply left the chamber when he was speaking.

3. NATIONAL CONSOLIDATION AND EXPANSION

The one man in Congress who could control Randolph, it was believed, was Henry Clay of Kentucky, the "Western Star," who was elected Speaker by his colleagues on his very first day in the House in 1811. He served in that office for six terms—the longest tenure as Speaker of the House in the 19th century—his popularity due in part to his ability to squelch Randolph. The Clay-Randolph feud began in 1812, when Clay refused to entertain Randolph's resolution against the declaration of war. In 1820, after the House approved the Missouri Compromise—which temporarily helped maintain a balance between slave and free states—Clay again thwarted Randolph, this time refusing his motion to reconsider the bill. Not that Clay thought the action would change the vote—he simply didn't want to give Randolph the satisfaction of seeming to control the business of the House. At every turn, the two men butted heads. In 1826, they finally faced off in a duel.

Randolph—who despised Clay, but also secretly admired him—accepted Clay's challenge, declaring that he preferred "to be killed by Clay to any other death." But after two volleys, with the only injury a hole drilled through Randolph's flowing white coat, the two shook hands. ("You owe me a coat, Mr. Clay," Randolph said, to which Clay—then the Secretary of State—replied, "I am glad the debt is no greater.") It was, according to Senator Thomas Hart Benton (who had taken part in a few duels himself), "about the last high-toned duel that I have witnessed."

We think of duels as being fought with pistols or swords, but at least one Congressional duel was fought with rifles at a distance of 100 yards. After this particularly tragic encounter, dueling was outlawed in the capital. In 1838 Jonathan Cilley, a freshman Democratic Representative from Maine, made some comments in session that offended another first-termer, Whig William Graves of Kentucky. As was the custom, Graves challenged Cilley to a duel. The whole matter might have ended with everyone's honor and health intact, had it not been

for a Tyler Democrat named Henry A. Wise, who represented the state of Virginia.

A fiery defender of slavery, Wise—who later, as governor of Virginia, would have John Brown hanged—was, by all accounts, an angry, abrasive fellow. According to Benjamin Brown French, the Clerk of the House, Wise had "shot his former friend, Coke, through the arm, in a duel. His wife and brother have died, his house has been burned, he has been either a principal, or second, in three duels, in each of which blood has been shed."

Wise was even more riled up by Cilley's comments than was Representative Graves, and offered to serve as second to Graves, encouraging him to "kill that damned Yankee." On February 24, 1838, the two contestants met on the old dueling grounds in nearby Bladensburg, Maryland. Each took two shots at a distance of 100 yards. Both missed. That would have satisfied honor had not Wise insisted the duel continue. On the next round, Graves killed Cilley.

Congress, and the public, were shocked. The newspapers made much of Wise's murderous role. The next year, Congress passed a law banning the giving, delivering or accepting of a challenge to a duel in the District of Columbia.

Over the next ten years, Congress continued to lose its insularity. In 1848 a telegraphic network called the Associated Press began flashing accounts to newspapers all over the Eastern Seaboard. A few years later, the new Pitman system of speed stenography allowed Capitol Hill reporters to capture every word of Congressional debate. Transport and accommodations improved. Wives and families came to Washington, and a whole new, somewhat more decorous, social life expanded. The boarding-house life was fading. By 1850, less than half of the Senators still lodged in the old communal fashion.

Despite all the altercations, the early Congresses managed to cover a considerable amount of legislative ground, ranging from what paintings should hang in the Rotunda to a tariff on imported pasta to the construction of a national road (from Maryland to Illinois) to the settle-

ment of international boundary disputes with Spain and Britain. Congress also brought increasing order to its dealings in the form of a growing body of precedents, committees and subcommittees—during a period when the country, and its Congress, more than doubled in size and complexity.

Yet the ire of the men Dickens called "desperate adventurers" did not fade, especially as the struggle over the ratio of new slave states to free states began to burn hotter still. During debates on the Compromise of 1850—through which Congress hoped to avoid civil war—Senator Thomas Hart Benton of Missouri, who favored compromise, advanced in a rage on Senator Henry S. Foote of Mississippi. Foote pulled out a big pistol. Benton, safely restrained by his colleagues, shouted, "Let him fire! . . . I have no pistol! I disdain to carry arms! Stand out of the way, and let the assassin fire!" One Senator said that during the stressful 1850s the only members not carrying a knife and a revolver were those carrying two revolvers.

The Compromise—an attempt to resolve disputes over slavery in the Western territories lately gained in the Mexican War—allowed Congress to avoid the issue for several years, but in the end, it did not work. Six years after its passage, Representative Brooks brutally beat abolitionist Senator Sumner. It took three and a half years for Sumner to recover fully, and by then, the country was on the brink of civil war.

ADDITIONAL SOURCES

On the Hill: A History of the American Congress by Alvin M. Josephy jr., Simon and Schuster, 1979

Congressional Anecdotes by Paul F. Boller jr., Oxford University Press, 1991

Washington: A History of the Capital, 1800–1950 by Constance McLaughlin Green, Princeton University Press, 1962

Witness to the Young Republic by Benjamin Brown French, University Press of New England (Hanover, New Hampshire), 1989

The Great Triumvirate: Webster, Clay, and Calhoun by Merrill D. Peterson, Oxford University Press, 1987

Women at Large: Travel in Antebellum America

How easy or safe was it for women who travelled—often alone—in the new American republic? Patricia Cline Cohen charts their progress—and perils—and the way in which public transport helped shape the gender system.

Patricia Cline Cohen

Patricia Cline Cohen is Professor of History and Chair of the Women's Studies Program at the University of California at Santa Barbara. She is the author of A Calculating People: The Spread of Numeracy in Early America *(Chicago, 1982).*

In the sixty years from the 1790s to the 1840s, the United States experienced what has been aptly termed a 'transportation revolution'. Revolutionary it truly was, for the social, economic and political consequences of the changes in transportation were far-reaching and transformative. Usually historians identify activities such as the growth of markets and the flow of information as the most significant results of the growth of regularised stagecoach, canal boat or railroad routes. But equally important, the transportation revolution altered gender relations as well. The speed, convenience and regularity of travel (compared to earlier years) enticed many more passengers to take to the roads, among them large numbers of women.

Back in the 1770s, when travel depended on individual equestrian skills or access to the rare private coach, one young mother named Abigail Adams commented to a male correspondent on American women's low propensity to travel, which she framed in terms of women's weakness as well as sexual danger:

> Women ... inherit an Eaquel Share of curiosity with the other Sex, yet but few are hardy eno' to venture abroad, and explore the amazing variety of distant lands. The Natural tenderness and Delicacy of our Constitutions, added to the many Dangers we are subject to from your Sex, renders it almost imposible for a Single Lady to travel without injury to her character.

Having a husband for escortage hardly helped matters, Adams added, since married women 'have generally speaking obstacles sufficient to prevent their Roving', namely small children. Within her lifetime, Adams was to see the advent of a transportation revolution that made travel feasible, routine and even attractive. Women could now 'rove' to a degree unparalleled before; adventure beckoned, curiosity could be satisfied. But there was an inherent risk as well as benefit for women in the new forms of transport. Women did not move confidently into public space on the same terms as male rovers and travellers.

Consider, for example, the information about gender and travel embedded in this story, reported in several newspapers in January 1836. On a wintry day, a young Vermont girl visiting relatives in Boston accepted a treat from a man she had only recently met: a ride on the newly opened Boston and Worcester Road, a forty-four mile railway. Perhaps she did not see her decision as risky, since the train was a public space under the watchful eyes of a conductor, and she figured she would return within the day. Perhaps the sheer attraction of an exciting experience overcame her better judgement; there were no trains yet in Vermont in 1836. The fare was $2 each way, not something that a young girl could afford to spend on her own for a lark. A legal expert later called in to help adjudicate the resulting trial for abduction explained:

> Some will say, it *looks suspicious* for a young girl to come off with a man, comparatively a stranger; here she was imprudent, she sees and owns it now. I am told it is a common, fashionable thing to take the railroad to Worcester and return again in a few hours to Boston.

Unfortunately for the unsuspecting girl, her escort had ulterior motives. When the couple arrived at Worcester, the man informed her he had business to conduct in Hartford, Connecticut, a long day's travel to the south-east by stage. The girl protested, but the fact that she had no money left her no option. Once at Hartford, the man booked two rooms at the local Temperance Hotel for the night. Perhaps this sober and moral hotel allayed the girl's worst fears for the moment.

The next day the man insisted that the fastest way back to Boston was to travel to New Haven and catch a packet boat around the coast. The girl was by now sufficiently alarmed that she confided her circumstances to the hotel maids. Soon the hotel owner set off after the couple, but not in time to stop the man from embarking not for Boston but for New York City, America's capital of vice in the 1830s. Once there, the man forcibly took the girl to a hotel room where she encountered her true opponent, a fifty-three year old judge from her hometown in Vermont. The judge was a distinguished member of the bar, a recent candidate for Congress, and a reputed rake and libertine. Newspapers alleged that he paid his agent to procure the Vermont girl, bring her to New York, and set her up for a rape or seduction. The girl heroically resisted and escaped, aided by the timely arrival of the Hartford hotel owner.

This well-publicised story served as a cautionary tale about travel and gender in antebellum America. Newspaper readers were instructed about the potential dangers to women posed by fast-moving men. Abductors now had available new forms of transport which allowed them to spirit their unwitting victims far from the safety of home. This could happen in part because trains were new and enticing, an attractive lure for a naive girl, and seemingly rather safe. The fixed track, the short distance, even the spatial configuration of railroad cars offered assurance of safety. American-style multi-passenger cars were very open and public, unlike European compartment trains built to resemble contiguous stagecoach cabins, cloistered and private. But of course, without money a poor girl in the end was at the mercy of others for her safe passage.

The transportation revolution unfolded between 1790 and 1840 in four overlapping stages, each with its own particular contribution to make to the gendered etiquette of travel. Beginning in the 1790s, postroads and turnpikes were built and extended, making possible thrice-daily stage coach service between major destinations. By the decade of the 1810s, stagecoaches were utterly

The Morris canal with its inclined planes connecting the Hudson and the Delaware—a sketch from Frances Trollope's book describing her travels in America in 1832. Canal boats were a popular mode of transport by the early 19th century and generally contained a separate Ladies' Cabin.

common, rumbling along dirt or plank roads from Augusta, Maine, to Augusta, Georgia. The nine-passenger Concord coach quickly became the industry standard, and both male and female passengers crowded into them, elbow to elbow and knees touching backsides when the three seats—two facing front, one facing back—were entirely full.

Surviving passenger lists amply demonstrate that typical stagecoach assemblages were thoroughly mixed by age and sex. By custom and sometimes by company rule, women passengers did not ride on top with the driver. Inside the cabin, courteous men were supposed to yield the back-row seats to women, the row that both faced front and provided back support. Passengers of course were not free to move about in such a confined space and thus could not easily pick and choose conversation partners. Given the length of most trips, total isolation from other passengers was uncommon. Nowadays we combat stranger intrusiveness on the crowded underground or subway by looking past people and constructing a bubble of solitude. But early stagecoach rides enforced sociability, much more than did boats or trains, where onboard mobility

allowed for a degree of choice in interaction with strangers.

Even when sociability was high in a stagecoach, there were stil gender conventions in conversations: politics and current events were common subjects of talk among men but not women. As one young woman put it, in an 1828 letter to her mother describing a trip she took with a coach full of men, the conversation:

> . . . was upon subjects that ladies are not often consulted about, such as the presidential election, tariff, canals, slave trade, smuggling, &c &c. Some part of the time I felt somewhat more alone, than if alone.

Though excluded from conversation, this girl was not invisible. The close, fixed seating and the face-to-face configuration of the rows made every passenger quite visible. A woman passenger was subject to the gaze of others, but ultimately that visibility provided an additional safety feature, that every person's behaviour was under close scrutiny.

Canal boats came next in chronology and popularity. The completion of the 400-mile Erie Canal in 1825 marked the highpoint of this new form of travel.

When the tow-path was well maintained and the moon was high, animals could pull canal boats by night as well as by day, permitting a slow but steady 24-hour a day travel service. Night-time travel required an etiquette of public sleeping, so canal boats generally contained a Ladies' Cabin, with berths, settees, and sometimes a female attendant on duty. Men and boys slept on the deck of the boat, or in a room next to the ladies' cabin, which was never called the men's cabin, since during daytime hours, women could also occupy that space.

Commercial steamboats came on line soon after 1808, when the first steam-powered vessel, developed by Robert Fulton, went up the Hudson against the current. By the 1830s, steamboats prevailed on all the major and many of the minor river systems in the country. A traveller could leave New York City in a steamboat, disembark at Albany to pick up a canal boat, float to Niagara Falls and there catch a steamboat on the Great Lakes that churned all the way to Chicago. An alternate Grand Tour route traversed the Ohio and Mississippi Rivers to New Orleans. Pleasure journeys for people with money and leisure time came into style. As in the canal boats, Ladies' Cabins for sitting and sleeping marked out a space of retreat for women passengers, a retreat deemed unnecessary for men.

Railroads completed this transportation revolution. The 14-mile Baltimore and Ohio Road of 1829 was the first; by the mid 1830s a veritable railroad mania afflicted the country. By the end of the decade, some 4,000 miles of track webbed the eastern United States, and steam engines strewing ash and cinders pulled passengers along at the incredible speed of 30 miles per hour. There were no ladies-only railway cars in the antebellum period; gender segregation is, after all, costly to railroads, since there is no guarantee that sixty unescorted women will show up to purchase seats sufficient to fill a car. And many women did travel with men, which argues for a considerable space devoted to mixed-sex seating. Where railroads did honour gender was in the construction of major railway stations, which typically provided Ladies' waiting rooms, insulated places where women could wait for trains, nurse babies, and not be bothered by men.

An articulated concern to protect travelling women from unauthorised approaches by men seems to have materialised most clearly and fully in the 1830s and not earlier. The basic concern of course was never completely absent; the comment from Abigail Adams in 1771 to the effect that women were constrained from travel due to 'the many Dangers we are subject to from your Sex' manifests a realistic anxiety about the age-old power inequality between the sexes that posed risks for women in public without male protectors. But not all women abroad were equally at risk to the depredations of all men. Class and race status generally protected many travelling women from uncomfortable assertions of male sexual privilege.

What was new and different in the 1830s about gender relations in public was the fact that greatly improved, regularised, and cheapened public transport launched thousands of young girls and women not of the privileged classes out into canals and railways, in search of employment or on the path to far-flung relatives' houses to participate in a broadening circle of female waged and unwaged labour. In other words, not only were there more unescorted women, they were younger, inexperienced, and unprotected by class status.

The same economic factors of cheap transport and an ever-enlarging circle of employment opportunities put young men on the road too, men who increasingly saw young women alone as legitimate objects of fantasy and desire. Male sexual privilege could be shaped, constrained and policed by local customs in a small home community, but on the loose, in public with little accountability for their actions, some men began to exercise their imaginations more liberally. Male sexual privilege might be displayed in subtle ways, as in prolonged gazes, or in not so subtle ways, such as unilateral touching and in insistent and too-intimate conversation. At its worst, male sexual privilege assumed that unescorted women were open targets for sexual conquest.

Three kinds of sources disclose evidence of male sexual privilege as it was expressed in public behaviours. Most directly, young men themselves wrote about it, in letters, in travel diaries and in published accounts of travel, that exude a sense of entitlement to these attitudes. A second window comes from women who witnessed or experienced it.

Sometimes their references in letters and travel accounts are oblique, as if it were not their place to criticise men; so instead we get description of strategies undertaken to deflect male presumption and make the women less noticeable, strategies like pointed references to wearing hats with veils and unshowy clothes. A third window is provided by people who assumed the role of authority in policing inappropriate male behaviour and intervening in gender interactions. Sometimes these monitors were older, concerned women, who reported on their interventions in the anti-licentious columns of journals like the *Advocate of Moral Reform*. And sometimes the monitors were actually the police, called upon to arrest someone for criminal behaviour, as in the case of the gullible Vermont girl who merely fancied a daytrip by train.

For male accounts, consider this reverie elaborated by a young bachelor. Willis Gaylord Clark, writing in 1835 in the *Knickerbocker*, took a trip by steamboat up the Hudson River and crowed about the pleasures of staring at women:

I regard ladies in public masses, as I do a splendid gallery of pictures. I say, reader—just in your individual ear—did you never particularly relish a jaunt on board a steamboat, when you found beautiful women there? Tell me honestly, did they not, though strangers, materially enhance the delightsomeness of your journey? Have you not singled out some fairest One of them all, and directed a volley of desperately-agreeable looks to her-ward; greatly delectated, peradventure, when they met return? . . . It is one of those pleasures that nobody writes about, and every body feels.

Young Clark whispers in his (male) reader's ear about this fleeting and harmless fantasy that sweetens existence, as he called it. When a girl returns his volley of glances, his heart quickens; he never stops to consider that his attentions might make some young women a trifle nervous.

Other young men confessed to the hobby of girl-watching. A fellow grandly named George Washington Johnson kept a diary of a canal boat tour through New York in 1833, on his way to Dutchess County to ask a young woman to marry him. At every step he was alert to the presence of women and even fancied that young women were eager to make his acquaintance. At a hotel in Batavia, New York, for example, he imagined that 'five hundred women overran me at dinner. One, in particular, passed and repassed me three times to be seen of G. W. J.'. On the boat after Utica, he counted six likely women on board, out of forty passengers. 'I am shaved, dressed, and in all respects in fine trim', he boasted, ready for flirtation.

But alas, canal boating proved to be 'a dull way of travelling and less social than the stage, the ladies getting by themselves, and I being too shy to pursue them'. A clergyman was not too shy, he noted, and engaged the women in a checkers game. 'Ah, your parsons know the way to the women! Would that I did!' So uncertain was young Johnson about his prospects for success with women that when he got to his destination he failed to pop the marriage question to his young intended. On the trip home, he consoled his ego by again imagining his powers of charm. At Little Falls he wrote 'All civil to me. Am rather courted. Whence I infer I possess considerable powers of pleasing'. West of Utica he was still admiring his success with female strangers: 'Made myself a favorite again'.

Yet another example of a man taking pleasures that he unreflectingly assumed were harmless involved a young Scotsman who took a crowded overnight stage in Virginia in 1836. Robert Brownlee found himself seated next to a black woman, and as sleep overcame the passengers he found it easy and very pleasurable to lean close to the woman's body without seeming to raise her suspicions or her ire. Could Brownlee actually have been unaware of the racialised power differential that would have prevented the woman from raising a complaint? A black woman in the South, whether slave or free, could not claim the same privileges of gender as white women. Her experience of the Scotsman's night-time snuggling can only be imagined, and it seems unlikely that she slept as peacefully as he did—or that she slept at all.

Women travellers had varied reactions to clear signs of male interest in them. A number of them reported in letters that they took pains to remain reserved, so as not to invite undue intimacies. Hats with veils provided convenient barriers to eye contact. Real

All crammed in: an extraordinary coach assemblage on the Baltimore and Ohio Railroad in the 1830s, and (below) a later 1848 woodcut of a women's sleeping car on the railway. Segregated by night, by day mixed-sex seating was the norm.

or imaginary male escorts provided another level of protection. A young married woman from Brookline, Massachusetts, got on a stage in 1819 and invented a story that at once established her class position and named her protector. She looked around at the other passengers, all men, and asked aloud if any of them had a letter from her brother, Lewis Tappan, a leading merchant in Boston. 'The answer was no. I then observed to the gentleman on my right hand, that I was very much disappointed, for my brother had promised me a protector'. Her ruse worked to establish her own privileged position, on which none of those men would dare to presume.

Occasionally there is evidence of young women who welcomed and returned appraising glances from men. One such young woman was Sarah Mendell, twenty-six, from western New York State. Mendell travelled freely in the 1850s as an agent selling subscription books. She had a keen sense of the adventure of travel and a striking disregard for how ladies ought to behave. In one stagecoach interchange a rough Irishman called her a sweet creature. Mendell reflected:

I suppose discreet young ladies would have frowned at such a compliment; but how could I, when I was so pleased? I suppose I *should* have put all conversation bestowed on me to silence, by a decided mumness. But I have yet to learn, that woman can sustain her purity, or benefit her race most, by such seclusion of herself from those to whom she has not had a formal introduction.

Within a few months this same Sarah Mendell would learn the benefits of seclusion and suspicion. On a train to Washington, a man bent on undue familiarities began to chat her up. Mendell's letter to a friend elaborated in wonderful detail her shifting and ambivalent feelings as the man pressed his attentions. Even this adventuresome woman, normally unafraid to accept compliments from admiring men, sensed that something was seriously amiss:

I have seen a wolf! yes, a wolf— I'm sure he was—on the cars! What! a wolf on the cars, and in the passenger train? Yes; but he had on sheep's clothing, . . . It makes me shudder now with very fear, when I think how he turned his big eyes on me! I looked away, and hardly dared breathe. By-and-by, he took a seat nearer me. I kept looking out the window; then he offered me a newspaper . . . I looked very cross, and told him I never read when I was travelling; but he did not care, and took a seat just before me. O! dear! I thought I should scream with fright—I could scarcely sit still; and he said he had met me before. I knew I never had met a wolf before—how could I have forgotten it? . . . I did not say a word, but looked very intent upon the passing country. He said that he had met me when I was travelling, and that I talked with him. I could not remember meeting him . . . He said I was a book agent; and, he pitied me very much. . . . I did not need any pity, and told him so, but he talked on; he told me he had two lambs, one of them was his companion . . . — and that he had a young and tender little lamb—he was its father—and his eyes grew so beautiful as he talked of it. What! a father be a wolf? No, no; it could not be. I was sorry I thought him a wolf—how cruel! He did not look so like a wolf either,—no. I would talk, and make it up. How wrong to distrust! He told me that he lived in Washington. Humph! I have heard of wolves there, but he was not one.

I told him I was going to Washington. He said he could aid me there, and he advised me what was best to do,—for which I was thankful, and told him so. He said a warm heart like mine must be sad at times. I wished he had not said thus; but he looked so innocent, as if it was nothing to say. I told him if my friend did not meet me, I might be lonely sometimes. He said he would be my friend, and wanted me to trust him entirely; that he knew how I would want someone to trust, in a city like Washington, and talked much about his benevolence, and my having entire confidence in him. I told him my nature was very stubborn, and I could not trust, until I could not help it. But he said the same thing again, and more too— many things I thought very wrong, about admiring me; but he always looked so innocent, as if it was nothing bad. How dare I be angry, and too, when he had talked so well, and had thought he was not a wolf; but I wished he was away, be whatever he might. O! dear! He said I had beautiful eyes—so beautiful! O! just as the wolf talked to 'little Red Riding-Hood'. I looked as angry as I could, and my face grew red. He did not look at me, but kept on talking, and said I had a pretty little hand. What a falsehood! I knew then he was a wolf. O! how I trembled; I felt so grieved that a father should be a wolf. How dreadful! I shall never speak again to one that looks like a wolf at first.

Mendell's initial intuition about this man proved correct. She distrusted him on approach, but then softened as he discussed his family. However the insistent talk of trust, followed by a barrage of compliments, set off the warning bells again in her head. She did not reveal how she shook him off; perhaps her show of anger did the trick. Probably not very many young women of the mid-nineteenth century were as accomplished and assertive in dealing with strange men as was Sarah Mendell.

Older women of the New York Moral Reform Society took to policing the behaviour of men in public. Their newspaper frequently carried accounts of their protective actions on behalf of girls, who by age and dress appeared unable to fend off or recognise untoward attentions. Police authorities also got involved in cases, but only when a criminal act was alleged, as in the 1847 case of a girl raped by a train conductor. Strangely enough, however, rape was rarely mentioned as a threat to women. The concern in the period from the 1830s to the 1850s focused much more on seduction, on the artful conquest of women through deceit and trickery. Travel was a new, attractive, and yet also disorientating enough experience for women (and men too) that they were perhaps more open to offers of assistance and guidance than travellers today are. If gullible girls could be easily lured into the train out of Boston, if young women travelling to Washington freely expressed a need for advice about what to see and do in a strange city, then the way was open to clever men on the make to take advantage of women's apparent trust and helplessness.

The transportation revolution is a much overlooked and important source of change in the gender system in the early nineteenth century. As a newly emerging public activity, travel offered a cultural space for interactions that reflected negotiations in the power relations between men and women, even as it offered opportunities for some women and men to explore alternative behaviours and identities. Both Sarah Mendell and the wolf she encountered on that train were behaving in ways that would probably not meet with approval in the bosom of their home communities. The possibility of movement, both rapid and far from home, untied people from obligations, restrictions and expectations. For some, it led to experimentation with different styles of behaviour.

This rather worrisome possibility inherent in travel produced in response an etiquette of travel that emphasised rigid codes of conduct, rules of politeness and sex segregation where feasible. Public transport thus shaped the gender system by spurring the articulation of fairly rigid male-female codes of behaviour, even as it provided the very arena where those behaviours would be tested, challenged, and stretched by individuals emboldened by the freedom from convention that travel also provided.

FOR FURTHER READING:

George Rogers Taylor, *The Transportation Revolution, 1815–1860* (Rinehardt, 1951); Seymour Dunbar. *A History of Travel in America* (Tudor Publishing Company, 1937); Patricia Cline Cohen, 'Safety and Danger: Women on American Public Transport, 1750–1850' in Susan Reverby and Dorothy Helly, eds., *Gendered Domains: Public and Private Spheres in Historical Perspective* (Cornell University Press, 1992); Sara Mills, *Discourses of Difference: An Analysis of Women's Travel Writing and Colonialism* (Routledge, 1991); Mary Louise Pratt, *Imperial Writing: Travel Writing and Transculturation* (Routledge, 1992). Sarah Mendell, book agent, published her account under the title *Notes of Life and Travel* (New York, 1854) carrying the byline 'by the Misses Hosmer and Mendell'.

1846: The Way We Were— and the Way We Went

The year the Smithsonian was born, America picked up a million square miles of real estate and our westward destiny was highly manifest

Timothy Foote

It was a year when people were reading "The Raven" by a neurotic genius who had flunked out of West Point. It was the year when Melville scored a hit with *Typee,* his first South Seas adventure; five years later *Moby-Dick* stirred hardly a ripple. The first game of baseball (*not* invented by Abner Doubleday) was played with present-day rules. Walt Whitman, age 26, landed a job as editor of the *Brooklyn Eagle.* In Manhattan P. T. Barnum, already rich and famous for "exhibiting all that is monstrous, scaley, strange and queer," was pleasing crowds with the latest of his Fat Boys.

It was a year when, at a great industrial fair in the nation's capital, inventor Elias Howe showed off his amazing new sewing machine. The first telegraph lines had been strung between Baltimore and Washington. During an operation at Massachusetts General Hospital in Boston a dentist named William Morton administered ether in the first public demonstration of its use as an anesthetic. Thereafter the help of three or four men need no longer be required to amputate a leg or pull a tooth.

It was a year when some 20,000 Mormons, savagely driven out of Nauvoo, Illinois, a city they built as a New Jerusalem, crossed the icy Mississippi to safety in Iowa. They were abolitionists who had lately begun to practice polygamy; their prophet, Joseph Smith, and his brother had been taken from jail and

murdered. Now, under Brigham Young, they were on the point of heading farther west, not seeking any green and desirable place (where Young figured they would be attacked again) but some site where, with discipline and the help of the Almighty, they aimed to make the desert bloom.

To the south, in Independence, Missouri, several thousand emigrants, westward bound out of the United States for the Oregon territory and for California, then part of Mexico, were about to set off toward Fort Laramie and the Platte River, an early stop on what was to become famous as the Oregon Trail. Already at Laramie was an ambitious historian-to-be, 22-year-old Francis Parkman, Harvard '44, who intended to study Indians. He needed to know about them because he planned to write about the French and their Indian allies, but in his research back East the only Indians he could find were already completely corrupted by white civilization. The Indians around Fort Laramie turned up each day to cadge a handout of biscuits and coffee, and menace arriving wagon trains if the emigrants didn't give them richer fare. So Parkman was headed out to live in a remote Oglala Sioux village. The emigrants also disappointed him. They seemed to him "like a troop of schoolboys lost in the woods."

Also heading west was young Charles Stanton, who was exhilarated after crossing the Continental Divide at South Pass. "I have seen the Rocky Mountains," he wrote his brother, "and am now on the waters that flow to the Pacific! It seems as if I had left the old

world behind and a new one is dawning upon me." Stanton was traveling with the Donner Party. On December 21—snowblind, frozen, starving and alone—he died after trying to help others make it over the last few agonizing miles of the Sierra Nevada and down into sunny California.

The year, of course, was 1846. We are just now commemorating it hereabouts as the Smithsonian Institution celebrates its 150th birthday, complete with a traveling show and a special exhibit at the National Portrait Gallery. Quite apart from the Smithsonian's founding, 1846 was an astonishing year. It was the year the Mexican War began. The year when the country, taking a quantum leap forward, suddenly completed the westward course of empire that Jefferson had dreamed of when he sent Lewis and Clark out exploring 40 years before. As 1846 began, the Union occupied less than half of what is the continental United States today; when it was over we possessed, or were soon to possess, all of it.

This was accomplished by means that are controversial to this day—the canny use of cash, diplomatic deal-making, the threat of war and, finally, when the others failed, war itself. The war left us with 13,000 American dead—only 1,721 died in battle, most of the rest from disease. President James Polk's policies changed the contour of the country by adding more than a million square miles of territory. Some claimed they changed the content of our national character—and for the worse.

The author, on the Board of Editors, recently wrote about D-Day and the Irish "Troubles" of 1916–22.

From *Smithsonian,* April 1996, pp. 38–46, 48, 50–52. © 1996 by Timothy Foote. Reprinted by permission.

3. NATIONAL CONSOLIDATION AND EXPANSION

On May 3, 1846, down in steamy Fort Brown (now Brownsville, Texas), Ulysses S. Grant, a 24-year-old second lieutenant, heard enemy gunfire for the first time. The war he was about to fight, Grant figured (incorrectly, it turned out), would encourage the spread of slavery, and he wrote home, "I felt sorry that I had enlisted." In July, to protest that same war, Henry David Thoreau refused to pay his Concord, Massachusetts, poll tax. Characteristically, his aunt paid it for him, so after a night in jail he repaired to a nearby small lake to contemplate further civil disobedience and the changing seasons.

The war added place-names like Buena Vista and Chapultepec to the American vocabulary. It brought to the fore two generals. Zachary Taylor, fondly known to his men as "Old Rough and Ready," dressed like a tramp, believed in the bayonet but fortunately had light artillery. In 1848 he would parlay his fighting fame into the Presidency. Towering Winfield Scott, unfondly known as "Old Fuss and Feathers," for years unsuccessfully aspired to the Presidency. But Scott won victories while keeping casualties to a minimum, and he ended the fighting in 1847 by jumping off across Mexico from the coast at Veracruz, driving toward Mexico City. His soldiers were always outnumbered, but they defeated Santa Anna again and again until the capital fell, in a campaign still admired by military tacticians.

Alexis de Tocqueville regarded America as one of the hopes of the world but nevertheless noted that Americans were "slaves of slogans." The slogan of choice in 1846 was "Manifest Destiny." The term had been coined in 1845 by a New York publisher named John O'Sullivan, eager to encourage, or get out ahead of, the curve of national expansion. It has drawn much scorn of late. In the 19th century, belief in Manifest Destiny would lead to some deplorable policies and even more deplorable rhetoric. But at first it simply meant that Providence had a universal design for Americans to carry their democratic machinery and customs across the continent.

In 1846, the man who more than any other set all this in motion was James K. Polk. A Scotch-Irish lawyer from Tennessee, Polk was a dyed-in-the-wool Democrat, a Presbyterian and a compulsive political micromanager. Though he had served five years as Speaker of the House (then made up of only 228 Congressmen) he was so little known to the voting public that when the Democratic convention at Baltimore finally chose him on the ninth ballot in 1844, the rival Whig Party jeered happily, "Who is James K. Polk?"

When the jeering stopped, he was the 11th President of the United States, with 170 electoral votes to famous Henry Clay's 105, though there was only a 38,000-popular-vote difference between them. Polk worked a 10- to 12-hour day, kept a diary of everything that he did or said (it ran to 25 handwritten volumes), complained bitterly about how hard the job was, but quickly set about becoming the first President to keep all his promises. He said he would serve only one term. He said he would fix up the federal treasury. He said he would adjust customs duties—in an era when Southern states sometimes threatened secession over tariffs. He said he would acquire Oregon ("54-40 or fight!"), a huge, disputed territory claimed by both Great Britain and the United States since the joint-occupancy treaty of 1827. He said he would annex the Republic of Texas. He said he would acquire California. He did all that and more.

Oregon was simple. All he had to do was to make it seem as if Americans were willing to risk war over it, discover that the British weren't, outbluff the British a time or two, and get a touchy Congress to pass an aggressive bill abrogating the 1827 treaty. In the end Polk had to settle for everything south of the 49th parallel—which meant that he got part of Idaho and all of what are now the states of Washington and Oregon.

Texas and California launched him into the sort of high-stakes, peace-or-war diplomatic maneuvering that Americans like to think only Bismarck and the British foreign office were good at. California still belonged to Mexico; only ten years earlier Texas had won its independence by defeating strongman Santa Anna's forces at San Jacinto. Sporadically raided and threatened with war by Mexico, the breakaway Texas Republic was kept out of the Union because adding a slave state would disturb the uneasy political balance in the U.S. Senate. But before Polk's Inauguration, through an initiative taken by Polk's predecessor, John Tyler, Congress admitted Texas as the 28th state—with Wisconsin shortly added to balance. Overnight, the border dispute between Texas and Mexico became a problem for the United States.

Polk opened talks with Mexico to clear things up—as well as settle long-outstanding money claims on Mexico by U.S. citizens. He named John Slidell, a Louisiana trader, as special minister plenipotentiary authorized to offer Mexico $25 million for California and $5 million for New Mexico. Both Texas and the U.S. Government now claimed the Rio Grande as the western Texas-Mexico border. Mexico bitterly insisted the border was the Nueces River, 120 miles to the east (see map). Polk quietly moved 2,000 men under veteran Indian fighter Zachary Taylor toward the Nueces. The Mexican government kept Slidell (and Polk) waiting for weeks, then refused to receive Slidell, at least as minister plenipotentiary. By April, Taylor's army, considerably reinforced, had been moved on down to the mouth of the Rio Grande—either the southern tip of Texas or well inside Mexican territory—whichever way you saw it, a provocative move. Mexico saw it as invasion and again threatened war, this time with the United States.

Not only threatened. On April 25 a Mexican army crossed the Rio Grande with a view to cutting off Taylor's forces. It met with a startled American patrol, killed 11 troops, wounded 5 and took 47 prisoner. Stirred to action and outnumbered nearly two to one, Taylor's little army won two quick battles, then crossed the river, took the Mexican town of Matamoros and set up headquarters there. Taylor's dispatches did not reach Polk until May 8. On May 13, the President, declaring that Mexico had "shed American blood upon the American soil," signed a joint resolution stating that war had begun.

Polk was not a man to leave things to chance. When the unstable Mexican government was slow to come to terms, he got involved in a secret plot to bring the exiled leader Santa Anna to power—in return for a quick peace. Santa Anna double-crossed him. But Polk's aim had always been bloodless conquest. Whatever happened below the Rio Grande, he figured to stir up local revolutions in other restless Mexican territories. Weeks before the war, he had sent representatives to Santa Fe, in the huge Mexican province of New Mexico, to bribe its governor and to promise (correctly) that conditions would dramatically improve should revolution or a U.S. takeover occur. Now he ordered Gen. Stephen Kearny at Fort Leavenworth,

Kansas, to take a force of dragoons to Santa Fe. For years, far more American than Mexican goods had been offered for sale in Sante Fe, so Kearny reached New Mexico closely followed by a traders' wagon train. On August 18 he took the capital of New Mexico without spilling any blood.

California was, as it usually is, a whole story in itself. In 1846 it was a sleepy province of Mexico, almost empty and dramatically ill-governed to the extent it was governed at all. The most remote and underpopulated part of the collapsed Spanish empire, it ran itself without much help from distant, usually bankrupt and chaotic Mexico City. From time to time one genial California general would snatch power from a rival in a bloodless coup, which, as an observer reported, mostly meant "that the revenue [had] fallen into other hands." The total California population ran to about 6,000 Mexicans in addition to the local Indians, often reduced to devout near-servitude on behalf of religious missions. The land was controlled by Mexican cattle ranchers. There were some 800 ragtag Americans, most having come by ship around Cape Horn to trade for hides.

Polk being Polk, his cash offer to Mexico for California was not his only ploy. Early on he had sent secret orders to Commodore John Sloat, commander of our Pacific naval squadron, and to Thomas Larkin, a trader who served as U.S. consul in California. If war came, or if the British Navy made any move, Sloat was to occupy all California ports. Larkin was to cultivate his contacts with the lax local authorities and encourage any move on their part to declare independence from Mexico City. Mostly he was to impress on them not to accept the protection of any foreign power except the United States.

Polk's third secret message may have included orders to flamboyant John C. Frémont, at 33 a famous writer-explorer. Frémont always claimed it did, as did his father-in-law, Thomas Hart Benton, a powerful Senator from Missouri, and of course Frémont's wife, Jessie, whose editing of her husband's exploring accounts gave them much of their charm and readability. In any case, on the 9th of May, 1846, a messenger from the nation's capital, Marine Lieut. Archibald Gillespie, caught up with Frémont near Klamath Lake in Oregon. Frémont was bound east from his fourth mountain exploration. Whether from ambition or acting under orders, he abruptly turned back toward California, where he soon was fomenting revolution. He had raised a band of roughnecks. Creating a theatrical distraction, they captured the "microscopic hamlet" of Sonoma (it "could have been captured by Tom Sawyer and Huck Finn," says historian Bernard DeVoto) and, running a flag with a lumpily painted bear on it up the pole there, declared California an independent republic.

Frémont got himself made acting governor. In fairly short order, California was under the control of the United States of America. The fact was confirmed by the Treaty of Guadalupe Hidalgo, under the terms of which America got not only California but the land that today is Arizona, New Mexico, Nevada and Utah, as well as chunks of Colorado and Wyoming. Mexico got $15 million.

It is the custom now for Americans to judge the American past harshly and with a really notable lack of understanding, as if the people who lived then were exactly like us. But even the passionate abolitionists, pure spirits, and New England Whig politicians who bitterly condemned the Mexican War at the time, could not have imagined a country like our own, deeply concerned with the condition of its minorities, a country rich and secure enough even to debate whether wolves should be reintroduced into Yellowstone Park. The America of 1846 was nothing like that.

In that year the nation consisted of an uneasy union of 28 still very sovereign states. It had a population, including Indians and slaves, of less than 20 million, about as many people as live in New York State today. Its western border ran roughly on a north-south line from Wisconsin to Louisiana. Beyond that lay what maps referred to as the "Great American Desert."

Americans were not much given to the kind of self-criticism we now practice. Or to criticism of any kind. Chest thumping was more our collective style. We were already noted for being miffed by critiques from Europeans who were always coming over to tell us how rude, violent, greedy and tasteless we were, as well as ragging us for spitting tobacco juice on the carpet, keeping slaves and terminating Indians with extreme prejudice.

All that was more or less true, of course, but, according to the prevailing American view, beside the point. In 1846 Eastern and Midwestern Indians had been crushed or brushed aside with treaties, for the time being. They were treated deceitfully by the government and would be treated worse as the century wore on. But in the struggle, they had done things to settlers that were not forgiven or forgotten. This was especially the case with people who already regarded them as savages and had little reason not to regard them as entirely inimical to the creation of towns, schools, railroads and real estate deals, which then, as now, passed for the spread of civilization. Slavery was seen as a problem and, by some, as a sin, but we had tried to contain its divisive thrust with the Compromise of 1820: no slave states north of 36 degrees 30 minutes north latitude. If we kept expanding westward, we might keep it from splitting the Union for a while, and perhaps it would wither away.

THE FRANCHISE WAS STEADILY EXPANDING

In 1844, the antislavery candidate got just 62,000 votes; it was only in 1845 that Congress lifted a decade-long ban on debating slavery issues in the House. In 1848, the Free-Soil Party polled just 290,000. If women didn't vote, well, they didn't vote anywhere else either, did they? Europe, after all, was a place we'd broken away from by force of arms, a place governed by tyrants and frozen into rigid social classes. Meanwhile, over here, the franchise was steadily expanding. Almost anyone could walk into the White House and see the President. In 1846, America was the only place in the world where the people got to elect their head of state.

The country was not yet embarrassed by patriotism. Settlers rolling west in covered wagons read the Declaration of Independence aloud to each other on the Fourth of July. Americans were deeply religious. They had no trouble believing that God had created the world in all its infinite variety (Charles Darwin's findings on evolution were 13 years away) or that Providence was watching over America, the greatest experiment in freedom and democracy ever. It followed (and was mostly true) that any place annexed by America was likely to be better off than it had been before.

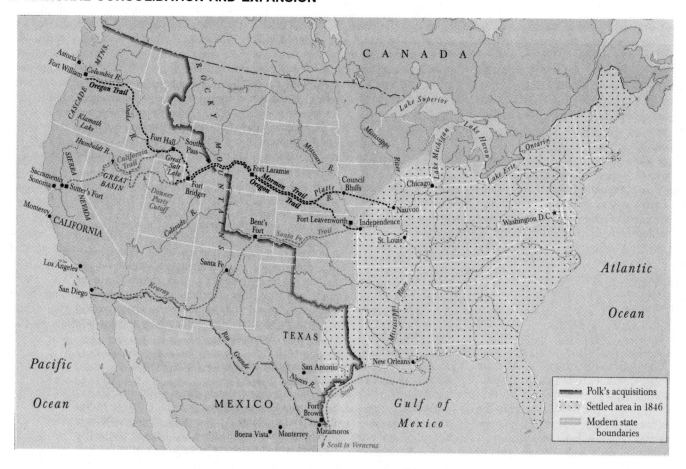

Map shows the United States in 1846—roughly the somewhat-settled eastern area—the vast lands acquired by war and Polk's diplomacy. Trails to Oregon, Utah and California all crossed the Rockies at South Pass.

By dog-eared tradition America's remarkable growth and prosperity depended on private liberty, more of it than any stable political system had tried before, and public land, more of it tillable and easily acquired than history had yet seen. Because of it there was no income tax; the federal government and those of many states ran mainly on the sale of public land. (Frugally, of course—Polk had only one private secretary to help him with his paperwork.) Land policy varied. Real estate scams abounded. But generally the old cliché of the American Frontier did apply: a family with grit could move west, carve a life out of the wilderness, squat there and have a good chance of buying the place, sometimes for as little as $1.25 an acre.

Because of land the immigrants came. Starting in 1846 the latest wave, more than a million, were refugees from Ireland's potato blights and killing famine. At first they did not go to the frontier; the only farming they knew was the cultivation of an acre or two of potatoes. Instead, they huddled in the seaboard

cities and soon were dying by the thousands of cholera. They displaced free people of color as servants to the rich and slowed incipient attempts to organize labor by their need to work at almost any wage. Most were Catholic and many spoke only Gaelic, and they sometimes found themselves treated as half-human. Thousands volunteered for the war (monthly pay $7). Of these enough deserted to the Mexican side to form the "San Patricio" battalion. The Mexicans promised 320 acres of free land and did not fail to point out that fellow Catholics should not be fighting alongside black-hearted Protestant gringos.

Zachary Taylor's volunteer soldiers struggling into Mexico and the hundreds of wagons creaking and bumping westward in the summer of 1846 were the vanguard and living proof that the idea of Manifest Destiny had taken root. New England Whigs lambasted the Mexican War as a betrayal of American ideals. A fair number of people today can hardly mention it without wincing as if for the transgression of a shady relative. But in

the South and West it set off a blaze of patriotic feeling. Though the peace treaty was slow to be signed, we had whipped the Mexican Army. Settlers were about to take on the Great American Desert.

A VAST EXPANSE, SAVAGE AND FORBIDDING

Entering it, you were emigrating outside the United States. Back East, people knew very little about it except that it was forbidding. A vast expanse of plains with Indians. Sometimes mountainous and hard to cross—like the Rockies and the Sierra Nevada. Sometimes flat, baking hot and waterless. Even the treeless, near-to-hand prairies, which eventually became the breadbasket of the nation, were little known. Westering settlers thus far had been used to cutting farms out of forest, braving Indians, running a few pigs as livestock. They figured that any place where trees did not grow wouldn't be much for growing anything else. Besides, without trees, how could you build a cabin?

It would be two decades before a rush of homesteaders settled these prairies and got used to grim sod huts and great corn crops. But in the early 1840s a few thousand farmers and homesteaders dared to try the grueling five-month trek across the often deadly 2,000 miles or so that lay between Independence, Missouri, and the alluring green of Oregon's Willamette Valley. In 1846, of some 2,700 people gathered for westward migration at Independence, more than 1,200 were aiming for California. They were the real start of a rush there that ran wild in 1849 after gold was found.

The allure of the place that year can largely be blamed on a best-selling new book by an unscrupulous real estate promoter named Lansford W. Hastings. Its title: *The Emigrant's Guide to Oregon and California.* Hastings, who had interests there, was high on California, a place of "perpetual spring," he wrote, where no "noxious miasmatic effluvia" existed. Oats grew eight feet tall and wheat yielded 70 bushels per acre—sometimes 120. Hastings' clincher for householders wheezing and freezing back East during the cold winter of 1845: in California you never had to build a fire, except to cook.

The trek continued for nearly 20 years. It became one of the set pieces of American history. The routes to Oregon and California were the same at first: up the south fork of the Platte River, over South Pass (at 7,500 feet) in what is now Wyoming, north past Soda Springs in Idaho, then down the Snake River. Those California bound turned south beyond the Great Salt Lake to follow the Humboldt River to the Sierra Nevada and Sacramento. The way west could be a great adventure. As the Donner Party proved, it could also be a season in hell. In any case it was a challenge taken mainly by people of substance. George Donner, leader of the ill-fated Donner Party, was rich; his wife was going to start a genteel girls' school in California. Fellow travelers came from all sorts of trades and professions, some scribbling poetry or collecting scientific specimens along the way.

It took considerable substance to get together the supplies thought necessary for a family of four, including: a covered wagon that could run you $200 even if you bought the cover in Missouri to save money; four yoke of oxen (more durable than horses and less often stolen by Indians) at $20 to $30 per yoke; for each male traveler a rifle, a shotgun and maybe one of Samuel Colt's new single-action revolvers (about $50); 200 lbs. flour; 75 lbs. bacon; 300 lbs. "pilot" bread, or hardtack; 10 lbs. salt; 20 lbs. sugar; 5 lbs. coffee; 2 lbs. tea; 25 lbs. rice, and a small keg of vinegar. At a rough total, from $700 to $1,500. Many people sold off all their land and livestock to get the cash.

Between 1845 and 1859 some 280,000 souls took the Oregon Trail; an estimated 30,000 died along the way. Many were babies and toddlers who, on the trail or off it, in the America of 1846 often did not live past age 5. Dysentery, fever, almost any sort of infection, swept them away. Cholera became a notable killer; settlers, not expecting to pass that way again, were slapdash about latrines and garbage, and those following them suffered. Women died in childbirth. But generally people were killed by carelessness; children fell out of wagons and were run over; guns went off accidentally, though some wagon trains required that most guns be kept unloaded during the day's run. The dead were carried along till evening, then buried. Next day all the wagons would roll over the grave to obliterate it and pack it down as a protection from marauding varmints. Until the 1860s, contrary to the impression given by the movies, Western Indians rarely killed migrating settlers along the trail, though they stole horses, shot poison arrows at oxen and sometimes fired on passing wagons.

Francis Parkman's famous *Oregon Trail* is sharper about Indians than about wagon trains. Because he was in search of groups uncorrupted by whites, stayed in the village of a notable Sioux warrior chief, and much admired his host's skill and bravery, he makes an interesting witness. Modern scholars note that Parkman was not a trained cultural anthropologist and was thus incapable, as one told me, "of recognizing differences in honorable cultures." Yet it is hard not to believe his low-key reporting when he watches a young woman catch, kill and skin a family puppy for a feast, adding that he himself later bought a white dog that had growled at him and had it cooked at an obligatory party for his host. The Sioux, he notes, will "sometimes give away the whole of their possessions." But they also routinely stole wives and ponies from each other and sometimes tortured captured enemies. What strikes Parkman as most troubling, though, is that the Sioux he knows are capricious in the extreme; honorable, perhaps, but not easy to integrate into busy, greedy 19th-century society. Crossing the plains, wood soon ran out; wagon-train women gingerly learned to use buffalo chips (known as *bois de vache*) for cooking. The stuff burned better than cottonwood. The travelers scratched brief messages for others coming behind, using cattle skulls and bones that gradually accumulated along the way. Those who too flagrantly broke the wagon-train rules were hanged from an upright wagon tongue (which must have been remarkably awkward) or were driven from the group to travel on alone. This happened to the Donner Party's James Frazier Reed after he killed a man in self-defense. As a result of his exile, he survived and heroically helped lead repeated rescue parties, the first of which found his 9-year-old daughter, Patty, barely alive in a snow-covered hut in February 1847.

Even in the best of times, except in highly disciplined groups—commercial traders, say, or the Mormons—progress was nothing like the orderly procession of white-topped prairie schooners, routinely circling for protection each night, that Hollywood has made part of American culture (along with stagy Indians in bad makeup who keep attacking and being shot down in droves). There were practical procedures about assignment of duties and places in line for the daily march, but the American penchant for exercising personal freedom at all costs caused all sorts of trouble. A "captain who wanted to camp here rather than there," Bernard DeVoto writes, "had to make his point by parliamentary procedure and the art of oratory. It remained the precious right of a free American . . . to camp somewhere else at his whim or pleasure." Or not stay in line. Strung out along the trail at "senseless intervals they traveled fewer miles a day than they might have, traveled them with greater difficulty than they needed to." They were ready enough to help one another through any emergency or difficulty, DeVoto concludes, but "were unwilling to discipline themselves to an orderly and sensible routine."

He is not here particularly describing the Donner Party. It came to almost unimaginable grief for reasons that discipline and common sense might not have avoided. The group tried a shortcut urged on them personally by Lansford Hastings: south of the Great Salt Lake, then across the salt flats, which even today drivers in air-conditioned cars are advised not to enter casually. That took weeks. Even so, they might not have become a grisly chapter in frontier history if in 1846 blizzards had not started a month early in the Sierra Nevada, burying the passes in 30 feet of snow. History has concentrated on cannibalism, but the group produced some heroes whose self-sacrifice is almost beyond praise. To read about them is to weep for us all. DeVoto is probably right, though, that the significance of the Donner experience is as a reminder of dangers that any wagon train might face if things went really wrong.

Critics of Polk and the Mexican War attacked the President with self-righteous passion and some Whiggish hypocrisy for nudging the country from domestic innocence to incipient imperialism. But it was, and is, hard for most Americans to believe it would have been better for the United States and the world if Mexico or some other country (Britain? Spain?) controlled much of what we now call our own. In 1846 even the most violent abolitionists hadn't a clue about how to free—or later deal with—some three million slaves. War was, in fact, the only way to abolish slavery in the United States. But like most people confronted by an unsolvable and shameful problem—and by such a destructive alternative—Americans generally tried not to face it, hoping it would go away. With all that new land, most of it not suitable for slave-worked crops, might not the tension ease? Instead Southerners and States Righters grew more desperate about their share of power and more politically aggressive, especially after an attempt in Congress to link the peace treaty to an agreement that no part of the land acquired from Mexico would permit slavery. Meanwhile the power of the abolitionists—who, as late as 1844, were widely regarded as politically insignificant and a bit nutty—increased. And, with a little help from the speeches of Daniel Webster, so did the cult of the quasi-sacred Union—to be preserved at all costs. The federal government, of course, had just got considerable practice in mobilizing for modern war.

James K. Polk did not live to see what happened. He died, exhausted, three months after the end of his term. Ambitious John C. Frémont lived to take part in it, ineffectively. In 1856 he became the first candidate for President put up by the new Republican Party—and lost. Four years later the Republican candidate was Abraham Lincoln. After the people of the Thirteen Colonies had won their freedom, and the French had disposed of their monarchy, British statesman Edmund Burke had this to say: "The effect of liberty to individuals is, that they may do as they please: We ought to see what it will please them to do, before we risque congratulations."

In June 1846, George Pickett of Richmond, Virginia, graduated from West Point last in a class of 59. For him the road to Gettysburg led through Chapultepec.

ADDITIONAL SOURCES

Year of Decision: 1846 by Bernard DeVoto, Houghton Mifflin, 1984

The American Heritage History of the Great West by David Lavender, American Heritage, 1982

Francis Parkman by Howard Doughty, Harvard University Press, 1983

The Oregon Trail Revisited by Gregory M. Franzwa, Patrice Press, 1988

The Presidency by Marcus Cunliffe, Houghton Mifflin, 1987

So Far From God: The U.S. War With Mexico 1846–1848 by John S. D. Eisenhower, Anchor Books, 1989

Forgotten Forty-Niners

The common perception is that only "women of easy virtue" took part in the California Gold Rush. But a careful examination of the historical record shows that thousands of women engaged in virtually every occupation and inhabited every level of gold-rush society.

JoAnn Levy

Los Angeles author JoAnn Levy specializes in writing about California and Western history.

If Concord, Massachusetts is remembered for the "shot heard 'round the world," Sutter's Mill, in the foothills of California's Sierra Nevada, is remembered for the "shout heard 'round the world"—"Eureka!" As that cry reverberated across the globe in 1848 (and echoed into the 1850s), a flood of humanity converged on the land of golden opportunity. This human tide irrevocably changed the West, opening up the frontier as no other force in the nation's history has, before or since.

One of the most common assumptions about gold-rush-era California is that it was almost exclusively a male domain—and that such women as could be found there were prostitutes. As recently as 1983, a California historian asserted that "it was, literally, mankind which participated in the gold rush, for woman kind, at least of the 'proper' variety, was almost totally absent."

A careful study of surviving diaries, memoirs, newspapers, and census records from the period refutes this longstanding misperception, revealing that the vast wave of migration to California included thousands of "respectable" women—and numerous children, too.

Many of these adventurous women accompanied or followed their husbands, fathers, or brothers to the golden land; others arrived entirely on their own. Once in California, enterprising women engaged in almost every occupation and inhabited every level of society. They mined for gold, raised families, earned substantial sums by their domestic and entrepreneurial labors, and stayed on to help settle the land—contributing a facet of gold-rush history that until now has been largely overlooked or forgotten.

In actuality, so-called respectable women outnumbered prostitutes in California, even in 1850, by four to one. While 25 percent represents a large number, even if not in this instance a "respectable" one, it is far from a majority.

BEFORE THEY COULD AVAIL THEMSELVES of the opportunities afforded by the gold rush, woman argonauts, like their male counterparts, had to undertake and survive the arduous journey to California. Many travelers chose the Cape Horn route, braving gale, storm, and shipwreck on a voyage that consumed from five to seven months; others shortened the ocean journey by making the difficult crossing of the Isthmus of Panama via small boat and mule. In 1849, more than twenty thousand gold-seekers arrived at San Francisco by sea, and nearly twenty-five thousand more followed in 1850. Many journals and letters mention the presence of women on these routes, which travelers generally regarded as being safer for families than the even more daunting overland crossings.

Despite the hardships and dangers involved, thousands of other wealth-seekers trekked overland by wagon or on foot, crossing plains, deserts, and forbidding mountain ranges while carrying with them—and then often abandoning for survival's sake—their worldly possessions. Trail-journal entries suggest that of the twenty-five thousand people traveling overland in 1849, at least three thousand were women and fifteen hundred children. Forty-four thousand people crossed the plains the following year, and, given California's census of 1850, about ten percent of these may be assumed to have been female. News of hardship, starvation, and cholera stemmed the tide of overland emigrants in 1851 to little more than a thousand, but in 1852 an estimated fifty thousand again surged across the continent. By July 13, 1852 the Fort Kearny register had tallied for that year alone the passage of more than seven thousand women and eight thousand children.

"The country was so level that we could see long trains of white-topped wagons for many miles," recorded one woman of her experiences on the eastern segment of the overland trail. "And, when we drew nearer to the vast multitude and saw them in all manner of vehicles and conveyances, on horseback and on foot, all eagerly driving and hurrying forward, I thought, in my excitement, that if one-tenth of these teams and these people got [there] ahead of us, there would be nothing left for us in California worth picking up."

ON JUNE 28, 1849, THE "BUCKEYE ROVers," a company of young men heading from Ohio to California's gold fields, camped near Independence Rock on the overland trail. One of the group, John Banks, wrote in his diary that night of seeing "an Irish woman and daughter without any relatives on the way for gold. It is said she owns a fine farm in Missouri." Two weeks later, on the banks of the Green River, their paths

From *American History Illustrated*, January/February 1992, pp. 38-49. © 1992 by Cowles Magazines, Inc. Reprinted through the courtesy of Cowles Magazines, Inc., publisher of *American History Illustrated*.

converged again: "Last night the Irish woman and daughter were selling liquor near us. . . . Fifty cents a pint, quite moderate."

Some distance beyond the Green River, near the Humboldt River, a woman named Margaret Frink recorded in her journal for August 12, 1850: "Among the crowds on foot, a negro woman came tramping along through the heat and dust, carrying a cast-iron bake oven on her head, with her provisions and blanket piled on top—all she possessed in the world—bravely pushing on for California."

Frink and her husband had begun their westward trek in Indiana. Along the way they stopped at the home of a Mr. and Mrs. McKinney near St. Joseph, Missouri. "Mrs. McKinney," wrote Margaret in her diary, "told me of the wonderful tales of the abundance of gold that she had heard; "that they kept flour-scoops to scoop the gold out of the barrels that they kept it in, and that you could soon get all that you needed for the rest of your life. And as for a woman, if she could cook at all, she could get $16.00 per week for each man that she cooked for, and the only cooking required to be done was just to boil meat and potatoes and serve them on a big chip of wood, instead of a plate, and the boarder furnished the provisions.' I began at once to figure up in my mind how many men I could cook for, if there should be no better way of making money."

These vivid images of independent and determined women are strikingly at odds with the stereotypical picture of the long-suffering and sad-eyed pioneer wife peering wearily westward while a creaking covered wagon carries her ever farther from the comforts of home. Perhaps more startling is the departure from the perception of the gold rush as an exclusively male adventure.

ALL TRAVELERS ENDURED HARDSHIPS EN route to California, but the lure of gold enticed and beckoned like a rainbow's promise. Upon reaching the golden ground, numbers of women, as eager as any male red-shirted miner, grubbed in the dirt and creekbeds for the glittering ore. Gold fever raged in epidemic proportions, and women were not immune.

The journal of schoolteacher Lucena Parsons, married but a year, reveals her infection's daily progress. On May 30,

1851, Parsons confessed to "a great desire to see the gold diggings"; she accompanied the men and watched them mine for gold. On May 31, she wrote: "This morning the gold fever raged so high that I went again with the rest but got very little gold. . . .". On June 2, "again went to the canion [sic] to find that bewitching ore"; and June 3, "a general turn out to the mines . . . we made 10 dollars to day." On June 4, she went again "and did very well."

Elizabeth Gunn, who had sailed around the Horn with four young children to join her prospecting husband in Sonora, observed to her family back East that "a Frenchman and his wife live in the nearest tent, and they dig gold together. She dresses exactly like her husband—red shirt and pants and hat."

The editor of the *Alta California* reported a similar sighting: "We saw last April, a French woman, standing in Angel's Creek, dipping and pouring water into the washer, which her husband was rocking. She wore short boots, white duck pantaloons, a red flannel shirt, with a black leather belt and a Panama hat. Day after day she could be seen working quietly and steadily, performing her share of the gold digging labor. . . ."

Many of the women who tried mining, however, found the prize unworthy of the effort it required. Eliza Farnham, famed for attempting to deliver one hundred marriageable women to California, wrote that she "washed one panful of earth, under a burning noon-day sun . . . and must frankly confess, that the small particle of gold, which lies this day safely folded in a bit of tissue paper . . . did not in the least excite the desire to continue the search."

Louisa Clapp, wife of a doctor at Rich Bar, concurred, writing to her sister in the East: "I have become a *mineress;* that is, if the having washed a pan of dirt with my own hands, and procured therefrom three dollars and twenty-five cents in gold dust . . . will entitle me to the name. I can truly say, with the blacksmith's apprentice at the close of his first day's work at the anvil, that 'I am sorry I learned the trade'; for I wet my feet, tore my dress, spoilt a pair of new gloves, nearly froze my fingers, got an awful headache, took cold and lost a valuable breastpin, in this my labor of love."

Mary Ballou, at the mining camp of Negro Bar, wrote her son Selden, left behind in New Hampshire, that she "washed out about a Dollars worth of

"I like my Voyage very much so far and anticipate a great deal of pleasure yet to come[.] I have seen some things that I never could at home."

gold dust . . . so you see that I am doing a little mining in this gold region but I think it harder to rock the cradle to wash out gold than it is to rock the cradle for Babies in the States."

THE LABOR WAS INDEED DISCOURAGING, and most gold-rushing women found it easier—and more profitable—to market their domestic skills in exchange for the glittering metal. As Margaret Frink had heard, if "a woman could cook at all," she could earn her living. Boasted one fiercely independent woman: "I have made about $18,000 worth of pies—about one third of this has been clear profit. One year I dragged my own wood off the mountain and chopped it, and I have never had so much as a child to take a step for me in this country. $ 11,000 I baked in one little iron skillet, a considerable portion by a campfire, without the shelter of a tree from the broiling sun. . . ."

Forty-niner Sarah Royce, who journeyed overland to California with her husband and three-year-old daughter, met a woman at Weaverville who "evidently felt that her prospect of making money was very enviable." The woman received one hundred dollars a month to cook three meals a day, was provided an assistant, and did no dishwashing.

In San Francisco, Chastina Rix supplemented the family income by ironing. In one week she noted that she had ironed sixty shirts, thirty-five starched and twenty-five plain, plus "hosts of other clothes & I have made twelve dollars by my labor." Her husband Alfred wrote to friends in the East that Chastina "is making money faster than half the good farmers in Peacham. She has just bought her another silk dress & lots of toggery & cravats & gloves for me and all the nice things & has quite a fund at interest at 3 per cent a month."

Laundresses were in especially high demand in the gold fields: during the early days of the rush some desperate

In a rare 1852 daguerreotype of a California mining operation, a woman visits diggings near Auburn—perhaps to deliver a basket lunch to her husband and his partners. Other even more free-spirited women participated actively at the sluice box and cradle. Among the more fortunate of these was a Mrs. H. H. Smith who, while working with her husband in French Ravine, discovered a nugget weighing ninety-seven-and-a-half pounds, "estimated by Langton and Company, bankers, at Downieville . . . to be of nearly $13,000 in value."

miners shipped their laundry to the Sandwich [Hawaiian] Islands and even to China, waiting as long as six months for its return. Abby Mansur, at the Horseshoe Bar camp, wrote to her sister in New England about a neighbor who earned from fifteen to twenty dollars a month washing, "so you can see that women stand as good a chance as men[;] if it was not for my heart I could make a great deal but I am not stout enough to do it."

WHETHER WASHING OR COOKING, MINing or ironing, women at work in frontier California toiled arduously. No labor, however, seemed more intimidating than keeping a boarding house. In 1850, about one out of every hundred persons gainfully employed in California ran some sort of hotel. Many were women, and none attested more eloquently to the labor involved than forty-niner Mary Jane Megquier, who had crossed the Isthmus from Winthrop, Maine to run a San Francisco boarding house.

"I should like to give you an account

of my work if I could do it justice," Megquier wrote. "I get up and make the coffee, then I make the biscuit, then I fry the potatoes then broil three pounds of steak, and as much liver, while the [hired] woman is sweeping, and setting the table, at eight the bell rings and they are eating until nine. I do not sit until they are nearly all done . . . after breakfast I bake six loaves of bread (not very big) then four pies, or a pudding then we have lamb, for which we have paid nine dollars a quarter, beef, pork, baked, turnips, beets, potatoes, radishes, sallad [sic], and that everlasting soup, every day, dine at two, for tea we have hash, cold meat bread and butter sauce and some kind of cake and I have cooked every mouthful that has been eaten excepting one day and a half that we were on a steamboat excursion. I make six beds every day and do the washing and ironing[.] you must think that I am very busy and when I dance all night I am obliged to trot all day and if I had not the constitution of six horses I should [have] been dead long ago but I am going to

give up in the fall whether or no, as I am sick and tired of work. . . ."

Although Megquier fails to mention how much she earned from these herculean exertions, another female forty-niner formerly of Portland, Maine earned $189 a week from her ten boarders, clearing about $75 after expenses. The accommodations she shared with them were minimal, if not spartan:

"[We] have one small room about 14 feet square, and a little back room we use for a store room about as large as a piece of chalk. Then we have an open chamber over the whole, divided off by a cloth. The gentlemen occupy the one end, Mrs. H—and a daughter, your father and myself, the other. We have a curtain hung between our beds, but we do not take pains to draw it, as it is of no use to be particular here. . . . We sleep on a cot without any bedding or pillow except our extra clothing under our heads."

California's inflated economy required that everyone work who could, as forty-niner Luzena Wilson, an overlander with her husband Mason and two young sons,

vigorously affirmed: "Yes, we worked; we did things that our high-toned servants would now look at aghast, and say it was impossible for a woman to do. But the one who did not work in '49 went to the wall. It was a hand to hand fight with starvation at the first. . . ."

William Tecumseh Sherman. a gold-rush banker before history called him to greater fame as a Union general in the Civil War, confessed to a friend that keeping his wife Ellen in California ruined him financially: "No man should have a wife in California. . . . Unless she be a working woman, no man can by his own labor support her."

Many women like Ellen Sherman, accustomed to servants and unaccustomed to labor, gave up and returned east. Those willing to work, however, received substantial rewards in an economy where a washer-woman earned more than a United States congressmen. Writing from San Francisco in 1850, one woman declared: "A smart woman can do very well in this country true there are not many comforts and one must

Instead of mining for gold, most women argonauts preferred to market their skills, cooking for the miners, doing their laundry, or running hotels. This 1850s view in Sonora includes several women and at least two children. Pioneering Californians found domestic work hardly less demanding than mining—and some found it discouraging. "Three times a day I set my Table which is about thirty feet in length," wrote boarding-house keeper Mary Ballou: "I would not advise any Lady to come out here and suffer the toil and fatigue that I have suffered for the sake of a little gold."

Women arriving in gold-rush California discovered the region almost totally lacking in civilized amenities. One of the first nuisances they had to cope with was the abysmal state of San Francisco's streets—"one vast fathomless sea of mud . . . Its composition is heterogeneous, its character antipellucid, its adhesive qualities immense and antagonistic to a composed state of nerves." Commenting on appropriate female attire for such conditions, one newspaper editor observed that "in one or two cases we have detected bona fide pantaloons peeping out from beneath the 'flowing skirts' . . . If ladies go out . . . no objection ought certainly to be urged to their appearance in boots and whatdycallems to protect them from the mud."

work all the time and work hard but [there] is plenty to do and good pay[.] If I was in Boston now and know what I now know of California I could come out here[.] If I had to hire the money to bring me out. It is the only country I ever was in where a woman received anything like a just compensation for work."

MANY OTHER GOLD-RUSHING WOMEN both affirmed the necessity to work and observed that there were "not many comforts." Those who had arrived via the overland trail, for example, often continued to make their beds in tents and wagons, like Mrs. John Berry, who protested: "Oh! you who lounge on your divans & sofas, sleep on your fine, luxurious beds and partake of your rich viands at every meal know nothing of the life of a California emigrant. Here are we sitting, on a pine block, a log or a bunk; sleeping in beds with either a quilt or a blanket as substitute for sheets, (I can tell you it is very aristocratic to have a bed at all), & calico pillow-cases for our pillows."

Harriet Ward, already a fifty-year-old grandmother when she journeyed overland, wrote happy descriptions of her roomy cabin and pine-stump furniture in

"Everybody ought to go to the mines, just to see how little it takes to make people comfortable in the world."

remote Sierra County. But of the beds she penned only, "Oh, such beds! I will say nothing of them!"

One report of a comfortable California bed does survive in the reminiscence of a guest at a celebrated gold-rush hostelry. The St. Francis boasted that it was the first San Francisco hotel to offer sheets on its beds. The lady confirmed that her bed there was "delightful." Two "soft hair mattresses" and "a pile of snowy blankets" hastened her slumbers. On this occasion, however, the California deficiency was not the bed, but the *walls:*

"I was suddenly awakened by voices, as I thought, in my room; but which I soon discovered came from two gentlemen, one on each side of me, who were talking to each other from their own rooms *through* mine; which, as the walls were only of canvas and paper, they could easily do. This was rather a startling discovery, and I at once began to cough, to give them notice of my *interposition* lest I should become an unwilling auditor of matters not intended for my ear. The conversation ceased, but before I was able to compose myself to sleep again . . . a nasal serenade commenced, which, sometimes a duet and sometimes a solo, frightened sleep from my eyes. . . ."

The walls of most early California habitations consisted of bleached cotton cloth stretched tightly and fastened to the dwelling's frame, then papered over. "These partitions look as firm and solid as they do made the usual way," noted Mrs. D. B. Bates, wife of a ship's captain, "but they afford but a slight hindrance to the passage of sounds."

California construction astonished Sarah Walsworth, a missionary's wife, who watched a house being built in Oakland: "Only a slight underpinning is laid on the ground, upon which rest the joists of the floor which is carefully laid down *first thing*. This looked so odd to me at first, that I could but laugh[.] Give a carpenter a few feet of *lumber*, a few doors, & windows, a few pounds of nails & screws a few hinges; to a paperhanger, a few yards of cloth & a few rolls of paper—to them *both* a *good deal* of *gold* & you may have a house in 6 days—perhaps in less time. You will have no trouble with 'digging cellars,' laying wall, having a 'raising' nor with dirty 'masons'—but after it is all done it is but an improved speaking-trumpet[.]"

At Santa Cruz, forty-niner Eliza Farnham built her own house. "Let not ladies lift their hands in horror," she wrote, "[but] I designed supplying the place of journeyman carpenter with my own hands." She succeeded so well, she confessed, "that during its progress I laughed . . . at the idea of promising to pay a man $14 or $16 per day for doing what I found my hands so dexterous in."

WHILE MOST WOMEN MADE DO WITH tents, cabins, and flimsily constructed clapboard houses, a very few enjoyed luxurious surroundings. "See yonder house," wrote a San Francisco chronicler. "Its curtains are of the purest white lace embroidered, and crimson damask. . . . All the fixtures are of a keeping, most expensive, most voluptuous, most gorgeous. . . ." Upon the Brussels carpet "whirls the politician with some

sparkling beauty," he added, "as fair as frail. . . ."

The house described is thought to have been that of Belle Cora, a beauty from Baltimore by way of New Orleans, who crossed the Isthmus in 1849 with gambler Charles Cora. Belle and a handful of other successful parlorhouse madams lived extravagantly, but such magnificence was the exception among California's demimonde population.

The first prostitutes to gold-rush California sailed from Valparaiso, Chile, where news of the gold discovery arrived in August 1848 via the Chilean brig *J.R.S.* Many of these women not only married argonauts, but enjoyed the luxury of choosing among their suitors.

Other Latin women, however, fared poorly. Hundreds, through indenture arrangements, were destined for fandango houses, the poor man's brothels. José Fernandez, the first alcalde at San Jose under American rule, wrote: "They did not pay passage on the ships, but when they reached San Francisco the captains sold them to the highest bidder. There were men who, as soon as any ship arrived from Mexican ports with a load of women, took two or three small boats, or a launch, went on board the ship, paid to the captain the passage of ten or twelve unfortunates and took them immediately to their cantinas, where the newcomers were forced to prostitute themselves for half a year, during which the proprietors took the bulk of their earnings."

China, like Chile, received news of California's gold discovery in 1848. By 1854, San Francisco's burgeoning Chinatown included hundreds of Chinese girls imported for prostitution. Typically, agents took arriving Chinese girls to a basement in Chinatown where they were stripped for examination and purchase. Depending on age, beauty, and the prevailing market, they sold from $300 to $3,000.

American women were not exempt from similar exploitation, albeit more subtly executed. In late 1849 and early 1850, several prostitutes in the East received passage to California by signing contracts as domestics. Some unethical agencies subsequently adopted the ploy of advertising that "servants" were wanted in California and receiving exceptional wages. A number of girls innocently responded to these procurement fronts that masqueraded as employment offices.

France similarly pounced on the fortuitous discovery at Sutter's Mill. Recruiting agents, as well as the French government, assisted the emigration of French women, who arrived in California literally by the boatload. Testified one eyewitness: 'They have done the wildest kinds of business you can imagine in San Francisco, such as auctioning off women in the public square. I got there when matters had settled down somewhat: a ship arrived with sixty French women, none of them had paid her passage, so they offered a girl to anyone who would pay what she owed. Next day they did not have a single one left."

"[True] there are not many comforts, and one must work all the time and work hard. . . ."

A knowledgeable Frenchman noted that his countrywomen profitably hired themselves out to stand at gaming tables: "All in all, the women of easy virtue here earn a tremendous amount of money. This is approximately the tariff.

"To sit with you near the bar or at a card table, a girl charges one ounce ($16) an evening. She had to do nothing save honor the table with her presence. This holds true for the girls selling cigars. when they sit with you. Remember they only work in the gambling halls in the evening. They have their days to themselves and can then receive all the clients who had no chance during the night. . . .

"Nearly all these women at home were streetwalkers of the cheapest sort. But out here, for only a few minutes, they ask a hundred times as much as they were used to getting in Paris. A whole night costs from $200 to $400."

PROVIDING THEATRICAL ENTERTAINment for lonesome miners offered a less notorious but equally profitable means of amassing California gold. Everywhere forty-niners could be found, from San Francisco's gilt-decorated theaters to the rough boards of a mining camp stage lit by candles stuck in whiskey bottles, actresses, dancers, singers, and musicians performed before appreciative audiences.

The pay varied as much as the venue. In Grass Valley, a black woman presented public piano concerts, charging fifty cents admission. The miners of

Downieville bestowed $500 in gold on a young female vocalist who made them homesick by sweetly singing old familiar ballads. A Swiss organ-girl, by playing in gambling halls, accumulated $4,000 in about six months. A Frenchwoman who played the violin at San Francisco's Alhambra gambling hall earned two ounces of gold daily, about $32.

In 1850, three French actresses opened at San Francisco's Adelphi Theatre. A critic observed that two of them "have been on the stage for a long time (I was about to write too long a time), and . . . have never definitely arrived." The women succeeded despite the quality of the performances, for the critic noted that they "have not done badly from a financial point of view, as they now own the building, the lot, and the scenery."

Renowned female performers willing to try their fortunes in far-off California achieved enormous success. Soprano Catherine Hayes, a tall blonde woman of imposing appearance, introduced costumed operatic presentations to the San Francisco stage and was rumored to have departed from the golden state with an estimated quarter-million dollars. Lola Montez cleared $16,000 a week for performing her titillating spider dance.

CALIFORNIA'S FREE AND OPEN SOCIETY also permitted women to pursue a variety of other employments nominally deemed unacceptable for their gender. The editor of the *Alta California* welcomed a female doctor with a cheerfully delivered jibe: "So few ladies in San Francisco that the new M.D. may attend them all. . . . No circumlocutions necessary. . . . Simply, as woman to woman: 'Saw my leg off!' "

The same newspaper advised "those wishing to have a good likeness are informed that they can have them taken in a very superior manner, by a real live lady, in Clay street, opposite the St. Francis Hotel, at a very moderate charge. Give her a call, gents."

The editor also boosted the business of a female barber with a shop on Commercial street by admitting that it was 'not an unpleasant operation . . . to take a clean shave at the hands of a lady fair."

Advertising her own skills in the San Francisco paper was "Madame St. Dennis—Late of Pennsylvania," who could be "consulted on matters of love, law and business, from 8 a.m. to 8 p.m. Office second brown cottage from Union street, between Stockton and Dupont." Similarly self-promoting was the linguistically talented Madame de Cassins: 'The celebrated diviner, explains the past and predicts the future. Can be consulted in English, French, Italian, Greek, Arabic and Russian . . . No. 69 Dupont st." And, at the site of the future state capital, "Miss Chick begs to inform the inhabitants of Sacramento, that she has taken a suite of rooms . . . for the purpose of teaching all the new and fashionable dances."

CALIFORNIA'S EARLY NEWSPAPERS ARE a mother lode of rich and often surprising information about female goldrushers; tidbits are as diverse as the experiences of these women.

Three women, for example, made one newspaper's December 14, 1850 listing of San Francisco millionaires: Mrs. Elizabeth Davis, Mrs. Fuller, and Mrs. Wm. M. Smith. And in September 1850, noted another article, a fire destroyed the capacious dwelling house of Mrs. Jane Smith, "erected a few months since at an expense of $10,000."

At the opposite end of the spectrum, on March 10, 1850, the *Alta* reported the particulars of a washerwomen's meeting at which laundry fees were discussed and jointly agreed.

Newspapers also reported what we would term gossip-column material today, such as an item appearing in the September 14, 1852 *Alta:* 'Forlorn: This was the charge written against Eliza Hardscrabble's name on the Recorder's docket. Unacquainted with the peculiar character of this offence, we referred to Webster, and found perhaps the proper definition, 'a lost forsaken, solitary person. Yes, Eliza is one of 'em. Whether blighted affection, harrowing care, or an erring be the cause, she is now an incurable rum-drinker, and is no longer fit to take care of herself."

Quite able to take care of herself was Dorothy Scraggs. Nonetheless, she advertised in a Marysville newspaper that she wanted a husband. She advised that she could "wash, cook, scour, sew, milk, spin, weave, hoe, (can't plow), cut wood, make fires, feed the pigs, raise chicks . . . saw a plank, drive nails, etc." She added that she was neither handsome nor a fright, yet an *old* man need *not* apply, nor any who have not a little more education than she has, and a great deal more gold, for there must be $20,000 settled on her before she will

> *"I get up and make the coffee, then I make the biscuit, then I fry the potatoes then broil three pounds of steak, and as much liver . . . after breakfast I bake six loaves of bread . . . then four pies, or a pudding . . . I make six beds every day and do the washing and ironing[.] you must think that I am very busy and when I dance all night I am obliged to trot all day and if I had not the constitution of six horses I should [have] been dead long ago . . ."*

bind herself to perform all of the above."

Court records, too, provide intriguing glimpses into the lives of gold-rushing women. In July 1850 Mrs. Mary King testified in the Sacramento justice court that persons unknown had stolen from her two leather bags containing gold dust and California coin worth about $3,500.

According to the record of *People v. Seymour alias Smith,* Fanny Seymour was indicted on a charge of assault with intent to commit murder when she shot stage-driver Albert Putnam for refusing to pay for a bottle of wine.

In *People v. Potter,* Sarah Carroll's case against William Potter, whom she claimed stole $700 in gold coin from her trunk, was dismissed because she was black and Potter was white.

Equally interesting are the surviving letters, diaries, and reminiscences of men who encountered women during their California adventures. For instance, Enos Christman, a young miner, witnessed a bullfight in Sonora at which a "magnificently dressed" *matadora* entered the arena: "She plunged the sword to the hilt into the breast of the animal. She was sprinkled with crimson dye . . . and greeted with a shower of silver dollars."

In Weaverville, Franklin Buck, a trader, was smitten by a young woman who owned a train of mules by which she delivered flour to the distant mining community: "I had a strong idea of offering myself . . . but Angelita told me she had a husband somewhere in the mines . . . so I didn't ask."

Lawyer John McCrackan met a woman who, while en route to California, brought fresh produce from a Pacific island as a speculative venture: She sold some pieces of jewelry . . . which cost her about twenty dollars at home [and] purchased onions which she sold on arriving here for eighteen hundred dollars, quite a handsome sum, is it not?" . . . She also brought some quinces & made quite a nice little profit on them."

Most fascinating, however, are the women's own observations of life in the gold regions. Wrote Abby Mansur from Horseshoe Bar: "I tell you the women are in great demand in this country no matter whether they are married or not[.] You need not think [it] strange if you see me coming home with some good looking man some of these times with a pocket full of rocks . . . it is all the go here for Ladys to leave there [sic]

Husbands[.] two out of three do it."

In fact, the divorce rate in gold-rush California was startlingly high. One judge, growing impatient with incessant requests for divorces under California's permissive divorce law, sought to deter further applications to his court by publishing his negative decision in *Avery v. Avery* in *Sacramento Daily Union*.

BY THE END OF 1853, A CONTEMPORARY historian estimated California's female population at more than sixty thousand, plus about half that many children. In San Francisco alone, women numbered about eight thousand.

By that time, energy and gold had transformed San Francisco from a city of tents into a booming metropolis. No longer a hamlet, the city reflected the changes taking place throughout the newly admitted state. Its people were no longer simply transient miners. Men were bankers and businessmen, lawyers and doctors, farmers and manufacturers. They intended to stay.

So did the women, as California pioneer Mallie Stafford later recalled. "Very few, if any, in those [first] days

contemplated permanently settling in the country. . . . But as time wore on . . . they came to love the strange new country . . . and found that they were wedded to the new home, its very customs, the freedom of its lovely hills and valleys."

Thus tens of thousands of women, through choice, chance, or circumstance, found themselves in California during the "great adventure." And, after the gold fever eventually subsided, many of them remained to help settle the land. Although they are today a neglected part of gold-rush history, the "forgotten forty-niners" were there when history was being made and they helped to make it.

Reading Notes: Author Jo Ann Levy's *They Saw the Elephant: Women in the California Gold Rush* (Shoe String Press, 1990) is one of only a few volumes devoted exclusively to women in early California. Firsthand accounts of the gold rush by women include Louisa Clapps's *Shirley Letters from the California Mines, 1851–1852* (Peregrine Smith, 1983) and Sarah Royce's *A Frontier Lady: Recollections of the Gold Rush and Early California* (University of Nebraska Press, 1977). Also see *Covered Wagon Women: Diaries & Letters from the Western Trails, 1840–1890* (Arthur H. Clark, 1983).

Christmas in 19th-Century America

'I'm Dreaming of a White Christmas'—symbol of American identification with the festive season. But before 1850 many US citizens did not dream of Christmas at all. Penne Restad tells how and why this changed—and played its role in uniting the States in social cohesion.

Penne Restad

Penne Restad is a lecturer in American History at the University of Texas in Austin, and the author of Christmas in America *(OUP, 1995).*

The Christmas that Americans celebrate today seems like a timeless weaving of custom and feeling beyond the reach of history. Yet the familiar mix of carols, cards, presents, trees, multiplicities of Santas and holiday neuroses that have come to define December 25th in the United States is little more than a hundred years old.

Americans did not even begin to conceive of Christmas as a national holiday until the middle of the last century. Like many other such 'inventions of tradition', the creation of an American Christmas was a response to social and personal needs that arose at a particular point in history, in this case a time of sectional conflict and civil war, as well as the unsettling processes of urbanization and industrialization. The holiday's new customs and meanings helped the nation to make sense of the confusions of the era and to secure, if only for a short while each year, a soothing feeling of unity.

In colonial times, Americans of different sects and different national origins kept the holiday (or did not) in ways they carried over from the Old World. Puritans, for instance, attempted to ignore Christmas because the Bible was silent on the topic. Virginia planters took the occasion to feast, dance, gamble, hunt and visit, perpetuating what they believed to be the old Christmas customs in English manors. Even as late as the early nineteenth century, many Americans, churched or unchurched, northerners or southerners, hardly took notice of the holiday at all.

By mid-century, however, new conditions had begun to undercut local customs and create needs for common and visible celebrations. Communication and transportation revolutions made once isolated parts of the country acutely aware of each other. Immigration vastly widened the ethnic and religious pluralism that had been a part of American settlement from its beginning. Moral, political and economic tensions mounted among east, west and south, raising new questions about the nature of the Union itself. Science challenged religion. New wealth and larger markets superseded old. Population swelled. The pace of life accelerated.

The swirl of change caused many to long for an earlier time, one in which they imagined that old and good values held sway in cohesive and peaceful communities. It also made them reconsider the notion of 'community' in larger terms, on a national scale, but modelled on the ideal of a family gathered at the hearth. At this crossroads of progress and nostalgia, Americans found in Christmas a holiday that ministered to their needs. The many Christmases celebrated across the land began to resolve into a more singular and widely celebrated home holiday.

This new 'revived Christmas of our time' afforded a retreat from the dizzying realities of contemporary life, but cast in contemporary terms. Americans varied old themes and wove new symbols into the received fabric to create something definitively their own. The 'American' holiday enveloped the often contradictory strains of commercialism and artisanship, as well as nostalgia and faith in progress, that defined late nineteenth-century culture. Its relative lack of theological or Biblical authority—what had made it anathema to the Puritans—ironically allowed Christmas to emerge as a highly ecumenical event in a land of pluralism. It became a moment of idealized national self-definition.

Not surprisingly, the strongest impetus for such a holiday came from those areas most profoundly affected by the various social, economic and technological revolutions of the *antebellum* era. Especially in the northern cities, where the intimacies of village and town culture had been most forcefully challenged by city and factory, the felt need for more explicit symbols of common purpose and shared past grew first. A number of writers came to see holidays as a tool to meet these ends and even to forge a national culture. New Year's Eve, the Fourth of July and, especially, Thanksgiving had their merits and partisans, but Christmas emerged as the most logical and affecting choice. By the 1850s, it had captured the Northern imagination and was making inroads in the South.

The Civil War intensified Christmas' appeal. Its sentimental celebration of family matched the yearnings of soldiers

3. NATIONAL CONSOLIDATION AND EXPANSION

and those they left behind. Its message of peace and goodwill spoke to the most immediate prayers of all Americans. Yet northern victory in 1865 as much as the war situation itself determined the popularity and shape of America's Christmas. Now unchallenged in the sphere of national myth-making and in control of the publishing trade, customs and symbols of Yankee origin and preference came to stand for the American Christmas.

We can see this as a broad and unified development only in retrospect. More interesting is the way details of the holiday appeared through accident and personal genius. Each custom had its own history, and only over time merged with others to create a full-blown, national holiday.

As early as 1832, Harriet Martineau had identified what would become one of the most familiar symbols of the American Christmas. She had 'little doubt' that the Christmas tree would 'become one of the most flourishing exotics of New England'. By the 1850s, many Americans, not just New Englanders, had fallen in love with the German custom. Some had seen Christmas trees for the first time when they had toured Germany and then recreated their experience of German Christmas celebrations for friends at home. Others viewed them first-hand in the homes of German Americans. The media introduced the custom even more widely, inspiring Americans throughout the nation to adopt the tradition as their own.

As the tree gained prominence in front parlours, it also assumed a place in the market. During the 1850s, town squares began to bristle with trees cut for seasonable profits. Seamlessly, the 'German-ness' of the tree receded as it became an icon of an American festival and, to some, an index of acculturation. Even in the homes of 'the Hebrew brethren', 'Christmas trees bloomed', noted a Philadelphia newspaper in 1877. '[T]he little ones of Israel were as happy over them as Christian children'. By 1900, one American in five was estimated to have a Christmas tree.

At first, the decoration of these fragrant evergreens reflected the whim of folk tradition. Celebrants added nuts, strings of popcorn or beads, oranges, lemons, candies and homemade trinkets. However, widely-read newspapers and ladies' magazines raised the standards for ornamentation. (One suggestion: cotton batting dipped in thin gum arabic then diamond dust made a 'beau-

An all-American Christmas: Stars and Stripes bedeck the Christmas Tree as St Nicholas strides to pay seasonal visits in this 1869 woodcut.

(RANGE PICTURES)

tiful frosting' for tree branches.) Homely affectations gave way to more uniform and sophisticated ones, the old style overtaken by the urge to make the tree a showpiece for the artistic arrangement of 'glittering baubles, the stars, angels, etc'.

Tree decoration soon became big business. As early as 1870, American businessmen began to import large quantities of ornaments from Germany to be sold on street corners and, later, in toy shops and variety stores. Vendors hawked glass ornaments and balls in bright colours, tin cut in all imaginable shapes and wax angels with spun glass wings. 'So many charming little ornaments can now be bought ready to decorate Christmas trees that it seems almost a waste of time to make them at home', one advertisement declared.

The rise of Christmas cards revealed other aspects of the new holiday's profile. R. H. Pease, a printer and variety store owner who lived in Albany, New York, distributed the first American-made Christmas card in the early 1850s. A family scene dominated the small card's centre, but unlike its English forerunner (itself only a decade older), the images on each of its four corners made no allusion to poverty, cold, or hunger. Instead, pictures of Santa, reindeer, dancers and an array of Christmas presents and Christmas foods suggested the bounty and joys of the season.

It took Louis Prang, a recent German immigrant and astute reader of public taste, to expand the sending of cards to a grand scale. Prang arrived in America in 1850 and soon made a name as a printer. By 1870, he owned perhaps two-thirds of the steam presses in America and had perfected the colour printing process of chromolithography. After distributing his trade cards by the thousands at an international exposition in 1873, the wife of his London agent suggested he add a Christmas greeting to them. When Prang introduced these new cards into the United States in 1875, they proved such a hit that he could not meet demand.

Behind Prang's delight in profits lay a certain idealism. He saw his cards as small, affordable works of art. Through them he hoped to stimulate popular interest in original decorative art and to educate public taste. In 1880, Prang began to sponsor annual competitions for Christmas card designs to promote these ends. These contests made Christmas cards so popular that other card manufacturers entered the market. By 1890, cheap imitations from his native Germany drove Prang from the Christmas card market entirely.

Whatever Prang's plans for democratizing art in his adopted land, the advent of Christmas cards in the marketplace soon served functions in keeping with the increasing pace and essential nature of American society. In a hurried and mobile nation, more and more Americans resorted to cards instead of honouring the older custom of writing Christmas letters or making personal holiday visits. The cards' ready-made sentiments drew together friends and families spread across a rapidly expanding national geography, making them a staple of December's mail. 'I thought last year would be the end of the Christmas card mania, but I don't think so now', one postal official complained in 1882. 'Why four years ago a Christmas card was a rare thing. The public then got the mania and the business seems to be getting larger every year'.

Christmas cards also made modest but suitable presents. '[W]orn out from choosing gifts' for old friends and school mates, one writer noted, 'we usually fall back on Christmas cards, which constitute one of the most precious and at the same time inexpensive contributions of these latter days to the neglected cause of sentiment'.

Decorated trees and cards, however, were only window dressing to the custom of Christmas gift-giving that blossomed in the 1870s and 1880s. Gifts had played a relatively modest role in Christmases of the past. Now they lavishly gilded the already popular holiday. Clearly a product

of the new world of commerce and consumerism, Christmas presents also served more subtle ends. The getting and giving of gifts provided a means of grappling with jarring social change. Through personal gifts, Americans mediated the fragile relationships of an increasingly fragmented society. Through charitable gifts, they sought at least symbolic solutions to the problems of extreme economic inequality that threatened

social peace and individual conscience. Gift-giving itself became controversial, sometimes perceived as a worrisome, materialistic perversion of a holy day.

Such fear has not stemmed the growth of Christmas commerce. Indeed, by our own day, Christmas gift-giving has become the single most important sector of the consumer economy. No wonder that some have read backwards in time to make the new Christmas almost a con-

Christmas Morning—an 1864 cover of *Harper's Weekly*. Present-giving, not just for children, but for friends and associates, was to become another aspect of the festive consumer economy.

(RANGE PICTURES)

Chairman of the Board: Santa as administrator in this 'Christmas Night' woodcut by Thomas Nast.

spiracy of retailers. Yet evidence suggests that the transition to a Christmas economy occurred only gradually, with both merchant and consumer acting as architects. In the 1820s, '30s and '40s merchants had noticed the growing role of gifts in the celebration of Christmas and New Year. Starting in the mid- to late-1850s, imaginative importers, craftspersons and storekeepers consciously reshaped the holidays to their own ends even as shoppers elevated the place of Christmas gifts in their home holiday. However, for all the efforts of businessmen to exploit the season, Americans persistently attempted to separate the influence of commerce from the gifts they gave.

What emerged was a kind of dialogue between consumers and merchants. Many gift-givers, for instance, ranked handmade gifts over purchased or totally manufactured ones. Retailers responded by marketing partially assembled goods to which givers applied the finishing touches. Americans also moderated the relationship between commerce and giving by wrapping the gifts they gave. The custom had once been merely to give a gift unadorned and un-

covered, but a present hidden in paper heightened the effect of the gesture, fixing the act of giving to a moment of revelation. Wrapping also helped designate an item as a gift. As gifts came increasingly from stores, factories and homes of cottage labourers, paper and string helped redefine an object to meet its social use. The commercial world comprehended the importance of this symbolic transformation of goods. Grander stores began to wrap gifts purchased from their stock in distinctive, coloured papers, tinsel cords and bright ribbons, as part of their delivery services. Thus, while paper might have blurred a present's association with commerce in some cases, in others it advertised a material status associated with patronizing the 'right' store.

The spiralling custom of giving and getting gifts did not simply reflect the materialism of the age. The felt need to demonstrate kinship ties and communal bonds more vividly helped to insure the importance of Christmas gifts. Some scholars have explored the important role that kinship plays in determining the value of an object. In what one ob-

server has called our 'materials-intensive way of life', gifts often serve as 'social statement[s]'. Given within families, another has commented, gifts 'provide continuity in one's life and across generations'. The Gilded Age, a time of particularly challenging social and economic upheaval, underlined the importance of family ties even as it threatened them. Gifts symbolized and helped secure these important relationships. The magazine *Harper's* gave early voice to the link between gifts and givers in 1856: 'Love is the moral of Christmas . . . What are gifts but the proof and signs of love?'

Charity functioned in a related manner, but more as a symbolic, cathartic exercise in selflessness. The same social changes that fostered gift-giving as a means of reinforcing familial and social attachments at the private level also inspired charitable gifts as a way of declaring, if only symbolically, a unity and safety in society that extended even to the most impoverished. It was but one more large step to extend those good feelings and generosity to the homeless, hungry and unemployed, and to target Christmas as the time for the amelioration of those conditions (or at least the assuaging of guilt over them). 'Nowhere in Christendom are the poor remembered at Christmastide so generously as they are in American cities, especially our own,' the New York *Tribune* contended.

In their comprehension of poverty and its solutions, most Americans moved little beyond Ebenezer Scrooge's personally fulfiling but ultimately narrow patronage. Their sentimentalization of 'worthy paupers' at Christmas time, especially virtuous but destitute women and vagabonds children, did not question the essential goodness of the market economy that had, directly and indirectly, produced the poverty. As in Dickens' evocation of charity, the rich man escaped condemnation if he recognized that his money meant little compared to his responsibility to humanity. That truth perceived and acted upon in highly public, seemingly generous fashion, the wealthy man could make his peace.

In this glow of self-congratulation, Americans persisted in seeing poor relief as a matter of individual action to be undertaken on much the same terms as gift-giving within the circle of family. The best and largest gifts, of course, went to those closest to the circle's centre. Lesser gifts, in descending order of value, went to relatives and acquaintances of decreasing importance. The deserving poor, as the outermost members of the larger community, received gifts too, though often the least valuable and certainly the least personal of all. An 1894 advertisement for Best and Company illustrated the hierarchy. It suggested that 'while busy buying "things for Christmas" the shopper might think of other children who are 'less fortunate than your own.' For them, the store advised that 'a gift of serviceable clothing', chosen from its special group of marked-down goods, 'would be more than welcome'.

This material means of salvation indicated a broader truth about Christmas and its gifts. In a world dominated by commerce, one important ritual of grace was spending money on others. Indeed, charity and gifts, and the increasingly munificent expenditures on them, emphasized the relationship between affluence, which many saw as a reward from God, and Christian duty. Mixing traditional Protestant and American doctrines of individualism with the newer vision of Social Darwinism, many in the Christian community felt that American prosperity was proof and extension of God-ordained success, a link confirmed by Christmas giving.

If gifts became the currency of an almost theological vision of affluence, their transcendent symbol was an updated version of an old saint. Santa Claus, with his fur-trimmed red suit, sackful of toys, reindeer, sleigh and home at the North Pole, emerged as a major folk figure. He first appeared in semi-modern form in the 1820s, in Clement Moore's *An Account of a Visit from Saint Nicholas.* By the 1850s and '60s, artists and writers had given wide circulation to the genial and generous American saint that Moore had introduced. Thomas Nast's fanciful Christmas drawings widened the sphere of Santa's rule in the late nineteenth century. Moore had already supplied eight reindeer to pull the sleigh. Nast gave him a workshop and ledgers to record children's conduct. He made him taller and dressed him in red. To this, Nast and others added a home at the North Pole, elves, a wife and even, by some accounts, children.

These amplifications imparted to Santa an ever more human and credible dimension and idealized troublesome aspects of the nation's material and spiritual life. For example, the charming notion that Santa and his tiny helpers supplied all the Christmas toys encoded

a highly romantic vision of American capitalism. This Santa reigned without opposition over a vast empire. In a world of practicality, he prospered as a highly successful manufacturer and distributor of toys. From his fur coat to his full girth, he resembled the nation's Gilded Age presidents and its well-fed captains of industry.

Labour conditions were idealized as well. A work force of skilled and reliable elf-labour helped secure Santa's place in the pantheon of American business. These North pole elves were not unlike immigrants working in the nation's sweatshops. Unassimilated, isolated from the rest of society, and undifferentiated by individual name or character, the best of them worked hard, long and unselfishly. Their existence made manifest a maxim that hard work and a cheerful attitude benefited all.

Yet any analogies that might be drawn between Santa's work and late nineteenth-century capitalism lay enmeshed in paradox, for, in significant ways, Santa Claus also represented values at odds with the system. He was a robber baron in reverse. Rather than acquire wealth, he shed it yearly. He never purchased gifts, but (with elf help) made his own to give away without regard for financial profit, rewarding best the most innocent and naive of all—the children. His world lay at some distance from the calumnies and banalities of everyday life. Santa Claus exemplified the realm of dreams, hopes, wishes and beliefs, not from the realities and compromises necessary to negotiate contemporary life.

So powerful a symbol did Santa become that a number of writers and preachers worried that he had become a substitute and rival to Jesus. Centuries earlier Puritans had expressed the same fear about saints in general. Although the faith not only of Puritan Calvinists but of all Christians had modified over the intervening years, America's Protestant culture still looked upon an iconographic, human-like embodiment of Christmas with great suspicion. An evangelical magazine gave a succinct illustration of the danger when it reported in 1906 that one little girl, when told that Santa did not exist, refused to attend Sabbath School. 'Likely as not this Jesus Christ business will turn out just like Santa Claus', she reasoned.

The fear that children might equate Santa with Jesus or God, however, missed an important point. In an age of science, Santa, while not a religious fig-

ure *per se,* represented a palpable medium through which children and adults in late nineteenth-century America could experience and act upon spiritual impulses. In that age (and ours) of material wealth and rational discourse, the ascetic saints of Christianity held no wide appeal, but Santa allowed one to give and get and also to believe.

Therein lay the significance of the *New York Sun's* famous discourse on the spiritual meaning of Santa. In 1897, Virginia O'Hanlon asked a plain question of the editor: 'Is there a Santa Claus?' 'Yes, Virginia, there is a Santa Claus', came the terse reply. The answer, though, was not a patent fib designed to placate a youngster, but an exposition on belief itself. 'Virginia, your little friends are wrong', the editor wrote. 'They have been affected by the scepticism of a sceptical age. They do not believe except they see'. Without Santa, he argued:

> . . . there would be no childlike faith then, no poetry, no romance to make tolerable this existence . . . Nobody sees Santa Claus, but that is no sign that there is no Santa Claus. Nobody can conceive or imagine all the wonders there are unseen and unseeable in the world.

The durability of the American Christmas may, in fact, rest on its ability to bring to our material and scientific world, against daunting odds, a broadly shared hint of the sacred. It is in the brief December season that Americans, using the language and objects of their culture, recapture ideals and act according to their better selves. In this sense, the nation's Christmas truly brings together the culture's two most disparate yet similarly unbounded projects—to seek wealth and to secure salvation.

FOR FURTHER READING:

James Barnett, *American Christmas: A Study in National Culture* (New York, 1954); Stephen Nissenbaum. 'Revisiting "A Visit from St. Nicholas": The Battle for Christmas in Early Nineteenth-Century America', in *The Mythmaking Frame of Mind: Social Imagination and American Culture,* by James Gilbert (ed), (California, 1992); Leigh Eric Schmidt, 'Joy to [Some of] the World. Christianity in the Marketplace: Christmas and the Consumer Culture', *Cross Currents* 43 (Fall, 1992); Phillip Snyder, *The Christmas Tree Book* (New York, 1976); Phillip Snyder, *December 25th, The Joys of Christmas Past* (New York, 1985); William Waits, *The Modern Christmas in America: A Cultural History of Gift Giving* (New York, 1993).

Eden Ravished

The Land, Pioneer Attitudes, and Conservation

Harlan Hague

Harlan Hague teaches history of the American West and American environmental history at San Joaquin Delta College, Stockton, California. He is the author of Road to California: The Search For a Southern Overland Route *and articles on western exploration and trails.*

In O. E. Rölvagg's *Giants in the Earth,* a small caravan of Norwegian immigrants stopped on the prairie, and the riders got down from their wagons. They scanned the landscape in all directions and liked what they saw. It was beautiful, all good plowland and clean of any sign of human habitation all the way to the horizon. After so much hoping and planning, they had finally found their place in the new land. One of the men, Per Hansa, still had difficulty comprehending what was happening:

"This vast stretch of beautiful land was to be his—yes, his. . . . His heart began to expand with a mighty exaltation. An emotion he had never felt before filled him and made him walk erect. . . . 'Good God!' he panted. 'This kingdom is going to be mine!' "

Countless others who went to the West reacted like Rölvaag's Per Hansa. They entered the Promised Land with high expectations, possessed the land and were possessed by it. They changed the land and in time were changed by it.

The influence of the West on the American mind has interested historians ever since Frederick Jackson Turner read his momentous essay in 1893 to a meeting of the American Historical Association. In the essay, Turner concluded: "The existence of an area of free land, its continuous recession, and the advance of American settlement westward, explain American development." Turner went on to describe in some detail the various ways the western environment changed the frontiersman, molding him into the American. The processes and result of this evolution were in the end, by implication, favorable.

Writing in the early 1890s, Turner did not detect one of the most important themes, if not the most important, of the westward movement, a theme which would have immense impact on the shaping of the American character. This was the belief that the resources of the West were inexhaustible. Henry Nash Smith, in his influential *Virgin Land,* caught the point that Turner missed:

"The character of the American empire was defined not by streams of influence out of the past, not by a cultural tradition, nor by its place in a world community, but by a relation between man and nature—or rather, even more narrowly, between American man and the American West. This relation was thought of as unvaryingly fortunate."

This cornucopian view of the West was the basis of the frontiersman's attitude toward and his use of the land.

The typical trans-Mississippi emigrant in the last half of the nineteenth century accepted the assumption of inexhaustible resources. Yet the view of the West as an everlasting horn of plenty had been proven false long before the post-Civil War exodus. For example, commercial hunting of the sea otter along the California coast, which had begun in 1784, reached its peak around 1815; by the mid-1840s, the numbers of the animals had declined alarmingly, and the otter was soon hunted almost to extinction. The beaver's fate was similar. Soon after Lewis and Clark told about the teeming beaver populations in western streams, trappers moved westward to harvest the furs. They worked streams so relentlessly that the beaver began to disappear in areas where it had always been plentiful.

By 1840, the beaver had been trapped virtually to oblivion. No mountain man in the 1820s would have dreamed there could ever be an end to the hardy little animal. Yet unbridled exploitation had nearly condemned the beaver to extinction. The lesson was lost on Westerners.

Pioneers were not noticeably swayed by the arguments of the naturalists, who publicized the wonders of nature or went further and pled for its preservation. William Bartram, a contemporary of Jefferson, wrote eloquently about the beauty of American nature in his *Travels.* Originally published in 1791, his book was more popular in Europe than in the United States, which had yet to discover its aesthetic environment. John James Audubon had more influence in this country upon publication of his *Birds of America* series (1827–1844) and his subsequent call for protection of wildlife. Francis Parkman, while not famed as a naturalist, wrote firsthand accounts about the scenic West and the Indian inhabitants who lived in harmony with nature. It is no wonder that Parkman, who was enthralled with the outdoors, admired Indians and mountain men more than the settlers he encountered during his western travels.

There was indeed a whole body of romantic literature and art during the first half of the nineteenth century that might have persuaded Americans that environmental values could be measured in terms other than economic. William Cullen Bryant wrote-with such depth of feeling about the simple pleasures of the outdoors that he is still known as one of our foremost nature poets. The founding spirit of transcendentalism, Ralph Waldo Emerson, wrote in his first book, *Nature:*

"In the presence of nature, a wild delight runs through the man. . . . In the woods, is perpetual youth. . . . In the woods, we return to reason and faith. . . .

The currents of the Universal Being circulate through me; I am part or particle of God. . . . In the wilderness, I find something more dear and connate than in streets or villages."

Emerson's contemporary, Henry David Thoreau, was even less restrained in his adoration of untamed nature when he wrote: "In Wildness is the preservation of the World." At the same time, Thomas Cole and the Hudson River school of landscape painters captured on canvas the essence of nature that the romantic writers had recorded in prose and poetry. And farther west, beyond the Mississippi River, George Catlin, Karl Bodmer, and Alfred Jacob Miller were painting the exotic wilderness that increasingly drew the attention of Americans.

Unmoved by praise of the aesthetic quality of the environment, frontiersmen were even less impressed by warnings that its resources were not without end. Every American generation since the colonial period had been told of the virtue of using natural resources wisely. An ordinance of Plymouth Colony had regulated the cutting of timber. William Penn had decreed that one acre of trees be left undisturbed for every five acres cleared. In 1864, only a moment before the beginning of the migration that would cover the West within one generation, George Perkins Marsh published his book *Man and Nature,* the most eloquent statement up to that time of the disastrous result that must follow careless stewardship of the land. "Man has too long forgotten." he wrote, "that the earth was given to him for usufruct alone, not for consumption, still less for profligate waste." That is, man could and should both cherish and use the land, but he should not use it up. The significance in Marsh's warning was the recognition that the land could be used up.

While American ambassador to Italy, Marsh had theorized that ancient Rome's fall could be traced to the depletion of the empire's forests. He predicted a like fate for the United States if its resources were similarly squandered. Marsh's book appears to have been widely read by American intellectuals and probably favorably influenced the movements for national parks and forestry management. In it, indeed, were the seeds of the conservation movement of the early twentieth century. Yet it is unlikely that many frontiersmen read or were aware of—or at least they did not heed—Marsh's advice.

Pioneers heard a different drummer. They read descriptions about the West written by people who had been there. Lansford W. Hastings's glowing picture of California and Oregon thrilled thousands:

"In view of their increasing population, accumulating wealth, and growing prosperity, I can not but believe, that the time is not distant, when those wild forests, trackless plains, untrodden valleys, and the unbounded ocean, will present one grand scene, of continuous improvements, universal enterprise, and unparalleled commerce: when those vast forests, shall have disappeared, before the hardy pioneer; those extensive plains, shall abound with innumerable herds, of domestic animals; those fertile valleys, shall groan under the immense weight of their abundant products: when those numerous rivers shall team [sic] with countless steam-boats, steam-ships, ships, barques and brigs; when the entire country, will be everywhere intersected, with turnpike roads, rail-roads and canals; and when, all the vastly numerous, and rich resources, of that now, almost unknown region, will be fully and advantageously developed."

Once developed, hopeful emigrants learned, the area would become the garden of the world. In the widely-distributed *Our Western Empire: or the New West Beyond the Mississippi,* Linus P. Brockett wrote that "in no part of the vast domain of the United States, and certainly in no other country under the sun, is there a body of land of equal extent, in which there are so few acres unfit for cultivation, or so many which, with irrigation or without it, will yield such bountiful crops."

Other books described the routes to the Promised Land. The way west was almost without exception easy and well-watered, with plenty of wood, game, and grass.

There was not just opportunity on the frontier. Walt Whitman also saw romance in the westward migration:

Come my tan-faced children,
Follow well in order, get your weapons ready,
Have you your pistols? have you your sharp-edged axes?
Pioneers! O pioneers!
For we cannot tarry here,
We must march my darlings, we must bear the brunt of danger,
We the youthful sinewy races, all the rest on us depend,
Pioneers! O pioneers! . . .
We primeval forests felling,

We the rivers stemming, vexing we and piercing deep the mines within,
We the surface broad surveying, we the virgin soil upheaving
Pioneers! O pioneers! . . .
Swift! to the head of the army!-swift! spring to your places, Pioneers! O Pioneers!

The ingredients were all there: danger, youth, virgin soil. Well might frontiersmen agree with Mark Twain who wrote that the first question asked by the American, upon reaching heaven, was: "Which way West?" Thoreau also thought a westward course the natural one:

"When I go out of the house for a walk . . . my needle always settles between west and south-southwest. The future lies that way to me, and the earth seems more unexhausted and richer on that side. . . . westward I go free. I must walk toward Oregon."

Emigrants felt this same pull but for different reasons. Thoreau's West was a wild region to be enjoyed for itself and preserved untouched, while the West to the emigrants was a place for a new start. The pioneers would conquer the wilderness and gather its immeasurable bounty. This did not imply that Westerners were oblivious to the beauty of the land. Many were aware of the West's scenic attractions but felt, with the influential artist Thomas Cole, that the wilderness, however beautiful, inevitably must give way to progress. In his "Essay on American Scenery," Cole described the sweet joys of nature—the mountains, lakes, rivers, waterfalls, and sky. The essay, dated 1835, is nostalgic. Cole closed his paean with an expression of "sorrow that the beauty of such landscapes are quickly passing away . . . desecrated by what is called improvement." But, after all, he added, "such is the road society has to travel!" Clearly, Cole, like most of his nineteenth-century readers, did not question the propriety of "improvement" or the definition of "progress."

THE BELIEF IN THE INEXHAUSTIBILITY OF western resources was superimposed on an attitude toward the land that Americans had inherited from generations past. In the Judeo-Christian view, God created the world for man. Man was the master of nature rather than a part of it. The resources of the earth—soil, water, plants, animals, insects, rocks, fish, birds, air— were there for his use, and his proper role was to dominate. It was natural then for God's children to harvest the rich garden provided for them by their Creator. They went into the West to do God's bidding, to use the land as he willed, to fulfill a destiny.

This attitude of man-over-nature was not universal. Like most primitive cultures throughout history, it was not held by the American Indian. The Indian saw himself as a part of nature, not its master. He felt a close kinship with the earth and all living things. Black Elk, a holy man of the Oglala Sioux, for example, believed that all living things were the children of the sky, their father, and the earth, their mother. He had special reverence for "the earth, from whence we came and at whose breast we suck as babies all our lives, along with all the animals and birds and trees and grasses." Creation legends of many tribes illustrate the Indian's familial attachment to the earth and his symbiotic relationship with other forms of life.

The land to Indians was more than merely a means of livelihood for the current generation. It belonged not only to them, the living, but to all generations of their people, those who came before and those who would come after. They could not separate themselves from the land. Of course, there were exceptions. Some Indians fell under the spell of the white trader who offered them goods that would make their lives easier, not to say better. As they became dependent on white man's goods, the land and its fruits began to assume for them an economic value that might be bartered for the conveniences produced by the white man's technology. This is not to say that the Indian attitude toward the land changed. Rather it illustrates that some Indians adopted the white man's view.

To European-Americans, the western Indians' use of the land was just another proof of their savagery. The pioneers had listened to the preachers of Manifest Destiny, and they knew that the nomadic tribes must stand aside for God's Chosen People who would use the land as God intended.

And so they returned to Eden. While some went to California and some to Oregon, the most coherent migration before the rush for California gold began in 1849 was the Mormon exodus to Salt Lake Valley. The latter was not typical of the westward movement. The persecuted saints entered the West not so much for its lure as because of its inaccessibility. In 1830, the same year that the Mormon

Church was founded, Joseph Smith announced a revelation which would lead eventually to—or at least foresaw—the great migration:

"And ye are called to bring to pass the gathering of mine elect . . . unto one place upon the face of this land [which] . . . shall be on the borders by the Lamanites [Indians]. . . . The glory of the Lord shall be there, and it shall be called Zion. . . . The righteous shall be gathered out from among all nations, and shall come to Zion, singing with songs of everlasting joy!"

Mormons who trekked to the Utah settlements in the late 1840s and 1850s knew they were doing God's bidding.

Other emigrants were just as sure that the Lord had prepared a place for them. "Truly the God in Heaven" wrote an Oregon-bound traveler in 1853, "has spread in rich profusion around us everything which could happily man and reveal the Wisdom and Benevolence of God to man." Oregon Trail travelers often noted in their journals that they were going to the "Promised Land." In A. B. Guthrie's *The Way West*, Fairman, who would be leaving Independence shortly for Oregon, proposed a toast "to a place where there's no fever." McBee, another emigrant, impatient to get started, responded:

" 'Y God, yes, . . . and to soil rich as anything. Plant a nail and it'll come up a spike. I heerd you don't never have to put up hay, the grass is that good, winter and all. And lambs come twice a year. Just set by and let the grass grow and the critters birth and get fat. That's my idee of farmin.' "

It seems that most emigants, in spite of the humor, did not expect their animals or themselves to wax fat in the new land without working. God would provide, but they must harvest.

Following close on the heels of the Oregon Trail farmers, and sometimes traveling in the same wagon trains, were the miners. This rough band of transients hardly thought of themselves as God's children, but they did nevertheless accept the horn-of-plenty image of the West. Granville Stuart wrote from the California mines that "no such enormous amounts of gold had been found anywhere before, and . . . they all believed that the supply was inexhaustible." Theirs was not an everflowing cornucopia, however, and each miner hoped to be in the right spot with an open sack when the horn tipped to release its wealth.

The typical miner wanted to get as rich as possible as quickly as possible so he could return home to family, friends, and a nabob's retirement. This condition is delightfully pictured in the frontispiece illustration in Mark Twain's *Roughing It*. A dozing miner is seated on a barrel in his cabin, his tools on the floor beside him. He is dreaming about the future: a country estate, yachting, carriage rides and walks in the park with a lady, an ocean voyage and a tour of Europe, viewing the pyramids. The dreams of other miners, while not so grand, still evoked pleasant images of home and an impatience to return there. This yearning is obvious in the lines of a miner's song of the 1850s:

Home's dearest joys Time soon destroys,
Their loss we all deplore;
While they may last, we labor fast
To dig the golden ore.

When the land has yielded its riches:

Then home again, home again,
From a foreign shore,
We'll sing how sweet our heart's delight,
With our dear friends once more.

Miners' diaries often reflected these same sentiments, perhaps with less honeyed phrases but with no less passion.

A practical-minded argonaut, writing in 1852 from California to his sister in Alabama, explained his reason for going to the mines: "I think in one year here I can make enough to clear me of debt and give me a pretty good start in the world. Then I will be a happy man." What then? He instructed his sister to tell all his friends that he would soon be "back whare (sic) I can enjoy there [sic] company." Other miners thought it would take a little longer, but the motives were the same. A California miner later reminisced:

"Five years was the longest period any one expected to stay. Five years at most was to be given to rifling California of her treasures, and then that country was to be thrown aside like a used-up newspaper and the rich adventurers would spend the remainder of their days in wealth, peace, and prosperity at their eastern homes. No one talked then of going out 'to build up the glorious State of California.' "

The fact that many belatedly found that California was more than worked-out diggings and stayed—pronouncing the state glorious and themselves founding fathers—does not change their motives for going there.

There was a substantial body of miners, perpetually on the move, rowdies usually, the frontier fraternity boys, whose home was the mining camp and whose friends were largely miners like themselves. They rushed around the West to every discovery of gold or silver in a vain attempt to get rich without working. Though they had no visions of returning east to family and fireside, they did believe that the West was plentifully supplied with riches. It was just their bad luck that they had not found their shares. Their original reason for going to the mining camps and, though they might enjoy the camaraderie of their fellows, their reason for staying, was the same as that of the more genteel sort of miner who had come to the western wilderness, fully expecting to return to the East. More than any other emigrant to the West, the miner's motive was unabashed exploitation. For the most part, he did not conserve, preserve, or enrich the land. His intention, far from honorable, was rape.

THE CATTLEMAN WAS A TRANSITION FIGure between the miner who stripped the land and the farmer who, while stripping the land, also cherished it. The West to the cattleman meant grass and water, free or cheap. The earliest ranchers on the plains raised beef for the eastern markets and for the government, which had decreed that the cow replace the buffalo in the Plains Indians' life-style. The Indians, except for a few "renegades," complied, though they were never quite able to work the steer into their religion.

It was not long before word filtered back to the East that fortunes could be made in western stock raising. James Brisbin's *Beef Bonanza; or, How to Get Rich on the Plains,* first published in 1881, was widely read. Readers were dazzled by the author's minutely documented "proof" that an industrious man could more than double his investment in less than five years. Furthermore, there was almost no risk involved:

"In a climate so mild that horses, cattle, and sheep and goats can live in the open air through all the winter months, and fatten on the dry and apparently withered grasses of the soil, there would appear to be scarcely a limit to the number that could be raised."

Experienced and inexperienced alike responded. Getting rich, they thought, was only a matter of time, not expertise.

Entrepreneurs and capital, American and foreign, poured into the West. Most of the rangeland was not in private ownership. Except for small tracts, generally homesteaded along water courses or as sites for home ranches, it was public property. Though a cattleman might claim rights to a certain range, and though an association of cattlemen might try to enforce the claims of its members, legally the land was open, free, and available.

By the mid-1880s, the range was grossly overstocked. The injury to the land was everywhere apparent. While some began to counsel restraint, most ranchers continued to ravish the country until the winter of 1886–1887 forced them to respect it. Following that most disastrous of winters, which in some areas killed as much as 85 percent of range stock, one chastened cattle king wrote that the cattle business "that had been fascinating to me before, suddenly became distasteful. . . . I never wanted to own again an animal that I could not feed and shelter." The industry gradually recovered, but it would never be the same. More land was fenced, wells dug, and windmills installed. Shelters for cattle were built, and hay was grown for winter feeding. Cattle raising became less an adventure and more a business.

In some cattlemen there grew an attachment, if not affection, for the land. Some, especially after the winter of 1886–1887, began to put down roots. Others who could afford it built luxurious homes in the towns to escape the deficiencies of the countryside, much as twentieth-century townsmen would build cabins in the country to escape the deficiencies of the cities. Probably most cattlemen after the winter of 1886–1887 still believed in the bounty of the West, but a bounty which they now recognized would be released to them only through husbandry.

Among all those who went into the West to seek their fortunes, the frontier farmers carried with them the highest hopes and greatest faith. Their forebears had been told for generations that they were the most valuable citizens, chosen of God, and that their destiny lay westward. John Filson, writing in 1784 about frontier Kentucky, described the mystique of the West that would be understood by post-Civil War emigrants:

"This fertile region, abounding with all the luxuries of nature, stored with all the principal materials for art and industry, inhabited by virtuous and ingenious citizens, must universally attract the attention of mankind." There, continued Filson, "like the land of promise, flowing with milk and honey, a land of brooks of water, . . . a land of wheat and barley, and all kinds of fruits, you shall eat bread without scarceness, and not lack any thing in it."

By 1865 the Civil War had settled the controversy between North and South that had hindered the westward movement, the Homestead Act had been passed, and the Myth of the Garden had replaced the Myth of the Desert. By the grace of God and with the blessing of Washington, the frontier farmer left the old land to claim his own in the new:

Born of a free, world-wandering race,
Little we yearned o'er an oft-turned
sod.
What did we care for the father's place,
Having ours fresh from the hand of
God?

Farmers were attracted to the plains by the glowing accounts distributed by railroads and western states. Newspapers in the frontier states added their accolades. The editor of the *Kansas Farmer* declared in 1867 that there were in his state "vast areas of unimproved land, rich as that on the banks of the far famed Nile, . . . acres, miles, leagues, townships, counties, oceans of land, all ready for the plough, good as the best in America, and yet lying without occupants." Would-be emigrants who believed this sort of propaganda could sing with conviction:

Oh! give me a home where the buffalo
roam,
Where the deer and the antelope play;
Where never is heard a discouraging
word,
And the sky is not clouded all day.

There was a reason for the sky's clarity, the emigrants learned when they arrived on the plains. It was not long before many had changed their song:

We've reached the land of desert sweet.
Where nothing grows for man to eat;
I look across the plains
And wonder why it never rains.

And, finally, sung to the cadence of a "slow, sad march":

We do not live, we only stay;
We are too poor to get away.

It is difficult to generalize about the experience of pioneer farmers. Those who continued their journeys to the Pacific Coast regions were usually satisfied with what they found. It was those who settled on the plains who were most likely to be disillusioned. Their experience was particularly shattering since they had gone to the West not just to reap in it but also to live in it. Most found not the land of milk and honey they expected, but, it seems, a life of drudgery and isolation.

The most persistent theme in the literature of the period is disenchantment. This mood is caught best by Hamlin Garland. In *Main-Travelled Roads,* Garland acknowledged two views of the plains experience when he wrote that the main-travelled road in the West, hot and dusty in summer, muddy and dreary in fall and spring, and snowy in winter, "does sometimes cross a rich meadow where the songs of the larks and bobolinks and blackbirds are tangled." But Garland's literary road is less cluttered: "Mainly it is long and wearyful, and has a dull little town at one end and a home of toil at the other. Like the main-travelled road of life it is traversed by many classes of people, but the poor and the weary predominate."

The opposite responses to the plains are more pronounced in O. E. Rölvaag's *Giants in the Earth,* one of the most enduring novels of the agricultural West. Per Hansa meets the challenge of the new land, overcomes obstacles and rejoices in each success, however small. He accepts the prairie for what it is and loves it. Meanwhile, his wife, Beret, is gradually driven insane by that same prairie. Where Per Hansa saw hope and excitement in the land, Beret saw only despair and loneliness. "Oh, how quickly it grows dark out here!" she cries, to which Per Hansa replies, "The sooner the day's over, the sooner the next day comes!" In spite of her husband's optimistic outlook, Beret's growing insanity dominates the story as it moves with gloomy intensity to its tragic end. It is significant that Per Hansa dies, a victim of the nature that he did not fear but could not subdue.

Willa Cather, the best-known novelist of nineteenth-century prairie farm life, treated relationships between people and their environment more sensitively than most. While her earlier short stories often dwell on themes of man against the harsh land, her works thereafter, without glossing over the severity of farm life, reveal a certain harmony between the land and those who live on it and love it.

Her characters work hard, and suffer; but they are not immune to the loveliness of the land.

The histories of plains farming dwell more on processes than suffering, but accounts that treat the responses of the settlers to their environment generally verify the novelists' interpretations. According to the histories, the picture of desperation painted by Garland and Rölvaag applies principally to the earliest years of any particular frontier region. By the time sod houses acquired board floors and women were able to visit with other women regularly, Cather's images are more accurate.

The fact that pioneer farmers were not completely satisfied with what they found in the Promised Land does not alter their reasons for going there. They had gone into the West for essentially the same reason as the trappers, miners, and cattlemen: economic exploitation. Unlike their predecessors, they also had been looking for homes. Yet, like them, they had believed fervently in the Myth of Superabundance.

THE IRRATIONAL BELIEF THAT THE WEST'S resources were so great that they could never be used up was questioned by some at the very time that others considered it an article of faith. George Perkins Marsh in 1864 warned of the consequences of a too rapid consumption of the land's resources. In 1878, John Wesley Powell attacked the Myth of the Garden when he pointed out that a substantial portion of western land, previously thought to be cultivable by eastern methods, could be farmed successfully only by irrigation. Overgrazing of grasslands resulted in the intrusion of weeds and the erosion of soil, prompting many ranchers, especially after the devastating winter of 1886–1887, to contract their operations and practice range management. Plowing land where rainfall was inadequate for traditional farming methods resulted in wind and water erosion of the soil. Before the introduction of irrigation or dry farming techniques, many plains farmers gave up and returned eastward. The buffalo, which might have numbered fifty million or more at mid-century, were hunted almost to extinction by 1883. Passenger pigeons were estimated to number in the billions in the first half of the nineteenth century: around 1810, Alexander Wilson, an ornithologist, guessed that a single flock, a mile wide

and 240 miles long, contained more than two billion birds. Yet before the end of the century, market hunting and the clearing of forest habitats had doomed the passenger pigeon to extinction. Examples of this sort led many people to the inescapable conclusion that the West's resources were not inexhaustible.

At the same time a growing number of people saw values other than economic in the West. Some plains farmers struggling with intermittent drought and mortgage could still see the beauty of the land. Alexandra in Cather's *O Pioneers!* could see it: "When the road began to climb the first long swells of the Divide, Alexandra hummed an old Swedish hymn. . . . Her face was so radiant" as she looked at the land "with love and yearning. It seemed beautiful to her, rich and strong and glorious. Her eyes drank in the breadth of it, until her tears blinded her."

Theodore Roosevelt wrote often of the "delicious" rides he took at his Badlands ranch during autumn and spring. He described the rolling, green grasslands; the prairie roses; the blacktail and whitetail deer; the songs of the sky-lark; the white-shouldered lark-bunting; and the sweet voice of the meadowlark, his favorite. Of a moonlight ride, he wrote that the "river gleams like running quicksilver, and the moonbeams play over the grassy stretches of the plateaus and glance off the wind-rippled blades as they would from water." Lincoln Lang, a neighbor of Roosevelt's, had the same feeling for the land. He called the Badlands "a landscape masterpiece of the wild, . . . verdant valleys, teeming with wild life, with wild fruits and flowers, . . . with the God-given atmosphere of truth itself, over which unshackled Nature, alone, reigned queen."

Even miners were not immune to the loveliness of the countryside. Granville Stuart, working in the California mines, was struck by the majestic forests of sugar pine, yellow pine, fir, oak, and dogwood. He described the songs and coloration of the birds and the woodpeckers' habit of storing acorns in holes that they meticulously pecked in tree limbs. He delighted in watching a covey of quail near his cabin each day. "Never was I guilty of killing one," he added. Bret Harte lived among the California miners, and his stories often turn to descriptions of the picturesque foothills of the Sierra Nevada. After the birth of "The Luck" in Roaring Camp, the proud, self-appointed godfathers decorated the baby's "bower with flowers and sweetsmelling shrubs, . . . wild honey-suckles, azaleas, or the painted blossoms of Las Mariposas. The men had suddenly awakened to the fact that there were beauty and significance in these trifles, which they had so long trodden carelessly beneath their feet."

Success of some sort often broadened the frontiersman's viewpoint. The miner, cattleman, or farmer who had succeeded in some way in his struggle with the land had more time and inclination to think about his relationship with it. Viewing his environment less as an adversary, the Westerner began to see what was happening to it.

At times, concern for the environment led to action. The mounting protests of Californians whose homes and farms had been damaged by the silt-laden runoff from hydraulic mining finally led to the outlawing of this mindless destruction of the land. Frederick Law Olmsted, who had designed New York's Central Park, initiated an era in 1864 when he and some friends persuaded Congress to grant to the state of California a piece of land in California's Sierra Nevada for the creation of a park, merely because the land, which included Yosemite Valley and the Mariposa Big Trees, was beautiful and the public would enjoy it. The idea took hold, and other parks soon followed, Yellowstone in 1872 being the first public "pleasuring ground" under federal management. The new art of landscape photography showed Easterners the wonders of the West, without the hardships of getting there, and revealed to many Westerners a land they inhabited but had never seen. With the improvement in transportation, principally railroads, more and more people ventured into the West to see these wonders firsthand.

A growing awareness that unrestrained exploitation was fast destroying the natural beauty of the West and that its resources, by the end of the nineteenth century widely acknowledged to be finite, were being consumed at an alarming pace led to considerable soul-searching. Frederick Jackson Turner, who had most eloquently described the influence that the great expanses of western land had on the shaping of American character, also hinted that the disappearance of available land was likely to cause some serious disruptions in American society. "The frontier has gone," he wrote, "and

with its going has closed the first period of American history."

If the first phase of American history, in which a dominant theme was the advance of the frontier, ran from 1607 to 1890, the second phase began with the emergence of the conservation movement which would lead to the alteration of fundamental attitudes toward the land nurtured during the first phase. While based generally on concern for the environment, the movement split in the early twentieth century into two factions. One faction argued for wise management of the country's resources to prevent their being wasted. This "utilitarian conservation" was not a break with the frontier view of exploitation. It was a refinement. While the frontier view was one of rapid exploitation of inexhaustible resources, the utilitarian conservationists rejected the myth of inexhaustibility and advocated the careful use of finite resources, without rejecting the basic assumption that the resources were there to be exploited. This view of conservation led to the setting aside and management of forest reserves, soil and water conservation projects, and irrigation and hydroelectric programs.

The other faction, whose ideology has been called "aesthetic conservation;' clearly broke with the frontier past when its members argued for the preservation of areas of natural beauty for public enjoyment. This group's efforts bore fruit in the establishment of national and state parks, monuments and wilderness areas. There are indications that the two factions are drawing closer together in the umbrella ecology movement of the 1970s, perhaps eventually to merge.

It is senseless to compare nineteenth-century frontier attitudes toward the land with today's more enlightened views. Faced seemingly with such plenty—billions of passenger pigeons, millions of buffalo, innumerable beaver, endless seas of grass, vast forests of giant trees, mines to shame King Solomon's—excess was understandable and probably inevitable. Excess in this case meant waste. Here the Turner thesis is most meaningful, for the belief in the inexhaustibility of resources in the West generated the unique American acceptance of waste as the fundamental tenet of a life-style. For this, the frontiersman is not entirely blameless. But certainly, he is less blameworthy than the neo-pioneer who continues, against reason and history, to cling hopefully to the myth of inexhaust-

ibility. Yet there were examples, however few, and voices, however dim, that the frontiersman might have heeded. It remains to be seen whether Americans today have learned the lesson their ancestors, four generations removed, failed to comprehend.

BIBLIOGRAPHIC NOTE

There are few comprehensive surveys of the evolution of American attitudes toward the environment. Three useful sources are Stewart L. Udall, *The Quiet Crisis* (New York: Holt, Rinehart, 1963); Hans Huth, *Nature and the American: Three Centuries of Changing Attitudes* (Berkeley: University of California, 1957); and Roderick Nash, *Wilderness and the American Mind,* rev. ed. (New Haven: Yale University, 1973), the last particularly concerned with the American response to wilderness. Frederick Jackson Turner's frontier thesis, which inevitably must be considered in any study of the reldtionship between Americans and their environment, is in his *The Frontier in American History* (New York: Henry Hoit, 1921). Invaluable to an understanding of what Americans thought the West was is Henry Nash Smith, *Virgin Land: The American West as Symbol and Myth* (New York: Vintage Books, 1950). The most influential book of the twentieth century in the development of a land ethic is Aldo Leopold, *A Sand County Almanac* (New York: Oxford University, 1949).

Selections from historical materials and literature were blended in this study to illustrate western emigrants' expectations for and responses to the new country. In addition to titles listed in the text, literary impressions of nature are in Wilson O. Clough, *The Necessary Earth: Nature and Solitude in American Literature* (Austin: University of Texas, 1964) and John Conron, *The American Landscape: A Critical Anthology of Prose and Poetry* (New York: Oxford University, 1974). Useful bibliographies of the literature of the westward movement are Lucy Lockwood Hazard, *The Frontier in American Literature* (New York: Thomas Y Crowell, 1927) and Richard W Etulain, *Western American Literature* (Vermillion, S.D.: University of South Dakota, 1972). Bibliographies of historical materials are in Ray Allen Billington, *Westward Expansion,* 4th ed. (New York: Macmillan, 1974), and Nelson Klose, *A Concise Study Guide to the American Frontier* (Lincoln: University of Nebraska, 1964).

Walt Whitman's Different Lights

In the long line of American radicals—celebrated in a book published by Routledge*—the figure of Walt Whitman stands tall as writer, poetic free spirit and a nineteenth-century prefigurer of the Beat generation. But as Robert Martin describes here in an extract from the book, the extent to which his philosophical and even sexual concerns challenged the temper of their times, has not been properly appreciated.

Off the cuff: Whitman's celebrated 'casual workman' pose; from perhaps his most famous poetic work *Leaves of Grass*, 1855.

Robert Martin

Robert K. Martin is Professor of English and chair of the department at the Université de Montréal. He is author of The Homosexual Tradition in American Poetry *(University of Texas Press, 1979) and editor of* The Continuing Presence of Walt Whitman *(1992).*

'I am as radical now as ever', Walt Whitman (1819–92) told his friend, the author Horace Traubel at the end of his life. A few months later he remarked to Traubel that 'there wouldn't be much wealth left in private hands—that is, if my say was final'. But Whitman's radicalism was individualistic; as he put it, he did not 'belong to any school'. In Whitman's earlier life he had been more willing to affirm party affiliations. In 1848 he had been a Brooklyn delegate to the Free-Soil convention, the anti-slavery coalition that split the Democrat Party, calling for unconditional backing for ex-President Martin Van Buren, and editing the new Free-Soil paper, *The Freeman*. He gave up the venture after the paper's office burned down, and after he had come to recognise the role of compromise in politics.

Whitman's radicalism had much in common with his age and his American roots. Radicals in America seem generally to have preferred the individual and the anarchistic to the collective and the socialist. Whitman might reject the idea of private property, but he cared too much about his sense of 'self' to be able to adapt to any political programme. Whitman's radical origins included the

This article first appeared in *History Today*, April 1994, pp. 45-49. © 1994 Robert K. Martin. Reprinted by permission.

(Below) the frontispiece from a later edition
to one of the poems 'Song of Myself'.

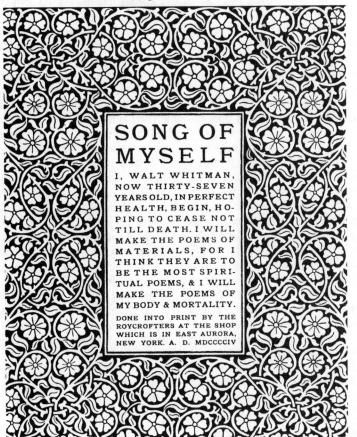

SONG OF MYSELF

I, WALT WHITMAN, NOW THIRTY-SEVEN YEARS OLD, IN PERFECT HEALTH, BEGIN, HOPING TO CEASE NOT TILL DEATH. I WILL MAKE THE POEMS OF MATERIALS, FOR I THINK THEY ARE TO BE THE MOST SPIRITUAL POEMS, & I WILL MAKE THE POEMS OF MY BODY & MORTALITY.

DONE INTO PRINT BY THE ROYCROFTERS AT THE SHOP WHICH IS IN EAST AURORA, NEW YORK. A. D. MDCCCCIV

(FROM *LEAVES OF GRASS*, 1855)

utopian movements that flourished in the American 1840s. He was a great admirer of Frances Wright, the British reformer (1795–1852), who had founded the Nashoba Community, an inter-racial utopia in West Tennessee, and collaborated with Robert Dale Owen on the New Harmony *Gazette*. Wright's talks on education, birth control, and the distribution of wealth, and her attacks on the church lie behind much of Whitman's poetry.

Another important formative influence on the young Whitman were the views of Quaker reformer, Elias Hicks. Hicks' transformation of American Quakerism brought it into line with a growing evangelism, replacing a strict code of unworldliness with an emphasis on the personal voice or 'inner light'. The appeal of Quakerism for Whitman was, as Newton Arvin put it, their 'spiritual independence and self-trust'.

The American 1848 was not a programme for political revolution, although it included a justification for resistance by individuals. It was instead a reaffirmation of American ideals of selfhood and individualism. Whitman imbibed these ideas above all from Ralph Waldo

Emerson (1803–82), in essays such as 'Self-Reliance'. It was that joining of the celebration of the individual consciousness with the celebration of the young nation that appealed to Whitman, who saw himself as the national poet Emerson called for. Nevertheless, however much Whitman was a spiritual descendant of Emerson's, there were significant differences. Just as Whitman knew and admired the actual radicals and utopians of his day, and had himself participated in some of the moral/social crusades, such as the temperance movement, while Emerson remained aloof, so too Whitman saw himself as providing a place for the body that was strikingly absent, or derided, in Emerson's Platonism.

Whitman's vision was not merely a product of the Concord philosophers (the group including Margaret Fuller, Henry Thoreau and Nathaniel Hawthorne that settled with Emerson in Concord, Massachusetts) of his time, but even more of an American radical tradition, an antinomianism (opposition to the obligatory nature of moral law) perhaps derived from the early Puritans and their dissenters, and from the revolutionary voice

of Thomas Paine. For Whitman, America's 'radical human rights' were in large part the work of Paine. They were also the product of his own childhood and young adulthood. Whitman was the first major American writer to come from a working-class background that was far from the privileged élites of Boston, Philadelphia, or Virginia. He was born in West Hills, Long Island, into a family of English and Dutch farmers. His father was part of the first Revolutionary generation, and subscribed to the hopes of a democratic future. A few years after young Walter's birth in 1819, the family moved to Brooklyn, where they occupied a series of houses, as Walt's father built frame houses he hoped to sell at a profit. In an age of speculation, he failed. By the time he was twelve, Walt Whitman had begun work as a printer's apprentice. After completing his apprenticeship at sixteen, he was unable to find work as a printer, and turned to rural teaching (for which he had no training and scarcely any formal education) for several terms until returning to New York to work as a printer. Whitman had lived in democratic America, in practice as well as in theory, and knew first-hand the dangers of a free economy as well as the possibilities of self-creation. He was also a remarkable autodidact, absorbing his reading and incorporating it into an eclectic, undisciplined body of heterogeneous knowledge. His poetry reflects his enormous storehouse of obscure information, as well as his disdain for 'official' knowledge: as he would write in his greatest poem, 'Song of Myself', 'I have no chair, no church, no philosophy'.

Whitman applied Emerson's theoretical democracy to the nation to the body, claiming a radical equality of body parts and functions. He expressed this not only as a statement of principle. 'Welcome is every organ and attribute of me, and of any man hearty and clean,/Not an inch nor a particle of an inch is vile, and none shall be less familiar than the rest', but in shockingly concrete terms, 'The scent of these arm-pits aroma finer than prayer'.

The Concord philosophers sought to escape experience by a withdrawal into a world of pure idea; nature was the site of a disembodied experience (Emerson's 'transparent eyeball') of an eternal world of forms. Whitman's celebration of the radically new self was based on a recuperation of the body, and a breaking down of a body/soul hierarchy or binarism. A crucial arm in the struggle against Western philosophical idealism was the recuperation of 'lower' forms. In this struggle the resistance to Western philosophy ran parallel to a struggle against Victorian prudery. In the famous section 11 of 'Song of Myself' Whitman allied himself with the lonely woman observer who seeks to join in the erotic celebration of the young men bathing. The gender boundaries that normally enforce the image of the 'lady' in nineteenth-century culture break down in a vision of the men touched by 'an unseen hand' until they give in to the anonymous sexual encounter and 'souse with spray'.

That final image of an undirected seminality is crucial to Whitman's programme of resistance to the antimasturbation campaign of his day. In a social context where masturbation was seen as an economic crime ('spending') as well as a moral transgression, Whitman celebrated the auto-erotic, as well as the homo- and heterosexual. Well aware that the status of women was connected to the cultural silence around sexuality, he argued that:

only when sex is properly treated, talked, avowed, accepted, will the

woman be equal with the man, and pass where the man passes, and meet his words with her words, and his rights with her rights.

A fervent believer in the equality of women, Whitman began the practice of inclusive language, insisting on 'the man or the woman' rather than the generic masculine. His adoption of such language also served to mask his own homosexual desires.

In his honesty about his physical sexual attraction to other men, Whitman found himself lacking a community. Sexual encounters were probably not difficult (his note books include many names of young men who spent the night with him), and 'bohemian' bars like Pfaff's may have provided some sort of place for fulfillment of homosexual desire, but Whitman found himself largely alone in his wish to understand his sexuality in a democratic culture. Nineteenth-century homosexuality was fundamentally classical, from Byron at the beginning of the century to Symonds at the end. Whitman learned about classical models of pederasty, since they were just about the only models available, but he also sought to

displace them. It was in his sequence of 'Calamus' poems that he sought to give expression to his desires and to theorise their nature and possible social place.

The sequence begins with that most famous of classical homosexual allusions, Virgil's second eclogue, but even here Whitman is making the landscape American and constructing a role for himself as the originator of 'athletic love' and the celebrator of 'the need of comrades'. Although 'athletic love' carries with it echoes of the Greek *gymnasium*, it is also being offered in opposition to a cultural assumption, both already existing and being constructed, of the homosexual as effete, decidedly unathletic dandy. Although Whitman's presentation of himself as the poet of homosexual love has made him a figure of enormous importance for later gay writers and readers, his position on desire between men has little in common with the 'minority' view taken by many sexual radicals in the 1960s. For Whitman homosexuals do not constitute a small group that requires equal rights; instead homosexuality is seen as the fundamental condition of a democratic society.

Wall Street in the 1850s – its panorama of docks and ships appealing to Whitman's love of the sea and the 'rank masculinity' associated with it.

(MANSELL COLLECTION)

Whitman's influence has been enormous, and has always included a recognition of his part in the redefinition of sexual desire. Homosexual writers including Garcia Lorca, Pesoa, Hart Crane, Jack Spicer, Allen Ginsberg, and many others have felt themselves enabled by Whitman's example. Women writers, too, although sometimes troubled by the almost exclusively male world of Whitman's imagination, have often responded enthusiastically to his affirmation of female desire and his insistence upon sexual equality. Kate Chopin's *The Awakening* (1899), in particular, derives its heroine's sexual awakening from Whitman's model. And black writers have found Whitman's influence on the novelist Richard Wright (1908–60) and poet Langston Hughes (1902–67) was considerable. Such writers saw beyond the sentimental adaptations of Whitman that had been offered by American liberals such as Carl Sandburg or Sherwood Anderson, and tried to enlist Whitman in a radically engaged struggle against racism and economic privilege.

In matters of poetic form Whitman was even more of a radical, although his transformations have turned out to be so lasting that it may now be difficult to recognise the magnitude of his accomplishment. As Ezra Pound put it, Whitman 'broke the back' of conventional metre, thus putting into practice Emerson's famous dictum that 'it is not metre but a metre-making argument' that defines poetry. There were other radical attempts at redefining English metre in this period, including notably Gerard Manley Hopkins' 'sprung rhythm', but they failed to take. Whitman invented the long unmetrical line that allows him to expand, to dilate. Avoiding prose by paratactic structures and parallelism, Whitman is able to shift the spine of the poem to its left-hand margin. Only such an open form could give voice to his inclusiveness, his refusal of principles or order and subordination. His famous 'catalogue' technique, or enumerative style, allows him to celebrate the thing itself, without a surrounding fabric of hierarchies of value. At the same time the very act of inclusion, in the genteel world of verse, amounts to a confrontation of the reader with the reality and diversity of experience, unfiltered by 'art'. His poetry is, as he put it in 'Song of Myself':

the meal equally set, . . . the meat for natural hunger,/It is for the wicked just the same as the righteous, I make ap-pointments with all,/I will not have a single person slighted or left away.

Whitman's self-presentation, as in the famous frontispiece to the first edition of *Leaves of Grass*, the book coterminous with the life that Whitman constantly rewrote and revised, was that of a worker in open-necked shirt, with hand jauntily on the hip. The poems, too, try to break away from the power of the *salon*, offering instead the outdoors of adventure and freedom. 'Song of Myself' proclaims the natural man of Romantic origins, now physically present in an American landscape. To go outdoors was also to liberate the self, to 'come out': 'I will go to the bank by the wood and become undisguised and naked'. Conventional life, like conventional sexuality was a disguise: nakedness was the condition of truth. 'Song of the Open Road' brought together Whitman's love for the natural world with his sense of political mission, as he adapted the French Revolutionary call, '*Allons*', into a call for a 'greater struggle' of the self for freedom from the fixed paths. Whitman's 'open road' created American space and possibility, later to be claimed by the Beats in the fifties, and it associated it with what Whitman called 'adhesiveness', adopting a term from the nineteenth century pseudo-science of phrenology and making it into a name for a love of men that was casual, spontaneous, and omnipresent, 'the talk of those turning eye-balls'.

Although Whitman's indifference to the proprieties alarmed many of his literary colleagues, he found a warm response among many readers. His work as a nurse in the Civil War brought out his qualities of friend and care-giver. The letters between him and the wounded soldiers are an extraordinary testimony to the power of his sympathy to cross lines of class, and in an age before the sharp demarcation of kinds of desire, to offer loving affection to the men in his care. These men, often barely literate, were moved by Whitman's attention and kept in touch with the poet even after they returned to civilian life and, in most cases, marriage. The war tested Whitman's faith in the power of the American democratic vision, but he emerged from it convinced that liberty cannot be obtained by legal documents, but only with 'manly affection' that can tie the states with 'the love of lovers'.

Whitman's dream of national unity and his vision of friendship across class lines made him a powerful attraction for English socialists of the late nineteenth century. The poet and reformer Edward Carpenter (1844–1929) did more than anyone to apply Whitman's ideas and poetic practice, and tried to develop a community of lovers devoted to social and sexual equality. In his Whitman-like poem 'Towards Democracy' and in essays such as 'Love's Coming of Age' and 'The Intermediate Sex', Carpenter developed a social critique based on the adaptation of feminist and socialist theory. The views of Carpenter and his colleagues in Sheffield, joining as they did, multiple reform movements and utopian strains, looked back to the same kind of radical impulse that had given rise to Whitman, but they were increasingly removed from a socialist movement now linked to trade unionism and uninterested in sexual reform. The last gasp of this line of influence, at least during this period, came in E. M. Forster, whose final novel *A Passage to India* records the impact of Carpenter on the young Forster and the novelist's attempt to imagine the power of an inter-racial intercultural male friendship to overcome imperialism and racism.

But Whitman's India, apparently untouched by the colonial experience, seemed unattainable. So too the poets of the 1950s could only look back to Whitman with a sense of loss. Allen Ginsberg could find 'the older man' only in 'a supermarket in California', the American dream gone sour. It would take a still later generation of poets such as Marlon Riggs to recapture something of Whitman's original sense of possibility. In his 'Tongues Untied' the ability to find a voice, to speak for the speechless and silenced, which Whitman had taken as his task, becomes real again. Whitman's lasting power has remained one of enablement, of allowing the excluded to speak:

I act as the tongue of you,/Tied in your mouth, in mine it begins to be loosen'd.

This article has been adapted for History Today *from Professor Martin's chapter in* The American Radical, *edited by Mari Jo Buhle, Paul Buhle and Harvey J. Kaye, to be published by Routledge this May, priced £40.00 hardback/£14.99 paperback.*

FOR FURTHER READING

Newton Arvin, *Whitman* (Macmillan, New York, 1938); Justin Kaplan, *Walt Whitman. A Life* (Simon and Schuster, New York, 1980); Paul Zweig, *Walt Whitman. The Making of the Poet* (Basic Books, New York, 1984).

The Civil War and Reconstruction

The debate over slavery came to dominate the political scene during the 1850s. Various efforts were made to strike settlements that would placate both sides, but these proved unsatisfactory and only forestalled an accounting. An agreement over tariffs, for instance, could be hammered out by splitting differences. Slavery was a moral question that proved unamenable to compromise even though some moderates tried. In "Dred Scott in History," Walter Ehrlich provides an example of how an effort to resolve the matter only exacerbated the situation.

The Whigs fell apart over slavery, and the Republican Party emerged from the wreckage. Drawing its strength almost exclusively from the North, it seemed to Southerners a direct threat not only to their interests but to their very way of life. Republican candidate Abraham Lincoln repeatedly stated that although he opposed the extension of slavery into the territories, he had no intention of attacking the institution where it already existed. Many Southerners believed that the spread of slavery was necessary to maintain their power within Congress and that Republicans sooner or later would try to destroy the institution completely. Lincoln's election in 1860 was the signal for Southern states to begin seceding, and his unwillingness to let them dissolve the Union led to war.

Many believed the war would last only a short while. Northerners clamored for a march on the Confederate capital of Richmond, hoping that this would smash resistance very quickly. Southerners were equally optimistic in thinking that inflicting military reverses on the North would destroy its will to continue. "First Blood to the South: Bull Run, 1861" by Brian Holden Reid describes the first large-scale battle of what became the bloodiest war in American history. John Talbott's article, "Combat Trauma in the American Civil War," discusses the debilitating effects protracted combat had on individual officers and men.

During the early part of the war President Abraham Lincoln insisted that it was being fought to preserve the Union rather than as a crusade against slavery. One of his reasons for this was that he was afraid of alienating crucial border states. In "The Struggle for Black Freedom before Emancipation," Wayne Durrill describes the role black people themselves played to gain freedom. The essay "Who Was Lincoln?" discusses Lincoln's character and his conduct during the war. Then, Richard Fraser, in "How Did Lincoln Die?" offers a rebuttal to the notion that Lincoln's wound was so massive that it would have been fatal even if he had received the best treatment available today. Fraser also provides information about the state of medicine at the time of the assassination.

To achieve its goals, the North had to conquer the South. For the latter, however, all that was necessary was to hold out long enough so that the North would lose its will to go on fighting. This almost came to pass by the early part of 1864, and Lincoln was pessimistic about his chances of reelection. Several important military victories restored Northern morale and the war continued until General Robert E. Lee surrendered his forces early in 1865. Historians have debated ever since why the North won the war, assigning varying degrees of importance to questions such as leadership, industrial output, and a larger population, among other things. "Why the South Lost the Civil War" by Carl Zebrowsk offers the brief views of 10 leading Civil War historians.

The Civil War has been the subject of countless books, articles, and movies. A lengthy television documentary that aired in 1991 attracted millions of viewers. James McPherson, in "A War That Never Goes Away," tries to explain why that conflict has retained such enduring interest.

After the fighting stopped, a struggle ensued over what status blacks would have now that slavery had been destroyed. Many Northerers, referred to as "radical" or "advanced" Republicans, wanted to guarantee freedpersons the full rights of citizenship. Some radical Republicans were motivated by morality, others sought to achieve political and economic goals. Most white Southerners, however, resisted changing their way of life and sought to keep blacks as near as possible in a state of servitude. "The War We Never Finished" by Richard McMurry describes the legacy of Reconstruction with particular emphasis upon the South. Finally, Eric Foner acknowledges that Radical Reconstruction failed in the short run, but he argues that its "animating vision" still has relevance in his report, "The New View of Reconstruction."

Looking Ahead: Challenge Questions

Analyze the significance of the *Dred Scott v. Sanford* decision with regard to the sectional struggle that was tearing the nation apart.

Discuss why the Civil War lasted as long as it did, and why the South lost in the end. What advantages did each side have? What disadvantages?

Why did Radical Reconstruction fail to attain its objectives? Could such lofty goals have been attained had the radicals used different tactics? Or was it more or less doomed from the start? Defend your answer.

What lasting effects has the war and Reconstruction had on many Southerners? What is relevant about the Reconstruction effort for today?

Dred Scott in History

Walter Ehrlich

Dr. Walter Ehrlich is Associate Professor of History and Education at the University of Missouri–St. Louis.

Dred Scott v. *John F.A. Sanford* stands as one of the most memorable and important cases in the history of the United States Supreme Court. Except for the celebrated *Marbury* v. *Madison,* which in 1803 established the Supreme Court's power to invalidate federal laws, perhaps more has been written about *Dred Scott* than about any other action of the American judiciary, either state or federal. Most of that literature deals with the controversial final decision, rendered on March 6, 1857, by Chief Justice Roger Brooke Taney. To comprehend the full significance and impact of that decision, it is imperative to understand clearly what the issues were; and to understand the issues necessitates an almost step-by-step unfolding of the litigation itself. It did indeed have a singular history.[1]

Born in Southampton County, Virginia, in the late 1790's or early 1800's, the property of Peter Blow, Dred Scott came with his master to Missouri, via Huntsville and Florence, Alabama, settling finally in St. Louis in 1830. Very little is known about the slave's early life. He was "raised" with the Blow children and apparently was close to them, performing menial labor one might associate with household slaves. Yet when Peter Blow found himself strapped financially, he sold Scott to Dr. John Emerson, a physician then residing in St. Louis. This was sometime before De-

Dred Scott, *by Louis Schultze, 1881. Courtesy of the Missouri Historical Society, St. Louis.*

cember 1, 1833, when Emerson embarked on a military career that took him, among other places, to Illinois and Wisconsin Territory (now Minnesota). Scott was with his master in both places until 1842, even though slavery was prohibited in Illinois by that state's constitution and in the northern Louisiana Purchase territory by the Missouri Compromise of 1820. Scott, however, made no effort to secure his freedom.

While Scott was in this service to Dr. Emerson, two weddings occurred which affected the slave's life. The first was Scott's, in 1836 or 1837, to Harriet Robinson, whose master, Major Lawrence Taliaferro, transferred her ownership to Emerson. This marriage was unique in American slave history, for it was a legal civil ceremony performed by a justice of

the peace. Dred and Harriet Scott had two daughters; Eliza was born in October, 1838, aboard the steamboat "Gipsey" while it was on the Mississippi River in "free," "northern" waters, and Lizzie was born about 1845 at Jefferson Barracks in Missouri. (Eliza never married. Lizzie married Wilson Madison of St. Louis, and through them exist the present descendants of Dred Scott.) The other wedding was Emerson's, on February 6, 1838, to Eliza Irene Sanford, whose brother later played a major role in Dred Scott's legal struggles for freedom.

In 1842 Dr. Emerson was posted to Florida where American military forces fought against the Seminole Indians. He left his wife and the slaves in St. Louis with Mrs. Emerson's father. The doctor

---

[1] For the best account of the case's chronology, especially in the Missouri courts, see Walter Ehrlich, *They Have No Rights: Dred Scott's Struggle for Freedom* (Greenwood Press, 1979). For further information, see Don E. Fehrenbacher's *The Dred Scott Case: Its Significance in American Law and Politics* (Oxford University Press, 1978) and David Potter's *The Impending Crisis, 1848–1861* (Harper and Row, 1976).

From *Westward,* Vol. 1, No. 1, Winter 1983, pp. 5-10. © 1983 by the Jefferson National Expansion Memorial Historical Association. Reprinted by permission.

returned from the wars in 1843, but died shortly thereafter at the age of forty, leaving a young widow with an infant daughter and the Dred Scott family.

The whereabouts of the slaves during these St. Louis years is unclear, except that they were hired out to various people, a frequent experience for city-dwelling slaves. Then on April 6, 1846, Dred and Harriet Scott sued their mistress Irene Emerson for freedom, initiating litigation in the local Missouri state circuit court that would take eleven years before culminating in the celebrated decision of the Supreme Court of the United States on March 6, 1857.

But what brought on that suit for freedom in 1846, when Scott had been "eligible" in free territory since 1833? The evidence is not exactly clear, but some facts are obvious. From 1833 to 1846 Scott was unaware of the law. (It should be noted that he was illiterate and had to mark an "X" for his signature, not uncommon for slaves.) Only after he returned to St. Louis was he apprised of the possibility of being free. But why, and by whom? Again all the details are not known, but it is now undeniable why the case was *not* brought. It was *not* instituted for political or financial reasons as many later imputed. The evidence is indisputable that Dred Scott filed suit for one reason and one reason only, to secure freedom for himself and his family, and nothing else.

But who told him now what he had been unaware of for thirteen years? Again the evidence could be stronger, but it points persuasively to several people. One was a white abolitionist lawyer, Francis Butter Murdoch, recently moved to St. Louis from Alton, Illinois, where as city attorney he had prosecuted criminal offenders on both sides in the infamous and bloody Elijah P. Lovejoy riots and murders. Another was Reverend John R. Anderson, himself a former slave and the black pastor of the Second African Baptist Church of St. Louis, in which Harriet Scott was a devout member. Like Murdoch, Anderson was an emigre from racial-torn Alton.

The exact sequence of events remains somewhat fuzzy; but it was Murdoch, on April 6, 1846, who posted the necessary bonds and filed the required legal papers which initiated the suit. Then, within a few months and before any further legal action occurred, Murdoch left for the west coast, where he lived the rest of his days in California. Having thus initiated the suit, he dropped out completely.

Now another group of Dred Scott's benefactors emerged: the sons and sons-in-law of Peter Blow, those "boys" with whom the slave had been "raised." Murdoch's departure left their ex-slave and childhood companion in limbo. Now the former owners stepped in, posted bonds, secured attorneys, and took over the process of seeking his freedom. They were to carry it through to the very end.

They anticipated no difficulty. According to the facts of the case and the legal precedents in Missouri, there is no question that Dred Scott was entitled to freedom; indeed, that it was such a patently open-and-shut case may even explain why the Blow family so readily came to their former slave's rescue. At any rate, two totally unexpected developments now changed the situation.

The first was the decision on June 30, 1847, in the trial court, denying Scott his freedom and ordering a new trial—not because of the law or the facts, but because of a legal technicality invalidating certain evidence introduced by Scott's attorney. The slave's freedom, which otherwise unquestionably would have been granted in 1847, now had to await a new trial. The second unexpected development was that it took three long years, until 1850, before that second trial finally occurred, a delay caused by events over which none of the litigants had any control. With that legal technicality of 1847 corrected, the court now, on January 12, 1850, unhesitatingly granted the slave his freedom. That should have ended the case.

But during that three-year delay more unexpected developments came into play. The first was Mrs. Emerson's departure from St. Louis and marriage to Dr. Calvin Clifford Chaffee, a Massachusetts abolitionist completely unaware of the litigation involving his new wife. When she left St. Louis, her local affairs were supervised for her by her businessman-brother, John F.A. Sanford. Among those affairs was the pending slave case.

A second development was monetary. Because Scott's eventual status was still undecided, the court had assigned the local sheriff as custodian of all wages the Scott family might earn, which would then accordingly be turned over to either a free Dred Scott or to his owner. The accrued wages, though by no means an inordinate amount, nevertheless made ownership of the slaves in 1850 much more worthwhile than it had been in 1846 or 1847. The result was, therefore, that Mrs. Emerson (actually her attorney hired for her by her brother Sanford) immediately appealed to the Missouri Supreme Court to reverse the freedom decision of the lower court.

This set the stage for the most consequential development yet, the injection of slavery as a political issue. Up to this point the legality or morality of slavery had never entered into the case to any degree. But by the early 1850's, stimulated by national discord over the seemingly uncompromisable slavery issues, and exacerbated by local Missouri factionalism centering on Senator Thomas Hart Benton, some judges of the Missouri Supreme Court took it upon themselves to reinterpret and reverse Missouri's longstanding legal principle of "once free always free," that a slave once emancipated in free territory would remain free even after returning voluntarily to the slave state of Missouri. By sheer coincidence, the case just appealed to the Missouri high court contained the necessary circumstances for such a ruling. This singularly irregular political partisanship on the part of the judges was abetted by an equally dissolute legal brief introduced at the last moment by Mrs. Emerson's attorney, Lyman D. Norris, a document characterized more by its vituperative pro-slavery tirades than by its legal reasoning.

The result was that on March 22, 1852, the Missouri Supreme Court reversed the lower court's decision and remanded Dred Scott to slavery. What the court now said in effect was, even though the law of a free state and a free United States territory may have emancipated a slave, the slave state of Missouri no longer would accept that status within its own borders. In other words, "once free always free" became "maybe once free, but now back to slavery." It was a radical change in Missouri law, overturning precedent and clearly endorsing the extreme pro-slavery point of view. What had been a simple and genuine emancipation case seeking only freedom for a slave under longstanding law and principle had been transformed into a matter focusing on the most divisive issue the nation had ever experienced.

This was precisely why the case appealed to the Supreme Court of the United States: to clarify "once free always free" and to determine to what degree, if at all, a state could reverse

Since it was rendered, the Dred Scott case has been one of the most discussed and written about court cases in American history. This booklet, containing the Supreme Court decision in the Dred Scott case, was published in 1857. It is preserved in the Jefferson National Expansion Memorial archives, located in St. Louis' Old Courthouse.

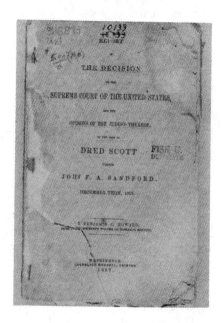

freedom once granted through the implementation of the Northwest Ordinance of 1787, prohibiting slavery in the Northwest Territory, and the Missouri Compromise of 1820. Note that this did not question the validity of granting freedom in a free state or territory; the power to prohibit slavery or to manumit slaves taken into free territory was universally recognized. In question was whether that freedom *once granted* could be lost by returning to a slave state. It was a highly controversial and delicate political and moral issue which the United States Supreme Court had deliberately sidestepped even when the opportunity to decide had been present. The Court had shown that judicial restraint as recently as 1850, in *Strader* v. *Graham*. Instead of deciding on the merits in that particular case, the Court took a procedural approach: it fell back on a long-standing and safe (albeit unpopular to some) prin-

ciple that the Court simply would abide by the decision of a state's supreme court as the definitive arbiter of that state's law, in this instance Kentucky.

Some time before the Missouri high court rendered its drastic decision, Dred Scott's situation came to the attention of Roswell M. Field, one of St. Louis' leading lawyers. A native of Vermont and an abolitionist, Field for some time had articulated the need for clarification of "once free always free." He realized *Dred Scott* v. *Irene Emerson* could be the vehicle through which to appeal to the Supreme Court for that clarification. But he also was aware of the *Strader* case. *Strader* v. *Graham* had gone to the Supreme Court of the United States on direct appeal from the high court of Kentucky. If Dred Scott's case were appealed the same way, directly, the Court could easily evade the controversial and delicate merits by using *Strader* as a precedent and then simply fall back on the Missouri decision, foredooming Scott to slavery. The only way Scott might attain his freedom was to get the Supreme Court to examine the case's merits; and the only way to do that was to institute a case in a lower *federal* court and appeal from it to Washington. In that way *Strader* might not be a precedent and it could open the door for an examination of the substantive issues.

Thus was born *Dred Scott* v. *John F.A. Sanford* in the federal Circuit Court of the United States, docketed in St. Louis in 1853 and tried on May 15, 1854.[2] Sanford was named defendant for two reasons. The first was to make the case eligible for the federal court system. A long-time resident of St. Louis, Sanford had moved to New York, though he still maintained business and social ties in St. Louis. Scott as a citizen of Missouri

---

[2]Contrary to widespread St. Louis tradition that all the local Dred Scott trials occurred in the historic Old Courthouse, this trial was conducted elsewhere, in an inauspicious upstairs room in what was then the Pap in Building on First Street between Chestnut and Pine Streets. Normally the federal courts sat free of charge in the Old Courthouse. But since that structure was state-owned, state courts had priority on use of the courtrooms, and if there was no room available then the United States marshall simply had to make other arrangements. This was the situation in May, 1854. And so the private room in the Papin Building was rented.

suing Sanford as a citizen of New York created a federal case on the grounds of diversity of citizenship. The second reason for naming Sanford as defendant was as executor of his brother-in-law's estate and thus the virtual, if not real, owner who was "holding" Scott in slavery.

As an interesting and fascinating side issue, the presumption of Sanford as executor was in fact not true. Sanford had been named in Dr. Emerson's will as executor, but by a unique set of circumstances he never legally qualified. For some curious and unknown reasons, though, neither he nor, apparently, his attorneys realized this, and he accordingly managed the estate as though he was indeed the executor. When Dred Scott sued Sanford, therefore, the latter could not and did not deny that he was at least "holding" Scott as a slave, and so whether he was the executor or the actual owner made no difference. What counted legally was that he was "holding" Scott as a slave.

And so *Dred Scott* v. *John F.A. Sanford* was instituted to clarify "once free always free." But again a new issue unexpectedly appeared. Sanford's attorney Hugh A. Garland (his partner Lyman D. Norris had died) now claimed that Scott was not a citizen of Missouri and therefore could not sue in a federal court. The reason, argued Garland, a native of Virginia with pro-slavery proclivities, was that Scott was "a negro of African descent." Now injected into the case was the right of a black man to be a citizen of the United States. As if "once free always free" was not delicate enough!

More was to come. It was a foregone conclusion that the lower federal court decision would be appealed to the Supreme Court, as of course it was. Moving to the highest court in the land brought more changes. One was that both sides acquired outstanding and nationally-reputed attorneys and spokesmen for their political and legal points of view. Another was that the case was now publicized throughout the country as one involving important and highly controversial issues.

Yet another change transformed this case from the obscure freedom suit it had been in 1846 to the *cause celebre* which it now became. It will be recalled that *Scott* v. *Sanford* came into the federal courts to seek clarification of "once free always free," and that the original right and power to emancipate a slave in a free

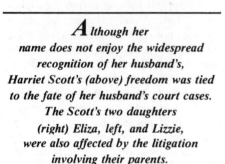

Although her name does not enjoy the widespread recognition of her husband's, Harriet Scott's (above) freedom was tied to the fate of her husband's court cases. The Scott's two daughters (right) Eliza, left, and Lizzie, were also affected by the litigation involving their parents.

(MISSOURI HISTORICAL SOCIETY)

state or territory was universally accepted. Now that too was changed, when Sanford's attorneys, Senators Henry S. Geyer of Missouri and Reverdy Johnson of Maryland, introduced the extreme pro-slave doctrine that slaves were private property protected by the Constitution and therefore Congress did not have the power to abolish or forbid slavery in the first place. In other words, the Missouri Compromise, and presumably any similar slavery prohibition, was unconstitutional. Applied specifically to this case, the issue was no longer whether Missouri could remand Dred Scott to slavery; the issue was whether he had ever been free in the first place.

This, then, was the case and these the issues thrust before the Supreme Court of the United States. At any other time these matters would have been difficult enough to deal with, for they could not be divorced from their political and sociological implications. In the tense and discordant national atmosphere of the 1850's, those political and sociological implications made an acceptable solution virtually impossible. In addition, the pressures on the Court were appalling. It was precisely because the issues were so delicate that many looked to the Supreme Court as the only institution which could

solve them, indicative of the esteem in which the Court was held.

Nevertheless, it appeared that judicial restraint would prevail, as the Court found a way to skirt the divisive substantive questions. Even though *Dred Scott* had come up from a lower federal rather than a state supreme court, *Strader* v. *Graham* still would be used as a precedent, and how the state (Missouri) supreme court had ruled on its own state law would be acceptable to the United States Supreme Court. This was a safe and long-accepted principle, and most important it would avoid dealing with the volatile substantive slavery questions. Justice Samuel Nelson of New York was assigned the task, and he began to write what apparently would be a very bland Court's Opinion.

Then all the unbridled forces of the time came to a head. The exact sequence of events is not absolutely clear, but the key event was the proposal by Justice James M. Wayne of Georgia that the decision be changed to include the two controversial issues Nelson was deliberately omitting, the citizenship of blacks and the constitutionality of the Missouri Compromise. Though Wayne made the specific proposal, responsibility for precipitating the drastic step falls on at least

four of his colleagues, Chief Justice Taney and Associate Justices John McLean, Benjamin R. Curtis and Peter V. Daniel. At any rate, a bare majority, all from slave states, concurred with Wayne. Chief Justice Taney would write the new Court Opinion. As delivered on March 6, 1857, it is the famous—or infamous—"Dred Scott Decision."

Dred Scott was declared to be still a slave, for several reasons. (1) Although blacks could be citizens of a given state, they could not be and were not citizens of the United States with the concomitant right to sue in the federal courts. Dred Scott's suit therefore was dismissed because the Court lacked jurisdiction. (2) Aside from not having the right to sue in the first place, Scott was still a slave because he never had been free to begin with. Slaves were property protected by the Constitution, and Congress exceeded its authority when it passed legislation forbidding or abolishing, slavery in the territories. The Missouri Compromise was such an exercise of unconstitutional authority and was accordingly declared invalid. (3) Whatever the status of an erstwhile slave may have been while he was in a free state or territory, if he voluntarily returned to a slave state, his status there depended upon the law of that slave state as interpreted by its own courts. In Scott's case, since the Missouri high court had declared him to be still a slave, that was the status and law which the Supreme Court of the United States would accept and recognize. "Once free always free" went by the wayside.

In the tense sectional-ridden atmosphere of the time, it is no wonder that the decision triggered a violent reaction. The Court had sought to solve the volatile slavery issue; instead, what it did has been recorded as the most ill-advised and unfortunate moment in its history. It unleashed irreconcilable passions, both North and South, that merged with those already building toward civil war. The press, the pulpit, the political stump and the halls of Congress now reverberated with scathing condemnations as well as vigorous defenses of the Court's action.

The intrusion of the Court into the slavery issue created an unprecedented political dilemma. *Dred Scott* appeared to give constitutional sanction to slavery. If so, that compromised the new anti-slave Republican party, whose very *raison d'etre* now seemed undermined. Existence as a national political party demanded respect for the law; but that existence also demanded the overturn of *Dred Scott* law. The political realities of the time offered little likelihood of either. Undoing *Dred Scott,* therefore, involved a hard new look at existing American institutions. To many in both North and South, any compromise over slavery now was impossible. The attack on slavery consequently was bound to involve action and measures more radical and drastic than anything the American democratic process had ever before experienced, and in like manner, the defense of slavery was destined to become equally inflexible. Once the Court had spoken, the two sections, irrevocably moved down a road that could lead only to disaster. *Dred Scott* might well have been the point of no return.

Anti-slavery forces now rose in righteous anger, determined to prevent the next fearful step, the legalizing of slavery everywhere. For that was the frightful specter which *Dred Scott* foreshadowed. If slaves were property protected in the territories, which was the consequence of the Missouri Compromise being declared unconstitutional, then they were also property which could be protected in the states. One more decision like *Dred Scott* and slavery would be a na-

tional institution. "Slavery national" rather than "freedom national" loomed on the horizon.

Forces intent on ridding the nation of slavery now mounted an unprecedented assault. Ironically, *Dred Scott* and Chief Justice Taney showed the way. Pro-slave states' rights Jeffersonian agrarians, for all their political philosophy, had utilized *national* institutional machinery to strengthen slavery. If that machinery was strong enough to *legalize* slavery throughout the nation (as some feared it now would), was it not also strong enough to *destroy* slavery throughout the nation? If Repub-

---

*D*red Scott's
final resting place is in St. Louis'
Calvary Cemetery. The descendents
of Scott's last owner, Taylor Blow,
paid to have this monument
erected in 1957.

(MISSOURI HISTORICAL SOCIETY)

licans could just hold the line on slavery and prevent any further expansion, all they had to do was gain control of the national machinery *without weakening it institutionally.* They could then use it to reverse whatever gains agrarianism and slavery had made. (After all, slavery was not the only concern of the new Republican party.) Gaining control of the executive and legislative branches had to come first; "proper" appointments to the federal judiciary would eventually follow.

In the meantime, the Court had to be prevented from legalizing slavery nationally, not by subverting its institutional

decision-making power, but by diminishing its influence and prestige *temporarily.* This was done by a vicious assault upon the *Dred Scott* decision. The charge of *obiter dictum* rang throughout the country, meaning once the Court had decided Dred Scott could not sue for lack of jurisdiction, then any incidental opinion on issues having no bearing upon the case was uncalled for. Legal scholars today overwhelmingly agree that Taney's rulings were not *obiter dicta,* but many contemporaries were convinced otherwise.

Taney and his concurring colleagues were derided and ridiculed to such a degree, not only for their legal abilities but also for personal matters, that confidence gradually eroded in their ability to render unbiased judgments. At the same time, Republicans and abolitionists heightened the fear of a "slave-power conspiracy" that purportedly included even members of the Supreme Court. This vicious attack on the Court was the spearhead of an unprecedented furious campaign to gain control over the national government, and then to run it under a centralized-power philosophy. It succeeded; in 1860, Abraham Lincoln was elected President of the United States.

The *Dred Scott* decision played a most significant role in those troubled days in still another way. As noted, individual judges were singled out for abuse and vilification because of their legal opinions. Inevitably, the assault on these individuals affected the institution itself, degrading it as a partisan body no longer capable of rendering justice without bias. Prior to *Dred Scott* there was a willingness—even an eagerness—to look to the Court to solve difficult constitutional problems, including slavery; after *Dred Scott,* confidence in the Court on such issues evaporated. Perhaps never before in the history of the United States was there so much need for the stabilizing influence, the sobriety, and the sound guidance that a respected Court might have provided. But it was no longer there. True, it would return later, but too late. Instead, bloodshed and violence prevailed.

The Dred Scott case, then, was of momentous consequence. Originating as an obscure open-and-shut freedom litigation, it literally was dragged by circumstances into prominence and notoriety. Little could that slave anticipate, when his benevolent friends went into St.

Louis' Old Courthouse to seek his freedom, that they were unleashing one of the most exciting and traumatic episodes in American constitutional history.

POSTSCRIPT: With the Taney pronouncement caught up in the dramatic events that exploded into bloody civil war, historians have largely overlooked what happened to Dred Scott the person. According to the Court, of course, he remained a slave. But whose? A careful examination of the record revealed that he still belonged to Mrs. Emerson, now Mrs. Chaffee, whose husband was a prominent Massachusetts abolitionist. Incredulously, though, Chaffee did not learn of his wife's association with the now-famous slave until only a few weeks before the Court rendered its final decision. His embarrassment was compounded because Massachusetts law considered his wife's property as his. The law also prevented him from freeing the slave until the pending legal action had been concluded. Once the Court announced its decision, however, Chaffee issued a quitclaim transferring ownership to Taylor Blow in St. Louis. (Dred Scott and his family had remained in St. Louis throughout the entire litigation.) Then, on May 26, 1857, in accordance with Missouri law, Taylor Blow formally freed Dred Scott, his wife Harriet, and their two daughters. That action occurred in the same courtroom in St. Louis where the case had started eleven years earlier in 1846. And so, despite the Supreme Court decision, Dred Scott and his family now were free.

Dred Scott worked as a porter in a St. Louis hotel for more than a year. But his popularity and new-found fame were short-lived. On September 17, 1858, he died of tuberculosis (some called it consumption). He was buried in the Wesleyan Cemetery just outside the St. Louis city limits. In 1867, as the city expanded westward, the cemetery was abandoned. Through the efforts again of Taylor Blow, Dred Scott's remains were reinterred in Calvary Cemetery in what is now northern St. Louis. For a long time the grave remained unmarked. In 1957, through the generosity of Taylor Blow's granddaughter, a stone marker was installed. It stands there today as a historical monument, a reminder of one of the most famous episodes in America's legal and constitutional history.

First Blood to the South: Bull Run, 1861

The rebel yell that dispelled hopes of a quick Union victory—Brian Holden Reid looks at the battle that set the scene for the American Civil War's protracted and bloody conflict.

Brian Holden Reid

Brian Holden Reid is Lecturer in War Studies at King's College, London and co-editor of American Studies: Essays in Honour of Marcus Cunliffe *(Macmillan, 1991).*

The First Battle of Bull Run, fought around a stream of that name on a boiling hot day on July 21st, 1861, in northern Virginia, was a salutary and traumatic experience for its participants. It was to date the greatest battle fought on North American soil. It has been the subject of two fine books, R.M. Johnston's *Bull Run: Its Strategy and Tactics* (1913), and more recently, William C. Davis' *Battle at Bull Run* (1977). Both works are examples of traditional campaign studies. The former was influential in examining the art of war within a narrative framework and expounding those elements upon which that art rested; the latter relies comfortably on archival research and is less didactic. But both books share a common characteristic which is the besetting sin of Civil War historiography, namely, that the military operations are studied in a vacuum. From the moment the campaign begins it is studied in isolation from those political and social issues that not only surrounded it, but governed it.

This campaign cannot be understood adequately unless it is connected with the social and political sources of warmaking in North America. It serves as a representative symbol, a culmination of the illusions and miscalculations, as well as the wisdom enshrined in the American military tradition. In the words of the late Marcus Cunliffe, the First Battle of Bull Run 'epitomised the variegated confusion of a century and more of American warfare'.

The campaign itself formed the climax of a dramatic series of events that began with the bombardment of Fort Sumter on April 12th 1861. Three days later Abraham Lincoln issued 'By the President of the United States, A Proclamation'. In this document Lincoln stressed his determination 'to suppress said combinations [of rebels] and to cause the laws to be duly executed'. In so doing he promised that 'the utmost care will be observed . . . to avoid any devastation; any destruction of, or interference with, property, or any disturbance of peaceful citizens in any part of the country'. He called for 75,000 volunteers for three months. On May 3rd, he issued another call for a further 42,000 volunteers for three years.

This political imperative governed the workings of the campaign—the need for a short, sharp victory over traitorous combinations of troublesome politicians. This political factor was accentuated by a decision of the Confederate government to give up its quarters at Montgomery, Alabama, to move to the more cosmopolitan surroundings of Richmond, Virginia, about fifty miles south of Washington. This decision, which brought the capitals so close together, led to an obsessive focus on the war in Virginia. Politicians are invariably of the opinion that the world revolves around their sayings and doings, and American politicians are more voluble than most. It

was a desire to occupy Richmond before the Confederate Congress reconvened there on July 20th that provoked the somewhat hysterical cry of 'On to Richmond'.

Most professional soldiers complain at some stage that their operations are hamstrung by politicians. But the position of Washington in 1861–62 was a special case. It is rare that a war of such scale and intensity was fought so close to the political heart of a country in which political decisions had such important strategic implications. Military action had been resorted to because American political mechanisms had broken down. From the outset, therefore, soldiers were exposed, not only to the political aspects of the war, but to the cut and thrust of political life. This was especially true of the opening months of war because the secession crisis had been such a painful experience that many politicians were infected by hysteria. The chairman of the Joint Committee on the Conduct of the War, Senator Benjamin F. Wade, was to write of this period that:

There was treason in the Executive mansion, treason in the Cabinet, treason in the Senate, treason in the House of Representatives, treason in the Army and Navy, treason in every department, bureau and office connected with the government.

This statement was a trifle exaggerated, but is a striking indicator of the sense of outrage and betrayal that secession had kindled into flame.

In May 1861 Brigadier-General Irvin B. McDowell was appointed to command the newly formed Army of the Potomac. He was a solemn and humourless man prone to over-eating, but a competent commander. McDowell laboured under the intense strain of political pressure for an immediate triumph over the rebels. This emanated from members of Congress, the administration and perhaps most important of all, the newspapers. Hugh Brogan has written that Americans are not schooled to the long haul; they expect everything to happen quickly. In 1861 both War Democrats, whose views on slavery were cautious (believing that Congress had no right to interfere with property rights in the states), and the more radical Republicans (who demanded its abolition), were impatient to see an early and decisive victory. The conservatives were anxious for an immediate end to the rebellion as a signal that there would be no change either to property rights or race relations in the Southern states. Before 1860 the South had been a fastness of the Democratic Party; its dominance of the presidency could not be restored until Southern electoral votes could be counted in its column. The Radical Republicans demanded an immediate overthrow of secession as a prelude to the destruction of the Southern plantocracy—the infernal 'Slave Power' that threatened to subvert democracy with its brutal, aristocratic mores. But whatever the aspirations of various party factions and their vociferous spokesmen in the newspapers, all assumed as a matter of course that the war would be short and that the Confederacy would be overthrown in one great, decisive, pitched battle. Congressman George Washington Julian, a Radical Republican, 'found everybody taking it for granted [that] when the first fight began our forces would prove triumphantly victorious'.

The expectations loaded on to McDowell's ample shoulders were therefore not light. He drew up a respectable plan to advance overland towards Richmond, outflanking the left of any Confederate forces he might meet, and advance on the city, whose fortifications were then infinitely weaker than they would soon become. Central to his plan was the need to pin down the Confederate forces commanded by General Joseph E. Johnston in the Shenandoah Valley. He could not risk any Confederate concentration against his forces north of Richmond.

McDowell was able but inexperienced. He was overworked and lacked a group of able staff officers to help him. The *Times* war correspondent, William

Howard Russell, met McDowell harassed and care-worn, as he arrived in Washington on July 16th. 'He asked where I came from and when he heard from Annapolis, inquired eagerly if I had seen two batteries of artillery . . . which he had ordered up and was waiting for, but which had "gone astray". Russell continued:

I was surprised to find the General engaged in such duty, and took leave to say so. 'Well it is quite true, Mr Russell; but I am obliged to look after them myself, as I have so small a staff, and they are all engaged out with my headquarters. You are aware I have advanced? No! Well, you have just come in time, and I shall be happy, indeed, to take you with me. I have made arrangements for the correspondents of our papers to take the field under certain regulations, and I have suggested to them they should wear a white uniform, to indicate the purity of their character'.

A sense of humour was not one of McDowell's strong points, and the irony of this last remark passed him by. But it is clear from Russell's account that the command system was chaotic, geared at the wrong level, and the commanding general was wasting his energies on trivia.

The same was true of the Confederate command system. General P.G.T. Beauregard commanding the Confederate forces north of Richmond (also confusingly called the Army of the Potomac) and General Johnston were hardly the two most modest men in the Confederate army. And much as Beauregard welcomed the arrival of Johnston's troops by rail the day before the battle, he did not welcome the arrival of their commander. He was jealous and suspicious of Johnston as a rival. Both men were under considerable pressure to justify the reputations they had either cultivated or built up on the basis of very slender experience. As Governor Pickens of South Carolina wrote of Beauregard, he was:

too cautious, and his very science makes him hesitate to make a dash. His knowledge of Batteries and cannon and engineering is great, but he relies nothing upon the spirit and the energy of troops, and has not experience in the management of Infantry. His Reputation is so high that he fears to risk it, and yet he wants the confidence of perfect genius.

Pickens expressed a widely felt view that war would be determined by moral, and not material, factors. William Howard

'Reading the War News in Broadway, New York' – an 1861 *Illustrated London News* sketch. Facile optimism (on both sides) about a speedy war began to recede in the aftermath of Bull Run.

(MANSELL COLLECTION)

Russell, became very irritated by the blithe Southern assumption of moral superiority. He asked, 'Suppose the Yankees . . . come with such preponderance of men and *matériel,* that they are three to your one, will you not be forced to submit?' 'Never [was the reply]. The Yankees are cowardly rascals'.

From the northern point of view the battle went well, at first. Beauregard had concentrated his forces in the centre and on the right along the Bull Run and neglected his left. But as the day wore on, mainly under Johnston's influence, Beauregard was persuaded to move more of his forces to the left so that he could counter McDowell's out-flanking move. This switch was greatly aided by the futile attrition of Federal strength on the right and centre. For example, within hours Colonel Ambrose E. Burnside's brigade had been reduced to one regiment, the 2nd New Hampshire, which Burnside personally commanded. All commanders, no matter how senior, felt happiest at this level of command. It was in this sector that General Bernard Bee's immortal remark concerning Jackson's 'stone wall' was coined—which had much more significance in Confederate folklore than as a turning point in this battle.

Even by the late afternoon, the battle had not gone badly for McDowell. But his plan was simply too complex for his untrained and raw army to implement. Because he lacked a good staff, McDowell was frequently absent from the main point of decision attending to other people's work, and co-ordination was lacking. Discipline broke down. 'No curse could be greater', concluded Colonel William T. Sherman, 'than invasion by a volunteer army . . . Our men are not good soldiers. They brag, but don't perform, complain sadly if they don't get everything they want, and a march of a few miles uses them up'. The crisis of the battle was reached shortly after 3pm. The Confederate army had virtually turned 90 degrees to face McDowell's outflanking force. Colonel Oliver O. Howard's brigade was severely mauled in an attack on Henry Hill and was driven back in confusion. It was symptomatic of the amateurish deployment on both sides that the success of McDowell's assault rested on one brigade, and that the arrival of three Confederate regiments, two from South Carolina and the 28th Virginia, was sufficient to steady the Confederate line. It was this movement, the repulse of one brigade and the arrival

Feeble Yankees – the Southern sense of moral (and physical) superiority over their Northern counterparts is reflected in this cartoon comment on the 1856 caning of Charles Sumner by Brooks in the senate, after the former's attack on South Carolina's policies.

(*HISTORY TODAY* ARCHIVES)

of three regiments that triggered off the Federal retreat. Some parts of this turned into a rout which swept up a number of important political personages who had come out to watch the crushing of the impertinent rebels. Thus ended, with such ignominy, the campaign of Bull Run, in which so much hope had been invested. What were the main factors that had led to this unexpected (but for the South welcome) Union defeat?

The main feature of this campaign was the complete lack of preparation on both sides for sustained military operations. During the secession crisis very little had been done to organise the United States Army for a punitive expedition against the rebels. Seven warships had been ordered by Congress to help the revenue service collect the duties and enforce the blockade of Southern ports. Some money had been voted by Northern legislators to improve the militia—but this did not amount to very much. After Sumter there was a burst of martial enthusiasm. The decision was taken to raise volunteers rather than to expand the regular army. In the South a plan was mooted to raise a regular army but here, too, the volunteer system was preferred. McDowell found the three month volunteers an embarrassment. If he had insisted on waiting until he was properly prepared and trained before attacking the

Confederates, then he would have lost 10,000 of his best men once their terms of enlistment had expired. In July 1861 President Lincoln called for a further 400,000 volunteers, again for three years.

These troops were undisciplined and poorly trained. As McDowell wrote in his report, Union troops were 'unaccustomed to marching . . . and not used to carrying even the load of "light marching order" '. The opinionated and obstreperous behaviour of American soldiers so struck observers that one recorded after Bull Run that 'I doubt if our democratic form of government admits of that organisation and discipline without which an army is a mob'. And it must be stressed that such was the novelty of seeing large bodies of uniformed troops drilling, that many of the favourable impressions recorded by politicians were exaggerated. Lincoln's friend, Orville Hickman Browning, described a regiment of Rhode Island volunteers in the following glowing terms: 'I have never seen troops to surpass [them] in appearance or perfection of discipline, or accuracy of drill'—but he had seen so few others to compare them with. On the Southern side, the secessionist fire-eater, Edmund Ruffin, was disgusted to find that there were as many men retiring from the victorious field of Bull Run as advancing. 'But I was struck with the strange fact, that of all these men reported as either wounded or worn down by exertion, not one was sitting or lying as if to rest'. They were, of course, making a rapid withdrawal from the scene of maximum danger.

Ruffin's comments are interesting because they contradicted a widely held view that the South was better equipped in every way to wage war than the North; indeed that the South had its own military tradition. This overlooked rather conveniently the fact that the Confederacy won a defensive victory and that it was much more difficult for the Union Army to organise offensive movement. But it was assumed that such a military tradition did exist; that Southerners were inherently superior at the profession of arms. It was also believed that the secession conspiracy had been years in the making—and not just an impulsive reaction to the election of a Republican president in 1860. This, too, was an assumption that was based on fragmentary evidence. The only evidence that secession had been carefully nursed was found in a novel published in 1836 by Nathaniel Beverley Tucker, *The Partisan Leader,* which predicted the coming of civil war as the result of the courageous Southern efforts to resist Northern tyranny. 70,000 copies of this work were circulated during May 1861. Conspiracy theories tend to proliferate when the evidence is fragmentary or non-existent. The commandant of cadets at West Point, Colonel (later Major General) John F. Reynolds, believed that when the Confederate President, Jefferson Davis, was Secretary of War in the Pierce Administration (1853–57) he had seduced Southern officers from their true allegiance and planted instead 'the poisonous weed of secession, . . . the depth of his treachery has not been plumbed yet', he predicted. But because public opinion in the South was convinced that the South had been well prepared for the battle, the meaning of Bull Run was misinterpreted. Far from seeing that chance had proved to be the decisive factor in a battle between two unprepared armies, many concluded that Southern martial prowess was the key.

These elements fitted into a vision of war that assumed it would be short. Consequently, there would be no need to train or prepare in the North because the South would be crushed quickly; and in the Confederate States faith in Southern martial prowess would suffice to bring a

rapid victory over the Northern masses. The model that fitted these preconceptions of what a future war would be like was George B. McClellan's advance in May and June 1861 into the Unionist counties of West Virginia who stubbornly refused to be coerced by the Confederacy. Lightning advances, striking gains, little fighting but pleasing victories advertised by bombastic Napoleonic pronouncements, were its prominent, comforting features, at least for the North. The occupation of these counties came as a shock to the South and threw a (temporary) cloud over the career of Robert E. Lee. Southerners were convinced, as Russell noted in a visit to the deep South, 'that the white men in the slave States are physically superior to the men in the free States'; their moral superiority had been proven by confrontations between politicians in Congress—especially the caning of Senator Charles Sumner in 1856. According to Louis T. Wigfall, this was an example 'of the manner in which the Southerners would deal with Northerners generally . . . [and] in which they would bear their "whipping" '.

Even taking into account that Wigfall was drunk during this conversation, it is a somewhat hazy description of the shape a future war would take. In the West Virginia instance, it had been the South that had been 'whipped'—though this verdict was reversed by Bull Run. Nevertheless, the view that the war would remain short persisted long after the battle. In January 1862, a wealthy Georgia planter, Edgeworth Bird, wrote to his wife, Sallie, 'I believe the war will not last long . . . England's interest unerringly points to an issue with them [the Federal Government], and it will surely come [and lead to British intervention on behalf of the South]. Let us keep our cotton and let not a single bag go, except in exchange for necessary articles'. Thus the illusion of a short war was buttressed by another illusion—that Great Britain would rescue the Confederacy because of her desperate need for cotton.

That the war did not take the expected form led to some confusion and a severe oscillation in morale on both sides. Before Bull Run, Congressman Joseph Medell was of the opinion that 'The idea of waiting until frost set in, and merely defending our capitol was a preposterous one in a political point of view, and our struggle is not a purely military one'. The main spokesman for this view was

Horace Greeley of the New York *Tribune* whose opinions were as impulsive as its chimerical editor. Before 1861 Greeley had seen no need for an army. After Fort Sumter Greeley urged 'condign punishment' on the South. The leader-writer, Charles A. Dana, sketched the headline 'Forward to Richmond'. This was just one more influential voice that swelled a chorus demanding swift and decisive action. It underestimated both the enthusiasm and determination of Southern soldiers. Commentators were too easily persuaded that the war would resemble an affray like Shay's Rebellion in Massachusetts in 1786, in which a body of discontented farmers were dispersed without effort. Consequently, the North was over-confident before Bull Run and the South over-confident after it. Russell was convinced that both sides in 1861 were too prone to boast about their martial prowess without experiencing the realities of war. Here Bull Run was a salutary shock.

The expected short war would be brought to an end by a great and decisive battle. This was a naive and romantic vision, that would rise again before 1914. In so far as it envisaged fighting at all (as opposed to picturesque movement and heroics), this involved hand-to-hand fighting. John S. Mosby convinced himself of Southern martial superiority when he noticed that the Federals 'never once stood to a clash of the bayonet—always broke and ran'. But bayonet fights were rare. Another Southern observer remarked that 'We were taken out into an open field and formed in line of battle where we made excellent marks for the enemy who commenced firing at us'. Other observers expressed frustration at not being able to see the enemy: 'The enemy can't see us and we cannot see them being covered by trees . . . Nothing but trees to fire at'. The concern with dash expressed in all of these comments—an obsession with reckless movement, led by officers of a feckless and histrionic mien, buttressed the supposition that the whole war would be over in one great battle—an illusion that would prevail for at least another nine months. It was revealed as foolish by the First Battle of Bull Run.

As Northern confidence was uneven, and oscillated between boastfulness and despair, so the defeat at Bull Run was followed by a search for scapegoats. McDowell was sacked and replaced by the hero of West Virginia, George

B. McClellan—prematurely dubbed the 'Young Napoleon'. After three months of hostilities the Federal Government was still on the strategic defensive. It would remain so—even after the Battle of Shiloh—until General McClellan set out on his ill-fated Peninsular Campaign in the spring of 1862. Thus the campaign ended with politicians blaming one another for urging McDowell on to his premature advance—even though he had no choice but to move when he did. The true significance of this somewhat unedifying controversy lay in its convenience as a pretext for discrediting the President and his cabinet. Attempts were made to reconstruct it in favour of one pressure group or another. Earlier efforts had failed before the firing on Fort Sumter, and they would be repeated during the Cabinet Crisis in December 1862 following the Union defeat at the Battle of Fredericksburg. Lincoln's dominance of his administration depended crucially on the progress of military events, mainly in the Virginian theatre.

Certainly, the Lincoln administration wanted the battle. There were some dissident voices, such as the general-in-chief, Winfield Scott, who always thought that untrained volunteers could not be trusted. But the campaign went ahead on the Northern side because of the overwhelming faith that the war would soon be over. Hardly anyone challenged this belief. The South similarly was inspired by the expectation that the war would be short. Success at Bull Run, despite the lack of a pursuit, fortified Southern confidence that their martial skills, now abundantly vindicated, would bring an early triumph. The First Battle of Bull Run had revealed starkly the illusions and false expectations cherished about the character of warfare in the mid-nineteenth century. This is a task often discharged by early battles. Yet these illusions persisted. So strong was the yearning for a dramatic, decisive victory that would bring the fratricidal conflict to an end, that in February 1862 William H. Seward, the Secretary of State, informed Senator Charles Sumner that he had 'authentic information from Virginia that the Rebellion would be over there in four weeks'. The source of this startling intelligence was not divulged. Four more years might have been a more accurate prediction.

FOR FURTHER READING:

Marcus Cunliffe, *Soldiers and Civilians: The Martial Spirit in America, 1775-1865* (Eyre and Spotiswoode, 1969); William C. Davis, *Battle at Bull Run* (Louisiana State U.P., 1977); William Howard Russell, *My Diary North and South* (ed.) Eugene H. Berwanger (Alfred A. Knopf, 1988); Kenneth M. Stampp, *And the War Came: The North and the Secession Crisis* (Louisiana State U.P., 1950); Michael C.C. Adams, *Our Masters the Rebels* (Harvard U.P., 1978); Brian Holden Reid, 'General McClellan and the Politicians,' *Parameters,* XVII (September 1987).

The Struggle for Black Freedom before Emancipation

Wayne K. Durrill

Wayne K. Durrill teaches American history at the University of Cincinnati.

The Civil War has recently become a hot ticket. The movie, *Glory,* the PBS series "The Civil War" by Ken Burns, and James McPherson's recent Pulitzer Prize-winning account of the conflict have all dramatized the continuing relevance of the war as a defining experience for a people and a nation. These stories, however, have often neglected an important part of that defining experience: the role of black people in securing their own emancipation. Most accounts of war date emancipation from Lincoln's famous proclamation and the military campaigns that followed. Even *Glory,* which traces the heroic deeds of black soldiers from Massachusetts, portrays slaves in the lowcountry of South Carolina as incompetent and ineffectual, persons who simply waited for Northern free black liberators to march South and rescue them from bondage.

However, even this relatively enlightened view of the role of black people in their own emancipation is historically inaccurate. As Ira Berlin and his colleagues have shown in their monumental multi-volume series, *Freedom: A Documentary History of Emancipation,* slaves throughout the South squeezed freedom in dribs and drabs from their own local situation as opportunities arose in wartime. In Kentucky, where blacks remained in bondage until after the Civil War, slaves fled to Tennessee where they could join the Union army as laborers and later as soldiers, and thereby free themselves and sometimes their families. Others stayed home, testing the limits of servitude in a volatile and dangerous situation, always with an eye toward establishing claims to property and

place, as well as to their own humanity. These black struggles for freedom within slavery are sometimes difficult to visualize. Indeed, they seem to be a contradiction in terms. Yet they did occur, and with an intensity and regularity that historians have only just begun to uncover. As an example of such struggle, let us examine the story of how one group of North Carolina slaves redefined the rules of slavery in the crisis of war so as to create for themselves a larger space in which to carry on a life separate from their white masters.

In September of 1861, after the fall of federal forces of Hatteras Island on North Carolina's Outer Banks, Major General John Wool, Union commander of the island, reported that "negro slaves" were "almost daily arriving at this post from the interior." They came in small groups, many traveling over one hundred miles from the counties bordering the Albemarle Sound. At Columbia, on the eastern edge of the Sound and about five miles from William Pettigrew's plantation, a certain planter had brought his slaves to town for "safekeeping." The militia had already mustered there and the town had a jail if he needed it. But shortly after their arrival, thirteen of the man's slaves quietly stole a boat and sailed for Hatteras, setting in motion a chain of events that quickly spread through counties all around the Sound. One planter complained that news of the escape had spread among slaves in the area, and he reasoned, "We may look for others to leave soon." In response, slave owners throughout the Sound region began to move to the upcountry, taking with them as many of their slaves as they could support on the land available to them.

William Pettigrew, one of the richest planters in Washington County, North Carolina, grasped the crisis early on and

resolved to remove his slaves before planting began the following spring. On 4 March 1862, the planter arranged for twenty-five Confederate cavalrymen to descend upon Magnolia plantation. The move took the slaves by surprise, and all were captured. That day, men, women, and children were loaded onto wagons guarded by armed troopers, and began a long journey upcountry. After a nine-day forced march, Pettigrew and the slaves came to Haywood, a small crossroads community about fifty miles west of Raleigh where the planter had located a small farm for sale. He purchased the farm as his base camp in the upcountry, but it was too small to support any but a handful of his slaves. The others he drove on foot fifty miles further west where he leased out eight-seven of them in nineteen groups to fifteen different planters.

The exchange of slaves for promissory notes, however, signified more than simply a purchase of labor. It included a broader transfer of power from one planter to another. For this reason, William Pettigrew insisted that persons who hired his slaves provide them with certain goods in the coming year, mostly food, clothing, and shoes. The planter might have provided the goods himself and factored the cost into his asking price. But he did not. Instead, he included in the contract detailed directions specifying what each slave should receive. In doing so, Pettigrew ensured that his slaves' new master would become the sole source of some crucial goods for them, thus giving the new master enormous leverage over the hired-out slaves. By his actions, Pettigrew produced not merely new employers for his slaves, but new masters.

Such contracts, however, did not settle all questions of a planter's dominance and a slave's submission in the upcoun-

From *OAH Magazine of History,* Vol. 8, No. 1, Fall 1993, pp. 7-10. Adapted from *War of Another Kind: A Southern Community in the Great Rebellion* by Wayne K. Durrill. © 1990 Oxford University Press, Inc. Reprinted by permission.

try. Planters and slaves, in fact, had always created their own mutual expectations, in part by contesting the rules by which they lived. Before the war, this had not been a conflict among equals, to be sure. Instead, the struggle between planter and slave presumed an unequal resolution; the master would rule and the slave submit. But in 1862, the relations between planters and slaves had changed dramatically, even in the upcountry. Many of the Pettigrew slaves worked for new masters who might or might not be skilled in managing human property. Would these men have the wherewithal to nail the meat-house door shut, call in the slave patrol, or face down a personal challenge? No one knew. But William Pettigrew's slaves were determined to find out.

Mary Jane, for example, decided early on to see just what kind of master she had been assigned. William Pettigrew had hired her out as a cook to a planter named George Foushee, along with a slave named Dick Lake, his wife Jenny, and their five children. Mary Jane complained "mostly of colick" during her first three weeks at Foushee's place. In that period, she rendered "very little service" in the planter's view. According to Foushee, "She don't seem to be very bad off, just sick enough to keep her from work." The planter further wondered if "a good deal of it is deception." To find out, Foushee asked Dick Lake about her, and the slave's answer confirmed the planter's suspicions. According to Lake, Mary Jane had "never done much the year she was in a family way." Mary Jane had a history of probing the limits of her master's power.

Similarly, Jenny took advantage of the change of masters to renew work rules she had known at Magnolia plantation. She had just borne a child and informed Foushee that she had "never been required to do any work until her child was eight weeks old." She also objected to Foushee's plan to put her to work in the fields. At Magnolia she always had labored as a cook and now complained that she "could not work out."

Mary Jane, Jenny, and their fellow slaves did not wish simply to avoid work by refusing to labor for their masters. Most, in fact, worked steadily and with a will. In late March, a friend of William Pettigrew's who saw some of the planter's slaves "most every Sunday" in church, reported them at work and "well satisfied" with their new circumstances.

Therefore, the action taken by Mary Jane and Jenny must be interpreted as having some more specific purpose. Mary Jane had succeeded in making pregnancy a privileged status at their old plantation. Here, she renewed the rule by making a public event of her refusal to work while pregnant. Similarly, she served notice upon George Foushee that Pettigrew slaves could not be required to work when ill, no matter how slight the planter thought evidence of any malady appeared. Jenny, for her part, sought to reinforce two rules. The first would give women a special status when pregnant. The second would renew a longstanding division between housework and fieldwork that served as the basis for some very important and very sharp distinctions among the Pettigrew slaves themselves.

George Foushee understood all of this on a practical level. Doubtless, he could never admit publicly, or perhaps even to himself, that Mary Jane and Jenny's actions constituted a challenge to the local rules that governed relations between masters and slaves. But Foushee did have the presence of mind to remain calm. He reported by letter to William Pettigrew the two slaves' failure to work diligently. But Foushee did not propose that either he or Pettigrew take any action. The planter concluded his account of Mary Jane's behavior by saying simply, "I hope she will be better hereafter."

Mary Jane did become better. After she had made her point, she returned to work as usual. Other planters, however, did not fully appreciate the give-and-take that an exercise of a master's power required, particularly when the power of masters had been so undermined by Union military activity on the North Carolina coast. Or perhaps some planters sensed in small challenges larger issues that George Foushee had overlooked.

A. E. Caveness is a case in point. Caveness had hired one slave family from William Pettigrew—Jack, his pregnant wife, Venus, and their six young children. The children must have been young because the entire family hired out for twenty-five dollars, less than the cost of hiring a single prime male field hand. Caveness got a good deal more than he bargained for, however, when he paid his pittance to William Pettigrew. When members of the slave family initiated the same contest that took place on the Foushee plantation, Caveness could not comprehend their actions for what they were. In his view, the slaves attempted to "over-

run" him. Finally, in a fit of ill-temper, the planter whipped the oldest child, a girl named Sarah, for what he considered her "laziness and disobedience."

The girl's parents objected violently to this. They "made a great ado about it," according to one account, so much so that Caveness felt compelled to "take Venus in hand." At that point, Venus "started off" down the plantation road and, as she walked, turned to the planter and told him off. What exactly she uttered that day remained a matter of dispute. Caveness claimed that she shouted, I am "going to the Yankees." Doubtless, she had no such intention—if she even spoke these words. Venus and her family had just made the nine-day trek from the coast on foot. She well knew that she needed food and extra clothing for such a journey, that Confederate troops blanketed eastern North Carolina and would demand a pass from her, and that William Pettigrew would hire a slave catcher to find her long before she reached federal lines. Later, Venus's husband claimed that she had said no such thing. By the slave's account, Venus told Caveness that she intended to walk to the plantation of William Campbell, Pettigrew's friend, presumably to lodge a complaint against her new master for his actions. Whatever the exact words, Venus had made her point in producing this small drama—pubicly and loudly. She feared no man, planter or otherwise, and if she chose to oppose that man, she would make her claim a matter of public debate.

Caveness "ordered her to come back," but Venus refused and continued walking down the road. The planter then got his whip and followed her. Some distance from the house, he finally caught up with her. Again, Caveness commanded Venus to return to the plantation. Once more, the slave refused and voiced her intention to leave. At that point, the planter lost all patience and good sense. Caveness began to whip Venus, at which time Jack, who evidently had followed the two, "got in between them." The planter then "fell to work on Jack, and drove both slaves back to the house."

But Venus had succeeded in her purpose even as she and her husband bore the lashes of the planter's whip. Caveness complained that "the fuss might have been heard all over the neighborhood." If he hoped to exercise any power over Pettigrew's slaves, Caveness now would have to submit to the scrutiny of his neighbors, both black and white. Each side in this conflict would mobilize its supporters. The battle between master and slave over who would rule the family, and particularly the children of Venus and Jack, became a public controversy.

The next day, Caveness traveled to William Campbell's plantation, where he hoped to make his case to the county's planters. To Campbell, he gave an account of the basic facts in the matter. But Caveness made no attempt to justify his actions. Instead he simply announced a solution. He demanded that Campbell, who had been charged with managing William Pettigrew's interest in Chatham and Moore counties, write to the slaves' owner seeking "permission to conquer them." If Pettigrew refused to grant him such authority, Caveness demanded that their master "take them away." By this ultimatum, Caveness cast the conflict in terms of fundamental issues—in this case, the interest of planters in dominating their slaves. Essentially, Caveness argued that all planters must stand with him, no matter what the specifics of this case, in order to preserve their power over slaves as a whole.

Meanwhile, Venus and Jack also made their opinions known throughout the neighborhood. The couple communicated their interpretation of the conflict to slaves belonging to William Campbell who, in turn, approached their master after Caveness returned home. They told Campbell that Caveness had "not been good" to Pettigrew"s slaves. They argued that Caveness was "a man of bad temper," and he acted "very ill" to Jack and his family. In particular Campbell's slaves charged that Caveness had refused to give Jack and his family "enough to eat," even though he had "plenty of meat and bread" to sell to other persons in the neighborhood.

During the next two weeks, Jack and Venus appealed directly to William Campbell. When Campbell visited the family, Jack accused Caveness of abusing them "without any just cause." To support the charge, the slave pointed out that recently Caveness had "knocked Edith [his youngest child] down with a hand-spike." The blow cut the little girl "severely on the head." And "since the first difficulty with Venus," Caveness had "knocked [her also] down with a chair." That piece of viciousness caused Venus to miscarry. On 10 June, she was reported "very bad off." Moreover, after he struck Venus, Caveness "threatened to kill her if she did not get up and go to work," according to Jack's account.

Jack therefore requested that Campbell write to William Pettigrew in order to give the planter the slaves' version of events. In the letter, Jack argued that he and his family had "worked harder" that spring than they had "ever worked in their lives," but Caveness could not be satisfied. Therefore, he implored William Pettigrew to remove them from Caveness's plantation. Jack declared his family "willing to live anywhere," even "on half feed," as long as they would "not be abused." We "did not want to put you to any trouble," Jack told his master, but we can "not stand it."

In the end, Jack and his wife prevailed. Their story had a ring of truth that even Caveness himself made no attempt to deny. Moreover, Caveness's poor reputation in the area precluded his attempt to mobilize planter opinion in his cause. Campbell considered Caveness "very hard to please" and "a very passionate man." Finally, Caveness did not help his own case when he admitted to Campbell that if he had carried his gun along, he would have "killed some of them."

But all of this might have come to nothing if Venus had not made the dispute a public event. By mobilizing local opinion, both black and white, Jack and Venus forged a means by which the Pettigrew slaves could shape their own destiny, at least in some small part. William Campbell considered his slave's version of events "only negro news" and therefore, "only to be used as such." Yet, he recommended to William Pettigrew that Jack and his family be removed from Caveness' plantation to a place where they would be "well cared for." "If Caveness is not willing to keep them and treat them humanely as other negroes are treated in this part of the country," wrote Campbell, "I should take them away."

In one sense, the customary rights of slaves acting within the rules of paternalism had been renewed. Yet, there was more to the story than a restoration of peaceable relations between masters and slaves. The abuse by Caveness of Venus and her children provided an unprecedented opportunity to challenge a slaveholder. Caveness had made certain guarantees to Pettigrew—physical safety and an adequate subsistence for the slaves—that he failed to fulfill. And ironically, by insisting on Pettigrew's rights in his property, Venus advanced her own claim as a human being. Indeed, she used those double-edged claims to turn Caveness's own class against him; she forced Pettigrew and others to recognize not only her right to safety and subsistence but also her right to be heard and recognized as a person. In doing so, Venus and Jack and all the other Pettigrew slaves participated in a much larger defining moment, the self-emancipation of America's slaves in the crucible of the Civil War.

Combat Trauma in the American Civil War

Shell-shocked—a phrase redolent of the Western Front and the Great War. But was it also a reality fifty years earlier on the killing fields of Virginia? John Talbott investigates.

John Talbott

John E. Talbott is Professor of History at the University of California, Santa Barbara.

When Civil War soldiers 'saw the elephant,' as they called going into action, some of them sustained injuries they could not name. Wounds to the mind left them open to imputations of malingering, allegations of cowardice or charges of desertion. For the Union army had no label like shell shock, battle fatigue or post-traumatic stress disorder to help explain and legitimise a mysterious condition, no category short of lunacy to account for peculiar behaviour. In late November 1864, for instance, Captain J. McEntire, a provost marshal, wrote of Private William Leeds, a prisoner in his charge:

> He has been strolling about in the woods, and has procured his food from soldiers . . . He has a severe cut on his nose and his eyes are in mourning for the loss of his character.

Since enlisting the previous January, Leeds had been trying to escape the Army of the Potomac: 'We have not been able to keep him a moment except in confinement,' his colonel wrote. On Christmas Eve 1864 Leeds was committed, under escort, to the Government Insane Asylum—St Elizabeth's Hospital—in Washington, D.C.

Perhaps Leeds was lucky. For men whom medical officers might have diagnosed for combat trauma in 1916, 1944 or 1968 were hauled before courts mar-

tial in 1864, and some of them probably wound up at the end of a noose or in front of a firing squad. The human response to stress did not change between the Civil War and the Vietnam War, but understanding and interpreting the response were transformed.

The evidence bearing on combat trauma in the Civil War is anecdotal, ambiguous and fragmentary. Traces usually appear in such narratives as soldiers' diaries, journals, and letters home. Sometimes evidence appears in stories written long after the war. James Thurber, for instance, often mentioned his grandfather's awakening from nightmares of the Federal retreat from Fredericksburg. An Ohio volunteer who spent a lifetime re-crossing the Rappahannock in his dreams probably suffered from combat trauma. Such mind wounds afflicted many fewer people and drew far less attention from either physicians or the public than 'nervous breakdown,' the Victorians' term for incapacitating depression. Combat trauma led an underground, phantom-like existence until bursting into full view, and grudging recognition, in the war of 1914–18. For all its elusiveness, it leaves tracks.

Consider the case of the James boys—William, Henry, Garth, or 'Wilky,' as he was called, and Robertson or 'Bob'. The two older boys, the philosopher and the novelist, did not serve in the Civil War; the two younger ones did. Wilky, an officer in the 54th Regiment of Massachusetts Volunteer Infantry, was twice wounded in the assault on Fort Wagner; Bob was an officer in the 55th Massachusetts, a less famous regiment that also saw some hard fighting.

A mysterious back injury sustained fighting a fire in Newport, Rhode Island, kept Henry out of the army that so many of his friends and contemporaries rushed to join. William James shared Henry's ambivalent feelings about military service but not the back problem that went with it. Later on, however, he became deeply interested in the relationship between psychological trauma and psycho-pathology. Henry James' 'obscure hurt' and William's debilitating bouts of depression are far better documented than the fate of the foot soldiers Wilky and Bob. While the older brothers emerged as two of the most influential men in American intellectual life, the two combat veterans dwelled in obscurity. Wilky moved from town to town, concocting grandiose financial schemes in which he repeatedly lost his shirt. Bob became an alcoholic. To ascribe the postwar fortunes of the junior members of the Jamesian quartet solely to their war experiences is too simple. Still, Wilky's chronic restlessness and Bob's alcoholism are tell-tale signs of combat trauma.

Other evidence bearing on mind wounds is more indirect. Combat is replete with episodes of anomalous, peculiar or unusual behaviour. Such behaviour falls within the pattern the psychologist Pierre Janet called 'dissociation.' As a response to traumatic events—indeed, as a defence *against* trauma—dissociation is an adaptive strategy. It allows a person under stress to continue functioning, although often in an autonomic and sometimes inappropriate way. Three such cases among many that might be adduced in-

(MANSELL COLLECTION)

Close combat: a skirmish between Union and Confederate soldiers during the so-called 'Battle of the Wilderness' in Virginia in May 1864. The bitter fighting over wild terrain precipitated an alleged episode of dissociation involving Union Brigadier General James Wadsworth, with disastrous results for the 20th Massachusetts.

volve high-ranking officers, not the infantrymen or 'grunts' who were at greater risk of combat trauma.

On June 30th, 1862, toward the close of the ill-fated Peninsula campaign and the sixth day of the ferocious Seven Days' Battle, General George B. McClellan, Commander of the Army of the Potomac, boarded the gunboat *Galena* and steamed up the James River, putting a great number of miles between himself and the responsibilities of his command. What could account for such behaviour? The judgement of McClellan's biographer, Stephen Sears, is harsh: the general 'had lost the courage to command'. This moral judgement might be softened by guessing that McClellan, never eager to commit his army to battle and chagrined by the consequences, was suffering from dissociation, a response to trauma rather than a loss of nerve. Indeed, Sears goes on to qualify his own remark: '[McClellan] was drained,' he says, 'in both mind and body.' This is a Janet-like acknowledgement of the psychosomatic consequences of stress. In any event, McClellan recovered his equilibrium, if not his fitness for high command.

The other two examples derive from eye-witness accounts. In late November 1862 Lieutenant Henry L. Abbott, 20th Massachusetts Volunteers, wrote to his father about the alarming behaviour of Raymond Lee, the colonel commanding his regiment:

Col. Lee . . . is undoubtedly very much shaken in his intellects, at any rate at times . . . It seems the horrors of Antietam, his previous fatigues and his drinking, completely upset him. After the battle he was completely distraught. He didn't give any orders. He wouldn't do any thing. The next morning he mounted his horse, without any leave of absence, without letting any body [know] where he was going, he set out alone. Macy, who was bringing up some recruits, met him about ten miles away from the regt. without a cent in his pocket, without any thing to eat or drink, without having changed his clothes for four weeks, during all which time he had this horrible diarrhea—just getting ready to turn into a stable for the night. Macy gave him a drink and some money and got him into a house, put him to bed stark

naked, and got his wits more settled and then came on. When the poor old man came back to the regt. they thought he had been on an awful spree, he was so livid and shaky. Macy says he was just like a little child, wandering away from home.

The third episode of dissociation is more ambiguous. Around mid-morning on May 6th, 1864, the second day of the Battle of the Wilderness, the 20th Massachusetts was dug in behind log and earthen breastworks hastily thrown up along the Orange Plank Road. During a lull in the firing, Brigadier General James S. Wadsworth came galloping up and ordered the regiment to advance toward a wall of saplings and scrubby pines believed to conceal rebel troops.

At fifty-nine Wadsworth was the oldest senior officer in the Army of the Potomac, a wealthy and well-connected New Yorker admired for serving competently and without pay in a position of great danger. Yet on the morning of May 5th, a 20th Massachusetts officer recalled, Wadsworth rode up 'in a very wild and excited manner' demanding to know who was in command. Told by Colonel George Macy that his own brigade commander had ordered him to hold his position at any cost, 'Wadsworth then said very excitedly,' according to the Massachusetts captain, '"I command these troops and order you forward."' In fact, Wadsworth commanded a division of the 5th Corps, under Gouverneur Warren. The 20th Massachusetts belonged to the 2nd Corps, under Winfield Hancock. In the confusion of battle Wadsworth had either lost or deliberately left, for a purpose known only to him (perhaps an attempt to impose order where he saw none?), his own division. In any event, when the jurisdictional issue was raised Wadsworth 'became still more excited,' according to our informant, 'throwing his arms in the air, and said something which I did not catch, but to which [Macy] answered "very well sir, we will go."'

Accounts of what happened next are markedly at odds. Either Wadsworth led the charge of the 20th Massachusetts or, as a survivor of the assault remembers it, the general 'immediately galloped off and disappeared' before regimental officers managed to pry their men loose from the breastworks and walk them into the muskets of the 8th Alabama, lying in wait on the ground. 'Great God!,' Macy told his captains, 'That man is out of his mind.' Shot through the head that afternoon, Wadsworth died a few days later. In the space of fifteen minutes, the

533 men who charged into the woods were reduced to the three of four officers and 110 men who eventually reformed on the Brock Road.

General Alexander S. Webb, who had anchored his brigade's line on the strong position occupied by the 20th Massachusetts, later called Wadsworth's command to put his twelve regiments at Wadsworth's disposition 'the most astonishing and bewildering order.' Indeed his actions on the morning of May 6th make little sense. Seeking to arrest the disintegration of the Federal line, Wadsworth accelerated it. Why was he so far from where he belonged? Why did he countermand the instructions of the experienced and able commander on the scene? Why did he so frantically urge a reliable, veteran regiment to assault an invisible enemy? This episode illustrates both the fog of war and the disorientation of Wadsworth. In the hours before the incident in question, the general admitted to an aide that 'he was exhausted and worn out' and wondered about his own fitness for command. Dissociation may help account for his 'most astonishing and bewildering' behaviour.

The best-known case of dissociation in the Army of the Potomac lived only in Stephen Crane's imagination. Despite his preternatural sense of the realities of warfare, when he wrote *The Red Badge*

of Courage (1895), a tale of a Union soldier's coming of age, young Crane had never been in combat. From what he had read and heard from friends and relatives, however, he created one of the truly great American novels. For verisimilitude, his 'Tattered Man' is unsurpassed. He embodies the straggler, a whole category of armed and uniformed refugees, soldiers in search of (or in flight from) an army. In a vast penumbra around every battlefield, I suspect, wandered many acute cases of combat trauma.

Crane's story of wounds physical and mental unfolds at Chancellorsville, virtually the same ground as the Wilderness and its equal as a scene of savage fighting. In the year separating the first battle from the second, the character of the Civil War changed drastically. From First Bull Run in July 1861 to Gettysburg in July 1863, weeks, often months, passed between battles. From the crossing of the Rapidan on May 4th, 1864, until the end came nearly a year later, however, the Army of the Potomac and the Army of Northern Virginia were seldom out of rifle shot, and scarcely a day passed when shots were not exchanged. Two different wars were fought: one (1861–63) looked back to European wars of the seventeenth and eighteenth centuries; the other (1864–65) looked forward to the twentieth—to the Russo-Japanese War, the First World War and beyond.

Different wars have created different hells. At one end of the spectrum lies the Greek hoplite way of war, a deadly and terrifying rugby scrum over in minutes and definitive in outcome. 'It was a *brief* nightmare,' its historian, Victor Hanson, emphasises. At the other end of the spectrum lies Clausewitz's 'absolute war,' a theoretical realm of unrestrained violence. Over the last two centuries, especially, warfare has lurched toward the Clausewitzian end. In studies of twentieth-century wars, psychiatrists and social scientists have emphasised duration and intensity as key variables in the incidence of combat trauma. 'There is no such thing as 'getting used to combat,' an official study of infantrymen in the European theatre in the Second World War found. 'Each moment . . . imposes a strain so great that men will break down in direct relation to the intensity and duration of their exposure.'

Combat veterans who forded the Rapidan in the spring of 1864 quickly recognised the war had changed. The new conditions struck them with over-

The execution of a Federal deserter in camp at Alexandria: how many of those dispatched for desertion were suffering from combat trauma will never be known.

(MANSELL COLLECTION)

whelming force. 'These last few days have been very bad', Oliver Wendell Holmes Jr wrote his parents on June 24th, seven weeks after the Army of the Potomac had crossed the river. 'Many a man has gone crazy since this campaign begun (sic) from the terrible pressures on mind and body . . . I hope to pull through but don't know.' Holmes left the army later in the summer, against the urgings of his father, when his three-year enlistment ran out. 'Doubt demoralises me as it does any nervous man,' he had written earlier by way of explanation, 'I cannot now endure the labors and hardships of the line.' Holmes, in fact, served as a headquarters staff officer during his last campaign, but as a member of the 20th Massachusetts he had been in the thick of many of the Army of the Potomac's battles since the autumn of 1861.

Indeed, scarcely any Union regiment was in the heart of the storm longer than the 20th Massachusetts. At the end of June 1864, Captain H. L. Patten reckoned the toll exacted on his outfit:

[The men] have been so horribly worked and badgered that they are utterly unnerved and demoralised. They are easily scared as a timid child at night. Half our brigade were taken prisoners the other day, in the middle of the day, by a line no stronger than themselves, without firing a shot. You had a campaign of one day, we of fifty-three days; *every day* under fire, every night either digging or marching. We, our brigade, have made fourteen charges upon the enemy's breastworks, although at last no amount of urging, no heroic example, no threats, or anything else, could get the line to *stir one peg*. For my own part, I am utterly tired and dis-heartened and if I stay at all, it will be like a whipt dog—because I think I must.

The diary of Private Austin Carr, 82nd New York Volunteers, of the same brigade and division as the 20th Massachusetts, catalogues the pressures to which Holmes alluded in his letters home. Carr joined up in August 1862, right before Antietam, so his perspective is that of a seasoned grunt—just how seasoned is apparent from his entry of May 1st, 1863, the eve of Chancellorsville:

Eight days rations in our knapsacks and haversack, one change of clothes, an overcoat, an oil cloth blanket, a woolen blanket and a shelter tent will make an awful load to carry . . . Ten rounds more of ammunition served out to us, making fifty in all, that's the way they load us down, so that when we come to march, we can't go but a short distance before we are tired out. Forty rounds is all I want to carry, so when we start, I will throw the extra ten rounds away.

Like all veteran infantrymen, Carr keenly sensed the relative usefulness of, to use the title of Tim O'Brien's book on Vietnam, *The Things They Carried*. New recruits, he discovered in the Wilderness, posed a greater danger to their own side than to the enemy. Wildly firing his rifle, a man named Clark hit one comrade in the head and nicked Carr in the finger. 'That riled me somewhat,' Carr wrote, 'So I put my rifle to his head and threatened to blow his brains out if he fired again.' Now the risk of being killed came not only from the front but from all sides. Following the refusal of Webb's brigade to obey his order to charge (by no means an uncommon occurrence in the Army of the Potomac that spring), two intermingled lines of infantry fired into each other, dissolving momentarily into a fleeing mob. 'The boys don't fight as they used to.' Carr lamented. Still more fearful than misdirected small-arms fire was an artillery bombardment, friendly or hostile. In most accounts from the incoming end, including the following from Carr, terror vies with helplessness:

We lay upon a knoll close to the enemies' works and under their artillery, which they didn't hesitate to use, they having perfect range of the knoll. A deadly fire of shells was poured into us, killing and wounding a great many, without our having the means to retaliate. It was a fearful spot, and the sights I was compelled to witness was horrible . . . Our feeling can better be imagined than described while we were laying out under that destructive shelling. I trust that I will never get in another such position as I have been in today.

Eighty years later, an American Marine found himself in another such position. 'As Peleliu dragged on,' Eugene Sledge wrote:

I feared that if I ever lost control of myself under shell fire my mind would be shattered . . . To be under heavy shell fire was to me by far the most terrifying of combat experiences . . . Fear is many-faceted and has many subtle nuances, but the terror and desperation endured under heavy shelling are by far the most unbearable . . .

W. H. R. Rivers, who treated countless British soldiers for shell shock during the Great War, was convinced that his patients' sense of helplessness contributed far more to their condition that the routine horrors of combat. Perched beneath balloons tethered high over the trenches, artillery observers were sitting ducks to the riflemen and machine-gunners below. These utterly helpless observers, Rivers pointed out, suffered the highest incidence of breakdown of any branch of the service.

Digging in offered Austin Carr and his comrades one means of escape from the intensity of small arms and artillery fire. 'We entrench ourselves as soon as we halt for the night,' he wrote on May 27th. 'That much despised weapon of McClellan, the spade, is constantly brought in use'—despised, perhaps, but long since become the foot soldier's friend. Satellite mapping of the Chancellorsville battlefield is beginning to reveal that pickets on duty in front of their regiments' positions in May 1863 had dug in, fully a year before the idea of entrenching battle lines had become generally accepted. Henry Abbott, Major of the 20th Massachusetts, had noted after Gettysburg in July of the same year that the failure of Pickett's charge 'demonstrates . . . that . . . a front attack over an open field against even the slightest pit cannot be successful . . .'

But if a trench gives shelter, it also imprisons, immobilising its occupants and inducing a powerful urge to escape. 'We have to lay all day in the [rifle] pits,' Carr complained:

. . . amongst the dirt and sand. We have dug places in the ground for water, and places to go to attend the wants of nature. We are packed in here rather close, making it rather difficult to walk; if we do walk it is in a stooping posture. We are covered with sand, eat sand, drink sand, and breathe sand, until we have almost become pillars of sand . . .

Straggling kept pace with entrenching. The provost guard, or military police, Carr noted, 'is getting very strict and ugly. It is rumored that two of them was shot this evening.' Although gloomily aware of his own fraying nerves, he never wrote of deserting. In any event, he was spared the temptation. On June 22nd, 1864, Carr fell into the hands of the rebels, who happened upon a regiment stuporous from drink. Whisky was to the Army of the Potomac what dope became for the American army in Vietnam: the favoured means of self-medication against the stresses of war.

The war of movement, or at least the war of two large armies stumbling and crashing into each other in the woods of northern Virginia, had become a stationary war even before Austin Carr was captured. Rifle pits hastily scratched in the dirt each day gave way to elaborate fortifications stretching around Petersburg as far as the eye could see. One infantryman wrote to his hometown newspaper:

> We are close up to the enemy's guns besieging his works. The breastwork against which I am leaning is not more than 200 yards from the enemy's lines . . . The field is open between us, but it is a strip of land across which no man dares to pass . . . An attacking party from either side would be mown down like grass. We have abattis in front of our works, and so have they . . . [T]hese snarly prongs extending outward are no very pleasant things to get over in the face of a murderous fire at close range. I believe if the enemy should attack us, we could kill every man of them before any could get into our works . . . a man's head isn't safe a moment above the protection of the breastworks. Our work here is built zigzag, . . . which gives us a chance to protect ourselves from a cross fire. We can only get from place to place . . . by walking in trenches that we have dug for that purpose. Relieving is accomplished in the night, and as slyly as possible.

In virtually every particular, the war being described here could be the war of 1914–1918: the war of shell shock. The evidence for combat trauma in the Civil War seems far more diffuse and ambiguous than the disorder this term suggests. Yet 'shell shock' is misleadingly precise. It expresses an inference drawn in the early months of the Great War, when the novel and alarming symptoms front-line British soldiers displayed were attributed to the concussive effect of exploding projectiles on their brains and spinal columns. As combat trauma revealed its protean character, medical officers challenged this organic Democrats who lose control of the U.S. Congress as 'shellshocked.'

In terms of the terrible pressures they endured, combat soldiers of the last year of the Civil War had more in common with those of the first year of the Great War than either had with civilians of their own times. In terms of mental disorder, the so-called 'Front Experience' reached not only between belligerents but across generations. What changed in the half century between the Civil War and the First World War was not the response of the human species to stress, but the cultural expression of the response. In 1914 far more was known and admitted about what went on in mind, brain and body than had been the case in 1861. Mental disorder had been re-constructed. And so it has been re-constructed since 1918. Yet a little cultural construction goes a long way. In the realm of the historical understanding of combat trauma, it can easily go too far.

It would be well to remember a premise drawn from evolutionary psychology, a discipline historians have not been especially eager to borrow from. 'The evolved structure of the human mind,'—the one we all carry around in our heads today—'is adapted to the way of life of Pleistocene hunter-gatherers, and not necessarily to our modern circumstances.' Modern war is a concatenation of hells, none of them good for hunter-gatherers.

FOR FURTHER READING:

Eric Dean, 'We Will All Be Lost and Destroyed: Post-traumatic Stress Disorder and the Civil war, *Civil War History,* 37 (June 1991); Mark de Wolfe Howe, ed. *Touched with Fire: Civil War Letters of Oliver Wendell Holmes, Jr., 1861–1864* (Harvard University Press, 1946); Abram Kardiner, *The Traumatic Neuroses of War* (New York 1941); James M. McPherson, *Battle Cry of Freedom: The Civil War Era* (Oxford University Press, 1988); Tim O'Brien, *The Things They Carried* (Houghton-Mifflin, 1990); Daniel Pick, *War Machine: The Rationalization of Slaughter in the Modern Age* (Yale University Press, 1993).

Who Was Lincoln?

*His name can be heard on politicians' lips, but the man and his times
are being lost to Americans today*

Every new generation of Americans needs to get in touch with Abraham Lincoln. He is the most written about figure in American history and the most mysterious; the most familiar of faces and the most evanescent in spirit. Endlessly invoked by politicians, he is "the great American story," in the words of a moving documentary scheduled for four hours of network prime time later this year. Our other Rushmore-size leaders had political careers that spanned decades; Lincoln occupied center stage for only a half-dozen years, from his famous debates with Stephen A. Douglas in late 1858 to his assassination in April 1865. Yet he was the most severely tested of our leaders, the most ravaged by time and care, as he held the nation to his principles, from Illinois prairie towns to battlefields where 600,000 Americans—he insisted that the Confederates always were, and must remain, Americans—met their deaths.

"Fondly do we hope, fervently do we pray, that this mighty scourge of war may speedily pass away," he said at his second inaugural, 42 days before his death. "Yet, if God wills that it continue until all the wealth piled by the bondsman's 250 years of unrequited toil shall be sunk, and until every drop of blood drawn by the lash shall be paid by another drawn by the sword, as was said 3,000 years ago, so still it must be said, 'the judgments of the Lord are true and righteous altogether.' "

The resonance of Lincoln's life and principles changes over time, however. A half century ago, as Americans faced the prospect of fighting another great war, Lincoln was a more familiar figure. Millions of Americans had living memories of the war—Harry Truman's mother remembered when Union troops burst into her farmhouse—and the flames of

passion aroused by that war still burned. A 1930s joint reunion of Civil War veterans almost broke up because the men of the Grand Army of the Republic could not abide the Confederates displaying the Stars and Bars. It was easy in that era to imagine living in Lincoln's day, for much of the technology of 1860—steam rail, the telegraph, black-and-white photographs—was still familiar, much more so than the everyday life of the Founders was to Lincoln's contemporaries.

Character issue. The moral basis of Lincoln's politics was familiar then, too. He was an upwardly mobile striver in times bursting with economic energy and a gloomy, introspective philosopher in a culture fragrant with romantic literature. Lincoln was both a wily political operator and a stern moralizer. The key decision of his political career was made on moral principle. In 1858, national Republican leaders wanted to leave Douglas unopposed for re-election to the Senate. Lincoln, insisting that slavery was wrong and that Douglas's Kansas-Nebraska Act, which would allow slavery in new territories, must be opposed, ran and pressed Douglas into their debates. Yet Lincoln always acknowledged that principle must be pursued within practical limits imposed by law and public opinion: He supported the fugitive-slave law and confessed he had no idea how to abolish slavery even if he had the power. In the end, he recognized that assertion of principle might require force and violence. "A house divided against itself cannot stand," he said in 1858. A year later, as the abolitionist John Brown was hanged, Lincoln told Southerners that if they rebelled, it "will be our duty to deal with you as old John Brown has been dealt with."

Today, the passions aroused by the Civil War are mostly extinguished. The

war is an object of interest, not ardor. The civil-rights revolution of the 1960s has replaced the war of the 1860s as the event determining the place of blacks in American life. Our everyday technology—airplanes, long-distance telephone and fax, television—has made Lincoln's time, and even FDR's, remote to us.

Principled pragmatism. Even more distant is Lincoln's insistence, as historian Harry Jaffa puts it, that democracy must be based not just on "mere opinion" but on a "moral purpose." In a situation with no precedent, through events of the greatest horror, with almost no truly faithful allies. Lincoln never lost sight of his principles and showed astonishing political skills—maneuvering the rebels into firing the first shot, holding Border States in the Union and then freeing the slaves, choosing Generals Grant and Sherman to lead his armies and manipulating political allies. Today's politicians, with their hair-trigger responsiveness to conflicting public demands and their issues carved into 24-hour news cycles, often seem unable to master Lincoln's principled pragmatism. They and the voters they represent have lost the tolerance always needed in a democracy for the tension between the moral principles for which it must stand and the practical realities it must respect. Half a century ago, the American people and their leaders had confidence their country stood for great moral principles even as they understood its government must compromise with tawdry practical realities. In the turmoil of the 1960s, that confidence seemed to vanish, along with much of our knack for practical politics: no leader, save for a while Ronald Reagan, has really recovered either one.

Lincoln, who persevered when those principles and realities led to war, teaches a final lesson: that in a tragic world we must have an energetic sympathy for everyone. After the searing words of the second inaugural comes its, and almost Lincoln's, last sentence: "With malice toward none, with charity for all, with firmness in the right, as God gives us to see the right let us strive on to finish the work we are in, to bind up the nation's wounds, to care for him who shall have borne the battle, and for his widow and his orphan, to do all which may achieve and cherish a just and lasting peace among ourselves, and with all nations."

BY MICHAEL BARONE

THE FURROWS OF HIS FACE

The outsize ears and nose. The dark beard. The somber eyes and shaggy eyebrows. The mouth set with determination and the skin weathered by prairie wind and political worry. History has known no face more famous—looking out from Mount Rushmore, from the Lincoln Memorial, from millions of 1-cent coins and $5 bills. Nature struck the icon, politics embellished it and the nascent art of photography enshrined the image forevermore.

A crucial enhancement came just before Lincoln's election to the presidency in 1860. An 11-year-old girl wrote to the beardless candidate urging that he grow whiskers ("You would look a great deal better for your face is so thin"). Lincoln was so pleased that for years he carried little Grace Bedell's letter in his pocket. No cannier advice was ever given a politician. Though the press teased him (one paper quoted a "cockney" as saying Lincoln was "a-puttin' on 'airs"), whiskers gave him a new mien of moral authority.

The framers. Mathew Brady and others took some 120 pictures of the president, making him the most photographed man of his era. He was often posed in postures of stony contemplation, his head high, his big paws at rest, a lion in regal repose. Convention dictated such for statesmen. So did wet-plate photography. The endless exposure time—up to a minute—induced premature rigor mortis in subjects, discouraging smiles or other displays of spontaneity.

The still camera caught the gravity of Lincoln, freezing the image for eternity. Yet it did not—could not—capture his earthy animation, a quality widely remarked by those who saw him in the flesh. "Graphic art was powerless," wrote his secretary, John Nicolay, "before a face that moved through a thousand delicate gradations of line, contour, light, and shade, sparkle of the eye and curve of the lip, in the long gamut of expression from grave to gay and back again from the rollicking jollity of laughter to that serious, faraway look with prophetic intuitions." Lincoln was much too homely ever to have succeeded in politics in the television age, it is sometimes said. And said wrongly. How television would have loved that magnetic, mobile mug.

THE ECHO OF HIS LAUGHTER

The commander in chief was also the storyteller in chief, the quipster in chief, a country ham that couldn't be cured. Lincoln joked more than any president before or since and did it at a time when statesmen were expected to be as solemn as churchwardens. "I laugh because I must not weep—that's all, that's all," he once said. Indeed, jokes drove the demons of melancholy back into the hidy-holes of his mind. Yet Lincoln's wit was more than a suit of mail against despair. One minute it was a feather duster tickling friends, another minute a velvet-tipped lance pricking foes, as when he pronounced Stephen A. Douglas's arguments as thin as a homeopathic soup "made by boiling the shadow of a pigeon that had starved to death."

Lines like that smacked of the lathe. Others sprang from his lips in an inspired instant. Hearing that a senator's brother-in-law was in trouble for peeping over a transom at a disrobing mademoiselle, Lincoln averred that the cad "should be elevated to the peerage." Introduced to an Indian named Crying Water, Lincoln couldn't help remembering his earlier visit with a certain Minnehaha (Laughing Water) and couldn't help asking, "I suppose your name is Minneboohoo." As another might walk a dog for recreation, Lincoln walked his wit.

Skunk work. Not least, the 16th president of the United States, who wrote the book on the political uses of humor, used jokes as exercises in evasion. Delegations often came to the White House with demands or questions Lincoln had no wish to hear. He would recite his stories with gusto, scratching his elbows and guffawing loudly as the punch lines neared. Soon the visitors were out the door of the White House, still laughing at good old Abe, happy to have seen him even if somehow they had never managed to bring up the topic taxing their minds. Once, when Lincoln fired a cabinet member, some senators pressed him to cashier the whole cabinet. That reminded the president of a farmer who confronted seven skunks. "I took aim," the farmer said, "blazed away, killed one, and he raised such a fearful smell that I concluded it was best to let the other six go."

THE WHISPER OF HIS AX

"Four score and seven years ago . . ." Abraham Lincoln spoke a little longer than two minutes at Gettysburg, 50 minutes less than Bill Clinton at the Democratic convention in New York, 52 minutes less than George Bush in Houston. Even more than our own age, the 19th century wallowed in prolixity, yet Lincoln labored long to keep his speeches short. His second inaugural address contained a mere 700 words, about as many as a syndicated newspaper column. Still, for all his pithiness, the totality of his collected writings is anything but scant. Shakespeare's legacy amounts to 1 million words; Lincoln's bulks much larger.

Myth teaches that Lincoln scribbled his 272-word Gettysburg masterpiece on the back of an envelope during the train trip from Washington, the deathless phrases fairly leaping forth. In fact, Lincoln wrote a large part of the message on White House stationery before leaving for the Pennsylvania battlefield, after almost surely brooding about it for weeks. He was not one to seek inspiration in a wide array of sources; he read newspapers, the Bible and the Bard (especially "Macbeth," "Hamlet" and "Richard III") but surprisingly little else for a man revered today as an intellectual giant. When Lincoln put on his wire-rimmed spectacles and wrote speeches, proclamations or letters, he was communicating with himself as much as anyone, thinking with the nib of his pen, discovering the path of logic. As a youth, he split logs with a single well-aimed blow from his ax. Later in life the sharp edge of his prose found its mark just as efficiently, laying the truth bare with poetic, resounding whacks.

THE POWER OF HIS MIND

Presidents today are so layered with policy wonks, pulse takers, public-relations smoothies and other White House bureaucrats that it is easy to forget it was not always thus. Abraham Lincoln, *mirabile dictu,* never had more than three clerks on his White House payroll to help him as he won the Civil War, secured the future of freedom in the world and dealt with sundry other matters. True, Lincoln had no vast federal bureaucracy to manage. He had the next worst thing, a cabinet of prickly, independent men full of advice—much of it unsolicited—and serving a variety of agendas, theirs and his. If his external resources for meeting the challenge were meager, his internal resources were demonstrably ample.

"The shop," as Lincoln called it, was on the second floor just down the hall from the first family's bedrooms. It consisted of a reception area, rooms for his private secretaries and his own office, which doubled as cabinet room. Here, twice a week, Lincoln also took what he called his "public-opinion baths," allowing almost any citizen, wartime or no, to wait his turn and claim his moment with the chief magistrate of the land. Partisans came to plead for federal posts, relatives to beg mercy for condemned men, crusaders to petition for causes. Some people came just to shake the president's hand, to take his measure (6 feet, 4 inches). When the throng was shooed out, Lincoln sank into a horsehair swivel chair and worked on documents plucked from the alphabetized pigeon holes in his high postmaster's desk. Or he slipped over to the War Department to read cables. At crucial junctures, he shot off queries to generals and paced as he awaited replies, his hands clasped behind his back.

Lincoln knew how to delegate. Need be, he also knew how to intrude. Because most of his generals hated change, especially technological change, he acted as his own R & D chief, quizzing inventors and ordering purchases of repeating rifles, the first machine gun, mortars, an explosive bullet and other new arms. At times a tall, stooped figure, sans stovepipe hat, was glimpsed testing weapons on or near the White House grounds.

In making important decisions, Lincoln the president, like Lincoln the lawyer, relied less on experts or books or reports than on his own intuition, which could be agonizingly slow in rendering its verdicts. Blocking out the hubbub around him, he withdrew into the jury room of the concentrated mind. When he re-emerged, a resolve would have formed, a resolve not easily shaken.

Text by Gerald Parshall

How Did Lincoln Die?

Everyone knows that the ball John Wilkes Booth fired into Abraham Lincoln's brain inflicted a terrible, mortal wound. But when a prominent neurosurgeon began to investigate the assassination, he discovered persuasive evidence that Lincoln's doctors must share the blame with Booth's derringer. Without their treatment the President might very well have lived.

Richard A. R. Fraser, M.D.

Richard A. R. Fraser, M.D., is a professor of surgery (neurosurgery) at the New York Hospital–Cornell Medical Center. He wishes to thank his three fellow researchers on the article: Aaron Zelman, Dirke Brunner, and James Dana.

Threat of assassination may seem the greatest risk a President of the United States must take upon entering office, but history suggests that until recently a Chief Executive's life was threatened more by his post-assault medical treatment than by his assassin's bullet. There have been at least eleven attempts on the lives of American Presidents, four of them successful. John F. Kennedy was shot with a high-velocity bullet that destroyed his brainstem, an instantly fatal injury that rendered any medical treatment useless. The three other victims did not immediately suffer fatal wounds.

Both James Garfield and William McKinley received substandard medical care after being shot, which probably contributed more to their deaths than the wounds themselves. Garfield, who was shot in 1881, died of sepsis, an infection that may result from any wound but in his case most likely resulted from a series of unsterile wound probes by his doctors. It is curious that while Garfield's doctors took every other antiseptic measure throughout the case, they explored the wound with naked fingers *fourteen times,* repeatedly engaging in a practice thoroughly condemned by medical texts of the day.

McKinley's death twenty years later also appears to have been the result of

his doctors' poor judgment. The surgeon who attended him, Dr. Mathew Mann, was an obstetrician-gynecologist who had never operated on a gunshot victim and should have declared himself unqualified. Dr. Herman Mynter, the first surgeon on the scene, was responsible for the hasty appointment of Dr. Mann. Mynter decided that the surgery must be performed as soon as possible, and Mann lived nearby. However, the time it took actually to begin operating would have been sufficient to bring the wounded President to one of the most advanced medical facilities in the country, the Buffalo General Hospital, which owned one of the first X-ray machines and employed doctors well qualified to perform the procedure. Instead McKinley was taken to an ill-equipped, unlit room in the Exposition Hospital and, like Garfield, died of sepsis.

Booth stood four feet behind the President and pulled the trigger; Lincoln's head dropped to his chest.

After having discovered the quality of medical care given to these two American Presidents, I thought it reasonable to investigate the care of their predecessor, Abraham Lincoln. Many details of the event that took place on the night he was shot are obscured by

misleading and contradictory accounts, but a consensus of various sources maintains certain facts.

On the evening of April 14, 1865, five days after General Lee surrendered his exhausted army, President Abraham Lincoln attended a performance of *Our American Cousin* at Ford's Theater in Washington. He arrived late, at approximately 8:15 P.M., and the play was briefly halted to welcome his entrance. Lincoln was accompanied to the President's box with his wife and his guests, Miss Clara Harris and her fiancé, Maj. Henry R. Rathbone. At around ten o'clock John Wilkes Booth, who frequently performed at Ford's Theatre and had a close rapport with most of the staff, walked into the theater's main entrance and approached the ticket taker, Joseph ("Buck") Buckingham, whom he knew very well. Jokingly Booth asked him, "You'll not want a ticket from me?" Buck laughed and told his friend, "Courtesy of the house." Booth headed up the stairs to the dress circle.

Sometime between ten-fifteen and ten-thirty, he entered the President's box. Lincoln, his attention temporarily diverted from the stage, was sitting with his head tilted forward and to the left, probably watching a musician in the orchestra. Standing about four feet behind the President, Booth pulled the trigger of his derringer and Lincoln's head dropped to his chest.

The first doctor to reach the wounded President was Charles A. Leale. He was the assistant surgeon of United States Volunteers and only twenty-three years old. The remainder of this account of

Lincoln's death is taken mostly from a report Leale rewrote from notes he made the day Lincoln died and submitted to the Congressional Assassination Committee in 1867. Directly after Leale saw Booth leap onto the stage, wave a dagger, and hurry toward the exit, the doctor heard shouts for a surgeon. Leale made his way to the President's box. "While approaching the President—I was told that—he had been murdered, and I sent for some brandy and water." He arrived at the box and saw Major Rathbone standing at the door. Lincoln was sitting on a high-backed armchair with his head leaning toward his right side, supported by Mrs. Lincoln. Miss Harris was at the left and behind the President.

When the surgeon reached Lincoln, he found him paralyzed, with his eyes closed. Leale placed his finger on the right radial pulse but felt no movement. With assistance Leale immediately placed the President in a recumbent position, and in the process his hand came in contact with blood on Lincoln's left shoulder. He thought that perhaps the President had been stabbed with the dagger, but found no wound. Continuing to examine the patient, Leale noticed that the pupils were dilated, and he discovered a large clot of blood about one inch below the superior curved line and an inch and a half to the left of the median line of the occipital bone in the back of the skull. He passed the little finger of his left hand through the hole made by the ball. Lincoln "was then apparently dead," Leale wrote in his report, but when he removed his finger, blood oozed out, and the President "soon commenced to show signs of improvement."

There is some question about what occurred next. Leale's account of the assassination submitted in 1867 made no mention of resuscitation, but in 1909 he delivered an address in New York giving a detailed description of practicing mouth-to-mouth resuscitation on Lincoln after he probed the wound. It is strange that Leale did not include this in his first account, which omitted no other important details of the President's treatment. I am more inclined to give credence to this earlier version, recorded in Leale's own hand the day Lincoln died.

In any event, this resuscitation, if it actually occurred, was directly followed by the arrival of an Army surgeon, Dr.

Charles S. Taft, and Dr. A. F. A. King of Washington, at which point the three doctors agreed to remove the stricken President. Leale was asked to put Lincoln in a carriage to take him to the White House, but he refused for fear that the President would die if placed upright. Instead Lincoln was taken across the street to the nearest house, which belonged to a Mr. William Petersen, and was placed on a bed—diagonally because he was too tall to fit lengthwise. Leale asked that everyone leave the room with the exception of "the medical gentlemen." After undressing the patient, Leale found that the President's lower extremities were quite cold "to a distance several inches above his knees." He sent for the surgeon general, J. K. Barnes, the family physician, Robert K. Stone, and the commander of the Armory Square Hospital, D. W. Bliss. The moment Dr. Stone arrived, Leale gave control of the President's care over to him. (Dr. Bliss is unique in being the only surgeon to participate in the care of two assassinated Presidents; he helped preside over President Garfield's post-assault care sixteen years later. The quality of his conduct in that case and that of his colleague Dr. Weiss, an anatomist, prompted one reporter's acid comment: "If ignorance is Bliss, 'tis folly to be Weiss.")

When Lincoln was first laid in bed, a "slight ecchymosis of blood" (a spot from a rupture) was noticed on his left eyelid, and the pupil of that eye was dilated. At 11:00 P.M. the right eye began to protrude, and this was followed by an increase of the ecchymosis, until it encircled the right orbit. The wound was kept open by the surgeon general with a silver probe. Dr. Taft remarked that at 11:30 a twitching of the facial muscles of the left side set in and continued for about fifteen to twenty minutes, and "there was artificial heat to the extremities." At 1:00 A.M. "spasmodic contractions of the muscles came on," and "at about the same time both pupils became widely dilated and remained so until death." Presumably at this moment Lincoln became decerebrate—brain dead.

At 2:00 A.M. a doctor's aide arrived with a Nelaton's probe, and an examination of the wound was made by the surgeon general. The probe was driven about two and a half inches when it hit

a foreign substance. This was passed, and then the probe felt another hard substance, which was at first thought to be the ball. However, when the probe was removed without a lead stain, the obstacle was thought to be another piece of bone. The probe was introduced a second time, and the ball "was supposed to be distinctly felt by the Surgeon General." Taft accounts for the ball's not making any mark on the probe by explaining that it "was afterwards found to be of exceedingly hard lead." Following the probes, "Nothing further was done except to keep the wound free from coagula." Taft remarks on the "great difference in character of the pulse whenever the orifice of the wound was freed from coagulum" and adds that "while the wound was discharging freely, the respiration was easy, but the moment the discharge was arrested from any cause, it became at once labored."

The probe hit a foreign substance and kept going until it felt another one, at first thought to be the ball.

During the night doctors counted pulsations, and at 6:50 A.M. respirations ceased for some time. Lincoln lived about thirty minutes longer, during which time Rev. Phineas Gurley said, "Let us pray," and everyone knelt beside the bed. At 7:22 A.M., Lincoln "breathed his last."

Ford's Theatre Museum, where the weapon is currently kept, gave me a detailed description of the gun that Booth used to assassinate President Lincoln. It is a single-shot muzzleloading Philadelphia derringer with a percussion cap. Its total length is $5^{27}/_{32}$ inches, but the barrel is only $1^{15}/_{16}$ inches long. The interior diameter of the barrel is 0.4375 inch, making the gun a .44-caliber pistol (caliber refers to the barrel and/or bullet diameter in inches). The derringer shot a round lead ball. Usually a gun fires a bullet or ball of approximately the same caliber, but the pathological examination of the ball that

Side View:

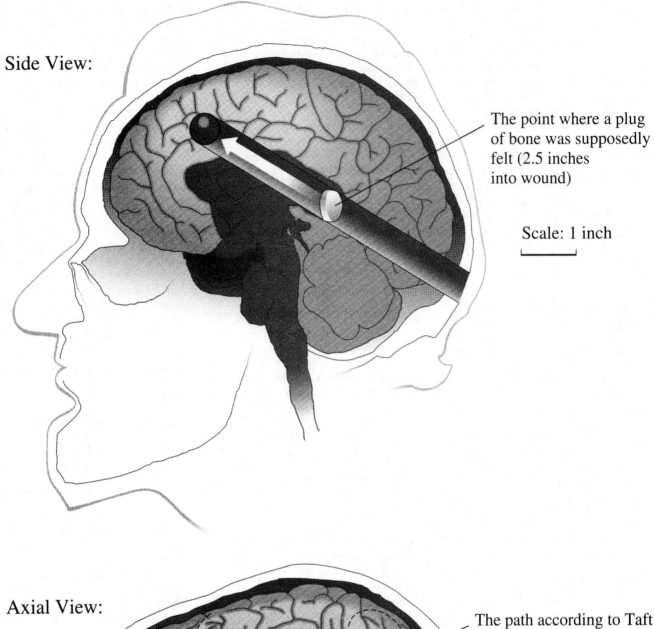

The point where a plug of bone was supposedly felt (2.5 inches into wound)

Scale: 1 inch

Axial View:

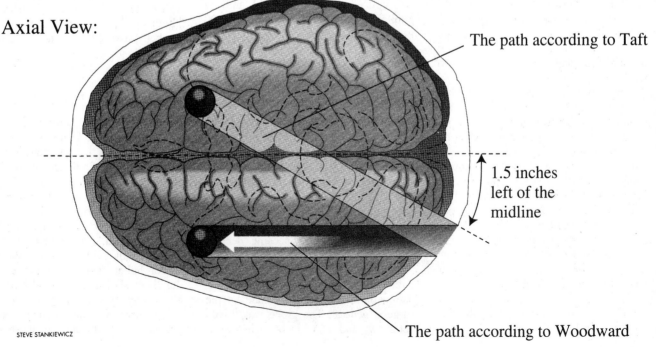

The path according to Taft

1.5 inches left of the midline

STEVE STANKIEWICZ

The path according to Woodward

killed Lincoln suggests that Booth used a .41-caliber ball in his .44 derringer.

The National Museum of Health and Medicine currently owns the ball that killed Lincoln. On April 6, 1971, the ball was examined. It weighed 6.314 grams and was found, by spectroscopy, to be principally lead. Its weight was not the same as at the time Booth shot it, for three reasons: the lead had corroded, and the corrosion was easily rubbed off in handling the ball; it had a small hole drilled into it prior to 1941 for mounting at an exhibition; and most significantly, part of the ball had been broken off by the skull when it entered the President's head. This fragment was found during the autopsy but was later lost. The ball was flattened by the impact of the shot; in 1971 it was measured at 13.3 mm in diameter at its widest and 12.1 mm at its narrowest point and was 7.2 mm from front to back.

The most widely accepted current theory that attempts to describe the extent of tissue damage incurred by a missile states that its wounding capacity is proportional to its kinetic energy, which may be calculated with the formula: $KE = \frac{1}{2} mv^2$. In other words, the kinetic energy of a missile is proportional to the missile's mass times the square of its velocity. The kinetic energy, and therefore the wounding capacity, of a bullet is much more dependent on its velocity than on its mass. If a bullet's mass is doubled, its kinetic energy is doubled; if a bullet's velocity is doubled, its kinetic energy is quadrupled.

The derringer fired by Booth had a very low muzzle velocity—around four hundred feet per second, which is about that of most of today's air guns. To calculate the ball's kinetic energy, the only further measurement needed is its mass. Since the ball was weighed after a significant amount of its volume had been lost, it seems sensible to estimate its original mass using the density of lead and the volume of a .41-caliber sphere, which would have been 6.7 grams.

From this it can be calculated that the kinetic energy of the missile that killed Lincoln was 36.7 foot-pounds. Today this magnitude of kinetic energy is associated with guns of a much lower caliber. A .22-caliber short revolver, for example, produces approximately 48 foot-pounds of kinetic energy. A pathologist describing the wound of a twenty-

year-old male who shot himself in the head with this type of gun noted that the bullet entered the brain in the right temporal lobe and perforated the left parietal lobe before lodging in the left occipital region. The bullet's track was straight and cylindrical, tapered at the entrance and lodgment areas, and about three centimeters wide in the middle. This wide area is the result of cavitation, a phenomenon common to missile wounds. Lower-velocity bullets will normally produce little or no cavitation, while high-velocity ones transfer more of their kinetic energy to the tissue and produce large temporary and permanent cavities. A temporary cavity is formed when the missile's kinetic energy separates the soft tissue around where it strikes, producing a wide opening for a fraction of a second before the tissue recedes back toward its normal position. If the tissue does not recede completely, a permanent cavity is formed.

The derringer had a very low muzzle velocity— around four hundred feet per second, about that of today's air guns.

The shape and size of this cavity also depend on variables other than kinetic energy, such as yaw—the wobbling motion of a bullet—and the effect of secondary missiles that form when the bullet's kinetic energy is transferred to bone, which fragments and itself becomes projectiles. When the bullet enters tissue, it chisels out a cavity much larger than its own diameter. A ball cannot produce yaw because it has no longitudinal axis to wobble on, and no secondary missiles were formed in Lincoln's injury because, other than entering the occipital bone, the ball encountered only soft brain matter. The occipital bone that was hit was driven like a plug and found in the autopsy about two and a half inches down the missile track. The hole made in the bone, wrote a witness to the autopsy, "was as cleanly cut as if done with a punch." The absence of yaw and secondary missiles combined with the ball's low velocity should have rendered the effect of cavitation in Lincoln's

wound minimal, and indeed, the autopsy report seems to indicate the ball's having made a fairly clean, narrow track.

Curiously there are two completely different versions of the autopsy report. The autopsy itself was performed by Assistant Surgeon J. Janvier Woodward, who hand-wrote a description the day Lincoln died. According to him, "the ball entered through the occipital bone about one inch to the left of the median line and just above the left lateral sinus, which it opened. It then penetrated the dura mater, passed through the left posterior lobe of the cerebrum, entered the left lateral ventricle and lodged in the white matter of the cerebrum just above the anterior portion of the left corpus striatum, where it was found. . . ."

Dr. C. S. Taft, who was present but did not participate in the autopsy, wrote an entirely different report: "The calvarium was removed, the brain exposed, and sliced down the track of the ball, which was plainly indicated by a line of coagulated blood extending from the external wound in the occipital bone, obliquely across from the *left to right* through the brain to the anterior lobe of the cerebrum, immediately behind the *right* orbit. The surface of the right hemisphere was covered with coagulated blood. After removing the brain from the cranium the ball dropped from its lodgement in the anterior lobe. . . ."

The last sentence of this version may explain why there was a discrepancy as to where the bullet lodged; it fell out after the brain was removed, perhaps before the doctors could get an accurate view of its location. It is odd that Taft describes the track of the ball as "plainly indicated," since Woodward obviously had an entirely different view. Both versions do agree that the two orbital plates were fractured, an occurrence common in gunshot wounds to the head.

The procedures used to treat Lincoln were obviously very different from what would have been done today. From the start his doctors were probably doing more harm than good. Dr. Leale's comment about first inserting his finger into the wound—"I believe that he would not have lived five minutes longer if the pressure on the brain had not been relieved and if he had been left that much longer in the sitting posture"—reveals a total misunderstanding of the pathophysiology of brain trauma. Although intracranial pressure may have been high, the sort of probe Leale delivered could have easily ruptured blood vessels that had not been hit by the ball. The blood that "oozed out" almost certainly resulted from fresh bleeding. After this type of low-velocity missile enters the brain, the tissue behind the ball will swell, closing up the track of the ball. A probe of this sort will therefore cause an *increase* in intracranial pressure, adjusting to the sudden increase in volume. When the finger is removed, whatever oozes out has been caused by a broken clot or perhaps a broken blood vessel.

When Lincoln's doctors again entered the wound with a porcelain Nelaton's probe to locate the ball, the surgeon general encountered a foreign object about two and a half inches down the track that was "easily passed" until the tip of the probe came in contact with the ball itself. More damage could easily have been incurred here. Furthermore, it was not necessary to remove the missile. Today the ball would have been left alone, unless it was easily accessible.

The question is, how many of these hazards were known in 1865? Surgical case records at New York Hospital from the early 1860s describe treatments of injuries of an invasive nature similar to Lincoln's. In most of these cases the doctors did very little for the patients. On December 4, 1862, a man was wounded by a buckshot "which entered outside of the left orbit exterior to globe of eye, and passing, backwards, downwards and outwards, lodged probably in the neighborhood of the mastoid portion of the temporal bone." The doctor made an opening behind and a little below the ear and, at a depth of three-quarters of an inch, reached the abscess and evacuated the contents. A few small pieces of bone were felt but could not be removed. Little else was done, and in less than a month the patient healed and was discharged. Another patient was wounded by a ball that entered near his right eye. The direction of the ball was backward and a little downward. "On passing a probe, it goes in about two inches but cannot detect the ball." After three more weeks in the hospital, the patient was discharged while the ball was never found. The doctor's only treatment was to "order a poultice."

There were several other incidents of gunshot wounds to the brain from the case histories dated 1859–1862. In fact, most of these wounds were found to be nonfatal—largely the result of the low-kinetic-energy missiles that were in use. The New York Hospital Archives reveal only one head wound admitted during the Civil War that underwent "passing a probe."

In none of these cases did the doctors report using their fingers or any other device to "relieve the pressure" on the brain. In fact, there were many doctors who explicitly warned against the practices that were administered to Lincoln. When Leale first probed Lincoln's wound with his unsterile finger, he was inviting sepsis, and had the President lived long enough, his wound would have become infected. Then, as now, infection was an issue. Around 1860 the discoverer of chloroform anesthesia, Sir James Y. Simpson, issued a survey to surgeons and found that of 2,098 amputations in hospital practice, 855 (40 percent) died, while only 226, or 10 percent, of the same number of patients died from amputations performed outside hospitals. Simpson concluded that "a man laid on the operating table in one of our surgical hospitals is exposed to more chances of death than was the English soldier on the battle of Waterloo." During the Civil War 110,000 Union soldiers died from wounds or were killed in action, while 224,000 died from disease; the figures for Confederates were roughly proportionate.

It was clear to almost everyone that something was flagrantly wrong with the hospitals and medical practices of the time. Ignaz Semmelweis, a Hungarian doctor working in Viennese maternity wards, attempted to address the problem. Everyone knew about the high incidences of fatal puerperal fever among postpartum women in maternity wards and that the lying-in wards attended by medical students and doctors had higher fatality rates than those attended by nurses.

Semmelweis observed that the doctors came straight from dissecting tables to these wards, and around 1846 he began to insist that all who came from the dissecting rooms wash their hands in chlorinated lime. Incidences of puerperal fever fell dramatically.

Most doctors did not heed Semmelweis's warnings, but there were medical men in this country who supported his assertions. Oliver Wendell Holmes in fact had already published an article advising physicians to wash their hands in calcium chloride after attending women with puerperal fever. At around the same time, Louis Pasteur, studying fermentation, had discovered that it could not take place without germs. Eventually he drew the first clear analogy between fermentation and septicemia. But Pasteur was not a doctor, and his principles were not applied to medicine and surgery until Dr. Joseph Lister read them and formulated a technique for performing antiseptic surgery.

The importance of antiseptic measures had been realized by many doctors by the time of Lincoln's assassination. Still, this was a minor concern and not a contributing factor in Lincoln's demise. Tissue damage incurred by the probe was likely much more harmful, and it, too, was an imprudent procedure given the standards of the time. Some doctors had known this as early as the 1820s. Dominique Jean Larrey, the surgeon-in-chief of the imperial armies of France under Napoleon, was emphatically opposed to this type of probe: "And I repeat this," he wrote, "if foreign bodies pass beyond the inner table of the skull into the substance of the brain, it is better to leave the patient to the results of expectant treatment than to attempt to explore the interior of this pulpy organ, as we have seen some practitioners do."

John K. Lattimer, the author of the 1980 study *Kennedy and Lincoln: Medical and Ballistic Comparisons of Their Assassinations,* wrote extensively on the topic of Lincoln's murder, and his is the most detailed account of the President's medical treatment. There are several points in Lattimer's book that I would question. Most important, he asserts that "there seems to be no reason to disagree with those who have stated that Lincoln could not possibly have survived this wound, even in modern times. . . ." He argues that "the principles of aseptic techniques and the concept of germs as the cause of wound infections were unknown in Lincoln's day; while occasional Civil War soldiers were reported to have recovered from bullet wounds of the brain, these were rare exceptions."

As we have seen, the role of germs in wound infections certainly was known in Lincoln's day. Lister did not publish his first papers until two years after the President's assassination, but his theories on the spread of infection by germs had been established two decades earlier. As for Lattimer's other assertion, research indicates that during the Civil War many soldiers as well as civilians *did* survive gunshot wounds to the brain. Among the cases I reviewed at New York Hospital, more patients survived these wounds than did not!

The damage done by the ball was significant but not devastating; many people have survived greater wounds.

Another point Lattimer uses to support his case is that the autopsy "does not take into account the further damage which is now known to result from the momentary creation of a large cavity in the brain when it is traversed by a missile traveling at the speed of a bullet." This is true for many of today's high-velocity bullets but not of the slow-moving lead ball that killed Lincoln. Evidence

for the derringer's extremely low muzzle velocity is shown in that the ball "lodged in the white matter of the cerebrum," a fact uncontested in all of Lincoln's autopsy reports; the brain's gelatinous consistency can impede only the very slowest missiles. The ball's kinetic energy would have been too low to form much, if any, of a cavity.

With all the speculation as to the correct path of the ball, I assert that regardless of whether it lodged above the right or left orbit, Lincoln's wound was not necessarily fatal. There are two errors in Lattimer's comment that "it is surprising that, if the bullet had indeed traversed the central part of the brain [stem] damaging it directly as it would if it crossed the midline, respirations could be maintained at all." First, if the bullet had damaged the brainstem directly, it would have been impossible for Lincoln to have lasted nine hours; he would have died instantly. Second, if the ball crossed the midline of the brain, it didn't traverse the brain stem. If the ball entered just above the left lateral sinus (a fact uncontested in Woodward's autopsy report) and traveled across the brain to lodge above the right orbit, it would have passed above the brainstem.

It would, of course, be unfair to hold Lincoln's doctors completely responsible for his death. It was at the time very difficult to understand the extent of

this type of injury and devise a procedure to treat it. Although excessive probing did probably have a negative effect on the President's condition, there was still the problem of raised intracranial pressure, for which there was no known treatment in 1865.

Nevertheless, there were doctors in Lincoln's day who knew better. If the principles of Larrey and others had been heeded, the doctors would never have probed as they did. There are reasons to believe that today Lincoln's life could have been saved. The damage incurred by the ball was significant but not devastating, and many people have survived wounds of a greater force.

When defending the constitutionality of the Emancipation Proclamation, Lincoln used a metaphor that is both ironic and relevant to this article: "Often a limb must be amputated to save a life. The surgeon is solemnly bound to try to save both life and limb; but when the crisis comes, and the limb must be sacrificed as the only chance of saving the life, no honest man will hesitate. . . . In our case, the moment came when I felt that slavery must die that the nation might live."

In the days before antiseptic surgery, Lincoln had foreshadowed his own demise; his efforts to preserve the life of the nation had been successful at the cost of its strongest limb.

Why the South Lost the Civil War

Interviews by Carl Zebrowski. Ten Civil War historians provide some contrasting—and probably controversial—views on how and why the Confederate cause ultimately ended in defeat.

Carl Zebrowski

Carl Zebrowski is associate editor of Civil War Times Illustrated, *another magazine published by Cowles.*

"The art of war is simple enough. Find out where your enemy is. Get at him as soon as you can. Strike at him as hard as you can and as often as you can, and keep moving on."

Put that way, the business of fighting and winning wars sounds simple enough. And perhaps it was simple in the mind of the man who so concisely described the complex art: General Ulysses S. Grant. After assuming command of all Union armies in March 1864, Grant crushed the Confederacy in about one year.

But the American Civil War, like any war, was not simple. The North and South engaged each other for four long years. More than half a million people were killed. Families were torn apart, towns destroyed. And in the end, the South lost.

For the past 130 years Americans have argued over the reasons for the Confederacy's downfall. Diverse opinions have appeared in hundreds of books, but the numerous possibilities have never adequately been summarized and gathered together in one place. So we decided to ask ten of the country's most respected Civil War historians: "Why did the South lose the Civil War?" Here (edited for length) are their answers.
—Carl Zebrowski

WILLIAM C. DAVIS

Former editor of Civil War Times Illustrated *and author of more than thirty books about the war, including the recent* "A Government of Our Own": The Making of the Confederacy.

Why did the South lose? When the question is asked that way it kind of presupposes that the South lost the war all by itself and that it really could have won it. One answer is that *the North won it.* The South lost because the North outmanned and outclassed it at almost every point, militarily.

Despite the long-held notion that the South had all of the better generals, it really had only one good army commander and that was Lee. The rest were second-raters, at best. The North, on the other hand, had the good fortune of bringing along and nurturing people like Grant, William T. Sherman, Philip Sheridan, George H. Thomas, and others.

The South was way outclassed industrially. There was probably never any chance of it winning without European recognition and military aid. And we can now see in retrospect what some, like Jefferson Davis, even saw at the time, which was that there was never any real hope of Europe intervening. It just never was in England or France's interests to get involved in a North American war that would inevitably have wound up doing great damage, especially to England's maritime trade.

> *"Despite the long-held notion that the South had all of the better generals, it really had only one good army commander and that was Lee. The rest were second-raters, at best."*

Industrially the South couldn't keep up in output and in manpower By the

From *American History*, October 1995, pp. 24–26, 28, 66–67, 69. © 1995 by Cowles Magazines, Inc. Reprinted through the courtesy of Cowles Magazines, Inc., publishers of *American History*.

end of the war, the South had, more or less, plenty of weaponry still, but it just didn't have enough men to use the guns.

I don't agree with the theories that say the South lost because it lost its will to win. There's nothing more willful or stubborn than a groundhog, but whenever one of them runs into a Ford pickup on the highway it's the groundhog that always loses, no matter how much willpower it has.

We can't fault the Southerners for thinking at the time that they could win when we can see in retrospect that there probably never was a time when they could have. The most important things they couldn't see was the determination of Abraham Lincoln to win, and the incredible staying power of the people of the North, who stuck by Lincoln and stuck by the war in spite of the first two years of almost unrelenting defeat. The only way the South could have won would have been for Lincoln to decide to lose. As long as Lincoln was determined to prosecute the war and as long as the North was behind him, inevitably superior manpower and resources just had to win out.

The miracle is that the South held out as long as it did. That's an incredible testament to the courage and self-sacrifice of the people of the South—both the men in the armies and the people at home who sustained them, with nothing but continuing and expanding destruction all around them.

The South lost the war because the North and Abraham Lincoln were determined to win it.

ROBERT KRICK

Historian and author of ten books about the war.

The South lost because it had inferior resources in every aspect of military personnel and equipment. That's an old-fashioned answer. Lots of people will be scornful of it. But a ratio of twenty-one million to seven million in population comes out the same any way you look at it.

The basic problem was numbers. Give Abraham Lincoln seven million men and give Jefferson Davis and Robert E. Lee twenty-one million, and cognitive dissonance doesn't matter,

(CIVIL WAR TIMES ILLUSTRATED COLLECTION)

European recognition doesn't matter, the Emancipation Proclamation and its ripple effect don't matter. Twenty-one to seven is a very different thing than seven to twenty-one.

BRIAN POHANKA

Consultant for the weekly series "Civil War Journal" on the Arts and Entertainment network, on-set history advisor for the movie Gettysburg, *a staff writer and researcher for Time-Life Books'* The Civil War *series, and a founder of the Association for the Preservation of Civil War Sites.*

The South certainly did not lose for any lack of idealism, or dedication to its cause or beliefs, or bravery and skill on the battlefield. In those virtues the Confederate soldier was unexcelled, and it's my belief that man-for-man there was no finer army in the history of America than the Army of Northern Virginia.

But of course the factors that enter into the South's ultimate defeat are those things that you hear time and time again, and with a great amount of validity: the North's industrial base; the North's manpower resources; the fact that for-

eign recognition was denied the Confederacy. In time these things would tell on the battlefield, certainly on the broader level. The North was able to bring its industry and its manpower to bear in such a way that eventually through sheer numerical and material advantage, it gained and maintained the upper hand.

That's when you get into the whole truly tragic sense of the Lost Cause, because those men knew their cause was lost, they knew there was really no way they could possibly win, and yet they fought on with tremendous bravery and dedication. And that's, I think, one of the reasons why the Civil War was such a poignant and even heart-wrenching time. Whether or not you agree with the Confederacy or with the justness of its cause, there's no way that you can question the idealism and the courage, the bravery, the dedication, the devotion of its soldiers—that they believed what they were fighting for was right. Even while it was happening, men like Union officer Joshua Chamberlain—who did all that he could to defeat the Confederacy—could not help but admire the dedication of those soldiers.

NOAH ANDRE TRUDEAU

Author of three books about the war's final year, including the recent Out of the Storm: The End of the Civil War *(April–June 1865).*

One main reason why the South lost (and this may seem offbeat because it flies in the face of the common wisdom) is that the South lacked the moral center that the North had in this conflict. Robert Kirby in his book on Florida's Edward Kirby Smith and the Trans-Mississippi suggests that the South's morale began to disintegrate in the Trans-Mississippi in about 1862.

The North had a fairly simple message that was binding it together, and that message was that the Union, *the idea of Union,* was important, and probably after 1863 you could add the crusade against slavery to that.

Ask the question, "What was the South fighting for; what was the Southern way of life that they were trying to protect?" and you will find that Southerners in Arkansas had a very different answer from Southerners in Georgia or Southerners in Virginia. And what you increasingly find as the war continued is that the dialogue got more and more confused. And you actually had state governors such as Joe Brown in Georgia identifying the needs of Georgia as being paramount and starting to withhold resources from the Confederacy and just protecting the basic infrastructure of the Georgia state government over the Confederacy. In the North you certainly had dialogue and debate on the war aims, but losing the Union was never really a part of that discussion. Preserving the Union was always the constant.

"The South certainly did not lose for any lack of . . . bravery and skill on the battlefield. In those virtues the Confederate soldier was unexcelled."

So, one key reason the South lost is that as time went on and the war got serious, Southerners began losing faith in the cause because it really did not speak to them directly.

JAMES M. MCPHERSON

Professor of history at Princeton University and author of nine books about the Civil War, including the Pulitzer Prize–winning Battle Cry of Freedom.

Historians have offered several explanations for the Confederate defeat in the Civil War. First, the North had a superiority in numbers and resources—but superiority did not bring victory to the British Empire in its war against the American colonies that were fighting for their independence in 1776, nor did it bring victory to the United States in its war against North Vietnam in the 1960s and '70s. While Northern superiority in numbers and resources was a necessary condition for Union victory, it is not a sufficient explanation for that victory. Neither are the internal divisions within

(CIVIL WAR TIMES ILLUSTRATED COLLECTION)

the Confederacy sufficient explanation for its defeat, because the North also suffered sharp internal divisions between those who supported a war for the abolition of slavery and those who resisted it, between Republicans and Democrats, between Unionists and Copperheads. And, in fact, the North probably suffered from greater internal disunity than the Confederacy.

Superior leadership is a possible explanation for Union victory. Abraham Lincoln was probably a better war president than Jefferson Davis and certainly offered a better explanation to his own people of what they were fighting for than Davis was able to offer. By the latter half of the war, Northern military leadership had evolved a coherent strategy for victory which involved the destruction of Confederate armies but went beyond that to the destruction of Confederate resources to wage war, including the resource of slavery, the South's labor power. By the time Grant had become general-in chief and Sherman his chief subordinate and Sheridan one of his hardest-hitting field commanders, the North had evolved a strategy that in the end completely destroyed the Confederacy's ability to wage war. And that combination of strategic leadership—both at the political level with Lincoln and the military level with Grant, Sherman, and Sheridan—is what in the end explains Northern victory.

GARY GALLAGHER

Professor of history at Pennsylvania State University and author, coauthor, or editor of eleven books about the war, including the recent Third Day at Gettysburg and Beyond *and* The Fredericksburg Campaign: Decision on the Rappahannock.

The principal cause of Confederate failure was the fact that the South's armies did not win enough victories in the field—especially enough victories in a row in the field—to both sustain Confederate morale behind the lines and depress Union morale behind the lines. In the end there was a waning of the will to resist on the part of Southern white people, but that was tied directly to the performance of the Confederate armies in the field; more than once they seemed to be on the brink of putting together enough successes to make Northern people behind the lines unwilling to pay the necessary price to subjugate the Confederacy.

The primary reason the Confederates did not have more success on the battlefield is that they developed only one really talented army commander, and that, of course, was Robert E. Lee. There never was a commander in the West who was fully competent to command an army—and I include Joseph E. Johnston and Albert Sidney Johnston and Braxton Bragg and the rest in that company. The almost unbroken string of failures in the West depressed Confederate morale. Lee's successes in the East were able to compensate for that for a good part of the war, but in the end there simply was too much bad news from the battlefield. And that bad news, together with Union advances into the South, the destruction of the Confederate infrastructure, and the problems of the Confederate economy that worked hardships on so many people, all came together to bring about Confederate defeat.

RICHARD MCMURRY

Historian and author of Two Great Rebel Armies, *which examines the Confederacy's defeat.*

If I had to pin the South's defeat down to one sentence, I would have to say it was due to very bad military commanders: Albert Sidney Johnston, P. G. T. Beauregard, Braxton Bragg, John C. Pemberton, Joseph E. Johnston, and John Bell Hood (and if you want to go down a notch or two in the command structure, Leonidas Polk, William J. Hardee, and Joseph Wheeler).

With people like Polk and Hardee you've got ranking generals in an army who deliberately sought to undermine their commanding general Braxton Bragg. With Wheeler you've got a subordinate general who on at least two occasions—in the fall of 1863 and the fall of 1864—went off joy-riding when he should have been obeying his orders from his army commander. With Beauregard and Johnston you had two generals who were unwilling to work with their government. With Hood and Bragg you had two generals who were basically incompetent as army commanders. And with Albert Sidney Johnston you had a general who underwent some kind of confidence crisis after Fort Donelson.

"One main reason why the South lost is that [it] lacked the moral center that the North had in this conflict."

Let me point out that every one of those generals was in the West. Any explanation that does not account for the West is irrelevant to your question. The war was lost by the Confederates in the West and won by the Federals in the West. I don't see how you could even question that. In the crucial theater of the war, the Confederacy did not have a competent commanding general.

MARK GRIMSLEY

Professor of history at Ohio State University and author of the upcoming Hard Hand of War, *his first book about the war.*

There are really two interesting questions. One is: Why did the South fail to

gain or maintain its independence? The other is: Why did the South not only lose its bid for independence but also its bid to influence the terms under which reunion would take place?

The answer to the second question seems to involve a combination of two things. First, the political culture in the South made it difficult for the many people (including those in leadership positions in the Confederacy) who wanted a negotiated settlement to make their will felt. Instead, Jefferson Davis, as president, was able to continue insisting on no peace short of independence. In a real two-party culture, Davis might have been pressured to compromise, or he might have been eased out, or the Congress might have been able to do something.

The other part of the answer is that while the key Confederate commanders—Beauregard, Lee, Joe Johnston—were trying to maximize their military position so as to influence any kind of peace negotiations and give the North an incentive to allow the South to reenter the Union on somewhat its own terms, military mistakes in the late winter and early spring of 1865 scuttled the Confederate military position in Virginia and the Carolinas. This precipitated a collapse sooner than might have happened, undermining any chance that the Confederate government might eventually pursue a negotiated settlement.

HERMAN HATTAWAY

Professor of history at the University of Missouri, Kansas City, and coauthor of Why the South Lost the Civil War.

My collaborators and I, in our book *Why the South Lost the Civil War,* laid out our theory, which is that the South lost the Civil War because it didn't really want to win badly enough. Defeat was ultimately due to a loss of collective will. But in other discussions with various learned groups, I've been induced to admit that in order for the Southern people to have a sufficient degree of will to win the war, they would have had to be a different people than they were. And so, in that sense, victory for the South was ultimately an impossibility.

Now certainly the course of the war, the military events, had a lot to do with the loss of will. The Southerners hoped that they would win spectacular victories on Northern soil, and they didn't. They hoped that they would be able to exhaust the will of the Northern people, and they didn't. And I don't know that all of the Southern people put a great deal of stock in their hopes that Abraham Lincoln would not be reelected, but certainly the key Southern leaders did, and this was their great hope and great strategy toward the end.

With regard to · military turning points, I'm not a fan of those, and I certainly don't think that Gettysburg and Vicksburg dictated the inevitable outcome of the war. We tend in *Why the South Lost* to imply that there was really still hope until March of 1865, but really I think the outcome of the war became inevitable in November 1864 with the reelection of Lincoln and that utter determination to see the thing through, and, of course, the finding of U.S. Grant by Lincoln and company. Grant was certainly the man to provide the leadership that the North needed.

EDWIN C. BEARSS

Former chief historian of the National Park Service and author of several books about the war.

The South lost the Civil War because of a number of factors. First, it was inherently weaker in the various essentials to win a military victory than the North. The North had a population of more than twenty-two million people to the South's nine-and-a-half million, of whom three-and-a-half million were slaves. While the slaves could be used to support the war effort through work on the plantations and in industries and as teamsters and pioneers with the army, they were not used as a combat arm in the war to any extent.

So if the South were to win, it had to win a short war by striking swiftly—in modern parlance, by an offensive *blitzkrieg* strategy. But the Confederates had established their military goals as fighting in defense of their homeland. In 1861, when enthusiasm was high in the South, it lacked the wherewithal and the resolution to follow up on its early victories, such as First Manassas in the East and at Wilson's Creek and Lexington in the West.

Despite the South's failure to capitalize on its successes in 1861, it came close to reversing the tide that ran against it beginning in February 1862. In the period between the fourth week of June 1862 and the last days of September and early days of October, the South did reverse the tide, sweeping forward on a broad front from the tidewater of Virginia to the Plains Indian territory. And abroad, the British were preparing to offer to mediate the conflict and, if the North refused, to recognize the Confederacy. But beginning at Antietam and ending at Perryville, all this unraveled, and the Confederates' true high water mark had passed.

In 1864, with the approach of the presidential election in the North, the Confederates had another opportunity to win the war. If the Confederate armies in Virginia, Georgia, and on the Gulf Coast could successfully resist the North and the war of attrition inaugurated by General Grant (with its particularly high casualties in Virginia), there was a good probability, as recognized by President Lincoln himself in the summer, that his administration would go down to defeat in November. But the success of Admiral David G. Farragut in Mobile Bay, the capture of Atlanta on the second of September by General Sherman, and the smashing success scored by General Sheridan at the expense of General Jubal A. Early at Cedar Creek, Virginia on October 19 shattered this hope, and Lincoln was reelected by a landslide in the electoral vote. With Lincoln's reelection, the road to Southern defeat grew shorter.

Judging from these responses, it seems clear that the South could have won the war . . . if. If it had more and better-equipped men, led by more capable generals and a wiser president. If it had a more unified purpose and was more aggressive. If it faced a different opponent.

The last condition should not be underestimated. By the end of the war, Lincoln and his powerful army were remarkably proficient at prosecuting war according to Grant's simple strategy. As historian William C. Davis has succinctly put it, "the North won it."

A War That Never Goes Away

More than the Revolution, more than the Constitutional Convention, it was the crucial test of the American nation. The author of Battle Cry of Freedom, *a most successful book on the subject, explains why the issues that fired the Civil War are as urgent in 1990 as they were in 1861.*

James M. McPherson

James M. McPherson is the Edwards Professor of American History at Princeton University. His most recent book is Battle Cry of Freedom *(Oxford University Press).*

"Americans just can't get enough of the Civil War." So says a man who should know, Terry Winschel, historian of the Vicksburg National Military Park. Millions of visitors come to Vicksburg and to more than a dozen other Civil War national battlefield and military parks every year. More than forty thousand Civil War reenactors spend hundreds of dollars each on replica weapons, uniforms, and equipment; many of them travel thousands of miles to help restage Civil War battles. Another two hundred and fifty thousand Americans describe themselves as Civil War buffs or "hobbyists" and belong to one of the hundreds of Civil War round tables or societies, subscribe to at least one of the half-dozen magazines devoted to Civil War history, or buy and sell Civil War memorabilia.

Above all, Americans buy books on the Civil War. This has always been true. More than fifty thousand separate books or pamphlets on the war have been published since the guns ceased firing 125 years ago. In recent years some eight hundred titles, many of them reprints of out-of-print works, have come off the presses annually. Nearly every month a new Civil War book is offered by the History Book Club or the Book-of-the-Month Club, often as the main selection. Many bookstore owners echo the words of Jim Lawson, general manager of the Book 'N Card shop in Falls Church,

Virginia. "For the last two years," he said in 1988, "Civil War books have been flying out of here. It's not [just] the buffs who buy; it's the general public, from high school kids to retired people."

Although we are approaching the end of the 125th-anniversary commemorations of Civil War events, the boom shows no signs of fading. As a beneficiary of this popular interest in the Civil War, I am often asked to explain what accounts for it—in particular, to explain why my own recent contribution to the literature on the war and its causes, *Battle Cry of Freedom,* was on national best-seller lists for several months as a hardcover book in 1988 and again as a paperback in 1989. I have a few answers.

The war did in fact pit brother against brother, cousin against cousin, even father against son.

First, for Americans, the human cost of the Civil War was by far the most devastating in our history. The 620,000 Union and Confederate soldiers who lost their lives almost equaled the 680,000 American soldiers who died in all the other wars this country has fought combined. When we add the unknown but probably substantial number of civilian deaths—from disease, malnutrition, exposure, or injury—among the hundreds of thousands of refugees in the Confederacy, the toll of Civil War dead may exceed war deaths in all the rest of American history. Consider two sobering facts about the Battle of Antietam, Amer-

ica's single bloodiest day. The 25,000 casualties there were nearly four times the number of American casualties on D-day, June 6, 1944. The 6,500 men killed and mortally wounded in one day near Sharpsburg were nearly double the number of Americans killed and mortally wounded in combat in all the rest of the country's nineteenth-century wars combined—the War of 1812, the Mexican War, and the Spanish-American War.

This ghastly toll gives the Civil War a kind of horrifying but hypnotic fascination. As Thomas Hardy once put it, "War makes rattling good history; but Peace is poor reading." The sound of drum and trumpet, the call to arms, the clashing of armies have stirred the blood of nations throughout history. As the horrors and the seamy side of a war recede into the misty past, the romance and honor and glory forge into the foreground. Of no war has this been more true than of the Civil War, with its dashing cavaliers, its generals leading infantry charges, its diamond-stacked locomotives and paddle-wheeled steamboats, its larger-than-life figures like Lincoln, Lee, Jackson, Grant, and Sherman, its heroic and romantic women like Clara Barton and "Mother" Bickerdyke and Rose O'Neal Greenhow, its countless real-life heroines and knaves and heroes capable of transmutation into a Scarlett O'Hara, Rhett Butler, or Ashley Wilkes. If romance is the other face of horror in our perception of the Civil War, the poignancy of a brothers' war is the other face of the tragedy of a civil war. In hundreds of individual cases the war did pit brother against brother, cousin against cousin, even father against son. This was especially true in border states like Kentucky, where the war divided

From *American Heritage,* March 1990, pp. 41-44, 46-47, 49. © 1990 by Forbes, Inc. Reprinted by permission of *American Heritage* magazine, a division of Forbes, Inc.

such famous families as the Clays, Crittendens, and Breckinridges and where seven brothers and brothers-in-law of the wife of the United States President fought for the Confederate States. But it was also true of states like Virginia, where Jeb Stuart's father-in-law commanded Union cavalry, and even of South Carolina, where Thomas F. Drayton became a brigadier general in the Confederate army and fought against his brother Percival, a captain in the Union navy, at the Battle of Port Royal. Who can resist the painful human interest of stories like these—particularly when they are recounted in the letters and diaries of Civil War protagonists, preserved through generations and published for all to read as a part of the unending stream of Civil War books?

Indeed, the uncensored contemporary descriptions of that war by participants help explain its appeal to modern readers. There is nothing else in history to equal it. Civil War armies were the most literate that ever fought a war up to that time, and twentieth-century armies censored soldiers' mail and discouraged diary keeping. Thus we have an unparalleled view of the Civil War by the people who experienced it. This has kept the image of the war alive in the families of millions of Americans whose ancestors fought in it. When speaking to audiences as diverse as Civil War buffs, Princeton students and alumni, and local literary clubs, I have sometimes asked how many of them are aware of forebears who fought in the Civil War. I have been surprised by the large response, which demonstrates not only a great number of such people but also their consciousness of events that happened so long ago yet seem part of their family lore today.

THIS CONSCIOUSNESS OF THE WAR, of the past as part of the present, continues to be more intense in the South than elsewhere. William Faulkner said of his native section that the past isn't dead; it isn't even past. As any reader of Faulkner's novels knows, the Civil War is central to that past that is present; it is the great watershed of Southern history; it is, as Mark Twain put it a century ago after a tour through the South, "what A.D. is elsewhere; they date from it." The symbols of that past-in-present surround Southerners as they grow up, from the Robert E. Lee Elementary School or

Jefferson Davis High School they attend and the Confederate battle flag that flies over their statehouse to the Confederate soldier enshrined in bronze or granite on the town square and the family folklore about victimization by Sherman's bummers. Some of those symbols remain highly controversial and provoke as much passion today as in 1863: the song "Dixie," for example, and the Confederate flag, which for many Southern whites continue to represent courage, honor, or defiance while to blacks they represent racism and oppression.

This suggests the most important reason for the enduring fascination with the Civil War among professional historians as well as the general public: Great issues were at stake, issues about which Americans were willing to fight and die, issues whose resolution profoundly transformed and redefined the United States. The Civil War was a total war in three senses: It mobilized the total human and material resources of both sides; it ended not in a negotiated peace but in total victory by one side and unconditional surrender by the other; it destroyed the economy and social system of the loser and established those of the winner as the norm for the future.

Civil War soldiers were the most literate up to that time. Their diaries and letters have had a lasting appeal.

The Civil War was fought mainly by volunteer soldiers who joined the colors before conscription went into effect. In fact, the Union and Confederate armies mobilized as volunteers a larger percentage of their societies' manpower than any other war in American history—probably in world history, with the possible exception of the French Revolution. And Civil War armies, like those of the French Revolution, were highly ideological in motivation. Most of the volunteers knew what they were fighting for, and why. What were they fighting for? If asked to define it in a single word, many soldiers on both sides would have answered: liberty. They fought for the heritage of freedom bequeathed to them by the Founding Fathers. North and South alike wrapped themselves in the mantle of 1776. But the two sides interpreted

that heritage in opposite ways, and at first neither side included the slaves in the vision of liberty for which it fought. The slaves did, however, and by the time of Lincoln's Gettysburg Address in 1863, the North also fought for "a new birth of freedom. . . ." These multiple meanings of freedom, and how they dissolved and reformed in kaleidoscopic patterns during the war, provide the central meaning of the war for the American experience.

When the "Black Republican" Abraham Lincoln won the Presidency in 1860 on a platform of excluding slavery from the territories, Southerners compared him to George III and declared their independence from "oppressive Yankee rule." "The same spirit of freedom and independence that impelled our Fathers to the separation from the British Government," proclaimed secessionists, would impel the "liberty loving people of the South" to separation from the United States government. A Georgia secessionist declared that Southerners would be "either *slaves in the Union or freemen out of it.*" Young men from Texas to Virginia rushed to enlist in this "Holy Cause of Liberty and Independence" and to raise "the standard of Liberty and Equality for white men" against "our Abolition enemies who are pledged to prostrate the white freemen of the South down to equality with negroes." From "the high and solemn motive of defending and protecting the rights which our fathers bequeathed to us," declared Jefferson Davis at the outset of war, let us "renew such sacrifices as our fathers made to the holy cause of constitutional liberty."

BUT MOST NORTHERNERS RIDICULED these Southern professions to be fighting for the ideals of 1776. That was "a libel upon the whole character and conduct of the men of '76," said the antislavery poet and journalist William Cullen Bryant. The Founding Fathers had fought "to establish the rights of man . . . and principles of universal liberty." The South, insisted Bryant, had seceded "not in the interest of general humanity, but of a domestic despotism. . . . Their motto is not liberty, but slavery." Northerners did not deny the right of revolution in principle; after all, the United States was founded on that right. But "the right of revolution," wrote Lincoln in 1861, "is never a legal right. . . . At most, it is but a moral right, when exercised for a morally justifiable cause. When exercised without such a cause revolution is no right, but simply a wicked exercise of physical power." In Lincoln's judgment secession was just such a wicked exercise. The event that precipitated it was Lincoln's election by a constitutional majority. As Northerners saw it, the Southern states, having controlled the national government for most of the previous two generations through their domination of the Democratic party, now decided to leave the Union just because they had lost an election.

For Lincoln and the Northern people, it was the Union that represented the ideals of 1776. The republic established by the Founding Fathers as a bulwark of liberty was a fragile experiment in a nineteenth-century world bestridden by kings, emperors, czars, and dictators. Most republics through history had eventually been overthrown. Some Americans still alive in 1861 had seen French republics succumb twice to emperors and once to the restoration of the Bourbon monarchy. Republics in Latin America came and went with bewildering rapidity. The United States in 1861 represented, in Lincoln's words, "the last, best hope" for the survival of republican liberties in the world. Would that hope also collapse? "Our popular government has often been called an experiment," Lincoln told Congress on July 4,1861. But if the Confederacy succeeded in splitting the country in two, it would set a fatal precedent that would destroy the experiment. By invoking this precedent, a minority in the future might secede from the Union whenever it did not like what the majority stood for, until the United States fragmented into a multitude of petty, squabbling autocracies. "The central idea pervading this struggle," said Lincoln, "is the necessity . . . of proving that popular government is not an absurdity. We must settle this question now, whether, in a free government, the minority have the right to break up the government whenever they choose."

Many soldiers who enlisted in the Union army felt the same way. A Missourian joined up as "a duty I owe my country and to my children to do what I can to preserve this government as I shudder to think what is ahead of them if this government should be overthrown." A New England soldier wrote to his wife on the eve of the First Battle of Bull Run: "I know . . . how great a debt we owe to those who went before us through the blood and sufferings of the Revolution. And I am willing—perfectly willing—to lay down all my joys in this life, to help maintain this government, and to pay that debt."

Freedom for the slaves was not part of the liberty for which the North fought in 1861. That was not because the Lincoln administration supported slavery; quite the contrary. Slavery was "an unqualified evil to the negro, to the white man . . . and to the State," said Lincoln on many occasions in words that expressed the sentiments of a Northern majority. "The monstrous injustice of slavery . . . deprives our republican example of its just influence in the world— enables the enemies of free institutions, with plausibility, to taunt us as hypocrites. . . . "Yet in his first inaugural address, Lincoln declared that he had "no purpose, directly or indirectly, to interfere with . . . slavery in the States where it exists." He reiterated this pledge in his first message to Congress, on July 4, 1861, when the Civil War was nearly three months old.

Civil War armies mobilized a larger percentage of volunteer manpower than any other war in our history.

What explains this apparent inconsistency? The answer lies in the Constitution and in the Northern polity of 1861. Lincoln was bound by a constitution that protected slavery in any state where citizens wanted it. The republic of liberty for whose preservation the North was fighting had been a republic in which slavery was legal everywhere in 1776. That was the great American paradox—a land of freedom based on slavery. Even in 1861 four states that remained loyal to the Union were slave states, and the Democratic minority in free states opposed any move to make the war for the Union a war against slavery.

BUT AS THE WAR WENT ON, THE SLAVES themselves took the first step toward making it a war against slavery. Coming into Union lines by the thousands, they voted with their feet for freedom. As enemy property they could be confiscated by Union forces as "contraband of war." This was the thin edge of the wedge that finally broke apart the American paradox. By 1863 a series of congressional acts plus Lincoln's Emancipation Proclamation had radically enlarged Union war aims. The North henceforth fought not just to restore the old Union, not just to ensure that the nation born in 1776 "shall not perish from the earth," but to give that nation "a new birth of freedom."

Northern victory in the Civil War resolved two fundamental, festering issues left unresolved by the Revolution of 1776: whether this fragile republican experiment called the United States would survive and whether the house divided would continue to endure half slave and half free. Both these issues remained open questions until 1865. Many Americans doubted the Republic's survival; many European conservatives predicted its demise; some Americans advocated the right of secession and periodically threatened to invoke it; eleven states did invoke it in 1860 and 1861. But since 1865 no state or region has seriously threatened secession, not even during the "massive resistance" to desegregation from 1954 to 1964. Before 1865 the United States, land of liberty, was the largest slaveholding country in the world. Since 1865 that particular "monstrous injustice" and "hypocrisy" has existed no more.

In the process of preserving the Union of 1776 while purging it of slavery, the Civil War also transformed it. Before 1861 the words *United States* were a plural noun: "The United States *are* a large country." Since 1865 *United States* has been a singular noun. The North went to war to preserve the *Union;* it ended by creating a *nation*. This transformation can be traced in Lincoln's most important wartime addresses. The first inaugural address contained the word *Union* twenty times and the word *nation* not once. In Lincoln's first message to Congress, on July 4, 1861, he used *Union* forty-nine times and *nation* only three times. In his famous public letter to Horace Greeley of August 22, 1862, concerning slavery and the war, Lincoln spoke of the Union nine times and the nation not at all. But in the Gettysburg Address fifteen months later, he did not refer to the Union at all but used the word *nation* five times. And in the second inaugural address, looking back over the past four years, Lincoln

McPherson's Basic Reading List

Allan Nevins. **Ordeal of the Union,** 2 vols. (New York: Charles Scribner's Sons, 1947). **The Emergence of Lincoln,** 2 vols. (New York: Charles Scribner's Sons, 1950). **The War for the Union,** 4 vols. (New York: Charles Scribner's Sons, 1959–71). These eight volumes are a magisterial account of the crisis-laden years from the Mexican War to Appomattox, covering social, economic, political, and military events in compelling prose.

David M. Potter. **The Impending Crisis, 1848–1861** (New York: Harper & Row, 1976). The best single-volume survey of the political events that led to secession and war.

Shelby Foote. **The Civil War: A Narrative,** 3 vols. (New York: Random House, 1958–74). A superbly readable military history by a novelist who did a massive amount of historical research.

Bruce Catton. **The Centennial History of the Civil War,** 3 vols. (Garden City, N.Y.: Doubleday and Co., 1961–65). Fast-paced chronicle of the fighting on the battlefield and the infighting in the political capitals of Washington and Richmond. **Mr. Lincoln's Army** (Garden City, N.Y.: Doubleday and Co., 1951). **Glory Road** (Garden City, N.Y.: Doubleday and Co., 1952). **A Stillness at Appomattox** (Garden City, N.Y.: Doubleday and Co., 1953). Catton's superb trilogy on the Army of the Potomac emphasizes the gritty determination of private soldiers despite the incompetent commanders who led them so often to defeat until Grant finally took charge.

Douglas Southall Freeman. **R. E. Lee: A Biography,** 4 vols. (New York: Charles Scribner's Sons, 1934–35). A classic study in leadership and command. **Lee's Lieutenants,** 3 vols. (New York: Charles Scribner's Sons, 1942–44). The story of the Army of Northern Virginia seen through the eyes of its principal officers.

Bell Irvin Wiley. **The Life of Johnny Reb** (Indianapolis: Bobbs-Merrill Co., 1943). **The Life of Billy Yank** (Indianapolis: Bobbs-Merrill Co., 1952). Thoroughly researched and superbly written studies of the common soldiers in both armies.

spoke of one side's seeking to dissolve the Union in 1861 and the other side's accepting the challenge of war to preserve the nation. The old decentralized Republic, in which the post office was the only agency of national government that touched the average citizen, was transformed by the crucible of war into a centralized polity that taxed people directly and created an internal revenue bureau to collect the taxes, expanded the jurisdiction of federal courts, created a national currency and a federally chartered banking system, drafted men into the Army, and created the Freedman's Bureau as the first national agency for social welfare. Eleven of the first twelve amendments to the Constitution had limited the powers of the national government; six of the next seven, starting with the Thirteenth Amendment in 1865, radically expanded those powers at the expense of the states. The first three of these amendments converted four million slaves into citizens and voters within five years, the most rapid and fundamental social transformation in American history—even if the nation did back-slide on part of this commitment for three generations after 1877.

From 1789 to 1861 a Southern slaveholder was President of the United States two-thirds of the time, and two-thirds of the Speakers of the House and presidents pro tem of the Senate had also been Southerners. Twenty of the thirty-five Supreme Court justices during that period were from the South, which always had a majority on the Court before 1861. After the Civil War a century passed before another resident of a Southern state was elected President. For half a century after the war hardly any Southerners served as Speaker of the House or president pro tem of the Senate, and only nine of the thirty Supreme Court justices appointed during that half-century were Southerners. The institutions and ideology of a plantation society and a caste system that had dominated half of the country before 1861 and sought to dominate more went down with a great crash in 1865 and were replaced by the institutions and ideology of free-labor entrepreneurial capitalism. For better or for worse, the flames of Civil War forged the framework of modern America.

So even if the veneer of romance and myth that has attracted so many of the current Civil War camp followers were stripped away, leaving only the trauma of violence and suffering, the Civil War would remain the most dramatic and crucial experience in American history. That fact will ensure the persistence of its popularity and its importance as a historical subject so long as there is a United States.

The War We Never Finished

The Confederate flag waves over a divided South. Some blacks demand that the banner come down. Some whites just don't understand the fuss. Perhaps a history lesson can help resolve the problem.

Richard M. McMurry

Richard McMurry teaches history at North Carolina State University in Raleigh, North Carolina. He is the author of the 1989 book, Two Great Rebel Armies.

Those of us who study America's great War Between the States frequently hear the shibboleth that "the Civil War still lives." More than any other event of our history, we are told, the war of the 1860s affects us. Such statements are often followed by a chain of explanatory truisms: "It was our war—American *versus* American;" "It was the last old style war and the first modern war;" and "It was the greatest of all our wars"—in terms of both the proportion of the population engaged and the number and percentage of Americans who died in military service.

If the Civil War does indeed "still live," however, it does so in a much less subtle way than the historical truisms suggest. Consider the following incidents, all of which took place in the past few years. In 1984, *Time* reported that some patrons of a national pizza chain were offended by the Confederate flags prominently displayed in the chain's restaurants. About the same time, controversy erupted in Greenville, North Carolina, over the flying of the Confederate flag on the town commons. The following year, black students at Alabama's Auburn University protested an all-white fraternity's displaying of a Confederate flag on campus. The protest, in turn, touched off a rush by whites to purchase Rebel flags and show them on houses, armbands and automobiles.

A few months after the incident at Auburn, another controversy boiled up when a black football player in Grand Prairie, Texas, refused to take the field under his high school's Confederate flag symbol—even after the flag had been redone in the school's red and gold colors. Over the years, other squabbles arose about flying the Rebel banner above the state capitol in Columbia, South Carolina, and over the courthouse in Caddo Parish, Louisiana. In Georgia and Mississippi there were calls for the removal of the Confederate battle flag from the flags of those states (to which it was added in 1956 and 1894, respectively).

In Wake County, North Carolina, in 1988, school officials barred a ninth-grader from class because of a Confederate flag on his jacket. A few weeks later a school in nearby Durham closed early for the weekend because 14 students wore Confederate flags to class for "Southern Pride Day."

In February 1988, a dozen or so black Alabama legislators were arrested as they attempted to climb to the dome of the state capitol to haul down the Confederate flag flying there. Several months later, black and white residents of Alexandria, Virginia, debated whether to resurrect a statue of a Confederate soldier that had been toppled from its pedestal by a truck.

Periodically across the nation, the Ku Klux Klan and similar groups display Confederate flags as they stage demonstrations protesting this or that action by blacks. From time to time, controversies erupt over the playing of "Dixie" or the showing of *Birth Of A Nation or Gone With The Wind.*

These incidents illustrate a major reason why "the Civil War still lives." For many Americans, it lives because it is still going on.

The war seemed to end in 1865, with the surrender of the Confederate armed forces; but in the Civil War things were not always what they appeared to be. The war was a complex struggle that involved four major groups which, for simplicity's sake, may be designated Confederates, Unionists, abolitionists, and egalitarians. While individuals sometimes shifted from one group to another, the groups themselves remained distinct throughout the crisis of the 1860s and 1870s—though some of them sometimes overlapped one another.

In 1861, Many Unionists Were Content To Let Slavery Continue In The South

---

The Confederates were the white Southerners who precipitated secession and then waged the war for Southern independence. Although individual Confederates acted from varied motives—especially from the desire to defend their homeland and protect their people—the fundamental reason behind secession and the establishment of the Confederacy was the desire to keep the South a white man's country through the perpetuation of Negro slavery. Secessionists realized the election of a Republican president (Abraham Lincoln) on a platform calling for no extension of slavery promised the eventual death of their "peculiar institution." Without slavery as a means of race control, they believed, white civilization could not be preserved in the face of a tide of semi-barbaric blacks.

The Unionists' goal was preservation of the American nation. To them, secession was the first step toward anarchy and the eventual destruction of the republican government. Slavery was of little concern to the Unionists. Most were as anxious to preserve white supremacy as any Confederate was, and when they talked about a "government of the people, by the people, and for the people," they usually meant *white* people. The typical Unionist opposed the expansion of slavery not because of any humanitarian concern about slaves' rights, but from fear it would harm the interests of non-slaveholding whites. In 1861, many Unionists were content to let slavery continue in the South, provided the South remained in the Union and did not use its political power to thwart the wishes of the Northern majority, which supported legislation to encourage national economic development.

The third group, the abolitionists, comprised those whose primary objective was the end of slavery. If forced to choose between emancipation and the Union, the abolitionists would have opted for the former. As it turned out, however, they could also be Unionists. At the war's outset, the abolitionists were few. As the conflict continued, however, and casualty lists lengthened, Unionist opinion expanded to embrace emancipation as a war measure necessary for victory.

"There is a desire," wrote Federal Colonel Augustus Auberne in January 1863, "to destroy everything that in *aught* gives the rebels strength. . . ." He vowed, " . . .this army will sustain the emancipation proclamation and enforce it with the bayonet," even though only a few of his men were abolitionists. "We must conquer the rebels or be conquered by them," noted Major General Henry W. Halleck. "Every slave withdrawn from the enemy is the equivalent of a white man put *hors de combat*."

Although the abolitionists would doubtless have preferred a more enthusiastic commitment to ending slavery, they were happy to cooperate with the Unionists, because by saving the Union they would also destroy slavery. By the midpoint of the war, abolition was inextricably linked with preservation of the Union, because by then most Unionists were

convinced that only by ending slavery could the United States win the war. The Abolitionists, therefore, swung wholeheartedly behind the Federal cause.

The egalitarians were those who envisioned an America free, not only of slavery, but of all distinctions based on race. They sought a society in which all Americans—at least all American *males*—would enjoy equal rights under the law. Most egalitarians were black, but a few whites marched in their ranks. The egalitarians had considerable clout with the "Radical" faction of the Republican party, but they were so small a group that only major blunders by their opponents offered them any hope of achieving their objective.

The military contest of 1861–1865 brought the triumph of the Unionists and abolitionists over the Confederates. Never again after 1865 would a state seriously contemplate leaving the Union. Never again would there be any serious challenge to the supremacy of the Washington, D.C. government. Indeed, in our century, the federal government has found in the power of the purse a far stronger force to wield against the states than the mighty hosts once led by Grant, Sherman, Thomas and Sheridan. The states—with the former Confederate states often in the lead—have repeatedly demonstrated that they will discard any vestige of their once vaunted self-government in the mad scramble for federal dollars.

The Unionists and the abolitionists won their war in spring 1865. Having triumphed, they were anxious to get back to normal life. The war between the Confederates and the egalitarians, however, had scarcely begun; it would continue on the new battlefield of Reconstruction.

The Confederates . . . Rushed To Enact A Series Of "Black Codes"

Ironically, in this new phase, the war followed a course that was, in many ways, the reverse of the military struggle of 1861–1865. Early in the battle of Reconstruction, the Confederates committed blunders every bit as egregious as those of McDowell, McClellan, Pope,

Burnside and Hooker in 1861, 1862 and 1863. In the initial engagements with the egalitarians, the Confederates, with no show of remorse, jubilantly elected former Rebel leaders to local, state and congressional offices; they adopted laws and resolutions indicating they would defy the Washington government; they publicly, and often officially, expressed great regret about the end of slavery; and they rushed to enact a series of "black codes" that placed the former bondsmen in conditions that differed little from what they had known under slavery.

This unrepentant conduct on the part of the Confederates, who, after all *had* started and lost the war, quite naturally provoked a reaction from the Unionists and the abolitionists. Those two groups rallied to the support of the egalitarians, lest the work of 1861–1865 be undone. For several years this revived Northern wartime coalition was strong enough to control Congress. It managed to pass a series of laws (the most important being the Fourteenth Amendment to the constitution) designed to secure the victory of 1865 by protecting the rights of former slaves. Those free, newly enfranchised blacks would serve as a counterweight to the Confederates in the Southern states.

Gradually, it dawned on the Confederates that their own belligerence threatened—or was perceived as a threat to—the Unionists and abolitionists. When the Confederates realized what damage they were doing to themselves, they began to moderate the tone of what they said and wrote for Northern consumption. They made it clear there would be no renewed effort to secede, to resurrect slavery, or even to repeal the pro-business economic legislation the Republicans had enacted during the war.

The Unionists and abolitionists came to accept the Confederates' assurances, and withdrew from the coalition with the egalitarians. By 1876 or 1877, the Unionists and abolitionists were back to the position they had occupied in the summer of 1865. Once again they were willing to abandon the egalitarians and allow the Southern states to govern themselves within the Union, but without any institution called "slavery."

Meanwhile, the Confederates were happily discovering slavery was not necessary to safeguard white supremacy. If the former slaves could be intimidated, denied meaningful education and kept in poverty, they would work for very low wages. That meant the labor slavery had provided was still available, and at an even lower cost, since employers had no obligation to provide for sick or aged workers. By the 1890s, black poverty, reinforced by custom and "Jim Crow" segregation laws, had assured white supremacy. The South of 1900 or 1920 was not markedly different from the South of 1840 or 1860, so far as race relations were concerned. White supremacy appeared about as secure in the early 20th Century as it had been in the mid-19th Century.

Students of war have long recognized that winning battles and winnings wars are different matters. No war is an end in itself; each is fought for some larger purpose, some perceived gain. Karl von Clausewitz, the 19th-century Prussian general and observer of war, remarked that war is merely "a continuation of politics by other means." If, then, a nation achieves the political objective for which it fought, it wins the war no matter what happens on the battlefield. This is true of any war, including America's Civil War.

The Confederacy lost the military struggle of 1861–1885. Given the South's historic commitment to white supremacy, however, one can make a strong argument that the South achieved victory in the larger war that lasted from the 1820s and beyond. Once the Confederates understood who their real enemies were—the egalitarians—and realized those enemies could be beaten if they were separated from the Unionists and abolitionists, it was easy from them to accept the struggle's military outcome and return to the fold as loyal citizens of the United States—as Americans who just happened to live in the South. Suddenly, the South found itself in fundamental agreement with the North on Union, abolition and white supremacy. This unwritten accord explains why North and South were able to reunite so completely in the years after the shooting stopped. In effect, both North and South won the war, because each got what it was fighting for. Everyone was a victor; everyone, that is except the egalitarians.

Reconciliation among the Confederates, Unionists and abolitionists left the egalitarians alone and forgotten in their ongoing war for equal rights. The confederates, moreover, managed to bury the egalitarian cause even deeper by editing history. They claimed (and managed to convince themselves) that they had been fighting not at all for the preservation of slavery, but to protect their "rights" or "states rights." This view became the "party line" among white Southerners, and traces of it still surface in various publications.

In truth, white Southerners would have been hard pressed to list more than one "right" that was under attack in 1860 by any outsider. No Northerner advocated the abolition of freedom of the press, or freedom of religion, or freedom of speech in the South. Only the right to own slaves was threatened. Within the context of their own time and place, the secessionists of 1860–1861 were acting rationally. They recognized a real threat to a valued institution, and acted to protect themselves and the way of life they had based upon that institution.

In Effect, Both North And South Won The War, Because Each Got What It Was Fighting For

Not until the mid-20th Century would another group of egalitarians rally for a successful assault on the bastion of white supremacy in the South. By that time, the ranks of the white supremacists had thinned, because science and education had eroded the old belief that blacks were innately inferior to whites, and personal experience (such as service in an integrated army) had led many Southern whites to abandon the ideas of their ancestors. The desire for industrial, commercial and financial development also operated to convince many Southern political and business leaders that white supremacy and the struggle to preserve it were major handicaps to their region. Nevertheless, the battle between egalitarians and the ideological descendants of the Confederates continues to this day. The eradication of distinctions based on race is not yet complete.

To acknowledge the facts of our nation's history—of how the war between the egalitarians and white supremacists has continued through slavery, secession, Civil War and reconstruction into the present—is not to claim that all white Southerners who display the Confederate flag today are racists. The overwhelming majority are not.

The Confederate Flag . . . Means Different Things To Different White People

The Confederate flag, as black *Washington Post* columnist Courtland Milloy pointed out in a February 1988 column, means different things to different white people. Most Southern whites use the Rebel flag as a kind of generic rallying point—an "us" *versus* "them" symbol of some mystic, visceral Southern-ness that, in its own peculiar way, has nothing to do with race. Others use the flag as a safety-valve protest against some vague outside force, or as something to use just to raise hell and provoke somebody. Some view the flag as a means to commemorate the bravery of their ancestors who served in the Confederate army. Some do use it as a symbol of their devotion to white supremacy.

Blacks, on the other hand, view the Rebel banner only as the symbol of a racist nation whose sole reason for being was the perpetuation of the institution that enslaved their ancestors. In effect, blacks see the flag for what it was originally; whites see it in a more complex way, and for those things it has become as well as for what it was.

Southern whites are as ill-informed about the past as are most other Americans. Most of those who are aware of their history at all have been immersed in the Confederates' version of the the events of 1861–1865. Because of that immersion, they honestly believe there were no racial overtones to the attempt to establish an independent Southern nation. They, therefore, cannot understand why blacks would be offended by the use of the Confederate flag as a symbol for a group that includes Negroes, or why blacks would object to a public ceremony honoring the men who fought for the Confederacy. To whites who wish to honor the memory of their ancestors as brave men who sacrificed a great deal for what they regarded as their country, such objections from blacks seem insulting, wrong-headed, and unnecessarily confrontational.

There are a few hopeful signs that we may be making progress in getting out of this mess of our own creation. Columnist Milloy reported that he received excellent service at a "Johnny Reb's" restaurant in Atlanta despite his race and the Confederate flags hanging in the dining area. ("It's rare," he wrote, "to be treated that well right here in Washington.") Perhaps, Milloy suggested, blacks should concentrate on dealing with more serious matters, and maybe even develop a flag of their own.

In spring 1989 a Confederate reenactment unit from Georgia participated, albeit without flags, in a parade and reburial ceremony in Beaufort, South Carolina. The ceremony was conducted in connection with the reinterment of the remains of several black Union soldiers of the 55th Massachusetts and 1st North Carolina (U.S.) regiments. The confederate reenactors honored the black Union troops by firing a volley over their graves.

Black cadets at the Virginia Military Institute in Lexington, Virginia, regu-larly take part in the school's famous New Market Day ceremonies honoring 10 VMI boys who were killed or mortally wounded in the 1864 Battle of New Market, in which the cadets fought as a Confederate unit. On occasion, black members of the VMI color guard have carried the school flag with its Confederate battle streamer.

The University of Virginia's Professor Ervin L. Jordan, a black, recently co-authored a history of the 19th Virginia Infantry Regiment, part of *The Virginia Regimental Histories* series published by H. E. Howard of Lynchburg, Virginia. While many people expressed surprise that a black scholar would write the history of a Confederate unit, others (more presciently, we might hope) remarked on how such ventures might help promote better race relations in the South.

Someday, if we are lucky, we as a nation will grow beyond the acrimonious squabbling about symbols now more than a century old. Someday, it may be possible for Americans of all races to understand the war of the 1860s without bitterness, to be fascinated by its many unique features and by its in-triguing personages. Someday, maybe all Americans will come to appreciate and honor the courage displayed by most people on both sides of that conflict, persons of all classes, many nationalities, and at least three races. Those people, after all, were caught up in a great struggle started by larger, less personal forces, a struggle in which most of them sought to do what they believed was right. Someday, perhaps all Americans will take equal pride in the bravery of Confederate Major General Patrick Cleburne and his troops as they advanced into the holocaust at the 1864 Battle of Franklin, Tennessee, and in the valor of Union Colonel Robert Gould Shaw and his men of the black 54th Massachusetts, as they forced their way to the parapets of Battery Wagner off Charleston, South Carolina, in 1863.

Perhaps those of us who study that "greatest of all our wars," the war that, regrettably, "still lives," can contribute to a better understanding, by all Americans, of all the people who experienced it. That better understanding may help bring the war to its long overdue conclusion.

The New View of Reconstruction

Whatever you were taught or thought you knew about the post–Civil War era is probably wrong in the light of recent study

Eric Foner

Eric Foner is Professor of History at Columbia University and author of Nothing but Freedom: Emancipation and Its Legacy.

In the past twenty years, no period of American history has been the subject of a more thoroughgoing reevaluation than Reconstruction—the violent, dramatic, and still controversial era following the Civil War. Race relations, politics, social life, and economic change during Reconstruction have all been reinterpreted in the light of changed attitudes toward the place of blacks within American society. If historians have not yet forged a fully satisfying portrait of Reconstruction as a whole, the traditional interpretation that dominated historical writing for much of this century has irrevocably been laid to rest.

Anyone who attended high school before 1960 learned that Reconstruction was an era of unrelieved sordidness in American political and social life. The martyred Lincoln, according to this view, had planned a quick and painless readmission of the Southern states as equal members of the national family. President Andrew Johnson, his successor, attempted to carry out Lincoln's policies but was foiled by the Radical Republicans (also known as Vindictives or Jacobins). Motivated by an irrational hatred of Rebels or by ties with Northern capitalists out to plunder the South, the Radicals swept aside Johnson's lenient program and fastened black supremacy upon the defeated Confederacy. An orgy of corruption followed, presided over by unscrupulous carpetbaggers (Northerners who ventured south to reap the spoils of

office), traitorous scalawags (Southern whites who cooperated with the new governments for personal gain), and the ignorant and childlike freedmen, who were incapable of properly exercising the political power that had been thrust upon them. After much needless suffering, the white community of the South banded together to overthrow these "black" governments and restore home rule (their euphemism for white supremacy). All told, Reconstruction was just about the darkest page in the American saga.

Originating in anti-Reconstruction propaganda of Southern Democrats during the 1870s, this traditional interpretation achieved scholarly legitimacy around the turn of the century through the work of William Dunning and his students at Columbia University. It reached the larger public through films like *Birth of a Nation* and *Gone With the Wind* and that best-selling work of myth-making masquerading as history, *The Tragic Era* by Claude G. Bowers. In language as exaggerated as it was colorful, Bowers told how Andrew Johnson "fought the bravest battle for constitutional liberty and for the preservation of our institutions ever waged by an Executive" but was overwhelmed by the "poisonous propaganda" of the Radicals. Southern whites, as a result, "literally were put to the torture" by "emissaries of hate" who manipulated the "simple-minded" freedmen, inflaming the negroes' egotism" and even inspiring "lustful assaults" by blacks upon white womanhood.

In a discipline that sometimes seems to pride itself on the rapid rise and fall of historical interpretations, this traditional portrait of Reconstruction enjoyed remarkable staying power. The long reign of the old interpretation is not difficult to

explain. It presented a set of easily identifiable heroes and villains. It enjoyed the imprimatur of the nation's leading scholars. And it accorded with the political and social realities of the first half of this century. This image of Reconstruction helped freeze the mind of the white South in unalterable opposition to any movement for breaching the ascendancy of the Democratic party, eliminating segregation, or readmitting disfranchised blacks to the vote.

NEVERTHELESS, THE DEMISE OF THE traditional interpretation was inevitable, for it ignored the testimony of the central participant in the drama of Reconstruction—the black freedman. Furthermore, it was grounded in the conviction that blacks were unfit to share in political power. As Dunning's Columbia colleague John W. Burgess put it, "A black skin means membership in a race of men which has never of itself succeeded in subjecting passion to reason, has never, therefore, created any civilization of any kind." Once objective scholarship and modern experience rendered that assumption untenable, the entire edifice was bound to fall.

The work of "revising" the history of Reconstruction began with the writings of a handful of survivors of the era, such as John R. Lynch, who had served as a black congressman from Mississippi after the Civil War. In the 1930s white scholars like Francis Simkins and Robert Woody carried the task forward. Then, in 1935, the black historian and activist W.E.B. Du Bois produced *Black Reconstruction in America,* a monumental reevaluation that closed with an irrefutable indictment of a historical profession

From *American Heritage*, October/November 1983, pp. 10-15. © 1983 by Forbes, Inc. Reprinted by permission of *American Heritage* magazine, a division of Forbes, Inc.

that had sacrificed scholarly objectivity on the altar of racial bias. "One fact and one alone," he wrote, "explains the attitude of most recent writers toward Reconstruction; they cannot conceive of Negroes as men." Du Bois's work, however, was ignored by most historians.

It was not until the 1960s that the full force of the revisionist wave broke over the field. Then, in rapid succession, virtually every assumption of the traditional viewpoint was systematically dismantled. A drastically different portrait emerged to take its place. President Lincoln did not have a coherent "plan" for Reconstruction, but at the time of his assassination he had been cautiously contemplating black suffrage. Andrew Johnson was a stubborn, racist politician who lacked the ability to compromise. By isolating himself from the broad currents of public opinion that had nourished Lincoln's career, Johnson created an impasse with Congress that Lincoln would certainly have avoided, thus throwing away his political power and destroying his own plans for reconstructing the South.

The Radicals in Congress were acquitted of both vindictive motives and the charge of serving as the stalking-horses of Northern capitalism. They emerged instead as idealists in the best nineteenth-century reform tradition. Radical leaders like Charles Sumner and Thaddeus Stevens had worked for the rights of blacks long before any conceivable political advantage flowed from such a commitment. Stevens refused to sign the Pennsylvania Constitution of 1838 because it disfranchised the state's black citizens; Sumner led a fight in the 1850s to integrate Boston's public schools. Their Reconstruction policies were based on principle, not petty political advantage, for the central issue dividing Johnson and these Radical Republicans was the civil rights of freedmen. Studies of congressional policy-making, such as Eric L. McKitrick's *Andrew Johnson and Reconstruction,* also revealed that Reconstruction legislation, ranging from the Civil Rights Act of 1866 to the Fourteenth and Fifteenth Amendments, enjoyed broad support from moderate and conservative Republicans. It was not simply the work of a narrow radical faction.

EVEN MORE STARTLING WAS THE REVISED portrait of Reconstruction in the South itself. Imbued with the spirit of the civil rights movement and rejecting entirely the racial assumptions that had underpinned the traditional interpretation, these historians evaluated Reconstruction from the black point of view. Works like Joel Williamson's *After Slavery* portrayed the period as a time of extraordinary political, social, and economic progress for blacks. The establishment of public school systems, the granting of equal citizenship to blacks, the effort to restore the devastated Southern economy, the attempt to construct an interracial political democracy from the ashes of slavery, all these were commendable achievements, not the elements of Bowers's "tragic era."

Unlike earlier writers, the revisionists stressed the active role of the freedmen in shaping Reconstruction. Black initiative established as many schools as did Northern religious societies and the Freedmen's Bureau. The right to vote was not simply thrust upon them by meddling outsiders, since blacks began agitating for the suffrage as soon as they were freed. In 1865 black conventions throughout the South issued eloquent, though unheeded, appeals for equal civil and political rights.

With the advent of Radical Reconstruction in 1867, the freedmen did enjoy a real measure of political power. But black supremacy never existed. In most states blacks held only a small fraction of political offices, and even in South Carolina, where they comprised a majority of the state legislature's lower house, effective power remained in white hands. As for corruption, moral standards in both

government and private enterprise were at low ebb throughout the nation in the postwar years—the era of Boss Tweed, the Credit Mobilier scandal, and the Whiskey Ring. Southern corruption could hardly be blamed on former slaves.

Other actors in the Reconstruction drama also came in for reevaluation. Most carpetbaggers were former Union soldiers seeking economic opportunity in the postwar South, not unscrupulous adventurers. Their motives, a typically American amalgam of humanitarianism and the pursuit of profit, were no more insidious than those of Western pioneers. Scalawags, previously seen as traitors to the white race, now emerged as "Old Line" Whig Unionists who had opposed secession in the first place or as poor whites who had long resented planters' domination of Southern life and who saw in Reconstruction a chance to recast Southern society along more democratic lines. Strongholds of Southern white Republicanism like east Tennessee and western North Carolina had been the scene of resistance to Confederate rule throughout the Civil War; now, as one scalawag newspaper put it, the choice was "between salvation at the hand of the Negro or destruction at the hand of the rebels."

At the same time, the Ku Klux Klan and kindred groups, whose campaign of violence against black and white Republicans had been minimized or excused in older writings, were portrayed as they really were. Earlier scholars had con-

Until recently, Thaddeus Stevens had been viewed as motivated by irrational hatred of the Rebels (left). Now he has emerged as an idealist in the best reform tradition.

NEW YORK PUBLIC LIBRARY, PRINT ROOM

EDWARD'S ELLIS, *The History of Our Country*, VOL. 5, 1900

Reconstruction governments were portrayed as disastrous failures (left) because elected blacks were ignorant or corrupt. In fact, postwar corruption cannot be blamed on former slaves.

SCHOMBERG CENTER, NEW YORK PUBLIC LIBRARY

veyed the impression that the Klan intimidated blacks mainly by dressing as ghosts and playing on the freedmen's superstitions. In fact, black fears were all too real: the Klan was a terrorist organization that beat and killed its political opponents to deprive blacks of their newly won rights. The complicity of the Democratic party and the silence of prominent whites in the face of such outrages stood as an indictment of the moral code the South had inherited from the days of slavery.

By the end of the 1960s, then, the old interpretation had been completely reversed. Southern freedmen were the heroes, the "Redeemers" who overthrew Reconstruction were the villains, and if the era was "tragic," it was because change did not go far enough. Reconstruction had been a time of real progress and its failure a lost opportunity for the South and the nation. But the legacy of Reconstruction—the Fourteenth and Fifteenth Amendments—endured to inspire future efforts for civil rights. As Kenneth Stampp wrote in *The Era of Reconstruction,* a superb summary of revisionist findings published in 1965, "If it was worth four years of civil war to save the Union, it was worth a few years of radical reconstruction to give the American Negro the ultimate promise of equal civil and political rights."

As Stampp's statement suggests, the reevaluation of the first Reconstruction was inspired in large measure by the impact of the second—the modern civil rights movement. And with the waning of that movement in recent years, writing on Reconstruction has undergone still another transformation. Instead of seeing the Civil War and its aftermath as a second American Revolution (as Charles Beard had), a regression into barbarism

(as Bowers argued), or a golden opportunity squandered (as the revisionists saw it), recent writers argue that Radical Reconstruction was not really very radical. Since land was not distributed to the former slaves, they remained economically dependent upon their former owners. The planter class survived both the war and Reconstruction with its property (apart from slaves) and prestige more or less intact.

Not only changing times but also the changing concerns of historians have contributed to this latest reassessment of Reconstruction. The hallmark of the past decade's historical writing has been an emphasis upon "social history"—the evocation of the past lives of ordinary Americans—and the downplaying of strictly political events. When applied to Reconstruction, this concern with the "social" suggested that black suffrage and officeholding, once seen as the most radical departures of the Reconstruction era, were relatively insignificant.

RECENT HISTORIANS HAVE FOCUSED THEIR investigations not upon the politics of Reconstruction but upon the social and economic aspects of the transition from slavery to freedom. Herbert Gutman's influential study of the black family during and after slavery found little change in family structure or relations between men and women resulting from emancipation. Under slavery most blacks had lived in nuclear family units, although they faced the constant threat of separation from loved ones by sale. Reconstruction provided the opportunity for blacks to solidify their preexisting family ties. Conflicts over whether black women should work in the cotton fields (planters said yes, many black families said no)

and over white attempts to "apprentice" black children revealed that the autonomy of family life was a major preoccupation of the freedmen. Indeed, whether manifested in their withdrawal from churches controlled by whites, in the blossoming of black fraternal, benevolent, and self-improvement organizations, or in the demise of the slave quarters and their replacement by small tenant farms occupied by individual families, the quest for independence from white authority and control over their own day-to-day lives shaped the black response to emancipation.

In the post–Civil War South the surest guarantee of economic autonomy, blacks believed, was land. To the freedmen the justice of a claim to land based on their years of unrequited labor appeared self-evident. As an Alabama black convention put it, "The property which they [the planters] hold was nearly all earned by the sweat of *our* brows." As Leon Litwack showed in *Been in the Storm So Long,* a Pulitzer Prize–winning account of the black response to emancipation, many freedmen in 1865 and 1866 refused to sign labor contracts, expecting the federal government to give them land. In some localities, as one Alabama overseer reported, they "set up claims to the plantation and all on it."

In the end, of course, the vast majority of Southern blacks remained propertyless and poor. But exactly why the South, and especially its black population, suffered from dire poverty and economic retardation in the decades following the Civil War is a matter of much dispute. In *One Kind of Freedom,* economists Roger Ransom and Richard Sutch indicted country merchants for monopolizing credit and charging usurious interest rates, forcing black tenants into debt and locking the South into a dependence on cotton production that impoverished the entire region. But Jonathan Wiener, in his study of postwar Alabama, argued that planters used their political power to compel blacks to remain on the plantations. Planters succeeded in stabilizing the plantation system, but only by blocking the growth of alternative enterprises, like factories, that might draw off black laborers, thus locking the region into a pattern of economic backwardness.

IF THE THRUST OF RECENT WRITING HAS emphasized the social and economic aspects of Reconstruction, politics has not been entirely neglected. But political studies have also reflected the postrevisionist mood summarized by C. Vann Woodward when he observed "how essentially nonrevolutionary and conservative Reconstruction really was." Recent writers, unlike their revisionist predecessors, have found little to praise in federal policy toward the emancipated blacks.

A new sensitivity to the strength of prejudice and laissez-faire ideas in the nineteenth-century North has led many historians to doubt whether the Republican party ever made a genuine commitment to racial justice in the South. The granting of black suffrage was an alternative to a long-term federal responsibility for protecting the rights of the former slaves. Once enfranchised, blacks could be left to fend for themselves. With the exception of a few Radicals like Thaddeus Stevens, nearly all Northern policy-makers and educators are criticized today for assuming that, so long as the unfettered operations of the marketplace afforded blacks the opportunity to advance through diligent labor, federal efforts to assist them in acquiring land were unnecessary.

Probably the most innovative recent writing on Reconstruction politics has centered on a broad reassessment of black Republicanism, largely undertaken by a new generation of black historians. Scholars like Thomas Holt and Nell Painter insist that Reconstruction was not simply a matter of black and white. Conflicts within the black community, no less than divisions among whites, shaped Reconstruction politics. Where revisionist scholars, both black and white, had celebrated the accomplishments of black political leaders, Holt, Painter, and others charge that they failed to address the economic plight of the black masses.

Painter criticized "representative colored men," as national black leaders were called, for failing to provide ordinary freedmen with effective political leadership. Holt found that black officeholders in South Carolina mostly emerged from the old free mulatto class of Charleston, which shared many assumptions with prominent whites. "Basically bourgeois in their origins and orientation," he wrote, they "failed to act in the interest of black peasants."

In emphasizing the persistence from slavery of divisions between free blacks and slaves, these writers reflect the increasing concern with continuity and conservatism in Reconstruction. Their work reflects a startling extension of revisionist premises. If, as has been argued for the past twenty years, blacks were active agents rather than mere victims of manipulation, then they could not be absolved of blame for the ultimate failure of Reconstruction.

Despite the excellence of recent writing and the continual expansion of our knowledge of the period, historians of Reconstruction today face a unique dilemma. An old interpretation has been overthrown, but a coherent new synthesis has yet to take its place. The revisionists of the 1960s effectively established a series of negative points: the Reconstruction governments were not as bad as had been portrayed, black supremacy was a myth, the Radicals were not cynical manipulators of the freedmen. Yet no convincing overall portrait of the quality of political and social life emerged from their writings. More recent historians have rightly pointed to elements of continuity that spanned the nineteenth-century Southern experience, especially the survival, in modified form, of the plantation system. Nevertheless, by denying the real changes that did occur, they have failed to provide a convincing portrait of an era characterized above all by drama, turmoil, and social change.

Building upon the findings of the past twenty years of scholarship, a new portrait of Reconstruction ought to begin by viewing it not as a specific time period, bounded by the years 1865 and 1877, but as an episode in a prolonged historical process—American society's adjustment to the consequences of the Civil War and emancipation. The Civil War, of course, raised the decisive questions of America's national existence: the relations between local and national authority, the

definition of citizenship, the balance between force and consent in generating obedience to authority. The war and Reconstruction, as Allan Nevins observed over fifty years ago, marked the "emergence of modern America." This was the era of the completion of the national railroad network, the creation of the modern steel industry, the conquest of the West and final subduing of the Indians, and the expansion of the mining frontier. Lincoln's America—the world of the small farm and artisan shop—gave way to a rapidly industrializing economy. The issues that galvanized postwar Northern politics—from the question of the greenback currency to the mode of paying holders of the national debt—arose from the economic changes unleashed by the Civil War.

Above all, the war irrevocably abolished slavery. Since 1619, when "twenty negars" disembarked from a Dutch ship in Virginia, racial injustice had haunted American life, mocking its professed ideals even as tobacco and cotton, the products of slave labor, helped finance the nation's economic development. Now the implications of the black presence could no longer be ignored. The Civil War resolved the problem of slavery but, as the Philadelphia diarist Sydney George Fisher observed in June 1865, it opened an even more intractable problem: "What shall we do with the Negro?" Indeed, he went on, this was a problem *"incapable* of any solution that will satisfy both North and South."

As Fisher realized, the focal point of Reconstruction was the social revolution known as emancipation. Plantation slavery was simultaneously a system of labor, a form of racial domination, and the foundation upon which arose a distinctive ruling class within the South. Its demise threw open the most fundamental questions of economy, society, and politics. A new system of labor, social, racial, and political relations had to be created to replace slavery.

The United States was not the only nation to experience emancipation in the nineteenth century. Neither plantation slavery nor abolition were unique to the United States. But Reconstruction was. In a comparative perspective Radical Reconstruction stands as a remarkable experiment, the only effort of a society experiencing abolition to bring the former slaves within the umbrella of equal citizenship. Because the Radicals did not achieve everything they wanted, histo-

COURTESY OF THE ATLANTA *Constitution*

KNIGHTS
- OF THE -
KU KLUX
KLAN

For Home,
Country and
Each other.

A High Class Order for
Men of Intelligence
and Character.

The World's
Greatest Secret, Social,
Patriotic, Fraternal,
Beneficiary Order.

Some scholars exalted the motives of the Ku Klux Klan (left). Actually, its members were part of a terrorist organization that beat and killed its political opponents to deprive blacks of their rights.

RUTHERFORD B. HAYES LIBRARY, FREMONT, OHIO

rians have lately tended to play down the stunning departure represented by black suffrage and officeholding. Former slaves, most fewer than two years removed from bondage, debated the fundamental questions of the polity: What is a republican form of government? Should the state provide equal education for all? How could political equality be reconciled with a society in which property was so unequally distributed? There was something inspiring in the way such men met the challenge of Reconstruction. "I knew nothing more than to obey my master," James K. Greene, an Alabama black politician later recalled. "But the tocsin of freedom sounded and knocked at the door and we walked out like free men and we met the exigencies as they grew up, and shouldered the responsibilities."

"YOU NEVER SAW A PEOPLE MORE EXcited on the subject of politics than are the negroes of the south," one planter observed in 1867. And there were more than a few Southern whites as well who in these years shook off the prejudices of the past to embrace the vision of a new South dedicated to the principles of equal citizenship and social justice. One ordinary South Carolinian expressed the new sense of possibility in 1868 to the Republican governor of the state: "I am sorry that I cannot write an elegant stiled letter to your excellency. But I rejoice to think that God almighty has given to the poor of S. C. a Gov. to hear to feel to protect the humble poor without distinction to race or color. . . . I am a native borned S. C. a poor man never owned a Negro in

my life nor my father before me. . . . Remember the true and loyal are the poor of the whites and blacks, outside of these you can find none loyal."

Few modern scholars believe the Reconstruction governments established in the South in 1867 and 1868 fulfilled the aspirations of their humble constituents. While their achievements in such realms as education, civil rights, and the economic rebuilding of the South are now widely appreciated, historians today believe they failed to affect either the economic plight of the emancipated slave or the ongoing transformation of independent white farmers into cotton tenants. Yet their opponents did perceive the Reconstruction governments in precisely this way—as representatives of a revolution that had put the bottom rail, both racial and economic, on top. This perception helps explain the ferocity of the attacks leveled against them and the pervasiveness of violence in the postemancipation South.

The spectacle of black men voting and holding office was anathema to large numbers of Southern whites. Even more disturbing, at least in the view of those who still controlled the plantation regions of the South, was the emergence of local officials, black and white, who sympathized with the plight of the black laborer. Alabama's vagrancy law was a "dead letter" in 1870, "because those who are charged with its enforcement are indebted to the vagrant vote for their offices and emoluments." Political debates over the level and incidence of taxation, the control of crops, and the resolution of contract disputes revealed

that a primary issue of Reconstruction was the role of government in a plantation society. During presidential Reconstruction, and after "Redemption," with planters and their allies in control of politics, the law emerged as a means of stabilizing and promoting the plantation system. If Radical Reconstruction failed to redistribute the land of the South, the ouster of the planter class from control of politics at least ensured that the sanctions of the criminal law would not be employed to discipline the black labor force.

AN UNDERSTANDING OF THIS FUNDAmental conflict over the relation between government and society helps explain the pervasive complaints concerning corruption and "extravagance" during Radical Reconstruction. Corruption there was aplenty; tax rates did rise sharply. More significant than the rate of taxation, however, was the change in its incidence. For the first time, planters and white farmers had to pay a significant portion of their income to the government, while propertyless blacks often escaped scot-free. Several states, moreover, enacted heavy taxes on uncultivated land to discourage land speculation and force land onto the market, benefiting, it was hoped, the freedmen.

As time passed, complaints about the "extravagance" and corruption of Southern governments found a sympathetic audience among influential Northerners. The Democratic charge that universal suffrage in the South was responsible for high taxes and governmental extravagance coincided with a rising conviction among the urban middle classes of the

North that city government had to be taken out of the hands of the immigrant poor and returned to the "best men"— the educated, professional, financially independent citizens unable to exert much political influence at a time of mass parties and machine politics. Increasingly the "respectable" middle classes began to retreat from the very notion of universal suffrage. The poor were no longer perceived as honest producers, the backbone of the social order; now they became the "dangerous classes," the "mob." As the historian Francis Parkman put it, too much power rested with "masses of imported ignorance and hereditary ineptitude." To Parkman the Irish of the Northern cities and the blacks of the South were equally incapable of utilizing the ballot: "Witness the municipal corruptions of New York, and the monstrosities of negro rule in South Carolina." Such attitudes helped to justify Northern inaction as, one by one, the Reconstruction regimes of the South were overthrown by political violence.

IN THE END, THEN, NEITHER THE ABOLItion of slavery nor Reconstruction succeeded in resolving the debate over the meaning of freedom in American life. Twenty years before the American Civil War, writing about the prospect of abolition in France's colonies, Alexis de Tocqueville had written, "If the Negroes have the right to become free, the [planters] have the incontestable right not to be ruined by the Negroes' freedom." And in the United States, as in nearly every plantation society that experienced the end of slavery, a rigid social and political dichotomy between former master and former slave, an ideology of racism, and a dependent labor force with limited economic opportunities all survived abolition. Unless one means by freedom the simple fact of not being a slave, emancipation thrust blacks into a kind of no-man's land, a partial freedom that made a mockery of the American ideal of equal citizenship.

Yet by the same token the ultimate outcome underscores the uniqueness of Reconstruction itself. Alone among the societies that abolished slavery in the nineteenth century, the United States, for a moment, offered the freedmen a measure of political control over their own destinies. However brief its sway, Reconstruction allowed scope for a remarkable political and social mobilization of the black community. It opened doors of opportunity that could never be completely closed. Reconstruction transformed the lives of Southern blacks in ways unmeasurable by statistics and unreachable by law. It raised their expectations and aspirations, redefined their status in relation to the larger society, and allowed space for the creation of institutions that enabled them to survive the repression that followed. And it established constitutional principles of civil and political equality that, while flagrantly violated after Redemption, planted the seeds of future struggle.

Certainly, in terms of the sense of possibility with which it opened, Reconstruction failed. But as Du Bois observed, it was a "splendid failure." For its animating vision—a society in which social advancement would be open to all on the basis of individual merit, not inherited caste distinctions—is as old as America itself and remains relevant to a nation still grappling with the unresolved legacy of emancipation.

Index

Credits/Acknowledgments

Cover design by Charles Vitelli

1. The New Land
Facing overview—Photo from the Smithsonian Institution National Anthropological Archives, Bureau of American Ethnology Collection.
13—HT map by Ken Wass.

2. Revolutionary America
Facing overview—National Archives painting by John Trumbull.

3. National Consolidation and Expansion
Facing overview—Photo from the National Gallery of Art.
166—Bowring Cartographic.

4. The Civil War and Reconstruction
Facing overview—Photo from the Library of Congress.

ANNUAL EDITIONS ARTICLE REVIEW FORM

■ NAME: _____ DATE: _____

■ TITLE AND NUMBER OF ARTICLE: _____

■ BRIEFLY STATE THE MAIN IDEA OF THIS ARTICLE: _____

_____

■ LIST THREE IMPORTANT FACTS THAT THE AUTHOR USES TO SUPPORT THE MAIN IDEA:

_____

_____

_____

_____

■ WHAT INFORMATION OR IDEAS DISCUSSED IN THIS ARTICLE ARE ALSO DISCUSSED IN YOUR TEXTBOOK OR OTHER READINGS THAT YOU HAVE DONE? LIST THE TEXTBOOK CHAPTERS AND PAGE NUMBERS:

_____

_____

_____

_____

_____

■ LIST ANY EXAMPLES OF BIAS OR FAULTY REASONING THAT YOU FOUND IN THE ARTICLE:

_____

_____

_____

_____

_____

■ LIST ANY NEW TERMS/CONCEPTS THAT WERE DISCUSSED IN THE ARTICLE, AND WRITE A SHORT DEFINITION:

_____

_____

_____

_____

_____

We Want Your Advice

ANNUAL EDITIONS revisions depend on two major opinion sources: one is our Advisory Board, listed in the front of this volume, which works with us in scanning the thousands of articles published in the public press each year; the other is you—the person actually using the book. Please help us and the users of the next edition by completing the prepaid article rating form on this page and returning it to us. Thank you for your help!

ANNUAL EDITIONS:
AMERICAN HISTORY, Volume 1
Pre-Colonial through Reconstruction
Article Rating Form

Here is an opportunity for you to have direct input into the next revision of this volume. We would like you to rate each of the 40 articles listed below, using the following scale:

1. **Excellent: should definitely be retained**
2. **Above average: should probably be retained**
3. **Below average: should probably be deleted**
4. **Poor: should definitely be deleted**

Rating	Article
	1. Mighty Cahokia
	2. Columbus—Hero or Villain?
	3. Laboring in the Fields of the Lord
	4. Bearing the Burden? Puritan Wives
	5. Colonists in Bondage: Indentured Servants in America
	6. Entertaining Satan
	7. How British Are You? An Interview with David Hackett Fischer
	8. Slavery and Insurrections in the Colonial Province of New York
	9. Editing the Declaration
	10. The *Radical* Revolution
	11. The Hessians
	12. 'It Is Not a Union'
	13. "To Form a More Perfect Union . . ."
	14. The Founding Fathers, Conditional Antislavery, and the Nonradicalism of the American Revolution
	15. The Bill of Rights in Its Context
	16. Hamilton's Legacy
	17. The Whiskey Rebellion
	18. The Great Chief Justice

Rating	Article
	19. John Quincy Adams and American Continental Expansion
	20. Indians in the Land
	21. The Lives of Slave Women
	22. The Secret Life of a Developing Country (Ours)
	23. Fenimore Cooper's America
	24. Congress Couldn't Have Been *This* Bad
	25. Women at Large: Travel in Antebellum America
	26. 1846: The Way We Were—and the Way We Went
	27. Forgotten Forty-Niners
	28. Christmas in 19th-Century America
	29. Eden Ravished
	30. Walt Whitman's Different Lights
	31. Dred Scott in History
	32. First Blood to the South: Bull Run
	33. The Struggle for Black Freedom before Emancipation
	34. Combat Trauma in the American Civil War
	35. Who Was Lincoln?
	36. How Did Lincoln Die?
	37. Why the South Lost the Civil War
	38. A War That Never Goes Away
	39. The War We Never Finished
	40. The New View of Reconstruction

(Continued on next page)

ABOUT YOU

Name _____ Date _____

Are you a teacher? ❑ Or a student? ❑

Your school name _____

Department _____

Address _____

City _____ State _____ Zip _____

School telephone # _____

YOUR COMMENTS ARE IMPORTANT TO US !

Please fill in the following information:

For which course did you use this book? _____

Did you use a text with this *ANNUAL EDITION*? ❑ yes ❑ no

What was the title of the text? _____

What are your general reactions to the *Annual Editions* concept?

Have you read any particular articles recently that you think should be included in the next edition?

Are there any articles you feel should be replaced in the next edition? Why?

Are there any World Wide Web sites you feel should be included in the next edition? Please annotate.

May we contact you for editorial input?

May we quote your comments?

ANNUAL EDITIONS: AMERICAN HISTORY, Volume 1, Fourteenth Edition